Anne Skjønsberg

WHAT TO BELIEVE?

About extraordinary phenomena and consciousness

*Translated by the author from the original
Norwegian edition with additional material*

Are we here by accident?
What is consciousness?
Can dust create poetry?
Do angels exist?

© 2008 & 2013 Anne Skjønsberg

This book is copyrighted under the Berne Convention.
All rights of the owner reserved. Except for brief quotations in critical articles or reviews, no part of this book may be reproduced in any manner without prior written permission of the owner, or publisher.

First edition published in Norwegian 2008 under the title
Hva kan jeg tro?
by Emilia Forlag, Oslo, Norway. (ISBN 978-82-7419-123-5)

Revised Edition published in English 2013
by
Saturday Night Press Publications,
England
snppbooks@gmail.com
www.snppbooks.com

ISBN 978 1 908421 08 1

Printed by Lightning Source
www.lightningsource.com

www.snppbooks.com

My deep felt thanks go to Ann Harrison for her dedicated work with correcting my English after my translation of the Norwegian version of the book, and for her many comments and suggestions for further reading, which have made this edition much more thorough and comprehensive than the Norwegian edition, for the understanding of life's enigma.

*Furthermore, I must express my gratitude to
Øystein Bernhard Mobråten
for letting me use a picture of his beautiful sculpture,
The Primeval Philosopher, on the book's frontcover.*

Front cover: The Primeval Philosopher.

A bronze sculpture by the Norwegian artist Øystein Bernhard Mobråten, which is on exhibition at Oslo University, Institute of Biology.
(The sculpture is approximately 1.5 metres high.)   Photo: Jon.

The artist describes the work as follows:

The picture represents an inner evolution. The Ape represents: The primitive in a human being, who, through mental acknowledgement, must try to reach insight and understanding as regards the laws of life. The Ape is sitting next to and leaning against the Tree of Knowledge. The fruit from the Tree of Knowledge will give the human being the ability to discern between good and evil. The Ape holds a leg bone as a weapon in the right hand, which refers to the left half of the brain, the part that controls aggression and violence. In the left hand the Ape holds a flower, which refers to the right half of the brain, that part which controls the soft, searching, wondering human mind. By containing such contradictory qualities, the human being must of necessity try to reach an understanding of its own nature.
                                        Øystein Bernhard Mobråten

Table of Contents

1.	INTRODUCTION	9
2.	RELIGION	14
2.1	The history of humanity and the development of religion	14
2.2	Short introduction to the world's great religions – Christianity not included	22
2.3	Christianity	29
	The Christian belief	29
	What do we know about The New Testament?	32
	Jesus	37
	The Book of Revelation – The Apocalypse	49
2.4	GOD	50
3.	EXTRAORDINARY PHENOMENA AND ABILITIES	63
3.1	Introduction	63
3.2	Some individuals with strange abilities	64
3.3	Mystics, saints and spiritual teachers	67
	Definition of a mystic	67
	Two great mystic-philosophers	69
	Some Christian mystics	70
	Non-eating Saints in the Western World	74
	The Canonization Process in the Catholic Church	74
	Spiritual teachers, avatars, prophets and the like	75
3.4	Magicians	77
3.5	Shamanism – people with healing power and clairvoyant abilities	78
3.6	Autistic savant syndrome	81
3.7	Poltergeist phenomena and psychokinesis	82
3.8	Predictions	86
	In General	86
	Dowsing with a twig or pendulum	89
	Astrology	91
	I Ching	103
	Tarot Cards	104
	Comments	105
3.9	Luck and strange co-incidences/synchronicity	106
3.10	Out-of-body experiences	107
3.11	Spirit contact and channelling	109
	Introduction	109
	Spirit contact through a medium	110
	Ectoplasm	115
	Other forms of spirit contact and spirit possession	120
	Spirit rescue	123

	Cooperation with Nature Spirits – the Findhorn Community	124
	Documentation of spirit contact	125
	Comments	130
3.12	Thought images that become manifested on the body	131
3.13	Thought form that takes on a life of its own	132
3.14	Like attracts like	133
3.15	Animal's inexplicable abilities	134
3.16	Other peculiarities	134
3.17	What is reality?	137
4.	RESEARCH AND THEORIES ABOUT PARANORMAL PHENOMENA	141
4.1	Various paranormal phenomena	141
4.2	Stanislav Grof's research with LSD and holotropic breath	144
4.3	Some physics and biology	147
4.4	Everything is part of everything else – about holons	150
4.5	The holographic universe	155
4.6	Are we only a point of reference?	157
5.	THE PSI FIELD – THE CELESTIAL ARCHIVE	160
6.	THE AURA AND THE CHAKRAS	163
7.	CONSCIOUSNESS, DREAMS AND VISUALIZATION	178
7.1	Introduction	178
7.2	The development of the human beings and the consciousness	180
7.3	Brain activity levels	182
7.4	The consciousness' functional areas	184
7.5	Consciousness bodies	186
7.6	Some other explanations of the human being's structure	193
7.7	The personality and the unconscious forces in the human beings	197
7.8	Dreams	206
7.9	Hypnosis and visualization	212
7.10	Memory and morality	214
7.11	Cosmic consciousness, spiritual awakening and visions	215
7.12	Thoughts	220
7.13	Who is thinking?	224
7.14	The holotropic consciousness	226
7.15	The human being's spirit and soul	227
7.16	The different parts of consciousness – a summary	235
8.	CONSCIOUSNESS LEVELS	237
9.	SPIRIT BEINGS	245
9.1	Introduction	245
9.2	Spirit beings according to the great religions	246
	Angels	246
	Spirit beings described in other great religions	251
	Revelations of the Virgin Mary	252
	The term "The Holy Ghost" in The New Testament	254

9.3	Evil spirits	256
9.4	Explanations of spirit beings	258
9.5	Is help available?	272
9.6	Comments	275
10.	DEATH	279
10.1	Introduction	279
10.2	Near-death experiences	281
10.3	Stories told about what happens when a human being dies	287
10.4	A summary of what has been told about death	303
10.5	When is a human being dead?	310
10.6	Suicide	312
11.	REINCARNATION	314
11.1	Introduction	314
11.2	The Bible and the teachings of Christianity	316
11.3	Buddhist doctrines and related explanations	318
11.4	The teachings of Hinduism	323
11.5	Theosophical teachings	324
11.6	Contemporary lives?	326
11.7	Reincarnation stories	332
11.8	Spiritual possession, spirit attachment or telepathic takeover?	333
11.9	Several persons remember the same previous life	334
11.10	Research	334
11.11	Various statements about reincarnation	338
11.12	Comments	346
12.	LOVE – The goal of humanity	352
13.	EVIL, ANGST AND CONSCIENCE	360
14.	DESTINY AND FREE WILL	368
15.	DISEASES AND HEALING	377
16.	PRAYER, MEDITATION, FORGIVENESS AND SPIRITUAL DEVELOPMENT	395
16.1	Prayer and meditation	395
16.2	Sin and forgiveness	412
16.3	Spiritual development	416
17.	MYTHS, SYMBOLS AND RITUALS	426
18.	THE UNIVERSE AND EVOLUTION	440
19.	CONCLUSION	452
Reference Notes		461
Bibliography		486
Index		500

Illustrations

Figure	Illustrations	Source	Page
1	Materialised form of Tom's Aunt	Tom Harrison	118
2	Materialised form of Granddad Bessant	Tom Harrison	118
3	Psychic photograph from *The Case for Spirit Photography*	Conan Doyle	121
4	The four Quadrants	Ken Wilber	153
5	The Heart's Electromagnetic Field	'Institute of HeartMath'	165
6	The Aura		167
7	The Chakra Centres	Powell / Moore	174
8	Consciousness Bodies		188
9	The Great Nest of Being	Ken Wilber	195
10	Consciousness Planes		238
11	Variations on the angelic hierarchy		247
12	The Virgin Mary in Cairo	Jerome Palmer	253
13	The Tree of Life	The Kabbalah	436
14	Sketch from *Talking with Angels*	Gitta Mallasz	444

The author and publisher would like to thank the following companies for use of their material:

Figures 4 and 9 from *A Theory of Everything,* by Ken Wilber, © 2000 by Ken Wilber. Reprinted by arrangement with Shambhala Publications Inc., Boston, MA. www.shambhala.com.

Figure 5 from *'Science of the Heart', 2001* is reprinted by arrangement with the Institute of HeartMath, Boulder Creek, California. www.heartmath.org.

1. Introduction

"Love is the goal of humanity." Marcello Haugen

Do we today know how the mind is functioning – what consciousness is? Can we believe everything people say about their experiences with paranormal phenomena, such as telepathy, precognitive dreams, ghosts etc., or is this fantasy going wild? Can we simply consider the great religions as myths, or disregard stories about unexpected healings, spiritual happenings or other similar rather exceptional stories as fiction or as coincidences? What is to be expected is that we listen and wonder or, at least, take a look at what parapsychologists have investigated and what others claim to know about such phenomena. Maybe we will learn something that will give us a better understanding in our quest about what life is and how life should be lived.

"I do not believe in God or in the Bible or in Jesus" – these are statements I quite often hear. But what is it that they do not believe? That they cannot answer. By wondering and looking around, I have found certain answers which have given me a good platform as to how I shall live my life.

To give a definition of the term religion which will satisfy everybody is quite impossible. The word religion derives from *religare*, which is the Latin word for to bind, or it comes from *religio,* which is the Latin word for obligations or bounds, alternatively to bind together or being conscious of. The British historian in religion, James Frazer (1854-1941) once said that there is probably no subject in the world about which opinions differ so much as the nature of religion.[i]

His definition of religion is that it concerns theories and activities which are aimed at propitiation and conciliation of powers superior to humans, which are believed to direct and control the course of nature and of human life. Therefore, he thinks that religion actually consists of two elements, a theoretical part and a practical part, respectively to believe in higher powers and an attempt to propitiate or please them. If the belief does not contain such a practice, then we do not deal with religion in his opinion, but in theology – that is the teaching about the Divine.

---

i. Frazer is considered the founder of *modern* anthropology, and his book *The Golden Bough* is esteemed as an encyclopedia for religious and mythological studies (the citation is from page 50 in his book).

Many people will probably follow the definition given by James Frazer when stating that they are not religious.

The Swiss psychiatrist Carl Gustav Jung (1875-1961)[i] is supposed to have said that religion is to show respect to and to take into consideration the forces in the unconscious.[1] That is to respect them and honour the processes going on in the unconscious, and to seriously consider the signals from this area, whether they come through dreams or in any other way, and to listen to the message given. To listen to the interior signals is, according to Jung, to have a religious approach to life.

A belief may also be a conviction that some people have, due to experiences acquired or because they want to build on other people's experiences. The Danish mystic Martinus Thomsen (1890-1981, who from here on will just be called Martinus, since he is known by this name in Scandinavia) has said that some people are born with the ability to believe, but others are not. I belong to the last category, as so far I do not know what to believe. I cannot accept, without further proof, what others tell me. I do not feel at home with any of the established great religions or church societies, and I have problems with many of the terms used within those circles when they explain what they believe, or the established rituals used in remembrance of what they consider the foundation of existence. However, in this book I have tried to put together what I can register with my senses, what I have experienced, what I have read and what I have been told. And I have come to the conclusion that there must be a spiritual dimension in our existence and a special purpose within our lives. It is possible to believe in a spiritual dimension of existence without having to follow a certain practice or a certain teaching, or having to try to appease the high powers. My belief is then based on the feeling or the experience that there is more to our existence than the physical.

In my opinion, the word religious ought to be used only as a general term for a person's belief in or being open to a possible spiritual dimension. Some people prefer using the word spiritualism in this regard, but to me, that is the same. So, what do we mean when using the term a spiritual dimension? For some, this may be a certain consciousness attitude which is not tied to the daily life, but which does not mean that there is a conscious existence after the physical life. For others, this means a belief in an existence after the physical – a sort of everlasting conscious existence.

---

i. Carl Gustav Jung was taking dreams seriously and was the founder of the so called analytical psychology, where terms like the archetype, the shadow, anima and animus etc. were central. This made a special approach to understand the psyche of humans, which later has been developed by the C.G. Junginstitutt in Zürich. This Institute is educating psychologists who, even as late as in 2008, were not acknowledged as such in Norway. Jung's ideas have, however, many followers around the world. His starting point is that humans are spiritual beings, and unless this is taken into consideration, it is impossible to try to understand them.

However, many people do not believe in an afterlife, and many deny that humans have other senses than the five physical ones. These are some of the subjects I will consider in this book.

Superstition is an expression I often hear and then always with a negative connotation. But what is belief and what is superstition? The term superstition does not tell me anything. The term is normally used when there is something people do not want to consider further and therefore reject, as for example phenomena which are unexplainable when applying the physical laws we know today and which are, therefore, called paranormal. However, I want to have a closer look at such phenomena. Maybe they can tell us something new of importance about our existence that go beyond our daily awareness. I will also take a look at the lives of the mystics and what they have tried to tell us, and also at people who have been working with spiritual questions without being dedicated a special religion. Someone has said that a philosopher, who is only using his thoughts as a tool, is not able to experience the spiritual dimension of existence. Only a person who is open to the mystical experience can do that. That there is such a spiritual dimension of existence, has, in my opinion, been demonstrated by many mystics through their way of living and the abilities they have shown. We should listen to what the mystics are trying to tell us if we want to understand ourselves and the world in which we live. The Danish author, teacher of meditation and consciousness researcher, Jes Bertelsen (b.1946) has also posed the question – why do we not listen to what the mystics and the people who are spiritually awake tell us.[2] Mystics exist today all over the world – and there have always been such people. If you doubt that some people have abilities which surpass the ordinary senses and have knowledge about the non-physical world, you should study the life of the mystics.

When you consider what mystics, channelled spirits (that is entities from another existence that make their presence known through physical persons) or other people have said or written, one must remember that what those individuals have told as the absolute truth, is not necessarily so. And, as will be shown below, you do not always get the same story in the different reports about the same thing. Both the German spiritual researcher Rudolf Steiner (1861-1925)[i] and the spirit Ambres (channelled by Sture Johansson, Sweden)

---

i. Rudolf Steiner was born in Kraljevic in the former Austria/Hungary. The family was catholics. For the most, he grew up in Austria. In the biography written by Colin Wilson, published in 1985, *The Man and His Vision*, Wilson states that Steiner was one of the most remarkable men from the twentieth century, and that it is impossible to overstate the importance of what he said (see page 170). Rudolf Steiner became the secretary general of the German section of the *Theosophical Society* when this section was established in 1902. This Society was founded in New York in 1875 with Helena P. Blavatsky, Henry S. Olcott and William Q. Judge as founding mothers/fathers. The goal of the Society was to study religion, philosophy and science, as well as doing research regarding the inexplicable laws of nature as well as the latent potentialities in humans. Annie Besant, who was president of the Society from 1907 to 1933, introduced a young Indian, Jiddu Krishnamurti, as a new Messiah of a sort, which Steiner clearly rejected *(cont. below)* have stressed that the reader must use his/her own good sense when considering the sayings of the mystics.

The British author, Colin Wilson (b. 1931)[i] has, for example, pointed out that the Swedish mystic Emanuel Swedenborg's detailed description of life on other planets (presumably those within our own solar system) and Rudolf Steiner's visions regarding King Arthur and the Knights of The Round Table, were quite wrong.[3] The founders of Theosophy, Helena Blavatsky and Annie Besant, obviously were not well grounded in all their activities and writings, but that must not lead to discarding everything they said. The same goes for others. It seems as if the mystics are sometimes cheated by their own fantasies, or maybe rather by archetypical pictures or the fantasies of other people. Therefore, there may be different opinions regarding some of the personalities and authors that I refer to in this book, but I cannot dismiss their sayings without further checking and quite a lot of it I do find of interest.

The American philosopher, mystic and author, Ken Wilber (b.1949)[ii] has pointed out that none of the worldviews (including his own) contains the total truth, but as more and more of these views can be placed within a greater understanding, a better explanation of the Cosmos can be reached. Most of these explanations are true, on condition that they are considered in accordance with the general understanding at the time they were given. As an example, he explains that both Christmas Claus and Apollo or Zeus are phenomenological realities in a mythical worldview, considered from a mythical plane. Even though we may believe the opposite, neither is our worldview today final, because we have to consider that humanity in the future will expand its horizon and understanding, from which follows, that great parts of today's worldview will be disregarded or rejected.

Among the people, who in my opinion have especially contributed to a better understanding of existence, and whom I will refer to extensively in this book, Jes Bertelsen[iii] and Martinus are of special interest. Also Ken Wilber and Rudolf Steiner will be quoted extensively. The British teacher in

---

(Steiner cont.) rejected. He broke contact with the Theosophical Society in 1913 and changed the name of the German section to the Anthroposophic Society.

i. Colin Wilson has a B.A. in linguistics from 1995 and PhD in cognitive science from 2000. He has written many books about subjects such as criminology, psychology and mysticism. Since 2000 he has been assistant professor at the University of Los Angeles. He is especially interested in phenomenological theory.

ii. Ken Wilber has a university degree in biochemistry and has studied under different Zen masters and Tibetan Buddhist masters. He has published many books about psychology, consciousness, the human soul and human development potential.

iii. Jes Bertelsen, PhD, is a Danish author, teacher in meditation and a consciousness-researcher. He has published many books about philosophy, psychology and consciousness. In 1972 he received a gold medal for a paper on the philosophy of Søren Kierkegaard, presented at the University of Aarhus, where he had studied and later lectured at its 'Idé-historisk Institut'. At the same time he gave individual consultations regarding the understanding of dreams and the individuation process. He obtained his doctoral degree for a thesis on *The structure of the Self*, based on the   *(cont opposite.)*

meditation Bob Moore (b.1928) (see further description in chapter 3.2), with whom Jes Bertelsen has had close cooperation, is also very interesting. I will also refer several sayings received through channelling from spirits in the other world – the spirit world. These spirits will be further described in the chapter regarding spirit contact and channelling.

I have written this book, partly to be able to remember what I have read and partly in order to see all this in a totality, and also in the hope that this book may be of help to others. In contains what I have found after many years of reading, and my reflections on these topics.

I am beginning with a short description of the history of religion and of the greatest written religions as a background for what comes next. Then I am recording several phenomena not explained in the religions, and what has been found and ascertained through research, both by parapsychologists and researchers within other sciences. Knowledge regarding this research is important when we consider what the mystics are telling us about consciousness, about spirit, about death and about reincarnation, among many other things.

All the mystics, and others that I refer to, maintain that love is the main goal of humanity. What is meant by this term, I have tried to explain in chapter 12. What I have otherwise found – apart from what I have written in the final chapter – may best be described by referring to the recommendation given by Sture Johansson. He has said that we must let life lead us; we must cooperate with life because we are neither independent nor free beings.[4] I have found that when life is difficult that is because I have not taken the signals given that I should do something else, change my course, get out of a situation etc. I have not accepted what happened as help, which it actually was, to get on with my personal development. I did not see that I was bogged down in something which had no future. And then, when change came, I used a lot of energy and strength to hold on to the old. Slowly I have come to recognize how important my actions and my thoughts are for me, and not at least in relation to others. What happens has a meaning, and I must try to understand what I can learn from it. When I let life be my leader, I find that the circumstances are adjusted and I get unexpected help just at the time when I have great need of assistance – and sometimes also in everyday life.

I would like to give thanks to everyone who has followed me a short or longer part of the way, and who have helped me move forward through questions, commentaries and wonderings. And thanks also to those who have crossed my path and forced me to reconsider – and by that, hopefully, helped me understand a little more.

(Bertelsen cont) psychology of Carl Gustav Jung. In 1982 he started *Vækstcenteret* (the word means the centre of growth) at Nørre-Snede in Denmark. This centre is an existential cooperation, a centre for development, the aim of which is to help people in their process of self-realisation (according to the centre's 7th Year's publication).

2. Religion

> Each one of us is free to go to which-ever teacher he/she wants. Each teaching is fresh. The teachers have approached the problems from different angles, but the source is the same.
> *Ambres[5]*

> When you start on the spiritual road, it is important that you choose the teaching that suits your mental development and disposition, as well as your spiritual standing. It is decisive that each one finds the spiritual praxis and belief system that suits his/her special needs. Only then will the internal changes come forward, the inner stillness which makes the individual a spiritual mature and warm-hearted, a whole, good and friendly person. This it is important to consider when looking for spiritual nourishment.
> *The 14th Dalai Lama[6]*

> The founders of religions are 'religious savants' who experience and decipher God's speech in new and original ways. When they get disciples and congregations who believe and translate the 'divine reality' in the way they do, then religions are born.
> *Kristian Schjelderup[7]*

2.1. The history of humanity and the development of religion

Throughout all of history, ideas about our existence have been passed on from one generation to the next. Most of these ideas are presented through the different religions, whether they have been world religions or sectarian offshoots. The American historian in religion, Joseph Campbell (1904-1987) has written extensively about this in his books *The Masks of Gods*, from which I have taken most of what is written in this chapter.[i] But philosophy, without a religious influence, has developed independent of the religions, even though not everything has been printed and many ideas have been supressed by the authorities in power. Among the oldest philosophical treaties which we have today, in writing or which have been passed on orally, many were written around the period 500 BCE. This must have been a

---

i. Joseph Campbell was a popular teacher, author and lecturer. He was educated at Columbia University, as well as at the universities of Paris and Munich. After 1934 he was engaged at the faculty for literature at Sarah Lawrence College, New York, and was during a period of 10 years member of the Board of Bollingen Foundation.

universal period of flowering, and makes us wonder why so much happened at that time. At this time Gautama Siddhartha lived in India, better known later as Buddha (or Buddha Sakyamuni, 563-483 BCE). In China there was Confucius (551-479 BCE) and Lao Tzu (maybe 50 years previously). Zarathustra (also called Zoroaster – 628-551 BCE) lived in Iran. In Greece we find Pythagoras (ca. 580-500 BCE), Socrates (died 398 BCE), Plato (427-347 BCE) and Aristotle (384-322 BCE). But thoughts about our existence existed long before those teachers lived. It seems that humans always have been religious beings. Stonehenge in England is well known, as well as the megaliths of Northern France and the grotto paintings in Southern France and Spain, just to mention some of the greatest wonders in Europe which are believed being dedicated religious praxis. Do they have any connection with our religious terms today? That I cannot answer. But the prehistoric artefacts which have been found indicate burial rituals and spiritual symbols which show that people have been concerned with understanding who they were and what life is, and to prepare a proper transition to a possible next world.

Humanity's cradle was in Africa, but the earliest humans then wandered out of Africa to Asia and later also to Australia. Skeletal-parts of Homo erectus have been found both in Java and in Africa, from about the same time. The oldest parts are considered being about 1.8 million years old, although some finds in Africa in the year 2000 are thought to be at least 6 million years old.

Homo erectus was the first being among humanity's predecessors who used complicated tools such as hand axes, but this did not happen until 500,000 thousand years ago. At this time we also have finds of animal bones which show that one forefather/mother for some sort of reason split open the head from the body of the animal. This individual clubbed its victims with a leg bone from a gazelle – a club with an enlarged end. From about 400,000 BCE individuals we call the Heidelberg-man and the Peking-man (Sinantropus) lived. From this period there are also finds of hand axes and fireplaces. Obviously, Peking-man was a cannibal.

The Neanderthals, who lived between 200,000 and 25,000 BCE approximately, were probably also cannibals. Finds show that the skulls of their victims were opened in a special way. Their name derives from a valley in Germany but there are similar finds in Java from the same period. Those individuals are not considered predecessors to today's humans – Homo sapiens, although some scientists think they may have been partly so. The finding of the skulls indicates that there must have been special rituals in connection with cannibalism. These individuals knew how to use fire, although there are no indications that fire was used for cooking. Such finds do not exist before about 30,000/10,000 BCE. Scientists presume, therefore, that such fireplaces were used only in connection with rituals, as fire was considered sacred. From this period we have the earliest findings of holy rituals. Graves with artefacts and sacred mountains with bear skulls indicate offerings of animals.

Scientists are not in agreement as to when the ability to speak first arose. Some think that it first happened 40,000 years ago, others – after discoveries in South Africa – that this may have occurred as early as 70,000 years ago.[8] Neither the jaw nor the throat was formed before this time as to be able to make different sounds in quick succession. The Human ability to speak, as we do today, could not be developed before this happened as that is a prerequisite for language. I wonder how the Neanderthals were able to communicate and develop a culture without having the ability to talk. Possibly, the artefacts mentioned above may have been from a later period.

The period called the Palaeolithic from about 30,000 to 10,000 BCE was the goddess-and-grotto period. The Crô-magnon-man is from this period. He belongs to the Homo sapiens group, to which today's people also belong. From this period we have finds consisting of large and small figures depicting fat, rounded women – the naked goddess or the immemorial mother.

Such finds have also been excavated from the Ukraine to the Pyrenees as well as eastwards to the Baikal Sea. The finest, and the earliest finds from graves, are from the Ukraine. A well-known example is *Venus from Willendorf* in Austria, which is 11 cm high. From this period you also have the elaborate grotto art, in grottos in the south of France and in Spain, of which the grottos of Lascaux, Trois Frères and Tuc d'Audoubert are best known. This art mainly depicts animals. Joseph Campbell considers this grotto art to be the first sign of a masculine spirit that slowly displaced the naked goddess.[9]

The next periods are called Epipaleolithic, Mesolithic and Proto-neolithic and cover the years from about 10,000 BCE forwards. These periods are also called the Caspian period. In this period we find the petroglyphs (stone drawings), especially in Northern Africa, in the Atlas Mountains, in Sahara and on both sides of the Gibraltar Straits, also along the Nile, in Israel at Mount Carmel (about 30 km northwest of Jerusalem). In Jordan, Mesopotamia, India and Sri Lanka we too find such stone drawings. In 1928 artefacts from around the year 6000 BCE were found on Mount Carmel. Petroglyphs from about 5000 BCE are also found in the southern part of Africa, in Zimbabwe and in Namibia. Many of these drawings depict hunting scenes as well as scenes of fighting, dancing and sacrifices. From this time on the bow and arrow were used as weapons.

From the oldest Neolithic period (about 7500 to 3500 BCE) we have finds in the city of Jericho in Palestine showing a defence tower made of stone. Jericho is the oldest example of a dwelling guarded by stone walls. The wall there is presumed to be from about 8000-6000 BCE. From this period we have finds showing cultures with animal husbandry and farming, and in the latter part, also crafts in elegant ceramic art with fine geometrical patterns. It is from this period we see the first figures of the Maltese cross, the swastika, the rosette and the double axe.

The birth of civilization, which began in the area called 'The Fertile Crescent', takes place in this period. The earliest city states were established around the years 3500 to 2500 BCE, and then we come to the period called 'the historical'. From this time on there are finds of small cities both in Mesopotamia near the great rivers Euphrates and Tigris as well as in Anatolia in Turkey, along the Mediterranean coast, in Egypt and in Iran. Sumer is one of the earliest and more advanced states among these city-states. Now we see the formation of greater states in these areas and the temple buildings are becoming steadily bigger. It is in this period we presume that the special temple complex in Malta was built. In these temples we find many figurines of well–rounded women of different sizes, as well as phalluses (the symbol of the male organ) made in clay.

Mesopotamia. From around 3200 BCE there is clear evidence that there were professional, initiated temple priests in Mesopotamia (the so-called Uruk B finds). It is from this time we find the first written signs (as from Ugarit), which is the base for documented history. The wheel came into use in Sumer. The great epic *Gilgamesh* is presumed coming originally from Uruk at around 2700 BCE. The city of Ur (which is supposed to be the birth place of Abraham) is presumed to have been established around 2600 BCE. Other city names that we know today are Lagash, established around 2550 BCE, Akkad which was the seat of King Sargon I who ruled from 2334 to 2279 BCE, and Mari which is considered established around 2550 BCE. In Mesopotamia there are finds from great temple structures, the so-called ziggurats, which presumably were built around 2500 BCE. Babylon had several glorious periods after 1900 BCE, especially during the reign of Hammurabi (who is especially known for his many laws) lasting from 1792 to 1750 BCE, and during the reign of Nebuchadnezzar II who suppressed Judea. He ruled from 605 to 561 BCE.

Egypt. King Menes made Upper and Lower Egypt into one state around 3100 BCE. From this time on we see the first signs of writing, both on wood, stone and in other materials. The oldest pyramid – Djoser's pyramid – was built at Saqqara around 2650 BCE as burial ground for the pharaoh Djoser. Between 2575 and 2465 BCE the pharaohs were Cheops (Khufu), Chephren (Khafre) and Mykerinos (Menkaure). Scientists believe that they built the three pyramids at Giza, near Cairo, which bear their names today. These pyramids lie next to each other with the Sphinx nearby. It is supposed that the Sphinx was built by Chephren. The book called *The Egyptian's Book of the Dead* is a collection of texts from the pyramids and from papyrus documents, mainly written between the years 2000 to 1750 BCE. Around the year 1630 Egypt was attacked and subdued by the people called Hyksos.

It is not certain from where those people came originally, but probably from Turkey. Their victory is partly due to their use of the wheel which helped them design quick and easily manoeuvrable war chariots. From about 1350 the pharaoh Akhenaton (with his queen Nefertiti) reigned, and after him came his son/son-in-law Tutankhamen. Akhenaton introduced the idea of one God, Aton, who should be venerated instead of the many gods of the Egyptians, of whom Amon was the leading deity. But Amon was reinstated by the priests when Akhenaton was dead. The great war-pharaoh, Ramses II ruled around 1250 BCE. In 663 BCE the capital city Theban was conquered by the Assyrian ruler Assurbanipal. From this time onwards iron came in use in Egypt. After Alexander had conquered the country, the Ptolemaic period began under Alexander's general Ptolemaios Soter. His descendants ruled, with Queen Cleopatra as the last, until the Romans, under Emperor Augustus (Octavian), dethroned her and her lover Mark Antony in the year 30 BCE. During the whole pharaoh period there were laborious and complicated religious rituals concerning the many Egyptian gods. The pyramids are supposed to have been tombs, but may also have served other purposes.

Judea. According to legend, Abraham should have walked the Earth around the year 1800 BCE. Moses is supposed to have left Egypt while Rameses II was pharaoh, which was around the year 1250 BCE[i]. According to the Bible, the great time for the Jews started with King David (about 1000-960 BCE) and King Solomon (from 960 to 935 BCE), although Judaism is not considered to be established until after the captivity in Babylon when the Persian king Cyrus permitted the Jews to rebuild the temple in Jerusalem (538 BCE). In the year 598 and again in 587 BCE Judea was conquered by King Nebuchadnezzar II (604-561 BCE) of Babylon and all the people of Judea were taken to Babylon. King Herod the great is supposed to have ruled at the time when Jesus was born, but he died soon after. He ruled from the year 37 BCE until 4 BCE. Many Jews consider him as one of the really great Jewish kings. He renovated the temple in Jerusalem as it had been devastated some hundred years before. The temple was again destroyed by the Romans in the year 70 CE after the Jewish revolt. After a new revolt in the years 132-135 CE, the city of Jerusalem was totally destroyed and Judea made a Roman colony. The Jews were forbidden to live there. Judaism was from then mainly preserved by Jews in the Diaspora – from places outside of Israel.

India. In Harappa in Punjab in India and in Mohenjo-Daro in Sind in Pakistan there flourished from around the year 2500 BCE two great cities.

---

i. Some researchers think that Moses actually was the pharaoh Akhenaton. Akhenaton's father was Amenhotep III and his mother was Amenhotep's wife Tiye who was not royalty. Presumably, she was the daughter of Yusuf of Yuha, the foremost minister of the pharaoh. Yusuf may have been the Joseph of the Old Testament, the son of Jacob. The book *Bloodline of the Holy Grail* by Laurence Gardner mentions this (see page 10). Nefertiti is said to be the daughter of Amenhotep III by another wife with full royal status. Tutankhamen is considered the son of Akhenaton and Nefertiti.

Both were situated on the great river Indus. Rather surprisingly, none of these societies show any form of development during their approximately one thousand years of existence according to the artefacts found. Those artefacts are rather monotonous although they have been found in quite large areas in India, from Punjab to Bombay. Presumably, the Indian deities Shiva and Kali were venerated at this time. Already from about the year 2350 BCE there were ships in the harbours of Mesopotamia presumably from India. But after the time of Hammurabi, about 500 years later – that is around 1750 BCE, no such contact seems to have existed.

China. Around the year 1500 BCE a rich culture arose in China under the Shang dynasty, with Honan as the capital city. This culture was based on farming but included also some cities. There are many beautiful bronze artefacts from this period. A special form of calendar and archives show that they had an advanced form of writing. The last part of this epoch, the Chou epoch, lasted from about the year 1000 BCE to 221 BCE. The first Chinese kingdom, The Chin dynasty, was established that year and lasted until 206 BCE. It brought prosperity and cultural growth, which continued under the next regime, the Han regime from 206 BCE to 220 CE. There are many important writings from this period. The Chinese book of divination *I Ching* and the collection of writings called *Shih-king* were supposed written before the year 600 BCE. Lao Tzu (about 600 BCE) was supposedly the emperor's counsellor in Loyang, the capital of the province Honan. His words of wisdom are well known and admired ever since his time, also in the West, and are collected in the book known as *Tao Te Ching*, which means *The Way of Life*. Whether the book is authentic or not is disputed, but it was supposedly written by one man. It has been said about this book that it is one of the most profound books in the world of philosophy, profound yet at the same time clear, mystical and practical. The teacher and philosopher Confucius probably lived from 551 to 479 BCE. Some of the discourses he had with his disciples have been written down by his students.

Europe. At around 1800 BCE the mighty stone monuments at Stonehenge in England and Carnac in France were built. We do not quite know how they were used, but religious burial rituals seem to have been the main purpose. Stonehenge may also have been used to predict the equinoxes and solstices. Around 1200 BCE the veneration of the great mother-goddess ended in Europe. About this time, the shepherd people, the nomads from the Russian and Arabian steps, pushed into farmland with settled populations. The Minoan culture in Crete, where the veneration of the goddess was strong, flourished around 2000 BCE. At Troy, which is situated at the western coast of Turkey, many artefacts are found with the oldest dating from around 3000 BCE. The Trojan War presumably took place around 1100 BCE. The great time of Athens was around 500 BCE. The Greeks had Zeus as the superior god and he supposedly lived on Mount Olympus. The gods in the Greek hierarchy were very human in their ways of living and acting. Zeus was the son of Cronos (Time - Saturnus in Roman mythology) and Rhea. Rhea was the daughter of Uranus and Gaia (The Earth). Rome is said to be founded in the year 753 BCE, but it was not until around 250 BCE that the great expansion started. The first Roman emperor, Augustus, reigned from the year 27 BCE until the year 14 CE. Emperor Constantine (died 337 CE) moved the capital from Rome to Constantinople. A short time later the empire was split in two. The West-Roman Empire ended when the last emperor was dethroned by the German headman Odovacar in the year 476 CE. There are mainly the same gods in the Greek and Roman mythology, although with different names, and this mythology has many of the same features that we also see in the Nordic mythology.

From the earliest history of the *North- and Middle-Americas* there are finds showing traces of a farming culture in the Ohio area dating from around 800 BCE, the so-called Adena culture. In Mexico finds from around 2000 BCE also show farming. The Olmec culture is from around 500 BCE. The Maya culture existed from around 300 CE until 1400 CE. This culture is well known due to the great pyramids, human offerings, hieroglyphic writing and knowledge of mathematics and astronomy. The Toltec culture is from the period 900 to 1300 CE, and the Aztec culture of Mexico, in which we see much of the same culture as the Maya culture, lasted from 1300 until 1521 CE when the Spaniards (and possibly also a deadly virus) destroyed it.

In *South America* the oldest traces of a civilization are from around 2300 BCE. The Inca Empire did not exist before about 1100 CE and was conquered by the Spaniards in 1532.

As this short survey shows, humans have through all times had relationships with the spirit world or the divine world – a supernatural existence. Offerings to the gods were performed in almost all cultures. Human offerings happened in many places and were done on an enormous scale especially in Middle- and South America. In order for the corn to grow, the seed must die. The old must die before the new can rise. The life energy was considered as something that could be transferred from one individual to the next. The gods had to be pacified, either with part of the crops or with human beings. If we can imagine how it is to live in a land that fairly often is devastated by great nature catastrophes where tens of thousands humans lose their lives without understanding the cause of the catastrophes, but believe this happens because of the wreath of the gods, it is easier to understand the religious praxis with offering human beings in order to appease the gods.

Karl Marx wrote: "Religion is opium for the people." In all the cultures here mentioned, religion has been used as an instrument for keeping groups of people together, with feasts, burial rituals and offerings. In many places, the foremost leader, whether this has been a king, a pharaoh or a headman, has from the earliest times been a combination of ruler and high priest, as the representative on Earth of the gods. Later on those functions were split.

Most religions are aiming at giving humanity an explanation as to what happens when we die. The former Norwegian university teacher Olav O. Aukrust (b.1912) wrote a three volume commentary called *Dødsrikets Verdenshistorie* (The World History of the Realm of the Dead), published in Norway in 1985, and gave there a thorough introduction to the ideas behind the different most important religions in the world. All of them seem to be based on an idea of some sort of a consciousness continuum. But as to how such a continuum might be – or even be possible, there has been little agreement. Researchers in religion usually point out that there is much influence from one culture to another nearby, and that there are many parallels in the development of theories throughout history. Because many believe that there are forces outside human beings with special power to influence or change the happenings in the world and in the life of humans, people have to find ways to attend to those forces through rituals and rules. This leads to thoughts about those forces which then turn into religion. The stories about those forces become myths. The rituals are also a form of reminder of important happenings, important periods of transformation in life, such as being born, coming of age, being married and dying. An individual must be initiated into what is to come and learn to be in contact with the subconscious and the unconscious layers in the psyche, as well as to learn to know his or her self. All the known mythologies may be understood from this way of viewing the story.

So what is the basic theme in the most important belief systems we see today? This is what I will consider next, although the presentation of necessity must be short – and probably also superficial. I will not say anything about the different groups within the different religions. Sectarianism is often due to strong personalities and their way of understanding words, sentences and phenomena. What I see necessary here, is to understand the main differences. Christianity is mainly a western phenomenon. But there are many parallel ideas between the different religions when you disregard the myths they are based on, the dogmas and the words used, and take a look at the deeper understanding of existence. As example, Hinduism is often said to be a religion that venerates many gods. But the many gods are just a picture of the all-embracing creating (divine) principle that, in so far as I have understood it, also is the basic in Christianity. A Jew once told me that Judaism actually is a way of life. Probably, this may also be said of the other great religions.

2.2. Short introduction to the world's great religions – Christianity not included

Hinduism

In Hinduism there are no creeds and no dogmas. Many consider Hinduism more like a philosophy than a religion. Hinduism supposedly arose when the Indo-European Arian immigration came to India (about 1200 BCE). The teaching was preserved for posterity in the books called Veda, such as Rig-Veda, Bhagavad Gita, Vedanta and Upanishad. No-one knows the origin of these books, but they are said to be revealed by the Rishis of old (that is sages, but the word Rishi might also mean archangel). The Veda books may have been written around 600 BCE, although their origin may be as far back as around 1700 BCE. The Rig-Veda is the oldest one and consists of 1028 songs praising the gods. There are some important common pillars of belief within the different varieties of Hinduism, such as the system of castes, the superiority of the Brahmans (the Brahmans are the cast of the priests and the highest caste in the system), the holy places of adoration, the holiness of cows, special rituals, the belief in *Karma*[i] and the continuity of the soul, among others. Hinduism denies the existence of an objective reality, maintaining that everything we experience is illusion or Maya. The word Maya can be translated as veil. The Hindus have an idea of a perennial non-material existence, the soul. This soul, however, can be delivered from the round of lives – called moksha.

The more advanced versions of Hinduism believe mainly in the one God. All other gods we meet in Hinduism are only pictures or symbols of the One. God is the only reality behind existence and the manifold which is *Brahman*. Brahman is the god of mysticism, without human sex and without qualities. The One God is all-knowing, almighty, merciful and the helper of mankind. In Hinduism you will also meet the One Woman – Mahādevī or the great-mother. This we can read in the Sanskrit text called *Devī-Māhātmya or Devotion to the Goddess*. The text has been known for at least fifteen hundred years. When this text is recited, the Great Goddess is called upon. She is said to be the greatest power of the Universe. Anyone being in distress will receive help from this Goddess.[10]

The gods are superior to human beings. They are creative and destructive. The goddess is not a woman in the same way that the gods are not men. The many gods of Hinduism may be considered as a personalization of Brahman without qualities. Then they will be seen as either male or female. Important male aspects of Brahman are the creator Brahma, the conserver Vishnu and the destroyer and renewer Shiva, who destroys everything at the end of the world

---

i. The term *karma* has been explained in different ways and I will return to many of the comments later. But at present, it can be said that a human being leaves a print on the astral plane, an astral pattern. A new individual may bring this print along into a new earth life. That is, the new human being must live a life that seeks to compensate for the negative in the astral pattern created by the previous individual.

period. These three gods are called *trimurti*, one god with three aspects. They are often pictured as one person with three heads or one figure with three sides. It is explained that the Cosmos only has one original power which is Brahma – the creator. The important womanly aspects are Brahma's spouse Saraswati, who is the goddess for learning, Vishnu's spouse Lakshmi, who is the goddess of wealth, and Shiva's spouse, Parvati. There are many aspects of Parvati, which are both positive and negative. She is, *inter alia*, responsible for cosmic violence. She is called Durga when she comes forward with weapon in her hands, or Kali when she is especially evil and destructive. When these aspects of the God are pictured in a human form, there are always four arms.

Two other important gods in Hinduism is Ganesh, with an elephant head, the god for wisdom and learning and the chief ape, Hanuman. Hanuman is the son of the god of the wind and is considered as the helper of the gods. On the next step downwards in the spiritual hierarchies, we find Krishna (who has a central role in the epic poem *Mahabharata*) and Rama (who is depicted in the epic poem *Ramayana*). Both these personalities are considered as reincarnations of the god Vishnu, and are so-called avatars. It is maintained that also Buddha is the reincarnation of Vishnu.

Holy places, such as rivers, lakes and mountains or trees and plants, are venerated. Many believe that a visit to such places, or that water at such places, will give healing. Brahma, however, has only one holy place, which a small lake in the city of Pushkar in Rajasthan. There, you will also find the only temple dedicated to Brahma.

Buddhism

Actually, Buddhism is not a religion; it is rather a way to understand human existence and a guide for the conduct of living. Therefore, it may be considered to be more of a philosophy than a religion. The ruling Dalai Lama[i] has explained that Buddhism is a way for living in peace, happiness and wisdom.[11] The word Buddha means The Awakened One or The Enlightened One. The founder of Buddhism is Shakyamuni Siddhartha Gautama. Shakyamuni means the wise one of the family Shakya. He is supposed to be born in Rummindei in Nepal in 563 BCE and lived until 483 BCE. When he was about 30 years of age, he had a profound religious experience. It was so profound that it completely changed his life. Such an awakening or acknowledgement is called bodhi in the old Indian language. Shakyamuni then became a Buddha after previously having been a bodhisattva. Bodhisattva is a Sanskrit word for one who has the potential of being a bodhi, one who has vowed to work for the enlightenment of all

---

i. Dalai Lama, who is number fourteen of the Dalai Lamas, was born in 1935. His original name is Tenzin Gyatso. He is the secular and religious leader of Tibet, who has been in exile since 1959 and lives in Dharamsala in India. He received the Nobel Peace Prize in 1989. He has written many books, and there are also several books arising from seminars he has attended.

human beings so they may become Buddhas, that is to obtain deliverance from the physical obstacles, which is to obtain Nirvana.

Buddha's view in regard to existence is that nothing is; everything is always changing, without pause and permanence. All concrete forms, all things, happenings, humans or ideas, are nothing but Maya (veil), but we believe it is real because of ignorance (*avidya*). Nirvana is the only real reality. But in Buddhism you also learn about karma. In Nirvana, karma is no more. Then *samsara* (that is the everlasting return of life) will end, and the flame will blow out. Ordinary people can only reach Nirvana after many rounds of life on Earth where progress is slow, but where a life with good deeds and perfect morals, progress takes a leap forward. It is also explained that Nirvana (the word actually means to blow out) is not disintegration, but liberation from suffering. Suffering is due to fantasy, greed and hate.

There is no god in Buddhism. That means that there is no superior being directing the existence. Many people think this is in contrast to Christianity, although the Christian's understanding of God is fairly diffuse. But there is one clear distinction between Buddhism and Christianity and that is that Christians believe in a personal saviour – Jesus Christ. There is no such saviour in Buddhism. Furthermore, Christians believe in God's grace – a help to be saved, a hope that you will not see in Buddhism. A central teaching in Buddhism is the road to no-self, *anatman* (also called *anatta*). This teaching explains that there is no permanent self. This is not a nihilistic doctrine. The teaching about anatman is the opposite of the view that there exists a self or atman. It is the belief in atman that is the cause of suffering, because one then clings to the idea of a self.

Buddhism consists of many different branches and sects. The most important of these are Theravada (also called Hinayana), Mahayana and Vajrayana. There are great many Buddhist books. One textbook or canon already existed in the third century BCE – and consisted of the works *Tripítaka, Vínaya, Sutta* (or *Sútra*) and *Abhidhárma*. An important doctrine in Buddhism is the teaching about The Four Noble Truths and The Eight Roads to Nirvana. By following these recommendations, all frustrations will cease. The Four Noble Truths are:

> 1. The world's central disease is frustration or suffering. The point is that human beings are suffering because they are trying to reach the unreachable.
>
> 2. The cause of suffering is that human beings are holding fast, clinging to or controlling. We stick to the exterior world because of ignorance or because we are not conscious. We believe that everything is permanent and do not see that absolutely everything is constantly changing. This relates especially to the fact that we stick to our ego, which is an illusion.
>
> 3. It is possible to end the evil circle that follows from the two previous truths. That is to obtain freedom through Nirvana. We reach

Nirvana when we stop clinging to life.

4. To reach Nirvana you have to follow The Eight Roads.

The Eight Roads are:
1. Right consideration (right view)
2. Right understanding
3. Right speech
4. Right conduct and action
5. Right way of life
6. Right diligence and struggle
7. Right mindfulness
8. Right contemplation

In addition there are the six virtues which is said to be the bodhisattva ideal. These are charity, moral, patience, enthusiasm, concentration and wisdom. There are many definitions as regards The Four Noble Truths within the different Buddhist branches. Neither is the term Nirvana agreed upon, even though it seems to be the same on the surface.

Judaism and the Old Testament

The leading principle in Judaism is the study of the Law and the obligation to follow the rules for right living. The main rules are to be found in the Law – that is The Five Books of Moses (respectively Genesis, Exodus, Leviticus, Numbers and Deuteronomy), also called the Torah or the Pentateuch – and the other writings in The Old Testament. Those writings are also called Tanakh or the Hebrew Bible. Tanakh consists of the Torah (which means teaching), Nevi'im (the writings of the prophets) and Ketuvim (the rest). The writings that we find in The Old Testament in the Christian Bible are not in the same sequence as in the Tanakh, and in some places the verses are numbered differently.[12] One important textbook is the Talmud (which means teaching or transmission), a compendium consisting of history, rules of law, precedence and commentaries. Two editions of Talmud exist. One is from Israel from around 400 CE and one is from Babylon from around 5-600 CE. In addition there is another source of the same sort, which is called Midrasjim or Misjan (which means repetition). This is the oldest writing of Jewish law and is from around 200 CE. Also within Judaism there are different branches and sects following different interpretations of the laws with disagreement as to which writings are to be venerated.

The Old Testament consists of many different types of books. Some may be read as stories about the history of the Jewish people. This may be said of The Five Books of Moses and the books on the prophets. Most of the prophets' books are written at a later date than the time of the prophet mentioned, often after many years of oral transmission, and they may also have been adjusted according to the real events. Quite a lot, but far from everything that has been told as being real historical events, has been documented by archaeological excavations and finds. The Book of Job may be viewed as a story about the fear of God. The Book of Psalms may, as the title indicates, originally have been a collection of psalms, written in honour of God, the author then later said to be David. The Proverbs and the Ecclesiastes (the speaker) are considered to be books of wisdom. Some of the texts in The Old Testament are taken from older writings or histories. Some of the songs in the Book of Psalms are very much like some songs found in an Egyptian tomb – a tomb dedicated the god Aton. Some researchers believe that those songs were written by Pharaoh Akhenaton (about 1350 BCE).[13] Since 1947 many documents from the time of the early Judaism have been discovered in mountain caves nearby Qumran, close to the western shore of the Dead Sea. In Khirbet Qumran several buildings have been excavated dating from the first century BCE, one of which is a big monastery-like building and a pool. Furthermore there are the remains of a defence tower and a forge. Several finds of historic interest have been excavated in the area. Presumably the place was founded around the years 150-100 BCE, and it might have been totally destroyed by the Romans in connection with the Jewish/Roman war that ended in the year 70 CE, although this may not have happened until the third Jewish revolt was brought to an end in the year 135 CE. No one knows for certain who lived in Qumran and who hid the documents in the caves there.[14]

Some documents from Qumran have also been found in the fortress Masada which was conquered by the Romans in the year 73 CE. This fortress is situated further south from Qumran on a steep mountain top at the west side of the Dead Sea. It was fortified by Herod the great. The more warlike part of the Jewish population in the first century were called zealots. It was a group of zealots who committed suicide at Masada (with their families) when they could no longer manage to stand against the Romans. The documents found there show close contact between the zealots and Qumran. This indicates that the Qumran society was not just a peaceful group of people. This is also ascertained by the document found in Qumran which is called the *War Scroll*. Another document, the *Copper Scroll*, has detailed description of buried treasures. It is supposed that those treasures were coming from the temple in Jerusalem, which also indicates close connections between the Qumran society and the temple. Those writings cannot date from less than 68 CE, which is the year of the Roman occupation there. More than 900 fragments of documents have been found, and of these more than 100 are from The Old Testament. Fragments from all the books in The Old Testament have been found, except the Book of Esther. The language is partly Hebrew. Unfortunately, much of the find consists of small bits of pieces which are difficult to put together so as to be readable. But one long scroll of twenty-three feet (about 8 meters) is the whole of the Book of

Isaiah, which is identical to the text we know today. This scroll can be seen on display in the archaeological museum in Jerusalem. The writings are supposed to have been written in the period from about 100 BCE until 68 CE. Before those scrolls were found, the oldest writings in existence from The Old Testament were considered to be from the fourth century CE. During many years, scholars fought over the ownership to the Dead Sea Scrolls and over the right to study them. All the documents were not released for other researchers until 1991. It was École Biblique in Jerusalem, lead by a team of scholars consisting of catholic priests, who kept the documents for themselves. Some people have indicated that the finds could be damaging to the teaching of Christianity.

Israel Finkelstein, (b.1949) professor at the Tel Aviv University, and Neil Asher Silberman, (b.1950) American archaeologist and historian, have in the book *The Bible Unearthed* shown that most of the Bible manuscripts were written during the reign of King Josiah in the seventh century BCE, "based on more than two hundred years of detailed study of the Hebrew text of the Bible and ever more wide-ranging exploration in all the lands between the Nile and the Tigris and Euphrates Rivers. ... At the same time, archaeology has produced a stunning, almost encyclopaedic knowledge of the material conditions, languages, societies, and historical developments of the centuries during which the traditions of ancient Israel gradually crystallized, spanning roughly six hundred years – from about 1000 BCE to 400 BCE."[15] In the year 622 BCE, when Josiah was king of Judah (the eighteenth year of his reign), *The Book of the Law* was found during temple renovations by the High Priest Hilkiah, according to 2 Kings 22. 3-8 . It was then presumed that the book was written by Moses. It is supposed to be the law code now found in Deuteronomy.

The oldest edition of The Old Testament is called the *Septuagint*. This term came about because of the belief that seventy-two Jewish scholars in The Old Testament made a translation from Hebrew to Greek independently of each other. All the translations were equal. However, this story is supposedly made up by a Jew from Alexandria around the year 130 BCE and is found in a document called *Aristea's Letter*. According to Wikipedia's Internet page, the first edition of The Old Testament is considered to have been written in the third century BCE (The Books of Moses) and the rest in the second century BCE. The reason behind Palestine being such a central area for the Jews is that some of the revelations recorded in the Bible, happened there and it is therefore revered as a holy land. However, a Jewish country did not exist between the years when the Romans banished the surviving Jews from Judea in 135 CE, which was the end of the third Jewish revolt, until the modern Jewish state Israel was established in 1948.

A common denominator for the Jews is the language. The revelations were given in the Hebrew language, and this language has since been in use in memory of those. The revelations are the happenings recorded in The Old

Testament, when Yahweh made himself seen by the patriarchs and made them choose the right path (such as the exoduses of Abraham from Chaldea and of Moses from Egypt).

The Jews believe in one god – Yahweh – who created the world and then also the human beings. God is not a person, but someone you relate to. God is an entity of awe-inspiring majesty – a being that is neither amoral nor uninterested. This god chose the people of Israel (the descendants of the patriarch Jacob) as his own people. The people of Israel are supposed to show humanity, goodness and righteous living. They should obey Yahweh, since Yahweh is love.

Because Yahweh is love, suffering has a meaning. Many Jews believe that Yahweh needs a group of people with whom he has a special relationship until the world is finally released – this group is God's warriors in the history of humanity.

Rituals have an important place in Judaism. The function of the rituals is to make life holy. Traditions are also important. So also is the remembrance of the history of the Jews as presented in The Old Testament. Judaism can be said to be a way of life. All the Jewish days of celebration are connected to important historical happenings for the Jews.

Islam

The word Islam is a denotation for the followers of Muhammad – the Muslims – and means to be devoted to or to surrender to. Muhammad Ibn Abd Allah (ca. 570-632CE) was the founder of this religion and is considered to be the prophet of God or his ambassador on Earth. The Quran, which is the holy book of the Muslims, is said to be the true reproduction of Muhammad's religious message. This message is supposed to be the words of God, as taken from Heaven's immemorial text which is with God or Allah, as transmitted through the angel Gabriel. The main prayer for the Muslims is "la ila'ha illa-l-la'h" which means "There is no God except Allah". A Muslim is obliged to follow the five main rules or pillars: to be ritually clean; to say the prayer five times a day at certain hours and a special prayer in a mosque each Friday afternoon; to fast each day from sunrise to sundown in the ninth month called Ramadan; to make a pilgrimage to Mecca and the holy site al-Ka'ba; and to give alms to the poor.

According to the American scholar in the history of religion, Huston Smith (b.1919), the most important theological terms in Islam are almost equal to those of Judaism and Christianity, which are its predecessors.[16] Everything in Islam concerns the most fundamental in religion, God. God is without a body and therefore invisible. The Muslims honour Jesus as a prophet and accept the virgin birth, but draw a line as regards the teaching about incarnation and the Trinity, as they consider that obscures the distinction between the divine and the humane.

Smith stresses that the word Islam also has another connotation, which is peace, and that the fear that Allah inspires is more than outweighed by the love he has for his creatures. The Muslims maintain, however, that the only real feeling in people, who are presented with the awful consequences of being on the wrong side of the uncompromising moral universe, is fear, and therefore the Muslims fear Allah. Smith also explains that Allah created the world on purpose and that the material world therefore is absolutely real. Foremost among the creatures that God created was the human being. Its nature is undisputedly good. There has never been any catastrophic 'fall' because of 'sin'. Even though the basic nature of the human being is goodness, humans forget their divine origin. They deserve respect and a good self image. The human beings have, however, two obligations. The one is to be thankful for the life they have. The other obligation is to surrender – that is to surrender to God. God, the creation, the human ego and doomsday – these are the most important theological pegs in the teaching of the Quran.

2.3. Christianity

The Christian belief

Christianity has its origin in the story we find in The New Testament of the Bible about the life of Jesus, his death and resurrection, and that he was later seen by the disciples and many others several times after his death. Jesus was filled with The Holy Spirit (God's power) when he was baptized by John and he was thereafter called Christ – the anointed one. Those events and what Jesus preached and what he showed through his way of living, are the central themes in Christianity. Jesus spoke about and showed in practice God's love to humanity. The disciples did the same after being filled with The Holy Spirit and having received the talent to prophesy and heal. This was the foundation that made Christendom spread around the Roman Empire.

Some theologians maintain that the origin of Christendom is due to St Paul – his travels around the Mediterranean and what he preached and wrote. The first Christians – the apostles of Jesus – had, however experienced the way Jesus behaved, and they tried to practise and teach this. Among them, the love for fellow man/woman, the society they had in common and the belief in God was the essential. The first Christian society is often called a Jesus movement. It was St Paul who taught that the crucifixion and resurrection were the most important events, and that Jesus died to atone for our sins. This may be called a Pauline theology. Later, the leading theologians – the church fathers – and the church councils have composed the dogmas in force today. The apostolic Christian confession of faith is as follows:

> I believe in God the Father, the almighty creator of the Heavens and Earth.
> I believe in Jesus Christ, God's only begotten son, our Lord, borne by

> the Virgin Mary, tortured under Pontius Pilatus, crucified, died and buried, went up to Heaven, is sitting at the right hand of God the Almighty Father and will from there return to judge the living and the dead.
>
> I believe in The Holy Spirit, in a holy ordinary church, the forgiveness of sins, the resurrection of the body and eternal life.

This can be said to be the basis for the Christian theology, because it was the followers' earliest attempts at a systematic understanding of the events that transformed their lives. The English Benedictine monk, Father Laurence Freeman (b.1951) has explained that God, Jesus and the Holy Spirit (the Trinity) is an expression of the Christian conception of God's nature, as a love connection one experiences in the mystery of the three individuals, who share one nature and in whom all living beings live and move and have their being.[17] Christianity's most important dogma may be the teaching that Christ is God, that is to say that he was not half human and half God, but that he was both fully. It was God who came to Earth and wore a man's body. Jesus' life is thus an image of the perfect man. Jesus' death on the cross freed people from sin. Sin is not to feel companionship with God. When one feels a relationship with God, one wants only good; the love of your fellow creatures will come before love for one's self.

The Roman Catholic Church (the term Catholic signifies general or universal) or the Holy Catholic Apostolic Roman Church claims to administer the correct doctrine. Huston Smith says about the Roman Catholic Church that it requires to be considered as both a teaching authority, as Jesus' teachings must be construed and preserved by the Church, and as sacrament steward. For the church to have absolute power there must be only one interpretation of the many double meanings that the Bible contains. This requires that the Pope is the Church's highest authority, and that everyone must bow to the Pope's interpretations – showing absolute obedience towards the Pope's Chair. Anyone professing the Catholic Christian faith must recognize the Tridentian Creed.[18] The Catholic Church has established seven sacraments (holy actions) that will help people to accept the Church Ordinances and to live properly. They focus on life's major passages. The sacraments are:

- Baptism
- Marriage
- Graduation ceremony
- Initiation of the Ministry
- The last anointment
- Confession
- The Eucharist

The Eucharist is a ritual to commemorate Jesus. (See Matt. 26.26-28 and Mark 14.22-24. Not mentioned in John's Gospel, but referred to by St Paul in 1 Corinthians 11.23-25.) This baptism is said to transfer power and grace from God to the soul, and to participate in the Eucharist should be just as important as eating. The other sacraments transfer grace to human beings. Rudolf Steiner's interpretation of the Eucharist was that this is a ritual that gives people an exoteric (outer) way to a spiritual encounter with Jesus Christ.[19] When you receive the blessed bread and wine, this is the expression that you want to live in fellowship with Christ. In earlier times people knew that spirit could be induced in matter through ritual handlings. Steiner believed that one participated in the spirit of Jesus by eating and drinking that which had been devoted Jesus. When people eat bread, which is grown out of the ground, or drinking juice, or eat plants, then they actually eat the body and blood of Jesus. The plant juices are the Earth's blood, which is the blood of Jesus. It is grown from the Earth, is of the Earth's body, which is the body of Jesus, since he is the spirit of the Earth. Steiner explained that through the Eucharist one is connected to the Earth's spiritual body, which is Christ.

The Greek Catholic Church, which, like the Russian Catholic Church calls itself orthodox, demands acceptance of the Nicene Creed (orthodoxy is a Greek word meaning right belief, strict adoption of the church's teaching, especially in an ecclesiastical society). This church celebrates the same sacraments as the Roman Catholic Church. It also has pretty much the same dogmas, such as the dogma about the Trinity and the teaching that Jesus was both God and man, but does not require the same obedience to certain biblical interpretations. It has no Pope and therefore requires no papal submission, but the Patriarch of Constantinople is the first among equals. This church broke with the Roman Catholic Church in the year 1054 CE. Jes Bertelsen has written that a significant difference between the Eastern and the Western Church is that the Eastern Church places the main weight on the transfiguration of Jesus on the Mount (see Matt chapter 17 – not described in John's Gospel), while the majority of the Western Church places the main weight on the crucifixion and that Jesus died for our sins.[20] That shows that the message of the Eastern Church is more about good news than a message about sin. In addition, the Eastern Church encourages members to mysticism through a contemplative life, to experience the joy of feeling God's presence.

Protestantism sprang out of the Roman Catholic Church in the 16th century, primarily thanks to the German Augustinian-monk Martin Luther's (1483-1546) activity to reform the Catholic Church. During the Reichstag (the German Parliament) of Speyer in 1529 a number of groups protested against the Parliament's attempt to stop the Reformation. From there came the name Protestantism. Huston Smith has suggested that the Reformation was also extensively due to political economy, nationalism, Renaissanceindividualism and dissatisfaction with the clergy. Some of the most important principles of Protestantism are what goes under the term 'justification by faith' and the disregard of idolatry. It is not the rituals that are important, but to set one's mind to love God – only then will we be able to experience the love of God and fulfil the will of God.

What do we know about The New Testament?

The Christian Bible or the Holy Scripture (as it says in my Bible) consists of the canonical books of The Old and The New Testament. That is, those that have been approved by the Papal see and therefore deemed holy and true. The Old Testament has thirty-nine and The New Testament twenty-seven writings. Most researchers believe that only seven of the thirteen epistles attributed to St Paul are genuine. These seven are – the letter to the Romans, letters 1 and 2 to the Corinthians, letters 1 and 2 to the Thessalonians, the letters to the Galatians and Philemon, as well as the letter to the Philippians.

The other epistles are the letter to the Ephesians, the letter to the Colossians, letters 1 and 2 to Timothy and the letter to Titus. The genuine letters are believed to have been written between the years 50 and 56 CE, and are then the oldest scriptures in The New Testament. The oldest known documents, however, are only from the end of the following century. The letter to the Galatians is the oldest scripture which has been found. It is a papyrus designated P-46 and dated to around the year 200 CE.[i] As to the Gospels and Acts of the Apostles (hereafter referred to as Acts), there is greater uncertainty, both of who the authors were, and as to the time when they were written. The oldest known handwritings are from 175-250 CE and are written in Greek. A small fragment of papyrus (6.4 x 8.9 cm) supposed to be from the year 125[21] may be from the Gospel of John, chapter 18, but it contains neither the name of Jesus nor Pilate.[ii] Many believe

---

i. Hermann Detering has in his book *The Falsified Paul: Early Christianity in the Twilight* presented very strong doubts as to who Paul was and suggests that much of what is in the Pauline letters were written by Simon Magus (who called himself the little one – the meaning of the latin name Paul is the little one) and edited by the archheretic, the Christian gnostic Marcion (85-160). See further Freke and Gandy, *Jesusmysteriene* (The Jesus Mysteries), chapter 8 and the footnotes mentioned there. Oskar Skarsaune has considered all of St Paul's letters to have been acknowledged by St Paul. See D*en ukjente Jesus* (The unknown Jesus) p. 128.

ii. In John's Gospel it is stated that it is "the Apostle whom Jesus loved" who wrote the Gospel (21.20-24). Rudolf Steiner argued that this was Lazarus, brother of Martha and Mary, who was called the apostle John in church history. Others have argued that this was the Lazarus believed to be the brother-in-law of Jesus and the brother of Mary Magdalene. Barbara Thiering suggests that the Gospel was written by Jesus himself. Timothy Freke and Peter Gandy have in the book *Jesus and the Lost Goddess – The secret teachings of the original Christians* written that this gospel probably was written by the Gnostic teacher Cerinthus at the end of the first century, but in the name of Mary Magdalene. Because of the church-fathers' phobia regarding women the author's name was modified and some of the text manipulated so it would be warped to fit a male disciple, see e.g. chapters 20 and 21. See also Internet: www:beloveddisciple.org.

that the Gospel of Mark was the first gospel written – in the 80's, and that the Gospel of Matthew then came in the 90's, and finally John's Gospel closer to the turn of the century. The Gospel of Luke and Acts, which many suppose were written by the same person, came in the second century. Luke cannot have been a disciple of Jesus, and he writes in the introduction to his Gospel that he has noted down what he has heard. He may have been the person who according to Acts, travelled with St Paul to Rome, a journey which assumingly took place around the year 60, though this is doubtful.[i]

One question is how the disciples, all or most of who must have been illiterate, have been able to remember and convey verbatim what Jesus said and preached. This must have then been told to others who also had to remember everything verbatim, and that was then written down at least fifty years after the time of Jesus. Today we know that many changes were made in all biblical scriptures by later scribes, as well as in citations, but we do not know the exact changes. Religion historian Professor Bart D. Ehrman (b.1955), PhD, University of North Carolina, has documented that many of the changes which we find in the Gospels have been made over time.[22] He has pointed out errors in writing that have been found in all later manuscripts after the first error; He has demonstrated deliberate changes made for the story to fit with the copyist's view, and he has pointed to directly opposite views in two otherwise identical manuscripts which have been found. Not least are the contradictions between much of what St Paul was writing about himself and the stories presented in Acts. Robert Eisenman, professor of religion at California State University, has pointed out that neither the Gospels nor Acts can have been written by Jews, because those writings show antagonism against the Jews, and they describe the situation of the Jews as seen from the outside. Among other things, he has mentioned that there are several places where it is maintained that the Jews killed their prophets, which they have never done (see Matt. 23.31 f., Acts 7.52 and Thess. 2.15).[23]

It is interesting to note that St Paul's letters are the oldest sources we have about Jesus (if not the letter of James, which some claim is older). St Paul does not write about the life of Jesus, but only of his death, the resurrection and the Holy Spirit. The four Gospels were written at least fifty years after the time of Jesus and seek to see him in a human perspective, but they do not always match. The Gospel of John is very different from the three other gospels. Acts has a few stories about the apostles and a lot more about Paul's travels, but nothing about the life of Jesus.

The word *apocryphal* means secret, hidden or disguised. The apocryphal gospels are writings which describe the life of Jesus and the apostles, but

---

i. Josephus describes in his biography a journey he undertook to Rome in the year 62 CE, which is almost identical to the story in Acts about the journey of Paul to Rome. Both journeys are said to have taken place around the year 62.

they are not accepted as part of the authorized Bible or canon. Many of these writings were central among the Gnostic-Christians. The oldest of those writings were written late in the second century. They were partly rejected and later on also condemned by the Orthodox Church as being against the right teaching, – that is teaching as designed by the church fathers. In 1945 key findings were made near Nag Hammadi, not far from Luxor in Upper Egypt. These findings turned out to consist of a total of fifty-two Gnostic writings, among them some writings that had been condemned by the Pope's Chair. In the past, some of these writings had been known of through letters and comments from believing Christians, especially through the condemnations from Bishop Irenaeus of Lyons as recorded in his book *Against Heretics* (Adversus Haereses) written in the years 180-185. The commentaries and the condemnations are preserved, but the original works that were criticized, were largely unknown until they were found at Nag Hammadi. The writings are interesting, especially the ones that give the impression of being Gospels, such as the Gospel of Thomas.

The papyrus on which these writings are written are dated to around 350-400, but the lyrics are believed to stem from the years 120-150. Some researchers have suggested that the Gospel of Thomas is from the first century, and perhaps earlier than the accepted Gospels (i.e. from around the year 50). Among the writings found at Nag Hammadi are the Gospel of Thomas, the Gospel of Philip, the Gospel of Truth, the Gospel of the Egyptians, the Secret Book of James, the Apocalypse of Paul, St Paul's letter to Philip and the Apocalypse of Peter. Who has written these and when they were written, is uncertain.[24] The Gospel of Mary Magdalene was found at the end of the nineteenth century. At the end of the twentieth century the Gospel of Judas was found in Egypt.

The word *gnosis* means knowledge or insight. According to a Gnostic teacher, Theodotus (c. 150 CE), a Gnostic is one that understands who we are, what we have been, where we have been and where we are going, what we will be released from, what birth is and what rebirth is. Knowing oneself is basically to know God. This can be said to be the view of the mystic. It should be noted, however, that many Gnostics had a special perception of the world's creation, which, inter alia, the great mystic-philosopher from the third century, Plotinus (205-270 CE) strongly rejected.[25] These argued that the creator of the Cosmos, called the Demiurge, was similar to the Jewish God Yahweh. The Demiurge was separated from his mother, Sophia (wisdom); therefore both the creator and the Cosmos were subject to evil. But the creator also had to have a creator, and that was the true God. It seems that the Gnostics' world view is part of the explanation regarding the strong resistance they faced in certain philosophical and Christian circles. The Christian Gnostics, who considered St Paul as the great teacher and who can be said to have a philosophy that is a mixture of Judaism and ancient mystery traditions, did not recognize Jesus as a son of God, who was crucified and resurrected from the dead. They were therefore considered heretics by the church fathers.[i]

In the nineteenth century a document, in Hebrew, was found in Cairo, which has become known as the Damascus document. Fragments of this have also been found in Qumran. This document has, besides many rules for the society, also a mention of a Teacher of Righteousness who took his companions who were faithful to the law into the wilderness to a place that was called Damascus. There they entered into a Covenant with God. This Pact is also discussed in other Qumran documents, including The Society's Rule. Researchers discuss why people there have used the term Damascus on a society which seems to be a Qumran community. Many of the rules in the Damascus document correspond to the rules of the Qumran-community, which is found in other documents. The authors of the book *The Dead Sea Scrolls Deception*, Michael Baigent and Richard Leigh, ask the question whether or not the term Damascus in Acts really is aiming at the Qumran community. So does also the Australian Bible researcher Barbara Thiering. They are, inter alia, pointing out that Paul would hardly have been allowed by the Romans to travel to Damascus in Syria to pursue different-thinking Jews there.

Another document, the Habakkuk-commentary, describes a controversy within the Qumran community, which at closest can be seen as a religious struggle. A person who is presented as the Liar has broken the Covenant, and there is a conflict between him and the Teacher of Righteousness. Another person, who is referred to as the Evil Priest, is also an opponent of the Qumran community. Many scholars are of the opinion that this struggle refers to the period of the Maccabees (164-63 BCE). In this connection it should be noted that many of the verses in the Habakkuk-commentary refer to the problems with the Kittims. The term Kittim is supposed, by most scholars, to mean the Romans, and they did not arrive in Palestine until 67 BCE. Baigent and Leigh are asking whether the Teacher of Righteousness might be Jesus (and later his brother James), and whether the Liar might be St Paul. In that case, Jesus must have had little to do with the religion that St Paul taught, or with the person St Paul described as Jesus. Something of the same has been suggested by Barbara Thiering. Robert Eisenman is of the opinion that the Teacher of Righteousness was James (i.e. the Lord's brother – which is the designation we find in St Paul's letters), not Jesus; and that the Evil Priest was the high priest in Jerusalem. He has, inter alia, pointed to St Paul's resistance to the Jewish practice of circumcision (see the controversy within the Jesus-congregation which St Paul has described in the letter to the Galatians, first chapters); St Paul's underlining that men

---

i. Timothy Freke and Peter Gandy have in the book *Jesus and the Lost Goddess* provided a detailed account of the philosophy of the Mystics which they call the Christian gnostics – those that relate to the inner Christ (Christ in you) and not an outer personality. In the book *The Laughing Jesus – Religious Lies and Gnostic Wisdom*, they have elaborated this further.

are justified by faith, not by works of the law (see, inter alia, Rom 3.28); as well as St Paul's arguments that he is not lying (Rom 3.7 and 9.1). Eisenman also mentions St Paul's many attacks on the Jewish dietary rules and other rules of life.

In 1993 a book with the title *The Lost Gospel – The Book of Q and Christian Origins* was published, the author was Burton L. Mack, professor in The New Testament at the School of Theology, Claremont, USA. He presents here the results that a number of theological scholars have found after ten years of scrutiny of similarities and differences in the four accepted Gospels. They have found approximately 225 verses that are equal in the Gospels of Matthew and Luke, and they assumed at first that these two were built on two common sources, namely the Gospel of Mark as well as a collection of Jesus' words, but then they discovered that Matthew and Luke had content that was not found in Mark. Eventually they came up with the theory that there exists a common source – in German *Quelle* (Q) – which they considered to be the basis for the three synoptic Gospels. (The word *synoptic* – meaning vision – is used to indicate that they have used mainly the same source.) This source consisted of Jesus-words and said nothing about the historical Jesus. Q is believed to have had three layers, or contained three different types of statements. The first and oldest created layer Mack calls aphoristic material, the next layer consists of prophetic statements, and the third layer has more mythological content. Statements in the first layer, said Mack, "proclaim practical ethics that was widely known as cynicism". He says that there is a long way for the imagination to go from the first layer of Q to John's Gospel during the short time that lay between them. The myth that the people behind the Gospels created, can only be called fantastic. Mack says, inter alia, that it was St Paul who created the Christian theology, as St Paul focuses on Jesus' death as a saving event and on Jesus' resurrection to cosmic dominion. St Paul uses the term Christ about the person who was crucified and who arose from the dead. By using the term Christ, St Paul created a congregation of Christ and not a Jesus movement. Professor of Church history at the Norwegian School of theology (MF) in Oslo, Oskar Skarsaune (b. 1946), however, disagrees with Mack's conclusion about Q. Skarsaune points out, inter alia, the puzzling fact that one cannot find a trace of this old Gospel in other writings among the huge amount of handwritten material we have. In addition, Matthew and Luke have special sentences which exist only in one or other of these Gospels, and sometimes also stories that are in Mark, but with important differences.[26]

It has often been said that the Bible is the word of God given directly to humanity. But how can that be maintained when the different Gospels are telling the same story differently? Such a statement can also be difficult to accept from what we currently know about The New Testament's conception. However, if you expect that nothing occurs at random, it is easier to accept the claim. Then any editorial change would be done for a particular purpose, whether the change was made, for example, in an English language edition or only in the latest Norwegian. Then it is the same consciousness that lies behind the selection of writings that are included in The Old and in The New Testament. Then it is perhaps the same consciousness that is now in our time causing us to find documents confirming the age of some Biblical texts, and which also gives us the Gnostic writings which were only known from negative reviews before. Perhaps we in the Western World are now ready for – and have knowledge enough – to receive more information about a spiritual world; yes to go one step further in the spiritual evolution that Rudolf Steiner and Martinus suggested would come.

The question of how the Bible was actually disclosed is one issue. Another issue is how ordinary people should read the Bible. Then you have to remember that the Biblical texts originally were written in languages other than the reader uses today – and often the term originally used may have had several meanings. The translators have therefore a problem of finding the true meaning of the words written. An example of this is the interpretation of The Lord's Prayer, which is discussed here in the chapter on prayer. Moreover, copyists of a biblical text may have written in personal opinions that differ from the true story that should be described. We can also interpret the Bible texts using a variety of ways: either with literal interpretation, moral interpretation, parallel interpretation, typological interpretation, metaphorically-allegorical interpretation, tropological or figurative interpretation, or anagogic interpretation (mystic, spiritual, or encouraging).

The biblical description of the person Jesus shows us a person who is the best inspiration we can have. The Bible also contains many words of wisdom, and it can therefore be read for encouragement and contemplation. But everyone must interpret it according to his own background and experiences considering that most of it was written for another culture and another time. No single interpretation can be the correct one. All of Jesus' parables are what they say to be, namely parables. And a parable has to be interpreted. Then there seems to be a good starting point to listen to the stories with your heart and try to understand the wisdom in them. Though perhaps one might as well drop the reading of the Bible altogether and instead say the same as Master Eckhart[27]: "To be emptied of everything is to be filled by God, and to be filled with the created is to be devoid of God."

Jesus

Christianity is considered a monotheistic religion (there is only one God), but at the same time the dogma is emphasizing that Jesus is God's son, see for example: John 10.30: *"I and the Father are one"*; John 1.34: *"I've seen it, and I have testified: he is the Son of God"*, and John 1.36: *"Behold, the Lamb of God."*

> Just think how these first words (in John's Gospel: *"In the beginning was the Word and the Word was with God and the Word was God"*) do not permit any other explanation than that in Jesus of Nazareth, who lived at the beginning of our time-reckoning, was an incarnated individual of a Supreme spiritual art. *Rudolf Steiner*[28]

The person Jesus is thus the centre of Christianity. Was he only a high-ranking spiritual person or was he also an incarnated deity?[i] The Muslims accept Jesus as a prophet, but not as God's son. The Gnostics rejected the idea of Jesus as deity, and they were later thrown out of the Christian Church community.[29] At the Synod of Nicaea in 325, it was determined as the right doctrine "that Jesus Christ was the true God, the same being as the Father."[30] But at the same time it was pointed out that he was an independent person. At the Synod of Chalcedon in 451, it was decided that Jesus Christ was true man and true God – as it is said in John 14.9: *"Whoever has seen me has seen the Father."* That is construed as if Jesus Christ was the true revelation of the Father – that is God. The Augsburg Confession says this (see Article III):

> The Word, that is God's son, took upon himself human nature ... therefore he has two natures, one divine and the other human. They are united in one person and cannot be separated.

According to The New Testament Jesus was born during the life of Herod the great and while Quirinius was the supreme Roman commander in Syria (see Matt 2.1 and Luke 2.2). It is assumed that Herod died in 4 BCE. There would have been a Roman army led by a general with the name Quirinius in Syria about 7 BCE. In order to clarify whether the myth of Bethlehem had some basis in reality, astronomers have noted that the planets Jupiter and Saturn had three conjunctions (close positions) in the star constellation Pisces in year 7 BCE. Many believe that the constellation Pisces also was the star and the constellation of the coming Messiah. A fish was later also used as a symbol for the Christians. It was further thought that Jupiter was a star for luck and a royal star, while Saturn was Israel's and the surrounding countries' star.[31] According to the astrological division of the sky, the Sun's position at the vernal equinox moved into the constellation Pisces just before the turn of this millennium.

The Gospel of Matthew tells us that Jesus' father was Joseph, son of Jacob, and that Jacob's family line goes back to David's son Solomon (Matt 1st chapter). Luke, however, says that Jesus' father was Joseph who was the son of Eli and that Eli's family goes back to David's son Nathan (Luke 3.23 f.). One can marvel over the difference and why this is explained if

---

i. Tertullian (160-220 CE) – who in the year 207 went over to Montanism (a form of Gnosticism) – wrote before this that he believed in the story of Jesus because the story was absurd.

Jesus is supposed to be the son of God and not by any other earthly human than Mary.

Professor of theology at the University of Oslo, Ragnar Leivestad (1916-2002) has confirmed that we do not know much about the historical Jesus.[32] St Paul's letters are the earliest writings we have where the name Jesus Christ has been found, but St Paul has no mention of a life or of actions of a person by that name. He never met Jesus. But he writes in his letter about Christ and his crucifixion, death and resurrection, and later emergence. He mentions the contacts he has had with "James, the Lord's brother" (Gal 1.19). Apart from the Bible and the apocryphal gospels, we have only four other reports to relate to. These are given by the historians Josephus, Suetonius and Tacitus and the Roman governor Pliny. However, all those reports are dubious as they have come down to us only thanks to Christian copyists.[i]

Josephus (37-c.100) was a Jewish author who wrote about the Jews' ancient history (published 93/94) and of the Jewish war against the Romans in the years from 66 to 73 (published 77/78). In the former work as we have it today Jesus is mentioned as a sage who was crucified by Pilate, and emerged three days after the crucifixion. Josephus also reports that John the Baptist was executed by Herod, and that Jesus' brother James was accused of transgressing the Law and was convicted to be stoned.[33] Robert Eisenman believes, however, that the sentence about Jesus was added in retrospect. The same is written by Timothy Freke and Peter Gandy in the book *The Jesus Mysteries - was the original Jesus a Pagan God?*[34] These statements of Josephus surfaced first in an edition of the fourth century, referred to by Bishop Eusebios, the first church historian. Oskar Skarsaune writes, however, that a growing number of scientists agree that the text is authentic.[35]

The Roman historian Tacitus (55-117) has written about the pursuit of Christians, which would have taken place in the year 64 under Emperor Nero. Nero attempted to place the blame for the fire in Rome on the Christians. Tacitus wrote that the founder of this sect was Christ (Chrestus), and that he had been executed by Pontius Pilate, who was procurator in Judea in Tiberius' imperial times.[36] (Pilate was not procurator, but the prefect of Judea from 26 to 36 CE.)

The Roman Governor in Asia Minor, Pliny wrote about the year 110 a letter to Emperor Trajan and asked what he should do with Christians who were singing praises to Christ as to a God. His report has not been found in the Roman archives, but has come down to us from Tertullian.

The Roman historian Suetonius (c. 69-130) also mentions the persecution of the Christians in the year 64. He wrote that under Emperor Claudius (emperor 41-54) the Jews were exiled from Rome for a time. This is believed

---

i. For further information see my book *Jesushistorien – Myte eller virkelighet?* (The Jesus story – Facts or fiction?), Kolofon Forlag AS 2011. ISBN 978-82-300-0873-7.

to have happened in the year 49-50, see Acts 18.2. Suetonius tells us that the expulsion was due to the Christians in Rome rebelling at the instigation of a Chresto (please note that Jesus should have been dead at this time). Umberto M. Fasola, who wrote about Peter's and Paul's stay in Rome, finds it odd that the name Chresto which Suetonius has used should not be referring to Jesus Christ.[37] The name Chrestus or Chresto also occurs in other documents from that time, according to him. However, this designation was supposedly a common name. It can mean the noble one or the good one. Josephus used the word about the Jewish King Agrippa I (died 44 CE).

Josephus tells of a conflict between the Samaritans and the Jews at the time when Cumanus was the Judean procurator (48-52). Then delegations, both from the Samaritans and from the Jews, came to Emperor Claudius in Rome. The Jews were allowed to return home, while the Samaritans and Cumanus were given a more unpleasant fate. Was it this story that Suetonius had heard about, but changed slightly? For a person in Rome, it was hardly easy to know the difference between the Samaritans and the Jews, both groups saw themselves as Israelites.

Another explanation could be the story that Justin Martyr (85-160) reported, and which applies to Simon Magus. Simon Magus was in Rome during Emperor Claudius' time and taught there. He was celebrated as a God (or maybe a Messiah or a Christ) by his followers. He, according to reports, declared himself to be the Christ, the Anointed One. Simon Magus was considered a great wisdom teacher by many at this time, but he had a philosophy that was contrary to the orthodox Jewish faith. It was probably he who was the cause of riots among the Israelites in Rome. Acts 8.9 f., see also Acts 13.8 f., tell a remarkable story of a Simon who performed magic. There is every reason to believe that this was Simon Magus.

The Jewish philosopher and author Philo (c. 10 BCE-45 CE), who lived in Alexandria, does not mention any person by the name of Jesus, in spite of describing the Essene society and having visited Jerusalem.

Jesus is the Greek form of the Hebrew name Joshua. This was a common name among Jews at the time. The name Joshua means king or saviour, and derives from Joshua who conquered Canaan for the Jews after Moses' death. The name was probably pronounced Jeshua in Hebrew.[38] The word salvation in Hebrew is yesha. The Hebrew word Messiah is the same as the Greek word Christ and means the anointed one. In old Jewish writings this designation was applied to the person who would liberate Israel from the occupying powers.

Most people assume that Jesus was crucified in 30 CE, approximately one year after the baptism in the river Jordan, which was performed by John the Baptist. According to Luke 3.1 the baptism of Jesus took place in the 15th year of the Emperor Tiberius' reign, which is the year 29. Luke writes that at that time Pontius Pilate was Governor of Judea (26-37), the tetrarch

Herod ruled in Galilee (until the year 39), his brother Philip (who died in the year 34) was the tetrarch in Traconities, and Lysanias was the tetrarch in Abilene (unknown time). Annas (between the years 6 and 15) and Caiaphas (until the year 37) were the high priests.[i] It is stated that Jesus was about thirty years old when this happened. But if he was born in the year 7 BCE, he must have been 37 years at the time of the crucifixion if that took place in the year 30. John the Baptist was killed by the tetrarch Herod (Herod Antipas) before Jesus was crucified (see Luke 9.7). However, it was only after John was thrown into prison that Jesus began to preach according to Mark 1.14. Matt 11.2 tells us that John heard of Jesus' preaching when he was in jail, and John is believed to have been killed around the year 36/37. Josephus recounts the execution of John just before he mentions that Emperor Tiberius was dead (that happened in the year 37) and after he mentions that the tetrarch Philip was dead. That John was beheaded by Herod Antipas is also stated by Matt 14.3, Mark 6.17 and Luke 9.9.

Crucifixion was a common method of capital punishment in Jesus' time. Josephus tells us that the Romans once crucified 7000 Jews on the same day as a result of riots (the figure is perhaps somewhat exaggerated). This method of execution was only used for people who were not Roman citizens, and who set themselves up against the Romans. One can ask why Jesus was crucified by the Romans if he was not regarded as a rebel against the Roman Empire. Timothy Freke and Peter Gandy write that there is no image found of the crucified Jesus in the catacombs of Rome older than from the fifth century. They suggest that the Roman mystery tradition which each year celebrated the god Attis' resurrection with a procession, in which the deity was carried tied to a tree, can be behind the story of the crucifixion of the god Jesus. Joseph Campbell has pointed out the similarity between the hero figures, as presented in the myths and stories from around the world.[39] He wrote that yesterday's hero will be tomorrow's tyrant, unless he is crucifying himself today. Here we recall the story of Odin, as presented in Hávamál:[40]

> I know that I hang
> on a windy tree
> nights nine,
> wounded by spear –
> given to Odin,
> self to myself –
> on the tree,
> no one knows
> where the roots grow.
>
> No bread was brought to me,
> Neither a drink
> Down I stared
> until runes I saw,
> Took them shouting
> and dropped from there.

We do not know the origin of these verses. Some scientists believe they have to be from the time before the coming of Christianity in Scandinavia.

---

i. The years stated here are not found in Luke's Gospel.

Timothy Freke and Peter Gandy have in the book *The Jesus Mysteries* made a thorough comparison of the stories about Jesus with other stories from antiquity. They have become convinced that what we read in the Bible about Jesus are not biographies but histories based on ancient mystery religions. They believe to be able to prove that there has not been any historical person named Jesus who grew up in Nazareth, and that the stories we have heard about this person's life is completely parallel with the myths and stories about other pagan divinities such as the Egyptian Osiris, the Greek Dionysus, the Roman Bacchus, the Syrian Adonis or the Persian Mithras, which all were divine, born of virgins, killed and re-emerged from the dead, and their sacrifice promised people eternal salvation.

Freke and Gandy compare the other stories in The New Testament with similar stories originating from different mystery traditions, or written about famous philosophers and mystics from antiquity – such as Pythagoras (580-500 BCE), Empedocles (490-430 BCE) and Plato (427-347 BCE), and have found many similarities. For example, Jesus selected twelve apostles, but it is unclear who these were. The number 12, however, can be seen in many connections. There are 12 signs of the Zodiac, 12 months a year, Hercules performed 12 labours, Plato mentions the 12 holy fixed elements, Israel has 12 tribes, etc. In esoteric circles the number twelve plus one has a special effect. Twelve people gathered under the leadership of a thirteenth meditating together, is said to create a very special atmosphere. It gives a concentrated energy, which can help those present in the practices of the mystics. The number twelve with an extra one as leader has been an important symbol since Pythagoras' time. It can be represented as twelve equal circles around a thirteenth of the same size, so that all of the outer circumferences touch each other's centre as well as the periphery of the inner circle.

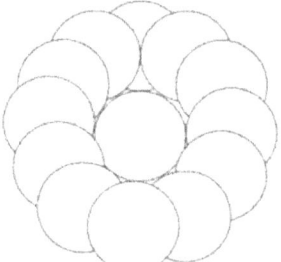

The Symbol for 13

The fish is a symbol that has been central to indigenous Christianity. According to John 21.11 Simon Peter received 153 fish in a net – a peculiar number. It is odd that this has been so important that it is mentioned in the Gospel, unless it had a specific meaning. This number is part of a powerful symbol of the ancient sacred geometry, attributed to Archimedes, and known as 'the fish's measure'. This symbol represents the sacred marriage of spirit and matter, and consists of two identical circles partly overlapping as part of the circumferences touch each other's centre. The shape of the overlapping area can look like a fish. The relationship between the height and length of this section is 153: 265. The word fish in Greek – *icthys* – had for many centuries been the name of Adonis in the Syrian mysteries, but was then used by the Christians as a symbol for Jesus. In the book *The Jesus Mysteries* many such strange coincidences have been pointed out – if we can call them that.[i]

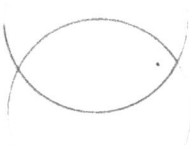

The Symbol of the fish

The authors of *The Jesus Mysteries* believe that most of what St Paul wrote in his genuine letters can be read as a mystic's inaugural report, and that his inaugural experience and the way of the mystics are what he was seeking to convey to the various churches he wrote to. These churches were located in cities that in his time were centres of mystery traditions. Moreover, Antioch, which seems to have been his main place of living, was a centre for the worship of Adonis; and his possible birthplace, Tarsus, was the original place for the worship of Mithras. Bethlehem was a sacred place dedicated to the God Adonis. The Gnostics may have perceived his epistles as a teaching on two planes at the same time. Those who were initiated understood the symbolic meaning in the letters, which they believed was St Paul's intent. The word Christ can be understood as the higher consciousness of the individual human being – the precious part of a human being or the human spirit. The term 'the Lord's brother' can have been added later by a copyist.

Barbara E. Thiering, PhD, (b.1930) has published several books about Jesus.[41] She is an Australian theologian with the old Hebrew language as speciality. She has argued that The New Testament must be interpreted according to a special code, and that the Gospels then show a completely different story than what has been told so far. She has evidently in-depth knowledge of the Dead Sea Scrolls, but she is not in compliance with other researchers in her interpretation of the relation between the Essene community and the rest of the Jewish community in Israel at the time, or how the Gospels are to be understood. In her books she presents the theory that Jesus was a

---

i. The number 153 is special also in other ways. It is the sum of all numbers from 1 to 17. Moreover, it is the sum of the third power of each of the numbers, as follows: $1^3 + 5^3 + 3^3$.

member of the Essene community. She believes that he was one of the leaders of this community, but a person who represented another teaching than the current one. He was, therefore, the leader of a faction that was opposed to the establishment. His message was essentially such as it is presented in the Gospels, but she believes that the description of the historical Jesus must be read in a completely different way from the traditional. Her most significant claim is that she believes Jesus' crucifixion took place within the Essene community, and that he survived. According to Thiering, he lived for many years after the crucifixion, founded a family with Mary Magdalene, came to Rome and died later than Peter and Paul. Everything that has been written about his re-emerging from the dead after the crucifixion, she relates to the fact that it was the physical Jesus who later met various groups of followers.[i] The foundation of Christianity fails if Barbara Thiering is right.

Jesus' early life as told in the Gospels, is virtually identical to the life story of the Tibetan Lama Garab Dorje who probably lived in the 6th century CE.[42] Also his birth was prefigured by a being of light according to the storytellers. He is said to have been born by a virgin, was exposed as a small child, appeared as a child with wisdom in the adult scholar's gatherings, performed miracles, was founder of a new spiritual movement, and was at his death turned into light. Being born without an earthly father was also repeatedly declared by the kings of antiquity to show that they were of divine lineage. Flavius Philostratos (170-245) has written a story about the life of Apollonios from Tyana. Apollonios was a person who lived around the time of Jesus, and of whom many of the same stories were told as those we hear about Jesus. However, some believe that his story was created by order of the Roman Empress Julia Domna (Empress in 193-211) in order to weaken the stories in circulation about the divinity of Jesus Christ.

Some of the wonders attributed to Jesus according to the Gospels are pretty unlikely, though wonders have occurred throughout the ages. Robert Eisenman has compared those stories with historical facts from that time, and with other documents from the first and second century, including the Dead Sea Scrolls and other ancient Jewish writings.[43] He thinks he is able to prove that it is something other than wonders attributed to a person by the name of Jesus, or the story of the first Jesus movement, that the Gospels and Acts are reporting.

He writes that these tales are similar to the apocryphal Gospels and must be considered more like fairytales partially built over well-known names (distorted) and historical events. For example, the entire chapter 10 of

---

i. Henry Lincoln (b. 1930 in London), Michael Baigent (b. 1948 in New Zealand) and Richard Leigh (USA) have in the book *The Holy Blood and The Holy Grail* indicated the same. It is also maintained by others, as in the book published in Norway with the title *Jesus døde ikke på korset* (Jesus did not die at the Cross) by Svein Woje and Kari Klepp, as well as the book by Laurence Gardner: *Bloodline of the Holy Grail*. See also Baigent and Leigh, *The Dead Sea Scrolls Deception*. However, both Oskar Skarsaune and Robert Eisenman are rejecting these theories.

Acts concerns the history of Cornelius – who is described as a God-fearing Roman leader of the Italic army-division in Caesarea. However, in Josephus, you can read about the Roman legionnaires' brutality prior to the revolt that led to the destruction of the Temple in Jerusalem in the year 70. Pontius Pilate was in the year 36 ordered home from Palestine because of excessive brutality. Is it likely that a Roman centurion was a God-fearing supporter of the new religion in Palestine? At the end of the century, the Romans introduced a law that forbade circumcision. This law was called Lex Cornelia de Sicarius. Josephus also mentions a messenger named Cornelius, sent to Rome from Palestine. Is that how the name came in to use in the Gospels?

Who was Judas Iscariot, Simon Iscariot's son (John 6.71)? Was he one of the foremost disciples, as the Gospel of Judas may indicate? Robert Eisenman thinks that the name can be linked with the word *sicarios* which Josephus uses on the dominant conservative party at the end of the first century. The term came in use because the members wore a dagger, which resembled the Roman *sica*. One of the companions of Jesus used a sword (Matt 26.51, Mark 14.47, and Luke 22.50). According to John 18.10 this was Simon Peter. The disciples were thus not without weapons, who returned evil with good![i]

According to St Paul, Christ died for our sins (1 Cor. 15.3). There was a strong Greek, not Jewish tradition, to praise an honourable death, and this comment in St Paul's letter may aim at such a tradition.[44] The Indian yogi Paramahansa Yogananda (1893-1952)[ii] tells in his autobiography that his own guru Sri Yukteswar explained (from the astral plane) that some major spirits can choose to come back to Earth to help people's spiritual

---

i. Jesus' disciple Simon (Luke 6.15 and Acts 1.13) is in King James' Bible termed Simon the Zealot (Zelotes). In Matt 10.4 and Mark 3.18 he is termed Simon the Canaanite. According to Acts 21.20 "they are all zealous of the law." The Jews who held stand against the Romans in the fortress of Masada until the year 73 CE were called zealots. Were some of the disciples of Jesus revolutionary?

ii. Paramahansa Yogananda lived in USA from 1920. In 1914 he became a member of the monastic order, the Swami Order (the word *swami* means *one who is at one with its own Self*) and he then received the name Yogananda. The word *ananda* means blessing, as the word *yoga* means to unite with the divine (I/262). I 1935 he was given the title *paramahansa*. He is considered as a *premavatar* or a love incarnation. In very young age Yogananda became a disciple of Swami Sri Yukteswar Giri (1855-1936) who lived near Calcutta. He is considered an *inanavatar* or a wisdom incarnation. (Yukteswar means *one with God*.) Giri is a branch of the Swami Order. (The word *giri* means hill/moutain. *Sri* means holy and is a title of honour. (I/133)) Sri Yukteswar was the disciple of Lahiri Mahasaya from Benares (1828-1895), who is called a *yogavatar* or a yogi incarnation. Lahiri Mahasaya (*mahasaya* means generous (II/63)) was the disciple of Babaji, who is called a *mahavatar* or a divinity incarnation, whom Yogananda calls modern India's great Yogi-Christ. It is told that he has lived through many centuries and is still living (?) in the Himalayas. Yogananda explains that a swami actually is a monk due to his membership in the Swami Order, and that anyone who is practicing a scientific technique in order to obtain a divine experience is a yogi. This technique was firstly mapped out by the old Rishis in India and later thoroughly tried out later by holy persons. In the USA Yogananda founded the organization the *Self-Realization Fellowship*. This organization is aiming at spreading knowledge about specific scientific methods leading to direct personal experience of God development. They can also choose to take on another person's karma burden. The Bulgarian mystic and teacher Omraam Mikhael Aivanhov (1900-1986), who worked in France, has said the same.[i]

Martinus has also commented on the question of whether Jesus died for our sins.[45] He explained that Jesus with the words that "our sins are forgiven" should only give the listener peace of mind. He could not exempt people from the consequences of their sins, because these consequences are one of 'the eternal Life's principles'. Martinus said that the greatest part of Jesus' deeds was not to give forgiveness of sins, but to declare and clarify the highest wisdom in the form of warnings against improper ways of life. St Paul wrote in 1Corinthians about the emergence of Jesus after the crucifixion (15.3-9; see also verses 12 and 32):

> For what I received I passed on to you as of first importance: that Christ died for our sins according to the Scriptures, that he was buried, that he was raised on the third day according to the Scriptures, and that he appeared to Cephas, and then to the Twelve. After that, he appeared to more than five hundred of the brothers and sisters at the same time, most of whom are still living, though some have fallen asleep. Then he appeared to James, then to all the apostles, and last of all he appeared to me also, as to one abnormally born. For I am the least of the apostles and do not even deserve to be called an apostle, because I persecuted the church of God.

According to Matt 28.9 Jesus showed himself first to Mary Magdalene and "*another Mary*", and then for eleven disciples in Galilee. According to Mark 16.9 Jesus showed himself first to Mary Magdalene, then for "*the two of them, while they walked out of the country*", and finally for the eleven.[ii] According to Luke 24.13 and 18 Jesus showed himself first to Cleopas and another one on the road to Emmaus, secondly, for those two plus the eleven. And according to John 20.14 Jesus showed himself first for Mary Magdalene, secondly for all the disciples except Thomas (verses 19 and 24), and then for all (number unspecified), and finally a third time for seven of the disciples (chapter 21). This is not consistent with St Paul.

Rudolf Steiner has a comprehensive explanation of Jesus' life, based on the idea that Jesus was the reincarnation of Zarathustra (Zoroaster). Zoroaster was

---

i. Omraam Mikhael Aivanhov (from hereon called only Aivanhov) lived and taught in France from 1937 and the rest of his life. He was a pupil of the Bulgarian mystic Peter Deunov who was the founder of the organization *The Brotherhood of Light*. Aivanhov's philosphy seems to be very close to that of Yogananda and other Indian yogis. Although Aivanhov did not come in contact with India until late in life, he had done thorough studies and knew most of the religious directions. Many books have been published about his life and teaching (but he did not write any himself).

ii. The oldest known editions of the Gospel of Mark are ending with verse 8 in chapter 16 (see *The Jesus Mysteries* p. 72). The verses 1-8 state only that it was Mary Magdalene, James' mother Mary and Salome who first saw the empty tomb. There is nothing there about the resurrection. What is written about the resurrection is added later. It should be noted that the Gospel of Mark is supposed to be the Gospel first written.

a prominent spiritual teacher in the ancient Persian culture who founded Zoroastrism. Steiner saw this incarnation as an important part of the Earth's and humanity's development – a cosmic event. Steiner believed that one of the most important moments in Earth's history was the moment when Jesus' blood flowed down to the earth during the crucifixion. That was a spiritual event. From then on the Earth was transformed; it was the Earth's initiation process.

Rudolf Steiner claimed that Mary Magdalene had a clear-sighted ability, because the Bible says that she saw two Angels – two spiritual figures – sitting in the grave (John 20.12). Steiner maintained that this was the astral body and the etheric body, both of which are in and around the physical body, and which slowly are freed to go over to the etheric World. When Mary then saw Jesus, she knew him not. Nor did the disciples recognize Jesus when he showed himself to them (John 21.4). This Steiner took as evidence that it was not the physical body they saw, but the spiritual one. If Jesus had been in his physical form, it would hardly be difficult to recognize him. But the disciples had to use something other than the outer vision, namely an inner psychic ability. Steiner wrote about the resurrection that it is correct that which is written in Matt 28.20: *"... I'm with you all days, until the end of the world."* He said that the people who have developed the right spiritual powers will be able to see Jesus when he returns, although that will not be in carnate form.[46]

Yogananda recounted meetings with deceased gurus where the gurus were seen in the physical shape they had during their last life on Earth.[47] He explained that to materialize the atoms of a physical form cannot be difficult for one who is united with God, and he refers to John 10.18: *"I have the power to give my life and the power to take it back again."*

Aivanhov explained that some advanced souls want to continue the spiritual work they were engaged in when they were in a physical body.[48] They can then return to Earth of their own free determination and take (it might be more appropriate to say occupy) a spiritual advanced physical person without reincarnating as a new body. This can happen as early as before birth. (A corresponding explanation was given by Rudolf Steiner.) He added that there are seven spirits of light at the highest level, who are love-giving spirits. The sunlight passes through six of these light spirits (Elohim, as he called them), who are sending powers of love down to humanity. The seventh light spirit is Yahweh, and this spirit caused the mature wisdom to flow down to Earth to prepare humanity for love. The human beings needed, however, someone to lead them in order to be able to see the loving nature of love physically, in the outer world. This happened when Jesus Christ came to Earth. He made the six Elohim – (or Logos –) forces corporeal. Aivanhov also explained that deep within every human being there is a contact with a divine power or entity, namely Christ. It is only by believing that this power exists that we can obtain the power, wisdom and love that Christ laid out in his earthly life. By having such faith, we will feel safe.

The spirit named Seth, who appeared through the medium Jane Roberts (1929-1984), was also asked about the person Jesus.[49] Seth then explained that particularly enlightened persons are on Earth in order to help people. He called them Speakers. He explained that the Christ unit was one very prominent Speaker and Buddha another, and that these entities are emerging in many incarnations, though they are just as active in a non-physical existence as in the physical. However, they are not always acknowledged or make themselves known in the physical world.

According to Martinus people have considered Jesus as a deity and worshipped him as such because of superstition, although he has only been one among the many redeemers of the World, i.e. a highly developed spiritual person, who has given the World a new impulse, but who has a long way to go before he can be one with the Deity.[50]

Levi H. Dowling (1844-1911) writes in the book *The New Age's Gospel about Jesus Christ* that the World's only salvation is love, and that Jesus came into the World to show this love.[51]

One of the great Christian mystics, Master Eckhart (1260-1328)[i], supposedly said that there is no difference between Jesus and us, except that Jesus was a very special human being.[52] The term the Son of God Eckhart also used about what we can say is the divine principle or the essence of God, because he often in his speeches mentioned God's son's birth in us. Such a statement from the master, however, was condemned heretical by the Church in 1329. But it was perhaps this which St Paul meant when he used the term Jesus Christ.

As we have seen, it is highly uncertain whether a person by the name of Jesus as described in the New Testament has ever lived. It seems that those who talk about him make from it mainly what they mostly want to believe, than from historical facts.

---

i. Eckhart was as a young man accepted into the Dominican monastery in Erfurt in Thüringen. From 1290, he was both vicar and prior in Erfurt. Later, he was in Paris where he studied for an MA degree – to become a teacher of the Holy Theology- that is a Meister. He then became the head of the Schlesian Order province, later also of the Bohemian Order province. Around 1313 he was sent to Paris as a teacher, but was already in 1314 back in Germany, now as prior and teacher in Strasbourg. He came as a teacher to Cologne in 1320 and was there until his death in 1328. Eckhart was condemned as a heretic by Pope John XXII, on the 27th March 1329, and many of his writings were condemned as heretical. Most of them are lost, but his sermons are preserved because they were written down by his audience. Jes Bertelsen (HI p. 111) writes about Eckhart that in him you will find the highest and ultimate mystic, and that there are not many places where this is so clearly reflected as in Eckhart and in his pupil Tauler. Jes Bertelsen says further: "This is also evident in the Indian Vedanta meditation, as well as in the higher forms of Zen meditiation, where it is almost word for word said the same as did Eckhart. Furthermore, in the form of the highest Tibetan Buddhism, the formulations might well have been Eckhart's."

The Book of Revelation – The Apocalypse

The Book of Revelation describes a vision which its author John says he received during his stay on the island of Patmos. This book is part of The New Testament. It is doubtful whether this John is the apostle John. The story is difficult to understand, and it is also difficult to understand why this text has been accepted as a canonical scripture. Several books and comments about how the Revelation is to be interpreted have been written, and the interpreters have a wide variety of solutions. Robert Eisenman has compared the language used in this book with the Damascus document and other Qumran documents, and have found striking similarities in the image usage. It may indicate that the author of the Revelation had good knowledge of the Qumran community.

Yogananda said that the Revelation contains a symbolic presentation of a yoga science which Jesus taught to John and the nearest disciples. Yogananda pointed out that the chakra system has seven centres in the spine, on the cerebrospinal axis. When the Revelation discusses the secrets of the seven stars and the seven churches, Yogananda is of the opinion that this refers to these centres.[53]

Rudolf Steiner believed that the Revelation is a mystic's explanation of life. The seven spirits of God, the seven churches, the seven stars and the seven candlesticks are images of the Earth and the Earth's evolution.[54] The seven churches are the seven post-Atlantis culture periods. The seven stars are the seven higher spiritual beings who are the spiritual leaders during those periods. The seven candlesticks are the spiritual beings that cannot be observed in the world of the senses. The seven spirits of God are the seven life bodies (the consciousness bodies) in the human being.

Former professor in ancient history at the University of Oslo, Egil A. Wyller (b.1925) who translated the Revelation from Greek to Norwegian and sought to interpret it, pointed to the special structure of the text.[55] It can be divided into five main sections with the addition of what Wyller designated as a coda (tail) and an epilogue. Thus, seven parts in total. The five main sections are about the seven churches, the seven seals, the seven trumpets, the seven bowls of wrath and the seven end of time sins. He wrote that the Revelation furthermore is made up in a very special way. When one looks at the development of the motifs and the ideas behind the parts and divisions, it is as if one is looking at a pyramid – with an ascending part and a descending part; where the ascending and the descending parts have corresponding actions. The first part leads to the presentation's vertex, which is in the end of chapter 11 (*"and God's Temple in Heaven was opened...."*), where upon one is slowly brought back to Earth and the starting point. Wyller's interpretation is essentially an explanation of the images and visions we meet in the Revelation, based on the assumption that these are Jesus' words in line with those found elsewhere in the Bible, and consistent with biblical symbolism in general as it is the usual way of interpretation. He does not explain why the number seven is so central in the story.

Helena Blavatsky has also commented on the Revelation in her book *The Secret Doctrine*. She says, inter alia, that it must be obvious that it is the hermetic (closed or hidden) teaching about humanity's development, such as she presents it in her book, that is explained in the Revelation. She referred, among other references, to Rev. 17.9-10: *"Here is needed sense and wisdom. The seven heads are seven mountains, and on them is a woman sitting. They are also seven Kings. Five of them are falling, one is now, and one is yet to come. And when he comes, he will stay only for a short time."* Helena Blavatsky explained that the text is here referring to that in the course of time, there will have been seven root-races of human beings on Earth, hence four have disappeared, the fifth is partly disappeared, and the two will come sometime in the future. The Revelation follows the occult symbolic language which occult teaching is following in all countries, according to Blavatsky.[56] Here the number seven is a key number.

2.4. GOD

> Therefore, it is said of Ptah: "It is he who has created everything and who has generated the gods. He is verily The Risen Land that brought forth the gods, for everything came forth from him. ... He had made likenesses of their bodies to the satisfaction of their hearts, and the gods had entered into these bodies made of every wood, stone, and clay thing that grows upon him, wherein they have taken form. And in this way, all the gods and their kas are at one with him, content and united with the Lord of the Two Lands."
> *Text from Memphis* ca. 2350-2175 BCE[57]

> Then God said to Moses: I am the one I am. This is how you should respond to the Israelites: "I am" has sent me to you.[i]
> Exodus 3.14

> God is simple, everything else is complicated.
> Yogananda[58]

> God is the heart of Cosmos
> Ken Wilber[59]

> It is possible to explain God's existence, but only to a certain extent. Even under everyday's conditions, we know that people do not know who is in control or why and how he controls. Yet they know that there is a Force that truly controls.
> Mahatma Gandhi[60]

In Buddhism there is no concept of God and neither do you find a corresponding central power as in the other major religions. For in Buddhism there is rather a particular way of being, or may be rather a type of non-being, that is the highest achievable goal. Buddha is supposed to have said that God's existence does not bring about the practical work needed to

---

[i]. I am – YAHWEH. The word YAHWEH may also be translated "I am the one I am" or "I am the one who brings into existence", or "I am the one who wants to exist".

liberate from ignorance.[61] The Buddha did not reject the term God, but neither did he talk about it.

In Hinduism the concept of God exists, not as a specific character, but as a force that manifests itself in many different ways, and ultimately in a variety of divine figures. In Juan Mascarós' introduction to the Upanishads the following is quoted from *Bhagavad Gita* XIII 27-28:[62]

> Brahman in the Universe, God in his transcendence and in himself, so is also the Human Spirit, the self that is in everyone and in all, Atman. The One who sees that everyone's Lord is always the same in all that is, immortal in the mortals – sees the truth. ... And when a man sees that God in itself is the same God who is in everything, that person will not hurt him/her self by hurting others; the person will truly achieve the highest level.

Christianity, Judaism and Islam have the same name on the highest power or force – namely God. How this term is understood will probably be defined differently in each of these three religions – and within the different religions. The highest attainable in Christianity is to stay close to God when judgment day comes – Jesus is sitting at God's right hand. Such as this is presented, there is a strong personalization of the God concept which I have difficulties in following. Most of the major Christian philosophers have tried with different definitions and sought to solve the question of whether one can acknowledge the existence of God, even though God cannot be proven.

Some people just know that God exists, while many others are dismissive. The latter is mostly dismissive without having studied the problem closer – and they are often not interested in going in depth on the issue. These must be allowed to remain where they are, just as we demand respect for what we believe in. But can you answer the question whether you believe in God or not before you have defined what you mean by God? The Augsburg Confession of faith, Article I says this:

God is creating and maintaining all things, the visible and the invisible.

All people have a yearning to understand why we live, even if many people choose not to think more about it. We who choose to acknowledge this longing, want to believe that our lives and what happens to us and around us have a meaning, and that there is a consciousness that governs the whole or that existence has a meaning. This Consciousness or Sense is what I understand as the concept of God in the different religions. But for me it is difficult to use the concept God, because the conventional definition makes me think that this Consciousness who is behind everything is a human-like figure. For me, it makes better sense to apply the concept The Divine Principle or The Divine Power of this all comprehensive

Consciousness. Master Eckhart used the concept The Deity when he talked about the power that cannot be impersonated.

It is important to be aware that we do have guides and mentors to show us the way when it comes to understanding the total reality, people who maintain that they have known such a Consciousness or Power, and who have given us their personal stories about the experience. I am thinking of the mystics of all religions. Those who refuse to acknowledge that there is a divine principle or rulings, should take a closer look at the mystics' reports. It is easy to dismiss their stories as something you cannot believe, or that their experiences do not represent any proper spiritual experience. But one should then take into consideration that the Catholic Church has pronounced as saints quite a number of people, by very careful scrutiny of what has been said about them and by them, and after a thorough review of what they have accomplished. This means that no other explanation has been found of their actions than that they have received help from above – from God. Occasionally, there are several witnesses who can confirm the unexplainable events taking place around the mystics, such as ecstasies, levitations and healing abilities. It is important to take a closer look at the reports about the contact with God that the mystics have experienced. Such contact has been achieved only after long periods of meditation and prayer, and has normally been experienced during a kind of trance. The following are some definitions of God that I have found. Not all of them are saying that God is a humanlike being.

Augustine (354-430) was bishop of Hippo in North Africa and was officially declared a church teacher in 1295. He is regarded as one of Christianity's greatest theologians. Augustine explained that he has sought in his memory for God without finding any trace of God outside of this, although he has been aware of the existence of God ever since he first heard about God and understood that God was the truth.[63] He has asked himself where in his own memory God is. But he concluded that God did not exist in that part of the memory that he has in common with the animals. Neither could he find God in the part where he can shape images or where his feelings can be said to live; nor in the part which he thought as the seat of the brain. He concluded that God cannot be in his brain, since God is the ruler also of the mind. But God must be in his mind because he remembers God, and it is in his mind that he finds God when he recalls God. Augustine also searched for God outside of himself without seeing God; he saw only God's creations. And although God was with him all the time, he was not with God. Despite the fact that God constantly sought contact with him, he was blind and deaf for this contact. But in the end Augustine woke up and thereafter he thirsted only after God and only desired God's peace. Augustine acknowledged that if he did not love God above everything, then he did not love God enough. Augustine furthermore stated that "if it can be understood, then it is not God".[64]

Hildegard von Bingen (see description in chapter 3.3) has in a letter to a bishop explained her understanding of the following theological thesis: "The eternity lives in the Father, the similarity in the Son, and in the Holy Spirit lives the unity of eternity and likeness."[65] She wrote in this letter, inter alia, that God is eternity and everlasting life, and the reason we call God the Father is that all things have their origin in Him.

Thomas Aquinas (1224-1274, declared a saint in 1323) claimed that all that can be said about God is that God is, but not what God is.[66] It is about the same as is said by most Christian mystics. Thomas Aquinas was the most famous church teacher of the medieval church, whose writings were declared to be the foundation for all Catholic theology.

Master Eckhart (1260-1328) was a prominent Christian teacher (Meister), though many of his theological formulations were declared heretical by the Church at the end of his life.[67] (He is now almost accepted by the Church. Pope John Paul II referred to one of his sermons in a speech at the end of the twentieth century.) Master Eckhart regularly used the term God in his sermons. But he was of the opinion that the Godhead is beyond time and space and every quality, and cannot be grasped. Eckhart said in a sermon that God is nothing and that God is a something. God is a being and contains all beings. And he refers to another master that is supposed to have said: "Whoever speaks of God using some kind of parable, speaks of Him in an impure way." When Eckhart used the term God then it is the face of the Godhead turned towards humanity – that which is active, or that part of the Deity which is close to human beings. Master Eckhart said, inter alia, that God is in the beings of all things. According to Jes Bertelsen, Eckhart's view is that God is behind all manifestations in the mind whatsoever, behind all sensing, images, and all matter, behind everything.[68] God is the source of all performances of consciousness. In a commentary about Master Eckhart written by Aasmund Brynildsen this is explained in this way:

> God is not something outside of us who can speak to us; He can only speak in us. We pray to our Father "who is in the heavens" – but the Kingdom of Heaven is within us.

The British nun *Julian of Norwich* (1342-1416)[i] sought to give a picture of God in her book *Revelations of Divine Love,* to the extent that it is possible

---

i. Julian of Norwich lived her final years as a hermit in a cell in the Church of St Julian in Norwich, England, hence the name. She was much used as a spiritual adviser. We do not know her background or her real name. She had a series of revelations when she was 31 years old. Then she was very sick and briefly thought to be dead. She wrote about this experience in a book with the title *Revelations of Divine Love*. (See the translation by Elizabeth Spearing from English of the 14th century into modern English). The book consists of two parts, a short text (ST) and a long text (LT), which has much in common. The latter is, in addition to repetitions of the short text, an exposition for understanding the revelations she received. (Please note that 31 years of age seems to be a year when many people have their divine experience.)

to describe God, who is not created.[69] She wrote that God is omnipotent, complete wisdom and fully good, and totally quiet in him/herself, without beginning or end. God is all that we find good and comforting. God is our clothes; God surrounds us with love and can never leave us. In order to love and possess God that has not been created, humanity will have to acknowledge that everything created is insignificant and actually nothing. Human beings can only obtain spiritual peace when they are totally filled with God. They have no peace as long as they seek satisfaction in trivial things, for there no peace is to be found.

The Norwegian mystic *Hans Nielsen Hauge* (1771-1824) has been characterized by his biographer, Dag Kullerud, as "the closest we come a Prophet on Norwegian soil in modern times". Hauge was a man with profound religiosity and he had a fierce energy for starting business activities, which was of great significance for Norwegian society from 1800 onwards. Dag Kullerud describes Hauge's God image, as follows:[70]

> Hauge's God is blessedly not very theological, yes, most profoundly considered and with exception of the necessity of repentance, very undogmatic. Hauge considers God as God even if all land lay deserted and all humans were dead. The definition given by Pontoppidan[i] is suitable here: "... a spiritual, infinite and inconceivable Being, who is almighty, all knowing, everywhere present, good, merciful, sacred, truthful and righteous." In his catechism from 1804, he gives an explanation to the first article with what must be considered a very modern "cosmological" proof of God: "But if you cannot see Him, then you can by all created things – as if by yourself, understand that there must be a higher being of a different sort and nature than us humans ... because we are born of something, or have a beginning and we will have an end, therefore there must be an eternal God, who always has been and who has no beginning and no end."

It is also interesting to look at what a Norwegian Christian bishop in recent times has said about God. *Kristian Schjelderup* (1894-1980) was in his time probably considered rather modern and radical by certain circles – while he is characterized as a Christian mystic by Jan-Erik Ebbestad Hansen, professor of history at the University of Oslo. Schjelderup was bishop of Hamar diocese from 1947 to 1964. He was ordained in 1945. He has described his view as follows:[71]

> In the human beings' deepest inner world there is hidden a secretive relationship with a world other than the one we live in with our senses. In that world we have our true home. Religion is the experience of this connection with a "different" reality, the experience of a world

---

i. Erik Pontoppidan (1616-1678) was born in Denmark and in 1673 became bishop in the Norwegian town Trondheim.

completely different from the ordinary, the embedding in the eternal.

Anyone who has had this experience knows that this reality exists and that only to live in that world makes him a human being in the deepest sense. Then the issue of whether the divine world is an 'objective' reality, simply no longer exists. This reality is spiritually at hand: the religious human being is living in it.

It is in a similar way as the world of aesthetic is at hand for the artist. He does not ask about its 'objective' reality, he lives in it.

Perhaps we may – metaphorically-speaking – say, as did Dean Inge – that the Divine is an atmosphere. God is the atmosphere in which the religious human being lives and breathes, and it is just as real and important for him as the air is for all organic life.

The Divine is not something that we 'presume' is. Man experiences God.

Mystery is probably the correct term for the deepest cause lying behind religion. The innermost experience defies in the end any description.[i]

Carl Gustav Jung must also be regarded as a mystic in addition to that he was an outstanding, though also highly controversial, psychiatrist, and is so even today. He is contested perhaps precisely due to that he was a mystic. The British author Laurens van der Post (1906-1996)[ii] has referenced Jung's statement about God as follows:[72]

> "I can't give you a definition of what God is," wrote Jung to me shortly before his death. "I can only say that my efforts have provided empirical evidence that God's pattern exists in every human being, and that this pattern has at its disposal the most powerful of all energies for reform and transformation of man's innate nature. This applies not only in relation to the meaning of life, but to human regeneration; and the renewal of humanity's institutions depends on the conscious relationship to this pattern in the collective unconscious."

The people who are quoted here must be characterized as mystics within the Christian tradition. However, the concept of God is also found outside of Christianity. It is therefore of interest to see what some other mystics have been saying, mystics with a different background for their views.

Yogananda wrote about God from his Hindu standpoint, but with reference to Christianity and Jesus' life and teachings.[73] He mentions that

---

i. Dean William Ralph Inge (1860-1954) was a professor in Cambridge and Dean at St Paul's Cathedral in London.
ii. Laurens van der Post was born in South-Africa and lived both in South-Africa and in England. He was author and farmer, and wrote many fascinating books about Africa, about nature and the culture there. He was a colonel in the British army during the Second World War and was imprisoned by the Japanese for many years.

a yogi, who through fully advanced meditation has combined his consciousness with the Creator, sees the profound essence of the Cosmos as light; to him there is no difference between the light rays that make up the water, and those that make up the land. Long concentration on the liberating spiritual eye makes the yogi able to annihilate all deceptions of the self-regarding the substance and its gravity; He sees the Universe as God created it: a fully undifferentiated mass of light. Great masters with insights gained from meditation understand that God both exists and can be known. He mentions that the sacred Hindu writings have thousand names for God, each with a different philosophical hue. Yogananda often used, among other things, the concept Divine Mother, who is God in the aspect of Mother Nature. He wrote, inter alia, the following:

> As the God's proper nature is blessedness, the human being, who is in unison with him, will experience a natural, boundless joy.
>
> These words of the Bible refer to God's threefold nature as Father, Son and Holy Spirit (Sat, Tat and Aum in Hindu scripture). God the Father is the Absolute, un-manifested, which exists beyond vibratory creation. His son is Christ-consciousness (Brahma or Kutastha Chaitanya), which exists within the vibratory creation; This Christ-consciousness is the 'only begotten' or the only reflection of the uncreated eternity. The exterior manifestation of the omnipresent Christ-consciousness, it's 'witness' – (John's Revelation 3.14), is Aum, the Word or Holy Spirit: invisible, divine power, the only creator, the only cause and life-giving power which sustains all creation through vibration. Aum, the blessings giver's Spokesperson that can be felt in meditation and disclosed to the seeker of God the final Truth, as he "reminds him of all things ..."
>
> As God is the eternal new, who cannot be predicted, we will never be tired of him.

Yogananda mentioned that the Indian sage Patanjali[i] described God as the true cosmic sound Aum, which is used in meditation and who is heard during deep meditation. He then explained this:

> His innermost being cannot be understood, even if you understand all the Trinity's mysteries, because his external nature, as manifests in the atoms' rule-bound constitutions and alterations, only expresses Him without disclosing Him. The final nature of God is only understood when "the Son rises up to the Father". The freed human being exceeds the vibratory realms and steps into the Vibrationless Original.

---

i. It is thought that Patanjali lived sometime between the second century BCE and the fifth century CE. He is supposed to have written the classical Hindu works the Yoga-Sutras, though many assume that those were written by different persons over several centuries.

For *Ken Wilber* God is no anthropomorphic father or mother figure, but more pure awareness, or rather consciousness as such. He thinks that that is what is and also all that is – an awareness that one cultivates in meditation and brings into one's daily life.[74] He points to the Eternal Philosophy when he answers the question of whether God exists, and the parallels between Christianity and Buddhism when it comes to this. He takes as a starting point that all belief-systems and philosophies consider that Spirit is a reality, that the Spirit is present in humans, but that most people do not acknowledge this because we live in a world of sin, seclusion and double life. With this last he thinks that we are living in an illusion. But it is possible to get away from this illusion or sin. If we follow a certain way, it will lead us to being reborn or enlightened. This is a direct experience of the inner Spirit, which gives complete freedom from sin and suffering. This liberation would lead to one actively wanting to act with compassion and companionship with all living beings. Wilber refers to Spirit and God being the same, that is, a superior reality (Supreme Reality). This reality is called Brahman, Dharmakaya, Kether, Tao, Allah, Shiva, Yahweh, Aton, depending on the culture one is in. This Spirit is experienced by mystics by direct experience and is not anything which can be reached by thinking. It is an experience that all mystics give the same description, wherever in the world they belong. Anyone, who will undertake the efforts to follow the spiritual path, will be able to gain the same experience. Wilber points out that it is in the same way as, for example, a mathematician, who must work hard in order to prove some mathematical formula – which cannot be experienced directly.

According to *Martinus* the part of God which you can see is simply the physical Cosmos. All physical life bodies are in a way the Divine's antennas, through which the Deity might experience the physical world. Each physical being is thus a part of the Godhead. Per Bruus Jensen, who has written about Martinus' cosmology, has given this explanation:[75]

> More exactly, the physical Universe plays the role as the structure of a Divine mother's uterus, which takes care of the development of new life forms and sensory methods; similarly, the physical beings may be considered as cosmic embryos in a more or less developed stage. With regard to the human beings, they are approaching that which, in connection with an ordinary embryo process, corresponds to the fully born stage.

God involves, however, also an invisible, non-physical reality. A spiritual world is included in this structure, in addition to all that is spiritual and invisible in the physical world. In the spiritual world there are spiritual beings, which thus become a part of God.

Bruus Jensen further explains:

> ... It is those spiritual beings, who as God's spiritual representatives, are registering or take notice of any prayer from the physical plane.

And it is those beings who, similarly, take steps to meet the person praying with sufficient help and support.

Martinus explained it in this way:

> As the movements of the Universe are reflected both in creations and in logical combinations of matter, so that they will be of benefit, joy and blessing for living beings, they also reveal that they are the result of thought, just as manifestations and creations by human beings. And in the same way as a human being's manifestations and creations reveal it as a living creature, so also the nature's or the Universe's creations reveal the Universe or the totality of the World as a living being. The Universe is thus an organism for an eternal 'I', in the same way as our organism is so for our own 'I'. The Universe is thus a living being's organism, in which we exist with our organism.
>
> We may by our way of acting be in discord with the structure of the Universe, which means discord with God's organism, and our fate will then be unhappy.

Plotinus also addressed the most high as God (Plotinus is mentioned later in chapter 3.3). Plotinus is supposed to have said:[76]

> We must recognize that other men have attained the heights of goodness; we must admit the goodness of the celestial spirits, and above all of the gods – those whose presence is here but their contemplation in the Supreme, and loftiest of them, the lord of this All, the most blessed Soul. Rising still higher, we hymn the divinities of the Intellectual Sphere, and, above all these, the mighty King of that dominion, whose majesty is made patent in the very multitude of the gods.
>
> It is not by crushing the Divine unto a unity but by displaying its exuberance – as the Supreme himself has displayed it – that we show knowledge of the might of God, who, abidingly what He is, yet creates that multitude, all dependent on Him, existing by Him and from Him.
>
> This Universe, too, exists by Him and looks to Him – the Universe as a whole and every God within it – and tells of Him to men, all alike revealing the plan and will of the Supreme.

Aivanhov has said that God cannot be described with words, and there is neither a philosopher nor a mystic who can do that.[77] God is the name we have given the Supreme Spirit, who created the Universe and is its only source and life-giving principle. We can refer to God as a certain polarized singularity by talking about the Universal Spirit and the Universal Soul. This is to state that there are two important principles that work in the Universe – an outward directed or masculine force (the Spirit) and a receiving or feminine force (the Soul). In all creation, these two forces are working.

Similar powers are within each human being, albeit of a different magnitude. (*As above so below*.ⁱ) If human beings were able to develop their souls and spirits, so that these become combined with the Cosmic Soul and Spirit, the human being would experience a boundless delight.

There are a number of messages coming to people from what are said to be spirits residing in a different dimension than our physical. We will now take a look at some such statements about the concept of God. Hungarian Gitta Mallasz (1907-1992) published in 1988 the book *Talking with Angels*.[78] Here she refers conversations from a period during the Second World War between spirits, channelled through her friend Hannah, and two other friends present. The spirits explained that the Divine is both here, there, everywhere and in everything, even down into the depths. Jane Roberts, who channelled the spirit Seth, wrote that Seth rarely used the term God, as he often said, "Everything that is" or "Primary energy entities". Everyone is part of "Everything that is" and has access to this, but "Everything that is" is more than the sum of all parts.[79]

"No one will be able to say: "Look here it is" or "There it is". For the Kingdom of God is within you." (Citation from Luke 17.21 as in my Bible from 1947.) The New International Version as well as the Norwegian Bible edition of 2011 has the following wording of Luke 17.21: *"... For behold, the Kingdom of God is in the midst of you."* The Norwegian priest Helge Hognestad, PhD (b. 1940), has pointed out that the wording of the oldest Greek edition is not to be misunderstood and has, like all former Norwegian Bible editions, the wording: *"For the Kingdom of God is within you."* King James' Bible also has the wording: *"The Kingdom of God is within you."* It is a big difference between being "in the midst of us" and "within us". However, the Norwegian bishop Per Lønning (b. 1928) has in a commentary printed in Aftenposten 6.4.2010 maintained that the Greek word used is *entós*, which can mean both within and in the midst, depending on the context. Joseph Campbell has in the book *Occidental Mythology* (p. 369) mentioned that the term within you requires the theological understanding that God is immanent, an understanding that the Church has never accepted, but considers as Gnostic heresy.

Father *Laurence Freeman* has explained that the word God is used as a term for the absolute with respect to being, meaning, truth and life.[80] God is greater than anything you can imagine, and therefore impossible to describe. God can only be recognized through love, not by thought. Laurence Freeman pointed out that Jesus extolled the inner life that is needed to get 'into the Kingdom of God', and that God's Kingdom, therefore, is both in us and

---

i. This is a statement that occurs in the book *The Emerald Tablets* attributed to Hermes Trismegistus (Hermes the third largest – Hermes was the Greek equivalent of the Egyptian God Thoth). The book is a collection of hermetic (secret) writings originally written in Greek and Latin, and is believed to derive from some time between the first and the third century CE. The book treats theological and philosophical questions as well as revelations regarding the occult or hidden.

among us, which the Gospel of Luke points out. However, scholars disagree even today as to whether God is something far beyond the human world, as a supreme being from which everything has emanated or is shining forth from – the teaching about emanation – or whether God is inherent in all beings – the teaching about immanation. In the first case, God has let him/herself be acknowledged through a stepwise ascent towards the top. In the latter case, it is about getting in touch with the innermost and deepest within yourself.

The British religious historian *Evelyn Underhill* (1875-1941) wrote that those who follow the doctrine of immanence are individuals who seem to experience God's touch most easily, rather than seclusion and sin, and therefore are more prone to love than to awe.[81] She said the following about the mystic experience:

> Unless safeguarded by limiting dogmas, the theory of Immanence, taken alone, is notoriously apt to degenerate into pantheism; and into those extravagant perversions of the doctrine of 'deification'; into which the mystics holds his transfigured self to be identical with the Indwelling God. It is this philosophical basis of that practice of introversion, the turning inward of the soul's faculties in contemplation, which has been the 'method' of the great practical mystics of all creeds. That God, since He is in all – in a sense, is all – may most easily be found within ourselves, is the doctrine of these adventurers, who, denying or ignoring the existence of those intervening 'worlds' or 'planes' between the material world and the Absolute, which are postulated by the theory of Emanations, claim with Ruysbroeck that "by a simple introspection in fruitive love" they "meet God without intermediary". They hear the Father of Lights "saying eternally, without intermediary or interruption, in the most secret part of the spirit, the one, unique, and abysmal Word."

The teaching about emanation assumes that God is the world's source. The farther away the world comes from the source, the less spiritual and the larger in scope and mass it becomes. Underhill referred to the following statement by Thomas Aquinas:

> As all the perfections of Creatures descend in order from God, who is the height of perfection, man should begin from the lower creatures and ascend by degrees, and so advance to the knowledge of God. ... And because in that roof and crown of all things, God, we find the most perfect unity, and everything is stronger and more excellent the more thoroughly it is one, it follows that diversity and variety increase in things, the further they are removed from Him who is the first principle of all.

The various Christian mystics and saints seem to belong to either one or other of these doctrines. This we should also have in mind when reading the above-referenced statements about what God is. After the Norwegian bishop Rosemarie Køhn held her accession sermon, in which she quoted from approved church teaching and pointed to the male and the female aspect of God, there were many protests from various people that neither could accept a female deity nor a deity with female characteristics. Many other people have trouble accepting God as Father, or that there is an anthropomorphic personality that controls our lives in detail both in regard to good and bad deeds.

The Gospel of John starts with these words: *"In the beginning was the Word, and the Word was with God, and the Word was God. The same was in the beginning with God."* (In the Greek version the term Logos is used.)[i] Aschehoug's encyclopedia (1958) explains the following regarding the word Logos:

> Logos (Greek) means 'word' or 'common sense' and is also used as a term for all expressions of opinion: thought, speech, learning, wisdom, etc. In the Stoic philosophy the word logos refers to the divine sense that is active, penetrating and expanding in the Universe. In the Jewish/Alexandrine philosophy of religion (see Philo) logos is partly an expression for the eternal, in itself resting divine wisdom, partly for the divine word of creation, whereby everything has come into existence. (John 1.1 and 1.14, John's 1st letter 1.1, and Acts 19.13)

Is it in these introductory words of John's Gospel, a suggestion that God is not a personality that a person can relate to, but a divine power? Many people may do things that cannot be explained by known physical principles. However, it looks as if the mystics might get such abilities when they have obtained complete recognition of the Divine after having followed the way of the mystics. This recognition is so dramatic that the personality is completely transformed. The Christian mystics who have been declared saints, have been very outstanding (standing alone) persons with an extraordinary love towards other beings that is incomprehensible for ordinary people. When we take into consideration what the mystics and sages from all cultures have been able to attain, we have to marvel over whether there is a deity, a divine energy that interferes in (or affects) a person's life. The description that Kristian Schjelderup has given of this God is, in my opinion, complementing the other sayings referenced here – that is that God cannot be regarded as a person, but more like an atmosphere. The problem for the modern human beings is to remember this. We should then have Buddhism in mind, where there is no concept of God. I think the spirit Seth has an understandable explanation in this regard. He explained:[82]

---

i. In a channelled message this wording can be found for John 1.1: *"In the beginning was the Thought and the Thought was with God and the Thought was God and without its help nothing would have been created of everything that has been created ..."* (Bente Müller, *Gjennom Lysmuren* (Through the Lightwall), Dreyer 1986).

> However, all individuals remember their ancestry and dream about "Everything that is" in the same way that "Everything that is" dreams about them. And they are longing for the source of abundance.
>
> There is no personal God in the Christian sense, but you have access to a part of "Everything that is", a part that to a large extent is directed on you ... Each individual has a part of "Everything that is" in their own consciousness, and this section is focused on it, and each consciousness has its own protection.

I will in a later chapter consider what some scholars have found out as a possible explanation for all paranormal phenomena, namely the holographic Universe. Their conclusion is that we have access to everything, and that each individual has a part of this in his/her consciousness. But the question that still remains to be answered is whether there is a spiritual dimension of life – are we spirits with a continued existence other than the physical? I will be returning to this later on.

3. Extraordinary Phenomena and Abilities

3.1. Introduction

My first encounter with parapsychological phenomena was some small personal experiences, which gave me cause for reflection. Then I read Øistein Parmann's book about the Norwegian mystic Marcello Haugen (see 3.2.below) which showed that my experiences were not especially uncommon. Later, I learned that there are and have been a number of people in Norway and elsewhere in the world that have some of the same capabilities as those of Marcello Haugen. I cannot find any reason to doubt that the stories told about Marcello Haugen or many other people with paranormal capabilities are true. There are too many eyewitness accounts and they are mostly trustworthy. What amazes me is that so many people still hold the view that such stories are nonsense and something they do not believe in, just because they do not have had the same experience. These experiences are quite common, but even today it is not acceptable to speak about them, or to recount dreams. Many people would rather not hear about paranormal phenomena because then they need to rethink their own view of reality. Therefore such stories are rarely told. Much of what is reported can also easily be considered as nonsense or rewritten as something trivial. But if we take a closer look at the large amount of such events and the research done in this area, we cannot be indifferent to them.

Christian saints and mystics of all faiths and cultures believe to have contact with what they consider to be a spiritual dimension – which they call divine. This we can choose not to believe in but many of them, thanks to this contact, eventually develop the ability to heal or to perform other miracles. We know all the Biblical stories about Jesus, where he heals the sick, restores the dead to life, transforms water to wine, feeds a crowd of people with only a few bread loaves and some fish. Others also have been able to perform such miracles according to the stories told. It is in this regard interesting to study many of the individuals who have been canonized by the Catholic Church, thanks to the miracles performed or occurring in connection with their lives. There is extensive research into such miracles before a saint is approved for canonization. One of these saints, *St Teresa of Avila*, described her experiences in her autobiography *Vida*. Much of what she recounts clearly goes under what we today call parapsychological phenomena, one of which is most amazing, namely levitation. That she, under intense concentration in prayer, actually sat in the air without anything beneath her, is hard to believe, but is confirmed by several contemporaries.

Has the development of civilization – or should we rather say the development of technology together with human greed – led us to forget that we have the capabilities to intuitively capture and understand everything around us? Have we forgotten that everything is energy, an energy that we can all use to our advantage? Maybe we can restore these capabilities, and ultimately live up to the visions of the American author *James Redfield*, presented as the nine insights in his book *The Celestial Prophecy*. I will come back to this in the final chapter.

But we must not overlook the fact that many people's willingness to accept others' stories, is great. Some of all that we hear, we can accept as true, while much may be false. How do we explain all the paranormal phenomena occurring and the strange abilities that some humans possess? Religions give no answer, except for the statement that some have 'special spiritual gifts'. Perhaps scientists are now beginning to approach an explanation? This we shall take a closer look at. However, I will first introduce some of the individuals who are known for their special abilities, amongst them some who are well-known in the Nordic countries. Then I will follow with reports of some strange phenomena, so it is clear what I am writing about.

3.2. Some individuals with strange abilities

Emanuel Swedenborg (1688-1772), Sweden, was a member of the Swedish Academy of Sciences (Kungliga Vetenskapsakademien) and thus a highly regarded scientist in Sweden in his time. He has been compared to geniuses like Galileo Galilei and Leonardo da Vinci but he was also a great mystic. Signe Toksvik, who wrote his biography, mentions that for a long time Swedenborg noted his experiences daily, what he saw, heard and felt. Most of this is published. One of the most famous stories about Swedenborg applies to his experience of the great fire in Stockholm which happened while he was in an official dinner in Gothenburg. The news of the fire arrived in Gothenburg only a few days later. (I will come back to some of the things he recorded below.) Former Chairman of the Norwegian Parapsychological Society, Sverre Martinussen (d.2012), has an interesting article about Swedenborg in the Society's journal, *Parapsykologiske Notiser* no. 46/1998. He referred to Swedenborg as 'the spiritual Columbus', who should have had a place in history in the same group as Aristotle, Plato, Newton, Kepler, and Bacon. Swedenborg wrote books about mathematics, astronomy, economics, anatomy, salt extraction, and more, and about his parapsychological experiences. Martinussen refers to a number of inventions, listed by Swedenborg in his various papers, for which others and later inventors have been given credit. As he became more and more concerned with parapsychological and spiritual phenomena, however, he was seen as a highly overwrought person and a preacher of the religion of the Devil. Colin Wilson has in his book *The Occult* mentioned that Swedenborg, out of his many seemingly reasonable considerations and factual information, had a fantasy that seemed very mixed up with dreams and fantasies. Wilson wrote that Swedenborg was sexually frustrated, and that in every textbook on abnormal behaviour today one will find many of his religious experiences described. But Swedenborg was not a charlatan, and Wilson frankly believed that he did have occult abilities, and that he was spiritually inspired by real insights and critical thoughts about existence.

Vis-Knut, Norway, his actual name was Knut Rasmussen Nordgard (1792-1876), was a well-known individual in the Gausdal valley. There were many who thought that Marcello Haugen was his reincarnated soul. *Vis-Knut* was psychic and was able to find people and animals that had been lost, as well as water and metals. He could also heal. Because of his religious activities and his healing practices, he came into conflict with the authorities and was once imprisoned for 14 days.

Johan Kaaven (1836-1918), Norway, is said to have been the last of the great shamans (Sámi wizards - noaide), and he was well-known by people in the district Finnmark and the northern part of Scandinavia. It was said that he could heal, but also help people find things, whether they were lost or stolen.[83]

Edgar Cayce (1877-1945), USA, is considered to have been the most prominent psychic in the US in his time. It is on record that more than 14,500 séances, readings, were given in his lifetime for approximately 6000 different people. Shorthand notes were taken of statements he made while he was in trance, dealing with individual people's lives and giving recommendations on how to cure their diseases or possibly solve other problems. Many books about these statements have been published, concerning reincarnation, healing, dreams, and much more. The reports of his abilities are unbelievable. But there is extensive evidence that the diagnosis given while he was in trance proved effective and appropriate. For example, he could recommend specific doctors or specific medication for a patient and say where this doctor worked, or how one could get hold of the medication. Such diagnosis could also be given for people he did not meet personally, wherever they were. It should be noted, however, that in retrospect it has been shown that several of the events that Edgar Cayce predicted, among others a series of catastrophes in the 1980s and a world disaster in 1997, did not happen. But Cayce did point out that these predictions implied that humanity was not able to change. Dr Harmon Hartzell Bro (b.1919) has written Edgar Cayce's biography. In 1943, when Bro was a theology student at the University of Chicago, he came in contact with Cayce and got the opportunity to collaborate with him. Bro reports that Edgar Cayce was in deep trance and lay on his back during his readings. He had a specific way of breathing and had restricted movement often characteristic of hypnotized people, though his speech and thought were clear enough. The condition was likened to a kind of death, so greatly were his physical functions reduced. The breath was very slow and the skin colour became whiter. It seemed as if he had out-of-body experiences, and when he mentioned certain sites it seemed as if he were there.

During the trance, he expressed himself very formally, perhaps rather sophisticated but not snobbish. And the voice had a different sound from normal. Bro meant that there was some sort of an active spirit or agent, with authority, which seemed to follow and lead the séances.

Marcello Haugen, Norway, (1878-1967) may well be described as the greatest known native Norwegian in regard to psychic powers. He was a mystic and healer. There are countless people who were helped or have a story to tell about him. There is only a small book by his hand plus a collection of notes known today. The Norwegian author Øistein Parmann (1921-1999) has written a fascinating biography, which now has been published several times and with new stories in each issue. Marcello Haugen was able to heal both directly and at a distance. He proposed herbal medicines as cures and also produced such himself. He was able to find objects and animals. He was able to make a painter paint images based on telepathic contact. He was for many confessor and spiritual advisor. Unfortunately, nothing is recorded about as to how he could explain his abilities.[84]

Martinus, Denmark, (his full name was Martinus Thomsen, 1890-1981), was a mystic who had a spiritual awakening when he was 31 years old and experienced, as he said, that he could look into eternity. He had then just received a book on Theosophy and in connection with reading this book he experienced what he called a 'baptism of cosmic fire' – an initiation. He had new sensory abilities which made him able to see the Universe's spiritual powers and eternal laws while being fully awake. He explained that this experience resulted in a permanently alert day-consciousness where he 'saw' the mystery of existence. He saw the spiritual powers, the causal contexts, the world's laws, the basic energies and principles that govern the physical world. He then devoted the rest of his life trying to explain and communicate this to humanity, by writing and drawing all that he had learnt in this way. What he explained is published in his major work, the seven volumes of *Livets Bog* (The Book of Life), and also in several booklets. He maintained that he had not read any book that could give him the information made available to him, and that after his spiritual awakening he was unable to read any book. He lived all his life in Denmark.

Anna Elisabeth Westerlund, Norway (1907-1995), who lived in Oslo most of her life, was able to say where an article originally came from and how it had been used (psychometry). She could also find artefacts that were missing, and sometimes people who had disappeared.[85]

Karl Tandstad (1868-1950) and his daughter *Olga Tandstad Skaue* (b.1912) from the Sykkylven district in Norway were both well-known for their psychic abilities.[86] They helped people find missing farm animals and artefacts. In some cases, they found people who had disappeared. They were also able to tell some people what awaited them in the future with regard to marriage, residency and children, though they normally avoided such themes. There is a story in connection with the development of the small place Aure, which is the community centre at Sykkylven. Karl Tandstad said at the time that they were building on the site of the former city – and it showed up during excavations that Aure in earlier times had been a power centre on the West coast of Norway. Karl Tandstad has explained that he saw this with his inner eye – almost as if he saw a movie. He did not see colours and the images were often unclear, though this obviously depended on whether he was tired or not. He saw the landscape as if he saw it from above and within a circle. Olga Tandstad Skaue explained her psychic sightings in the same way.

Bob Moore (b.1928) was born in Northern Ireland, but moved to Denmark in 1974. He has been teaching others how to develop greater awareness through meditation and spiritual exercises. Jes Bertelsen has said of him that he is centred in the higher consciousness and has clairvoyance, one who not only sees the physical and etheric energy field, but also the emotional and the higher astral level all the way to the mental-spiritual.[87] Randi Olerud has in her book from 1979, called *Flamme til liv – et skjebnemøte med helbredende hender* (Tongues of Fire making Life – a decisive meeting with Healing Hands), written about her meeting with Bob Moore and referring to much of his teachings. She described him as a person who conveys healing powers. He has had a teaching centre in Ringkøbing in Denmark, called Psykisk Center Aps., together with his wife Annie. This is an 'International Centre for Human Growth' – as it was written in an invitation to one of his courses. Bob Moore has been a teacher and an inspiration for a number of people both in Denmark and Norway. I have met many people who have attended his courses, and they have all told of his incredible capabilities, including telling someone something about his/her history and future (over the phone). In 1992 a book was published in Switzerland called *Conversations with Bob Moore* written by Anna & Alexander Mauthner, Switzerland, which refers some of his teaching. Bob Moore has not written anything.

3.3. *Mystics, saints and spiritual teachers*

Definition of a mystic

We usually use the term mystical about something that is strange and inexplicable; but a mystic is one that has a mystical experience, that is, a direct experience of God. A mystic may also be one with a spiritual world view. Mysticism is used as a term for belief systems where you are searching for direct contact with or think that it is possible to experience the Divine, God or the Supreme Reality, other than through the normal physical senses or by logical thinking. Within Catholicism a mystic is considered someone who has the highest form of religious life or has specific mystical experiences. Master Eckhart has said it in this way: "What comes to you in this way gives you pure being and durability ... In this birth you will nevertheless take part in the divine influence and all of its gifts."[88]

Ken Wilber has written that the essence of mysticism is that in the very deepest part of one's being, in the absolute centre of the pure consciousness, one is fundamentally in unity with the Spirit or Deity – The Totality, in a timeless, eternal and unchangeable way.[89] Many prominent scientists, such as Albert Einstein, Werner Heisenberg, Erwin Schrödinger, Louis de Broglie, Max Planck, Niels Bohr, Wolfgang Pauli, Sir Arthur Eddington and Sir James Jeans, have according to Ken Wilber a mystical cosmology, which is a deeply spiritual worldview. However, Wilber denies that modern physics is underpinning or proves Oriental mysticism.

The English professor of philosophy, Walter T. Stace (1886-1967) defined a mystic as a person who has had a mystical experience or who has a mystical awareness.[90] The mystical experience cannot be described by a sensory-intellectual consciousness. It is indescribable. But Stace mentioned certain characteristics of a mystical experience, as he had learnt it from mystics all over the world. The most important characteristic he believed was the experience of an ultimate non-sensuous unity in all things, which neither can be described through feelings nor thought.

Evelyn Underhill defined mysticism as an inherent tendency in a human being to long for complete harmony with the transcendental existence. This trend, she wrote, will in the great mystics gradually catch their total consciousness, it will dominate their lives, and, through what is called the mysterious union, Unio Mystica, reach its full extension. And whether this fullness is known as the Christian God, the soul of Pantheism or the Absolute within philosophy, the desire to achieve it and the struggle to reach it – as long as this is a real life process and not intellectual thought-play – is the real purpose of mysticism.

The mystics often get paranormal skills, such as the ability to do automatic writing, visions of future happenings, and hearing voices advising on their work. In addition, they often get healing abilities to cure both mental illness and physical damage.

There are many people today who have had a kind of a transcendental experience, a so-called peak experience, perhaps only for a few fractions of a second. Such an experience does not provide them with a deeper understanding of existence and the Divine, nor permanent psychic powers. But they will then often have received a deeply religious view of life – that is, they have obtained a feeling for the meaning of life. In this book, however, I will use the designation mystic only on those few people who have had a profound religious experience and who have expressed this in writings or been referenced in other people's writings. The term mystic may also include people who have capabilities that go far beyond the capabilities of ordinary people. These are people who often have knowledge of the unexplainable and in particular about conditions that are not part of the physical, understandable world – that is, about spiritual matters. We find mystics of all religions and all over the world, but they are few. Many of them have described their experiences and lessons learned, and many of their actions have been witnessed by others, who then have written down what was observed. I think there is every reason to note what these people have said, or what have been said about them.

Two great mystic-philosophers

Plato (ca. 429-347 BCE) left many writings which we know to be original. We can read the following in Aschehoug's encyclopaedia (1961):

> Greek's most outstanding philosopher ... Plato's learning we know mainly through his writings, all of which (one near) is as conversations, and in those conversations Socrates is the main character, who is leading the investigation; In this way Plato gives his beloved teacher an imperishable golden memory. ...
>
> Platonism is not a concept of one meaning, but certain themes are recurring in the stream of thoughts that derives from Plato; above all, the teaching about ideas or the opinion that above the world which we can grip with our senses, there is a more perfect world that comprises the norms, patterns or icons for thinking and action. Platonism is turning the attention to the spirit's invisible world; it claims the intangible nature of the soul and 'the absolute good' as the highest idea ...
>
> Strong elements of Platonism we find with the church fathers such as of Clement of Alexandria, Origen and Augustine; in the middle ages, from 12th century onwards as counterweight to Aristotelianism.

Plotinus (205-270) was a non-Christian mystic and philosopher. Ken Wilber considers him as one of the greatest mystics who ever lived. His philosophy was close to Plato's thoughts. Plotinus' teaching was the beginning of the direction later termed as Neo-Platonism. Plotinus was born in Egypt and studied philosophy in Alexandria for a decade. In the year 244 he travelled to Rome, where he taught philosophy and became a very renowned personality. He had the support of the Emperor Gallienus (253-268). Plotinus theories are brought together in what is known as the *Enneads* (the word indicates that it is a collection of nine units). The work consists of six books, each containing nine treaties with various chapters in each. The books were compiled by his disciple Porphyrios. Plotinus here explains the human soul, the relationship between mind and body, the Cosmos, time and life. It is told that he had several very strong spiritual experiences, which helps making his explanation of the Totality very compelling. His teachings involved that the soul has several levels. All levels are part of the individual human being. It is our own choice if we want to ignore the higher levels of the soul. When we are at the lowest level of the soul, we are only in contact with the needs of the physical bodies.[i]

Some Christian mystics

Hildegard von Bingen (1098-1179) lived most of her life (seventy-three of a total of eighty-one years) in a monastery. From 1136, she was the leader of Benedictine monasteries in the Rhine Valley, starting in Disibodenberg, then a few years later in St Rupert and finally in Rupertsberg. When she was forty-three years old, she started to dictate her visions, which were interpretations of religious texts. She had healing powers, composed music and wrote poems. She also painted some of her visions. She was very passionate about plants and their health-creating capabilities. Hildegard recounts in her diary about an experience she had when she was 56 years old, which gave her extraordinary abilities. She was then ordered to write down what she saw in her visions. She had an extensive correspondence with contemporary scholars who wrote to her for advice in religious matters. She is considered one of the greatest intellectuals of her day and one of the greatest mystics of the Western world, but she has not been canonized by the Christian Church.[91]

St Francis of Assisi (1181-1226), whose full name was Giovanni Francesco di Pietro di Bernardone, lived and worked most of his life in his native city Assisi in Italy. He was canonized in 1228, just two years after his death. When he was twenty-four years old, he was told in a dream to await a calling other than the one he had sought. Partly as a result of intense prayer after this dream and after a pilgrimage to Rome, he saw a vision of Christ. In a later vision he experienced that the crucifix in the chapel of St Damiano outside Assisi ordered him to repair the damaged chapel, which he then did. He also restored several other chapels in the area. During a mass the reading was from Matt 10.9-11 where it says that Jesus ordained the disciples to live in poverty, he decided to follow these words. He came from a wealthy family, but gave up all property and went about as a penitential preacher. In 1224, two years before he died, he saw in a vision a figure coming down to him from heaven. According to one of his friends, this figure was a seraph with six pairs of wings. It had two wings that arose above the head, two that were

---

i. When referring to Plotinus here, it is from the Enneads (referenced with chapter and verse number). Quotes are from the translation of Stephen McKenna, around 1960. The translation is, however, criticized by Lloyd P. Gerson in *The Cambridge Companion to Plotinus*, 1996/1999, who also maintains that the words of Plotinus in the Greek edition from Porphyrios are so ambiguous that almost every sentence gives opportunity for discussion.

stretched out as if to fly and two that covered the body. The seraph was attached to a cross, its arms were stretched out and the legs were together. Francis realized that his prayers to serve God in the most appropriate way had been heard, and that he would be like the crucified Christ. When the vision disappeared, he noticed the stigmata – he had been given the same wounds as Jesus received when he was crucified. At the same time, he experienced an overwhelming feeling of love. The stigmata that emerged on his hands, feet and in his side, were strong and gave constant pain. It has been said that when Francis was dead, it looked as if he just had been taken down from a cross. (It is said that more than 400 people by now have experienced having the stigmata. According to C. Bernard Ruffin, who has written a book about Padre Pio from Italy, this phenomenon was not known before the stigmata of Francis of Assisi.)

St Caterina of Siena (Caterina Benincasa, 1347-1380), who in most of her life lived as a Dominican nun in Siena in Italy, was canonized in 1431.[92] Caterina had healing powers and clairvoyance. She experienced ecstasies, such as Teresa of Avila described them, and also levitation. Ecstasies and visions were, literally, as daily food for her. The ecstasies came quite frequently within a period. During these times Caterina's body was always stiff and without feeling, she then saw and heard nothing. Sometimes many words came, and it also happened that she dictated letters while she was in ecstasy. Caterina had secretaries in attendance who were told to write down everything she said during the ecstasies. One day when they were eating, there was not enough food for everyone, for they had forgotten to go begging for food. Caterina said that they should start to eat anyway and it turned out that it was more than enough bread for everyone. During the entire meal Caterina was on her knees in her chamber, praying. Several times she healed psychotic people. When the plague ravaged in Siena and also at other times, she cured many diseases. Caterina is said to have lived without taking any kind of nourishment except the little she received through the Sacrament (which she received every day) and even though her body became thinner and thinner, she had an unbelievable strength when there was something that had to be done. Caterina also showed the stigmata, the first time happened during an ecstasy when she was twenty-three years old. These stigmata were not visible to others, according to the references, but they caused strong pain. Caterina had great influence over her fellow human beings and the foremost Christian leaders of the time, from the Pope downwards, even though she was only thirty-three years old when she died. According to what has been written Caterina was once examined by three of the most learned priests at the French court at a time when she stayed with the Pope in Avignon, to clarify how she could have such great influence on the Pope. They reached the conclusion that she had deeper insight into spiritual relationships than any doctor of theology. There are many people who have testified, both by word of mouth that has been later written down by others in her time, and through written statements from eyewitnesses, about the marvels she performed. Some of the stories were written by her confessor, Raimondo della Vigne, who later published his notes as a book.

St Teresa of Avila (1515-1582) is Spain's second Patron Saint (the first is Santiago the Apostle – Jacob the older, brother of John). She was considered a great mystic and a master of prayer. She reformed the Order of the Carmelite nuns and established several Carmelite monasteries where the nuns did not to possess anything but lived exclusively on alms. She was canonized in 1617 (along with Ignatius of Loyola and Francis Xavier). Teresa in her autobiography described the difference between being united with the divinity and being in ecstasy.[93] Although she tried to resist what was happening during the ecstasy, she had the feeling that her soul was lifted up and she was filled with delight. Sometimes she experienced that her body was lifted, which she was very unhappy for because it happened in someone else's presence. Teresa described what we in other words would call levitation – that she was being lifted up in the air by inexplicable powers. Her levitations were witnessed by several people, and they took place on different occasions. She reported the feelings she had during the levitations, the purely physical experience of being lifted. She believed that the experience began with the fact that she had a special wish, which probably must be interpreted as a desire, for unity with God. I find no reason to question her experiences, nor that did she actually levitate. This is said to have happened to other saints also, among them the contemporary of Teresa, John of the Cross (Juan de Yepes y Álvarez, 1542-1591, canonized in 1726). It has been said of Josef of Cupertino (1603-1663) that he could fly through the air, from the furthest back in the church and up to the Altar, which was witnessed by several people present.

St Padre Pio (Francesco Forgione, 1887-1968) was a monk of the Capuchin Order and lived most of his life in the Capuchin monastery La Madonna delle Grazie (The Madonna of Mercy) in San Giovanni Rotunda, Italy.[94] He was canonized in 2002. Padre Pio from a very young age wanted to become a monk, and in 1903 was accepted into a Capuchin monastery as a novice. In the same year, at the age of fifteen years, he had what might be called a 'light' experience when he witnessed a violent supernatural light. It is possible that he already at the age of twelve, when he was confirming to be a Christian, had his first spiritual experience. He has recorded that it was an unprecedented and unforgettable day, and that when he thought of that day later, he was always very touched. The Capuchin Order is very strict and conservative, and its tradition goes back to Francis of Assisi. Padre Pio has been canonized because of his strong commitment to God and the paranormal phenomena and miracles connected with him, especially his healing capabilities. Very early on he got the stigmata in his hands, in his side and on his feet. The first few signs came and went over short periods of time, and appeared as early as in 1910. They became permanent in 1918, when he was thirty-one years old. He had for many years prayed to God asking to suffer in the same way as Jesus suffered on the cross, despite the fact that he for a long time had been greatly affected due to unexpected illnesses, which, among other things, made it difficult for him to take nourishment and he was often bedridden.

A special paranormal characteristic of Padre Pio, which many people have confirmed, was his ability to appear in another place to that where he actually was – almost an out-of-body phenomenon. This phenomenon is called bilocation. Another strange phenomenon associated with Padre Pio is that people occasionally perceived his presence, in that they noticed a heavenly scent, which is described as a mixture of rose and violet. This was especially prominent when one was physically close to him, and it is assumed that it was due to the blood from the stigmata, though many people did not notice anything. Many experienced Padre Pio's fragrance without him being physically present, he could be miles away, and it was then connected with unexpected healing. Even after his death this was noticed. It appears that many holy personages have such a smell around them – it is generally known as an odour of sanctity. Many of the stories told about Padre Pio show that he was to some extent able to see into the future, and in addition to that, he could also tell a person about his/her life without having any previous knowledge of him/her. He could at times understand foreign languages that he had never studied. It is said that he sometimes gave information about deceased persons, whether they were well and had arrived in Heaven or not.

It should also be noted that he had initiated a hospital next to the monastery – a hospital that eventually became very large and much recommended, thanks to donations from Padre Pio's friends all over the world. Because of the many pilgrims and tourists that came to the monastery (essentially to Padre Pio), the town closest to the monastery – San Giovanni Rotondo – increased greatly in size – and the entire district had a strong economic up-turn. Originally, this was a very poor and isolated area. Even today, the flow of pilgrims to the monastery is great – there is said to be more people going there than to Lourdes.

Therese Neumann (1898-1962) is known for the strange events that are related to her life. She lived all her life in Konnersreuth in Bavaria, Germany. After a severe and prolonged illness period she was suddenly well and approximately one year later she began to get stigmata, similar to those of Francis of Assisi. Bishop Kristian Schjelderup, who visited Konnersreuth several times, has in his book *Under åpen himmel* (Under the Open Sky) provided an in-depth description of these stigmata, and the sufferings that Therese Neumann went through almost every Friday throughout the rest of her life. In addition to experiencing Jesus' sufferings, she also had visions from his life which accorded with the Biblical stories; and she was able to render words which in the beginning were incomprehensible, but which turned out to be the Aramaic, Greek, or Latin language that was spoken at Jesus' time. Another noteworthy aspect of Therese Neumann was that she from this time onward did not take any food or drink except a *hostie* (the little biscuit one gets in the Eucharist) and some liquid to swallow it down with. In spite of this, her weight was unchanged. Schjelderup has given a detailed report from the thorough examination and control which lasted the fourteen days that Therese Neumann underwent, in an attempt to uncover whether fraud could be behind the stories that were being told about her. Despite intensive surveillance, no cheating could be proved.

The Indian guru Yogananda also paid Therese Neumann a visit, and in his autobiography has described some of the same as that mentioned above. C. Bernard Ruffin wrote in his book about Padre Pio that Therese Neumann had out-of-body experiences. When that happened she was obviously somewhere other than where she was physically seen to be.

Kristian Schjelderup mentioned that Therese Neumann's consciousness could change, and that it involved four different awareness-related consciousness levels. The most common was the normal one, in which she was as other people and you would not imagine that there was something special about her. However, she could get into an ecstatic visionary state where she seemed to be without contact with the outside world. It was in this state she experienced visions of Jesus' life, and also visions of other important events in Church history. A third state was one that Schjelderup described, as if she really experienced what she saw, and could render what she saw and heard. He mentioned that she then expressed herself like a five year old child. The fourth state, Schjelderup called the elevated resting state. Then she seemed to be united with Christ, and at the same time having contact with her environment and being able to answer questions. Then it seemed as if she knew everything. When she was back in the normal consciousness, she did not know what she had said while being in the other states.

Non-eating Saints in the Western World

Also many other people apart from Caterina of Siena and Therese Neumann have lived without taking any kind of nourishment, according to what has been reported. Among those are the following Christian saints: Lidwina of Schiedam, Elizabeth of Rent, Dominica Lazarri, Angela of Foligno, Louise Lateau, Nicholas of Flüe and Brother Klaus.[95]

Martinus has explained that the human development in the future will allow people to replace the physical nourishment (the consumption of food) with another nutritional source which he called the respiratory nutrition. He has said that eventually people will come to live only on air.

The Canonization Process in the Catholic Church

The Roman Catholic Church recognizes that miracles in the form of visions of heavenly beings or deceased persons, unexpected healings, stigmata, bilocation, precognition, mind reading and maybe also other unexplained phenomena, do happen. A wide range of people have been declared saints by the Catholic Church, and many others have been declared blessed – the beatification process. The Catholic Church has established committees whose task it is to determine whether a person is to be declared *Blesséd* or a *Saint*. This is a long and circumstantial process.[96] In Padre Pio's case C. Bernhard Ruffin has told that it took six years to collect the information that led to the beatification on 5th May 1999. There are a number of requirements that must be met before a beatification takes place. First, the candidate must be considered holy, not only by his hometown. Furthermore, in order to be declared *Venerable*, the candidate must have led a life of faith, hope and charity, as well as having exhibited prudence, justice, fortitude and temperance. Then, for the Pope to declare the candidate for *Blesséd* (beatus or beata), all members of the Theological College of cardinals and bishops must recommend such a statement.

In order for the candidate to be declared 'Blesséd' proof is required that miracles have happened after the candidate's death. Preferably, any such miracle ought to happen in the form of inexplicable healing which takes place after it has been prayed to the candidate for healing.

The healing must have taken place immediately and spontaneously after such a prayer, and it must be lasting. The healing must be confirmed by medical experts and by a group of theologians. The latter will seek to determine whether the healing happened as a result of divine intervention thanks to prayer to the candidate. In Padre Pio's case the miracle happened to a lady with a very serious illness which required speedy operation of a tumour in her neck. The operation was scheduled for 3rd November 1995, but on the 1st November she contacted one of the brothers in the monastery, Padre Pio's monastery La Madonna delle Grazie, and asked him to pray for her. This he did by Padre Pio's grave. The lady said that she sensed Padre Pio's special odour while she was in the hospital. Anyway, she felt better. The tumour in the neck turned out to have disappeared and the operation could be cancelled. In order for a person to be canonized, another miracle must happen after the beatification process is ended. Only then can the candidate be declared a saint.

Spiritual teachers, avatars, prophets and the like

> Watch out for false prophets. They come to you in sheep's clothing, but inwardly they are ferocious wolves.   Matt 7.15

Although there are false prophets, there can be no doubt that there are people with great feelings for charity, extensive wisdom and extraordinary abilities. The capabilities which the Catholic saints have obtained, are normally a result of a strong commitment to God and Jesus. However, there are and have also been many other persons with strong spiritual basis and special capabilities.

In Hinduism there are stories about *avatars* incarnating on Earth as supervisors. An avatar is considered an incarnation of the deity. The word 'avatar' according to the ancient Hindu Scriptures means God's descent in the flesh, which means that God took human form and lived on Earth. At regular intervals avatars are said to have come to the Earth, but they do not always make themselves known. According to Yogananda an avatar is an individuality that stands outside what Yogananda calls 'the universal accounting' – outside of maya (people living under the veil) with its bondage and reincarnation cycles, but one who chooses to come back to a physical body.[97] They know the truth about life and death. Yogananda explained that Krishna, Rama, Buddha and Patanjali were avatars who emerged in India. In addition, there is an individuality that Yogananda called a *mahavatar* (a great avatar), namely he who is called Babaji. (The term actually means revered father or grandfather.) Babaji presented himself to Yogananda in 1920 and told him that he should travel to America and work there.

Aivanhov has told that he met Babaji, who appeared as a handsome young man, when he was in India in 1959.[98] Yogananda mentioned that a mahavatar always stands in relation to Christ, and that they together are working for humanity and its development.

A *bodhisattva*, which is a Sanskrit word for one who has the potential of a *bodhi* within, is one that is committed to work so that all human beings can become buddhas, which is to obtain liberation or Nirvana. It is said that they incarnate on Earth again and again as persons of great spiritual power and wisdom. Sogyal Rinpoche believes that the current Dalai Lama is a bodhisattva, an incarnation of Avalokiteshvara, the Buddha of eternal compassion.[99]

According to the *Tibetan Book of the Dead* a departed will meet bodhisattvas as helpers in the period just after the physical death.

An *adept* is an individual who has been through many incarnations and who eventually has acquired magical powers and a lot of wisdom. Rudolf Steiner believed that Apollonius of Tyana was an adept.[100]

Prophets are human beings who have a special contact with God, and who are being told by God what people should know. The prophets are not considered to be incarnations of the deity, nor necessarily incarnated spiritual beings.

Spiritual teachers are people whose commitment it is to help people to find the right way. They are people with extensive knowledge and profound spiritual insight. Rudolf Steiner must be considered a spiritual teacher. The same applies to a number of other people referred to in this book, such as Martinus, Aivanhov, Yogananda and Bob Moore.

Gurus are spiritual teachers who have disciples or students to whom they give direct teaching. In India they distinguish between gurus and *pandits* (former prime minister of India Jawaharlal Nehru (1889-1964) was referred to as Pandit Nehru). A pandit is a great teacher who does not have disciples. Ken Wilber may perhaps be said to be a pandit. *Mahatma* is an Indian honourable title given prominent spiritual leaders, a kind of saint, sage or guru. Mohandas Gandhi (1869-1948), the great Indian liberation and peace promoter, was called Mahatma Gandhi.

Aivanhov has explained that there are four categories of people that reincarnate on Earth.[101] The lowest category is people who commit crimes and incur heavy karmic burdens.

The next category, which includes most people, is for those who are seeking to develop themselves spiritually, although they do not get so far that they manage to free themselves from the karma they have incurred. The third category is people who come to Earth to perform certain tasks. These are often so developed that they do not have to come back to Earth when they die. The last category is individuals that have such compassion for people that they voluntarily return to Earth to help mankind. These individuals can even accept to be killed. He said that the latter (Aivanhov used the word creatures) can take possession of a highly developed physical human being without having to incarnate, to work with him and in him. Aivanhov mentioned Jesus in this connection. He referred to John 14.23: "*Jesus answered and said unto him. 'If a man loves me, he will keep my words: and my Father will love him, and we will come unto him, and make our abode with him'.*" (This is what Rudolf Steiner thinks happened to the person Jesus, that the Christ took residence in him.)

3.4. *Magicians*

Colin Wilson wrote in the book *The Occult* about a number of people with supernatural abilities and about many strange phenomena (occult means hidden). He is commenting on phenomena such as synchronicity, astral projection, telepathy, levitation, reincarnation, discovering water by dowsing, astrology, telekinetic, flying saucers, vampires, werewolves, ghosts, witches, magicians, shamanism, predictions and divination. He has given in-depth descriptions of people who were renowned magicians of their day, such as Nostradamus, Rasputin, Gurdjieff, Ouspensky, Crowley and many more. It should be noted that some of these also were mystics, although they did not appear as such. Most of the people Wilson reviews practised what he calls white magic – magic that did not hurt other people. There are however people who practise black magic, which aims at harming others. This is what we normally associate with witches and magic. Wilson wrote that black magic is real enough.

The British author George Bernard Shaw, according to Wilson, experienced being a victim of black magic himself, which resulted in an excruciating pain in his back. This he attributed to hate from a special woman. Black magic is usually performed by an individual and directed towards another individual. If the magic is hidden, it must be the practitioner's consciousness that manages to influence another's subconsciousness.

Wilson has in his book an analysis of the witch hunting that took place during the Middle Ages, and mentions a few books in which he has found acceptable explanations regarding this phenomenon. Poverty, wars, pestilence, boredom and sexual frustration, along with an imagination that ran wild, are some of the backgrounds. At the same time, the Church greatly contributed with its myths, symbols and descriptions of the devil, as well as its prosecution of people of 'different' thinking. At that time they did not understand psychiatry – cases such as hysteria. It was believed that insane persons were possessed by the devil. Many people are, however, easily suggestible and can easily lose their self-control. This is particularly true in large crowds and often results in violent actions. There are many examples of such behaviour from pop-concerts and soccer matches, not to forget Hitler-Germany's national mass meetings. The manipulation of people's minds that occur in such situations is a kind of black magic.

There is a big difference between a mystic and a magician. A magician has often paranormal abilities, either congenital or learnt, and can often perform many of the miracles that are attributed to mystics. However, according to Evelyn Underhill, there is an essential difference between the mystics and the magicians. A mystic will always be led by the heart and has a charitable quality that is difficult for ordinary people to match. A mystic will also have a deeply spiritual outlook on life. A magician, on the other hand, is following his/her intellect, and is not particularly concerned with the spiritual dimension of life. Many magicians use their abilities for the benefit of their fellow beings. But as often happens with those who have special paranormal abilities without a strong spiritual anchoring, these capabilities are being used for demonstration and show and the main purpose is to attract an audience and to make money. This might inflate the ego, so that the show and the publicity arising from it are what is important.

3.5. Shamanism – people with healing power and clairvoyant abilities

Shamans or medicine men/women are people usually known for their healing abilities, but they often also have the power of divination.[102] The word shaman is mostly used in connection with the Inuits and the nomads in the world's northernmost regions. It is believed to derive from the Russian Tungisi people, and seems to be related to similar words in many other Asian cultures. A *noaide* is the name of a Sami (Lapp) medicine man/woman. The term 'medicine man' has mostly been used in ethnic groups or people from the southern part of the world. Most ethnic groups, including those under the influence of the major religious systems, have in their midst people who act as magicians and healers within a spiritual system. Shamanism seems to go back to prehistoric times. A cave painting in Lascaux in France (from before the year 10,000 BCE) is interpreted by many as an image of a shaman performing a ritual.

The Icelandic history writer Snorri Sturluson (1179-1241) wrote in the *Ynglingasaga* (the story about the group of people called Ynglinga) that the leader of the group (later the god) Odin was *seidman* or *galdre-smith*. This is the same as being a shaman. Odin knew people's destiny and could tell what would happen in the future, according to Snorri. He was able to inflict death and disaster or disabilities on people. And he could take away people's senses and give them to others. These are powers that are attributed to shamans in primitive societies. The following description of Snorri is typical for shamanic stories: Odin often changed his physical figure; then his body would seem to be dead or dormant, while he himself could be a four-footed animal, a bird or fish or worm, and flew away to distant lands in the blink of an eye, on an errand for himself or others.

A person becomes a shaman either as a result of the profession being inherited, or as a result of the gods having chosen him or her. The latter may, for example, be if he/she is struck by lightning; or a dramatic dream is experienced as an appointment; being born with a handicap or disease; having psychotic attacks, epilepsy, or something that causes loss of consciousness for a short period of time, or a similar dramatic episode. As well as such a selection, it may be that he or she is required to undergo a long period of training and to sustain extreme hardship.

The Romanian-American historian, professor of religion Mircea Eliade (1907-1986)[i] has in his book *Shamanism – Archaic techniques of Ecstasy and Patterns in Comparative Religion* written that the typical characteristic of a shaman is not to physically represent a spirit, but that he/she during ecstasy is able to rise up to heaven or down to the land of the dead. There he will meet souls and either manages to bring a soul back to its earthly body, or to learn what is required for healing the person. However, certain shamans are able to channel spirits or allow a spirit to take residence in his/her body, but that is not really a shaman's task. In order to achieve the ecstatic state the shamans have used different techniques and different types of equipment.

These methods have changed through the ages, mostly due to the influence of religious thoughts and rituals from other ethnic groups nearby. The shaman's dress code shows that he identifies himself with for example an eagle (by including in his dress an eagle's feather), or a horse (by having artefacts considered to represent a horse for example a rod with a horse's

---

i. Eliade moved to Paris in 1945 and taught at École des Hautes-Études, Sorbonne. In 1958 he moved to the US, where he was the head of the Institute of religious history at the University of Chicago.

head). The shaman's use of artefacts will likewise be representative of his activity in the hereafter, or be the means by which he gets there. A rope hung up in a tree, for example, will represent his ascent to Heaven. A tree represents the connection between the Earth and the Heaven – The World Tree. When a shaman climbs the tree, it represents the contact between Heaven and Earth. A drum is a widely-used instrument for achieving the ecstatic state. The drum's design, its material and the symbols plotted on it, are also important. The shaman needs such articles to get the right associations during the ecstasy.

Colin Wilson has referred to studies of African Shamanism and witchcraft, showing that humans have strong unconscious abilities. As an example he mentions the rain dance, which has actually resulted in rain, or a leopard dance which resulted in living leopards appearing just outside the circle of dancers. The phenomenon of the rain dance shows that the subconscious is in contact with nature or matter and can affect this, which psychokinesis and the poltergeist phenomena also show. The English biologist and author Lyall Watson (b.1939)[i] in the book *The Lightning Bird* writes of Adrian Boshier (1939-1978), a South African who as a very young man went alone into the African interior. He was accepted by a primitive tribe and became a disciple with the tribe's medicine man. He was later hired by the archaeological museum in Johannesburg. Lyall Watson recounts Boshier's life and how he and the tribe actually managed to influence the weather through a rain dance. The explanation in regard to the effect of the rain dance may be that intense mental and physical concentration affects the air currents, so that a low pressure area is formed, which involves the inflowing of moist air. Both Wilson and Watson also refer to a strange phenomenon occurring in the Pacific Ocean, where certain people could call on turtles and get them to come to the beach. This shows that people can be in telepathic contact with animals.

The Russian psychiatrist Olga Kharitidi has described her meeting with Siberian shamans in the book *Inn i sirkelen* (Into the Circle). Her experiences are from the Altai region in the South-Eastern Siberia. She begins the book by referring to a dream experience, where she is a spirit that is called during a shaman séance to revive a dead woman. Her story is consistent with the descriptions that Mircea Eliade has given about Shamanism from various places in the world.

---

i. Lyall Watson is a researcher and author. He has a university degree in biology and zoology as well as a PhD in ethology (the study of animal behaviour). He grew up in South Africa and worked for a time as a professor in England. He has participated in mediumistic séances, gathered material concerning automatic writing and speech, anecdotes and histories regarding hypnotic regression. He has listened to voices without apparent physical sources, which is recorded on audio tape. For many years he has collected all possible sorts of stories from people who have experienced something paranormal6. This is done in order to seek to understand the phenomena, and he has commented on them in his books.

Mircea Eliade concludes his study with the comment that the shamanistic ecstasy could be considered a re-actualizing of the mythical time before the beginning of time, when people believed they were able to communicate with Heaven, where they felt that there was a celestial Supreme Being. Then there should also be a First Shaman, who was sent to the Earth by the celestial Supreme Being or his deputy to help humanity against diseases and evil spirits. This later changed to the worship of ancestors and divine or half-divine entities who took over the contact with people. Stronger emphasis was then put on the contact with these beings, and successively also for a contact with the realm of the dead. Still later the phenomenon of the shaman being possessed by spirits emerged. Eliade thought that much of this was due to influence from Buddhism and Lamaism, and also from the Iranian religion. However, Eliade emphasized that the shaman's ecstasy in many cases can be compared to the ecstatic experiences of the real mystics. And as these, the shamans have in many cases gained the ability to heal.

3.6. Autistic savant syndrome

Researchers have established that retardism caused by a defective gene, a disease similar to Down's syndrome, can give extraordinary abilities within a narrow range, despite the fact that the person is greatly retarded.[103] Often such people have autism and suffer from what is called the autistic savant syndrome. The American Kim Peek had this disease, but was able to memorize by heart all the books in his library – more than 6000. In addition, he remembered the post numbers of all the cities in America and all the local telephone area codes (see the Movie *The Rain Man*). Also the Scottish artist Richard Wawro (b.1952), who is internationally famous for his paintings, fits this description. Other examples of such extraordinary abilities in persons who are not able to attend to their daily necessities, was shown in a TV program on the Norwegian TV channel NRK1 sometime in the 1980s. The three people presented in this program could neither read or write and they needed assistance for most of the daily cores. However, the following tasks were resolved without difficulty:

Person A could in a few seconds tell which day in the week a particular date was, whether it was for example one, two, forty-six or one-hundred-and-fifty years forward or back in time. A person, sitting with a calculator and who knew the years when there was an extra day, was unable to find the proper day of the week as quickly. Person B did not know notes, but could play the piano without any problems. He was self-taught and could render difficult melodies after having heard the tune just once. Person C could, after having studied a building for a short time, such as the Houses of Parliament in London, render it perfectly in the smallest detail by drawing. This was Stephen Wiltshire, London, who is a very renowned artist today. He has, thanks to his drawing engagement, managed to get rid of most of his autism.

He was also presented in a BBC television program that was shown on the Norwegian channel TVNorge on 18th May 2008 titled *Autism and drawing genius*. In another Norwegian television program they showed a person who could see the square root of a large number faster than the reviewer was able to write the equation on his calculator.

Person A used only his head and mouth to give the correct answer. Person B used his ears and hands, as well as the piano. Person C used his eyes and hands, as well as the drawing paper and pencil. Person A could hardly be said to have used his memory, in which case he had to have all the dates and days stored in his head, but he must have obtained this information from somewhere. B and C could either have phenomenal memories, or else they would have to have the sounds and images ready for the inner eye. In addition, they must have had quite unusual abilities to convey to the piano and the paper what they heard and saw. Brilliant composers like Mozart and Beethoven must also have had a consciousness filled with completely different experiences from other people.

I have to presume that those people are using their brains in ways completely different from most people; they must have quite a different type of consciousness. Researchers have been able to show that such peoples' brains differ greatly from the brains of people who are categorized as normal, as some parts of an autistic person's brain have evolved much more than normal while other parts are less developed. One question concerns the physical parts of the brain, another is how they manage to manipulate the data required to perform intricate mathematical operations. That it is possible in a short period of time to say the day in the week of a date far back in time, where one has to take the extra days in consideration, is to me quite incomprehensible.

I would think that somewhere deep within us there is an opening, a channel, to a collective knowledge base. (Perhaps it is this that is called, by Helena Blavatsky, the Akashic records.) When this opening is of a certain size, the ability to convey what we are receiving from there in the form of stories, pictures and music will be correspondingly strong. The three people we saw on TV must have had an opening to this collective knowledge store, but that must have occurred at the expense of what we call normal consciousness.

3.7. *Poltergeist phenomena and psychokinesis*

A poltergeist (the word is German and means a knocking spirit) is a relatively well-known phenomenon within parapsychological research, and sufficiently researched that there is justification for giving it its own section here. This is a phenomenon which includes everything from articles flying through the air for no apparent cause, to strange sounds and much more. In some cases, it has been maintained that there is no other explanation than that it must be spirits triggering the strange events. This is discussed further in the section about spirit beings. But in many cases these phenomena are associated with a specific person. Often, there is a youth in puberty, who at first does not understand that he or she is the cause of the phenomena. The English healer Matthew Manning (b. 1955) has spoken about the poltergeist phenomena that occurred in his vicinity as he grew up – and there were several incidents and of very different natures. He mentioned in particular the issue his school principal had to face – whether to expel Manning due to the spirit activity (which meant that he thought this was real phenomena, with the publicity this would involve), or to let Manning continue at school and let the phenomena also continue (there would still be publicity, thanks to the fellow students).[104]

The events surrounding the Icelandic medium Indridi Indridason (1883-1912) at the beginning of the twentieth century was very special.[105] During a four-year period many séances were held with him at the centre. Everything that happened was witnessed by trustworthy people and thoroughly checked. They experienced all those classic poltergeist phenomena that are associated with physical mediums, such as loud tapping sounds, levitation of furniture and also of the medium, strong air currents, light phenomena, inexplicable smells, strong voices, movement of objects and furniture, remote playing of musical instruments and unknown materialized figures, as well as the short term dematerialization of an arm. During a séance the medium was dragged up in the air with his feet facing the ceiling and the head hanging down. However, the strange voices did not give any clear answers to the questions posed, or they gave wrong answers.

David Fontana (1934-2010), professor of psychology at the Cardiff University and visiting professor of transpersonal psychology at the John Moore's University in Liverpool, in 2005 published the book *Is there an Afterlife? - A Comprehensive Overview of the Evidence*. Here he discusses among other subjects the poltergeist phenomenon that goes under the name of The Cardiff Poltergeist Case. He himself had observed this phenomenon several times. It did not seem to be attached to any particular person, just to a particular house, in a workshop, in Cardiff. The phenomenon went on for about two years, from 1989 to 1992. Then the workshop closed down and the house shut up. The phenomenon began with rocks thrown on the roof of a shed that stood on the property. Then objects were thrown about indoors, such as stones, screws, pens and keys of unknown origin. Moreover, they found coins that were eighty years old, dated 1912. Objects moved. Blue flames were seen. Wooden planks were thrown in from the garden. Banging was heard. The ghost, which they called Pete, did sometimes react on request to throw something. With encouragement, one-pound banknotes turned up – in all, they found more than seventy pounds in this way. On three occasions the house's owner, Paul, observed, a boy of about twelve years of age, but only for a moment each time – as in the blink of an eye. The last time the boy waved to him – on this occasion Paul was in the house to lock it up for good. Investigations showed that a little boy had been killed in a car accident nearby a few years before the phenomena began. But further explanations as to a possible connection were not found. Similar poltergeist phenomena have been experienced and described by many others.

William G. Roll (1926-2012), professor of psychology at the State University of West Georgia, USA, has devoted much time to researching these phenomena. In particular, he studied a young woman – Tina Resch (b.1969), and the phenomena that came with her in 1984. They experienced candlesticks, lamps and pictures moving without anyone touching them. A shower-head on the floor above began to drip without anyone nearby. No one has been able to present an explanation as to how these phenomena could occur, but many have expressed scepticism about their authenticity. The Tina Resch case is to be found on the Internet. There you can also see a picture of her while a phone cable is suspended horizontally in the air in front of her. William G. Roll was interviewed in a television documentary about the case that appeared in the US in the 1990s.[106]

Colin Wilson has a long review and analysis of the poltergeist phenomena in his book *Mysteries*, citing among other cases the experiments with Matthew Manning and Uri Geller, who showed that they were able to affect matter mentally. (It must be noted that Uri Geller has been caught cheating in some experiments and some scientists are today maintaining that he always cheated.) Wilson believes that people have capabilities that go far beyond what we ourselves are aware of. When he considers all paranormal phenomena and is searching for a common denominator for them, he comes to the conclusion that everything goes back to the consciousness or psyche.

What to believe about this? Many of the poltergeist phenomena had such strict control protocols in place when they were examined, and especially those which took place around Indridason, that cheating must have been impossible. Can it be that everything is hallucinations – in this case shared by the many people present – experiences that include vision, hearing and more at the same time? I have difficulty believing that it is so. It is also a fact that articles and heavy furniture have moved and that articles have been materialized. This indicates that there must have been a strong force or energy associated with the phenomena – but what kind of force? Some of it may perhaps be explained as activities from nature spirits, although we do not understand what that is. But it also has to be some sort of psychic energy – this is known as psychokinesis – which, under special circumstances, is transformed into physical energy.

Helena Blavatsky has explained that psychokinesis is the phenomenon that occurs when a medium somehow manages to evoke a force that causes things to move or to make other unexpected physical phenomena to happen, as the poltergeist events show.

I am convinced that mind can affect physical processes, although scientists today have not been able to document this in a satisfactory manner. I (and others) have experienced that computers and copying- or writing machines 'crash' without any natural explanation other than that I have been in strong emotional state, either because of being stressed with things that I was in a hurry to get done, or because I was faced with difficult professional tasks or due to complicated personal relationships. Why do such things happen when you are most stressed? I suppose that the imbalance or tension that might be in my mind affects the environment, whether this is people or machines. That means that there must be some sort of electromagnetic radiation, as Helena Blavatsky has mentioned, which affects the machines.

At Princeton University in the US, Professor Robert G. Jahn and clinical psychologist Brenda Dunne have over many years repeatedly sought to prove that the mind can control physical processes by so-called random number generator experiments – also called RNG experiments or micro-psychokinesis. One such experiment was conducted on a live TV show from the BBC with the famous British hypnotist Paul McKenna leading the show. The program was shown on Norwegian television in March 1998 under the title *Det skjulte* (The Occult). The equipment used were computers that were electronically controlled and where random binary number combinations (i.e. built on two possible states, plus or minus, zero or one) formed the background for the movement of the generator. The hypothesis was that, on this basis, the change in the number combinations movement of the machines may be affected mentally – by the test person's mind power. In the television program the audience was asked to try to bring up the image of an astronaut on a TV screen, instead of a different image that the screen also could show. Both images looked rather fuzzy when the experiment started. The astronaut came clearly up after a few minutes. One of the scientists at Princeton University has said that they do not know how this phenomenon could be explained other than by use of the term psychokinesis – which is not understood either. The scientists suggest that there is a kind of resonance between the consciousness of the audience and the computer.

Psychologist Jane Henry, who heads The Open University Experiential Research Group at The British Psychological Society's Consciousness and Experiential Psychology Section, has, in an article from 2005, commented on the published reports from psychokinesis research, including the RNG experiments at Princeton University. More than a thousand such tests have been performed at this university with more than one hundred people in millions of individual tests.

Jane Henry mentions that in 1987 a meta-analysis was made of 832 such micro-psychokinesis experiments carried out by 68 different researchers, of which 258 were control studies. There emerged a small deviation from what was expected, which could not be attributed to coincidence – as the odds that this was accidental was calculated to a trillion to one. Jane Henry's conclusion of this analysis and other similar meta-analyses she had considered, was that a weak micro-psychokinesis effect was shown, which cannot have been caused by errors in the methods used, or because there were few researchers or participants in the projects. However, when it comes to repeated spontaneous macro-psychokinesis experiments, she did not regard the results as compelling. The associate professor of physics at the University of Athens, Dr Fotini Pallikari, however, is very sceptical of the conclusions of these meta-analyses. She argues that the experiments do not show any particular deviation from what can be expected from statistical calculations – the results lie close to a Gaussian curve with 50/50 result as mean value. If more experiments were made, the marking of this mean value will be stronger. She points out that according to probability calculations one positive result very often will be followed by more of the same sort and vice versa, this is the so-called Markovian effect. This may explain the observed deviations from the standard. She is of the opinion that so far not enough experiments have been made for the meta-analyses to provide a reliable picture. It requires a prodigious amount of tests in order to be able to draw the appropriate conclusion from these efforts.[107]

3.8. Predictions

In General

Researchers have conducted repeatable experiments that show that prior knowledge is a real phenomenon. Some of these are discussed by Dean Radin, PhD[i], in his book *Entangled Minds*. But the application of this is an open question, and can we rely on information we receive about the future? We want to be better acquainted with ourselves, but without it costing too much in tears and pain. And we would love to get help with difficult decisions. Many people contact psychics or someone who can predict the future through the help of cards, stars, coffee beans, intestines, or otherwise. Many believe that they are getting help; otherwise it would not be such a good business for those people who provide such assistance but it might be sensible to consider the human propensity for being gullible. Five different ways of fooling the spectator into believing something different than what actually is happening, have been identified. These apply to techniques that could fool the senses, mind, memory, attention, or simply by providing incorrect or untrue information. One way is to ask leading questions, so that the answer appears to originate from the spectator/client and not from the questioner. Another technique is to use visual clues such as the client's appearance, clothing, wedding ring or something similar, and then through the initial conversation draw out further details to build on. You can then

---

i. Dean Radin has been the head of the laboratory for consciousness research at the University of Nevada, Las Vegas, and is now (in 2008) the leader of a similar laboratory at the Department of Noetic Science in Petaluma, California. He holds a PhD in psychology.

move on with a personality description that seems personal, but which is representative for the vast majority of people. Some such statements are mentioned by Paul McKenna in his book *Our Mysterious World*. The medium will often have long experience in judging clients and good knowledge of people's behaviour, and can therefore draw the right conclusion on this basis and from the conversation with the client.[108]

The starting point for both parties in a divination situation will usually be an understanding that what is being said is from a paranormal source, and that it therefore is correct. It turns out that the client, furthermore, has a tendency to emphasize and remember all the statements that seem to be right, while those that do not fit are easily overlooked. That means that the client believes that the predicament is more appropriate than it actually is. There are also many mistakes that can be made in attempts to confirm or disprove a theory. Such errors can be anything from a deliberate attempt to twist the outcome as to being careless when setting up a test or during the actual test. In particular, the subconsciousness is good at twisting results in the direction wanted or hoped for (consciously or unconsciously). Even in control surveys using assistants to collect information, the results seem to go in the direction expected by the planners of the survey. It may seem as if this expectation somehow is picked up by the assistants or the test person. Moreover, researchers have now come to the conclusion that those who believe in paranormal phenomena often obtain more positive results in a test situation than the sceptics.

People have throughout all time used different methods to try to predict what will happen in the future. The most well-known predictions are those that have come down from the oracle in Delphi in ancient Greece. Many of these were ambiguous, whereas others – if the quotes as we know them today are correct – display an amazing prior knowledge, even if a great deal of imagination is required to interpret the oracle's saying. The Greek historian Herodotus (c. 485-425 BCE) quotes the answer the oracle gave King Croesus, when asked whether the King should go to war against King Cyrus of Persia. The response of the oracle was that if the King started this war, a large kingdom would perish (although it did not say which). A somewhat clearer answer was given when the Persian king Xerxes with a great army approached Athens in 480 BCE. The remaining free Greek city states would be threatened if the Athenians were defeated and the city of Athens taken. The oracle stated that the Athenians should withdraw from the enemy, but that they one day should meet the enemy face to face. It was further said that then the wall of trees would not fall, and that the divine Salamis would bring death to women's sons. The Athenian population therefore withdrew to the island of Salamis and left Athens to the enemy. The wall of trees was interpreted to mean ships. That Salamis was denoted divine, had to mean that the Greeks would win the upcoming sea battle, which they did.

The predictions of the French doctor and astrologer Michel de Notredame (1503-1566), known as Nostradamus, have been subject to much discussion.[109] Not everyone who has studied them agree that they predict what the different interpreters see in them. The disasters that Nostradamus predicted would take place at the beginning of the year 2000 have not happened. One verse (Nostradamus presented all his predictions in verses consisting of four lines) which many persons from his own time interpreted as a prediction about King Henry II of France's imminent death, was, however, correct. Although the King's name was not mentioned, the prediction about the way he died was accurate.

Another well-known story concerns the prediction that foretold or at least helped the Spaniard Hernán Cortés with his conquest of Mexico. Part of the story comes from the Franciscan monk Sahagún who lived in the middle of the sixteenth century. Some of it is told by the history writer Tezozomoc. The rest comes from the memoirs of the Spanish conquistador Bernal Díaz de Castillo, who accompanied Cortés during the whole conquest and who died in 1581. Cortés himself sent many letters about his experiences to the Spanish Emperor Charles V, and a state in the area (Tlaxcala) sent a letter begging for mercy to the Emperor about 1540, which consisted of fifty sheets with pictures detailing the conquest. The story was published as a book in 1632.[110] Thus there are a great deal of contemporary sources to relate to. The Mexicans' second main god, Quetzalcoatl had, a very long time before the Spanish conquest, been expelled. It was predicted, however, that he would come back and recapture his kingdom and impose his religion. He was against human sacrifices, which was a very important part of the Mexicans' religious practice and was performed on a large scale. It had been predicted that this god would come back across the sea from an unknown land to the East and aboard a magical vessel. It was expected that this would happen in the year 1519. The god would have a black full beard and white skin and be dressed in black, with a distinctive hat on his head. In addition, the Mexicans' king, Montezuma II, had in a vision seen "Reeds who moved as if they were people, armed for war, riding on animals of the deer family". (It is maintained that the Mexicans had never seen horses.) Furthermore, there were lots of nature signs indicating that a disaster was approaching: a comet appeared in the sky, there had been a strong Northern light, there had recently been earthquakes, as well as some other abnormal events. All these predictions were fulfilled by Cortés. In addition, it came to pass that he came on shore on the god's name day which was 21st April. This god expectation, in content part religious and part magical, could explain that it was possible for Cortés to conquer the strongly fortified and populated country with a very small army.[i] It should also be noted that the Europeans had firearms

---

i. It is possible that this myth is due to the landing of a Chinese fleet in Mexico around 1422 – see the book 1421 by Gavin Menzies, concerning the circumnavigation of the world in 1421-1424. The Chinese had brought horses.

and that the Mexicans were fighting each other, although I cannot see that this should have effect on the conquest of the capital. (But it is also possible that the easy conquest was due to a plague that decimated the population by almost sixty percent – a conclusion scientists have reached in 2012.)

There are plenty other reports from dreams and visions, which show that many have a prior feeling or have received a warning, about something that is going to happen in the future. But it is perhaps more correct to say that it is a prediction about something that may happen in the future. The future does not seem to be totally destined. The person, who has a vision or a dream, can in many cases change the prediction if appropriate steps are taken. There is also a matter of interpreting what one sees. And when it comes to interpretation, it is important to remember all the different types of information that one unconsciously can take into the consideration.

Dowsing with a twig or pendulum

There are many people in Norway who have found water wells by way of dowsing. A dowsing twig is a soft branch shaped like a Y, where the dowser holds the ends of the two arms in a special way and with the sharp end pointing horizontally forward. If the dowser passes a water steam the sharp end will be pushed down (or up) in spite of the dowser's determination to keep it steady. There are special copper rods on sale that can be used, although not in quite the same way. Many dowsers also use a pendulum when searching for water or other substances such as metals or minerals. Dowsing has also been used to discover earth radiation, and in search for people disappeared in an avalanche. Several attempts have been made to test the reality of dowsing.

Professor Rolf Manne, Norway, has in an article from 1999, commented upon some such attempts (where he also referred to a statement from Professor Jan Frøyland, Norway, who has rejected the concept of earth radiation).[111] Rolf Manne has pointed out that the twig is held in suspense in a position that is highly unstable, and that a tiny muscle impulse is sufficient to move it. Manne mentioned further that some people do not have to use dowsing, because they can demonstrate a source of water by sensations in their body. He also mentioned that there have been a number of so-called double-blind trials, where neither the applicant nor those who were present along with the applicant knew the correct answer. Another such test was that different dowsers should try to find the same water or article, or that the same person should find places which he or she previously had found. All such tests are said to have been negative. That is, the dowser did not find what he or she searched for. Manne's conclusion was that such methods only work when the applicant knows the answer.

Professor Hans-Dieter Betz at the University of Munich, however, around 1990, arranged some tests regarding the use of pendulum when searching for water, where more than 40 dowsing-experts participated. His conclusion on these trials was that this is a real phenomenon. In America many oil companies are supposed to have used pendulum experts to find oil wells, with successful results.[112]

Colin Wilson has devoted an entire chapter in his book *Mysteries* to experiments with the pendulum (dowsing) conducted by the British archaeologist Thomas C. Lethbridge (1915-1971) as described in Lethbridge's books.[113] Lethbridge has also written several books on non-sensual perception (ESP, extrasensory perception). Colin Wilson wrote that he is convinced that Lethbridge is the only scholar of the paranormal who in the twentieth century has provided a comprehensive and compelling theory of the paranormal. He performed many experiments with pendulums and found that the pendulum responded to water, minerals, materials, thoughts and feelings according to the length of the string the pendulum was held in. Slowly there emerged that there was a reaction for several things at the same length of the string, but that the number of swings of the pendulum differed for each article. By using the pendulum, he learned that all objects have a kind of field around them, and he believed that it was this field that the pendulum responded to. Water seemed to have a very active field. The length of the radius corresponded to the pendulum's string length. Lethbridge created a diagram for the different reactions of the pendulum. He discovered, inter alia, that if he put the various lengths into the figure of a circle, the opposite qualities could be found on opposite sides of the circle. He found furthermore that the same article reacted on different lengths, but with exactly forty inches (101.6 cm) increase each time. The peculiar thing was that the reaction was not directly above the article, but a little to the side. He tried this with spirals instead of circles, and got the same result every time he increased the pendulum's length with forty inches – it was like a new twist on the spiral. It was as though he registered several dimensions, and he suggests that there may be multiple spirit worlds that he got in touch with in this way. Colin Wilson pointed out that this may sound unlikely, but that anyone who takes the trouble to try can achieve the same results.[i]

Colin Wilson, and several other people to whom he referred and who were practicing the use of the pendulum including Thomas Lethbridge, assumed that the reactions may be due to the user of the pendulum and his

---

i. In the Norwegian newspaper Dagbladet of 9.4.2011, in its week-end journal Magasinet, there was an article with the title *Kvistmannen* (The Twig Man) concerning Sverre Øksne, Oslo, (then age 85, a chemist with university degrees also in physics and botanics and a former researcher at the Norwegian Research Institute for the Norwegian Department of Defence at Kjeller). He has performed many experiments with the copper rods and believes he has some good explanations as to why it works. He explained that when there is a positive charge in the Earth's atmosphere this will induce a negative charge on the surface of the Earth and create a slight electric current through a body. The body will try to compensate for this by moving ions. Chlorine-ions and sulphur-ions are negative, while calcium-ions and sodium-ions are positively charged. Water and minerals among other things, all have an electric field which intersects the electric field in a body. The body will respond to this interaction by moving a nerve which will give a small reaction in the hands holding the copper rods.

or her superconsciousness – a special part of the consciousness that is a skill which Colin Wilson calls *Faculty X*. Since matter can be explained from the vibrations it produces, it should not be unlikely that different vibrations can come also from paranormal phenomena such as telepathy, ghosts and the usage of the pendulum. Lethbridge believed that everything in the Universe has its own wavelength, in the same way that the chemical elements have their special atomic weight.

Astrology

Astrology is said to be based on experiences recorded through thousands of years. The Babylonians around the year 700 BCE began to divide the Zodiac (the Sun's path in the sky) into 360 degrees, and about 600 BCE placed those parts of the Zodiac in twelve sectors of the same size. Each was named after the star constellation that was in each sector at that time.[i] Around 300 BCE they knew so much about mathematical astronomy that they were able to calculate the motion of the Moon and the closest planets.[ii] When the telescope was invented in 1610 and empirical science became the norm, astrology was no longer accepted as a university course of study in Europe. The Theosophists (around 1900) used, however, astrology, and it then became fairly popular, primarily in the United States.

Lyall Watson has suggested that astrology must be much older than the Babylonians, and pointed out that a 30,000 year old leg bone with signs and drawings suggests knowledge of the Lunar rhythm. He wrote that we do not have any knowledge about when astrology first came in use as the oldest signs are found on the great pyramid in Egypt – ca 2650 BCE.[iii] He believed that it has not been possible to arrive at the theories of astrology by trial and error, nor to have satisfactory proof of these theories in historical times.

---

i. See the symbol for the number 13 and its description on page 42. This was an important part of the sacred geometry.

ii. From Wikipedia: "The Antikythera mechanism is an ancient mechanical computer designed to calculate astronomical positions. It was recovered in 1900/01 from the Antikythera wreck. Its significance and complexity were not understood until decades later. Its time of construction is now estimated between 150 and 100 BCE. The degree of mechanical sophistication is comparable to a 19th century Swiss clock. Technological artefacts of similar complexity and workmanship did not reappear until the 14th century, when mechanical astronomical clocks were built in Europe."

iii. According to Lucie Lamy (see her book *Egyptians Mysteries – New light on ancient knowledge*, pp. 11 and 21) the periods of ancient Egypt may be divided such: The age of the Scorpion (the oldest known king had a scorpion as his mark and was called the Scorpion King) lasted from ca. 8400 to 6300 BCE. In the age of Gemini (the twins), from ca. 6300 to 4200 – the protodynastic time, Egypt was split in two monarchies, each with its own capital. In the age of Taurus (the ox), from ca. 4200 to 2100, the main religious cult had the ox Mentu as its centre. Egypt is supposed to have become one Kingdom around 3200 BCE. The god Amun, who had the goat Aries as symbol, became the dominating godhead from around 2000 BCE. Then Pisces was the central star sign from around the start of our era. This indicates that the division of the sky in 12 star signs started before the era of the dynastic pharaohs. (Note that this sequence of signs is not in accordance with today's astrology.)

Then there is only one possibility, namely, that astrology has emerged as a living organism from the matter it is based on.

Even if astrology is from antiquity, interpretations have been extended and continually modified, also because new planets and other celestial bodies (Uranus was discovered in 1781, Neptune in 1846 and the planetoid Pluto in 1930) have been discovered. The interpretation of a horoscope is, at a minimum, based on the twelve celestial sectors or star signs, the twelve daily sectors or houses, and (mainly) the motion and placement in those sectors of the ten heavenly bodies, as well as the Northern and the Southern Lunar node. This indicates at least 1728 (12 x 12 x 12) factors affecting each other. You must have a pretty good memory to determine the correct relationship between them. The interpreter's imagination and psyche will strongly influence the result. The star signs are Aries, Taurus, Cancer, Leo, Virgo, Libra, Scorpio, Sagittarius, Capricorn, Aquarius and Pisces. Every second character is masculine (beginning with Aries) and every other character feminine, or respectively outgoing or inward-looking.

The Sun as seen in the sky is passing through the twelve star signs during a year, and the year begins with the vernal equinox (Aries). These signs have no relation today with the constellations of the stars, only with the seasons of the year. The Sun is passing through the twelve houses during the twenty-four hours of a night and day. When a horoscope is drafted, the starting point is the constellation that is coming up over the horizon in the East at the moment when the child is born. (This assumes that the Sun moves from below the horizon to up above the horizon. For long periods of the year this does not happen near the Poles, north or south of the Polar circles.)

The ten celestial bodies are the Sun, Moon, Mercury, Venus, Mars, Jupiter, Saturn, Uranus, Neptune and Pluto. Each of these represents certain types of energies and each star sign has one of those celestial bodies as ruler. The energies are both positive and negative. If you know the Greek/Roman gods and their segments of activities, you will know what each planet represents.

> The Sun represents the personality or the 'I'.
>
> The Moon represents the emotional aspect of the 'I'.
>
> Hermes/Mercury represents the mental – the ability to think, the intellect, to communicate. He is also god of the thieves.
>
> Aphrodite/Venus is the caring, the fair and harmonious. But also lust, infidelity and thoughtlessness.
>
> Ares/Mars is the god of war, and stands for action, willpower and strength. But he is also raw, vicious and destructive.
>
> Zeus/Jupiter is charming, outgoing, generous and doing others well. But he is also ambitious, vain, and self-promoting.
>
> Cronos/Saturn was the god of sowing and harvesting as well as time. You harvest according to what you have sown, so Saturn is the strict

teacher, patient, dependable, curious. But he holds also bitterness, intransigence and sadness.

Uranus (father of Cronos) stands for new energy and new opportunities, but also for difficult transitions.

Poseidon/Neptune is the god of the ocean and stands for the imaginative and creative, but also the dreamy, foggy and unconscious.

Hades/Pluto is the ruler of the Underworld, the realm of the dead. He stands for suddenly changes and transformation.

The four elements, fire, earth, air and water are central in astrology along with the positive (masculine) and negative (feminine) forces. These elements and forces are distributed among the individual star signs, as forces that work through the star signs. The masculine and feminine forces can also be said to correspond to buoyancy and gravity. (The English physicist, Professor Stephen W. Hawking (b.1942) has mentioned that this breakdown of the Universe into four substances – fire, earth, air and water – and forces– gravity, as well as the air's and fire's tendency to rise –, is in use even today.[114]) Each sign has also one of the following adjectives as a guideline: leading, fixed and movable.

Aivanhov has explained that even though the physical sky-objects are located far away from each other, their auras are touching each other or overlap.[115] He said, furthermore, that the Earth is a living organism with an etheric, an astral and a mental body in addition to the physical. All living organisms have both soul and spirit, and this also applies to the planets. One of the aura's tasks is to communicate with everything surrounding it. Humanity is created in the cosmic image so therefore a human being mirrors the Cosmos. That means that we have an inner sun and inner planets circulating around this sun, just as in our solar system. And that is the explanation as to how anyone believing in astrology can argue that human beings are affected by the planets. The outer planets affect our inner planets – so that the qualities astrology attributes to the outer planets are reflected in our interior. But how they work in our interior, depends on our aura. And the aura is a mirror image of our inner life, our health, our thoughts, our feelings and our spiritual development. Like attracts like: a planet's good energy affects good human efforts, while bad attracts the bad. People should learn to develop their best abilities, to obtain a positive aura in order to attract positive energy from the planets. That alien conditions affect people on Earth, is indisputable. The Sun's light causes photosynthesis in plants, which are important elements for life on Earth. Light affects the mood and energy of human beings. The Sun's nuclear explosions produce the so-called solar wind, the magnetic storms which can be observed as the Northern and Southern lights on Earth, and affects the climate. The Moon is causing the tides of the ocean. When the Moon is full many people are unable to sleep or they are sleepwalking. The planets affect each other's orbit around the

Sun. Before Neptune was discovered in 1846, this planet's existence was known because Uranus had an irregular path. The Sun's altitude in the sky, as well as the fact that the Earth's axis is not at a right angle relative to the Earth's orbit plane, gives us the seasons.

Lyall Watson writes in the book *Supernature* that every drop of water on the Earth is influenced by the Moon and the Sun, and that all animals and plants react to these celestial objects. The Moon influences both the tides and the air masses that pass over the ocean. In North America it is established that there is a tendency for most rainfall to happen in the first and third week of the synodic month – that is, in the days just after the full moon and at the time of the new moon. But he says that there is much that indicates that it is the light that has the main influence on living organisms. Another important source of influence is magnetism.

There are changes in the Earth's magnetic field associated with the Moon's and the Sun's position. Living beings seem to have a built-in clock and compass, which every navigation system is based on. The special properties of water (which in people make up 70% of body mass) make the body especially susceptible to the Sun's influence. Scientific experiments have shown that a chemical reaction that takes place in water is affected by cosmic energies, which means that the water or chemical is susceptible to electromagnetic radiation and sensitive to electromagnetic fields. Watson writes that we must acknowledge that the Sun and the other cosmic forces affect everything alive.

Watson refers to an interesting relationship between the planets' positions and the sun-spot activities, which John Nelson discovered in 1951.[116] When the planets were in a so-called beneficial aspect, that is 60 and 120 degrees, there was little activity on the Sun. It was in the aspects 90 and 180 degrees that the sun-spot activity increased. Strong sun-spot activity provides, inter alia, radio disturbances. All the planets are sending out powerful radio waves.

The stars and galaxies in space are doing the same. The so-called black holes emit powerful gamma rays, which can penetrate lead. Watson suggests that cosmic radiation may have been a major factor in evolution, and that the Earth several times has been exposed to radiation so strong that all life has been killed. He writes that all life is sensitive to the pattern the cosmic forces procure, because all life contains water which is unstable and easily influenced. Watson argues that all constituents in all substantial material have their special wavelengths, since they are made up of the same basic substances. All information passes on in waves and reaches the recipients in waves. When two waves of different frequency are placed on top of each other, there may be points where they come together. He says that such peaks create a particular rhythm, and that everything in the Cosmos moves according to such rhythms. In a survey conducted by the English philosopher John Addey, to see if there was any rhythm in human births, showed a steady rhythm with 120 peaks a year; that is, every third degree of a circle of 360 degrees.[117] Lyall Watson mentions further that statistics have showed that births have a clear correlation with the Moon. According to a survey in New York City concerning a half million births, the majority of the births took place at a decreasing Moon and the peak was just after full Moon. Its lowest point was at the new Moon. But other such surveys from elsewhere in the world showed no such correlation. Watson claims that there is a correlation between births and the tide, though it is not the tide that is the cause, but the Moon. The Moon affects the contraction of the uterus. He refers to surveys regarding menstruation cycles, indicating that the bleeding usually begins at the new Moon and reaches the peak at the full Moon. There are also many others surveys showing a relationship between human activity and the Moon.

Lyall Watson has pointed out that the Sun has a direct impact on some bodily functions, and that the human behaviour is controlled by physiology. Many body functions are sensitive to changes in the magnetic field around the Earth, which in turn is influenced by the Sun. He wrote among other things, that mining accidents and car accidents seem to happen especially at times when there are explosions on the Sun. Diseases caused by deficiency of lymphocytes (small cells that make up between 20 and 25 percent of the white blood cells) seem also to have correlation with solar activity. The same goes for blood clots and tuberculosis. He suggested that cosmic rays affect us in different ways. There are short wave rays and long wave rays. Both types of radiation seem to have their origin outside our solar system. There are radiations with wavelengths of millions of kilometres of weak and almost immeasurable energy, but which affects us anyway. Some of the short wave rays are ionizing the air in the higher atmospheric layers. Other rays convert carbon-dioxide in the atmosphere to carbon 14-isotope.

Some of the ionized air lower down becomes ozone, which in microscopic amounts can kill many bacteria. Such air is experienced by people as fresh air. If it is negatively charged it feels stimulating, while positively charged air seems depressing. This means that people are electrically charged. Human energy fields are positively charged at the full Moon, as we are then stimulated by negative ions. The Moon influences the water, air, earth and the Earth's magnetic field, which in turn affects a person's force field. The cosmic radiation can amplify our reactions.

Colin Wilson has mentioned Rodney Collin in his book *Mysteries*. Collin (1909-1956, his baptismal name was Rodney Collin-Smith) was a disciple of the mystic P. D. Ouspensky and has written the book *The Theory of Celestial Influence*. Here Collin claims that there is a correlation between the endocrine glands and the chakras. He also believes that there is a close relationship between the human aura (or magnetic field) and the Sun's magnetic field. He also sees a connection between the planets' magnetic track and the different systems of the human body – that is the nervous system, the arterial system, the lymphatic systems and more. If you draw a regular spiral through all the glands, starting with the thymus, you will see that they are placed symmetrically on the spiral – just like the planets orbiting the Sun, and the Sun circling in the Milky Way and the galaxies in the Universe. He suggests that the glands are converters of the energy produced in the body, and that they are also the receiving apparatus for planetary influence on the individual human being, as each of the glands is sensitive to one of the celestial bodies. It indicates that the celestial bodies are important sources of influence for the human child's temperament and character at birth, especially the Sun and the celestial body that is on the eastern horizon – rising over the horizon. Collin's grading of the glands does not quite match with the Oriental chakra systems, as he has thymus as the lowest and slowest energy transmitter and the sexual glands as the highest or fastest – while it is the opposite in the Oriental chakra system.

Two prominent British psychologists and scientists, H. J. Eysenck and D. K. B. Nias, have written a book on astrology (first published in 1982) in which they consider the question of whether this is science or superstition.[118] They accept some trials and publications that show a remarkable correlation between the constellations of the planets and life on Earth. Among other things, they refer to the fact that the middle point between Jupiter and Neptune in motion around the Sun, affects the Sun's sun-spot activity. According to some investigations, the Sun's sun-spot activity seems to affect, inter alia, the Earth's temperature and rainfall, even though the relationship between solar activity and the Earth's weather has not been finally resolved.

Eysenck and Nias mention that many researchers have sought to find a correlation between occupation and the star signs, with no positive result for astrology. But the Norwegian professor Odd Lingjærde at Gaustad psychiatric hospital in Oslo has stated that collected data show quite clearly that the more creative personalities seem to be born in the winter or spring, while more structured individuals are born in the autumn.[119] He suggested that this may be caused by the D-vitamins being more easily accessible to the mother in early pregnancy for the spring born.

Eysenck and Nias have examined a number of so-called scientific trials to document the veracity of the astrological doctrine, and believe that these are not of a scientific standard. They furthermore refer to several of their own and others' trials, where the conclusion is that there is no relationship between the personality and the star signs. Among those are analyses made by Michel Gauquelin (who has a Ph.D in psychology from the University of Sorbonne) in 1979, where he concluded that, no rule of classical astrology has been confirmed by statistical analyses, neither by astrologers nor scientists. One of these analyses was to see if the planet Mars had a somewhat similar position in each of the horoscopes of 623 murderers (most of them had been executed). It did not. (Mars has been associated with war, violence and blood.)

In another analyses from 1978 Gauquelin checked whether 1995 French generals mainly were born in Aries (the sign that has Mars as the leading planet), but it turned out that there was no special sign that was typical for them as a group. In a survey made in 1973 on 16,000 army officers in the UK (by Cooper and Smithers), there was a certain preponderance of people born in summer and autumn, contrary to what statistics show for the general population, where most births occur during spring and fewest in late autumn. A similar study of 12,000 US army officers showed a similar result as in the UK, but where the pattern of births for the whole community shows that there are most births in August and September and fewest in April and May. (How are vacation patterns for officers in these two countries? This is not mentioned in those statistics.) The conclusion is that the investigations show no unique results that may be used in other relations.

Michel Gauquelin has performed a number of other analyses, which are referenced by Eysenck and Nias. The analyses fully satisfy the requirements of statistical science. Gauquelin could see positive results for astrology when considering the planetary positions at the moment of birth (based on the equal House principle). A preponderance of prominent doctors was born with Jupiter, Mars or Saturn in the Twelfth House or in the upper culmination (Ninth House). Other controls also showed that the position of the planets at the moment of birth corresponded with the person's success in life. It was related to their personality type. That is, those that did have success were outgoing and with iron will, and had been born with Mars or Jupiter in the aforementioned positions. The inward-looking and cautious had Saturn there. In a survey which included 46,485 people, it turned out a preponderance of Mars, Jupiter, Saturn and the Moon in the appropriate positions for people in professions which were ruled by those planets.

Two more analyses were made by Gauquelin where he looked at the position of the nearest planet at the moment of birth for approximately 15,000 parental couples (in each trial) and their children. He noted that the astronomer Johannes Kepler (1571-1630) had previously claimed that if one or both parents had been born with a planet in the Twelfth House or highest in the sky, it would be very likely that their children also were born under this special planet.

The question was whether this was the case even when the birth was initiated. Eysenck and Nias did not find anything wrong with these analyses, and wrote as a comment to the result: "A child's fate is to some extent known to depend on genetic pre-dispositions. Maybe it is this pre-destination that allows a child to choose to be born when a particular planet has just appeared over the horizon or culminates. In other words, a child seems to initiate its own birth process in response to a particular planetary configuration." But they put a lot of question marks at such a conclusion, and called for an explanation as to how planets could affect a birth that way.

Lyall Watson has mentioned the investigations made in 1959 by the American psychologist Vernon Clark, where several horoscopes were shown a number of astrologists for interpretation. The astrologists gave remarkably similar responses. Watson's conclusion, on the basis that space is a chaos of wave patterns, was that astrology is our best chance for the time being to understand the harmony between the chaotic Cosmos and organized life.

However, there are contradictions, vague claims and questionable interpretations, but astrology seems to touch something fundamental, according to Watson. Many tests have been tried in order to assess the credibility of astrology. Shawn Carlson, Institute of Physics at the University of California, in 1985 arranged a test in which astrologers were asked to compare 116 people's horoscopes with responses derived from their personality tests, where each astrologer was presented three such responses. The result was no better than what one would expect as a result of chance. David Groome, lecturer in psychology at the University at Westminster, England, who has written about this survey and some other surveys concerning astrology, concludes that there are no scientific clues for the claims of astrology.[120]

Colin Wilson referred to some analyses that Jeff Mayo (astrologer) and A. White did in 1978. They found that people who were born in a water sign (Cancer, Scorpion and Pisces) had a tendency to be fairly emotional; that people born under a masculine sign seemed to be outgoing, as people born under a feminine sign seemed to be inward-looking.[121] David Groome argues, however, that no such correlation has later been proved.

Lyall Watson, as a biologist, finds it unlikely that planetary positions influence a child in the moment of birth, as a birth never happens in an instant.[i] He mentions further that the radiation a mother is exposed to during pregnancy affects the embryo just as strongly if not more strongly. His theory is more in the direction that the cosmic powers are best able to influence a person by affecting the foetus very early, so that the embryo develops in step with Cosmos and perhaps even determines when the birth should take place. The inherited potentialities that the embryo has, can give it special sensitivity towards certain cosmic impulses. Watson is here referring to the banana flies that always hatch out at dawn. He also mentions that if a cosmic force can exert a certain influence, it is not unreasonable to believe that this force is enhanced at the moment the Sun rises up over the horizon. (The star sign depends on the Sun's position in the sky – on the Zodiac. The exact time when a child is born is only in rare cases of significance for the star sign. That is only when the Sun is in transition from one sign to another. Watson's reasoning may be appropriate when it comes to the meaning of the ascendant in the horoscope. In that case, it must be the cosmic forces or radiation from that part of the sky where the ascendant is.)

---

i. It should be noted that the moment of birth as officially registered is when the whole baby is out of the womb.

Plotinus has rejected the thought that the stars could affect the life of a single human being.¹²² The Indian Sufi mystic Hazrat Inayat Khan (1882-1927)ⁱ, whom Marcello Haugen admired, has said that everything a clairvoyant person considers is like an open book, the truth can be found everywhere. All divination methods are therefore appropriate for a seer.¹²³

Yogananda explained that a birth horoscope can only be properly interpreted by people who have intuitive wisdom, and of them there are not many.¹²⁴ Carl Gustav Jung believed that there was something in it.¹²⁵ Rudolf Steiner said that people in our time do not have the true knowledge of the stars.¹²⁶ He mentioned, however, that a human being exists in a certain planet's sphere between the physical existences. Edgar Cayce referred frequently to the planetary spheres. A person's temperament was described as the effects of his or her soul's existence in a specific planet's sphere between the incarnated earthly lives. (This was about the same as what Rudolf Steiner taught.) A planet's sphere, however, was not a particular physical location, but a kind of open dimension where souls were given a certain type of experience. The description of the planets given in astrology was similar to the energy or teaching that the souls were supplied with in that special sphere. This influence would have consequences for the soul's subsequent earthly life, unless it had made choices that reduced this influence. Ken Wilber has, with reference to controlled attempts to test the astrological statements, concluded that all evidence so far have been strongly in astrology's disfavour.¹²⁷ He assumes that people are longing for a connection to the cosmos, so instead of working for a spiritual connection to the Cosmos (which he writes with a big C – that is the universal totality, including the spiritual, the subtle and the causal worlds), they rather try to believe that the material cosmos is linked to their personal egos. He thinks that belief in astrology is one of a variety of world views that have their origin in the mythic realm of consciousness. This belief has a purpose on this level as it gives a meaning to life and a sense of cohesion with the Cosmos.

Colin Wilson maintains, however, that anyone who gives some time to astrology will see that there is something in it.¹²⁸ He points out that the Earth is a living entity and that its forces increase and decrease in accordance with the heavenly bodies. The same is true for all living beings on Earth. He refers to the efforts of the physicists Burr and Northtrop (mentioned in the chapter about the aura) which show that all living beings have a life-field that is affected by changes in the Earth. He assumes that it is possible that sensitive people can detect the importance of the planets, without this having any relation to the physical gravity they exert.

---

i. Hazrat Inayat Khan was for a time professor of music at an Indian University. But he became more and more of a philosopher and mystic, and ended as the Supreme Grand Master of the Western Order of the Sufis. He settled in Geneva, and gave lectures over large parts of Europe and America. He was in Oslo in 1924. The goal of the Sufis is mutual understanding between different religions and cultures, unity and peace between people.

The whole solar system is perhaps a wave of powers and influences or purposes that have nothing to do with what is physically measurable. If the Earth's forces are affecting the biological and psychological structure, astrology cannot be rejected on the grounds that it is an early and distorted form of astronomy. And it is fully possible that those, who through its thousands of years of existence have designed the astrological system, registered the sky objects' impact on themselves and their fellow human beings.

Colin Wilson refers, however, to the theory of the Irish poet and mystic William B. Yeats (1865-1939), who described the Moon's influence on people in his book *A Vision*. Yeats described twenty-eight types of personalities, one for each day of the lunar month. The first fourteen types show the human being as expanding and the next fourteen as contracting. Yeats believed furthermore that people are balancing between the four fundamental forces in nature, comparable to Jung's term fundamental properties, respectively – thinking, feeling, sensing and intuition. (This is in accord with the four elements of astrology – air/thinking, water/feeling, earth/sensing and fire/intuition.) Colin Wilson says about Yeats' book that it is fascinating, and that this system appeals to the intuition.

According to Aivanhov, everything is predestined.[129] He explained that there is a kind of a cosmic computer which has all the data about the past, present and future, and that it is spirit beings which ensure that that which is going to happen, really happens. Nothing happens by chance. A child is born precisely when it should. The astrological sign, the ascendant and the planetary positions are given in advance, and conception occurs according to this. (Note that he mentioned conception and not the moment of birth.) Everything is determined by how the individuality has evolved in the past and what it is supposed to experience in this incarnation. The task of the human being in this incarnation is to work with its mind. That is, to control, clean and spiritualize the instinctive way of life. You have to identify yourself with your spirit – that is to take advantage of your free will. That is to seek to approach the world of light and charity, which will affect how the next incarnation will be. Most astrologers do not understand the significance of the horoscope, he said. What really can be read out of a horoscope is whether a person has the ability to successfully develop the spiritual, that is, to perform certain tasks, do the will of God and take on divine tasks. There is really nothing else of interest in a horoscope. You cannot avoid fate, but you can learn how to meet it in the right way.

When I, after much doubt, in 1988 took courage and consulted an astrologer, I came home as a great question mark – how was it possible that a person I had never met before could say so much about me that I felt was quite right? I could not forget this meeting and the questions it raised with me. I bought and read lots books about astrology. I drew horoscopes and engaged in interpretations. I found everything that the astrologer had told me in the books. Moreover, I realized that I could say something about other people based on their horoscope, which they felt was right. Is this sufficient to convince me of the accuracy of astrology? Unfortunately, I must answer no. In the beginning I was wondering why the horoscope I received fitted so well with my perception of myself. I have had the opportunity to study many print-outs from recordings from other people's meetings with astrologers, and each time been equally amazed at how accurate the descriptions were. Descriptions of one person did not in any way fit another's. However, I must mention that the horoscopes that fitted best were for the persons who talked most during the interview with the astrologer, and did not fit the person who was fairly silent. And there are always some questions. What I could not see fitted the system was as follows:

- How to determine the ascendant for people born north of the Arctic Circle, where the Sun in some periods does not go down at night and at other times does not come above the horizon during the day. The ascendant is the place in the east where the ecliptic cuts the horizon at the moment a person is born. The ecliptic is the path of the Sun on the sky, also called the Zodiac. It is tilted relative to the Earth's north/south axis. That is to say that it is only at the vernal and autumnal equinoxes that the ecliptic cuts the horizon exactly in the east in relation to the place one is born.
- As most people have observed, the Sun is going up and down in different places depending on the time of the year.
- The astrologers operate with a concept called houses. From the point where the ascendant cuts the circle of the horoscope, the circle is divided into twelve zones, and these zones are called houses. (The star signs, of which there also are twelve, also cut the circle in twelve parts. However, the signs will always start at zero degrees in the sign of Aries.) There are different systems for sectioning the houses and that varies with the various astrologers. I have received my horoscopes from three different astrologers, and they all used different house systems, respectively Koch, Placidus and the equal equal house system. I asked one astrologer how this was possible, and got the answer that one house system will work for one type of astrologers and another for another. Another responded that while one is young the system that is best suited is Placidus, but later it is Koch. But what really surprised me was that these three systems placed my birth planets in different houses. Either I got almost all of them in the 3rd and 8th house, or almost all in the 2nd and 7th house, or almost all in the 4th and 9th house. And if the houses are so important for the interpretation, how can each of these astrologers find the correct description of me? I need a better explanation than that one house system is best for one astrologer and another for someone else, whether this may apply to the interpreter or to the one being interpreted. If one were to adhere to such an explanation, it is my conclusion that astrology is based more on the interpreter's intuition than on the importance of the constellations in the sky.

- Even though the Sun, Moon and the planets follow the ecliptic, their paths are not always identical to this one. If that was the case, we would have lunar and solar eclipses much more frequently. In 2004 the planet Venus passed in front of the Sun, but it is a long time between each such event. How can you argue that such a planet and the Moon are in conjunction, when there is a height difference (above the horizon) of many degrees? Should not this have significance in the interpretation of a horoscope?

- The astrologers are not in agreement about which house can be said to represent the mother in the horoscope and which the father. Some say that the 4th house and 10th house respectively are the father and mother, and some say the opposite.

- When can an event be said to occur according to astrological interpretation? Here is the so-called orb of importance, that is the distance from an exact location (such as for example 30, 60, 90 or 180 degrees from the Sun's position) and to the point where the planet actually is. It can be a great deviation, which nevertheless is interpreted as such an important aspect. Some astrologers claim that deviations of up to 10 degrees must be given proper weight. This also applies in relation to the so-called transits. When such a degree of deviation is acceptable in the interpretation, I find it difficult to accept the result.

- Mercury and Venus have paths around the Sun which are closer to the Sun than the Earth's orbit. I have not seen that the astrological interpretations take into account that these planets sometimes can be in front of and sometimes behind the Sun. Also it ought to have an impact on a planet whether it is closest to the Earth in its orbit or farthest away from it. I have not seen this commented on either.

The birth horoscope seeks to provide a picture of a person's psyche, as it was likely to be when the person was born. Later, however, much can happen that affects this psyche. As a consequence, the astrologer will provide a horoscope for the consultation day to understand how the person has it that actual day or can expect to have it in the future. I doubt that one can obtain a trustworthy picture from what you can read out of a horoscope.

There may be reason to believe that there is something in astrology, but one should be wary of the interpreters. But we should not for that reason completely abandon astrology – it does have a mission, as all other forms of divination. What I am experiencing is that the horoscope, with its different descriptions related to the planets, signs, houses and the forces between them, is helping the imagination to put words on that which is perceived intuitively. Moreover, it provides a basis for communication with the clients that also give them associations of importance for the on-going conversation. Anyone seeking the help of an astrologer is doing it primarily to obtain better self-knowledge. The horoscope is a good tool for such a conversation as it is a neutral system that both parties can relate to. This it is important to remember, whether one is the interpreter of a horoscope or the one seeking help.

I Ching

The Chinese book of wisdom *I Ching* is also known as *The Book of Change*.[130] It is used as a book of divination. It is supposed to be written around the year 1000 BCE. Some of the hexagrams, however, have been mentioned as early as around 2200 BCE, so they are very old. The British author and psychologist Stan Gooch (b.1932) considers the book as a living miracle.[131] The times he has consulted it, it has provided remarkably accurate and informative replies, both about the past, present and future. This he thinks indicates that there is an inexplicable legality which has no relationship with the known scientific laws. Colin Wilson explains that the man who created the system, King Wên, had meditated on these symbols and come to the conclusion that they represented archetypal human situations.[132] He wrote further that if the requester is strongly concentrated on the question he asks when the coins are thrown (if coins are used, see below), he will receive a relevant answer. Wilson refers to Jung's theory of synchronicity (convergence of events), namely, that what is happening is in some way related to the subconscious. The subconscious knows the answer and causes the coins to fall accordingly. This explains why divination is possible, even to predict something for the future, and phenomena such as clairvoyance and foresight. Wilson mentions that he considers this book as the very best of the different systems of divination, and that it has yielded remarkable results the times he has consulted it. Both what Colin Wilson and Jung have written about *I Ching* is recommended for anyone to read who wants to study the book.

I Ching consists of sixty-four hexagrams. Each hexagram consists of six lines placed under each other. Each line is a symbol consisting of either one long or two short dashes. One long line represents Yang and the two short lines represent Yin. Yang and Yin are the two opposing forces of nature. The sign for Yang is then as follows: '—' and the sign for Yin such: '--'. There are eight basic elements of nature, and each of these is symbolized with three such dash-lines, like this:

Tui/sea	Chên/thunder	K'un/earth	K'an/water
--	--	--	--
—	--	--	—
—	—	--	--

Kên/mountain	Sun/wind	Ch'ien/sky	Li/fire
—	—	—	—
--	—	—	--
--	--	—	—

When each of these eight basic symbols is set in conjunction with one of the others, we get a total of sixty-four images or hexagrams, each with six dash lines. Each image has its history, and the composition of two images provide a new story. This gives the basis for the interpretations and predictions. Two hexagrams put in succession give the basis for predictions about what is to come.

In order to use the hexagrams as basis for divination, you must have a system where the person to be predicted for can bring up one or two lines by chance. Normally coins are used. You use three coins, each with sides called here respectively heads and tails. For each throw you either get two heads (twice '—') or one tails (once '- -'), or vice versa, or three of the same kind of either heads or tails. This reflects one of the basic symbols. You throw six times. On the basis of a number system that is described in the book, which converts what you have thrown, you then get one hexagram. Then, from this number system, you will see that one hexagram turns into another; or by throwing a second time you get a new hexagram. Then you have two hexagrams to relate to for the prediction. This transformation from one hexagram to the next is what has given the book the name The *Book of Change*.

Tarot Cards

The Tarot Card set consists of seventy-eight cards, split in two groups, the twenty-two Major Arcana cards and the fifty-six Minor Arcana cards. The minor cards consist of the usual four card suits, which here are called sword (spade), chalice (heart), pentagram (diamond) and wand (club), each with thirteen cards. In addition there is the Knight card, which is located between the Queen and the Jack card. The major cards are numbered with Roman numerals from I to XXI. In addition there is the Jester as card 22. The major cards have always a title, as the Queen, the Devil, Strength, etc. The meaning of the cards for divination emerges when they are placed in a certain way, and you then look at the relationship of the cards to each other. It is maintained that the images of the cards are evoking emotions and thoughts which help whoever is predicted to relate to him/herself.[133] The Tarot cards were allegedly created by the Italian upper classes in the 15th century, and were during the first 300 years used as regular card games. A French priest named Antoine Court de Gebelin then claimed that the symbols were from an old Egyptian wisdom book that some wise men had disguised as card games. From this originated the interest in using them for divination.

The British psychologist Dion Fortune (1890-1946), who has written a book about the Kabbalah (see chapter 17), explained that the Tarot cards and their divination effect have close relationship to the Kabbalah and the symbol The Tree of Life (Kabbalah's symbol).[134] In The Tree of Life there are twenty-two paths between the main signs – similar to the twenty-two major Arcana Tarot cards. She wrote that the Tarot is the most accurate system of divination and that this system is derived from and finds its explanation in The Tree of Life. In order to use the Tarot cards in a satisfactory manner, it is therefore necessary to know the signs in The Tree of Life and the interpretation of these symbols. She wrote further that The Tree of Life, the Tarot cards and astrology are three aspects of one and the same system, and that the one is incomprehensible without the other.

Comments

There are also many other types of divination, such as palm-reading and interpreting handwriting (graphology). The lines in the hand are said to be due to nerve impulses that occur according to what you think or do, or possibly from the abilities you are born with. Graphology can be said to have the same cause. I have received interpretations both from palm-reading and graphology. The impression I am left with, however, is the same as I have from meetings with astrologers. Somethings match and somethings do not match. What I did not recognize may have been right, but what was said was too vague and with so many words that it was impossible to say anything for sure about the result. I have also noticed that people who are known for being able to predict the future, have presented quite specific statements about what would happen, which did not come through. So you need to take predictions with a very large pinch of salt.

Here we are at the core of what I think concerns all types of divination, whether it is astrology, Tarot cards, tea-leaf-divination, or whatever, that it is the intuition – the subconscious – which is at work and which comes up with interpretations that the conscious mind then provides. The use of dreams and dream cards can be seen in the same way. It has been said about Nostradamus that he went up on the roof of his house when he wanted to look into the future. There he sat down and looked at his own countenance in a bucket of water, and saw the visions that were the basis for his predictions. Dion Fortune explained that the initiate's purpose with the use of The Tree of Life was to call pictures up from the subconscious, into an artificial constructed awake-dreaming that is related to the topic in question. The same must apply to other forms of divination. For example, I was once trying to guess something about a person I did not know. He was sitting opposite me and we were holding hands. My mind was blank and I was staring out of the window. Outside was a big park. All of a sudden I saw a car pass by, although no actual car was passing outside. I mentioned this and it turned out that the person was very passionate about cars. I have experienced similar situations more than once. If you are very intuitive, you will be able to receive a lot of information in this way.

The shapes that are seen in the object used for divination give the interpreter associations. These are guides for the intuition, which thereby gets information for the seeker. There is no doubt that human beings have capabilities far beyond what we acknowledge. Some persons are very intuitive and you can often get good help by seeking advice from someone who can foretell the future. Many people need help to talk about themselves in order to understand what is going on in their own psyche and in their relationships to other people. This can help the seeker to obtain better self-knowledge, and initiate greater efforts for further work in that direction. A diviner is a person who uses his or her time professionally to talk with people. They thereby develop a profound understanding of the human psyche, which then may help other people.

The essentials in an astrological interpretation, as in any other interpretation, are the astrologer's compassion, intuition and telepathic ability. It is these abilities that help one see and emphasize certain aspects of the picture being studied. When it is being interpreted the one being analysed will also recognize some aspects. Moreover, I suppose that if you recognize approximately 50% of what is said, you will feel that the interpretation is right despite the fact that most people probably will recognize themselves in most of the conversation anyway. As a rule, people's self-knowledge is rather poor, and an unbiased control is difficult to obtain.

Colin Wilson wrote that because we have forgotten how important intuition is, we look at magical systems such as shamanism, alchemy, the Kabbalah and any other divination art with indulgent contempt. But if people have a form of expanded consciousness – a more outreaching self – and if this self is able to receive much more information than the ordinary me, these systems are not more mysterious than the normal consciousness. The problem is that it is forgotten knowledge, because the modern human being uses his or her mind power more than the intuition.[135] The question that arises is what intuition really is.

3.9. Luck and strange co-incidences/synchronicity

It is perhaps not entirely coincidental that particular cards, with a certain limited meaning, will be pulled out when a question from a particular human being is considered. This particular phenomenon, which also can be of importance in predictions, is the phenomenon that Carl Gustav Jung called co-incidences – that is that events may have a strange relationship both in regard to place, time and matter. He used the term synchronicity of events that are directly connected in regard to content and time, but which are separate in regard to location.[136]

Lyall Watson has recounted some particularly strange co-incidences. In one case it was one of the greatest ice lumps that ever happened to come down from the sky, which accidentally ended up at the feet of a physicist who was researching whether ice could be generated by lightning. In another case eight fish of four different species, the largest of almost 23 cm, fell down around an ichthyologist (fish expert).[137] Watson posed the question whether such celestial gifts – and he mentioned many more than these two examples – may come as a consequence of oppressed unconscious desires, and can yield strange results similar to events in a dream. He also drew a parallel to the poltergeist happenings. When it comes to co-incidences, I can recall my own experiences with telephone calls. As a general rule almost the phone will ring when I am near water, such as in the shower or using the toilet. It is debatable whether this is a chance happening or whether other people have a mentally easier access to me in such a situation – the water may facilitate telepathy. It can also be that it is I who is intuitive and respond in advance by seeking water. The truth is I am not extra irritated when I get a call in such a situation, so that I give more attention to these phone calls than I otherwise would have done. It happens too often – and I do not receive many phone calls. Human beings have a tendency, however, to place more emphasis on random events than what is reasonable, and we might see strange correlations where none such exist.

Other examples of co-incidences are that several good things often occur at the same time. All good things come in threes, is a well-known saying. It suggests that people have the experience that good luck is followed by more luck. The opposite may, unfortunately, also be true – that bad luck is followed by more bad luck. Many people are acquainted with the strange phenomenon that things happen as they should, and that we get unexpected help from others just when we need it most. Many will dismiss such happenings as chance, but it seems to me that this happens so often that it cannot be attributed to chance. "When the need is greatest, the help is nearest" is hardly a saying that has arisen from nothing. Many people are so closely psychically bonded that one person's acts or thoughts in some way or another are picked up by another person or by someone in this other person's surroundings. It can also happen that several quite similar events occur at the same time. Jes Bertelsen has suggested that when we live our lives in accordance with the laws of nature, life is laid out for us in a good way.

Stanislav Grof (see chapter 4.2) wrote about synchronous events that occurred in connection with holotropic breathing séances and psychedelic therapy. Among other things, he found that when a person experienced an animal in a shamanistic-like vision, an animal that seems to act as guide or helper, such an animal would often show up in the person's real world as well. For example, a person experiencing a deer in a vision happens to meet a deer in real nature soon after. Grof reported that people, who engage in charitable projects inspired by a dream or a vision, often experienced incredible synchronous events that considerably facilitate the work. This is in line with what Jes Bertelsen said about living in accordance with the laws of nature.

3.10. Out-of-body experience

> "I know a man in Christ who fourteen years ago was caught up to the third heaven. Whether it was in the body or out of the body I do not know – God knows. And I know that this man – whether in the body or apart from the body I do not know, but God knows – was caught up to paradise and heard inexpressible things, things that no one is permitted to tell." (2 Cor 12.2-4)

Has St Paul here described an out-of-body experience? There are many books that describe the out-of-body experiences.[138] A number of people have had such experiences, which does not necessarily arise in connection with a life-threatening situation. Some of them are similar to what St Paul described as a relationship or association with a higher existence[i]. That is what the mystics are said to experience when they have an ecstatic Unio Mystica experience of God. Another term used for that phenomenon is a light experience. Other similar events can for example be that a person who is physically located in Oslo can see everything that happens in a room in London, although the persons being there are not seeing or sensing anything. But the one in Oslo can describe everything that happens in London, such as whom are present and what they are talking about. It is as if one is physically present. There are also stories about persons actually being seen and talked to as a physically real person, although he or she really is in quite a different place. It has also been told that articles have been moved during such a visit. The phenomenon that a person can be seen in a materialized figure at another place than where he or she is physically located – a kind of double presence – is called bi-location. As mentioned, it is said that Padre Pio was able to visit people in need, through spiritual distress or illness, in a materialized shape. It has also been said that he was actually seen after his death.

The question is whether this is a real double presence, or whether it is a form of spiritual vision that is experienced. In a special case it is said that there was a man who was born blind, but who actually saw Padre Pio and could describe his actual appearance. A strange phenomenon in this connection was that those who experienced seeing Padre Pio, often at the same time experienced a special smell. In Padre Pio's case, the smell was, as we have heard, a scent of roses.

A light experience is very similar to what is termed a near-death experience. Near-death experiences are discussed in more detail in the chapter about death. Any clear boundary between a light experience, an out-of-body experience and a near-death experience is difficult to draw. An interesting phenomenon, related to the out-of-body and near-death experiences, is that even people who are born blind can describe what happens during such a séance, as what is described above about Padre Pio. Professor of psychology at the University of Connecticut Kenneth Ring (b.1936) has studied what he called mind, sight or psychological vision, and has found that such experiences are not uncommon among the blind. This shows that there is no physical sensory organ used, and what is it then?

Stan Gooch, however, is very sceptical as to whether the out-of-body experiences are real phenomena – he thinks these are just fantasy visions. But then he should explain how such fantasies can be perceived both by a person

---

i. Was this really his own experience? Most people would think that this is the experience St Paul had on the road to Damascus as described in Acts, although that is not what St Paul reported. In Galatians 2.2 he reviews a revelation that happened fourteen years earlier after a visit to Jerusalem. But that visit occurred three years after the revelation that gave him the mission to preach the Gospel among the Gentiles (Gal. 1.16-18).

being out of the body and by someone seeing the other in question, and how objects can be moved at the same time. The experiences can be explained if you accept that consciousness is not related to the physical body, that consciousness can move with the speed of thought, and also that consciousness is able to materialise a body.[139]

3.11. Spirit contact and channelling

Introduction

In the Gospel of John we read that Jesus appeared to Mary Magdalene outside the tomb where he was laid after the crucifixion. Later the same day he appeared to his disciples. Then he came again eight days later and once again at the lake of Tiberius. (See John chapter 20 and 21.) But the New Testament is not the only place where you can read about meetings with people who no longer exists on the Earth. Both Emanuel Swedenborg and Rudolf Steiner talked about such contacts, and said that they could walk around in the spirit world. There is a story about Emanuel Swedenborg in which he passed over the threshold and got information from the deceased brother of the Swedish queen, information which he then passed on to the Queen; information which none other than the Queen and her brother could have known. The shamans explain that they can travel in the spirit world under certain circumstances. Others believe to have had visions of spirit beings and also of more tangible experiences with these.

Many people have experienced a departed spouse or relative in the form of an apparition. Often the figure seems quite diffuse and disappears after a short time. Sometimes an important message is received. Often you also hear of dying persons who see and talk to deceased close relatives, angels or a being of light just before death occurs, which is understood to be that these are coming to fetch or receive them.[140] The strange thing also is that individuals near the death bed may experience an out-of-body happening for a short while. Then they will see the death scene from above, with their own body and the deceased's body. And they see the deceased's soul at their side. They may also observe that other deceased souls are present. They take the final goodbye with the dead in this state.[141] People who have had out-of-body experiences or near-death experiences report that they are met by beings of light.

Some mystics seem to talk with spiritual beings when they are in deep prayer. Padre Pio reported that he both saw and had conversations with Jesus and the Virgin Mary. These talks were sometimes overheard, and some were recorded by his closest associates. They heard Padre Pio's remarks, but not the answers he received. He often asked the celestial beings to save or heal a person who had sought his help. Other times he was begging Jesus to give him the stigmata, so that he could be a victim so that others could be saved. Such talks often took place in what the listeners or viewers perceived as trance, but this was not a form of trance in which Padre Pio changed personality. Sometimes it was Padre Pio's personal angel – his guardian angel – he talked with. What his closest associates then noted, was that he was not quite so respectful in his speech as he was when he spoke with the higher celestial beings. Other times, it was deceased persons, such as Francis of Assisi, who Padre Pio saw and talked to. Padre Pio once explained that when a man far away sought his help through prayer, he saw the man's guardian angel as if he saw the man directly. He maintained that everybody has a guardian angel, and that this angel is always nearby.

Yogananda has said that his teacher Sri Yukteswar came to him in his physical likeness after his death – and explained to him everything about the existence after the physical.

Spirit contact through a medium

A form of spirit contact is communication with the spirits through a physical person – a medium – as intermediary. It is said that the departed often wants contact with their relatives or friends on the Earth and tries to obtain contact in this way. Normally the medium will be fully awake when such a communication takes place. In recent years a series of books about such contacts have been published. This is information that comes from something outside the normal consciousness of the person who writes the message down or speaks about it. Most people perceive that the information comes from a non-physical being and not from the medium's subconsciousness. In some cases, it may seem as if the medium has a conversation with a non-physical being, where the medium can see and experience the spirit, although others do not see or hear anything in particular. It happens that the medium can experience the discarnate entity's emotions directly, such as feeling sadness or horror, although without losing touch with his/her own personality. These types of spirit contact are also known as spiritism or spiritualism. In many countries there are now spiritual societies accepted as church societies, where people regularly meet to seek contact with the spirit world.

The American author David Scott Rogo (1950-1990) has told about some strange spirit contacts.[142] During a dispute regarding inheritance from 1925 (the so-called Chaffin Will Case, North Carolina, US), the deceased's spirit appeared several times and told them where the last Will could be found. In another case the murdered woman, Teresita Basa, communicated with a medium and said who had murdered her. Scott Rogo also mentioned other phenomena that can be said to be some sort of contact with dead people, such as some special dreams, apparitions, telephone calls from dead people and spirit voices on tape.

Many people have been able to perform automatic writing and produce good literature by automatic writing, which is when the hand writes or draws without the owner's awareness of it what he/she is writing. Matthew

Manning said that he for a time wrote short pieces in Greek and Arabic, a language he did not understand. He could also draw and sketch in the same style as some deceased artists such as Albert Dürer, Goya, Picasso, and others.[143] It should be noted, however, that these were not new creations, rather reproductions. Scott Rogo wrote further of cases where people maintained that they had inherited their special abilities from a departed spirit, or that they had received guidance from, or were possessed by a departed person and painted as this one did. He mentioned some such people by name: Rosemary Brown, England, who composed music; Emma Conti, Italy, who wrote poems in Emily Dickinson's style and won awards for her poetry; Frederic Thompson, United States, who at the beginning of the twentieth century painted in the same style as a departed landscape painter. These last cases might seem to be examples of spiritual possessions. During the explorations and excavations of Glastonbury in England, archaeologists were helped via automatic writing by a spirit, a former monk, who called himself Johannes.[i]

The case of 'Patience Worth' is rather special. When Pearl Curran (b.1883) was in trance, a personality introduced herself claiming to be a spirit named 'Patience Worth', who said she had been physically born in 1649. She appeared over a period of twenty-five years and could dictate a long poem the one moment and in the next dictate on a novel. She could take up the thread of a dictation from several days earlier during the dictation of something else. This literary production, which was very extensive, more than twenty-nine volumes, was completely unique, and could hardly be due to Pearl Curran's knowledge or background. Pearl Curran went to school only until she was fourteen years old. But is it likely that this spirit being could possess such phenomenal abilities? Perhaps it was several spirit beings involved.[144] Anyway, this production did exceed ordinary human capabilities.

In the biography of Carl Gustav Jung Laurens van der Post recorded a story about two good friends of Jung.[145] The story concerns the Professors James Hervey Hyslop (1854-1920) and William James (1842-1910). They were both greatly concerned with paranormal phenomena. Hyslop and James agreed that the first one to die should try to contact the other after death. William James died first. Several years passed without incident. But then one day a letter was received by Hyslop, from a person in Ireland who regularly practiced spiritism. The writer explained that a spirit who had

---

i. Glastonbury had a large church and monastery, which was plundered and destroyed by Henry VIII. The place is one of England's oldest mystical and sacred sites. Excavations at the site took place mainly in the beginning of the 20th century under the leadership of Frederick Bligh Bond. Bond had the help of a friend who through automatic writing got in touch with someone who claimed to be a deceased monk who had previously resided on the spot. Essential information of importance to the excavations was received. This is described in a book published in 1918 by Bond entitled *The Gate of Remembrance*. As a consequence, Bond was excluded from the better part of society and lost his job. (I read about Glastonbury – for the first time – the same day as there was a programme about Glastonbury on the Norwegian television in the series Lonely Planet which I then happened to watch.)

called himself William James constantly had interfered with the séances and insisted that they should contact a Professor Hyslop and give him the following greeting: "Remember the red pyjamas?" After a lot of endeavour they had managed to establish Hyslop's identity and delivered the message. Hyslop spent a long time trying to understand the message. But then he remembered that he and James one day had arrived in Paris without their luggage. The most urgent priority needed at the time were pyjamas and the only thing Hyslop found in the stores were special red pyjamas, which caused mocking from James. Van der Post pointed out also the symbolism with the pyjamas could point to the current situation, as James supposedly was in a place where there were no earthly goods, he was without luggage.

In some cases a spirit seems to control the persona of the medium in order to convey a message to humanity. The medium will then be in a trance and usually not remember anything of what was happening during the séance. In these cases it is not always a being with a previous physical life that appears, at least not from recent times. It has been suggested that spirits who are using mediums to express themselves, are coming from a higher sphere, and are beings of light. The reason that they contact people is that they want to guide humanity to a better understanding of life. What is common to many people providing trance messages is that they change their personality when the message is presented. They begin to talk and move in a completely different way from usual. The Theosophists explained that the medium withdraws from his/her physical body and only resides in the astral body, while the physical body is taken over by the spirit. This can supposedly only happen for a short period of time, lest the physical body is damaged.

I will in the following refer to some of what I have read regarding descriptions of such channelling. The order in which the individuals are mentioned here is somewhat arbitrary and involves no grading. Channelled information is nevertheless far more extensive than what is here discussed. There are a number of different kinds of channels and mediums, and there are many different types of messages. Some of what we receive as such information, I think, is especially interesting. In this book I will mention this in several places, for example what has been transmitted from the spirit Seth through Jane Roberts, from the spirit John through David Spangler and the spirit Ambres through Sture Johansson. What the medium says in a channelling séance often involves knowledge that the medium hardly can have acquired. Profound knowledge is presented about science, geographical conditions, contemporary political situations, as well as historical events, and sometimes in, for the medium, unknown languages.

Helena Petrovna Blavatsky (1831-1891) was one of the nineteenth century's most special personalities. She was of a noble Russian family, born in Dnepropetrovsk (formerly Jekaterinoslav) and died in London. She was one of the founders of the Theosophical Society, which was founded in the United States in 1875. She travelled widely in India and Tibet and elsewhere in the world, and came to the United States in 1873. She had an unusual ability to register extra sensory phenomena, and had done in-depth studies of these in the Orient.[146] Helena Blavatsky claimed that the books she wrote emerged by channelling. At a later date she partly rejected the first book she wrote, *Isis Unveiled*, maintaining that she was under influence of untrustworthy spiritual forces at the time when she wrote it. She therefore published a new book, *The Secret Doctrine*, which is an adapted version of the first. Her teaching has partly been the basis for theosophy. Geoffrey Farthing (1910-2004), who was a member of the Theosophical Society's general Council, has published several books in which he presents Blavatsky's doctrine, as she maintained it was received from her Master – without further explanation.[147]

The book *Talking with Angels* is a special document – a report from channelling that took place during the Second World War in Hungary. Gitta Mallasz (who was not a Jew) and her three Jewish friends – Joseph, Hannah and Lily, who all died in German captivity during the war (Joseph's fate is unknown, but Hannah and Lily died of starvation, exhaustion and disease) – had over a period of seventeen months, a remarkable conversation (with Hannah as the medium) with some beings that were perceived as angels. Through these conversations they acquired an incredible mental strength to face the atrocities they were later subjected to. Gitta Mallasz took notes from the conversations and managed to keep those through the war. But it was not until several years after the war, that she had enough vitality and time to rewrite the notes. A first edition of the book was published in 1976 in France – this was not possible under the communist regime in Hungary while she lived there. Gitta Mallasz begins the book with a brief account of what happened the first time Hannah started channelling. All of a sudden Hannah said that it was not she who spoke, and so she gave many statements which she afterwards did not remember. In the preface to the English edition the translator writes that the angels taught Gitta and her friends that the earthly existence is only part of a whole, and if we are aware of this, we no longer need to fear anything, nor death. Eternity is no longer the eternal repetition, but the eternal new. We are encouraged to be aware of the perpetual movement, the undogmatic Light. The more we are able to accept this light, the more aware we will become and the closer we will come to our highest point – the meeting point with our own Angel. At the same time, this Angel will try to come down to us in order to meet us at the same point. We are not alone in our endeavours, although we all have our individual ways to go.

In 1963 the American author *Jane Roberts* (1929-1984) began to channel messages from a spiritual consciousness, a teacher, from another dimension.[148] She has published numerous books with abstracts from these séances. I find that what is presented here is sensible and in good accord with my view of reality and what I have read elsewhere. One day, as Jane Roberts sat down at her writing table, she felt that her head was filled with thoughts and fantasies pouring in from a source outside of her. From a non-physical plane of consciousness this 'energy essence', who presented itself as *Seth*, would regularly lead conversations with those present, answering questions and dictate a number of books to Jane Robert's husband Rob. When Jane went into trance, it was as if her body was taken over by Seth. Her voice became deeper and her eyes darker, gestures and mimic changed. From the other world Seth gave answers to questions that people have asked at all times: Is there a life after death? Who is God? Is reincarnation a reality? What do our dreams mean? Can all people develop mediumistic capabilities? This is referenced in the published books about Seth. Seth is in these books stressing that what he explains is much simplified in order for people to understand as he resides on another plane of being.

David Spangler (b.1945) is a well-known American mystic with close connection to the Findhorn society. He has written several books, given lectures and held courses. He has contact with a spirit being named *John*. During a stay at Findhorn in 1991 I was given a booklet authored by David Spangler with the title *Co-operation with Spirit – Further Conversations with John*. Quotes from some of John's explanations on the spiritual and earthly existences were included in this booklet. About the contact between people and the spiritual world, John explained that such contact could be mutually enriching when it occurs as a result of a fellowship with God. What are here expressed are mostly recommendations given from the spirit's greater perspective, not statements about specific events or happenings. In regard to the latter, people will normally, as a rule, have the best knowledge, conditioned that they make some effort to get the correct understanding.

Ambres is a spiritual master or consciousness who since 1975 has presented himself through the Swede *Sture Johansson* (b.1940). Sture Johansson has explained that when he started with this channelling he could hear that he said something, but he could not control it.

He felt as if he had an inner 'I' who pushed forward and used his ordinary 'I' like a tool.[149] Ambres has stated that he lived in Egypt in his last incarnation which was 3000 years ago. He has said that it is today's people who are the cause of his emanation, and that he is here in order to help people obtain an insight they actually already have. What he says is, therefore, important, but in order to understand what he says, one must listen with feelings and not with the intellect. He recommends, however, that you do not blindly believe in what he says, but compare it with what you know or what you learn from others. The American film star and author Shirley MacLaine (b.1934) has described meetings with Ambres in several of her books regarding spiritual development. Among other things, she has referred to the filming of her autobiography where part of a séance with Ambres was also filmed, and, quite unexpectedly, it contained a personal message for her.[150] What she has recounted here seems to be typical for what people experience in meetings with Ambres.

Kevin Ryerson, USA, is channelling both a spirit by the name John, and one that calls itself *Tom McPherson*. Ryerson changes his personality completely when he is channelling the spirit of the one or the other. Ryerson has led many courses and workshops where the nature of personal reality is studied. Shirley Maclaine writes in her books about many séances with Ryerson (and mentions also one episode where he performed a variety of tasks blindfolded, as if he saw clearly). Kevin Ryerson also cooperates with David Spangler. He said in an interview that there are many forms of channelling, and that his mission is to help people to live in a more spiritual way and to bring out their talents and resources. He is also coaching a group of architects in order to obtain a better flow of the life energy through the landscape or the indoor environment. Ryerson mentions in the interview that some mediums often exaggerate their message in order to get people to understand what is happening and to get them to respond. He stressed that the messages should not be interpreted too literally.[151]

Ramtha is supposed to be a 35,000 year old soul from Atlantis. Ramtha is channelled through an American lady, J. Z. Knight (or Judith Darlene Hampton), and what was said during some of the séances has been written down and published in a book by Steven Lee Weinberg. The channelling began in 1977. J. Z. Knight had her blood pressure and cerebral activity measured during a séance and this showed remarkable changes. In addition, her body swelled and her voice changed. She remembered nothing afterwards. According to the advertisement for the Norwegian edition of the book about Ramtha, the purpose of life is to find the divinity in oneself, and to discover that we are ourselves masters of life's opportunities. There is not one truth, we must create it ourselves. All human beings are part of the deity, and the deity is a part of them. By loving yourself, you can control your life. Only then can you take responsibility for your own happiness.[152]

Edgar Cayce' extraordinary séances, the so-called *readings*, took place while he was in a trance. This was a self-inflicted trance in which he did not seem to be under control of some spirit contact, although his voice and language changed quite a lot during the séances.

Ectoplasm

A very special phenomenon that happens during some spiritualistic séances is the materialization of spirit beings, voices, sounds or items, the latter also called apports. This phenomenon is termed ectoplasm and requires the presence of a specially gifted medium, as the materialization is due to a substance that emanates from the medium's body orifices, most often from the mouth or nostrils. It must return to the medium's body at the end of the manifestation, otherwise the medium will suffer serious injuries. The same might happen if the substance is touched by an unexpected movement by any of the persons present or is being confronted with white light. A soft red light can, however, be used. Sometimes there is an unpleasant smell in the beginning. It was the French professor in physiology and Nobel Prize winner in medicine in 1913, Charles Richet (1850-1935), who first coined the term ectoplasm from the Greek word *ecto*, which means exteriorizing, and the word *plasma*, which means substance. Richet studied paranormal phenomena over many years and was in 1905 president of the English Society of Psychical Research. In 1919 he became honorary president of the French Institut Métapsychique International and its full-time president in 1929. The following about his observations of the medium Eusapia Palladino (1854–1918) is taken from his book *Thirty Years of Psychical Research*, 1923:[153]

> Many curious facts on the genesis of the materializations are observable, for only very rarely do materializations appear abruptly. They form by a concentration of matter around a central nucleus; much as a planet forms in a nebula or cells by concentration of aprotoplasmic material. ... There first appears a more or less formless mass, which may not even be visible, but which can be felt and seems capable of mechanical action. One can hardly help help imagining that movements of the table are due to mechanical energy, this half-visible hand ... whose resistance can be felt ... these are the formations which I call ectoplasm, for they seem to emanate from Eusapia's actual body. I have seen an almost rectilinear prolongation emerge from Eusapia. Many curious facts on the genesis of the materializations are observable, for only very rarely do materializations appear abruptly. They form by a concentration of matter around a central nucleus; much as a planet forms in a nebula or cells by concentration of as body, its termination acting like a living hand. ... At the Villa Carmen I saw a fully organized form rise from the floor, and a few minutes later it rose up in a straight line and became a small man enveloped in a kind of white burnoose, who took two or three halting steps in front of the curtain and then sank to the floor and disappeared as if, through a trap door. But there was no trap door. ...
>
> It has been asked how there can be materialization of clothes. This objection is somewhat naive, for the materialization of the hand is no easier to understand than of the glove that covers it. It is clear, however, that materialization may be of inanimate objects and not of the human body only.

An interesting and good description of a materialization where clothes and spectacles were clearly observed can be found in the book *Alec Harris: the full story of his remarkable physical mediumship* by Louie Harris. Alec Harris was a highly respected medium active in Wales and South Africa from the 1940s to the 1970s. Quotation:

It proved to be a very good circle. The highlight of the evening was the materialization of Mahatma Gandhi who came especially for Sir Alexander [Cannon]. The little Indian holy man was exactly as he had been on earth. He was painfully thin, almost emaciated, through many long fasts. Gandhi wore his customary loin cloth and the well-remembered steel-rimmed spectacles. He conversed at length with Sir Alexander in Hindustani, a language familiar to the doctor, but certainly not to Alec. Our eminent sitter was 'very impressed' with the manifestation, particularly at the accuracy of detail in the materialised form, and the timbre of his voice. Sir Alexander knew Mahatma Gandhi extremely well. Gandhi's conversing in his vernacular tongue was even more convincing evidence as far as he was concerned.

The French physicists and the Nobel Prize winners in 1903, Pierre (1859-1906) and Marie Curie (1867-1934) participated in experiments at the Institut Général Psychologique on physical anomalies surrounding Eusapia Palladino. Pierre Curie has left letters and both published and unpublished reports of these experiments. The Institut Général Psychologique was in the beginning under the leadership of Charles Richet and Pierre Janet.[i] Eusapia Palladino gave forty-three séances there over a three-year period. The following quotations are from an article by Renaud Evrard, *Pierre Curie, a Foot in Parapsychology?*, the Bulletin of the Parapsychological Association – autumn 2011:

> "They emphasized the need for introducing mechanical devices to record and corroborate the effects most often witnessed in the séances (changes in temperature, the movement of objects, sounds, apparitions) as well as to identify phenomena beyond the range of human perception (X-rays, electrical fields, magnetic fields, radioactivity, sonic vibrations). The equipment was intended to eliminate the possibility that the phenomena, as observed, were influenced by errors in perception resulting from fatigue and inattention in the observers as well as from the poor conditions of the séance room." (Brower, 2005, pp. 182-183).

As well as monitoring the physical events of the séance, the group gave special attention to the physiological status of the medium. The examination of Eusapia was to be continuous throughout the séance, with equipment (hidden in another room) and observers in place to note the medium's circulation, blood pressure, respiration, secretions, temperature, electrical potential, electrical resistance, autonomic reflexes, visual acuity and field, muscular capacity, reaction time, cutaneous sensibility, and mental processes (Courtier, 1908, pp. 479-480).

Curie confided to his friend the physicist George Gouy in a letter of July 24, 1905, that he expected to get a better idea in other sessions,

---

i. Pierre Janet (1859-1947) was psychiatrist and philosopher, professor at the Sorbonne University from 1895 and at the Collège de Franc in the years 1902-1936, as well as a member of Institut de France from 1913.

because he was not fooled: "We had at the Society of Psychology a few sittings with the medium Eusapia Palladino. It was very interesting, and really the phenomena that we have seen seem nexplicable by trickery. Tables lifted four legs. Appearances of distant objects. Hands that pinch or fondle you. Luminous apparitions. All in a room prepared for us with a small number of spectators all known and without possible accomplice. The only possible trick could result from a medium's extraordinary skill as a conjurer. But how to explain the phenomena when we hold the feet and hands, and when the lighting is sufficient for us to see what happens?" (in Blanc, 2009, pp. 583-586).

In 1989 Tom Harrison published his booklet *Visits by our Friends from the Other Side*. He tells of his mother, Minnie Harrison, who was a very special medium. She could produce ectoplasm when in trance and in this substance the sitters could often see their family and friends materialize. A few materializations were photographed, and some of those pictures can be seen on Internet as well as in the book. In 2004, with an extended edition in 2008, he published the book *Life after Death: Living Proof – A Lifetime's Experiences of Physical Phenomena and Materializations through the Mediumship of Minnie Harrison*. In this book, with foreword by Professor David Fontana, he gives details and presents pictures from séances where many different beings from the other side materialized and talked with and hugged the sitters present (he witnessed more than 1500 full materializations). The following pictures are from this book:

Figure 1. Tom's Aunt Agg, the main spirit communicator

Figure 2. Tom's Grandfather, (Minnie's father)

Notice the grandfather's beard. Tom Harrison was invited to feel the beard during the materialization and he reports that it felt as soft 'hair', but fairly dense and fairly long. His mother later explained that her father had been very proud of his beard when physical. No wonder he wanted to show how it was now. In his book Tom records how several men who had had beards materialised with them and the texture was different, as it would have been in life.

Peggy Barnes[i], a veteran medium, has in a booklet entitled *Psychic Facts: A series of fifteen lessons on the laws governing mental and physical mediumship* described ectoplasm. She writes:

> This substance [ectoplasm] in its many forms is used as the basis of all physical manifestations. It forms the body and clothing of a materialized spirit; it forms into rods and masses, strong and fibrous, to be used in all feats of ectoplasmic telekinesis; through its power the trumpet is levitated and the ectoplasmic hands and rods are formed that produce independent and automatic writing; in fact, even the tiniest of spirit raps could not be produced without the aid of a physical body from which is drawn the necessary ectoplasm. Spirits without the use of a material instrument are powerless to produce a sound or anything that comes into the range of our five physical senses, for they live in a higher range vibration of which we are unconscious. ...
>
> Ectoplasm is an elusive substance which emanates from the body of a medium; it exudes from all the natural orifices the mucous membrane and the skin ... it comes in many different forms, colors and conditions
>
> ... it may be gaseous, liquid, or fibrous; it may be soft as velvet with a moist, sticky surface, or it may be rough and solid; it can assume different colors or be of a soft white, grey, or black; it can be invisible, although it has weight and gives sensation on contact and can make an imprint on plastic substances; in materialization, it sometimes takes on gorgeous colors from the flowers and gowns of those in the room, and the manifesting entities are able to bring out a beautiful pattern on the ectoplasmic gauze which forms their robes. It is extremely sensitive to light and deteriorates when subjected to its rays. The spirit teachers tell us that the chemicals in the light rays tear down the ectoplasm, so that they are at this time experimenting to find a chemical to add to the ectoplasm that will enable it to withstand the devastating power of light.
>
> This substance, which is the basis of all manifestations of physical mediumship, is sometimes called ideoplasm, because it is sensitive to the thoughts and ideas of the sitters and the spirits. To be a physical medium the body must contain a superabundance of certain chemicals. One of our greatest scientists has made the statement that only one in 100,000 human bodies contains a sufficient amount of these

---

i. According to John R. Crowley, Peggy Barnes, the author of *Psychic Facts* and of twelve other small books, was the close associate and cabinet attendance of one of the outstanding physical mediums of the twentieth century, Rev. Ethel Riley Post-Parrish. She founded the Temple of Truth in the late twenties and in 1932, with the name changed to Camp Silver Belle after her doorkeeper, set up in the Mountain Springs Hotel and its spacious grounds in Ephrata, PA. This organization, which has resumed the name Temple of Truth, continues under the leadership of her grandson, its Spiritual Director, Rev. Joseph Riley.

chemicals to present a full-form materialization. Just what the necessary chemicals are we do not know. ...

...ectoplasm is an outer layer of protoplasm, an etherialized protoplasm, we might say. As we know, protoplasm is the basis of all plant and animal life. (It is safe to assume that physical mediumship requires either a superabundance of one of the chemicals contained in protoplasm or the addition of an unknown chemical built up by spirit power.)

Other forms of spirit contact and spirit possessions

Spirits (or as some may term them – Ghosts) may be photographed. If you search for spirit photography on Internet, you will find lots of pictures where there is something in the picture in addition to the physical people photographed. This may be an extra hand, an extra face or the shadow of a complete figure. Very often this face resembles a deceased family member or friend of some of the people attending the event. Arthur Conan Doyle has in a chapter in his book *The History of Spiritualism* dealt with this phenomenon and has there referred to several reports given by trustworthy eyewitnesses as to the circumstances when the photos were taken. They guaranteed that no fraud or trickery could have been the cause. The photographer obviously had mediumistic abilities. One such photographer with whom Conan Doyle worked was William Hope who developed his mediumship in what became known as the Crewe Circle. When the researcher Harry Price made, what Conan Doyle considered an unfounded attack on Hope, he wrote the book *The Case for Spirit Photography* (1925) which contains many photographs and unsolicited reports from people throughout Britain in support of Hope. In the book Conan Doyle says of one of his experiences:

"At the annual meeting of the Society for the Study of Supernormal Pictures, I being present, a photograph of the members was taken in the normal way as a souvenir. As Hope was present, it was suggested that a second photograph be taken by him in the hope that we might get some psychic effect. The plate was taken from an unopened packet in the pocket of the secretary, and some fifteen of us were witnesses of the whole transaction. Hope had no warning at all, and could have made no preparation. The plate was at once developed by one of our own members, and a well-marked extra, amid a cloud of ectoplasm, appeared upon this picture. This extra was claimed by one of our members as a good likeness of his dead father. The result, which is illustrated by figure 5,[*opposite*] was obtained before an audience of experts, if any men in this world have a right to call themselves experts upon this subject. How can it be explained by fraud and how can such a case be lightly set aside? Granting for argument's sake that the sitter may have been mistaken in the recognition, how can the actual psychic effect be accounted for?"

Figure 3. The photograph here is the 'figure 5' referred to in the quotation opposite from 'The Case for Spirit Photography', showing the psychic face in the centre of the picture, at 90 degrees to the sitters (highlighted by the white outline). Conan Doyle himself is seated, middle row next to the lady on the left of the picture. (We apologise for the screening marks but we did not want to 'doctor' the picture apart from adding the outline -Publisher)

In another chapter in the first mentioned book, Conan Doyle discusses voice mediumship, a phenomenon that often occurs during séances, when no materialization takes place. In some instances there are several voices heard at different places in the room and voices clearly distinct from the medium's, who may or may not be in trance. Sometimes a so-called trumpet is used, but that is not always needed. Messages may be given in different languages, languages unknown to the medium. Conan Doyle refers to an explanation as to how this phenomenon can take place – an explanation "corroborated by communications received from the spirits themselves". "It appears that ectoplasm coming chiefly from the medium, but also in a lesser degree from the sitters, is used by the spirit operators to fashion something resembling a human larynx. This they use in the production of the voice."

We hear a lot about ghosts and apparitions or 'spooks' who appear in many, especially older houses in most countries. In some houses there are so many disturbances that people do not want to live there. England is known to have a ghost in almost every old castle. This is said to be either a deceased previous owner of the castle who walks around and look after his/her property, or one that has suffered an untimely death and has not managed to leave the site. The ghosts can be either of an evil, neutral or well-intentioned disposition. They can cause a lot of noise and disturbance in a house. Some says that ghosts love to haunt.

Also what people may experience is the phenomenon called spirit possession. Then a friendly or non-friendly being from the other side possesses – that is takes control of – a physical person, as in the description given below of a so-called adhesive spirit, and in the account of Caterina of Siena who was said to be fighting evil spirits who had possessed physical human beings. Then a person's personality seems completely suppressed for a short or longer period of time, and the personality of a spirit seems to have full control. Professor Ian Stevenson (1918-2007), USA, has studied and written about some such cases where a child suddenly changes character completely and claims to be a different person, belonging to a different family and with a different name.[i] A possible explanation of these cases is that the person really was possessed by a deceased entity that still existed in a sphere close to our physical existence, as a spirit being. These stories fit George G. Ritchie's experience which he had during his near-death experience (see the chapter on Death) and with what Rosemary Altea (see below) has described in her book about spirit rescue.

It is an unclear boundary between what can be called an adhesive spirit and spirit possession. In both cases, the experience may be explained as a

---

i. Ian Stevenson was professor of psychiatry and Head of the Department for Personality Studies at the University of Virginia, United States. See the Journal of Nervous and Mental Diseases, September 1977, which discusses his work until then. He has researched reincarnation phenomena since 1960, and written many books on this subject.

negative spirit will seek to influence a physical human being, so that the person complies with the will of the spirit, instead of having his/her own will. The victim usually does not realize what is going on. Traditions within some religious groups – also among Christians – with exorcism or expulsions of devils are based on the conviction that some persons actually are possessed by evil spirits.

The Norwegian television channel TVNorge showed a program in the summer of 2003 from a Danish television series which was called *Spirit Power*. One of the programs showed a man who unconsciously had brought a spirit home with him when he returned from a pub. All of a sudden the apartment, where this man had lived for some time, began to be haunted. Both this man and the person with whom he shared the apartment, saw in their dreams a man who seemed crude and nasty, unkempt and with a large beard. At the same time strange things happened in the apartment, such as inexplicably flapping of curtains and objects falling on the floor and shattering. A so-called medium (spirit saver or spirit exorcist) believed that the tenant had been joined by a spirit of the type called an adhesive spirit – a spirit that would not continue further on into the 'other side', but would take over the tenant's individuality so that the spirit could continue his pub-going, drinking life, as he had done while alive. The medium saw the spirit exactly as the residents of the apartment had seen him in dreams. The tenant admitted that he now could drink up to two bottles of red wine in a short time without feeling drunk, and there was an open bottle of red wine in the apartment. The medium sensed strong red wine odours in several places in the apartment. He explained that everything is energy, and a spirit will be able to efficiently use the energy that a human being exudes, for example, as a result of alcohol intake. The story ended with the medium managing to expel the spirit, but he asked for a sign from the spirit that it really would disappear. And at that moment a glass table in the apartment cracked with a great sound - a glass surface so solid that it could support an adult man. This story shows that it is not always only old houses or what we might call old sites that are haunted.

In another program from the same television series, the man in the house had a knee problem which started at the same time as the haunting began in the house. Under the exorcism séance the man suddenly felt nausea and became dizzy but he got better after having received some healing from the exorcist. The pain in the knee was gone the moment the spirit disappeared. The exorcist explained that the spirit had sought to influence the man as well as his wife so that they should do what the spirit desired, and it was when this energy withdrew from the man as a result of the séance, that the man felt so unwell.

Spirit rescue

A variety of mediums are today engaged with what they call spirit rescue – they are seeking to help deceased souls from being bound to the physical, so that they may go on to other spheres, a place where it is said that one should be after the physical life or between the physical lives. It is said that what we experience as a ghost or as an evil spirit's possession of a physical person, normally will be a soul who has not been able to leave the physical plane.

Rosemary Altea, England, is helping deceased individuals to accept their new existence. What she says is pretty much the same as stories told by other exorcists, and what is experienced in many near-death experiences. She has published a book about her personal development and her activity as a helper of spirits, as well as about her work as a medium and mediator of conversations between living persons and their deceased relatives.[154] She is also a healer. For her work she gets help from a spirit – *Grey Eagle* – who was an American Indian when he lived on Earth. The physical people she helps are never in doubt that what is conveyed is correct, as it conveys details such as only the deceased could be familiar with. Regardless of whether one believes in her story or not, there are certain things that are difficult to explain away. Some of the things one should take note of when it comes to contact with the deceased are that the deceased, allegedly, are more interested in having contact with the family members or friends left behind, a desire that normally is stronger than the others' need for contact. For Rosemary Altea contact with the dead is quite natural; she sees and hears the deceased as if they were incarnate people. The only difference is that the colours associated with the deceased are stronger. She sometimes experiences the spirit world as more real and of firmer material than the human world.

Co-operation with Nature Spirits – the Findhorn Community

Everywhere in the world and throughout time, there have been people who believe that everything in nature has a soul or spirit, whether this applies to minerals, plants, trees and animals, and that existence is developed from minerals to people and later to pure spirit. By co-operation with these spirits it is maintained that the incredible can be achieved, while the opposite will be the result if the spirits are not pacified. The spiritual community at Findhorn in Northern Scotland claims to have achieved their fabulous agriculture results by collaborating with some special spirits, who are called nature spirits or Devas there. This is, inter alia, described in the book *The Secret Life of Plants* by Peter Chr. Tompkins. Eileen Caddy (1917-2007) and her husband Peter Caddy (who died in 1994) were the Findhorn Community's founders, along with Dorothy Maclean. Peter and Eileen Caddy and their three children moved to the Findhorn campsite in 1962 when the couple lost their jobs as managers of the Cluny Hill hotel. As more people joined them, the Caddy family settled on the campsite. Dorothy Maclean, who at one time had been Peter's secretary and had long spiritual training, followed the Caddy family to Findhorn.

During the most dramatic years of Eileen Caddy's life an inner voice grew in her, which comforted her and gave her good advice. This voice became slowly stronger, and she began to consult it in meditation when she needed coaching. Peter Caddy began to consult this guide through Eileen, and eventually it was frequently. In 1962 it was the voice that showed the way. Eileen Caddy has published several collections of words and poems that she received through her meditation.

The community became particularly famous because this small group was able to grow vegetables and flowers which normally would not have grown in such a cold place and in the barren earth of that part of Scotland. The vegetables were in addition of unusual size. It was Eileen's inner voice that was behind the founding of the garden, but it was Dorothy Maclean who had contact with the Devas. She sensed the Devas as thoughts or thought patterns that sought fulfilment. As she learned to listen to them, she received instructions about where and how the seeds were to be planted, and how the earth was to be prepared, etc. She made contact with the light beings of all the flowers and vegetables they planted, and also with a superior landscape angel. She learnt that the plants were very attuned to human radiation. If you are aware that plants have some form of consciousness, you will contribute to the well being of the plants.

Today, the Findhorn Foundation is established as a spiritual charitable organization, with the purpose of being a centre for education and a role model as how people can live together. There are several thousand visitors each year attending courses and conferences or living in the community for a short or longer period of time. The community is founded on the principle that God, or the Source of life is available for all of us at any time, and that nature, including his planet, has intelligence and is part of a much larger plan. The organization has no formal doctrine or religious confession, but those who join the organization believe that an evolving extension of consciousness takes place in the world, creating a human culture built on spiritual values. Author Paul Hawken writes in the book *The Magic of Findhorn* that Findhorn's mission is to create energies with new types of vibration, which is the first atunement for a 'mass planetary initiation'.

Documentation of spirit contacts

1. *Treatments at a sanatorium for mentally disturbed patients.*

A fascinating book about spirit contact and spirit exorcism is Carl Wickland's book *Thirty years among the Dead* from 1924. Carl August Wickland (1861-1945) was chief psychiatrist at the National Psychopathic Institute of Chicago from 1909 to 1918 and then founded the National Psychological Institute in Los Angeles, a non-profit corporation for the research of psychology. This Institute operated a sanatorium, where at any one time up to ten patients would be treated until they could be brought back to sanity. He administered electro-shocks to patients he thought to be possessed by spirits, a treatment which dislodged the spirits. His wife, Anna, was psychic and a trance medium; and he and his wife, together with some good friends, held séances every week for spirit contact. Very often the dislodged spirit appeared at a séance after the electro-shock treatment of the patient. After having been explained its true condition, the spirit normally continued on its path in the spirit world. Detailed reports of hundreds of spirit contacts were stenographically made in order to record the exact situation of the communicating entity. His fascinating book contains many such records, also from meetings with spirits who had not possessed a human being, such as Helena Blavatsky and Mary Baker Eddy, the latter was the founder of Christian Science, who now said she regretted her former teaching. The purpose of the Wicklands' work was primarily to restore the patients' health, but also to obtain reliable and incontestable evidence at first hand regarding 'after death' conditions, and, not the least, to free spirits from their earthbound existence. Wickland warned, however, against fraudulent psychics and deceiving spirits. In his book *The Gateway of Understanding*, 1934, he writes the following:[155]

> "While there are many earnest students of the interrelationship of the two worlds and many excellent psychic intermediaries who do great credit to the cause of psychic research, yet there are also many individuals, nondescript and illiterate, who possess psychic powers, but are dominated largely by designing and deceiving spirit entities. These entities, seeking to please the vanity of ambitious psychics, may assume the names of great personages, especially those of renown and fame, but their twaddle and inconsistencies are entirely foreign to the original characters they represent themselves to be. Many such pretentious assertions have come to our notice. ... A certain medium, whose husband is declared to be Jesus Christ reincarnated, claims that she is the reincarnation of the Virgin Mary, yet she swears, smokes and drinks like a man. A young man of quite ordinary intelligence informed us that the great Socrates was his spirit guide, and we were recently invited to attend a circle to hear Jesus talk through a trumpet. (We did not, however, accept the invitation.)"

2. The Cross-Correspondences.

In the archives of the Society for Psychical Research (SPR) in London you can find information about the events that go under the title of the Cross-Correspondences. After one of the founders of SPR, Frederick W.H. Myers (1843-1901), died, the Society received over a period of more than thirty years messages from mediums living in different parts of the world. The messages were incomplete, some were written in English and others in Latin or Greek, but all involved a request to send the messages to SPR. The messages were not understood by the mediums, who sometimes received them in trance or as automatic writing, and sometimes between other kinds of information. The messages often consisted of quotes from the Greek classics. As it turned out, the various quotes gave a meaningful context – something that some of the messages also gave hints about. It was claimed that the reason for these complex procedures was that Myers wanted to prove that there was an existence after physical death where conscious thinking and planning also could occur, and that the information he sent to the living should not be interpreted as telepathy between the living or as knowledge that these could have acquired otherwise.[156] It is possible that this phenomenon was special for the group around Myers. Some claim that the information can be attributed to the medium's close contact with this group, and with people who had in-depth knowledge of classical literature.

3. Experiments with mediums.

Professor at the University of Arizona, Gary E.R. Schwartz (b.1944), and Linda G.S. Russek, PhD, have over many years done research on mediumistic contact with deceased individuals.[157] They have had several well-known American mediums in sittings (readings) in which participants have received messages from deceased relatives. These séances have been filmed, and that which has been said has been extensively analyzed. Several mediums have had sittings with the same person, and the mediums' statements have been remarkably alike and correct. The mediums did not know who the attendees were until after the trials. The experiments were, inter alia, set up as blind meetings, where the medium and the attendee did not see each other, in some cases did not talk together, and in some other cases only had contact over the telephone without having any previous conversation. In some cases, the medium had already received paranormal impressions of the participant or his or her deceased relatives before the meeting had begun, information that was written down and later checked. Sometimes it is information that the participant did not know, but which was confirmed by subsequent research. Perhaps the most amazing thing with some of these sittings was that the participants sometimes denied that the received information was coming from a deceased relative, at which these relatives protested and affirmed their statements – which were later confirmed. Schwartz believed that the last mentioned event indicated that the medium could not have taken the information from a kind of archive in the atmosphere or from the attendee's memory or mind. He found it difficult to draw any other conclusion than that these studies show that the mind and the brain are not the same, and that the mind or the individual's awareness continues after the physical existence, although his deep-seated scepticism of such an explanation is still there. However, not everyone agrees with his interpretation or see the value of these experiments.

Professor Emeritus of psychology and statistics at the University of Oregon, Ray Hyman (b.1928) has strongly criticized some of the trials. Comments are to be found on the websites of CSICOP (The Committee for the Scientific Investigation of Claims of the Paranormal, USA).[158]

4. The Susy Smith Project.

The problem with many of the stories about spirit contacts is that they remain anecdotes and they are rarely taken seriously. Therefore Gary Schwartz and Linda Russek started a project where they collaborated with the medium and author Susy Smith (1910-2001), hoping to be able to document a life after the physical and the possibilities for contact with the deceased. At the University of Arizona they started The Susy Smith Project, where anyone who wanted to could leave a message in the University's computer memory bank. The message was encrypted, and only the one entering it knew the code. In order to read the message, one must first know the code – and the idea was that the one who deposited the message would after death convey the code to the person that should read it. The code should, of course, not be known by anyone living.[159] I do not know whether anything can be reported from this project yet.

5. Instrumental Transcommunication – ITC.

The Portuguese diplomat Anabela Cardoso PhD explained, at a meeting in March 2008 arranged by the Norwegian Parapsychological Society, that Instrumental Transcommunication (ITC) is communication with *The Other World*, a term which covers all types of paranormal messages received either in form of speech (although also pictures have been seen) by means of electronic media such as tape recorders, radios, fax machines, video recordings, telephones and computers. She maintained that evidence for such voices coming from the *other side* is now overwhelming, and that such information is received under strictly controlled circumstances. She mentioned in her talk that analysis of the voices showed acoustic peculiarities that do not occur in normal human speech, which proves that these cannot be earthly human voices. The voices answer questions posed to them, showing that there is real communication. Although she stressed that more research is highly desirable, she concluded by saying that the indications are that these are voices from people who have lived on Earth, and that they have a strong desire to show that they still have some form of existence and want to tell people about this existence. This phenomenon has received increased attention in recent years. Previously the term Electronic Voice Phenomena (EVP) was used, as only one-way information took place. One of the earliest recordings of such voices occurred when one of the pioneers on this side, Friedrich Jürgenson, Sweden, in 1959 was out in the forest to record birdsong and instead heard voices on the tape when it was re-played. This is described in the book *Liv etter døden?* (Life after death) by the Swedish psychiatrist Nils-Olof Jacobsen (b. 1937).

Thanks to experimentation with such contacts during the last fifty years, many people today experience direct communication with *the other world*, or with *the other dimension*, which are the terms used by the voices heard in the recordings, about the location where these exist. Since 1997, Anabela

Cardoso has made great efforts to clarify the phenomenon and she is behind the publishing of *The ITC Journal* with two editions per year. Together with the Board for the publication, she has organized conferences, the first one in 2004, where the experiences and problems are discussed. She collaborates with researchers in many countries. You can read more about this on the website http://itcjournal.org/journal.htm, where you can get a lot of information and also hear voices recorded on audio tape. Professor David Fontana has devoted an entire chapter of his book *Is there an Afterlife?* to this phenomenon. He visited Anabela Cardoso and experienced such communication in her studio. He felt confident that the voices were not coming from terrestrial beings.

On the website mentioned one can read that it was *the other world* that began with this form of communication. Those on *the other side* wanted contact in order to tell people that there is life after the physical death, that life is eternal and that the physical existence has a meaning. It is now supposed that this contact has been so successful that those on the other side no longer are dependent on mediums to establish contact. This means that the messages conveyed are not restricted by a medium's ability to understand and to redistribute what is received.

The best equipment for establishing such contact is a simple audio tape recorder, which is recording in front of a radio tuned in on a shortwave band where no broadcasting can be heard, only the so-called white noise. One can ask questions while the recording takes place, but will normally only hear a response during the playback of the tape. For those who are not trained to listen to such recordings it can be hard to perceive that something is coming through, but by training or repeated playback of the recording, this will improve. Anabela Cardoso has experimented with this for many years and she now receives more and better contacts. She has even experienced messages from *the other side* coming through on her telephone answering machine, and also that a radio is suddenly sending such information without her having done anything other than having the radio on with a faint noise. She has collaborated with electro-technicians in several countries with the aim of improving the receiver equipment and also to find better ways to eliminate the background noise in the recordings. She has also tried to find out what sort of conditions could provide the best response. Among other things, she has noted that water, such as gentle dripping from a spring, gives clearer voices on the tape. On the other hand, she cannot have other electronic equipment, mobile phone or a computer turned on, when recording is in progress.

There is one special individual in particular that she has had contact with in this way – one that calls itself Carlos de Almeida. It appears that contact with *the other side* must take place through a sort of central station there, where a special spirit is trying to improve the communication. This central station is termed *Rio do Tempo* (The River of Time). The voices that Anabela Cardoso hears speak mostly Portuguese. The language of the messages that other operators receive will normally be in the recipient's native language. A message received by Anabela Cardoso in this way is the following: "*Always remember our world. Anyone who is thinking of our world reduces the distance.*"

Comments

In many places in the world people sacrifice to the spirits. In the Norwegian tradition from olden times it was the custom to give porridge to the gnomes during Christmas, so that they would not make mischief. Whether spirits have to be appeased or not is an open question. Many believe that people themselves are clever enough to create havoc, so they do not need the help of non-humans or non-physical beings. However, as the stories about ghosts suggest, problems or disturbances might occur if a spirit is not aware that it no longer is physical. Then it needs help, not offerings.

In recent years many serious books on the issue whether life continues after the physical death, have been published. These in-depth references and analyses are coming from the best documented séances with proven mediums. I will mention two such books where we can find many references to other books of interest about the same. Professor of philosophy Stephen E. Braude (b.1945) at Maryland University, Baltimore, USA, published in the 2003 the book *Immortal Remains – The Evidence for Life after Death*. Professor David Fontana in his book *Is there an Afterlife*? has described much of the same. They have no other explanation for all those strange cases they describe, than that there must be some sort of existence after the physical death. Arthur Conan Doyle's work in two volumes titled *The History of Spiritualism* (1926) is also of importance. He has here given extensive reports from spirit contacts, thoroughly witnessed and described by trustworthy people.

So are all the stories we hear about sufficiently compelling for us to believe in a spiritual world or an after death-existence? Most people will probably reject their credibility or find other explanations such as hallucinations or dream experiences, although I do not see how one can disregard the messages obtained through instrumental transcommunication or the ectoplasm phenomenon. There are also other types of phenomena that supplement those mentioned here, and that is the near-death experiences and what they report about an existence on the other side. A book on this last topic is Michael Newton's *Journey of Souls – Case Studies of Life between Lives*. Michael Newton is a regression therapist and authorised hypnotherapist. He has hypnotized hundreds of people and brought them back into the existence between the earthly lives, and made them afterwards tell what they were experiencing. The accounts are similar to Plato's description given in the book The Republic about the soldier Er's experiences. Another book, which tells much the same as *Journey of Souls,* is the book *The Road to Immortality* by Geraldine Cummins. This book was written in trance, allegedly communicated by Frederick W.H. Myers, the aforementioned, co-founder of the Society for Psychical Research in England. However, it takes too long to render a description of life on *the other side* here, but I will come back to some of it in the section about death in chapter 10. The near-death experiences, I will also write about in the same chapter. In chapter 9 which is about spirit beings, I will review explanations of what the various spirit phenomena can be, but first we must try to understand what is said about some other aspects of life.

3.12. Thought images that become manifested on the body

As mentioned above, there are several Christian saints who have experienced stigmata in the form of wound marks on the body such as those Jesus suffered at the crucifixion. Stigmata can be said to be thought images manifesting physically on the body. Such stigmata are supposedly not mentioned in written historical sources before they emerged on Francis of Assisi. In some cases the wound on the hand is straight through it and has taken the form of a nail piercing it (Francis of Assisi and Therese Neumann). The stigmata of Padre Pio did not entirely match with those of Francis. Among others the wound in Francis' chest was on the right side, while it was on Padre Pio's left side. Furthermore, any trace of the stigmata disappeared from Padre Pio just before he died, while Francis' were prominent even after he was dead. All the stigmata are very painful, but not all have bleeding. Padre Pio's stigmata were thoroughly investigated by several doctors, who could not find any explanation for the phenomenon.

Also other types of thought images have been manifested. The heart of the Italian nun St Veronica Giuliani (1660-1727), who was sanctified in 1839, is said to have had imprints of a cross and a sword, which was seen during the autopsy of her body. Something similar happened to Teresa of Avila. She had a vision of an angel who pierced her heart with a sword. After her death, it turned out that the heart had a deep cut. She described her experience as follows: [160]

> I saw beside me, on the left side, an angel in human form - a form of vision I do not usually experience, only very rarely. Although I often see symbols of angels, the experience of those is on the mental plane. ... I saw in his hand a long spear of gold, and at the point there seemed to be a little fire. He appeared to me to be thrusting it at times into my heart, and to pierce my very entrails; when he drew it out, he seemed to draw them out also, and to leave me all on fire with a great love of God. The pain was so great, that it made me moan; and yet so surpassing was the sweetness of this excessive pain, that I could not wish to be rid of it, and one's soul will never be satisfied with anything less than God. It is a spiritual and not a bodily pain.
>
> (*It is reported that Teresa's heart showed signs of penetration, which was observed when she was autopsied after her death.*)

There is also a well-known story about a twelve-year-old girl in France, who in 1913 caused huge newspaper headlines because she managed mentally to produce different kinds of images on her the body. The American author Michael Talbot (b.1953), who wrote about these last phenomena in the book *The Holographic Universe,* believes that this kind of miracles can be explained by psychokinesis – that is, the psyche is able to produce physical reactions. He refers to David Scott Rogo's book *Miracles*, where such a hypothesis is presented. He further points to David Bohm's (1917-1994) theory on holo-movement.[i] Talbot wrote that a thought not only has mental consequences, there are also a number of physiological reactions from an experience. We react both physically and biologically to everything we experience. Often, the biological reactions are coming before the thought is acknowledged, such as a flight response when we believe we are threatened.[161]

3.13. Thought form that takes on a life of its own

Some people or several people together have managed to produce visions or phantom figures. The French-Belgian adventurer Alexandra David-Néel[ii] (1868-1969), who has written about her experiences from Tibet around 1925, has told how she was able to bring forth such a shape – in this case a monk – by strong concentration. Other people also saw it at times. The figure was at first friendly and nice, but changed character after some time and became quite unpleasant. She then tried to get rid of it, but that took a long time and required much effort before it disappeared. The phenomenon called *Philip* was a spirit that was created by a pilot group in Canada around 1970 under the direction of Professor George Owen, and which eventually caused real physical phenomena. (One such séance can be seen on Youtube – *The Philip Experiment.*)

Dion Fortune has recorded how she by her imagination once created a large wolf which materialized next to her, and which required much effort to get rid of. This shows that the power of the mind is great. She explained the incident by saying that a strong mind can create a form that takes on its own life – a so-called elemental (a thought-form). (As I have explained in chapter 9.4 Helena Blavatsky used the term 'elemental spirits' for nature spirits such as gnomes. They are not the same as elementals.) This means that a separation of energy from the etheric body or astral body takes place. She believed that this happened in her case because she wanted revenge over a particular person for a specific reason. When she used this thought-form in

---

i. David Bohm, American-born, was professor of quantum physics at Birkbeck College, London University, from 1961. His book *Quantum Theory* (1951) and the book *Causality and Chance in Modern Physics* (1957) are still authoritative textbooks. He was also strongly spiritually engaged and had close contact with Krishnamurti – an Indian spiritual teacher.

ii. Alexandra David-Néel author of, inter alia, the book *My Journey to Lhasa*, 1927 such a way, she would be doing black magic – something which also would create problems for herself. Anyone practising black magic will damage his or her own character.

You should therefore be careful not to use thoughts in a negative way – they can backfire on you. Arthur E. Powell, author of a variety of Theosophical writings, including the different consciousness bodies, has in his book *The Etheric Double* described such thought-forms and shown how they arise, a description that matches Dion Fortune's story.[162]

3.14. Like attracts like

Accidents rarely come in ones. Most people have probably learned the truth of this saying to a greater or lesser extent. Sometimes there seems to be a situation that can be compared with a low pressure atmosphere where a storm has increased strength. Due to the absence of air pressure, a low pressure centre attracts air from all sides (and the air is then pushed up into higher altitudes). Anyone without confidence in him or herself and who is thus without radiation, is sending out signals about their insecurity, to which others – who recognize this insecurity in themselves– are attracted. Seeing another's insecurity has the consequence that one can forget one's own and thereby feel safer. The one who has withdrawn into his or her self, as into a black hole, attracts the environment's energy and attention – especially energy from those who feel that black holes are threatening. It is a saying that old people gather strength from small children – they suck in that energy (and the young have more than enough to give). This probably explains the phenomenon of energy exchange between people, although this does not let like attract like, but is a levelling of one person's surplus energy against another's lack of energy. James Redfield gave in the book *The Celestine Prophecy* some examples of energy exchange between people. It seems that our energy radiation also affects our environment and our unconscious, so that we are attracted to places corresponding to something or other within ourselves. Laurens van der Post has in his book *Dangerous Journey to the Interior* given a description of what can happen when one is not completely attentive and does not take responsibility for the feelings and thoughts one has inside. He recounted a series of events that resulted in a young man losing his life, and he suggested that all the events were actually initiated by the young man himself. After having read the book, I have the feeling that we unconsciously steer ourselves into the events we go through, whether it is to learn something in particular or to die (as in the aforementioned case, but then also for others to learn something from that). Laurens van der Post wrote that accidents and disasters outside of us are feeding on accidents and disasters inside us. He thought that the patterns of our outer life reflect and confirm our deepest and most personal intentions.

Jane Roberts (Seth's channel) wrote about the same as Laurens van der Post.[163] She maintained that thoughts have a magnetic attraction on other people's similar thoughts, or procure repulsion if anyone's thoughts feel threatening. Perhaps it is not so odd if one accident is followed by another, or that a peculiar event is followed by similar events within a short period of time. There seems to be something in our structure, as explained by Seth, which sets events in motion. If that is correct, the most important thing one can do is to work with oneself and one's personality – and be careful as to what and how one thinks.

3.15. Animals' inexplicable abilities

Most people who have pets or other animals, have experienced that animals have unexpected paranormal abilities. My family's dog howled when my mother died at a different place from where the dog was. Another dog in the family had an incredible sense of direction and showed the right direction home in thick fog. A third dog found the way home over a distance of approximately ten kilometres without having walked the way before, as he had been driven to the starting point for the trip (a bitch was the bait). Rupert Sheldrake (b.1942) has researched and written a book about animals' unexpected capabilities.[164] He describes not only dogs' special abilities, but also the corresponding capabilities of cats, horses and other animals. He also comments on the incredible abilities of birds to fly vast distances, and the matching skills in butterflies, turtles, salmon and eels. Science has not found any adequate explanation as to how they get around, although they consider the Earth's magnetic field to be of great help. Sheldrake attributes the phenomenon to what he calls morphological fields, a phenomenon he described in detail in the book *The Hypothesis of Morphic Resonance – A New Science of Life*. It is possible that this field must be considered identical with the psi field, which I will describe later.

3.16. Other peculiarities

Michael Talbot explains in the book *The Holographic Universe* some peoples' incredible ability to withstand pain and injury on the body. He refers to reports that were recorded about what happened in Paris immediately after a prominent Jansenist, François de Paris (1690-1727), died. Many people fell into trance while following the mourning ceremonies and inexplicable healings occurred. Among the trance-individuals there were many who sustained the most awful attacks and injuries from the bystanders without seeming to notice anything or getting lasting damage. You can hear similar stories from some Asian cultures today, where people are celebrating Jesus' crucifixion or other religious events. Among other things, some have iron hooks fastened to the body and pull heavy platforms or vehicles with these devices. They show no pain and have no physical damage afterwards. Michael Talbot also discusses a wide range of strange phenomena, some of which are mentioned in this book, and all of which are well documented.

There has been a great deal of research on identical twins who were separated soon after birth.[165] Oddly enough, there is often a strange correlation between their life cycles, despite the fact that they do not know each other. One such pair of twins in the United States trained in the same profession, married women with the same name and divorced at roughly the same time, got married again, and again to women with the same name.

In the book *The Gold Leaf Lady* Stephen E. Braude writes about two people with quite exceptional paranormal capabilities. He has even been able to check the phenomena he writes about, and guarantees that all possible precautions were taken to prove that cheating did not occur. In both cases, the person in question had to undress completely before the experiment could begin and put on the clothing which the experiment leader provided. The first case deals with a lady named Katie, in Florida, USA, who had several types of paranormal capabilities. She experienced thin gold leaves (actually brass) suddenly emerging, many times, in different places on her body. The flakes were usually about 1 cm^2 and covered often large areas. This was not a one-time phenomenon. It was observed many times, but was not a phenomenon that Katie was able to control. The phenomenon was both uncomfortable and embarrassing, since gold leaves could occur at anytime and anywhere. Katie usually got itching skin wounds when this happened. The gold leaves could also pop up on her clothes or on objects within a certain distance from her.

Braude sought to arrange a TV recording of the phenomenon, but the TV team was spending so much time recording everything else about Katie, that when they got far as to try to film the purpose of the recording, Katie was both tired and fed up with them, whereupon nothing happened.

The second case concerns the American Ted Serios (1920-2006). In the 1960s there were countless trials in which he provided thought images on film using a polaroid camera. Serios did not touch the camera during the experiments, and the photos were immediately developed as soon as the photographs were taken. A peculiarity of these experiments was that the images often were twisted. For example, if he tried to create an image of the Chicago Hilton Hotel, what emerged on the polaroid-film was the image of the Denver Hilton Hotel and then from a slightly strange point of view. In another case the picture that emerged appeared to be of a particular building from an earlier time, and not the building as it looked that day. The American psychiatrist and psychologist Jule Eisenbud (1908-1999), who for many years was associate clinical professor at the medical school in the University of Colorado, watched thousands of tests in the period 1964-1967, and has described these in the book *The World of Ted Serios*. Images from these tests are now kept in the library of the University of Maryland, Baltimore County.

This is not the place to give a detailed mention of Atlantis or Lemuria or decide whether or not there have been countries or kingdoms by those names. But it should be noted that in addition to Plato's comment that a kingdom could have existed west of Gibraltar (Hercules' pillars) in ancient times called Atlantis, there are a number of mystics who mention this realm. Rudolf Steiner mentioned two such kingdoms, the oldest one he called Lemuria and the youngest Atlantis, and he explained that these were the precursors for the empires of the Earth. Also, Helena Blavatsky, Edgar Cayce, Seth and Aivanhov refer to Atlantis, and their descriptions are relatively congruent. Cayce often mentioned that a person's special problems could have been caused by the person's experiences in the Atlantean period.[166] This period should have been in existence for approximately 200,000 years and ceased to exist about 10,000 years ago. Cayce described Atlantis as a land area in today's Atlantic Ocean, where there was a civilization technically very advanced. It had used crystal-induced energy, misuse of which eventually caused the country's self-destruction and flooding. Large groups of survivors settled both in the Central and South America, in the Pyrenees and in North Africa.

Colin Wilson and Rand Flem-Ath have written a book about Atlantis.[167] They indicate many peculiarities when it comes to the placement of various mythical places and strange structures, such as their location, as well as the measurement and purpose of the Cheops's pyramid, which seems to indicate that Atlantis must have been a reality. They have suggested that Atlantis was located in Antarctica before the continent was covered by ice.

An area that has received increasing attention in our days is the UFO-phenomena (Unidentified Flying Objects). This is such an extensive and special subject, that I cannot go further into it here. There are many books and reports of UFO sightings, and a lot of information can be obtained from the Internet.[168] Some people, like Michael Talbot, have suggested that these visions and experiences are holographic projections of people's thoughts. Others, who report encounters with alien beings, experience these beings just as real as physical human beings, though with different appearances and with odd attire.

Another strange phenomenon – that many believe only can be caused by visits from outer space – is the crop circles. These are geometrical figures that occur in large fields of cereal crops just before the crop is cut, and they disappear naturally when the corn is harvested. No one can explain how they occur, in spite of thorough studies of the circles. The shapes are immense – some the size of a football field. Some are just simple circles, while others are spirals, geometric patterns or incredibly beautiful geometrical shapes. In one such phenomenon (at Chilbolton, England, at the 14th and the 19th of

August 2001, close to a Space Observatory) a pattern appeared the first day which could be interpreted as a face, and, a few days later next to this, a pattern which was almost identical to a message that a number of scholars (including Carl Sagan and Frank Drake) had sent in 1974 out into space in the form of radio signals from the world's largest radio telescope in Arecibo in Puerto Rico. Much information can also be collected from the Internet and from books about these phenomena. Many believe, however, that all such phenomena are fantasies (how something that is visible to all can be explained as fantasies, is not explained) or produced by human beings for the purpose of deception, without giving any plausible explanation as to how people have been able to bring forth these wonderful shapes.

3.17. What is reality?

Our sensory apparatus perceives only a small bit of reality.

Even though we apparently have limited receiving devices, we are continually receiving an endless stream of information. We do not need all this information, and we unconsciously filter away everything we cannot use. We use only what we are interested in – and we are therefore actually living only in our own illusion. If not, we would not be able to function in the world. Lyall Watson recounts, however, that memory studies show that we are still storing enormous quantities of information, but no one knows yet how we preserve them.[169] It seems to him that the memory store is in the brain as a whole, and he points out that even if parts of the brain become damaged, we will still be able to evoke memories of the life that has been. This is not a passive repository, it is constantly being turned around and we have direct access to all of it.[i] Sometimes we dive down into the archive, as in a dream, either when awake or in a sleeping state. We also have more senses than the five we normally know. Emotions in the form of moods and the feeling for what is good and beautiful, as well as intuition, are also senses. In addition, the body has memory, instincts and automatic functions – and people have the ability to think. Where does that ability come from?

Stan Gooch has written about the autonomic nervous system (1980), which is controlled by the cerebellum. It controls the balance and muscle coordination. He thinks that the cerebellum also is the place where the unconscious, the intuition, and the paranormal phenomena take place. He pointed out that the cerebellum has an exterior mass equivalent to 2/3 of the cerebrum (the big brain), even if the weight is only 11% of the cerebrum. In

---

i. A question in this regard is whether the memory store is in the physical brain or in a non-physical part which is what we call the mind. Chapter 7 deals with consciousness. In chapter 7.7, which has the heading "The personality and the unconscious forces in the human beings", the terms – brain, mind, spirit etc. are explained, as these terms are often used interchangeably. And as mentioned above, Gary E.R. Schwartz believes that his experiments with mediums show that the mind and the brain are not the same.

his view, the cerebellum is the most complex body that exists, because the cerebellum's cells can create far more connections than the cells of the cerebrum. He mentioned that if one cuts through the middle of the cerebellum, the foldings show patterns as a tree. He is asking whether the authors of the old legend of the Tree of Life, which also the Kabbalistic system is based on, were acquainted with the construction of the cerebellum. He mentioned that both Emanuel Swedenborg and the British court physician with the English name Jerome Cardan (actually Gerolamo Cardano, 1501-1576) argued that their paranormal abilities were due to the cerebellum. Another thing that Gooch mentioned is that the cerebellum receives a vast amount of information from the pre-cortex, something he found interesting, since we do not know the function of a large part of the pre-cortex, as this part does not react to electrical stimulation.

Human functioning ability seems not affected if this part of the brain is removed. It is possible that this is the area that gives us the intuitive or artistic skills. Gooch wrote that the cerebellum is closely associated with the autonomic nervous system, as mentioned, which in turn is closely connected with emotions and paranormal experiences. Furthermore, the autonomic nervous system controls sleep, heartbeat, digestion and more. Dreams and hypnosis influence that system – as meditation also does. The unconscious side of the consciousness is as important as the conscious, but it operates in an opposite way. Often you will suppress or deny that part of you which you do not accept. For example, researchers will often not recognize the unconscious or intuitive part of their psyche; men will reject their feminine side, while women will reject their masculine side. However, many scientific innovations are disclosed precisely as a result of unconscious work.

Stan Gooch has introduced the concepts that he calls RealityO and RealityS, which stands for the objective and the subjective reality. The actual reality is the universal reality – RealityU.

When talking or writing about different situations, it is necessary to know clearly whether one is subjective or so-called objective, or speak on the basis of a universal reality. What we experience need not be in compliance with what is actually happening around us.

Hallucination is a known phenomenon where people hear or see something that is not physically detectable. Through hypnosis you can get the test person to experience a totally different reality than the real one. Our senses are not to be trusted.

Emphasizing the role of the subconscious in this way is to underline that the paranormal is nothing supernatural, but a natural part of human consciousness and abilities. Gooch is therefore of the opinion that much of what is referred to as paranormal capability is not that, but the subconscious' incomprehensible ability to produce dreams and fantasies. On the other hand, he acknowledges that precognition and telepathy are realities, and he gives instructions as to how to develop these paranormal capabilities. He believes, however, that Human beings do not have a Higher Self, but an Inner Self – which is the cerebellum. Although many will disagree with this theory, there are also many people that maintain that each of us has an important Inner Self.

What I perceive as reality is not necessarily the same as other people's reality. So what is subjective reality and what is imagination? Some manage to notice more than others, but they cannot convey more to another person than that person can understand. Many are afraid if they are told about a different reality than the one they can relate to, it is seen as a threat to their world view and beliefs. We are still strongly influenced by what others think and feel, and will be easily induced to believe in what the majority seems to agree upon. Thoughts structure our reality. The line between genius and insanity can be difficult to draw. From where do the thoughts, dreams and images come? A thought is expressed in words and phrases that are based on images, feelings and moods but words, phrases and images are dependent on what we have experienced. They are also dependent on the symbols and opinions we have learned, and on the culture we have grown up in. Dreams are important and can help to shed light on why we feel, think or behave as we do. Fantasy images can provide us with answers to situations, problems and difficulties. Maybe the imagination gives us access to a 'truer' reality, to a transcendental realm or a cosmic consciousness which is more far-reaching than the one we usually have access to.

Since some people (and animals) have special abilities, then everyone ought to have equal opportunities latent in the genes, although perhaps with varying degrees; in the same way that some people are exceptionally musical, while others cannot hear the difference between two tones. The question is whether those who are unmusical can develop a similar musicality as the best musicians.[i] Probably the right answer is that the potential is there, but to get hold of it may be harder for some than for others. I have heard say that all infants are born with absolute pitch, but that capability will for most individuals fade as they grow up.

Humans have far greater potential capabilities than we use in our day-to-day life – they are only forgotten or maybe not 'un-wrapped'. We cannot use them for our daily tasks but perhaps we can use some of them to make life richer for ourselves and others – to give life meaning? The first step is to acknowledge that such abilities exist. The next step is to begin to practise. And the first exercise is to be conscious of what we are doing – do not let things be done with half attention. In the Japanese Zen tradition it is

---

i. A good example that confirms this theory is the story of Anthony Cicoria, Md, PLLC, (born 1952), which can be found on the Internet. He was hit by lightning and thereafter got a passion for music, which eventually made him a composer and a concert pianist. His story is described in Oliver Sacks' book *Musicophilia: Tales of Music and the Brain* (2007).

important to practise presence – whether that is in ceremonies such as serving tea, in flower decoration or otherwise.

Most people expect to be entertained, that something will come to them which demand all their attentiveness. This is in a way an escape from daily life. They are not present in the now. By being aware of what we do, how we do it and what is happening around us, we will increase our awareness ability. We will then see more and more signs which show that there are patterns in what is happening. We will be able to register internal signals and experience connections with outer events. We will expand our awareness – in a way we will expand our senses to a higher level, so that we register more of what is happening around us. We will, in short, experience a different reality.

4. Research and Theories about Paranormal Phenomena

4.1. Various paranormal phenomena

Maybe it is best not to ask questions about weird happenings, so we do not have to be confronted with an existence which comprises more than the daily struggles (which we are striving towards and against), and that the world is something completely different from what we want to believe. Some believe that most things can be explained. The question is how. Is there a spiritual dimension behind many of the strange phenomena that occur, which is overlooked in the explanations drawn from research?

The American astrophysicist Carl Sagan (1934-1996), who at the time of his death was the David Duncan professor of astronomy and space sciences and director of the laboratory for planetary studies at Cornell University, argued in the book *The Demon-haunted World – science as a candle in the dark*, that there is no scientific evidence for the paranormal.[170] He terms everything that is not scientifically proven (based on his criteria for science) as pseudoscience and superstition. To this unscientific group Sagan assigned most of the phenomena I have mentioned in the previous chapter. He considered his list as incomplete but here are just some of the things he mentioned: astrology, ghosts, multi-coloured halo-like auras which are said to be around everyone's heads, extrasensory perception such as telepathy, precognition, telekinetic and distance vision, Nostradamus' prophecies, hand reading, numerology, Edgar Cayce and other prophets (awake or 'sleeping'), near-death experiences and out-of-body experiences. He mentioned a number of cases that have been revealed as fraud or questionable when it had not been possible to check the allegations afterwards. He referred, to the British psychologist Susan Blackmore (b.1951) and the American magician James Randi (b.1928) as two people who have made it their life mission to expose charlatans. The rest of the book is used to promote what he thought was scientific research, but he did not recommend research on the paranormal. Sagan did not mention the serious efforts, both in the United States and in other countries, to prove paranormal phenomena. He did not explain, and neither was he interested in, cases such as Edgar Cayce and his unique ability to help people. On the contrary, Sagan used most of the book to write about witchcraft from the Middle Ages and about some contemporary UFO stories, to substantiate his assertion that anything that is not scientifically proven is nonsense. His book is, in my judgment, good evidence that one begins with a conclusion, ignores everything that does not fit the bottom line, and underscores the conclusion with appropriate material.

In fact, there has been extensive research on paranormal phenomena, although Carl Sagan did not find it opportune to mention this. Sagan is in his book referring to the organization CSICOP [i] whose purpose is to expose sham and promote critical thinking but he does not mention the British and the American parapsychological societies, both called Society for Psychical Research, and the extensive material gathered by these bodies. Neither does he mention the parapsychological research done in the twentieth century. The University of Edinburgh (Scotland), the University of Utrecht (The Netherlands) and the University of Freiburg (Germany) have, among others, special institutes for parapsychological research. The University of Lund (Sweden) got in 2006 a professor of psychology with parapsychology and hypnology as special fields. Much research has been done at many other universities as well, especially in the United States, regarding the abilities of the mind and on many paranormal phenomena.

Parapsychological researchers are now maintaining they have been able to verify (but not to explain, although both Arthur E. Powell and Michael Talbot have tried to explain how many of those strange phenomena occur) the occurrence of the following special phenomena:

ESP - Extra Sensory Perception - such as:
- telepathy (thought transference)
- clairvoyance (including vision, hearing, smelling, touching and tasting)[ii]
- precognition (visions of the future)
- retrocognition (visions of the past)
- remote viewing (visions of distant places)
- psychometry / mental archaeology (reading an asset's history)

Poltergeist phenomena / psychokinesis (see chap. 3.7)

Out-of-body and near-death experiences

Healing

Metal bending

Levitation (to be lifted up in the air without any physical means)[171]

Telepathy is perhaps the paranormal phenomenon that most people have experienced. Marlo Morgan tells in her book *The Real People* that the

---

i. Stephen E. Braude has in the book *The Gold Leaf Lady* written that CSICOP has a poorly hidden agenda. That is to promote its own kind of thinking, which is both dishonest and sloppy (p. 186).

ii. Clairvoyance actually applies only to seeing; hearing is clairaudience; smelling, touching and tasting are given other names but usually are termed clairsentience.

aborigines in Australia communicate with each other via telepathy, though they can be many miles apart. Also author and scientist Ervin Laszlo (1932) mentions this, and refers to both Marlo Morgan and to the antropologist A.P. Elkin, in his book *Revolution in Science – the Emergence of the Holistic Paradigm*.[172] Rupert Sheldrake also refers to these capabilities, as referenced in the section on animals' strange capabilities. Laurens van der Post wrote the same in his book *The Lost World of the Kalahari*, describing how those who were at home in the camp, a good time before the hunters came home with prey, knew what had happened and also what type of prey it was.[173] John Hasted (1921-2002), Professor of experimental physics and institution leader at Birkbeck College, London University, has written the book *The Metal Benders* and has submitted extensive documentation on people's ability to bend metal by the psyche alone. The medium Daniel Dunglas Home (1833-1886) was a very famous medium in the nineteenth century, who was known for his ability to levitate. He was never caught cheating. Several times he was observed up in the air by credible witnesses – once he floated, as it was described, in full daylight horizontally out of one window and in through another.[174]

I am not going into detail on these phenomena, but refer the reader to parapsychological research. Dean Radin has written extensively about this research in the books *The Conscious Universe* and *The Entangled Minds*. A thorough review has also been made in the book *The ESP Enigma – The Scientific Case for Psychic Phenomena* by Diane Hennacy Powell, MD. I will also strongly recommend the book *Irreducible Mind: toward a Psychology for the 21st Century* by the researchers and authors Edward F. Kelly, Emily W. Kelly, Adam Crabtree, Alan Gauld, Michael Grosso and Bruce Greyson. This book is dedicated to Frederick W.H. Myers and his book *Human Personality and its survival of Bodily Death,* which was published after his death in 1903. Myers' book is still highly interesting, and was re-released in 2005. Myers referred to a number of reports about paranormal experiences that both the English and the American Societies for Psychical Research received from people. Myers commented on those and tried to explain them. A lot of information about parapsychological phenomena may, inter alia, be found on Internet, in the Norwegian Parapsychological Society's publications, and in publications issued by The Society for Psychical Research.

Some parapsychological phenomena may belong to the category hallucinatory sensations.

Former professor of botany at the University of Oslo and chairman and board member of the Norwegian Parapsychological Society for many years, Georg Hygen (1908-1996), has in the book *Telepati - Vår Medfødte Mobiltelefon* (Telepathy, our Inner Mobile Telephone) used the term 'psychosomatic effects' in this regard. In this book he retells a number of telepathic stories that he has found reliable. He concluded by saying that theoretical deliberations about how telepathic communication can happen at all, must wait until we know more about the paranormal phenomenon. Under the designation psychosomatic effects he mentioned all of the phenomena affecting the normal five senses, such as seeing (vision), taste, hearing, smell or touch, of which most of the best known stories concern sight-hallucinations. But in addition, one might have feelings such as grief reaction, fatigue and the like, which without an outer obvious cause most probably must refer to a specific event buried in the unconscious. Such happenings, i.e. psychosomatic experiences, can also be attributed to telepathic transmissions. Hygen also raised the question of whether out-of-body experiences can be attributed to telepathic transmissions, in this case, vision and/or hearing hallucinations. The near-death experiences are, however, so very similar to the out-of-body experience – in some such cases the brain has been declared dead – that one cannot argue that this is a vision or hearing hallucination. Georg Hygen has also written the book *Vardøger – Vårt paranormale nasjonalfenomen* (Vardøgr – Our paranormal national phenomenon). He supposed that the *vardøgr fenomenon* actually is telepathy – the expectation or presumption that someone is coming, which makes one see or hear the person before he or she actually arrives. He mentioned that he had only heard of the *vardøgr fenomenon* in Norway. But the word vardøgr is now used in several English language publications according to Parapsykologiske Notiser no. 58/2004.

4.2. Stanislav Grof's research with LSD and holotropic breathing

The Czech-American professor of psychiatry, Stanislav Grof (b.1931) has dedicated his life to a special form of psychological research and psychotherapy. He started with the use of psychedelic drugs in his experiments and later with the help of what he calls holotropic breathing (*holos* is a Greek word meaning whole, while *tropos* means turn, direction, road, and is of the same root as *trepein*, to move towards) which procures mental experiences in order to learn to know one's own Self.[175] This method is also known under the term hyper-ventilation, liberating breath or circular breathing. Psychedelic drugs were used until they were banned. Before that he found that using LSD was the best way to obtain mental experiences. However, since 1975 he has used holotropic breathing, which he considers as the best alternative after the experiences with LSD. This is a technique that is performed while lying totally relaxed on the floor and at the same time breathing in and out deeply and quickly. It often produces strong mental experiences and at the same time strong bodily reactions also. Because of this, it is essential that anyone participating in such an experience is not alone, but has one or more people in attendance to give any help necessary, but without disturbing the psychological experience of the breather. Good results require a lot of practice. Stanislav Grof and his various collaborators, both in Czechoslovakia and the United States, have gathered many stories from people who have participated in these exercises. Grof has sought to organize the reports and has published several books about what he has found. People who are in such a breathing situation, have often come to a very unusual state of consciousness that he calls holotropic consciousness, to distinguish this condition from what in psychiatry is called psychoses or delirium. This holotropic consciousness state is not the same as dreaming. You do not lose contact with your personality, you are fully aware of what is happening around you and you can at any time stop the experience.

From a psychological point of view it is claimed that no child can remember what has happened before it is at least two years old. The extraordinary thing with what Grof has registered is that people not only can experience their lives from the time of birth, but also emotions, pain and reactions from the embryo state – the so-called transbiographical area. Grof believes that the existence during this period can be divided into four clearly distinct episodes.

The first – which he calls the BPM I (Basic Prenatal Matrice) – is the condition the embryo experiences in most of its existence. Then it is in full symbiosis with the mother, hopefully in a pleasant and quiet condition. This condition can almost be compared with paradise, provided the mother is living a harmonious and healthy life. The next phase, BPM II, starts when the birth begins. The uterus then begins to contract, everything becomes tighter and there is no way to avoid the suffering that then begins and there is no way out. In the third phase, BPM III, the birth channel begins to open. There seems to be an opportunity to escape the pain. In the final phase, BPM IV, the child is delivered and – let us hope – welcomed with love. Each of these phases – the existence as an embryo, the time of delivery, and not the least, the reception you get – will often give associations to archetypal images and stories, and mark the individual through life and also condition how it will relate to what happens in the physical world.

These prenatal (near birth) experiences are not the only peculiarities from these exercises about which Grof has received reports. Many people have had insights into their own diseases and into their own minds, which can have an incredible healing effect. But also every conceivable experience, from all types of living creatures and any cosmic activity, is described. In many cases, it has not been possible to have known in advance the information that would appear, and which has been verified later from other sources. These experiences show that consciousness goes far beyond the body's limitations. The new areas that consciousness may reach, Grof calls transpersonal areas. This includes experiences in which the person identifies himself or herself with other people, animals, plants and minerals; has visions of archetypes, mythological beings and worlds, or of the Cosmos; communication with ancestors and aliens and much more. Some people feel that they are moving far away from their earthly existence and are becoming one with the Cosmos, and are thereafter able to give information about cosmic processes. During such an experience not only are the experiences of the individual exceeded, but also the experience of time and space. For example, one may feel as though they are another person, one may experience being one's own parent (whether the father or mother is alive or not) or one's own ancestor. Some have near-death experiences or out-of-body experiences, which are almost identical with other such happenings experienced by people who have not participated in holotropic breathing or LSD exercises. Some people get a feeling as to how the cells in our bodies are functioning – a cell awareness. Some experience a group consciousness. Not only that, some also experience being one with a beast or any other kind of a living creature on Earth, also with plants and minerals. Reports are given concerning processes in plants and minerals and also the feelings that animals have.

Many experiences match the stories that are told about the shamans' and mystics' experiences, wherever they are in the world. These have recorded trance states, ecstatic or extraordinary consciousness states; states they achieved through the use of drugs, possibly with the help of singing, dancing, sound, meditation, fasting, fearful happenings or isolation and it is not as though the mind experiences this in the same way as when watching a movie, with a certain detachment. It seems to be one's own experience. Grof says that it seems as if something extraordinary occurs when one goes down into the memory field of the prenatal psyche. It appears then that one suddenly goes from an introspection (that is, looking into one's own psyche) to an experience of the Universe in general, through extraordinary, inexplicable senses. Grof points out that in this way we may obtain inexplicable insights, not only about conditions in earlier times and cultures, but also about animals' special habits, reproductive cycles and behaviour, and about anatomical, physiological and biochemical factors. He says that this research shows that every one of us possesses knowledge about the entire Universe and of all existence.

Is it possible to understand or explain what is happening in these experiments, or how it is possible to have such experiences? Is each one of us a hologram, where each part reflects the totality? Perhaps it is not possible to understand people and what consciousness is, unless we acknowledge that we are holograms. And maybe this theory explains all the strange phenomena that are reported. In addition, Grof believes that with such an understanding we will get a very different attitude to psycho-pathology, and we will be able to offer new therapeutic treatment methods that may revolutionize traditional psychiatry. Grof points out that with the specificity of this type of research we need to expand our understanding of the psyche to new areas, if we want to be able to understand human emotional problems. These cannot be explained if we stick solely to what has happened to the person from birth onwards, or are seeing the individual person's consciousness in isolation.

Stanislav Grof also mentions a phenomenon he calls transpersonal experiences of a psychoid type, which some people have under these séances. By psychoid he means the experiences which are coming from a region between awareness and matter, and he thus goes further than Carl Gustav Jung in his use of the word. Synchronous events belong to this area. As an example of psychoid events Grof mentions numerous cases where electronic equipment crashes when used in parapsychological experiments, as well as stigmata, strange radiations from saints, spiritualistic phenomena, sightings of ghosts, poltergeist phenomena and much more. Grof mentions further that psychedelic drugs can have marvellous healing effects on psychiatric patients, although it should be noted that the use of the psychedelic drugs often leads to abuse of such substances. Some of the drugs give intoxication with strong sensation and fantasies, which fit into the definition of psychoses. Psychosis is a mental illness which shows a lack of an understanding of reality, misconceptions or hallucinations (sensory deceptions) where you have visions or hear voices. The use of drugs must therefore be restricted and only be used when doctors prescribe them. However, Carl Gustav Jung had no confidence in drugs as a means to obtain enlightenment.

In the book *Psychology of the Future* Grof draws parallels with reports from scientists in many other research areas, such as anthropology, psychology, sociology, history of religion, quantum physics and much more. Grof refers to Ken Wilber's construction of consciousness and believes that the data that is disclosed through the holotropic research essentially corresponds to Ken Wilber's consciousness theory, called *The Great Chain of Being*, which I shall come back to later. Both suggest that the human mind is like a holon or hologram; we have all access to 'all there is', at the same time as we are separate biological entities – as above, so below. Perhaps we also are all that is, as the wise people of the Orient always have maintained. *'Tat vam asi'* is a famous Tibetan term which means 'you are that'.

It must be mentioned that the authors of the book *Irreducible Mind: towards a Psychology for the 21st Century*, Edward F. Kelly et al, are very sceptical about Grof's research, although they have not investigated this further. In their book they give Grof praise for having focused on an important area for research on the mind, but find that his conclusions are not satisfactorily scientifically based. They believe that most of it is Grof's own impressions, not so much first-hand information.[176] This is not, however, the impression I have. Primarily he refers to reports from others about their mind travels.

4.3. Some physics and biology

Many brain scientists believe that all our thoughts, visions and fantasies have a physical cause. But do they? Physics and chemistry can today explain what is happening between the individual cells in the brain and where in the brain there is activity, but not what makes the 'mind' work. Although modern science is very advanced, there are still many unsolved issues. And every time a problem is solved, new issues, which have not previously been imagined, arise.

Where do thoughts, feelings and moods come from? Why do we perceive something as good or beautiful? Who or what gives impulses to the 'pacemaker' that keeps us going?

A human being is so infinitesimal in the context of Cosmos that we cannot imagine it. A picture of the Milky Way shows the solar system as a dust spot. A picture of our solar system shows the Earth as a dust spot. A picture of the Earth from space shows no hint of life. The light from the furthest objects we have seen left the galaxies about eight thousand million years ago (the speed of light is approximately 300,000 km per second). With modern telescopes, there are seen to be about one hundred thousand million galaxies, and every galaxy contains at least a hundred thousand million stars. Light consists of waves or swings in the electromagnetic field. The frequency (or the number of waves per second) in light is extremely high. Visible light ranges from four to seven hundred million million waves per second. Some of these light frequencies are what our human eyes perceive as different colours.[177] Is it possible that there are energy structures that scientists have not yet been able to measure? Although quantum physics today is very advanced, no theory has yet been presented that encompasses everything that happens in the Universe, at the macro level or at the micro level. The general theory of relativity and quantum mechanics refer to different conditions in nature but perhaps the psi field that Ervin Laszlo has described, and which some people call the heavenly archive, covers most of it.

The relativity theory put an end to the idea of absolute time. Physicists say that time does not exist, everything is 'an eternal now'. What we are experiencing as past and future is just our way to take in the experience, because we are not able to perceive everything at once. The Indian-American doctor and author Deepak Chopra once said that Einstein, with support from other great physicists, has shown that reality can be described as a dam where the rings are ever-spreading.[178] Time is then 'possibility' waves, and space is composed of possibilities – clouded regions where a piece of matter may once have occurred or may be expected to emerge.

And these waves in this possibility pond will be spreading, not only on a horizontal surface, but in all directions. Chopra explained that in Einstein's wake, we have now got superspace, an area that explodes in new dimensions, new geometries and so many facets of time as it is possible to imagine. The stars are no longer separated by empty space. There are energies that pulsate through space. Time can be sucked into black holes and sent out again from singularities (specific points in space), which are space/time cores tightly compressed. In superspace time has no fixed direction as it might go back to the future as well as forward. Time was perhaps introduced with the *big bang* (if the big bang theory is correct, which some people today believe it is not). Master Eckhart's words about time from the 14th century ought to be remembered in this context:[179]

> The Now, wherein God created the first human being, the Now, when the last human eventually will die, and the Now, in which I am speaking here, are all one with God and is only one contemporary Now.

Padre Pio has also said that for God everything is an eternal now.[180] The same is said by Martinus: "On the highest level there is no is time, only an ever existing Now."[181]

In recent years astronomers have started contemplating the possibility that there is not only one universe, but multiple or even an infinite number. And that those universes together form what is called a multi-universe, and that it could also be infinitely many multi-universes. And that is not all – within those one may expect to find infinitely many universes similar to the one in which we exist.[182] These are called parallel universes. In some of these there may be existences like those on Earth, and events happening in the reverse order of what is going on here.

Physicists believe that there are connections between people and events outside of time and space and have introduced the concept of *non-location* – alocality. Such an alocal connection can be seen in the strange relationship between identical twins and in the phenomenon of precognition. The idea of a non-local connection was first presented by the physicists Einstein, Podolski and Rosen (later called the *EPR paradox)*. This theory has since been confirmed in experiments (the first one by the so-called Aspect Group and later by many others). In the experiment two interrelated photons were sent in opposite directions, after which an experimenter changed the so-called *spin* or wave-swing polarization of one of the photons. It turned out that the second photon immediately reacted with an opposite spin, regardless of the distance in time or space between the photons. Still today one cannot explain how this is possible.

Deepak Chopra has written that the physicists have set time and space into a new form of geometry that has no beginning or end, no circumference and no substance. Each specific particle in the Universe can be considered a ghostly energy cluster that vibrates in an infinite space. The pathologist Olav Hilmar Iversen (1923-1998), professor at the University of Oslo, explained in a newspaper article in 1994 that the body can be seen as a lake with nearly stable form, but with ever changing new water.[183] The cells are replaced all the time but also inside the cells is there replacement as the ions and molecules die and are renewed. Some cells renew quickly, while others take more time. In the course of a year, most cells are changed. Even in cells that have a permanent structure, such as those in the skeletal muscles, there is a metabolism that causes the cells to be altered. Thus, we are not formed of the same cells as those that were in our body only a year ago. Iversen wrote: "The body dies and is renewed every fraction of a second. Somewhere in each cell is an organizational plan and a regulatory mechanism that determines its form and function."

However, each cell must be aware of the whole – otherwise how could the individual cell adapt? What is it that determines a single cell to develop into a heart, another into a brain and a third into a hand? The fact is that the whole individual comes from a single cell which begins to divide. *Who is the body-designer in the cell community that becomes an individual*? It is not the individual that presents itself as an 'I', because the 'I' has no awareness of what is happening in the body.

4.4. Everything is part of everything else – about holons

> Humanity is one organism. Martinus

Both Martinus and Ken Wilber explained that everything that exists does so as part of a larger entity. All living beings are complex organisms, composed of millions of entities that live and work within their specific system. They create and perish. If they did not perish, everything would be static. Then nothing would be able to grow and evolve. The entire organism is dependent on its environment, whether it is the smallest single-cell entity or the whole we call a human being or an animal. We cannot consider the individual organism regardless of the environment. We may then ask whether it is appropriate to look at the individual being as something separate from the rest of its world, or for that matter as something separate from another human being. The boundaries we perceive are artificial, such as our skin being the outer limit for the human beings we are. We are sending a lot of information to the outside world, while we breathe in air and send used breath out. The waste substances we get rid of goes to the outside world. Behind the 'I' there is no unit which is an isolated phenomenon, but a fellowship with all life. Why do we then have such a strong perception of our 'I' as an isolated unit?

Human beings are made up of cells and micro-organisms, small micro-societies. People are parts of families, of city communities, country communities and the Earth. The Earth is part of a community of planets, and so on indefinitely. Author Fritjof Capra (b.1939), PhD in theoretical physics, has written about life's development and the theories and scientific discoveries made regarding life's evolution on Earth.[184] He has pointed out that it is now acknowledged that all life is due to collaboration, on cellular levels as well as in human society. He emphasizes in particular the work of two scientists at the University of Santiago, Chile, Humberto Maturana (b.1928) and Francisco Varela (1946-2001). They devised a theory of *autopoiesis*, which means self-creating, and which was first presented in

1974. This way of organising is the same for all living systems. Fritjof Capra writes of this theory that there is a network of manufacturing processes, where each component's function is to participate in the production or the transformation of other components in the network. In this way, the entire network is continually shaping itself. It is shaped by its components, which in turn creates these same components. Capra explains that according to this theory, we bring forward our 'I' in the same way as we create articles. Our 'I' does not have any independent existence, but is the result of coordinated activities in our internal structure. He says that we are self-administering individuals, "created by our own history of structural change. We are self-conscious, aware our individual identity – and yet, when we are looking for an independent self within our world of experiences, we cannot find such an entity."

Ken Wilber explains that everything that exists is part of what he calls a holon, a hierarchical development that he would rather have called holarcic because the higher unit includes the lower unit and transcends the lower unit. Life's development has gone from matter to body to mind, and most mystics and philosophers believe that this development will continue further to soul and to spirit– we can say that it goes along a vertical axis. But at the same time, according to Wilber, it will be what we might call a horizontal interaction that takes place between an 'I' that is experiencing and reacting based on what happens with it, and other's similar 'I's that it is communicating and exchanging experiences with – that is a cultural unit or what we might call a 'We'. These, in turn, are organized into different groups, where the other groups will be the 'They' and finally we have what the individuals physically consist of, how the biological system is functioning and on what the existence is based, that is the 'That'. None of these units can stand by themselves; they are all dependent on each other.

Wilber has designed a figure, in which he seeks to show the development in each of these four areas, respectively, the I, the We, the They and the That, and how the four areas are interrelated (see figure 4)[i]. He thinks that one must have these developments and this interaction in mind continually when seeking to understand and describe life. He has placed these four areas each in a part of a square, and has called them the four quadrants. Each step in the evolution of existence consists of a subjective purpose oriented step which he calls 'I', a cultural intersubjective step he calls 'We', a social observable step he calls 'They', and an objectively observable step he calls 'That'. From a single starting point (the centre of the square), Wilber has drawn up four lines (each in the direction of one of the four corners of the square and each within a quadrant), which shows the development step by step (roughly outlined) within each area, and the correlation between each line.

---

i. In the diagram Wilber has called the upper right quadrant 'IT' where I have preferred to use, when describing the diagram, the term 'That', and in the lower right 'ITS' (plural of IT) where I have used 'They', as I feel this is easier for us to follow.

The upper left quadrant (the 'I' – the subjective purpose oriented) seeks to describe the evolution of the one who is experiencing – the mind or consciousness development. It goes from the quite simple reactions such as irritations to impulses, to emotions, to conceptual understanding, just to name but a few points along this line. In order for something to respond to anything beyond the purely chemical reactions, it requires an individual that can perceive, sense, register or make thought constructions regarding what is – depending on the individual's level of development, whether it is a cell, plant, fish, bird, reptile, mammal, or a human being. The 'I' stand here for the individual with its senses, feelings, experiences and thoughts, including that of the super sensing, such as intuition. What is perceived as beautiful, precious and correct belongs here.

The lower left quadrant (the 'We' – the cultural intersubjective) covers the cultural relationships which the individuals or the 'I's are forming. An 'I' cannot live without a close relationship with others. In order for such an interaction to work, one needs a common understanding of the surrounding world and a common morality and ethics. One must be able to communicate with other similar individuals, and thereby use some sort of language. But also fragrances, sounds and movements give specific meanings or signals for the individuals, both people and other species. Within the different groups these forms of communication develop differently. People within a group are sharing the understanding of words, concepts and actions, and create their special explanations about life in the form of myths and religions.

Points along the axis, which, if we start looking only from the point where the human societies occur, Wilber terms them respectively as archaic, magic or mythical, rational and existential (centauric) cultures or societies, also illustrate the various world images these societies have created.

The upper right quadrant (the 'It' or 'That' – the objectively observable) covers the physical and biological evolution, from the start in the form of atoms to molecules and then to more and more complicated compounds, which the points along this line show. The human brain is perhaps the most complex system we know in our time, and is the last point on this line. It is this that the traditional sciences relate to – anything that can be observed, measured and weighed.

The lower right quadrant (the 'Its' or 'They' – the social observable) includes composites from star clusters to more and more closely knit physical units, ranging from planetary systems and ecosystems, down to family groups. This then provides opportunities for greater and greater collaborative groups and communities, such as cities, nations and perhaps eventually 'One World'. This reflects the way people try to organize themselves in order to obtain food, from hunter-gatherer cultures to horticulture, agriculture and industrial production. The horizontal interaction between 'I', 'We',

Figure 4. The Four Quadrants
From Ken Wilber, A Theory of Everything (page 70)

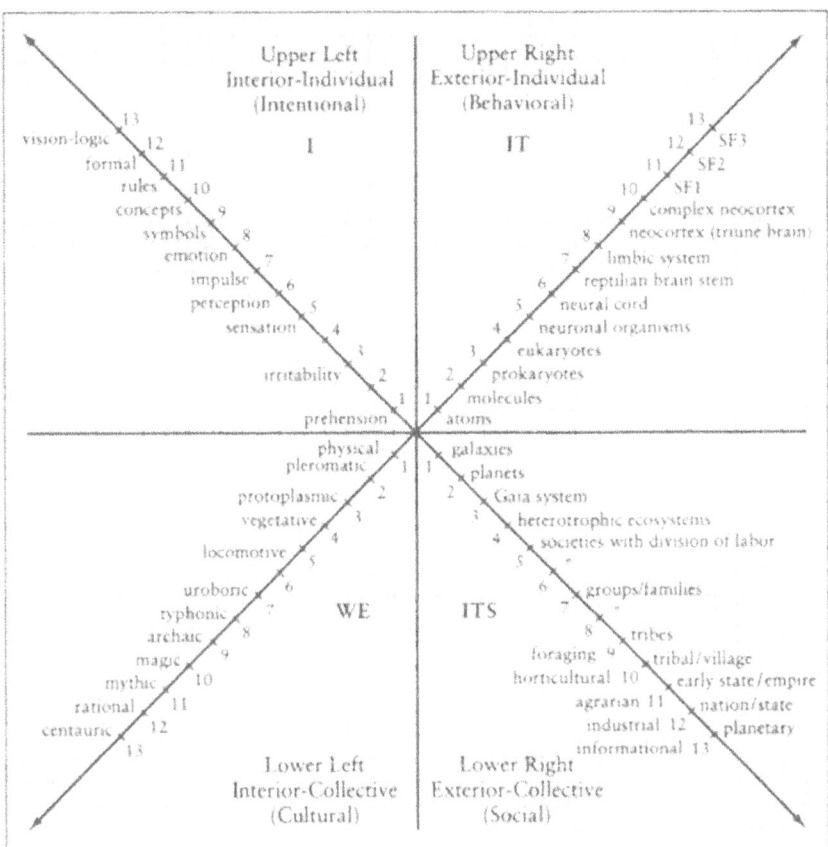

THE TRUE - Science / Matter / Society- Upper and Lower right quadrants
THE BEAUTIFUL - Art / The experience of oneself / The 'I' - Upper left quadrant
THE GOOD - Theology / Compassion - Lower left quadrant

'They'and 'That' implies a certain development level within each of these four branches. For example, to obtain:
  a) a certain level of the ability to think, as well as sensory ability and responsiveness, and
  b) a communication level, such as the abilities to produce sounds or language, and
  c) a certain form of social interaction,
     will require
  d) a certain capacity of the brain

- An individual who does not have the ability to think, but still has the ability to experience emotions and lower impulses, and whose responses are based on that (from a specific level in the Upper left quadrant – a),
- requires the limbic brain (a similar level in the Upper right quadrant – d),
- which in turn leads to a certain level of social organization (the same level in the Lower right quadrant – social organization in the form of a group or family, as with most animals today – c),
- which in turn leads to a certain understanding of life (same level in the Lower left quadrant – b).

The two right quadrants are all that can be verified through objective research and observation. This is the TRUE. *This is the domain of physics and biology.*

The upper left quadrant is also known as the BEAUTIFUL, that is, our valuations and our experience of art and beauty – the recognition of what is good and beautiful. We must have reached a level where we experience emotions to get emotional reactions to what we are experiencing, seeing and hearing. We must have a conceptual understanding and perhaps also have concrete operational thinking to understand what we see and to be able to manipulate this further. T*his is the domain of psychology.*

The lower left quadrant can be considered the GOOD. It is in co-operation with others that we can share our experiences, learn to understand our environment and improve our conditions. We are shaped by, and are completely dependent on the community in which we live. The community requires a certain morality from the individuals to make it work. The individuals develop an awareness of each other, and evolve from being ego-centric to be socio-centric. Eventually, they will also become ethno-centric, perhaps even Gaia-centric, and perhaps eventually Cosmos-centric (if the trend continues). *This is the domain of anthropology and theology.*

The True, the Beautiful and the Good are essential items at any stage of life, regardless of the level of consciousness, according to Wilber. The problem with most scientific theories to date has been only to construct the existence based on what is True – everything that can be measured and weighed. We have forgotten the person interpreting the detected data or making the hypothesis which is to be tested and the cultural context in which that person lives, which is essential for such things as language and conceptual understanding. In societies dominated by religious explanations, it is the accepted religious interpretation that has been crucial for the understanding. The Good has alone had thus the final word. History has shown that theologians have not accepted the results presented by science when these results do not match their own interpretation of the Holy Scriptures (cfr. Galileo Galilei). In many societies, this still happens. But neither the places where the True has been at the centre, nor places where the Good has been the determining factor, have they bothered to look at who is the interpreter. The Beautiful has, therefore, not been taken into consideration. We have not *differentiated and integrated* the three areas. Without accepting these as equally important and without co-ordinating those in the approach to the understanding of life (they must be differentiated, not dissociated), we cannot get any further. These three parameters must be taken into consideration at all stages of development, something which Wilber's four quadrants are trying to show.

4.5. The holografic universe

David Bohm believed that absolutely everything exists in a built-in order (*an implicate order*) that can be called spirit. He has proven mathematically that each electron in a metal expresses the movement and context of the totality.[185] That is, the whole is organizing the parts. Bohm used the term 'hologram' on some parts of his perception of reality, and denotes the interactions in the Universe as a *holo-movement*. He used the river as an image of this movement. The river is a totality, a meaningful abstract pattern that flows through everything – the built-in order. It is the overall movement of reality but it is made up of water particles which are never at rest, creating swirlings and currents, which seem stable, but are always changing – the unfolding or expressing order (*the explicate order*). All the separate parts must be seen as an expression of the whole. That also applies to the individual consciousness, which must be seen as an expression of the total consciousness, or a higher dimension. But because we are not willing to see that everything is bound together, we are creating problems both for ourselves and for society.

In order to understand a hologram, one must understand what the term interference means. If two stones are thrown into a pond at the same time, both will cause waves – where they meet they will create interference, which is a pattern that is different from each of the previous waves. All wave-like phenomena will result in interference when they meet, whether it is light waves, sound waves or radio waves. A hologram occurs when a single laser beam is split and sent in different directions, and then brought together again (using mirrors) on a photographic plate so that they collide there. One beam has meanwhile been directed toward an object, such as an apple, which then hits the photographic plate. Then there is a pattern of interference on the plate. If a light is then directed towards the plate, you will there be able to see a three-dimensional picture of the apple. The strange thing is that if you then split the plate in two, each part, when it is lit, will show the image of the entire apple. You can continue to split the plates and the whole apple will still be visible on each part. Even small bits of a holographic film will be able to show the entire object. It was the Nobel Prize winner Dennis Gabor

(1900-1979) who formulated the theory in 1947 which made the construction of the hologram possible.

In his book about the holographic universe, the author Michael Talbot used this experiment as a starting point to then thoroughly explain both David Bohm's theory and the principle of the hologram.[186] He believes that the hologram theory may explain all paranormal phenomena. In the book he has given a thorough review of the majority of these phenomena, among others, several of which are referenced here. Talbot wrote that scientists, under the leadership of the Austrian neuro-physiologist Emeritus Professor Karl H. Pribram (b.1919), at Stanford University, USA, since about 1970 have reached the conclusion that memory can be explained holographically. The same goes for vision, hearing, smell, taste and even feelings on the skin.

Memory cannot be localized at a specific place in the brain, but seems scattered throughout. Experiments with rats show that although some parts of the brain are removed, their memory is intact. A hologram can be used to store endless amounts of information, because by changing the angle of the laser beam, images can be saved on top of other images. It has been suggested that our ability to remember or forget may be a capability equivalent to a laser hologram – by slightly adjusting the angle of the beam, memory can bring new images into consciousness. This idea has been developed further to explain the body's ability to transfer skills from one part of the body to another, or how we are able to recognize a face, no matter from which angle we see it, and to explain the individual's ability to recall situations almost photographically from memory.

Scientists are starting to term the brain 'the holographic brain', and use terms such as recognition-holography and interference-holography. Pribram has come to the same conclusion as Bohm – that the whole Universe is a hologram. And if the whole Universe is holographically organized, it means that there will be no local characteristics, only so-called *non-local properties*, and neither will reality have any local characteristics on a sub-quantum level. If absolutely everything consists of frequencies and wave movements, one might ask how the body can register anything as solid matter. To answer this, Pribram has explained that the brain's perception of objects may be compared with the pains coming from a limb cut off from the body – so-called 'phantom pains'. Everything is a hologram, which in one case can be perceived as something fixed and in the next as an interference pattern. We are in our thoughts constructing what we perceive as reality, including time and space.

As out-of-body experiences seem to show, the consciousness can be outside the physical body and experience things far away. Michael Talbot believes that the idea of a holographic universe can explain this phenomenon. In this universe locality is an illusion. Furthermore, the phenomenon of materializing or phantom figures – that can be seen both with and without clothes, or with specific clothing – might be holograms which can assume many different forms. These apparitions are without substance and can disappear into walls or pass through physical objects. Talbot mentions that several people, who have written about their out-of-body experiences, believe that the figure they have in this out-of-body existence can be attributed to their thoughts and beliefs.

If the human body can be regarded as a hologram, then every human being – and maybe even every cell – is to be regarded as a universe in miniature. If our thoughts can be considered as holographic images – which we shall consider further when we read about the aura – that may explain how the mind can also perform miracles and it explains most of the remarkable cases discussed in the preceding chapter. Talbot believes that the hologram theory can explain such phenomena as synchronicity – which can be due to strong emotional experiences that affect the finer energetic levels in a holographic universe. He further suggests that if consciousness has its origin in the Universe, in its internal order, then consciousness must have access to all that is and has been through the holographic register. One needs only to shift focus to take notice of other times and places.

4.6. Are we only a point of reference?

Is consciousness entirely an influence from external stimuli in the form of electrical impulses, or is there something in (or around) the brain (or body), or something far outside the visible person, which affects each individual – which is the single individual? Deepak Chopra has said that the 'I' is only a point of reference that is made up of memories, only a set of experiences. But I am recognized by friends and family due to some characteristics, such as voice, way of walking, facial features and more. The weird thing is that this is true even if it may be thirty or forty years since they last saw me. So my memories and experiences are not enough to define me. There is also something else. It is a kind of basic pattern which the cells adjust to in order to recreate, and it is this pattern, with the memories and lessons that I have acquired, which is me. The so-called out-of-body experiences and near-death experiences indicate that the mind and the human brain are not the same. But is there something beyond the physical body that knows and has wisdom, and that affects or controls the single individual? What actually are intuition, impulse action, thought and memory? Olav Hilmar Iversen has said that what we perceive as stable – that is the body – is highly unstable, while the spiritual reality is really what is stable.[187]

Ken Wilber has sought to integrate modern science and spiritual knowledge. His standpoint is that there is a spiritual reality, something that goes beyond the rational thinking. He has demonstrated, inter alia, that all knowledge, whether it is nuclear physics, biology, psychology or mysticism, is based on *experience* – experiences that people have gathered through their ways of acknowledging existence. This experience can be *tested* by anyone who takes the trouble to study and use the methods by which experiences are gathered. It is thus not only the science of matter that is credible (as maintained by, inter alia, Carl Sagan). Wilber argues that people have a tendency to reject and deny everything they do not understand.

All developments show, however, that *expanded* knowledge, not greater *specialized* knowledge, means that one includes and understands the more narrow view. For example, he shows that Sigmund Freud did not understand Carl Gustav Jung's consciousness standpoint, he therefore rejected the essential in Jung's teachings, while Jung understood Freud's teaching and developed it further. Wilber points out that the same applies to scientific development. Science today largely rejects spiritual knowledge, because most natural scientists do not understand nor will study what that is. But the acquisition of spiritual knowledge has taken place for as long as human beings have existed, and this knowledge has been passed on and is today increasingly conveyed worldwide. All the world's spiritual masters present this knowledge in more or less the same way. Cognition can only take place through either a human being's ability to see and feel using the body's five senses, by abstract thinking using the mind or by spiritual experience, which is achieved with the help of the deeper levels of the mind – known as 'the spirit'. It is maintained that only the spirit envelopes everything. The body by itself cannot think. The thought or the mind cannot explain why something is beautiful or good or why charity is needed, this requires a higher cognition. Ken Wilber mentions the three terms used in this context – the Good, the True and the Beautiful. The Good is theology, the True is science, and the Beautiful is art. All three parameters are equally important for human life and at all levels of consciousness.

Ken Wilber has said that all the major religions describe the human body as consisting of the following five units:

Matter – Life – Mind – Soul – Spirit

He has pointed out that the science of nature today deals only with matter and biological processes (life). Psychology has during the last century collected material concerning the mind. But the stories about soul and spirit have not been accepted by the modern Western society. There is, however, a lot of material regarding such experiences – the experiences of the mystics. Those experiences can be achieved by anyone who has the patience required to make contact with their own inner being – the so-called Soul or Self.

(Some mystics have a far more detailed and nuanced specification of the human body than the five units mentioned here.)

We have now constructed a reality, based on what the majority of scientists accept – that is what we today can measure and weigh with the instruments that science so far has been able to create, and which give the same result for several equal tests. Everything that does not fit this understanding of reality is not accepted. Paranormal events are seldom repeatable, and that makes any type of investigation into most of these phenomena impossible. Some people however, are experiencing a reality other than what, so far, has been accepted. Those other experiences may in some cases so strongly influence a person that he or she has difficulties participating in the acceptably normal reality, and is unable to care for him or herself. If one is in a special type of mood, one may come in contact with forces or energies that expand the mind and make existence more intense. This type of experience may be conceived as an expansion of consciousness, as a divine experience, and may be of such an overwhelming nature that it leaves one longing for more. This is something far more basic than rapture or ecstasy. Many religious or meditative experiences fit this description. This is what we often call a *light experience*, cfr. St Paul's experience 'on the road to Damascus'. It is important to know that there is an indefinable divide, between what we see as reality (whatever we experience with our five senses) and other experiences of the mind, when we are trying to describe and draw boundaries within the topics we are discussing in this book. There may be another dimension of existence other than what physics has shown so far, and which is not explained by the theory of a holographic universe. That means that we need to learn more about mysticism – that is about the religious and the spiritual. If there is a spiritual dimension of existence, does that mean that the specific individual or entity is also a spiritual entity which survives death? The answer to this last question is what this book is seeking, and I believe that it is possible to find some clues.

5. The Psi Field – The Celestial Archive

Helena Blavatsky explained that our soul belongs to the invisible part of reality, which she termed the astral light. She called this light *akasha* or *anima mundi* (the world soul).

Everything that happens and everything that has happened will be stored in this light. Anyone with the ability to see it will be able to recount everything that has happened as a person's astral soul lives in unity with the astral soul of the Universe. Akasha, she said, refers to the subtle super-sensous spiritual essence, which transcends everything. According to Joseph Campbell the word akasha actually means space, the cosmic space. Geoffrey Farthing, however, has distinguished between akasha and the astral light. Akasha is the substance of everything that is – or rather, according to him – the only substance. The astral light is that in which absolutely everything is mirrored, – the living, plastic essence of the inner worlds.[188] Arthur E. Powell explained that the Akashic records represent the divine memory. On the astral plane they mirror the reflections from an even higher level, and are therefore imperfect and fragmented.[189] He wrote that the actual records exist on the mental plane, but that it requires quite special skills to be able to see the records on the mental plane. The founder of the Buddhist church in London in 1924, the lawyer, Christmas Humphreys (1901-1983) mentioned in his book *Karma and Reincarnation* that this is the substance of the manifestations in the finest form, a fingerprint of nature that can be read by those whose spiritual abilities are well enough developed in this direction.[190] Edgar Cayce said that he examined and interpreted the archive material that was written in time and space, which he termed the Akashic archive, when he went into trance to find information about a person.[191] This archive exists as a fine print in the ether. Cayce explained in a lecture that once he was aware that he was leaving the physical body during a séance. He then felt that he was moving through a shaft of light to an altitude where there was a temple. Inside the temple there was a large room which resembled a library. Here were the books that contained the lives of the human beings, all nicely recorded. He needed only to retrieve the records concerning the person about whom he sought information. Cayce's biographer, Harmon Hartzell Bro had difficulties understanding what was said about the archive, but he understood even less how Cayce was able to keep track of all the information that he brought forward to his audience, for, as Bro described it, he could give them information from the French crusades, from the Ming dynasty in China, from Galileo Galilei's Italy, or from the life of the American settlers. Cayce never contradicted himself, not even when he talked about four and five incarnations for the more than two thousand people who sought his help.

Levi Dowling's book *The New Age Gospel of Jesus Christ* is an account of Jesus' life, which is said to be recorded from the Akashic archive. Dowling maintained that he received this information during an altered state of consciousness. He explained that the actions and thoughts of every living being are stored in the cosmic archive, which he has described as subtle vibrations – the finer ether's sensitivity. According to the preface to his book, akasha is a Sanskrit word meaning archaic substance, which is the substance or the force which is at the basis of all creation and therefore is present everywhere in the Universe. It is said that every vibration anywhere in the Universe will form its own indelible pattern in this subtle archaic substance – even the thoughts and actions of the human beings. A person who is fully coherent with these fine vibrations, which means that he or she is enlightened, can obtain information from this archive.

Anna Elisabeth Westerlund has explained how she saw.[192] She compared her experience with that of using a camera or a satellite, which she had placed high up in the air, and which she could control. By using this 'eye' she was able to focus on the areas from the present or past which she wanted to investigate. Images from the site appeared as soon as she was prepared. Impressions of situations from the present, she attributed to telepathy. In regard to images from the past, she said that all matter on Earth has radiation that leads to waves of infinite duration being sent out. Everything that has happened in the world and all of the world's knowledge she thought were stored in atomic nuclei in the Earth's mass and in the Earth's atmosphere – a kind of Earth's memory. Anyone with the proper ability can capture those waves, in the same way as a radio or television station can capture radio waves and transform them into sounds or pictures.

Is this what Ervin Laszlo calls the psi field? He suggests that this field, which he thinks may be the same that the Eastern mystics have called the Akashic archive, controls everything in the Cosmos, both galaxies and cells, and he writes that research within various disciplines are now pointing in the direction that such a field must exist. He points out that despite the fact that the Cosmos contains myriads of stars and galaxies there is a marvellous coherence through the whole, which indicates that there must be a connection between these. In whatever direction you are looking from the Earth, you will see the same structures and the same radiation coming from deep space. The so-called *EPR* paradox (see chapter 4.3) shows that some particles (called entangled) are not individual units as they can react spontaneously to each other regardless of distance and time. This suggests that there is a fundamental field that connects them. Laszlo writes that within the field of physics it is now accepted that there is a virtual (possible, not observable) ocean of energy called the quantum vacuum, where everything has its origin and is exchanging information with this vacuum and also with everything else. In addition everything that happens will leave tracks in this field and anyone with the proper ability can bring this information through.

When there is such a unity on both the macro and micro levels, this suggests that the same must be true of all intermediate levels. Laszlo writes that the organisms are living in a super context which requires a comprehensive and dynamic interaction between each entity.

Living organisms are probably a macroscopic quantum system. All elements are in instantaneous and continuous communication, with access to information about all that is and has been; an access that is achieved through this field. This field is also called *The Zero-Point Field*. In her book *The Field – the Quest for the Secret Force of the Universe*, Lynne McTaggart (b.1951) has given a description of the zero-point energy and referred to the research that has been done in this regard.[193] She writes:

> The Field is the Zero Point Field, a subatomic field of unimaginably large quantum energy in so-called empty space. If you add up all the movement of all the particles of all varieties in the universe, you come up with a vast inexhaustible energy source all sitting there unobtrusively in the background of the empty space around us, like one all-pervasive, supercharged backdrop. To give you some idea of the magnitude of that power, the energy in a single cubic yard of 'empty' space is enough to boil all the oceans of the world. The Field connects everything in the universe to everything else, like some vast invisible web. The papers published by these scientists written about in The Field show that the solid stable stuff we call matter is an illusion and is simply subatomic particles constantly moving and being gripped on by the background sea of energy. Everything in our world, no matter how heavy or large, boils down to a collection of electric charges interacting with the Zero Point Field.

Laszlo's theory fits the idea of a holographic universe. In addition, this theory supports the thought that every cell, in both the body and the mind, is a hologram so that each cell has access to everything that is, cfr. Karl H. Pribram's and Stanislav Grof's research.

6. The Aura and the Chakras

The body's electrical radiation and registering ability

The author Carlos Castaneda (1925-1998) explained, in the books about the Yaqui-Indian Don Juan, that the human being actually is egg-shaped.[194] He wrote that outside the physical body there is an egg-shaped field which is the aura. Aivanhov explained that the aura is comparable to the skin. The skin protects the physical body, while the aura protects the finer bodies and makes the exchange of information with other people's auras possible. It filters the information stream that comes from other people, from other entities, from the planets and from the Cosmos. How well the aura is functioning depends on the individual's spiritual development. A good strong aura provides good sensitivity and a weak aura the opposite. Aivanhov therefore stressed the importance of working for a individuals. The difference is said to be due more as to what that person considers important, or his or her ability to 'see', rather than to any real differences in the aura. Jes Bertelsen has explained that perception of the aura depends on the meditative training of the person looking, and at the interplay between the aura of the person who is looking and the one being observed (the interference). Aivanhov explained the phenomenon in almost the same way as Jes Bertelsen.[195]

Michael Talbot wrote that people who are skilled psychics see shapes or pictures in a person's aura, and that maybe this is a sort of hologram. Such images are of people or ideas that have a prominent place in the person's thoughts. I have experienced being presented with such images from someone who was reading my aura, which did fit with thoughts I had. Some psychics will be able to see pictures of places and events associated with a person's life, as if you were watching a movie. Sometimes, it is as if you are in the centre of the event – on a stage, because everything takes place all around. It should, however, be noted that some psychics see such events with their internal eye and not in the aura of another person, for example, when they hold their hands above or on another human being. This is called *body reading* and is a kind of psychometry. But it can also be said to be telepathy – the capturing of images of something which have been associated with a specific person. Some people, such as Marcello Haugen, can see right through a human being, and can tell them about the diseases they have or have had. This can be said to be a kind of X-ray vision. All this indicates that it is not only the aura which is providing information, and also that the aura can be understood mentally. The nerve cells can trigger self-reinforcing electrical signals, the nerve impulses. Where there are electrical signals there will also be an electrical field. There is, inter alia, such a field around people's heads. The patterns in this field vary according to how the brain works. Today, most people have probably seen coloured images produced as result of brain scanning where the electrical activity in the brain is measured, a research method used to detect defects in the brain and also for the study of how the brain functions.

Both Colin Wilson and Lyall Watson refer to the two Yale-physicists, Harold Saxton Burr (1889-1973) and F.S.C. Northtrop (1893-1992), who in the 1930s published the paper *The Electrodynamic Theory of Life*, where it was suggested that all living beings are held together by a magnetic or electrical field, in the same way as the field around a magnet.[196] They called this the L-field (the field of life). They found that this field increased in size when a female ovulated. When a voltmeter was connected to a tree, it turned out that the electric field changed with the seasons, during a thunderstorm, and when there was great activity on the Sun.

Lyall Watson has explained that the L-field is affected by disease disorders in the body and by cosmic rhythms. The field is organized along the body's length axis. The strange thing is that this field also may be noticed around an unfertilized egg, so it seems that the embryo cells organize themselves after a pattern in an electrical field which existed before the individual began to exist. The L-field can be used by the chromosomes to present the pattern and changes in the pattern to the protoplasm. The protoplasm is the living substance inside the cells and consists of cytoplasm and the cell nucleus. The field changes in response to internal and external factors.

Watson relates that at the University in Saskatchewan, Canada, a detector has been constructed that can measure changes in the field at a distance of twenty feet (ca. 6 metres) when there are human emotional changes. Watson suggests that this field can be freed from the physical body, and that this may be the explanation behind the out-of-body experiences. A general theme in the out-of-body experience stories from totally different cultures, is that the physical body is associated with its double (i.e. the force field which can leave the body) with a thin thread, which is a luminous ribbon or a silver thread. If this thread is broken, it is said that the physical body will die. This bright thread is associated with the pineal gland. However, Watson finds it unlikely, both physically and biologically, that this energy body could survive physical death for a long period of time. When the body starts to decay, the energy body will also dwindle. He believes also that any other energy systems that might be attached to the body will disappear when the body disappears, although this has not been proven. But neither is the opposite proven. A split between the body and the mind seems to occur during the out-of-body experience. Such a split can also be said to occur when one dreams. It is not unreasonable to think that such a splitting takes place when the body dies, although maybe only for a short period, according to Watson.

At the *Institute of HeartMath*, United States in recent years, experiments have been carried out that show the heart's energetic or cardio-electromagnetic communication.[197] It has been established that the heart is the strongest generator of electromagnetic energy in the human body, and thereby also creates the greatest energy-rich field of all the body's organs (see figure 5 below). This field's amplitude is about 60 times larger and produces a magnetic field more than 5000 times stronger than that produced by the brain. The field can be registered several feet (a foot is 30.48 cm) outside the body in all directions, and is affected by changes in emotion, at the same time as it affects every cell in the body. Moreover, it is also noted that this field may provide information to and from other people, whether they are in direct contact with each other or just emotionally close to each other, and that synchronicity may be shown between the two peoples' heart and brain rhythms. Many people have probably experienced the latter, namely that coherence occurs when they are together. For example, often women's menstruation periods start at the same time when living together. Golfers can find that their golf balls are going to exactly the same place after a certain period of time when two or more players are together. Our minds are obviously sending out impulses that can be perceived by other people and also by computers and other types of machinery.

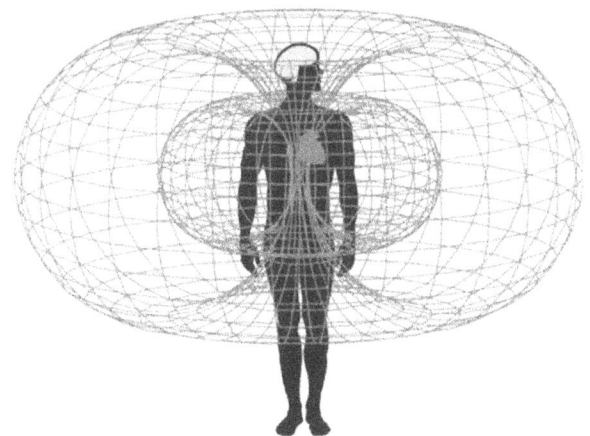

Figure 5. The Heart's Electromagnetic Field
from the book
'Science of the Heart', 2001 -The Institute of HeartMath USA

Gary Schwartz has described laboratory experiments on the relationship between the heart and the brain, carried out by him and Linda Russek in 1994.[198] They measured the electromagnetic signals of the heart of one person, and at the same time the brain signals of another person sitting close by. This was done using advanced computer equipment that Schwartz had developed specifically for this purpose. It emerged that people who had loving relationships with their parents during childhood, registered the heart signals of the other person better than others. They assumed that this also applies in general, in that those people are more sensitive to others than those who do not have a loving background. They called this relationship energy-cardiology. They believe that the energy patterns created during childhood are not forgotten, and that they also might exist after the physical body has decayed. Schwartz has also discovered something remarkable with respect to gamma rays, which are signals of very high frequency, which for the most part are registered as coming from stars far away, and which pass through material objects, bodies, and even lead plates. He has found that these rays are both absorbed by the human body and also sent out again, at the same time as the body also is sending out high-frequency X-rays. This happens all the time. Although his research so far has been focused on the heart and hands, he thinks that such radiation occurs from the entire body. Both gamma rays and X-rays are photons, which, when they are sent out from the body, are called bio-photons. He believes that further research will show that when people deliberately send energy to another person, especially someone with whom you have a close and loving relationship, there will be an increase in both the sending and the absorption of gamma rays and increased issue of X-rays. He raises the question whether these rays, as well as those which emerge on an electrocardiogram, and brain waves, all of which are invisible to our normal senses, perhaps are reflecting the connected energy of universal love. He points out that Sir Isaac Newton in his time, believed that the universal energy was love, and that the gravitational force, perhaps, was the best picture for this force.

In addition to the body's electrical radiation, all organic material will emit heat and humidity. So also does the human body – although that is sometimes perceived as coolness.

This radiation can be registered and it can also be seen or felt by sensitive people.

The human energy field is said to become more and more refined the further away it is from the physical body. When light is reflected in the field, it will – for those who have the ability to see – have varying colours, as in a rainbow. Therefore, many will say that there is more than one field. These fields are said to reflect the many different aspects of consciousness. The colours of the aura will vary according to what people think and feel.[199] The colour combinations seen in the fields are said also to show diseases in the body. There are currents between the fields, and these are particularly strong through the chakras. (See figure 6 - below and figure 7 p.174.)

Shafica Karagulla (1914-1986), former associate professor of psychiatry and neurology at Downstabe Medical Centre in Brooklyn, New York, has after extensive interviews with doctors in general practice (GP's) who were psychic reached the conclusion that the emotional field (the astral body) has an extension of some 45 cm and the mental field (the mental body) a further 60 cm or more out from the body.[200] She explained that there are eight major light swirls in connection with the glands and many smaller swirls in the field that surrounds the body. Five of these larger swirls are located along the spine and are comparable with the oriental chakra points.

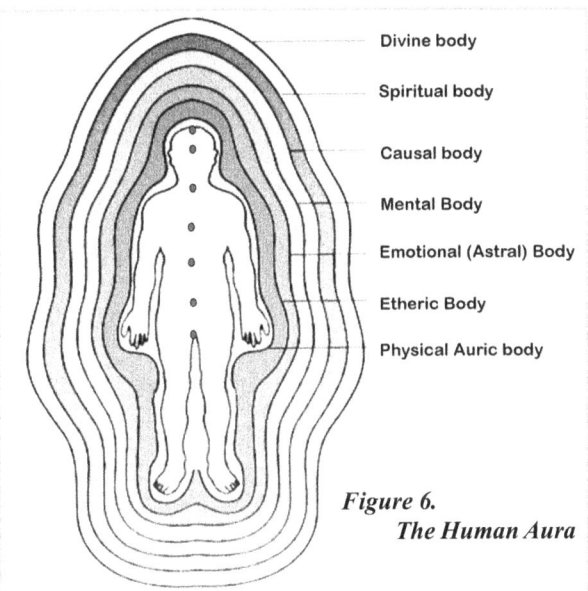

Figure 6.
The Human Aura

The aura is supposed to consist of certain main structures or levels that make up the real, total human being. It is maintained that there are seven main structures. In addition, the theosophists teach that within each of these structures there are seven new layers.

Barbara Ann Brennan (b.1939), MA, PhD, teaches healing in New York, and can give very accurate diagnoses based on what she sees in the aura.[i] Apparently she can also read the auras of people who are in a very different place from where she is. In the book *Hands of Light – A guide to healing*

---

i. Barbara Ann Brennan is an American healer and therapist. She has a MA in atmospheric physics and a PhD in philosophy and theology. She worked for a time for NASA at the Goddard Space Flight Center. Due to her psychic abilities, she started as a healer and coach. She has written several books about the chakra energies and about healing. Michael Talbot has written about Barbara Ann Brennan and about Valerie Hunt's research.

through the human energy field she explains that matter is only one form of energy, referring to Einstein's theory of relativity. She has expressed that what best explains that which is experienced as aura and as healing abilities, is the theory of the holographic universe: these phenomena are caused by energy frequencies that are independent of time and space, therefore, she believes that it is not especially strange if someone manages to capture or affect the energy structure that the human body consists of or emanates. In her account of the historical testimonials of the aura, Brennan refers to the *prana* energy, which is described in the oldest Indian scriptures, by the Chinese in their oldest documents (the *chi-energy*), and also in a wide range of esoteric papers from the earliest times to the present day. She refers to the observations and experiments that have been made in the twentieth century to map this energy, including Wilhelm Reich's experiments with what he called the orgone energy, which he tried to catch with the help of the specially constructed orgone cabinet.

Barbara Ann Brennan also refers to the attempts made by Professor Valerie Hunt (b.1916) and others at the University of California, Los Angeles – *A Study of Structural Neuromuscular Energy Field and Emotional Approaches* – confirming that the aura can be registered. In these experiments they used an electro-cardiogram (ECG) and an electro-encephalogram (EEG), as well as an electro-myograph (EMG). The last type of measurements captured an energy field around the body with a much higher frequency, but with smaller amplitude than the two other instruments. This field had the strongest radiation around the places that are categorized as chakras. Valerie Hunt concluded that there are certain points on the body that have specific colours. Using an oscilloscope (which can transform electrical waves to visible patterns on a screen), she found concordances between what a psychic person could see in the aura and the registrations of the electro-myograph, as she learned to identify a particular frequency pattern with a specific colour. Another strange phenomenon she registered during these trials was that she saw certain concordances between the frequencies of the energy field and a person's talents and abilities. The stronger an individual was linked to the material world, the lower the rate of energy radiation from the energy field; while a person with strong mental abilities would have an extremely quick rate, and an even faster rate the more spiritually developed the person was. Valerie Hunt believed that the holographic theory could explain the findings, since both the EEG measurements and the ECG measurements could be done also in a toe or a finger. Her data shows a chaos pattern in the biological system – which also has been noted in many other systems. She has shown that a disease can be recorded in this energy field before it breaks out and may then be diagnosed.

Many believe that the electric field around the body can be photographed by a method developed in 1939 by the Russian, Professor Semyon Kirlian and his wife Valentina Kirlian by means of an instrument that generates a high frequency electric field.[201] In the following years they photographed a number of patterns around everything from leaves to small animals and people. The patterns changed in accordance with changes in the health and mental condition of the person being photographed. Lyall Watson, who wrote about this type of photography, mentions that it is not clear what kind of energy it is. He believed that it can be registered as an electrical high frequency discharge. Watson suggested that the field seems to correspond to what the theosophists call the etheric double or the etheric twin. Some people call it the biological plasma body or bio plasma. Lyall Watson defined plasma as a gas where all the electrons are removed from the atom cores. Stan Gooch claimed, however (in 1978), that the Kirlian photography is cheating. He referred to attempts made by Professor William Tiller and his assistant David Boyers at Stanford University's Department of Materials Science, which proved that the Kirlian photography did not reach a scientific standard. Also Professor Arthur J. Ellison (1920-2000), UK, rejected the Kirlian technique, see the book *Science and the Paranormal - Altered States of Reality*.[202] Information about this technique can be found today on the Internet.

The psychiatrists Thelma Moss (1918-1997) and Ken Johnson (b.1948) at the Neuro- psychiatric Institute, University of California, Los Angeles, in 1973, performed the so-called 'radiation field photography'. They made special high frequency apparatus to photograph the aura. They found that each human being has a unique, identifying base pattern that changes a little from day to day according to their mood, and depending on what the individual has eaten or drunk. They have also shown that a person's energy could be transferred to another person, for example, under hypnosis.

The presence of electrical energy in people is proved, according to Colin Wilson among others, by the strange phenomenon of spontaneous combustion where some people suddenly ignite and can burn themselves to death without any outside influence. He indicated that we are living in a sea of energy, and that the most vital energy source may lie outside the physical body – in the Cosmos. Most organic substances also have a natural fluorescent essence. This essence cannot normally be seen in ordinary light but at the Sandia-laboratory in Albuquerque in New Mexico people are working with this phenomenon, and are seeking to develop a device that can capture the essence. It has been suggested that for the criminal police, such a device will be of great help in investigations.[203] Maybe this too is part of what can be said to be the aura, which some people can see.

If you search the Internet, you will find announcements for several techniques for aura photography. One of these systems, *Aurastar 2000*, has been found by many to be quite accurate in its ability to capture the existence of physical problems. The measurement is carried out exclusively from the hand. You place one hand on a number of small entry points that are connected to a computer system. There are said to be a number of meridians in the hand, and also certain zones (see the acupuncture teaching and hand zone therapy) which are connected to the body's different organs and glands. Skin resistance and pulse (cfr. Tibetan /Ayurvedic doctors often use the pulse in their diagnoses) are measured in the hand using advanced electromagnetic technology. It is maintained that this technique provides information about the energy levels in forty-five body organs, as well as the energy in each main chakra. The technique is supposedly developed with the help of medical knowledge, of individual's intuitive and clairvoyant (clear-sighted) capabilities, and also on the basis of traditional Eastern medicine, including Ayurvedic medicine. By the use of a computer, whatever is recorded is inserted into an image of a human figure (Leonardo da Vinci's drawing of the so-called Vitruvius man is used) wherein the circumference of the aura is plotted. The image is coloured according to the energy registered in the individual organs, and the colours are placed in the aura where a clairvoyant person normally sees the organs – as each organ has its special place in the aura. The image should thus be able to say a great deal about the health of the individual organ.

The Chakras

The word chakra is an old Sanskrit word meaning wheel, vortex or disc. Sogyal Rinpoche[i] (b.1947) has in his book about the Tibetan's understanding of life and death, *The Tibetan Book of living and dying*, explained that according to Buddhist teaching the human body has 72,000 subtle channels, of which there are three main channels. Those three are the central channel which goes alongside the vertebra and the ones on each side of this one. The two side channels are twisted around the central one and meet at several points. In addition to those, there are many energy centres along the central channel and from those a lot of smaller channels spread out almost like an umbrella's ribs. Those energy centres are the chakras according to Sogyal Rinpoche. A psychic person sees those energy points as vortices and the higher up the body, the tighter the vortices.

Aivanhov has explained that that which people in the East call chakras is the same as what the people in the West call plexuses – a collection of nerve threads around central organs.[204] The solar plexus is one such collection. The sympathetic nervous system is part of the autonomic nervous system. The main part of this consists of two lines of nerves stretching out on each side

---

i. Sogyal Rinpoche was born in Tibet, but had to flee in 1959 when China occupied Tibet. (Rinpoche means 'venerable' and is used as title for Buddhist teachers.) He was only 6 months old when he was placed in a monastery to be an apprentice of the great master Jamyang Khyentse Chökyi Lodrö. This master is considered as the reincarnation of Tertön Sogyal, a well-known mystic who was the teacher of the 13th Dalai Lama. Sogyal Rinpoche has studied at universities in Delhi in India and in Cambridge in England. He arrived in England in 1971 to study comparative religion. He has lived in the West for many years and has taught Tibetan Buddhism in Europe, USA, Australia and Asia. He is the founder of and the spiritual leader of RIGPA, an international network of centres and groups around the world which practice Buddhism under his guidance. In his book, of which more than 200,000 copies have been sold all over the world, there is an easily understandable description of Tibetan philosophy. (See page 248.)

of the vertebrae from the neck and down to the pelvis. On these lines of nerves there are many ganglia (knots with bunches of nerve cells) with extensions to the outer part. The outer part is a collection of nerve threads around the central organs. Aivanhov explained further that there is one main collection around the trigeminal nerve; one which is connected to the heart; one connected to the lungs and solar plexus; one connected to the solar plexus and from there also down to the intestines in the abdomen; and one collection connected to the sexual organs, the rectum and the bladder. Those collections are further connected to, respectively, the divine world, the spirit world and the physical world. So, the chakras are not connected to the endocrine glands, but to the sympathetic nervous system and the collections which are in this system.

Aivanhov mentioned that the brain is not able to influence the body directly, as all influences happen through the sympathetic nervous system. The solar plexus is the most important organ in this system. This is the true heart in the human being. It is the solar plexus that gives the brain energy. It is this organ which receives and understands the great cosmic truths, not the brain. It is the solar plexus which is the seat of the subconscious and which (together with the *hara* [*sacral*] centre in the abdomen) makes the human being able to be connected to "the universal ocean of life", as Aivanhov has put it. The human being should therefore see that there is balance between the activity of the brain and the activity of the solar plexus. Aivanhov wrote that there are 26 ganglia in the solar plexus and that this is not due to chance because the Kabbalah teaches that 26 is the sum of the four letters in the word for god (YHVH) in Hebrew: Yod=10, Hé=5, Vav=6 and Hé= 5. This is how this is written: ה ו ה י.

(This may be wishful thinking on his side, because the *Encyclopaedia Britannica 2001* explains that there are thirty-one and not twenty-six ganglia.)

Some people believe that the chakras are connected to endocrine glands. Harmon Hartzell Bro has mentioned that this was the opinion of Edgar Cayce.[205] Cayce called the chakras the seven delicate centres. He maintained that each chakra was in cooperation with the most important glands, and that it was through these that the aura influenced the physical body, its moods, emotions, alertness, fantasies and spiritual condition. Bro mentioned in this connection that it is these centres which were described by Ezekiel as wheels within wheels, and which John's Revelation describes as churches. In the aura there are also fields which accord with the energy fields of the body, and which especially influence the body's development, health and also partly its activities. Maybe these fields are the same as the etheric body, which is, by some, described as the energy field closest to and around the physical body, which also is very much like the physical body.

The British parapsychologist Serena M. Roney-Dougal, PhD, (b.1951) explains in her book *Where Science and Magic Meet* the following:[206]

> The crown chakra is connected to the cerebral cortex.
>
> The pineal chakra is connected to the pineal gland and the pituitary gland, and is therefore to be considered as the command centre of the body.
>
> The throat chakra is connected to the thyroid gland and to the parathyroid gland.
>
> The heart chakra is connected to our emotions. (But she mentions that some people are of the opinion that the heart chakra is connected to the thymus gland.)
>
> Solar plexus has some connection to the production of adrenalin.
>
> The two lower chakras (the hara chakra and the root chakra) are connected to the sexual glands.

As mentioned in the chapter about astrology, Rodney Collin has pointed out the close connection between the chakras and the endocrine glands, as well as the connection between the human aura and the magnetic field of the Sun.[207] However, Stan Gooch, in 1980 and before Valerie Hunt's research was published, mentioned that there are no facts which indicate that such energy centres, as the chakras are maintained to be, exist in the body. Firstly, he pointed out that only in some places in the East is such a theory is presented, but in China and among the American Indians as well as among the Aborigines of Australia there is no similar view. Furthermore, he says that there is no agreement in regard to the number of chakras, and he is very sceptical of everything where the number seven is said to be of importance – as this number is often seen in myths. It is completely wrong, he wrote, that there are seven endocrine glands in the body to which the chakras are connected, since there are more than seven such glands and some of those are even double; he mentioned hypothalamus, pineal, thyroid, parathyroid, thymus, the pancreas, the kidneys and the endocrine sexual glands. Gooch also referred to the fact that different people see different colours around the chakras, which indicates that the opinions about what is really seen, differ.

So what are actually the chakras? As many people are seeing some sort of energy concentration around certain points on the body and this must be considered documented by the research of Valerie Hunt, there is good reason to take a closer look at what is explained in regard to the chakras. There are said to be seven main chakras (and in addition there are twenty-one smaller chakra points, but those will not be considered here). The main chakras (see figure 7) are:

> Crown, white on top of the head.
> Pineal, violet on the forehead between the eyes
> Throat, blue on the throat
> Heart, green near the heart, almost in the middle of the chest

Solar Plexus, (spleen) yellow on the diaphragm, where the breast bone ends
Hara (sacral), orange just beneath the navel
Root, red almost at the end of the vertebrae

The colours given here are those mentioned by the theosophists, as well as by Jes Bertelsen and Bob Moore.[208] Others have reported other colours (which may not be especially peculiar since some people are unable to see some colours – most colour blind people do not see the colour green). Colours are aspects of white light, which means that they are energy vibrations. The chakras are connected to the following feelings according to Jes Bertelsen (the definitions given by Ken Wilber are here given in parenthesis[209]):

Crown: The soul, the contact with the Divine (the luminous spirit, formless mysticism)

Pineal: Wisdom, knowledge, intuition (the subtle consciousness, gnosis, real archetypes and god mysticism)

Throat: Thinking, conceptional understanding, intelligence (possible clairvoyance, creative visions, early stages of mysticism, transcending consciousness)

Heart: Love, compassion, unselfishness (higher mind, good sense, noble sentiments)

Solar Plexus: Strength, extroversion, determination, selfishness (the lower mind, force and purpose energy)

Hara: Sexuality, dreams, fantasies (life force, prana, emotions, sexual energy)

Root: Food, safety, the material (the material)

The chakras are representing different forms for energy. This is demonstrated in our daily speech: we have a good 'gut' feeling; we feel that our strength is in the solar plexus; we are hearty (heart-like). The different chakras are seen where the central glands are located: the pineal gland, the thyroid, the thymus, the adrenal and the ovaries/testicles, although they are not identical with those glands. The energy in the individual chakra may be too strong or too weak. Neither is good, so therefore it is important to work with oneself in order to find the right balance in each chakra.

The root chakra represents food, safety and the material side of our life. This is our connection to the earth, to the physical of existence. We must have food, housing and clothing. We must have the ability to provide a minimum of material goods in order to comply with the society in which we are living and in order to survive – but not too much. If there is too much energy here, we will collect treasures, or eat or drink too much, or over-reach in some other way. This is often due to a feeling of insecurity.

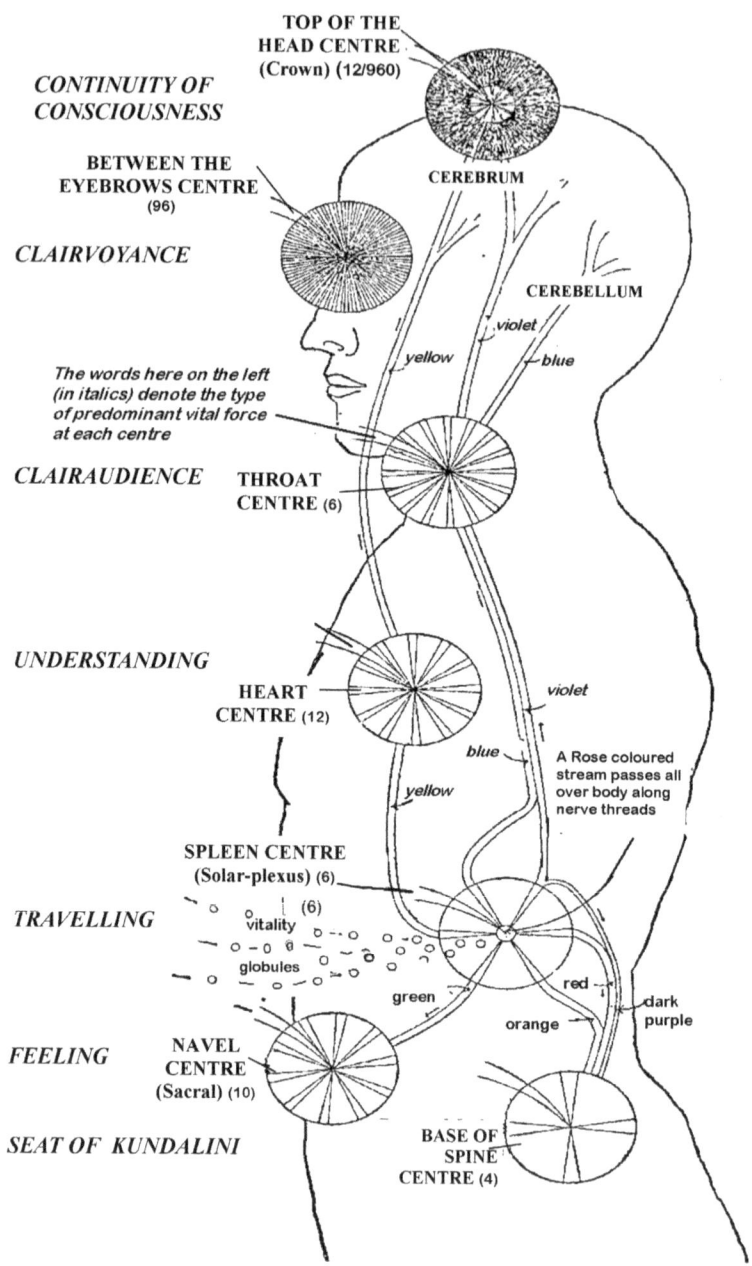

Figure 7. The Chakra Centres
From Arthur E. Powell, The Etheric Double (page 64). The same figure can be seen in the book 'Flammer til Liv' (Tongues of Fire making Life), page 98, by Randi Olerud, where she refers Bob Moore's explanation.

The hara chakra (the sacral/navel chakra) represents sexuality and spontaneity. The sexual energy is actually our strongest life force. In this chakra our emotions are shown, and the emotions are the instinctive reactions of our experiences, such as crying, happiness, fear or aggression. Our hopes, wishes, dreams and fantasies can also be seen in this energy centre. Too strong an energy here may cause that we lose contact with reality, so that we will be living in our dreams and in our cravings. For example, we may be driven by our sexual lust without consideration of other people's wishes or desires. Strong emotional feelings may give rise to depression, rigid self-control, over-dependency or uncertainty. A too weak an energy may lead to withdrawal from society, autism, narcissism or the loss of the desire to live.

The solar plexus chakra gives us the strength to meet the world, to reach out to other people, or to work for an idea or a goal. It gives force, outgoingness and self-certainty. Too much energy here may lead to single-mindedness, so that we are not open to meeting other people or that we dominate other people. Too weak an energy may lead to passivity or subservience, and that we too easily are controlled by other people.

The heart chakra gives balance in love, both to oneself and to others, compassion, unselfishness, the feeling of fellowship with others and the feeling of sanctity. Too much energy here can lead to us taking on other people's suffering, so that we do not let them learn from their own experiences or develop of their own accord. Too little energy indicates that we are not feeling enough or we have a lack of empathy, but also have too strong self-criticism or a constant pessimism which can lead to depression and also to a weak bodily defence system.

The throat chakra shows our ability to communicate with the rest of the world, to be understood (through the use of language). Intelligence in the form of creativity or rational thinking is represented in this chakra, as well as the ability to store information in the brain and to use this information via a proper connection. Too much energy here makes a person have problems with communication, to listen to what others have to say, or to meet another person on the level of this person's understanding. One may be too consumed by one's own thoughts or ideas and totally engaged by these, and therefore unable to open up to other people or to other's ideas or objections. Too weak an energy here, leads one to being afraid of expressing one's own feelings or thoughts, or considering oneself as dumb.

The energy in *the pineal chakra* (the pineal gland) shows a person's wisdom and ability to understand other people and also understanding one's existence. (This is the place which is considered as the seat of the soul – see Descartes, the Veda literature and others.[210]) The pineal gland is supposed to have developed from an eye, a central organ with light sensitivity which can still be seen in primitive reptiles. It has also been called the third eye. According to Lyall Watson, this organ produces melatonin which is procured by serotonin, which is very similar to the LSD molecule. He has suggested that LSD can influence serotonin so that it greatly changes the ability to see and understand the occurrence of reality, something which again may lead to visionary conditions. Good energies here are not connected with rational thinking, but to wisdom, life experience and the understanding of humanity. Contact with the intuition, the inner voice and the super consciousness goes through this centre. People who are clairvoyant, yogis, shamans or saints have strong energies here.

The crown chakra represents the soul, the contact with the Divine and formless mysticism. This chakra is well developed in people with spiritual contact, such as mystics and saints.

Sogyal Rinpoche has explained that the work of the spirit takes place through the chakras, and that a good flow of the energy in these centres is important for the human's psychic well-being and existential consciousness. The chakras are the connection points, not only between the physical body and the etheric body, but also between the different structures and layers in the aura. The best possible flow of energy between the different levels in the aura requires that the chakras are open, which means that the vortices (the movement of the energies) in the chakras are working optimally. This, however, is not so in most human beings, as the psyche is not well enough developed or has been blocked, possibly due to traumatic events but it is possible to improve the energy flow in the chakras through meditation. Human beings of today have not come far in regard to spiritual development, and the chakras are therefore not especially developed. There are, however, some exceptional people who have all the chakras in balance, but for most people some chakras are too strong while others are too weak. Some people need a lot of reassurance (the root chakra), which leads to weakness in the ability to feel compassion (the heart chakra). Others are using their ability in rational thinking (the throat chakra) together with the solar plexus chakra, without any strength in the heart chakra, and may, therefore, become dictators, either on a small or a grand scale (the psychopaths).

In relationships between couples there is often an unbalance that the couples are not able to understand. If you know about chakra energies and how they function, you will be more able to understand your own reaction and your partner's reaction and way of acting. A partnership should not only be based on the sexual energies, which is the hara energy. The energies in the heart and in the throat are equally important. Both partners must be on the same wave length in regard to those energies for the partnership to be able to function properly. A partnership based solely on the energies in hara and solar plexus makes no companionship. The companionship must be based on the energies in the heart (to feel and to take into consideration the partner's wishes and needs) and the energies in the throat chakra (in order to be able to communicate one's inner feelings and thoughts). A good root chakra must be developed at the same time to create a trusting relationship but also outside of a partnership it is important to know those energies in oneself. The heart energy is often mistaken for the hara energy, the sexual energy. But the clean heart energy has nothing to do with the sexually-directed partner energy. To love another person does not have to mean that you want a sexual relationship. A well-developed hara centre does not necessarily mean that you have strong sexual demands. The sexual energy is a life energy which may be directed towards other goals than the sexual orgasm. The Kundalini force, which is what the sexual energy is called in certain places, is – if it is used in the right way – a spiritual force. We ought to be aware of our imbalances and try to adjust them. That will give us a more harmonious existence.

By reading about some of the saints of the Catholic Church, such as Frances of Assisi and Teresa of Avila, I understand more fully Rudolf Steiner and Bob Moore when they talk about the energy consumption of human beings. Those saints have obviously managed by hard work to improve the lower chakras of their physical body and have thus strengthened the mental and spiritual energy bodies. This they have achieved through intensive prayer and meditation. It may be difficult to see where the individual saint actually has been in its spiritual development, but something may be perceived if we understand how the chakras are functioning. It may not be without reason that saints and the Buddha figures are depicted with a halo around their heads. The halo shows that they have a very special and strong radiation from the head and from the higher chakras. This is in accordance with measures taken of the structure of the aura, and with that which people maintain they can see there.

7. Consciousness, Dreams and Visualization

> Consciousness is the basic stuff in the All.   *Jeremi Wasiutynski* [211]

> Consciousness is the archaic, basic reality ... we are only at the very beginning of a complete understanding of consciousness.
> *Eugene Wiegner*[212]

> If there is a natural body, there is also a spiritual body.
> (1 Cor 15.44)

7.1. Introduction

We do not know what consciousness is, and we use the word with different meanings. Is consciousness the ability to think or is it the ability to acknowledge yourself as an independent individual? "Cogito ergo sum" – "I think, therefore I am", said René Descartes (1596-1650). However, it is not only human beings who think. Animals have the ability to think, to combine, to use tools, to show joy, to play and to grieve. Paleontologist and Jesuit priest Pierre Teilhard de Chardin (1881-1955)[i] believed that the superiority of human beings above animals was due to the human beings' ability for reflection, that is not only to know themselves, or not only to know, but to know that one knows.[213] Some believe that the ability to choose between different options demonstrates consciousness, and if so, all living creatures, even from the cell level, would have consciousness. It is maintained that to become a mystic an important step on the road is to learn not to think – only to be. Then you will reach past the ego. You will transcend

---

i. Pierre Teilhard de Chardin was also a geologist and philosopher. He took part in scientific expeditions in the East, especially in China, in Africa and also in America, and he wrote books and taught. However, because of his view on evolution and hereditary sin, his religious leaders imposed a ban on him teaching, and in 1947 he was also forbidden to write about philosophical topics and to seek a professorship in France. In 1938 he was appointed head of the laboratory for advanced studies in geology and palaeontology in Paris, but did not start working there because of the Second World War. In 1951 he moved to New York where he lived and worked until his death and where he wrote several important books. The Norwegian author Aasmund Brynildsen wrote in the introduction to the Norwegian edition of Teilhard de Chardin's book *About the future of humanity* that he ought to be characterised as an eclectic and says further: "... his lifework brings together ideas and thoughts that may seem to be in contention against each other, or be far away from each other, but which with him become a unity – and this unity is the really new with Teilhard de Chardin".

the ego. You will then be able to gain intuitive knowledge. You must, however, be conscious that you are thinking in order to be able to stop the thought.

Colin Wilson has said that the human consciousness is a powerful microscope, but the microscope has a limited field of view. People need to develop a different type of consciousness that can match the telescope.[214] He considers that people have a sort of sixth sense, which he calls Faculty X. This is a sense of the meaning of life. It is directed and not to be influenced. He believes that people are not aware that they have such a sense, therefore, it is not used. But it shows up in strange occurrences, and is also seen in savants and mystics in varying degrees.

Ken Wilber speaks of thirteen different approaches to the study or the description of consciousness.[215] These are:

- Cognitive science or science of self-knowledge
- Introspection or self-experience
- Neuropsychology or organic brain knowledge
- Individual psychotherapy
- Social psychology
- Clinical psychiatry
- Development psychology
- Psychosomatic medicine, such as bio-feedback
- Unusual consciousness states such as dreams and the like
- Eastern and contemplative traditions, who believe that yoga or meditation develops higher states of consciousness
- Quantum consciousness or the ability of consciousness to influence the physical world
- Subtle bio-energies which overreach the four recognised physical forces (respectively the strong and weak nuclear force, the electromagnetic force and the gravitational force)
- Development psychology and its close relative socio-biology

He believes that all these approaches are important for an integrated view of consciousness.

However, these approaches do not individually give any clear understanding of or an introductory perspective to understand the phenomenon. One must consider the individual's development level, the individual's social relationships, cultural context and physical development. In addition, you must have in mind the progress that each of these relationships has undergone over the course of time. And he stressed that consciousness has no locality.

The Norwegian author Erik Dammann (b.1931) has in his book *Bak Tid og Rom* (Behind Time and Space) described his extensive interviews with researchers in parapsychology, physics, chemistry, and psychology. He has come to the conclusion that consciousness has a range in excess of the limited time-space dimension, and that it has contact with an all-embracing immaterial *niveau*.[216] With reference to famous scientists such as Karl H. Pribram and David Bohm and to the research and philosophy of other quantum physicists, he suggested that 'awareness' is a term for this immaterial overall plane. He then finds it unreasonable to limit the existence of the mind to the body, as that which is part of something timeless cannot be terminated. He noted that a number of research projects indicate that consciousness is not only a product of the material brain processes, but co-operates with and interferes with these. This is also supported by more recent research.[217] There is thus no reason to ask where consciousness has its seat.

Ervin Laszlo says in his book about the psi field that consciousness neither seems limited by time or space, and is subtly connected with everyone else's consciousness. A person's consciousness can affect another person's mind and body, and also objects. We are not isolated objects, but are living in a sea of energy where everything affects everyone.

However, there is something that is not mentioned in these comments, and that is the human beings' and the animals' ability to feel love and care. Is this due only to the genes – a necessity for the survival of the species, or is it something else? This I will comment on later. But first, let us look at how human consciousness, or perhaps rather the human being's acknowledged ability, has been described by the mystics through the ages. Most mystics – as well as the great religions – seem to be in agreement as to the understanding of consciousness, when going into the details. The way it is explained may, however, be different due to different languages and ways of expression.

7.2. The development of the human beings and the consciousness

The development of life can, according to prevailing theories, be described in that the Earth first consisted of pure matter, then life slowly began to develop through the plant kingdom, then the animal kingdom came into being and finally the human kingdom. I question whether the human realm is the end of development – which I doubt when I look at evolution through time. But what might come? Maybe we can find an acceptable theory by looking at the structure of consciousness. People are made up of organic material, instincts and automatic skills, and they need to eat and drink, to multiply and to keep warm. The human beings differ from animals in that they have a more developed brain, a more advanced mind – an awareness of their own existence. Abilities that distinguish human beings from animals especially are those of speech and constructive thinking, as well as the ability for conscious self-sacrifice. Most people, however, do not yet know much about pure love, and not many are showing much charity.

Ken Wilber has explained, with reference to a number of research results that the human development is, in a way, parallel to the development of the Earth. He uses mythical figures to show this. He thinks the first hominids are best compared with snakes. He calls these the *Uroboros*, which was the mythical serpent biting its own tail – identical to the Midgard serpent in Nordic mythology. They had a 'sleeping' existence and were sufficient within themselves, in a perpetual existential circulation. In the next stage he calls the human being – *Typhoon*. Typhoon was a giant. He had a hundred dragon heads instead of fingers and from the waist down he was covered with snakes. Typhoon was thus half snake/reptile and half human. That is, he saw himself as separate from other beings, as standing apart. The dragon heads were perhaps necessary to keep other creatures at a distance. "Where there are others there is fear," according to Ken Wilber. (The next step should, in my judgment, be the *Sphinx*, which Wilber did not mention. The Sphinx has a lion's body, but a human head. It has intelligence, but the lion's has a need for flesh as food and thus its killing instinct.) The next step for Ken Wilber is the *Centaur*. The centaurs have a horse's body, but a human head (intelligence) and torso (heart?). They had four horse legs, but also two human arms. The centaurs lived in social communities; they were grass eaters so they had no need to kill. But the centaurs were wild and violent, and took easily to fighting. However, there was one centaur that was different from the others, namely *Kheiron* (Chiron) (whom Wilber does not mention). He was wise, knowledgeable and mild. He had knowledge of medicine and music. It is said that he was the teacher of Asclepius.

He is also said to have been the teacher of Heracles and other heroes from ancient myths.

Kheiron can be considered to represent the advancing human being – who acknowledges its animal body, but who has empathy, compassion, wisdom and clairvoyance. Martinus wrote that people now have developed their intelligence enough, but that they are still animals in a human body. It is only when the emotions, the ability to show true love, are fully developed, that the real human being will emerge. Only then will the *human beings* have developed the ability to recognize the Divine.

When we consider a human being's development from birth to death, it has many similarities with this mythological portrayal of humanity's development. The baby can be compared to the stage of Uroboros. It is dormant and enough in itself and unconscious about others' existence. Small children are more at the level of Typhoon. They see others as a threat to themselves – 'mine' is a word that is often used. Jealousy and assertiveness are strong feelings at this age. In young people – when the child enters puberty – the lion body becomes prevalent and the need for independence is strong. At the same time it does not know who it is or where it is going. This is the sphinx. As a young adult the human being becomes a centaur. The animal body is still strong and wildness dominates, though the ability to think increases. The feeling of relationship with others is becoming more prominent. The need for spouse and children arises. Eventually it is to be hoped that the human being will be more like Kheiron. It will still have an animal body, but the ability to love and its intelligence may develop so that wisdom becomes prevalent. Each individual must grow through the same stages that humanity has passed through to reach the level where most human beings are today, though there seems there is a long way to go for most people before they reach the wisdom stage.

Many psychologists and philosophers operate with a much more detailed description than the one I have presented here. Ken Wilber uses, for example, a scale with nine stages, which he designates as the transition stages or fulcrums in human development. He includes stages from the infant level to the most advanced mystic. His last three steps correspond to the consciousness levels of shamans, yogis, saints and sages. Each of these nine stages, he says, has its special characteristics, its opportunities for development – and their special potential pathologies.

The first people on Earth probably lived in small family groups, sufficient in themselves. These were the hunter-gatherer societies. They did not have to cooperate with those beyond their group in order to acquire food. This matches the Uroboros stage and the Typhoon stage. Later, they formed larger units as tribes or clans. Such larger social groups required organization. This resulted in the need to kill larger animals and to protect the group against intruders into the area that they considered their own. This is the sphinx stage. Slowly agriculture developed, which required more organization and regulation. As this often gave a surplus of most necessities, division of labour and barter was the next stage in development, and later again more trade. Thus small farming communities and village communities came into existence. Urban communities emerged where the conditions and the economy allowed such settlements. They again grew into small states and later, as greed took the upper hand, to larger states and kingdoms. Here we have reached centaur stage, where the right of the strongest is the prevailing law. Today we are seeing a trend towards confederate states and a society that tries to take care of everyone. Perhaps we in the near future will have one state – a One World Society. This is the vision for the future of humanity of Martinus and Ken Wilber. Then, let us hope, we will have reached the Kheiron stage.

7.3. Brain activity levels

The brain has different activity levels, which are respectively deep sleep, the dream state, the half-awake state, the awake state and the meditative state. In addition, there is a special state when under the influence of drugs or other intoxicating substances. These can intersect. We can dream while awake. Some can walk while sleeping, and some can work or walk in a meditative state. Brain activity can be recorded as small electromagnetic voltage variations in the brain by the so-called EEG measurements (electro-encephalogram), which measures the voltage fluctuations per second (Hertz, shortened to Hz). The various fluctuations can indicate whether you are sleeping or awake, or what kind of mood you have. The normal ranges are the following:[218]

Delta	0.5 - 3 Hz Deep dreamless sleep and unconsciousness
Theta	4 - 7 Hz Deep sleep, meditation and trance
Alfa	8 - 12 Hz Light sleep and dreaming, fantasy
Beta	13 - 22 Hz Active awareness

A normal level of activity for the awake state is the beta level. The level at which it is said that the brain is most susceptible to influences is the alpha level. This is not only the state for light sleep, but also for a totally relaxed awake condition. Thinking is then reduced to a minimum. This is the ordinary meditative state of the non-mystic. At this level one can easily be hypnotised (if one is susceptible to hypnosis) or dream in the awake state, and one can easily visualize – i.e. imagining images or events. When you are at this level, you may be able to program yourself so that you can get rid of bad habits or become more constructive – a form of self-hypnosis. It is said that by using this method you might improve your memory, improve your mood, obtain increased confidence and thereby an improved quality of life. This can also be used to improve, that is reduce, negative psychosomatic thoughts.

Colin Wilson wrote about the readings recorded of the brain activity of Matthew Manning while his psychic powers were being tested.[219] When Manning was trying to bend a key, his brain showed strong theta activity. (Wilson explained that theta rhythms are associated with violence, aggression and frustration. These rhythms are also believed to show up when you suddenly get an idea or an inspiration while in a half dreamy state.) The puzzling point with Manning was that there was a linear relationship between the peaks of the theta, alpha and beta states. Normally, the alpha rhythm becomes weaker or disappears when the beta rhythm increases. Wilson thought that it was as if the brain of Manning was holding the balance between aggression, concentration and relaxation. Wilson pointed out that poltergeist phenomena occur particularly in connection with frustrated youths. This has led him to suppose that psychokinesis may be a form of controlled poltergeist activity.

Ken Wilber's brain waves have also been tested during meditation, for both the left and the right hemisphere of the brain.[220] When he was in a normal state, the computer showed both alpha and beta brain waves in both hemispheres, though he also had some delta waves. When he then sought a total mental standstill in deep meditation, the computer showed that all the waves almost ceased. There was no alpha, no beta, and no theta waves, but a maximum of delta waves. Ken Wilber has explained that it looked as if he was brain-dead. When he then started a mantra-visualization, the theta waves emerged. Wilber thought that this was remarkable. He was completely awake during this meditation, but the computer showed theta waves, which normally only occur when one dreams and perhaps also in cases of intense creativity, and delta waves, which only occur when one is in a deep dreamless sleep.

He pointed out that the alpha waves come when one is awake, but in a relaxed awareness situation. The beta waves come during intense analytical thinking.

Alpha and beta can therefore be said to belong to the basic physical plane, theta the subtle plane, and delta the causal plane. That Wilber produced all the waves during deep meditation should imply that he was conscious at the same time on the physical, the subtle and the causal consciousness planes. Although we today have come so far that it is possible to detect where in the brain particular activities take place and also the brain's activity level, so that we can see from a machine whether a person is asleep, awake or in deep meditation, we still do not know what it is that creates consciousness or thoughts. We cannot see what a person is thinking by the use of computers.

7.4. The consciousness' functional areas

In order for a plant or an individual to function, there must be a number of chemical and physical processes. What is it that sets these in motion? This I shall return to in the section about the various consciousness bodies. Here I shall seek to classify the functions, all of which must come from some form of consciousness. I consider the division of a cell as a consciousness process.

We have a variety of *automatic internal functions*. Most of the activity of the physical processes in the body, we do not feel; although we are aware of some of them when focusing on them – such as the breath and heartbeats. Some of these automatic functions we can control, such as breathing. Many yogis train themselves so that they obtain extreme mastery of the body; some maintain that they even can control their heartbeat. The animal kingdom and the human kingdom have automatic functions in common with the plant kingdom, though the former two have a lot more, as well as more complex processes, in the body than plants. Usually we do not consider the automatic functions as human senses, but they are inner physical senses.

The five outer physical senses probably do not need any closer review. Vision, hearing, smell, taste and feeling are the body's outer senses. That is, all receive impulses through the body's external areas. It is said that even the equilibrium senses (the balance ability and the ability of orientation) and the motion sense or the kinesthetic sense are part of these physical senses, although we usually do not think of them as so.

We have also a variety of *instinctive actions*. Instincts are inherited species-related tendencies to perform certain actions or reactions and they are not subject to conscious thought. Jes Bertelsen has maintained that this is the ability to understand what benefits and what does not benefit the individual, which people have in common with animals.[221] That small birds hide when they see the contours of a predator in the sky, is an example of an instinctive action. Protection and the feeding of oneself and one's offspring is another example. The mating drive or sexuality is also an instinctive action. It is not the conscious part of the mind that controls the sexual reactions. It is debatable whether these and other instincts are anything other than chemical reactions in the body, or whether they are automatic reactions as a result of experience, either one's own or the species' experiences acquired through generations. In essence they can be said to be learned response patterns that are stored in our genes as a result of the species' development, and which thereby have become automatic chemical reactions in the body. These reactions may be described as *etheric* senses. This is also a form of consciousness.

Feelings and emotions are also senses. People may feel happy or sad, they may feel safe or anxious. And what is it that makes me think that something is beautiful and something else is ugly, or that something is right and something is wrong? I have a sensitivity which is mainly learned but there is also something very fundamental in this assessment. Martinus has said that emotional energy is one of the main energies that is slowly coming forward in humanity, and that people do not have this ability equally well developed. For example, not everyone has capacity for empathy – the ability to take part in another person's experiences. Animals too have emotions and different moods. They can be sad or happy, playful, loving or aggressive. They can be grateful, trusting or jealous. However, emotional energy is more strongly developed in people than in animals. But where is the seat of these feelings? What is it that gives us such reactions? These senses can probably be described as *astral* senses.

Intelligence and understanding language are said to be abilities unique to human beings. Parrots and crows can, however, be taught to say a few words; and experiments have shown that pigeons, parrots and monkeys have conceptual understanding, and that many animals and birds use tools to obtain food. But who and what is it that is thinking? According to Martinus intelligence is another of the main energies that is highly developed in today's humans. This is a *mental* sense.

Intuition is a sense not all people know. I would define intuition as the ability to know something immediately, a cognition that comes without thinking and without the use of the body's other senses. That is, one can see, hear and notice – become conscious of – something, thanks to the intuition, but this information comes from within oneself, not from the outside. Intuition can be said to be due to memory or instinct, but that is not what I would call proper intuition. The concept intuition, I reserve for cases where we receive knowledge that is not available in a way we would denote as normal. This is a *spiritual* sense.[i]

It seems that the mystics, when they have come far enough in their development, have an additional sense, or maybe rather a radar or antenna that reaches beyond their immediate surroundings. This antenna is by many called the *higher consciousness*. This is a spiritual or *causal* sense.

If you are really advanced, you will be able to see all existence. Then you have what is known as cosmic consciousness. It is said that some people can achieve or have achieved *cosmic consciousness* in glimpses, while others can experience it for longer periods. Martinus maintained that he had cosmic consciousness, which enabled him to write down all the things he has recorded in his books about what he called "The Divine World Order."

Consciousness can thus be said to have seven functional areas, respectively on the physical, etheric, astral, mental, spiritual and causal plane, as well as the total or cosmic plane. But these functional areas are not necessarily available in the normal state of the daily alert consciousness. According to Martinus, it is only when both the intelligence and the ability to unconditional love are sufficiently developed that the human being can gain access to the main energies which give the individual contact with the spiritual level, which then bring wisdom and intuition.

7.5. Consciousness bodies

Lyall Watson has written that the stories that have been collected about special abilities and inexplicable events, cannot lead to any other conclusion than that the body must operate on one other plane at least in addition to the physical plane we know.[222] This the mystics have also tried to explain throughout history. Bob Moore has explained that energy is everything we can perceive operating.[223] Thoughts are energy. Actions are energy. Feelings and emotions are energy. This energy has various grades. Consciousness' functional areas correspond to what the spiritual masters have described as

---

i. Rollin McCraty, Mike Atkinson and Raymond Trevor Bradley have researched people's ability to receive and process information by intuitive perception. Ref. *The Journal of Alternative and Complementary Medicine: Electrophysical Evidence of Intuition – The Surprising Role of the Heart*. The article is available on the Internet at the Institute of HeartMath. The project aims to contribute to a scientific understanding of intuition, that is, the process by which information, which is usually located outside of the usual consciousness area, is perceived by the psycho-physiological system. The first goal of the project, which was presented in two papers (part 1 and part 2) was to replicate and expand the results from previous experiments, which showed that the body can react emotionally to a stimulus seconds before it is actually experienced. The second goal of the project, as presented in the third treatise (part 3), is to formulate a theory that can explain that the body receives and relates to information which comes from the intuition.

the human beings different levels of consciousness or the human beings' different bodies, and these can be said to operate on different planes of existence. As mentioned in the chapter about the aura, Valerie Hunt has conducted experiments showing that the more strongly a person relates to the material world, the lower the frequency of the energy radiation from the aura, while a person with strong psychic abilities has a faster frequency – and even faster the more spiritually developed the person is. This seems to confirm what the mystics have always known – that consciousness can exceed the material level where most people are today. With a faster rate or increased subtlety in our information exchange with the outside world, we will become more able to perceive the world in a different and more comprehensive way than otherwise. If we can develop the etheric and astral senses, we will be able to understand much more of the sea of energy in which we live.

Jes Bertelsen has said that the human being has the following seven *consciousness levels* or *consciousness bodies:*[224]

The physical, which presents itself as the ego
The etheric
The astral or the lower mental
The higher mental

The spiritual   -   The Self   -   The Mary consciousness
The cosmic field   -   The open field   -   The Christ consciousness
The unity field   -   Nirvana   -   The Light

According to Rudolf Steiner the main structures in the aura are the same as here stated, but he uses slightly different terms, namely:[225]

The physical body
The etheric or living body
The astral body
The ego

The spiritual self or manas
The spirit of life or buddhi
The spiritual human being or atma

However, this is a slightly different sectioning of the various layers of the consciousness structure than that which Ken Wilber uses, (see about *The Great Chain of Being* in chapter 7.6). Aivanhov's terms are respectively the physical, the etheric, the astral, the mental, the causal, the buddhistic and the atma body.[226] As is shown in figure 8, in which the different mystics' sectioning of the various consciousness bodies is compared, they put the emphasis on different levels, and therefore the sectioning becomes somewhat different. For example, it seems as if Jes Bertelsen has placed a completely different emphasis on the spiritual level, or the Self, from what Rudolf Steiner did. Rudolf Steiner operated only with the physical, the etheric and the astral bodies, and so the ego.

Figure 8. Consciousness Bodies

					ADI ANUPĀDAKA
	THE UNITY–FIELD THE TOTAL 7th plane	**THE SPIRITUAL-BEING ATMA**	**THE ABSOLUTE-ONE THE DIVINE**	**THE SUPER-MIND THE DIVINE**	**THE SPIRITUAL-BEING ATMA** Self-existence VII
Spirit	The Cosmic field 6th plane The Christ - experience	The life spirit BUDDHI			The life spirit BUDDHI Blessedness VI
Soul	The Self The Spiritual 5th plane The Mary–consciousness	The spiritual Self MANAS	Nous— the subtle and intuitive mind Soul World Soul	The intuitive mind Super mind Enlightenment The World Mind	THE EGO THE CAUSAL BODY Wisdom Intelligence V
Mind	The higher mental 4th plane	The 'I'	Creative thinking Logic ability Concept and meaning	The higher mental Logic ability The concrete mind	THE MENTAL BODY Manas IV
	The astral 3rd plane	The astral body	Imagination happiness, pain Emotions Sensing ability	The lower mind The vital emotional Sensing	The astral body III
Life	The etheric 2nd plane	The etheric body	The vegetative life function	The vegetative	The etheric body II
Matter	The physical 1st plane	The physical body	Matter	Matter	The physical body I
Main Religions	*Jes Bertlesen*	*Rudolph Steiner*	*Plotinus*	*Sri Aurobindo*	*Theosophists*

Jes Bertelsen has said that the three former levels along with the mental level constitute the 'I', and that it is only the Self (the higher stages) that continues after the physical death. Jes Bertelsen has further suggested that the three last levels are comparable to the Holy Spirit which is the Mary consciousness (the susceptible consciousness), the Christ consciousness as well as the Divine. Arthur E. Powell explained the same as Steiner, but used other terms on some of the levels. He further explained that within each of these main levels, there are seven sub-levels. The Indian mystic Sri Aurobindo (1872-1950) and Plotinus mention even more levels of the consciousness, but these can be fitted within the above seven main levels according to Ken Wilber.

Rudolf Steiner has explained that the clairvoyant will see *the physical body* as a core in the middle of the different consciousness bodies. This body is what people have in common with the creatures of the mineral kingdom, that part of their being one can see with the eyes and touch with the hands. It is the lowest part of the human being, that which at death is left behind as the deceased's corpse. Steiner said that the nervous system in the physical body is linked to the astral body and the blood is linked to the 'I'. No creature has in its physical body a nervous system which is not pierced through by the astral body. And no creature has in its physical body a blood system that is not imbued by an 'I'. Jes Bertelsen has said that we have borrowed everything physical from the planet.

The etheric body, which Rudolf Steiner also termed the life body, he described as something that permeates the physical body, which is especially evident around the head, where it is seen as a clear light reflection. Further down, the etheric body becomes increasingly indistinct according to Steiner, and eventually loses the form of the physical body. The mineral kingdom's creatures have no etheric body. However, all beings of the Earth's plant kingdom have. The etheric body of every human being is its guard against death. Between birth and death the etheric body holds the human physical body intact, although its parts are tirelessly striving away from each other. At physical death, the etheric body will be withdrawn from the physical body.

Lyall Watson has written that all physical bodies seem to have a double, an etheric twin, which is a life-force.[227] This force is referred to as *prana* in yoga context or *chi* in acupuncture and qigong. He has also mentioned the bioplasma body, an organizing field that contains the individual memories and experiences, and which Harold Saxton Burr has described in detail, see chapter 6 about the aura. Watson wrote that this body, which can be said to be an organizer that arranges patterns in living matter without undergoing any change, survives the removal and destruction of the somatic system. However, he thought that it would dissolve after a while, as it depends on the energy that the physical body creates. He referred to the Irish psychic author Joan Grant (1907-1989) who said that all bodies consist of a physical and a super-physical part. She explained that when the energy-exchange between these parts ends, the physical body will die, while the super-physical continues its existence. This last part cannot die. It is an entity which she calls *The Integral*, which is the sum of all that we have collected through our different incarnations. She further said that a ghost or an apparition is a dissociated fragment of a personality with a limited amount of energy. This is probably the same as that which the Theosophists call the elementals (see the chapter about the spirit beings).

Arthur E. Powell explained that according to the Theosophists the etheric body (or the essential double, as he called it) is a true copy of the physical body, but consists of finer particles of physical substance.[228] The task of the etheric body is to collect the life force or *prana*, and distribute it to the physical body. Also, it is the intermediary between the physical body and the astral body, and in addition it is the connecting link between the physical brain and the higher consciousness. Geoffrey Farthing used the term the etheric double as another designation for the astral body, which he said is the consciousness body closest to the physical body. As the third aspect, after the physical and astral body, he mentioned the life force, while the fourth he denoted as the lower mental, where lust and passion have their seat. There are thus different descriptions in two Theosophical sources.

Jes Bertelsen has called the energy in the etheric field – *bioenergy*. It is this field which provides all cell activity in the body and causes the chemical and electrical impulses between the cells. He also designated this field as the dimension of life.

Bob Moore has explained that it is very important that we have a strong and complete etheric body in order to feel physical well-being. The etheric body is made up of atoms and has a nervous system similar to the physical body. The etheric body is surrounded by a closely knit web. The purpose of this web is that the rays and the bombardment of energies from the outside cannot flow too quickly and unobtrusively into the etheric body. The web of the etheric body has the same function for this body as the skin for the physical body. It provides protection from the world that surrounds us, a shielding from all the impressions with which we are bombarded. All types of energy must pass through this thin tightly knit etheric web. A certain penetration of the web is both important and necessary, but if the energy bombardment is too strong the web may be damaged, and thus damage the etheric body. The blood circulation will then be affected, because all influences on the etheric body will be transferred to the physical body. Too great and too many emotional problems such as stress can harm the web. A clairvoyant person will be able to see the effect of, for example, jealousy on the etheric body, as disturbances in the nervous system emerges as grey shades in the aura.

Ambres has explained that the soul, or what he calls The Rider, creates an *etheric fluidum* where the astral and mental body eventually emerge. It is this etheric substance that surrounds the physical body.

All living beings (except plants) have what is called an *astral body*. This is similar to the physical body, but is more comprehensive and has even finer particles of physical stuff than the etheric body. In addition, the astral body has sparkling colours, which mirror the person's physical and mental condition. Arthur E. Powell has said that the astral body of advanced individuals has its own life and has powers which the physical body can take advantage of. Among other things, many people have maintained that whoever has a 'developed' astral body, can use this to astral travel – for example, to visit people and places in other parts of the world. Both the physical body and the etheric body are enclosed in the astral body. This is surrounding the physical body and has a luminous form in the shape of an egg.

Rudolf Steiner suggested that the light rays in the astral body seem to come from the outside and go inwards and permeate the physical body. He explained further that in the astral body a great variety of different shapes can be seen, all possible kinds of lines and rays, some like lightning, some in peculiar spirals. All this surrounds the human being in a great diversity of shades. The astral body is the expression of the passions of human beings, their instincts, lust and desires, but also all their thoughts and beliefs. Everything one calls spiritual experiences can be seen illustrated in the astral body by a clairvoyant person, from the lowest drives and up to the highest moral ideals. The human being has this body in common with all animals. Rudolf Steiner said that the astral body remains linked to the ego during the first period after death, which he called the kamaloka period *(kama* means desire and *loka* means place in Sanskrit).

Then this body is a kind of power body that keeps whatever is stored from the last incarnated physical life of moral, intellectual and aesthetic achievements. In addition, it is said that diseases are also reflected in the astral field as dark shadows or lumps. These are attached to the chakras related to the specific diseases. Bob Moore has explained that the astral body is outside of the etheric body. There are several levels of the astral body. A lower level in the astral body he calls the *emotional plane*. He has pointed out that our emotions often govern our actions, confuse us and can lead us astray. We must learn to understand when we react with our emotions, rather than by logic or sense. He said that a clairvoyant person will see that the effects of the emotions are visible in the aura for a long time. Ambres explained that the astral body is made up of emotions, those we experience and those we create. Jes Bertelsen pointed out that also animals have an astral consciousness – they experience images, dreams, have sympathies and antipathies, they have emotions and instincts.

The fourth body is the *mental body* – the higher mental (the lower mental is the same as the astral body) – representing the thought world according to Jes Bertelsen. This is probably the ego in Rudolf Steiner's terminology, which makes the human being the crown of creation, makes it stand above all other earthly beings. This ego allows the human being – within the Earth's atmosphere – to develop into an individual and self-conscious being. Rudolf Steiner said that it is this ego that goes from one incarnation to the next; others maintain that it is the higher part of the 'I', also known as the Self that does this. Ambres explained that the mental body is composed of thoughts, those we have been given and those we have created.

Jes Bertelsen mentions three other consciousness bodies in addition to the four previously mentioned, that have contact with ever finer spiritual planes. These planes are respectively The *spiritual plane* where the Self (which he refers to as the Mary-consciousness) operates, The *cosmic* or *open plane* (where what he terms the Christ-consciousness operates), and The *unity plane*, also known as Nirvana or the Light. The spiritual plane is the first level that can be said to transcend the four consciousness levels which most of today's people use in their everyday lives. The Self is what most people consider as the Soul. A human being, who is using his or her abilities also on the spiritual level, is the proper or complete human being – the real living creature as expressed by Martinus. There are, however, only a few people who have contact with this level, because it requires that they do not let their minds be distracted by anything that happens in the physical life. The Theosophists use the term the *causal body* for the first of the higher consciousness bodies, while others reserve the term causal for an even higher level (Ken Wilber among others).

Jes Bertelsen reports that the monks on the Athos peninsula in Greece visualize the Virgin Mary while praying. They eventually reach a form of identification with Mary, a development which also affects their physical bodies as they become more feminine. Through this identification they obtain an opening towards the mystical process. Jes Bertelsen describes the Mary-state as a receptive emptiness where the mystery can take place. This state means that one should be as the Virgin Mary, open and receptive in order to obtain the Christ-consciousness. The Christ-consciousness is an experience of unity with everything in life, an experience of the divine power flowing into one's consciousness. Jes Bertelsen refers to Master Eckhart, who has described this condition. The dynamic of this process is what Bertelsen calls the Holy Spirit. Something similar is also said by Yogananda.[229] The Christ-consciousness is only obtained when one's own ego is dissolved. This may be said to happen to Jesus when he became Christ by baptism in the river Jordan, according to the story in the Gospels. From this date he identified himself with the transcendent Father beyond the created.

Rudolf Steiner also mentioned what he called the *phantom body*. That is a kind of spiritual body – a transparent power body. It is the shaping body or a person's spiritual structure; it is what does the preparatory work, the forming of the physical substances and energies, and the body that keeps the material parts together.

7.6. Some other explanations of the human being's structure

Martinus has a slightly different description of the situation of mankind than most other mystics. He mentioned 'the living entity's' eternal structure. He was also putting emphasis on the consciousness stages in the human being's structure, but he called these energy levels. He operated with seven such levels. These energies, which he called the basic energies, are almost similar to the seven consciousness bodies. He said that people develop through several incarnations, depending on what they have learnt and how they have changed during a specific life on Earth, so that the main weight will slowly move from one energy level to the next in the order they are listed below. There will always be one level that is at the top, two that are expanding and two that are contracting. There will always be one at rest. The seventh level, which is the maternal energy, is constant.

Martinus has mentioned the energies and their colours in the following order (compare this with the description above of the consciousness planes and the colours of the chakras – the names of the chakras have been included here, but Martinus does not mention these centres):

The instinct energy	(the plant realm)	Red	Root
The gravity energy	(the animal realm)	Orange	Hara
The emotional energy	(the human realm)	Yellow	S. plexus
The intelligence energy	(the wisdom realm)	Green	Heart
The intuition energy	(the divine world)	Blue	Throat
The memory energy	(the realm of blessedness / the mineral realm)	Indigo	Pineal
The maternal energy	(the eternity plane)	Violet	Crown

Living creatures have the most significant part of their consciousness concentrated at one energy level at a time, according to Martinus. People of today are mainly living in the gravity energy that corresponds to the energies of the animal realm, except that the emotional energy and the intelligence energy are much more developed than those of animals. He emphasised that what the human being must seek to develop is the energy of love – which is the emotional energy. It is only when the emotional energy is developed enough, that is, when people understand and abide by the message of charity that the real human realm will arise. Only then will 'the living entity' be able to acquire the intelligence energy or wisdom, and only then will we be able to develop the intuition energy needed to be able to (again) obtain conscious contact with the divine world.

It is only the gravity energy that lies within the conscious, physical world. The five other sensory areas (the maternal energy is not counted here) are only experienced slightly instinctively, because those basic energies are not especially prominent in today's human beings. These areas belong to the spiritual life. In some individuals, however, some of these spiritual levels may be more advanced than those of the vast majority.

Ken Wilber has said that all the major religions describe the human beings as comprised of the following five levels, or layers, often referred to as bodies, which correspond to the individual sections in what he calls *The Great Chain of Being*:

matter	(1)
body (life)	(2)
mind	(3)
soul / psychic / subtle	(4)
spirit / causal	(5)
And above it all, or comprising all those five levels, we have the All or the One, the Non-dual.	(6)

As mentioned, others describe seven such layers where the Unity field is included. The difference is not great. Wilber's 'mind' is by Jes Bertelsen divided into the astral and the mental mind, respectively.

What is important in this context, increasingly emphasised by Wilber, is that the higher level integrates and transcends the lower level, but not vice versa. The higher level is not ahead of a lower, it *builds* on the lower. The lower has the *potential* for the higher, but the higher must be developed, it was not there before. The higher level is not PRE, as Wilber says, but it is TRANS. This is so for each individual and for the totality of existence. If you visualize *The Great Chain of Being* transferred into a kind of Chinese box, we get *The Great Nest of Being* – 'Life's great interaction'(see figure 9).

Then we will have matter (step 1) at the base and in the centre. Beyond this, the physical and biological substance (step 2) will evolve – first the plants, then the animals, then the human beings. Without matter, the biological will not occur, but pure matter does not function biologically. Therefore the biological integrates and transcends matter, but not vice versa. Then the mental capabilities or the mind occur (step 3) – in the same way. Then the psychic occurs in the same way (step 4) – though this concerns only a few persons so far. And finally the spiritual (step 5) – something that lays in the future (I hope) for all mankind. The outer layers are based on and incorporate the layers that are within, but the inner layers are not aware of the outer. If an inner layer disappears, also those further out will disappear, while the outmost layer may disappear without any of the inner layers being affected. Development requires that what is new transcends *and* integrates that which has gone before. The outermost layer, penetrating everything and unaffected by anything, is the All – the Eternal, the Unchangeable, which often is referred to as God.

The potential for all those five layers being activated is there and all human beings have this potential. But how far each individual has come or will come in this Earth life, depends on many factors. The contact the human beings have with the different layers is essential, and whether they are working to get in touch with the higher layers. It is also so that we may experience shorter or longer glimpse of a higher level than the one we normally reside in, either during sleep, under the influence of narcotic drugs or during the waking-dream state. The possibilities are there, but the learning process is arduous, and the ability or willingness to work with one's psyche is rarely present in most people. Some prominent individuals, who from birth may have already had a greater potential for spiritual experiences than most other people, have obtained pure spirit, which is a feeling of pure being, that is to be one with the deity during a short or longer glimpse (Unio Mystica).

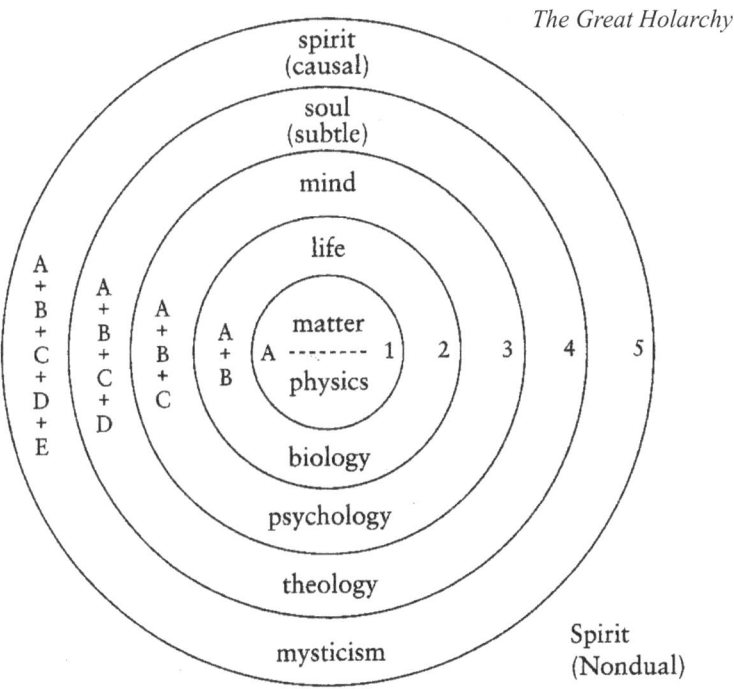

Figure 9. The Great Nest of Being
The Great Interplay of Existence from - 'A Theory of Everything' by Ken Wilber (2001)

The American psychoanalyst Dr John Lilly (1915-2001) has in the book *The Centre of the Cyclone*, which is based on his experience with the use of LSD, described a total of nine consciousness levels, four above the ordinary consciousness and four below.[230] The ordinary consciousness is at the physical level and can almost be compared to a robot, as we are only reacting to stimuli from the outside (response speed 48 – commented on further in the section below). The first level above this one is reached when we are concentrating intensely or occupied with something (speed 24). The next level (speed 12) he compares with blissfulness, such as the feelings when falling in love. The third level (speed 6) is the level where we have paranormal experiences, astral travels or meeting angels. The fourth level (speed 3) is the unity with the Divine or the Universal mind. The four levels on the negative side are mirror images of the four positive levels. The first is where we are when we are experiencing pain, shame and guilt. The next one gives the feeling that life is without meaning and of isolation. The third level is a kind of purgatory and the fourth level is like hell – where there are evil powers and negativism.

The speed numbers specified here John Lilly has borrowed from the mystic George Ivanovich Gurdjieff (1866-1949).[i] Gurdjieff explained that human beings are only responding to impulses from the outside – and that they really are in a deep sleep. However, he mentioned only seven levels and said that these levels have different vibrations, which match those found by Thomas Lethbridge with his pendulum experiments (see chapter 3.8).

Gurdjieff claimed, inter alia, that the Earth is subject to forty-eight laws, while the planets only have twenty-four, the Sun has twelve, the stars have six and the galaxies three. The Absolute or The One is subject to only one law. The absolute lowest level Gurdjieff called the Moon level, which has a vibration of ninety-six. Gurdjieff said further that the fewer laws that people are subject to, the freer they are; or the higher the consciousness level you have, the freer you are.

Gurdjieff also mentioned the human being's four consciousness bodies as, respectively, the physical, the astral (emotions and desires), the spiritual (the mind and intellect) and the causal (the master, the will or the real 'I'). The physical is subject to forty-eight laws, the astral to twenty-four, the spiritual to twelve and the causal to six. It should be noted that also Gurdjieff saw the Cosmos as a Chinese box, with each lower world within the higher. He said further that micro-cosmos reflects the macro-cosmos, and that everything vibrates, but with different frequencies – human beings cannot register the finer frequencies.[231]

---

i. Gurdjieff was a world-renowned Russian mystic, spiritual teacher and philosopher, born in Alexandropol in Transcaucasia, Armenia. He died in Fountainebleau near Paris where he lived and taught for many years. It is said that anyone who came into contact with him were impressed by his knowledge and communication. Colin Wilson characterised him as an outstanding psychologist, in line with Nietzsche. Wilson wrote that Gurdjieff had separated himselves from other magicians as he was entirely down-to-earth, very disciplined and self preserving, with no hints of eccentricity. However, he needed disciples, though this may be due to his perception that any people working together can achieve more than a single person alone.

7.7. The personality and the unconscious forces in the human beings

With the term 'personality', one usually thinks of each individual's way of being and acting; that means all the properties which the outside world perceives of a physical being. As stated above in the description of the human being's different bodies, Jes Bertelsen used the term *'I'* about that which *makes itself known* as a physical figure. That is, the 'I' consists of the physical, the etheric, the astral and the mental body. Both oneself and any outsider will normally experience this as a unit – that which makes itself known, both to oneself and to the outside world. This is a complex collection which is connected to identity and self-esteem, with interests, desires, weaknesses and strength. (Rudolf Steiner used the term the spirit-self and the Theosophists called it the ego, which Jes Bertelsen denotes as the higher self or the Self. In this book I have chosen to follow Bertelsen's use of the concepts.) The 'I' will normally use a *mask* or a *character type* in daily life, which it has adopted while growing up. Carl Gustav Jung used the term *persona* about this behaviour type. We are all wearing different masks or playing many roles, just like actors. For example, I am at one time the serious responsible physician or craftsman, the next a submissive son/daughter, only to be, at another time, the sparkling centre of attraction in a party. It is all part of the same personality, and within what is considered as normal. It is when the personality becomes fragmented or controlled by a trauma that is stored in the unconscious that disease conditions occur. There are many people who experience multiple personalities within themselves, personalities which are completely independent of each other. The books *Three Faces of Eve* (by Thigpen and Cleckley – the book was also made into a film) and *When Rabbit Howls* by Truddi Chase tell of people with multiple personalities. The first book is about a woman with three clearly distinct personalities. The personality that appeared first did not know the other two, but the two behind had full knowledge of the one in front. In the second book the person had more than 200 personalities which arose as result of extreme abuse in childhood.

Colin Wilson recounts several cases of multiple personalities in the book *Mysteries*. He points out that people are not clear-cut or unchangeable personalities. A child develops into an adult personality, and deep down in the personality the child is still there; but that child has never possessed the capabilities this person has acquired through their life. The child has capabilities, but whether they will be realised only time will show. In the adult all the different stages of the child is contained – and sometimes these emerge on the surface and behave as independent personalities. This happens especially when the individual comes into a stressed situation – all of a sudden it may be behaving as a seven-year-old, with the same movements, language and behaviour. But it could also be the other way round. The individual may, for example, stop its conscious growth when fifteen years of age, while the subconsciousness continues to experience and systematize the experiences. Suddenly one day, the experienced, mature personality steps forward and takes over the reins, without the fifteen-year-old being aware of what is going on. However, the explanation behind the behaviour of people with multiple personalities is not that simple. Michael Talbot recounts that these people may have completely different diseases or bodily symptoms. For example, one personality is of a woman menstruating, while the other personality that emerges during this period is not; one personality can suffer from diabetes, but not the other. It has also been shown that the various personalities have different patterns of brain waves. This shows at least two strange conditions. One point is that a personality is not something which is unchangeable and made once and for all. The second point is that there is something other than the brain that controls the personality, and what can that be?

How is a personality formed? Lyall Watson has maintained that there is little reason to doubt that the differences in personality and psyche are biologically based.[232] He has explained that it is partly genetic factors, partly environmental factors and partly personal experiences that shape the personality, as there is a selection of certain factors from the environment and an adaptation to these. A functional error, a chemical change or an alteration in the biological environment, can change the personality dramatically. Ageing can also result in big changes in the personality. All this shows that the personality is very much dependent on the body, so that when the body dies and disappears there is reason to believe that the personality also disappears. Watson wrote that if there is something in the organism that can survive death, consciousness must exist independently of the body and in a different kind of medium. But according to him, there is no reasonable biological explanation which should indicate that the personality can survive death. He mentioned, however, that the peculiar composition of dreams may indicate that there is such a different system, which is organised in such a way that is characteristic for each individual but he doubted whether such a different system can be completely independent of the body. He referred to the importance of dreams for an individual's mental equilibrium (dreaming seems to be something that only happens to warm-blooded vertebrates). If a person is prevented from dreaming, this can lead to loss of memory, dissociation and sometimes to epileptic attacks. Watson said that it has been established that some consciousness has its centre at a certain place in the cerebral cortex, so if this is removed by surgical intervention or is being damaged in any way, the individual may continue to eat, drink and defecate, but seems to be doing this sleeping – that is without the ordinary daily awareness or being awake. Watson asked how a creature can have experiences without using the body's sensory organs. Only to function by the use of telepathy or psychokinesis, he thought, was far removed from everything we know about life's development.

In psychology the term *'I'* often also goes under the term 'ego'. The ego is the individual human's assertiveness-need. It is important that we develop this need and have the abilities and powers to mark who we are, otherwise we can be easily overrun by our fellow beings. In the first, perhaps thirty years of our life, we must develop a strong ego. We must learn to stand on our own two feet, manage an independent life, master a profession and possibly also find a partner. In a partnership each of us should function as one of two equally strong individuals, otherwise we may be dominated by our partner, or the other way round. The next, possibly also thirty years, should be used to relinquish our adapted patterns, our urge to assert ourselves, and try to get away from all which is binding, such as the need to show off in a nice car or house, etc. That is to say that we should deliberately seek contact with the subconscious. Only then can we approach a higher or deeper dimension of our consciousness – a super consciousness or what is known as the Self.

However, 'Man' is functioning from more than the personality (or multiple personalities). But before we look into this, there are some concepts that should be understood. These are terms often used interchangeably or in a way that can make it difficult to understand the meaning of what is being said. These are the concepts the brain, the mind, the spirit, the essence, the soul and the Self.

The Brain: This is a *physical* organ where the chemical processes that control the body's activities take place. It is also said that it is this organ that filters out or blocks all impressions from the outside that we do not need. The Norwegian astrophysicist Jeremi Wasiutynski (1907-2005)[i], who has written the book *Det kosmiske drama og drømmer om den kongelige vei på terskelen til en ny tid,* (The Cosmic Drama and Dreams about the Royal Road on the Threshold of a new Era), believed that the brain is not the centre of the consciousness, but the organ that restricts the consciousness within time and space.[233]

The Mind: The thoughts, the imagination, the emotions and the intuition are brought forth in the mind. The *psyche* is a Greek term for the mind. Experiences are stored in the mind. It is debatable whether this is an organ that has a specific location in the brain or elsewhere, within or outside of the body, or whatever it is. Here the thoughts are formed and the experiences evaluated. Here the sum of life's experiences is stored – the wisdom of life.

---

i. Jeremi Wasiutynski was born in Warsaw, but lived in Oslo from 1937. He wrote several books which were published by the Norwegian Academy of Science and the Norwegian Research Council. The book *The Cosmic Drama and Dreams about the Royal Road on the Threshold of a new Era* provides an analysis of dreams that the author thought followed the same laws that apply to the Universe. His synthesis shows a correlation between in-depth psychology and theoretical physics. The book's cover says this, inter alia, about this synthesis: "An extended mathematics which includes all other sciences and is an à priori construction of the total reality, as a drama of consciousness and existence."

This includes both the body's *etheric, astral* and *mental* spheres. This is the total of our life experiences – the data bank, to use a modern term.

The Self: The 'Self' can be termed as the super consciousness – a consciousness that is more comprehensive (and inclusive) than what human beings normally use of their consciousness. This is the *spiritual* level. This is the manager behind our earthly life – our cosmic contact and awareness.

The Soul: The soul in the physical body can be said to be the contact between the spirit and the 'Self', which conveys deeper knowledge to the 'Self'. It is this unit which might be the carrier of the essence from the human life of a departed forward to a new existence. The soul is thus a deeper aspect of the 'Self'.

The Spirit: The spirit is the non-physical quality that is attached to the physical body. It is probably the same as Martinus called talent-seeds. This is our wisdom, sensibility (not knowledge, although our approach and way of thinking often is based on knowledge), an ability for unconditional love, compassion, and similar qualifications. The spirit of the individual human being is in contact with the spirit of the Universe.

The Essence: The core. I believe that deep within all people there is the same core of positive qualities and skills. However, this core is often covered by sediments that we ourselves have caused in this life or that which we have brought into it, and which it is our task to change for the better in this life.

Consciousness in a human mind or psyche normally operates in one of the following ways – *consciousness areas*:

> The daily consciousness: A surface consciousness.
>
> The nightly consciousness: Sleep. Where are you, and what are you doing, when you are sleeping?
>
> The unconsciousness: That which governs the body functions and which also stores the experiences from daily life and brings them forward when required.
>
> The subconsciousness: Intuition, the dream controller.
>
> The super consciousness: The sensibility and the higher spiritual levels; Clairvoyance; telepathic ability; the contact with everything that is happening and has happened.

As stated in the description of the different human bodies, it is especially in the astral body (the lower mental) and the mental body (the higher mental) that the ordinary consciousness, i.e. the daily consciousness and the nightly consciousness of the mind or psyche, is active. The unconsciousness and the subconsciousness also have their domain here.

The super consciousness will in addition also function in the higher consciousness bodies.

As mentioned in the chapter about the functional levels of consciousness, the consciousness could be in one of the following states:

sleeping – dreaming – partly awake – awake – trance/intoxication – meditation.

These consciousness states can be active on any of the above mentioned consciousness areas, and will there be able to use any of the consciousness bodies to a greater or lesser degree. You can, for example, in a half-awake, fantasizing state (where you are in contact with the astral level), suddenly have a feeling of blessedness, which might indicate that you are in contact with a higher (spiritual) level of the psyche. But the most significant activity will, for the vast majority of people today, be in the lower or higher mental body.

There are many unknown forces that affect much of what we are doing through the subconsciousness. Carl Gustav Jung has introduced the term *archetype* in order to explain some of these forces. According to Jung the archetypes are universal symbols. These symbols are collective in the sense that they are derived from the collective unconscious. That means that a newborn child has a brain that is equipped with instincts and ancient images that throughout time have been at the core of human thinking, as endless repetitions have printed the experiences into our psyche. The archetype is thus a kind of guiding principle belonging to the subconscious, in the same way as instinct. Jung said that there are as many archetypes as there are people. When a situation occurs that is reminiscent of an earlier experience, its archetype, which is a kind of form without content, will be activated, usually in the form of a figure or image – most often in a dream.[234] (Dion Fortune's term 'materialised ideas' may equal the term archetype.) Jung said:

> The term archetype... has been derived from the many times that we have noted that for example the myths and fairy tales of the world's literature contain specific motifs which always and everywhere appear again and again.

Astri Hognestad (b.1946), a Norwegian Jungian analyst educated at the Jung Institute in Switzerland, has explained that when we feel possessed by something that lifts us out of our daily experience of ourselves, we are in touch with what are known as archetypal forces. She said further that the term is related to the *super personal forces* that people throughout time have imagined, such as gods, spirits, trolls, etc. These are images of the original, that which can be said to be the psyche's pre-form or inherited structure. She wrote:[235]

> It is, rightly enough, a hypothesis that human beings have a layer within themselves which can be called the collective unconscious. Some experiences show, however, that it is possible to understand a person's psyche in this way. ... The archetypical images that occur spontaneously in the waking state or in dreams tell us something about what kind of forces we are in contact with.

People react in much the same way in specific situations and have mainly the same dream images in regard to certain conflicts. Fairytales recount such psychological situations, as drawings and paintings often do in a dream situation. By interpreting dreams and images from this point of view – that is from fairytales and myths and the archetypes the Jungians have shown us – we will often be able to understand dreams and thoughts that might otherwise seem incomprehensible. Central archetypes are the Self or the Wise one, the Shadow, the Animus and the Anima. It is helpful to know these concepts:

The Self or the Wise one: When an individual human being is experiencing the spiritual worlds – albeit only in a flash – it is in contact with the Self or the deepest forces in the consciousness. It is probably this that Martinus called 'The living Creature'. This is the manager of our earthly life – our cosmic core and consciousness. Ambres explained that if in a dream a personality shows a way out of a difficult situation, or is explaining a situation, then this is the Self, or the basic personality in Ambres' terminology. It knows the cause of all traumas and how to get out of the traumas and the difficulties. It is this entity Ambres also called the *Rider*.[236]

The Shadow: The shadow is the part of our personality that we do not want to recognize and which we reject. For example, we feel shame when it comes to the bodily functions. We do not like to think about them, or their requirements, but their needs are still there. Here we are denying some aspects of ourselves and project them on to others instead. For example, we can see that some people are passionate about sex, which we condemn. What we are condemning in others are, as a rule, the same hidden aspects of ourselves – our shadow. The shadow is the synthesis of all our traumas, according to Ambres.

The Animus and the Anima: The animus is traditionally dubbed the masculine character traits in a woman and the anima the feminine character traits in a man. For example, a woman can have both creativity and strength, which traditionally are regarded as masculine traits. That is the animus forces. Often these forces are not used because tradition and social convention have suppressed them. When they are not being used, frustration and problems occur. The anima represents feelings and sensitivity, as well as the irrational. These forces are often oppressed in men but without both archetypes being actively in use, one is not a whole human being.

Ken Wilber is critical of Jung's use of the term archetype.[237] He has pointed out that Jung and his followers use the term in at least three different contexts. The most common interpretation is to see the archetypes as archaic images, of which the world's mythology is the most typical. In the next context it is a 'form without content', and in the third context the archetype is seen as the first shape in 'the involution' or the infolding of consciousness in matter and form. The word archetype comes from the Greek *arche typon* meaning the archaic pattern or the original pattern. For the advanced mystics

– Wilber mentioned especially Shankara, Plato, Augustine, Eckhart, and Garab Dorje – archetypes are the first, subtle forms that appear when the world manifests itself out of the amorphous and unmanifested spirit. It is these patterns all other forms are based on. These subtle, transcended patterns are the first forms of manifestation, whether it is on the physical, biological, or the mental level, or any of the higher levels of consciousness. In most branches of mysticism these archetypes are nothing but brilliant patterns or bright dots, audible performances of lights, shapes and light figures of brilliant colours, rainbows of light, sound and vibration. It is from this that they say that the material world manifests itself. However, according to Wilber, Jung's use of the term archetype is mainly based on basic mythical structures that are collective for human experience, such as the jester, the shadow, the sage, the ego or persona, the great mother, the anima and the animus, etc. Wilber pointed out that these figures are not transcendental, but *existential*. They are simply variations of human experiences in daily life. They have nothing to do with higher awareness and there is nothing mysterious with them. According to Wilber, Jung is mixing the transcendental with the collective, i.e. what people have in common. Wilber maintained that there are collective pre-personal experiences, just as much as there are collective personal experiences and collective transpersonal experiences. You have to keep these different types of experiences from one another in order to understand human actions and reactions.

In today's language the word archetype refers normally to Jung's most common use of the term. One should then remember what Wilber said, that this is not to be associated with higher consciousness or transcendental awareness, but with the astral and the unconscious. Wilber agreed with Jung that certain archetypes point beyond the ordinary consciousness, such as the Sage, the Old one, the Animus and the Anima.

The archetypes, however, are not the only forces that are playing with us. In transactional analysis therapy the concepts Parents, Adult and Child are used.[238] *Parents* are the rules and decrees and the expectations that are instilled in us while we are small, whether they come from parents, teachers or the community around us. What we receive of impressions and impulses from our parents, have often been received by them from their parents or grandparents. It means that certain patterns of action or response patterns recur from one generation to the next. *Child* refers to our types of reaction which we resort to as small children when we are trying to get our will through. We also often take refuge in these forces as adults, when we do not wish to behave, or are unable to face a situation, in a calm manner. The *Adult* is the mental state we are in when we use the mind, by balancing the various experiences against each other and making decisions or are communicating from well-considered thoughts.

If we are to achieve a harmonious existence, we must seek to find the Adult in us. We must learn to understand when our instincts, the primitive and/or the irrational, govern our emotions and actions, so that we can adjust our behaviour with the help of our sensibility. The true sensibility is the Self. When we stop letting outside things and events control us, and instead follow the intuition and the deeper purpose of our lives, harmony and the understanding of life will come. Master Eckhart emphasised the concept of "gelâzenheit" (a German word) as an important maxim. The Norwegian professor of philosophy, Jon Wetlesen (b.1940), who has written a book about Eckhart, translated this word as relaxation, and said that the term has its roots in the verb *to let*.[239] I associate this with to let things happen, to go with the energies. That means that it shall not be so that my energies and needs control me, but that I should follow what I intuitively feel is appropriate. If we have a relaxed approach to life, to what is happening with us and around us, much will be arranged for us. We will still experience hardship and resistance in order to grow, but we must not let the emotions take the upper hand.

As we have seen, everything can be considered as consciousness, and our thoughts can manage all types of life processes. Magic relates to the psyche's hidden area, as Colin Wilson said.[240] What we have discussed above about strange abilities, shows that human beings have an enormous potential to experience and act, which goes far beyond what we encounter in everyday life. The mystics are striving to get in touch with the astral and the mental consciousness levels, and to use this type of consciousness to become better individuals and to help others to the same. On these levels there are obviously no limitations. Probably, by the full exploitation of consciousness' possibilities, we might experience something like the near-death experiences. Many people have special abilities, and some are born with strong mental or transcendental powers but, as Colin Wilson pointed out, many seem to have obtained that kind of ability after a serious illness or a great shock, this last may for example be due to an electric shock in childhood. He suggested that by such a shock, an internal locking mechanism – a safety valve – may be destroyed. The etheric body may be damaged, so that more information from the outer world gets through[i]. The purpose of such a safety valve is to prevent the inflow of too much information – otherwise we would be totally confused and bewildered of what we can use and what we can ignore. One type of such information experienced by some people is information about accidents and disasters just before they happen, which is very disturbing. The unfortunate thing is that many who have special abilities, have not always come far enough in regard to intelligence and charity to use these powers in humanity's best interest. Without being in possession of the ability for unconditional love, such powers may be too easily used in the wrong way – which would be greatly detrimental to oneself. The best explanation in this regard, I think is the one given by Martinus. Human beings need to

---

i. As probably was the case with Anthony Cicoria (b. 1952) who was struck by lightning, as mentioned above in a footnote in chapter 3.17.

develop the ability to love in order to achieve wisdom. It is only then that we are on the right path.

Most people undergo various life crises, of which the worst often happen when one is about forty years of age. It is maintained that these life crises are trying to bring the individual on to a better path in cases where one is stuck in a particular way of living or life pattern. A marriage may break up around this time, or one might have a serious illness. One decides to work in something completely different, or to move to another location. Usually it is something that has long been contemplated, maybe only unconsciously, which breaks out as a conflict or crisis – a crisis that may have been unconsciously provoked by the person's own self.

This is how it is explained astrologically, Uranus – which introduces turmoil and change – is in opposition to its position at birth (i.e. where it stood in the birth chart of the individual) after forty-two years. Major changes, strangely enough, happen around the age of twenty-nine or fifty-eight, as Saturn then having had a spin around the Sun and has returned to its position at birth. I cannot see that the conscious 'I' is arranging such events. When I look back on my own life, it seems that there is someone/something outside of me that controls or directs what happens to me at times when I am not following a signal to change direction. All of a sudden something, which I cannot understand that I am responsible for, happens. It throws all my previous plans and life patterns into disarray and in extremely difficult situations people have appeared who have thrown a life-belt out to me and prevented me from drowning (to use a phrase metaphorically). It has also happened that conditions are suddenly adjusted so that the changes, when considered in retrospect, are for my own good. Why have I had exactly the experiences I have had? I feel that something in the reincarnation theory can explain my experiences in this life. That feeling is reinforced by some regression experiences I have had regarding possible past-life experiences. This proves, however, by no means that reincarnation is a reality, or that there is some regression reality or that there is a connection with previous lives in such experiences. I will look further into this later. But it seems to me that sometimes I am pushed both into and through crises and then it is not my consciousness that is leading me. Arthur Koestler has in the book *The Sleepwalkers* proven that people who are changing the world, often do so thanks to sudden impulses that give them the solution to a specific problem or question. From where do these ideas come? Sometimes people in different places in the world get the same ideas simultaneously and independently of each other. How is that possible?

If we consider the individual human child's development, the development of the imagination and the ability for rational thinking, we see that the higher level must integrate with the lower in order for development to take place – as Ken Wilber has pointed out. For example, an infant does not have mental or spiritual abilities – these abilities are, at that stage, not yet developed, while an adult person has lived, integrated (hopefully) and grown on the infant's adventures and experiences. Although today's human beings have little or no contact with the spiritual, and might be more concerned with the physical requirements than the intellectual, they are not one hundred per cent dominated by the consciousness level from which they usually act and react. For example, they can experience a flash from a higher level, as in an intuitive happening. In addition there are different consciousness levels, which we experience differently whether we are awake, dreaming, sleeping or meditating, or under the influence of drugs.

Ken Wilber mentioned that there are at least a dozen different development lines in growth from infant to wisdom. As examples of such development lines he mentioned 'the cognitive, moral, affective, love, concern, attention, self-identity, defence, interpersonal, artistic and kinestetic', and these lines will develop independently of each other through the different levels of Life's great interaction.[241] For example, he mentioned that an individual, who has come fairly far in spiritual matters, does not necessarily have to be equally well developed with regard to coping with its psychiatric bindings or its sexuality. In addition, there comes what may be said to be a horizontal interaction in life, which is about the relation between what he calls the Beautiful, the Good and the True (see figure 4). He uses the term integral psychology when all this is considered together. He believes that meditation is not the way to go in order to process all the different conditions that must be taken into consideration in self-development, as meditation alone does not bring you in close contact with the subconscious – it only helps in opening the higher levels. He recommends psychotherapy combined with meditative practice if you want to work towards higher levels – which you consciously should do, no matter where you happen to be existentially, because everyone has within themselves a longing to reach the higher levels. That is, we should strive to develop body, mind, soul and spirit within the areas of the 'I', culture and nature. Then we will be approaching the Beautiful, the Good and the True. There are, as we have seen, several layers of consciousness that must be taken into consideration. Which layer will be activated in the form of an 'I'-decision will depend on the individual human being's stage of development.

7.8. Dreams

> Dreams are the meeting place between the conscious and the unconscious.
> *Jeremi Wasiutynski*

Why do we sleep and dream? Professor Montague Ullman (1916-2008), New York, who has done research on dreams and written books about this, thought that we do not know why we sleep or why we dream, but he stated that experiments have shown that if we do not sleep or cannot sleep undisturbed, the body gets indisposed, which may cause irritability, confusion, and in extreme cases psychoses.[242] The need for sleep varies greatly from individual to individual. The transition from sleep to an awake state leads to significant psychological and physiological changes.

Martinus explained that dreams are real thought reactions, with experiences that are as realistic as adventures in the awake state – the day awareness.[243] The difference between physical experiences and dream experiences is that the dream experiences are not felt through the physical body. He pointed out that human beings are living in two worlds, and the dream experiences he considered as proof of the existence of the two worlds. He asked how we otherwise can explain the predictive dreams, the out-of-body experiences and clairvoyance. He explained further that sleep is necessary for the well-being of the physical body. It is a resting state for the physical nervous system's wear-and-tear or its fatigue, which enable it to be repaired. Such fatigue occurs as a result of the human being's activities and mental state when it is in its day awareness. When sleeping, the day awareness is transferred from the physical body to the emotional body, according to Martinus. Dreams, he said, are flashes of light from the other world that have entered into the earthly entity's day consciousness.

Seth explained dreams much in the same way.[244] Because the day-consciousness is so strongly associated with the body and what is going on around and in it, we seldom remember our dreams. However, the consciousness, or what Seth called the dream ego, leaves the body when we are asleep and goes to another dimension. He called the physical ego a fleshy projection of the dream ego. The dream ego has memories of everything encountered or experienced in the dream world, and it can have contact with other people in completely different parts of the world, which we in the awake state are not aware of. Dream experiences are on purpose directed as the day experiences, and just as meaningful. It is in the dream world that the vitality and the creative force behind the physical existence are generated. However, we do not perceive our dream ego's full reality when awake. The dream ego is much richer and includes so much more than the physical personality we think we are. But to describe it in understandable terms is difficult. Part of the dream ego provides the physical existence of the individual, some provides communication and creativity, some for what we call the soul, and all in all it covers something that can be called the multidimensional self, according to Seth.

Lyall Watson believes that dreaming is a continuous process, which in itself is as important as being conscious.[245] In the embryo state the dream is the embryo's mental activity. Later there is an alternating effect between dream and awake consciousness, though the consciousness is also active in the dream. Watson pointed out that even when a person is unconscious, such as during an operation, he/she is in many cases able to tell what happened during the operation and what the doctors were talking about. He thinks that sleep is just a sort of continuation of awareness, but under a different control. The dream is therefore something that comes from the mental activity, but now without conscious control. Night dreaming is due to the individual's need for safety. Watson mentioned that the first mammals were already dreaming, and that this dreaming ability was an alarm system that was built into the brain. The best surveillance guard is the nightmare. But the animals that became predators did not have to be alert in the same way. They could sleep more and dream more and feel safer without nightmares. They could therefore have wishful dreams, for example about food and hunting.

One theory of dreams is that they are reconsidering the daily experiences and are sorting out what we have to remember and what we can forget. (Who has not woken up in the middle of the night and seen or understood the solution to a difficult problem, or remembered something not identified in the awake state.) Lyall Watson also mentioned that Barbara Lerner, from the Mental Health Centre in Chicago, has suggested that an important part of the dream function could be to integrate the personality by letting us live out our fantasies in dreaming.

Watson suggested that the independence of the consciousness of genes and environment indicates that it is only in dreams that the conscious thought, any perceptions, unconscious reactions, involuntarily physiological processes and the organelles special application can sort out their conflicting interests and needs (an organelle is a structure in the cell with special functions). And he wrote that perhaps this is on a 'time sharing basis', which permits our complex system to work at all.

Human beings have always known that dreams can convey something of interest and that it therefore may be of importance to take dreams seriously and try to understand them. In The Old Testament we have examples of prophetic dreams, such as the stories about Joseph's dreams as told in Genesis and King Nebuchadnezzar's dreams as told in the Book of Daniel. A papyrus from Egypt, from approximately 2000 BCE, presents an explanation of dreams which shows that in ancient times dream interpretation was important. Some people today have designed dream cards to help dreamers interpret what their dreams may mean. Many people think that a spirit will influence you to choose a special dream card for interpreting a dream. There are many explanations regarding the meaning of a dream. Dreams can tell us something about the following:

What will happen	Future events, prophecies
What happened the day before	The day's residue
What happened in the past	Some nightmares may be due to past experiences
The problems of the subconsciousness	Conflicts, the individuation process, daily problems
What happens with others	War, catastrophes, etc. (telepathic dreams)

Spiritual dreams	Encounters with a deity or spirit
Dreams such as near-death experiences	Meeting with the unconscious
Dreams about other lives in this or any other type of existence	

The Norwegian psychologist Eva Røine (b.1928), who established the Norwegian psychodrama school in Oslo in 1986, has tried to diagnose diseases on the basis of dreams.[246] When the dreamer is settled in bed in the evening, he or she should request to have a dream that can tell about his/her condition and give a hint as to what can be done about it. Eva Røine has explained how she analyses a dream so that in a three-part dream the first part represents the actual problem, the second part how the problem is expressed, and the last part contains the solution or dissolution of the situation. Jeremi Wasiutynski has said almost the same. He explained that the first part shows the dreamer's internal situation or conflict, the second part the consequences of the situation and the third part the possible solution. However, these three parts may also be split on a number of dreams. The dreamer will in this way be guided by his/her own unconscious mind.

Ambres explained that dreams speak to us in symbols, which can be said to lie between an abstraction and a subjective experience.[247] (An abstraction is not something concrete that we have named or something of which we have a picture, but something of which we have an emotional understanding.) Dreams have no clear conclusion, and it is the dreamer who is best placed to interpret a dream. Ambres said that when we want to interpret our dreams, we have to work through our emotions – we must try to find the most important thing in a dream (the dream subject) and look at what it says. In his dream interpretations he took as a starting point the roles the human beings are playing. Every human being may be considered playing a variety of roles, which we act out according to what the situation requires. Sometimes we play the naughty child (perhaps several types), sometimes the angry parent (or another such character), and sometimes a school child being scolded, etc. In a dream these different roles will appear as different personalities. Each individual's personality, which consists of all these roles, is considering its world, based on an interpretation of what it sees and experiences. But there are many factors that affect the interpretation of dreams. One consideration must be based on the culture to which the dreamer belongs or has as social background. Another is the feeling that the dream produces and the thread of the dream. It is only the dreamer who knows whether an interpretation is correct or not.

Montague Ullman explained that he strongly rejected the notion that anyone can become an expert on another person's dreams, but we can help others to become experts on their own dreams. He is thus fully in line with Ambres here. But he said it was important to work with dreams, because they can help us to deal with the life we live, and to come to a deeper understanding of ourselves. Nan Zimmermann (Ullman's co-author of the book *Use your dreams*) said that dream images are part of an inner self-healing process which is at our disposal, and that their significance can be brought forward by hard work. But both claim that the content of the dreams is derived from our experiences in real life. Montague Ullman found it doubtful that a dreamer's subconscious is using universal symbols in a dream to get the dreamer to understand a message. He believed that it is only the dreamer who can say what the meaning of a dream image is. If, for example, the dreamer sees a cow, and usually has a negative understanding of the term cow – such as a silly being – then that is what the dream is about and not about the ancient mythological/religious symbol of a cow. But Ullman did not deny that the dreamer may have used symbols in the way his or her society uses it, so that a cross may mean suffering or salvation for those who belong to the Christian culture. Our dreams are in symbols and not in a common language, which Ullman meant was due to our use of symbols in general. We are using symbols to metaphorically reflect on reality and for our understanding of reality. Ullman compared his view on dreaming with Freud's and Jung's and gave in his book a good overview of the differences. These differences also include the interpretation of the symbols that appear in dreams.

Edgar Cayce highlighted that dreams have their limitations, but that certain rules govern what and how to dream.[248] A dreamer can only dream about that which is relevant to him or her. We can also dream about things on which we deliberately want to get information. The dreamer's mental condition and health condition affect dreams. If we are too ambitious, the dream quality will decline, while a calm mind increases it. Dreams can also come from different levels of the psyche, and in order to interpret a dream we have to understand from what level the information comes. We can get help from our inner voice or intuition if we ask for help either in the dream or immediately afterwards. Cayce believed that an important part of dream interpretation consists in using the ancient art of *urim*[i]; that is, we have to recognize symbols with relatively universal significance such as we know them from myth and art. Fire often means anger. Light means insight or help from the Divine. A child may mean a helpful beginning, while a horse or knight may refer to information from a higher consciousness level.

Jeremi Wasiutynski explained that dreams are one of the means which the subconscious or the Self is using to point out human neglect towards its spiritual and religious nature.[249] He believed that dreams are not exclusively a psychological phenomenon, but a phenomenon that encompasses everything human, such as physiology, religion, physics and metaphysics, as well as cosmology, poetry, ethics and art. The keys to a worldview and a life philosophy are hidden in the dream symbolism. Wasiutynski mentioned,

---

i. Urim is mentioned in Numbers 27.21 and described in the Talmud, Yoma 73B.

inter alia, that in the human being's subconscious is a factor that works to bring people into contact with their spiritual nature, whose main function is to get in touch with the All or the cosmic process. The same symbol can stand for opposite ideas, such as for both life and death. A figure in a dream may represent both a person in the outside world and that part of our own psyche which we have projected upon that person. Among other things, he said: "A 'real' dream symbol, which is an archetypical image, can be interpreted both according to its original spiritual meaning, and in a degenerated, material meaning. ... When it comes to the newly formed symbols, the interpretation possibilities are virtually limitless. The meaning of an image is dependent on the circumstances."

Jes Bertelsen holds that the vast majority of dreams are shadow dreams or emotional dreams.[250] The Shadow contains the unconscious, uncontrollable part of the emotions or personality. The purpose of the emotional dreams is to bring forward into the conscious mind the emotions which either have not been well enough acknowledged or not sufficiently expressed, or which have been too excessively expressed. Emotional dreams are dreams that are dominated by one or several emotions such as anxiety, aggression, desire, sorrow, sadness, emptiness, excitement or determination. As long as a human being has not acknowledged and integrated the Shadow, the dream mechanism will constantly be forced to compensate in order to rebalance the emotional instability and adjust projections of the unknown part-personalities. The content of the dream is the atmosphere, the feelings and the emotions that are in the dream or which are seen in the dream. These feelings and moods are partly atmospheric, which means that they are lightly spread throughout the elements of the dream, they are partly concentrated in terms of people, trees, houses, animals and more. Self-development is to work with the dreams and integrate what the dreams are trying to portray. Jes Bertelsen placed great emphasis on the dream's symbols, and has in his book about dreams explained the most common symbols. He noted that both Freud and Jung worked to expose the legality in the symbol language, and he refers those who want to study this language more closely to their textbooks, as well as to a series of recent books on dreams. Jes Bertelsen said, inter alia, that a person who is controlled by his or hers emotions and thus in the deeper sense has not realised and integrated the shadow sides, will through the dreams be confronted with the emotions in order to rebalance them. An individual is thus forced to become aware of his/her shadow. Wisdom dreams occur when a person in his or her development process begins to interact with the deeper layers of the personality, with an overall control and insight. If we do not follow the instructions given in such dreams, the development process is hampered.

Ken Wilber believes that dreams must be interpreted from the development stage (Wilber is operating with a total of nine such stages) or the *fulcrum* where the dreamer is, just as Edgar Cayce explained.[251] (A fulcrum can almost be compared to a consciousness body, and the question then is in which consciousness body the essentials of the person's energy are.) Especially in psychotherapy, it is important to be aware of this, so that the interpretation of a dream starts with a consideration from the lowest point, and then proceeds from there if necessary.

Sigmund Freud, in 1900, published his famous book on dreams (*Die Traumdeutung*). Freud considered wish-fulfillment as the central driving force behind dreams. He placed strong emphasis on the sexual, and believed therefore that many symbols had a sexual meaning. Carl Gustav Jung believed, however, that many of the symbols the dreamer was meeting in a dream were the most ancient symbols which he called archetypes, which shed light on the individual's individuation process and the limitations which at the time of dreaming was to be found in the dreamer's ego, the awake or unconscious bindings. Many people who have worked with dreams for longer periods of time have followed Jung's understanding. The colours observed in a dream are said to have an equivalent meaning. Many of the symbols in dreams can be found in fairy tales and myths. Jeremi Wasiutynski has on this basis interpreted many dreams, and his book *The Cosmic Drama* provides some interesting interpretations. When we try to interpret the people or the symbols that appear in a dream, we should remember that dream symbols can provide some guidance, but only to a certain extent. If we consider what different authors have said about the different dream symbols, we will see that they are fairly vague and inconsistent – and to some extent give quite different interpretations. The conclusion must be that it is impossible to provide a general interpretation of a dream based on the figures, colours, or actions that occur in it. Everything must be interpreted according to the dreamer's situation, culture, feelings and surroundings. The dreamer's personal situation is the essential and the dreamer is always the best dream-interpreter. We can get some help with the interpretation by using associations, which may take the archetypes as a starting point, as well as cultural images and fairy tales. But you are yourself the best interpreter of your dreams.

7.9. Hypnosis and visualization

Lyall Watson believes that hypnosis is one of the best ways for getting in touch with the unconscious and to receive information from it, which would otherwise not be available.[252]

Watson has referred to trials in England and Russia in which subjects are taken back to childhood, and also to the pre-birth period as well as to the time around and even before conception. Performing artists have used hypnosis in their creative work. For example, Rakhmaninov's (1873-1943) second piano concerto was supposedly composed in this way.

However, some people are easily hypnotised, others are not.

Human beings do have paranormal capabilities, although many do not acknowledge this.

Many people are very sensitive. That is, they may know something before it has happened; or they can understand other people or know something about other people before it is clearly stated. Some people have healing abilities. The ability to self-hypnotize (i.e. the ability to reprogram one's own feelings and actions), as well as a strong sensitivity and a good intuition are due to the use of special areas in the mind which most people leave unused. A person with a good intuition is using his or her paranormal ability. I assume that everybody has these capabilities to a greater or lesser extent, although very few know how to use them. Thoughts are important. They can be of significance both for oneself and for others, even if the thinker does not believe that this affects other people. What we have learned about the aura and the body's radiation indicates that thoughts and feelings can be transmitted directly from one mind to another. In literature we read stories about people who become ill and may die as a result of someone else's evil thoughts, although anyone with good mental health is unlikely to be influenced by others' negative thoughts. Occasionally, the unconscious mind may, however, destroy a person's mental health through frightening thoughts – for example in the form of an invisible threatening monster.

Thoughts may also have a positive effect, as noted by the saying 'you can be whatever you want'. Today there are many methods to inspire people to greater confidence, reduce stress, improve memory etc. There are many books available about self-hypnosis and visualization. Most of them tell you to be in a relaxed mood and try to go down into the alpha level of consciousness, to reprogram yourself with something positive, such as to be able to remember better or to get rid of a disease. It is maintained that if you learn to meditate actively, as at this level the mind will be more receptive and easier to control. Positive thinking is most effective at this alpha level. A relaxed mood is best achieved by breathing deeply and slowly while slowly counting down from ten to zero. After a bit of practice this counting alone should be sufficient. Then you are in a state receptive to instructions, such as visualizing the goals you want to reach and to give yourself positively charged sentences (affirmations). In order to achieve success you must practise daily, and you must be intent on performing well and to let go of all the negative thoughts you have about yourself. It is emphasised that you must express abundant joy at the thought that all will be well, as excitement usually is an integral part of these techniques. Different visualization techniques may be used to improve your health and to improve performance in general. Those who are able to bend metal spoons and the like, say that they instil in themselves an altered state of mood and visualize that they enter the material and displace the atoms. The same method is advocated for someone practicing healing, either for themselves or others. According to them you should imagine that you are entering the body or the structure and there try to influence the cells or change the structure of the atoms. For example, you can imagine that cancer cells are attacked by an army of healthy cells and are killed. Lately many different methods for reprogramming the mind have been presented, in order to get away from negative thoughts and obtain more positive attitudes toward life and the environment.

7.10. Memory and morality

Plotinus is supposed to have said that memory has its seat both in that part of the soul that presents itself as the living human being and in that part which has its origin in the All.[253] However, when they separate, each soul part will soon forget that which the other part was concerned with, but maintain the memory of its own part longer. The human related part of the soul will only remember what has happened in this human life. When death occurs, memories from previous lives will slowly arise, as time goes by, while some experiences from the last life will be pushed away as of no concern. Much will disappear into oblivion. Plotinus referred to what he called The Intellectual Principle, which is in the All, both as part of the All and derived from it. The soul is one with this Principle when it is one with the All, without thereby losing its identity. But the soul wants change and removes itself from the All, and thereby receives its own memory. That part of the memory which is associated with what Plotinus called The Intellectual Plane (perhaps the same as the mental plane), seeks to influence the soul so that it remains on that plane; while the part that is associated with the earthly plane, leads the soul down to this level. Plotinus believed that a part of the memory which feels connected to the celestial sphere, binds the soul to this sphere. Whatever the soul keeps strongest in its awareness influences the soul. The consciousness at this level will either be the intuition which is something with which the soul is identifying, or something imagined.

Plotinus mentioned in this regard the following two spheres: the intellectual region and the celestial region. It is firstly in the celestial region that the memory begins to be felt. In this region the soul will be able to recognize other souls it has met before, provided that it remembers these meetings. Plotinus believed that such recognitions would be natural if the souls had bodies that matched the bodies they were in at previous meetings. If not, the recognitions must be based on the soul's character or quality, or on previous thought exchanges. This is the same as Martinus' teaching. Martinus explained inter alia that the memory energy in today's human beings is only instinctively weakly felt, since this energy belongs to the spiritual existence. In some individuals the spiritual levels may, however, be more advanced than that of the vast majority, so that they will remember more.

If a group of people manage to live together, they must have certain rules for conducting their lives. The oldest such rules that we are familiar with are Hammurabi's laws from about 1790 BCE and the Ten Commandments which, according to the Bible, Moses was given by the Lord on Mount Sinai, probably around 1400/1200 BCE. The more complex a society becomes the more complex its laws and regulations will be. A society expects its members to follow the given rules, whether they find them purposeful or not. Often what makes sense to a group as such will not be beneficial for each individual, wishing to keep its freedom intact. Individuals will have different degrees of submission capability and willingness, and the community must therefore have the means to force individuals into submission, although this is not always sufficient to get the strongly ego-centred individual to adapt. Others, however, may have so much respect for their community that they have no trouble following the given directives. And even where there is no given directive, most people clearly understand what is for the community's benefit and are working for it. They acknowledge the community's best interest – they have what is called good morals. Why does someone so easily feel guilty, while others seem to be completely devoid of conscience? I believe all people have the same degree of conscience; the problem is only that some are better than others at suppressing their feelings and thereby also their conscience. I think that the conscience is the soul's spokesperson to the day-awareness. Life is a school where our mission is to constantly learn more and constantly improve our character – not in the way of cleverness, but the degree of love – the capability of compassion. Sooner or later we must take stock of how we have managed this task in this earthly life. This is part of the purpose of the Catholic Church's institution of confession. If we are not able to ease our conscience while we live, we may have trouble later – if there is an existence later where we are conscious and with the memory intact.

As we have seen, there is much which indicates that there is such an existence. Perhaps there is a basic moral attitude in all people, as in all things living, as expressed by Fritjof Capra:[254]

> All larger organisms, including ourselves, are living proof of the fact that destructive practices do not work in the long run. Finally, aggressors will always destroy themselves, and pave the way for others who know how to collaborate and live together.

Without co-operation nothing is achieved. But without seeing and understanding what lies behind other peoples' actions, we cannot collaborate properly.

7.11. Cosmic consciousness, spiritual awakening and visions

All human beings have the potential to have contact with the different consciousness bodies, but it requires long training to get past the lower, tighter structures. You can – if you manage to get past these – reach Unio Mystica. As mentioned before, this is a state of conscious unity with the Divine, or even a consciousness state that gives all knowledge – enlightened consciousness or cosmic consciousness. Some of the great spiritual masters, like Jesus and Buddha, are said to have had such awareness, they would have been permanently in the finer consciousness bodies – in touch with the divine world.

According to Acts, Saul (St Paul) on the road to Damascus experienced that Jesus stood in front of him in the form of a very bright light, and questioned why Saul persecuted him. The experience made Saul blind and he was blind for three days. Saul therefore became an adherent to the Jesus movement and called himself Paul.[i] Francis of Assisi had in 1205 (when he was twenty-four years old) a dream where he was asked to return to Assisi from Spoleto, where he lived, and there await a call to a kind of new type of chivalry. He then began to pray and lived alone, in order to prepare for this call. Many people have had such special experiences, light experiences, which can make such a deep impression that they get a spiritual life view and it changes their personality. Often such an experience is an introduction to the approach to life for which the mystics are especially known. The experience may last only a second, but also longer. It has been maintained that some people may be permanently in such a state.[255] This condition is called *enlightenment*. As mentioned, a lot of people have told of so-called out-of-body experiences and near-death experiences. Sometimes these experiences are closely related to light experiences – perhaps they are actually the same kind of experiences, only that there are differences in the intensity of the experiences.

Sogyal Rinpoche has explained that in every mind there is the essence that the Buddhists call the Buddha-nature.[256] He said that this is the same as that which the Christians and the Jews call God, and the Hindus call the Self or Brahman, Shiva and Vishnu (the three main aspects of the Godhead), or what the Sufis call the 'hidden essence'. The person who has contact with this essence is not affected by death. This essence is the original, the Rigpa, the pure consciousness which is all intelligence, all knowledge, total cognition, always brilliant and awake. All human beings have the possibility to attain this contact; something that Sogyal Rinpoche thought that saints and mystics from every corner of the world have shown is possible. The road to go is meditation, and with that he means the technique which follows his words 'leading the mind home'.

Yogananda explained that when a yogi achieves union with the divine world, or a higher consciousness, his life force will in the beginning be withdrawn from the physical body, which thus seems to be dead. But the yogi is fully conscious of his bodily condition.[257] Yogananda described the

---

i. In chapter 3.10 above I have referred 2 Cor 12.2-4 where St Paul gives a completely different description of the experience.

various stages towards such a divine union. As the yogi obtains contact with the higher spiritual stages, he will be able to hold onto this cosmic consciousness without losing contact with the physical body. Yogananda said that an individual needs about one million years in a normal evolution to achieve cosmic consciousness, but this can be abbreviated by using specific exercises and on-going endeavours. An ordinary human being cannot hold on to the energy which the cosmic consciousness needs, but by careful and regular exercises over a long period of time, the body might be trained in that regard. Yogananda recounted his first, wonderful experience of cosmic consciousness, which lasted for a few seconds. His sense of identity was no longer restricted to the physical body. He was given a spherical vision. He saw everything, even things that were hidden from the physical eyes. He wrote that a celestial glory was emanating from his nucleus to each part of the universal structure.

In the Bible there are many accounts of visions. In The Old Testament we find several descriptions of prophets receiving revelations from God about what is going to happen, or instructions to perform certain actions. In these stories it is normally God who contacts the prophets, without showing him/herself. In The New Testament it is the angels that usually are seen – as the angel Gabriel's visitations to Mary and Joseph. Revelation is probably the most famous Christian vision. Hildegard of Bingen has described her visions and she also painted some of them. She also heard music which she has left on record. She said that she was not in ecstasy when she had these visions, nor in deep meditation or contemplation.[258] Nor were they as dreams during sleep. She felt that she was awake and fully present, with open eyes, and reviewed what she saw carefully with a clear intellect. The visions were in a way illuminated from above. But it was with an inner sight and an inner ear that the visions were received. She also had impressive dreams, partly nightmares, where many people or souls sought her help without her being able to do anything for them. These dreams were very different from the visions.

Muhammad was approximately forty years old (around the year 610) when he had a vision of what he identified as the archangel Gabriel. Gabriel declared that Muhammad was God's messenger or prophet. Later, he regularly had visions, and it is the messages that he received through these visions that have become the Quran.

Padre Pio had many visions while he was in deep prayer. These visions could be voices who talked with him, but also characters whom he could see such as the Virgin and Jesus. He saw Jesus at the last supper or in the Garden at Gethsemane or on the cross. Padre Pio has explained that it was not possible to fully explain the visions because language is too limited. After each vision, he felt a tremendous amount of joy, and he felt an ever stronger desire to come closer to God and serve God. However, he also often met demons in these visions.

Edgar Cayce was in a trance when he gave his *readings*. Also many mediums who perform channelling usually do this in trance. They remember nothing of what is said or done while they are in this trance state. The same is true in many cases of the shaman's trance states, although these can often recount their travels in the spiritual world when they are back in a normal mental state. These kinds of trance states are not necessarily providing contact with the higher spiritual worlds, or give any experience of unity with the Divine.

Plotinus is supposed to have experienced Unio Mystica many times.[259] He explained that he felt himself lifted out of the body so that he felt outside of everything, but still centred in himself. He experienced an incredible beauty and felt unity with the Divine. However, he could not stay for long in this state, so he had to come down from this supreme existence of consciousness to normal consciousness or thinking. And he had to ask himself how the soul, which obviously is somewhat elevated, could come down into the body again.

Here he referred to Heraclitus and Empedocles who both explained almost the same, but he said that it is Plato that best describes this, although he believed that it is not easy to understand Plato at this point (he did not elaborate further on what Plato had written)[i].

The experiences of Stanislav Grof's patients or clients can be considered as a sort of trance condition, at least as a different type of consciousness state than the one we are in during our daily activities. Some had mystical experiences or ecstasies without losing touch with what was happening around them. Stan Gooch, who had a mystical experience when he was channelling in a trance state, mentioned, however, that what is typical of such an experience is that you lose your sense of orientation and the ability to be active for a shorter or longer period of time.[260] You feel that your awareness is expanded; you experience a strong light and have contact with some sort of spiritual existence. Many people develop paranormal abilities, such as the ability to heal others, clairvoyance and precognition, or have paranormal experiences. Such experiences are reported from many countries and religious societies. Stan Gooch had this experience when he was in his twenties. Later, he experienced so-called *lucid dreams* (dreams where you are aware that you are dreaming), which he considered as hallucinations (which may include sight, hearing and smell). He believed that such

---

i. In the book *The Republic*, part 10, Plato wrote about the near-death experience of the soldier Er. He there describes the souls' experiences in the 'other world'. When the souls were returning to Earth and had prepared themselves for this return, and had chosen the life they would live, they came to the River of forgetfulness. Depending on how much they drank of the water in that river, they forgot what they had experienced and fell asleep. Suddenly, they experienced thunder and earthquakes, and were led away to the point where they were to be reborn as if they were shooting stars. Er, who was destined to come back to Earth and tell about his experiences, could not understand how he came back to his body, as he suddenly woke up at the pyre. He had then been 'dead' 11 days.

experiences cannot be construed to be more than subjective experiences, which provide a more direct access to the subconscious and its magic world. For example, he mentioned that one morning early his room was for a short time brilliantly lit by a kind of light beam that came out of a hole in the wall. He emphasised strongly that such experiences must not be given importance at the expense of the objective reality in which we live, and to which we need to relate. But the subconscious must be taken into consideration and can be used constructively for anyone who accepts that its reality must be equal to the objective reality.

Huston Smith has written the following about the teaching of the Sufis:[261]

> In order to avoid separation from Allah the Sufis have designed the teaching of *fana* (annihilation). They did not believe that it was their consciousness that would be annihilated; it was their self-consciousness – their consciousness of themselves as a distinct self, filled by private, personal purposes – that would be brought to a close. If the termination was complete, they would not find anything of themselves when they looked into the empty shells of their selves which now were emptied. They would only find God.

As mentioned previously, Walter T. Stace has described what mysticism is, and has referred to the experiences of various mystics. His starting point was the mystical experience or consciousness state, and he explained that this is a non-intellectual open consciousness state. The typical of such an open consciousness state is that it does not contain any form of thoughts, visions, sensing or hallucinations. The condition cannot be described properly with words. Stace pointed out that even if the mystical experience is described differently by the mystics around the world and from different denominations, there are certain characteristics which are common to all these descriptions. The most essential with those experiences, which all fully developed mystics are in agreement on, is that you gain the understanding that everything is one; it is a non-dual existence that cannot be acknowledged with the usual senses or explained with words, thought or sense. Stace quotes a description given in the *Mandukya Upanishad*:

> Mandukya says that it (the inward-looking mystical consciousness) is "beyond the senses, beyond understanding, beyond all expression. ... It is the pure unitarily consciousness, where the consciousness of the world and about the diversity is completely eradicated. It is infinite peace. It is the Maximum Good. It is One without a second. It is the Self."

Stace stressed that he had cited a Hindu source, but Christian mystics have given exactly the same description, and he mentioned the great Flemish mystic Jan van Ruysbroek (1293-1381) as an example. He wrote in this regard that this shows that people in different cultures have the same experience, but that the description of it will depend on the culture of the individual. Christian mystics explain the experience with the Christian notion of God and the teachings about the Trinity; the Muslims explain it by using the Quran's teaching about God or Allah; while the Hindus explain it with the doctrine of the impersonal Absolute, and the Buddhists explain it with Nirvana. They all agree that the experience gives a sense of peace, blessing and joy.

Evelyn Underhill stressed that the true mystics are active and practical, not passive and theoretical in their behaviour.[262] This is not an intellectual attitude. The mystic's goal is purely transcendental and spiritual, and it is the heart and not the intellect that governs the mind. The object of the heart's feelings is the unchanging ONE. This One is not just the 'One reality' consisting of everything there is, but also a living, personal object of love. To live in communion with this One is a clear condition or type of exalted life. It is only through a demanding psychological and spiritual process – the so-called mystical way, which means a total change of character – that you reach this state. Underhill pointed out that the mystical life has nothing to do with occult knowledge, it is not a philosophy, nor a religious belief, and has nothing to do with religious doctrines. It is an organic process that involves a total consummation in God's love, or a deliberate contact with the Absolute. She stressed that the purpose and the method of the mystics is Love, which is the true, pure, generous love, not the superfluous devotion or emotion which often is termed love. In this connection we should remember St Paul's description of true love as that which can sustain everything. Jes Bertelsen has written about the spiritual evolutionary road from the ordinary everyday consciousness state and to the state which the advanced mystics have described.[263] He mentioned that all the major religions' esoteric kernel uses the same basic training, and that anyone who seeks to enter the spiritual path, must go through the same seven stages.

7.12. Thoughts

Professor Olav Hilmar Iversen wrote in 1994 that we do not understand the connection between the body and the soul.[264] Although we know that the central nervous system works by the use of electrical impulses and chemical transmission of substances, we do not understand how this leads to thought activity and experiences. Nothing in the physical body, such as molecules, cells and substances is stable, while the 'I'-experience or the personality, however, is quite stable. Brain researcher Per Andersen (b.1930), professor at Oslo University, has, in an article from 2001, stated that there is no other way to understand consciousness than as a result of electrical impulses in the brain, and that there must be a neurobiological explanation of what consciousness is and how it comes into being.[265] Both the sensory impressions and the subjective feelings he thought were encoded in the brain cells. He pointed out that the brain consists of fifty-billion cells which are in continuous activity. These are programmed differently, all based on humanity's and the individual's experience. The researchers can see which area of the brain is activated by a specific type of sensing or thinking. All human behaviour and thought activity he believed could be attributed to the work of the brain cells. Professor of mathematics Roger Penrose (b.1931), England, however, has pointed out that a computer never will be able to act as a human being, even if it is possible to program it to communicate like a human being. See his book *The Emperor's New Mind*.

In the book *Irreducible Mind – toward a Psychology for the 21st Century* Kelly et al review most of the known documentation and research regarding paranormal phenomena.

In this connection they refer to the different theories presented by a series of prominent researchers regarding the correlation between brain and mind. But no theory has so far been put forward that satisfactorily answers their questions, although they very strongly emphasize Frederick W.H. Myers' research and thoughts which were presented at the end of the nineteenth century. Myers was intensely interested in paranormal phenomena. Also highlighted in this book is the American psychologist and philosopher William James (1842-1910), who is considered one of the foremost thinkers of the Western world, and who was a strong admirer of Myers' way of thinking in this area. It is highly regrettable that these two geniuses have been largely ignored by psychologists in the twentieth century. The authors' conclusion is the same as the one Olav Hilmar Iversen presented in his time, namely that we do not yet understand how the mind works. They suggest that the mind is, in a way, acting 'outside' of the brain, such as we at present understand how the brain is working. But it requires a lot more research – and research that is willing to consider paranormal and metaphysical questions compared with what so far has been the case in the field of psychology, to find, if it is possible, the final answers to the question of what the mind is.[266]

Seth has said that the brain is a meeting point of electromagnetic relations that we do not understand. These can be compared to a controlled storm, where there is a continuous exchange of energy between the brain and its environment.[267] He explained that people react not only to the weather; they are actually participating in forming it, as both emotions and thoughts have unstable electromagnetic potentials. (This explains the phenomenon of the rain-dance.) By simply breathing air and sending air out again, individuals affect their environment. Seth said that thoughts have a structure similar to cells. They react to stimuli and organize themselves. They flourish on associations, that is, they attract other thoughts that are similar to themselves – and they repel thoughts that are threatening to their own existence. The human beings' problems, to a large extent, are due to the fact that they do not accept responsibility for what they are thinking. The mental life and the emotional life give a frame that affects cells in the body. The consciousness can change beliefs and also largely the bodily experiences if the person in question is sensitive enough. Seth mentioned that human beings are on the Earth in order to expand their consciousness by creative thinking.

Martinus explained that experience is the same as consciousness. Experience is movement. It is a living being's desire for change that creates movement.[268] Movement is thus an expression of life, or a result of will and intelligence. Desires for change result in ideas on how you want things to be. All of an individual's thoughts and ideas present themselves on the spiritual plane, and are there just as real as physical objects are on the earthly plane. He said that what an individual is thinking or doing through the day-consciousness, which is the seat of the will, will have impact on its future welfare – both bodily and spiritual, either in this life or in one coming later. He used the term cosmic chemistry on the actions and reactions that arise as a result of human thoughts and actions. He compared this with the meteorological climate of the Earth. He mentioned that the living entity is living between two heavens, one internal or spiritual and one outer, physical heaven. It is the individuals who are creating all the clouds, air currents and atmosphere in the interior world, while the macro entity or the Earth (Gaia) directly and indirectly is creating the earthly meteorological climate. The living entities must work to create harmony between the interior world and the earthly world.

Deepak Chopra has argued that some researchers now have reached the conclusion that every cell in the body thinks and acts like a mind.[269] The mind is not restricted to the brain, it works everywhere in the body. In the right mood, you can get the body to produce the kind of molecules you need. He agreed with those researchers and maintained further that the mind is non-local and resides anywhere in time and space. He suggested that maybe it is the consciousness that creates the physical body; not that the physical molecules are there first. He asked whether a human being can rather be considered an intelligence field which has its source in the same unit that is the origin of the stars and the galaxies, but that we have forgotten this origin. (This is presumably the same as Ervin Laszlo has explained with what he called the psi field.)

Professor Roger D. Nelson at Princeton University, New Jersey, USA, has along with a research group placed special measuring apparatus at various sites around the world (The Global Consciousness Project).[270] The machines generate continuously random numbers of zero and one. The distribution of those numbers are mostly located within the normal statistical expectation when one looks at the curve in the main machine in Princeton resulting from the data from all the machines, to which it is connected. But a couple of times this curve has given abnormal results. A very odd result occurred 11th September 2001 and the subsequent days. Another abnormal result occurred on 4th March 1999 when NATO began bombing in Yugoslavia. The same research group has also checked the weather in Princeton on the 4th May for the last 50 years, the day on which the University holds its annual outdoor anniversary party. It turns out that it rarely rains in Princeton on this day. In the chapter on the aura, I have described trials made at Princeton University by professor Robert G. Jahn et al regarding psychokinesis. The mind has obviously a tremendous amount of mental energy. Was it the enthusiasm of the Norwegian population that contributed (or was the cause) to the good weather which was so amazingly nice just during the fourteen days of the Olympic Games at Lillehammer in Norway in 1994?

A curious phenomenon often occurring in parapsychological research is what the psychologists call the goat/sheep phenomenon. 'Sheep' is the designation given to trial leaders who believe that paranormal phenomena occur, while the term 'goat' refers to those who do not believe. In repeated laboratory experiments the sheep often get positive results in the direction of verifying the paranormal phenomena, while the goats on the contrary often get negative results. This is startling, for if only coincidence was the determining factor, the result should be zero. It indicates that the trial leader's consciousness in some way affects the outcome.[271]

In this context, I offer a thought I had after a TV program about birds on the Galapagos Islands. Some finches were blown to an isolated island, from which they did not escape. After a dry period they were no longer able to find the kind of food they were accustomed to eating. What was available were nuts, but the ordinary finch beak was unable to penetrate these nuts. After some time the finches developed a much tougher beak, and they then continued to eat these nuts even when they could find other food. With reference to Darwin's doctrine, it was suggested that it was the birds that basically had the toughest beaks who survived the drought period, and that was why the beaks had become tougher. I wonder if this is correct. Perhaps it was the birds' consciousness that saw the need for coarser tools, and thereby caused the genetic blueprint for the bird's beak to change. Maybe that is how evolution actually takes place, given that all existence is due to consciousness, as is maintained by the mystics. Ervin Laszlo has maintained that scientists now doubt whether everything is controlled by genes and only by genes. He has pointed to the well-known Russian biologist Lev Beloussov's view of genes as obedient servants who carry messages from the whole organism. Laszlo wrote that an increasing number of biologists consider the living organism as a macroscopic quantum system.[272]

Lyall Watson believes that all kinds of supernatural or unexpected phenomena, such as UFO experiences, spirit possession and reincarnation can be explained as the amazing abilities of the mind.[273] He considers that hypnosis has shown that the unconscious part of the mind has a vast, seemingly limitless capacity to gather and structure information. The unconscious has access to material stored in our genetic code, in the pre- and post-natal experiences, and in the collective unconscious. And Watson assumes that human minds can get in touch with each other over great distances, without any known physical connection. This is confirmed by the reports Stanislav Grof has received from his clients, as well as by the theories about the holographic universe and the psi field.

Ken Wilber wrote that both time and space are factors that consciousness has created, although he denied that matter exists only in our consciousness.[274]

The American author Gary Zukav (b.1942) has explained that the quantum physicists have posed the question: did anything exist before anyone thought of measuring it.[275] There will always be an observer behind any observation. Did the researchers unconsciously create the articles with which they were experimenting? If all observations depend on the observer, will we ever be able to understand reality or understand what is happening? We are also so incomprehensibly small in an unimaginable universe.

Thought is the constructor, according to Edgar Cayce.[276] The mind has a tremendous capacity. If we could acknowledge that our thoughts affect our surroundings; if we could learn to make full use of our intuition; if we could accept that dreams have something to tell us, as they are bringing daylight into that which takes place in the subconscious; and if we could learn to exploit our waking-dreams; then we would be as open to each other as if we were watching a movie. We could not then hide ourselves from others. We would have to present ourselves as we actually are. We might be better able to understand ourselves and others would relate to the person we actually are and not to the one they think we are. There is then no longer any use in lying or pretending. *Then we could talk to each other with the heart.*

7.13. Who is thinking?

Deepak Chopra once said that researchers have not been able to answer the question: where is the source of our decisions, where are they made.[277] They can only answer the question where in the brain the decisions are made. This indicates that it is not the brain that is thinking. The brain is only a body for thinking and for collecting our experiences and emotions. But where is the decision-maker – that which I perceive as 'I'? Deepak Chopra responded by saying that the decision-maker is everywhere and nowhere. That is, each human being is everywhere and nowhere. We are not limited to the physical body. Are we then limited to an 'I'? Who else is behind what is happening just to me? To be able to answer that question, I think we have to acknowledge that the existence builds on a community within a society within another society etc. I am a part of a larger community, both physically and spiritually and I am made up of smaller similar societies. My everyday consciousness is only aware of just a small bit of the totality of which I am a part.

Sogyal Rinpoche has said that life and death is in the consciousness and nowhere else.[278] He said that consciousness consists of many hues. Part of the consciousness is the one who thinks, wants, has feelings and emotions, incessantly shifting and continuously affected by external impression. This part experiences changes and death. Another part is the consciousness' real nature, its innermost essence, which is untouched by change and death. This is often called also the pure consciousness. It remains, however, unnoticed because the thoughts and feelings completely dominate the picture, except maybe in the short flash of inspiration or in a sense of something divine.

Colin Wilson has pointed out that people need to concentrate on the everyday issues in order to tackle them.[279] They are thereby limiting their awareness and thereby also their vitality. By such focusing, everything else becomes less visible; that is, we are losing the understanding of the meaning of life. Because so much needs our attention, our concentration is reduced. We get digestive problems that can be sufficient to give us a sense of pointlessness. Wilson said, however, that if we can muster all our attention and focus on one single subject or idea, we will experience a special increase of inner power, similar to the way in which a laser beam builds up strength by being reflected from one mirror to another. We will eventually be able to focus on things that usually leave us unmoved, and understand their inner meaning. Perhaps it is such concentration that makes healing work?

Consciousness can be controlled by others through hypnosis and by electrical impulses.

Researchers have shown that schizophrenic individuals who hear voices are actually hearing their own thoughts or subconsciousness in the same way as other people hear voices and sounds that clearly are coming from the outside. This is because the impulses are received by the hearing organs and passed on in the same way as they would with actual sound. It is also proven that by stimulating specific areas of the brain with electrical impulses, hallucinations such as dreams, images, memories and pain could be induced. We understand only what we let our sensory apparatus understand or what our consciousness is programmed to understand. We see colours only because our visual nerves split light in a certain way.

The most important consciousness level for today's people is the level of higher consciousness, the super consciousness – also known as the Self. The Self is an unconscious force which my ego can access. The Self transcends the ego, however, which means that my personal identity (the ego) is part of the Self. The Self is aware of a much larger part of the totality. We can get in touch with the Self, as the saints' mystical experiences show us; but most people are not able to get this far, mainly because they do not know that they have a super consciousness. To me it seems that it is the Self that is the director, who arranges the play and engages other players (these are other people who need to have their special experiences, but for reasons other than mine) so that the Self through the ego can have its special experiences. The ego, however, has its free will, and does not have to listen to the Self. If it chooses not to, the ego will be going no further in its development and will often face the same problems over and over again. However, there is much that indicates that help will sometimes come from somewhere. That is, there must be some powers – powers that I will designate as helpers – which are in cooperation with the Self about the education of the ego. *Katha Upanishad* explains the human being in this way:[280]

> Know the Atman (the essence of the soul) as Lord of a chariot; and the body as the chariot itself. Know that reason is the charioteer; and the mind indeed is the reins. The horses, they say, are the senses; and their paths are the objects of sense. When the soul becomes one with the mind and the senses he is called 'one who has joys and sorrows'.
> ...
> The man whose chariot is driven by reason, who watches and holds the reins of his mind, reaches the End of the journey, the supreme everlasting Spirit. Beyond the Spirit in man is the Spirit of the universe, and beyond is Purusha, the Spirit Supreme. Nothing is beyond Purusha: He is the End of the path. The light of Atman, the Spirit, is invisible, concealed in all beings. It is seen by the seers of the subtle, when their vision is keen and clear. The wise should surrender speech in mind, mind in the knowing self, the knowing self in the Spirit of the universe, and the Spirit of the universe in the Spirit of peace. ...
>
> The Atman is beyond sound and form, without touch and taste and perfume. It is eternal, unchangeable, and without beginning or end; indeed above reasoning. When consciousness of the Atman manifests itself, man becomes free from the jaws of death.

Deepak Chopra has said that you will be in a blessed condition if you experience being in contact with Atman.[281] This condition does not have any particular cause. You then experience life as if both the body and the Universe are inside you and not that the Universe is outside of you. It removes all illusions about death as a cessation of existence. For most people, I believe, it must be sufficient to stick to common sense and try to acquire wisdom. Not everyone is destined to be either a saint or a yogi but in order to have contact with wisdom, you must master your emotions, and you must work to develop the love ability – which is unselfishness. Then the sorrows and worries will have no control over the mind, and you will learn to see that life has meaning.

7.14. The holotropic consciousness

Stanislav Grof has, as mentioned above, for many years been researching anomalous consciousness states in human beings. Such states of consciousness are conditions which are often characterised by strong emotions, curious thought activity or behaviour, or other psychosomatic reactions. However, some such states have therapeutic significance and also what he calls heuristic meaning – something that can bring the person in question to new knowledge through independent thinking. These conditions he calls holotropic states. The specificity of them, in relation to delirium and similar trauma, is that the person does not lose their senses. They will have their normal mental functions intact.

Michael Talbot suggested that if the human body is holographic, then we are all in a way the Universe in miniature. (This was also Gurdjieff's teachings.[282]) This theory may explain the otherwise inexplicable phenomena such as miracles, synchronicity and much more. He pointed to David Bohm's suggestion that consciousness has its source in the implicate order. This must mean that both the human mind and the holographic preservation of everything that has happened are in the same domain. That is, if you can open your mind for impressions from the paranormal, everything from the past will be available – both in terms of vision, hearing, smell and sensing. It explains everything from déjà vu experiences to clairvoyance – and perhaps also what many people experience as memories from their past lives in the so-called reincarnation experiences. That explains what many psychics say about how they experience information from the past – in many cases it is as if they are ensconced in a scene where the actions take place all around them.

So the question is how is this theory in accordance with the mystics' teaching about the different levels of consciousness and the various consciousness bodies. If we return to Ken Wilber's *Great Chain of Being*, and his theory of the different *fulcrums* (stages in the consciousness development) and the individual's spiritual development (to the mental and spiritual level, and more) and compare this with Stanislav Grof's experiences, then the stories reported by Grof can be explained in this way – you are sending a beam into – or projecting a part of yourself into – a higher plane of consciousness or into a holographic domain. You do not have to have your consciousness rooted in such a plane to have such experiences – only some advanced mystics can do that. How far you are able to go – or for how long you can be on this higher level – will vary. On the highest plane you will be experiencing unity with the All. At a lower level, such as the astral plane, you may encounter other peoples' astral bodies and thereby understand their thoughts and stories.

7.15. The human being's spirit and soul

Rudolf Steiner has said that Jesus' coming to the Earth gave the impulse so that man could evolve from having a group spirit to be an individual soul, that is to have an 'I' or a Self.[283] Jes Bertelsen has also explained something similar. In certain circles of mystics it has been maintained that animals have no individual soul, only a group soul. They will therefore not appear as individual beings in a non-earthly existence. Philosophers have thought and written extensively about the concept of the soul, what it is and where in the human being it is located. An understanding of the term is intertwined with what we understand as consciousness, and is essential if we wish to be able to accept that there is an existence after the physical death. In that case, there must be something, what we usually call the soul, which has a continuing existence. Some, philosophers among others, term this unit the monad. Ambres called it 'the Rider'. Martinus used the term the 'living entity'. For many, it is natural to use the term soul on this entity, while others may want to reserve that word for something else. The soul is of a somewhat finer structure than what many term the Self, while the Spirit is of an even higher and more refined structure.

It is maintained that anyone who has consciousness in the Self, will not die – that is, they will retain consciousness through the physical death. But it also means that they then are not attached to the personality and the material world, nor do they have bindings such as most people have to the material world. We all know that physical units are made up of smaller units; and that atoms become molecules, which develop to cells, which develop to the bodies which are all of the plants, insects, fish, and all amphibious and animal species that we see on the Earth today. These species joins in groups, which for the human beings become families, communities, cities, countries and states. Does each of these units have a soul? We say that a country or a city has character, but does it also have a soul? In all types of co-operation there must be decision-making organs or entities – does that also exist in the individual human being? A city or a country disintegrates if its people are expelled or perish, or the decision making powers disappear. Is this true also for the individual human being or animal, or is there something else for the collection of cells that we call a living creature? I will now take look at what the mystics have said about the soul and how it is described by some of those.

The ancient Egyptians had the concept *ka* and *ba*. Olav O. Aukrust described these terms as follows:[284]

> *Ka* is the divine life force that is the origin of all life.
>
> ... The human being brings his *ka* with him at birth. *Ka* represents both the ancestors, which brings the force of life, and the descendants, who are continuing life. ... The *ka* of the Egyptians reminds us of the Greeks' heroes and the Latin genius. ... *Ka* is everything that makes life, and is also present in all types of nutrition. ... Both gods and humans have their Ka. Steindorff saw in Ka a guardian angel, like the Latin genius. Erman considered it as the personified vitality. ... The *Ka* term is too wide and fluid to be defined. Ka cannot be described as a special force; it is a bodily entity similar to the human being in form and growth and takes part in the individual's development phases. When the body dies, the *Ka* does not change; but *Ka* is like an immortal part placed in an individual.

Ba may be defined as the human soul as the closest, although that is not completely adequate according to Aukrust:

> ... From being a revelation of various powerful beings, Ba is now becoming an 'entity' closely related to the human being and its fate, an entity that preserves the strength of the dead, when it is "coming out of their flesh's fluids", as a group of texts from The Middle Kingdom express it.

Nothing which is composed consists of life itself, said Plotinus.[285] That which gives something life, he called the soul. He explained further that there is no living body without a soul. It must therefore be two components, body *and* soul. Actually there is only one soul – the All. There are, however, smaller and smaller beings, because a part of the One Soul sheds more and more of itself. It is constantly being divided into smaller units. When a soul removes itself from the All and experiences itself as separate from the All, it becomes a part and forgets the whole. When a soul wants to individualize itself away from The One, it becomes a Self in Time, away from the Eternal. When it is in the Eternal, it knows everything and does not need a memory. Memory occurs with the individuality, either in the spiritual realm or on the Earth. What it recalls, is whatever it wishes to identify with. The soul is thereby not without connection to the All; it still belongs to the All, but is a minute part of it. And in the All everything is known – there is no need for any individual memory there. Wisdom is to acknowledge this. Furthermore, you have to look in the opposite direction from the body to see the soul. No living creature will ever cease to exist, but many individuals may be incarnations of the same soul. That is, a physical person is not necessarily one individual soul.

Master Eckhart also saw the human being as two-fold, that it consists respectively of all the things we see as a normal human being as the one part and the soul as the other part.[286] When it comes to what we see of a human being, we see what Eckhart called the outer human being, which is what we perceive with the five regular senses (sight, hearing, smell, taste and touch), as well as the three lower soul forces (these are the lower intellect, desire and anger). Then, in addition, comes what he termed the inner human being, consisting of the three higher soul forces (memory, the higher intellect and the will). As regards the soul, Eckhart often used the term the very inner human being. He also called this the soul's base. It cannot be acknowledged in a reflective, thematic sense. When you are in contact with the soul, the mind rests in itself, where everything pertaining to the common human being is omitted. That is, it is an altered consciousness state or ecstasy. In an ecstasy the mind has no sense of the body; you are without thought, without sense of space or time. But there is a vigilant awareness. You are nothing. But where nothing is, there the God consciousness can come in. Eckhart called this "the birth of God in the human being's soul".

The German philosopher G.W. Leibniz (1645-1716), who first introduced the concept of the monad about the innermost unit in each creature, had a philosophy about this which is close to what the mystics explained. The following description is taken from Carl Grimberg's history books:[287]

> Leibniz's philosophy is especially known for the theory of the monad, a word of Greek origin, meaning unit. "These monads are nature's real atoms", he writes, "and shortly said, the thing's elements." But they are not atoms in our normal use of the word, for their behaviour is like an active force. As a result, they do not receive impressions from the outside: the monad has no windows." Each monad is a small world, a micro-cosmos mirroring the entire Universe. But each monad reflects the totality of the world differently "because nature cannot make two beings that are fully identical". Not even two blades or two hairs are exactly the same. Nature never repeats itself.
>
> Between the monads, there is no essential difference, only a degree of difference. The highest monad is God. To Him alone it is given to have clear and distinct ideas. But below Him there are monads of higher and lower degrees of perfection. God created them all, so that their imaginative worlds match each other, but they differ from each other by the degree of clarity and distinction with which they sense the universe. The lowest standing monads have only a vague and unconscious imagination. They spend their lives as in a dream. If a monad raises itself up so that it has conscious ideas and common sense, it has earned the designation *soul*. And if its ability to perceive is expanded to self-awareness and common sense, it becomes a *spirit*. The spirits are in a conscious fellowship with God. In this endless chain of monads, there is a continuing transition from the lower to the higher, for as little as nature repeats itself, it does sometimes make leaps. It is the development idea Leibniz is anticipating here.
>
> The human organism is made up of a ruling soul monad, surrounded by a complex of lower, serving monads. A person's death does not mean destruction, only that the connection between spiritual and bodily monads dissolves.
>
> This in brief is the major content of Leibniz's peculiar monad teaching, which has been characterised as "a mathematician's dream" or as "a draft of an ingenious engineer who is planning a universal computer".

Martinus has said that a being's spirit is the 'I' and its thought world.[288] This is the same as the individual's consciousness, and the consequential psychological state constitutes its psyche. This spirit exists in the being's superconsciousness. He said further that it is this spirit that makes an organism alive and which is the origin of the brain and of all the body's organisms. This is the 'something' that is behind the phrase that "I go", "I am doing this and I am doing that". When the spirit leaves the physical body, the body will remain like a corpse and disintegrate – a body without spirit. The

'I' can, however, leave the body without completely disrupting the connection; the body is then sleeping or is unconscious for some other reasons.

The being is immortal, although it is undergoing development and reincarnation. All beings exist as 'something of God'. It is the being's spirit that creates the appropriate matter for the different bodily organs, such as vision, hearing, heart, lung etc., through which the being can manifest itself and meet the physical world. To believe that there is no creator behind the created, whether on the micro level, in the world of the human beings, as a cosmos in between, or at the macro level, is like believing that whatever the human beings have created by the use of their intellect, are not generated by them, but by coincidence. The being must, however, be developed from the deepest darkness to existence's lightest and most delightful level. It has to go through all good and evil – nothing human should be unknown. It must learn the difference between good and evil, and must learn to understand that only by being in compliance with the Universe's basic principle, which is charity, will it be able to approach the light. This is why Martinus said that everything in our destiny that deviates from this basic principle is due solely to our own being, and that our own Self or the 'I' is the real cause behind every event. But the being is unable to understand more than what it has experienced, and must therefore undergo a series of experiences, so that the soul will be formed and shaped, and make what Martinus called the experience and talent cores.

Ken Wilber explained it in this way:[289]

> So the Vedanta version of five sheaths is almost identical to the Judeo/Christian/Muslim version of matter, body, mind, soul, and spirit, as long as we understand 'soul' to mean, not just a higher self or higher identity, but higher or subtler mind and cognition. And soul also has the meaning, in *all* the higher mystical traditions, of being a 'knot' or 'contraction' (what the Hindus and Buddhists call the ahamkara), which has to be untied and dissolved before the soul can transcend itself, die to itself, and thus find a supreme identity with and as absolute Spirit (as Christ said, "He cannot be a true disciple who hateth not his own soul").
>
> So 'soul' is both the highest level of individual growth we can achieve, and also the final barrier, the final knot, to complete enlightenment or supreme identity, simply because as transcendental witness it stands back from everything it witnesses. Once we push through the witness position, then the soul or witness itself dissolves and there is only the play of non-dual awareness, awareness that does not look at objects but is completely one with all objects (Zen says "it is like tasting the sky"). The gap between subject and object collapses, the soul is transcended or dissolved; and pure spiritual or non-dual awareness – which is very simple, very obvious, very clear – arises. You realize that your intrinsic being is vast and open, empty and clear, and everything arising anywhere is arising within you, as intrinsic spirit, spontaneously.

The Czech professor Milan Ryzl (1928-2011), a parapsychologist with a doctorate in physics and chemistry and professor at the University of California from 1967, said in a lecture in 1997 entitled *The Quest for Recognition of the higher Dimensions and a different World* that he is convinced that modern parapsychological research (in particular the tests regarding ESP – extra sensory perception) has verified the existence of a non-material reality outside time and space, so that our physical world is not the only one.[290] He thought that both worlds exist in parallel and are complementing each other. He referred in this context to the understanding of our physical universe that researchers have now reached: A complicated swirl of force fields that penetrate each other, and that in regard to space have no clear borders. He presented the following hypothetical model about what reality actually is:

> The material world in space and time
>
> The non- material (spiritual) world *without* space and time
>
> The hypothetical connecting joint, which enables their alternating effect.

Ryzl believed that the properties of ESP are part of the spiritual world that can be considered as a special human sense. He believed ESP works in two phases. In the first phase the transferred information will be received in the subconsciousness of the recipient. In the second phase this information will be acknowledged, either by a motor reaction or through dreams, visions or other senses such as hearing. Depending on the recipient's mental state and other psychological factors, such as desires, thoughts and parapsychological abilities, the message is clearly received, as a dream, or vision or something similar which is difficult to interpret. Often the message or experience is difficult to decipher because of our limited experience and linguistic constraint. Often the spiritual experience happens during a trance, which might be received during prayer or meditation. He thought that experiences that are portrayed by mystics and spiritual adepts have confirmed this understanding. He pointed out that in traditional understanding human beings are composed as follows:

> The material body (which is in time and space)
>
> The soul (which is a conveying component) – the life energy
>
> The spirit (the divine inspiration) – the divine spark in the human being

He then said the following:

> When we understand spirit as something that is raised beyond time (or is timeless), it cannot simply possess our well-known consciousness, as this 'linear consciousness' runs through time as thinking consists of a sequence of individual awareness and thoughts in time.

I find that the ancient Egyptians were not so far removed from what I experience as reality. For me, there is sufficient evidential material presented so I feel I am right when saying that there must be an existence beyond the physical: and that people can acquire skills that are difficult to accept by those who do not comprehend this. However, as we have seen from what is referred to in this book, there is much that speaks for the existence of one or more spirit worlds – which will be further clarified when we learn more about what the mystics and other special people say about what happens when we leave the physical life.

Let me recapitulate: Human beings have a physical body. It changes all the time with cells that grow, die or change but it consists of genetic material that has the ability to renew itself, such as a salamander can make a bone or grow a tail and be whole after it has been torn off. The problem for human beings is that we are not mentally in contact with this genetic factory (although may be some people are). We need the physical body in order to be able to live in the physical reality but we do not need this body to exist in a spiritual world. Moreover, the human beings have an etheric body, an etheric energy or etheric consciousness. This controls the life energy and the sexuality. These forces are also called Eros. We often see that the stronger the life energy, the stronger the sex drive and the desire for dominance. However, these forces can also be controlled mentally in a direction that does not cause the individual to dominate other individuals. We can observe that people on a high spiritual level have in a way managed to tame these forces so they may be utilised in a spiritual direction. The life energy is a necessity in the physical reality in order to meet physical challenges. The sexual drive is necessary for the physical reproduction, but this is part of the life energy and can be channelled and transformed into a life quality and a spiritual energy, which the life of the mystics has affirmed. Those *who wish* to obtain spiritual consciousness will seek the life of the hermit, and most will live sexually abstinent. The mental body is composed of the lower mental or astral energy, and the higher mental energy. The former gives us dreams, fantasies, creative skills – all that which help us to survive in the physical world, but which are not necessary in a spiritual existence. The higher mental energy is the energy of the thoughts, the heart and the intuition. Here we find the memory. If there is something that should be transferred to a spiritual existence from a physical existence with the law of karma as background, it ought to be this energy. In my judgment, there must be this energy which the monad or soul takes with it into a spiritual world, if a spiritual existence is of any purpose.

However as we have seen above, everything exists as part of something greater. This must also apply to the individual human being, who is not only part of a family, a city, a country, a world, but who also must be part of a larger entity. The Earth is part of the Universe. If everything is consciousness, then the human beings must have a consciousness in common, the Earth must have a consciousness and the Universe must have a consciousness. Some mystics think that the spirit of a human being is part of a spirit being, which in turn is part of a higher spirit being. In the book *Talking with Angels* seven persons per one spirit being is mentioned, who in turn is one of seven beings controlled by a higher spirit being, and so on indefinitely (see figure 10). Here there is a split – an increasing physical concentration downwards and increasing spirituality upwards, to infinity. This is not easy to understand – and my 'I' becomes very insignificant in this context. Maybe my 'Self' is the second level on this spiritual scale but then what is my Self? The *Upanishads* provide a clarifying description of the human mind, soul and spirit. The following is from *Maitri Upanishad*:[291]

> Since the body is like a chariot without consciousness, who is the Spirit who has the power to make it conscious? Who is the driver of the chariot? ...
>
> There is a spirit who is amongst the things of this world and yet he is above the things of this world. He is clear and pure, in the peace of a void of vastness. He is beyond the life of the body and the mind, never-born, never-dying, everlasting, ever ONE in his greatness. He is the Spirit whose power gives consciousness to the body; he is the driver of the chariot. ... Master, how does this pure Being give consciousness to the unconscious body? How is he the driver of the chariot? ...
>
> Even as a man who is asleep awakes, but when he is asleep does not know that he is going to awake, so a part of the subtle invisible Spirit comes as a messenger to the body without the body being conscious of his arrival.
>
> A part of Infinite consciousness becomes our own finite consciousness with powers of discrimination and definition, and with false conceptions. He is in truth Prajapati and Visva, the Source of creation and the Universal in us all.
>
> The Spirit is consciousness and gives consciousness to the body: he is the driver of the chariot.
>
> The poets say this is the Spirit who wanders on this Earth from body to body, free from the light and darkness which follow our works. He is free because he is free from selfishness, and he is invisible, incomprehensible, hidden in darkness. He seems to work and not to be; but in truth He works not, and he is. He is in his own Being, pure, never-changing, never-moving, unpolutable; and in peace, beyond desires he watches the drama of the universe. He is hidden behind the veil of the three conditions and constituents of the universe; but in the joy of his law of righteousness he is ever ONE, he is ever ONE.
>
> ... Master, you have spoken to us of the greatness of the Atman, the Spirit, the Supreme Soul; but what is the soul who is bound by the light or darkness which follow works, and who, born again from good and evil, rises or falls in its wanderings, under the impulse of two contrary powers? ...

There is indeed the other soul composed of the elements of the body, the *bhutatman*, who is bound by the light or darkness which follows works and who, born again from good and evil, rises or falls in its wanderings under the impulse of two contrary powers.

And this is the explanation:

There are five subtle elements, *tan-matras,* and these are called elements. There are also five gross elements, *mahabhutas*, and these are also called elements. The union of these is called the human body. The human soul rules the body; but the immortal Soul is pure like a drop of water on a lotus leaf. The human soul is under the power of the three constituents and conditions of nature, and thus it falls into confusion. Because of this confusion the soul cannot become conscious of the God who dwells within and whose power gives us power to work. The soul is thus whirled along the rushing stream of muddy waters of the three conditions of nature, and becomes unsteady and wavering, filled with confusion and full of desires, lacking concentration and disturbed with pride. Whenever the soul has thoughts of 'I' and 'mine' it binds itself with its lower self, as a bird with the net of a snare.

7.16. The different parts of consciousness – a summary

As shown above, the human being has thus (at least) seven different consciousness levels or bodies. Moreover, we have the following five states: half-awake, awake, meditating, dreaming and sleeping and then it is possible for the different areas of the consciousness, such as the super consciousness or the subconsciousness, to be in activity. We can be under the influence of powers in the subconsciousness even when we are awake, powers we cannot control. No wonder we often feel confused. Our mind is in a sense multi-dimensional. Consciousness is not in one particular mood, it may be in three or four moods at the same time, which is quite normal.

One way to become more aware of why and how we react is to feel from where in the body the reaction comes. A better understanding of the chakra system and the energies that are associated with each chakra (both positive and negative), will give an indication. By concentrating on the chakras through energy exercises, we may gain better control of the psyche. This is in line with what Master Eckhart has said about understanding our self and our attitudes.[292] He pointed out that the human being has a variety of needs and inclinations that partly are due to the physical body, partly to the lower soul capabilities and partly to the higher soul capabilities, and partly to what he called the very inner human being. This may be compared with what other mystics called the physical, the astral, the mental and the spiritual part of the human being. If you identify strongly with one of those areas at the cost of others, you will be wrongly developed. For example, a strong fixation on the body (the physical part) may cause greediness and desire for power as result. You may develop addictions that you might suffer because of later. Anyone heavily engaged on the astral level, may lose touch with daily life.

Rudolf Steiner's description of future human development is that the human being will, from its ego (which for him equals the higher mental level), gradually process and refine the lower parts of its being, thus making it master over its ego. When the ego has developed the astral body and made it its property, so that the unconscious and unguarded drives, instincts or passions no longer exist, then the 'I'-power has become what he called the *spirit-self* or *manas* (the Self). When the ego later transforms the etheric body, the buddhi or *life-spirit* will be achieved. And when the ego at some point in a distant future has transformed the physical body, so that this, through the 'I'-power will be completely spiritualised – which is the most difficult task because the physical body is the densest of the three essential parts – then the physical body has evolved to the human being's highest stage, the *atma* or the *spiritual human being*.[293] What Rudolf Steiner has here described, seems to be consistent with how most mystics perceive the individual person's total being.

8. Consciousness Levels

> The Mystic, the Gnostic and the Theosophist speak of a soul and spirit world, which is just as real for him, as the one you can see with your physical eyes and touch with your physical hands. *Rudolf Steiner* [294]

Many mystics tell us that in the same way as the human mental structure consists of several layers, or levels, so the spiritual dimension consists of several layers, planes or worlds. Most mystics say that there are seven main planes (see figure 10). These spiritual planes or worlds match those of the various levels of consciousness, and a person who has his or her consciousness at a certain level has access to the equivalent or lower levels – but not necessarily to the higher level. Each level is, according to Arthur E. Powell, composed of a variety of sub-planes – there are said to be seven sub-planes for each main plane. It is further explained that while the physical plane is three-dimensional (with the exception of time), the astral plane is four dimensional and the mental plane five dimensional. (Some physicists suggest that the Cosmos is multidimensional, but it is hardly likely that they also include the spiritual planes.) However not all explanations about the spiritual world are the same. It might be interesting to recall that the ancient Egyptians only mentioned two planes – Osiris' Realm (the Moon's sphere) and Ra's Realm (The Sun's sphere). In Osiris' Realm the being expected either to be reincarnated on Earth, or to undergo a process that would lead to a new death in which the subtle body would disappear; whereby the being would move to the Sun's sphere – which would be a kind of celestial existence.[295]

The spirit John (channelled through David Spangler) has said that there are several spiritual worlds.[296] In all the worlds, we may have experiences of being close to the Divine. Everything is created by God, and everything is part of God's life. The various spirit worlds can be defined by their functions, although any definition would be incomplete. When it comes to the worlds that are directed towards human interests and experiences, these are best described as the formative world (this can be Rudolf Steiner's so-called phantom body-sphere), the physical world, the psychological world, and the transcendental and transforming worlds. The formative world lies *ahead* of the physical realm and is invisible. Here are the instinctive and unconscious

	THE PLANE OF ONENESS 7th plane—The All	THE DIVINE'S CONSCIOUSNESS
Spirit	The Cosmic plane The Christ experience 6th plane	
Soul	The Self The Spiritual The Mary consciousness 5th plane	The Causal plane The light experience Formlessness

Mind	The higher mental	The Mental plane Heaven The forming world
	The astral	The Astral plane
Life	The etheric	The Etheric plane Feelings, emotions, Dreams
Matter	The physical	The physical plane

Religions   ***Jes Bertlesen***   ***The Theosophists***

Figure 10. Consciousness Planes

forces; forces that build and maintain the physical bodies either in terms of physical beings or globes or planets. (This seems to correspond to the etheric plane in someone else's terminology.) A formative world, as explained by John, is comparable with Plato's world view. Plato explained that beyond our world of the senses, there is a world that comprises the norms, patterns and role models for thinking and action – the spirits' invisible world.[297] John's psychological world is the one we know from our emotional and mental experiences, which is the same as the lower astral and mental planes according to John. He said that of consciousness.

Ambres (in a lecture[298]) explained that different spiritual levels do not exist in the spiritual life in the manner that esoteric teaching has described. Everything is one. However, existence is experienced according to how we think and when we are trying to understand how the spiritual life is; the description of the spiritual planes is a guide or a picture that is easy to relate to. We have only to remember that there are no fixed boundaries between the described spiritual planes, and that it is impossible to give a correct representation of these. Ambres said that everything is consciousness, and where you are will depend on what your consciousness is concerned with. But according to the book *Meeting Ambres (Møte med Ambres)* he nevertheless uses the plane concepts referred to above when explaining the existence on the spiritual side.

Seth explained that he is on a different plane than the one people are going to just after the physical death.[299] His surroundings are very different from the earthly existence. He said that there is not only one dimension of non-physical consciousness; and that it is consciousness that creates form and not the opposite – there is no objective reality. His existence is much more rewarding and challenging than the physical existence. The description that Yogananda's teacher Sri Yukteswar gave of the existence in the non-physical dimension is consistent with Seth's description.

In the book *Talking with Angels* the author Gitta Mallasz writes that she and her friends perceived it as though they each had their own angel who talked to them through their friend Hannah, and that it was the Divine, in the book called Ö (Ö is a Hungarian personal pronoun in third person which is neither masculine nor feminine), which was the cause behind the beginning of the conversations. Her angel explained that there are two kinds of worlds, the created world and the creative world. The created world is composed of the mineral kingdom, the plant kingdom and the animal kingdom. The creative world consists of an angelic world, a seraph world and the seventh world. The human being stands between the two types of worlds, and its mission is to unify spirit and matter. It is only through the human beings that the angels can influence the Earth.[300]

The Danish psychologist Henrik Lauridsen-Katborg (b.1952) has in a book about his personal meditation experiences described what he calls "the structure of the heavenly consciousness", with which he was able to get in touch through some kind of consciousness pipeline that went from his body up through the various layers of heaven.[301] He wrote about zones of intense white light, which correspond to the white light reported from the near-death experiences. These zones are located between different consciousness layers in Heaven's consciousness. One such layer is a reincarnation layer, which is a belt, forming images where the 'I'-consciousness is presented with its personal history. Another consciousness layer consists of images and stories that are more like fairy tales and might be designated an astral zone. He thought that this zone showed that there are other worlds than the Earth's. In a third consciousness layer there are beings like the human beings on Earth, but these are without a physical body. He suggested that these may be spiritual guides, messengers or guardian angels. You can see the differences between the beings you meet, you can talk to them, and they can give advice and answer questions.

In the book *The Road to Immortality* by Geraldine Cummins there is a description of the different consciousness levels, which is very similar to those described by Henrik Lauridsen-Katborg and gives depth to others' explanations. Geraldine Cummins (1890-1969), was a well-known Irish author and trance medium. This book is said to have been given through trance writing, recorded in the period 1924-1931, and allegedly originated from the deceased F.W.H. Myers. The first plane, which the Myers-spirit named the *material plane*, includes not only Earth, but all forms of existence in which matter is dominant. The next plane (the etheric according to the term used below) Myers called the *plane of illusion*, or the dream plane. This plane is supposed to be emotionally directed and connected to physical forms. The plane above this last one is termed the *plane of colour* (the astral plane). It is controlled by thoughts and consists of extremely fine matter in a kind of physical form. Then comes the *fire plane* (the mental plane). Here, you will be aware of the pattern which the spirit is weaving and the spiritual fellowship. On the next plane, you will be aware of the soul group's existence through all the physical lives. This plane is called the *plane of white light* (the causal plane). If the soul goes further it will experience the true reality, where it becomes one with the highest consciousness and conscious of all existence. This should be the true reality, the timeless reality also known as the consciousness of the Divine.

Many philosophers and theorists seem to believe that consciousness cannot exist in different planes. One of the pioneers in the field of parapsychological research, Hans von Noorden, has reviewed, however, what he called the field of souls.[302] He referred to Plato's idea of the world's soul, and Gustav Theodor Fechner (1801-1887, German physicist and philosopher) who further developed this, in his own way, in the book *Zend Avesta*. According to Fechner, every thought that occurs in people will merge into the world's soul and will there be closely woven into a sort of universal consciousness. Von Noorden also referred to the German philosopher,

Professor Hans A. E. Driesch (1867-1941) and his teachings about the soul field, as well as to several other philosophers. These theories can help explain telepathic and extrasensory perceptions. Driesch believed that there is a non-spatial and super personal frame for what takes place between souls. This is comparable to the Akashic archive or the world memory, an idea which is also supported by William James.

We shall now take a look at the different consciousness planes as described by Rudolf Steiner, the Theosophists and some others.

The *physical plane* we know – and, as most of us know it as the only thing that exists, a more detailed description should be unnecessary. According to Rudolf Steiner this plane is composed of atoms that strive to get away from each other.

Then there is said to be a structure that keeps the physical together, which is called the etheric body. It has contact with the *etheric plane*. This plane can also be considered as the biological plane, as a living cell has all the information needed to build a living organism. It is not inconceivable, however, that it may be gravity that is behind this plane. Lyall Watson mentioned that Professor William Tiller has suggested that matter on this plane has the same character as a hologram, and that it might work on magnetic principles, not electrical.[303] Watson found this explanation interesting, because according to his thinking it must be a physical principle that can explain phenomena such as telepathy and psychokinesis, and also cosmic and mystical experiences.

The *astral plane* is called *kamaloka* by Steiner and the Theosophists. (as already mentioned in chapter 7.) On this plane 'live' the human archetypes and the unconscious has access to this plane. Also the human subconscious or its automatic functions and instincts are supposed to have their cause in this plane. In addition, all feelings and emotions are shown here. Jes Bertelsen has suggested that the astral plane is a level that all human beings have in common.[304] Whatever you experience here, he believed, is not identical with the spiritual life consideration and dimension. In order to reach the spiritual dimension (the dimension of the Self), you have to work your way through the astral level, which consists of both deterrent and demonic adventures and sublime and divine images, according to Bertelsen. In the astral dimension you will meet the personal and the collective unconscious. Thus the astral realm seems to be a thought world or a world of imagination and images. This view is supported by Edgar Cayce, who has said that the first astral plane is primitive and resembles the Earth plane.[305] Thought forms from retarded or undeveloped souls exist there, among other forms, which can easily take shape as threatening figures, such as those we experience in nightmares.

The astral plane can be found in philosophical thinking and mystical doctrines throughout the ages, and traces of this are also found in orthodox physics according to Evelyn Underhill. She mentioned that this plane might be seen as the true or spiritual form of everything that has been created and all that exists.[306] She explained that the astral plane has been considered as the cosmic memory, where images of all creatures and events are saved in the same way that they are preserved in human memory. (It is possible that this is the Akashic archive, although spirits have never been mentioned in relation to the Akashic archive.) On this plane exist also the spirits of the deceased, according to her. Evelyn Underhill mentioned that the astral plane is the same as the archetypical world or Yesod in the Jewish Kabbalah, and 'the perfect land' in the ancient Egyptian religion, where the true or spiritual form of all created exists. She referred to *Bhagavad Gita,* where it is written: "Above this visible world there is another, invisible and eternal, which, when everything created has disappeared, does not disappear." She said further that there are descriptions of such a plane, or whatever we call it, in most of the world's cultures. According to the Kabbalists this should be "the seat of life and vitality and that which feeds the entire world". The patterns for future creations and events are present there, resting in the eternal now, before they are brought to birth in the physical world. This, she thought, could explain prophecies and clairvoyance, as such psychic abilities are said to be aroused when the mind is focused on the astral world. John (David Spangler) distinguished, however, as mentioned, between the formative world and the astral realms. So those explanations are not quite consistent. But this may be due to Evelyn Underhill's mentioning of apparently only one plane, not several.

Sri Yukteswar explained that there are many astral spheres with plenty of astral creatures.[307] The astral universe is created by fine vibrations of light and colour, and is many times larger than the physical Cosmos. This astral universe is exceptionally beautiful, rich in colour-radiating seas, shining oceans and rainbow-coloured rivers, and there is harmony and equality for all. There are myriads of beings coming from the Earth for a shorter or longer period of time. There are also fairies, mermaids, fish, animals, dwarfs, half-gods and spirits. And there are different spheres for good and evil spirits. This master mentioned that there are wars and quarrels between the fallen 'black' angels, but these are located in separate regions in a lower sphere where they must try to dissolve their evil karma. Astral, ostensibly fixed, materials can be converted into a different consistency by the force of the inhabitants' own will. The anatomy of the astral beings includes, according to Sri Yukteswar, an astral brain, also known as the thousand leaf lotus of the light, and six centres in what is called the *sushumna* or the astral cerebro-spinal axis. In most cases the astral form is a true copy of the last physical body, but in a young (and complete) form. However, the beings are able to alter this form at will. The intuition is the most important sense, and all the earthly senses operate through an intuitive sense. The forehead chakra (the third eye or the pineal) is the main eye. Communication between the individuals is done through telepathy and astral television.

The *mental plane* is called *Devachan* by the Theosophists; by some of the other mystics, especially the Christians, it is called Heaven. Arthur E. Powell said it is in the mental plane that the intelligent thoughts are formed by the 'I'.[308] The human being's 'I' consciousness with its thought activities dwells in the mental plane. All contact with the surrounding world is due to electrical impulses at this level, which then pass down through the other levels until they are 'translated' for the physical brain – which makes people act according to the impulses that come from without. These thoughts are accessible for people who are conscious on this plane. The mental plane is described as a sea of candlelight, surrounded by all 'conceivable wonders in colour and form'. Everything changes according to thought.

Concrete thoughts present themselves in the form of things, whereas abstract thoughts appear in geometric patterns. Here is experienced an intense happiness, vitality and strength.

In the spiritual dimension, also known as the *causal plane,* is the human being's Self, its higher consciousness. This is then the plane of the Selves. Some people have had contact with this plane as a light experience. Jes Bertelsen calls it the Mary-consciousness or the 5th plane. Sri Yukteswar said that the causal world is indescribably subtle and difficult to understand. If you were able to see this world, you would be on the border of a fusion of mind and matter. He said that you will see there all created things as consciousness forms.

There are even *higher spiritual planes*. Arthur E. Powell wrote about two higher levels above the causal plane. He referred to those as the consciousness of the Godhead. Jes Bertelsen calls the 6th plane the Christ-experience and the 7th plane – the All. Rudolf Steiner has a slightly different term for them, and the Theosophists have a third term. Jes Bertelsen mentioned, inter alia, that when human beings are viewed from the three highest levels, the meaning of being human is love and higher consciousness. These higher consciousness planes, which are called spiritual or religious, are hidden in the ordinary consciousness. This is not some sort of belief. According to Bertelsen, anyone with sufficient patience will be able to reach these higher consciousness planes. Ken Wilber has said the same. Those who reach these levels of (higher) consciousness will not experience something special in the form of sightings or visions, but they will get a very different attitude towards everyday events and experiences. Thus higher consciousness denotes more a posture than content. The 14th Dalai Lama is said to be an example of a person with higher consciousness. Jes Bertelsen has described the connection to the different levels like this:

> 1. The ordinary consciousness of the 'I' has its basis in the first plane, in the physical world, through the root centre.
>
> 2. In the second plane the 'I'-based instincts and sexuality are through the hara centre.
>
> 3. In the third plane the 'I' emerges through the emotions, expressed through the lower solar plexus and the lower astrals.

Most people function only in these three planes. To be able to be free from them, the human being must comply with the fundamental monastic vows, which are owning nothing, sexual abstinence and unconditional obedience.

> 4. The fourth plane is the plane of the heart and of the mental.
>
> 5. The fifth plane is the spiritual plane where you may have a glimpse of higher consciousness. This is perceived as grace. (It is probably on this plane that many people today have what is called a light experience.)
>
> 6. The sixth plane is the cosmic plane. Here you will find a true fusion between subject (i.e. the person meditating) and the object (which is the Divine). But the meditator will continue to experience itself as an 'I'. St Paul's experience (on the road to Damascus, according to Acts) was perhaps an experience on this plane. He wrote that he was caught up in the third Heaven, which he termed Paradise (2 Cor 12.2-4).
>
> 7. The seventh plane is the Unio Mystica, where you unite with God. Christ and the Buddha are considered to have been conscious on this plane when they lived. That is, they were fully enlightened. The mystics who have described this condition have only been there in brief glimpses.

Jes Bertelsen has written that the fifth, sixth and seventh planes are continuous structures, which exist not only in one life-time, but operate over infinite time. He says about this:

> These three higher levels infold through a human being's incarnation in, respectively, the mental, the astral, the etheric and the physical. Thus the Divine individualizes, and the result is people like us all, with the Divine as the innermost essence.

9. Spirit Beings

9.1. Introduction

Those who believe in a spiritual existence normally believe that there are spirit beings that are helping mankind, either by reincarnating on Earth (as Jesus Christ is said to have done), or that there are angels or good spirits who assist from the other side. In the Christian, Jewish and Islamic traditions there are angels and prophets who tell people what to do and how to live. In other religious traditions there are other ways the deity or the spiritual world provides assistance to the human beings. In the more primitive religions this often happens through the ancestors, who exist in the spiritual world, who may be contacted. The transcommunication, that is conveyed through some mediums today – the so-called channelling – between living persons and their deceased relatives, indicates that many people also in our modern society believe that there is a continuation after the physical life, and that those relatives can help the living.

As I have mentioned above, there are several planes of consciousness that belong to a spiritual world – a world that does not consist of physical matter, and where spiritual beings exist. People have seen and reported many different such beings and the term spirit has been used for different types of visions and phenomena. The following is a possible list of such encounters, with the most prominent mentioned first:

The Unity	-	The All
That which creates life	-	The life-giving principle
The Holy Spirit	-	Cfr. the Christian Trinity teaching
The Spirit or Causal body	-	The Christ-consciousness
The Self or soul	-	The higher 'I' of the human being
Angels	-	Non-physical helping spirits
Good spirits	-	Physical and non-physical spirits
Neutral spirits	-	Physical and non-physical
Nature spirits	-	A sort of consciousness in nature
Deceased persons	-	Forefathers, -mothers and others
Evil spirits	-	Physical and non-physical

| Shells of deceased persons | - Their astral image or thought form |
| People with higher consciousness | - Sages and mystics |

The human beings' mind or psyche, thoughts or inner world

The human beings' abilities and potential

The sustainable force or meaning behind a picture, sculpture, culture, country and the like

Although the term spirit, in general, refers to a human being's mental life or thinking ability, there are many who want to combine it with something beyond the physical person. Good spirits, neutral spirits and demons are often referred to as fairies, ghosts, apparitions, phantoms, witches, trolls, and much more. This includes phenomena where people experience to see, hear, or communicate with other identities which are not real physical people. In the chapter about spirit contact and channelling, I have described a variety of such encounters. I will now report what has been said about these beings. The beings that are designated as deities are not included here.

9.2. Spirit beings according to the great religions

Angels

The word angel comes from the Greek word angelos (Latin angelus), which means messenger. The word is generally used to mean God's messenger. In the Bible we find angels mentioned quite often, although there are also other spiritual beings mentioned there. You do not find the word angel in religious traditions other than the Christian, Jewish and Islamic religions, but within these there is an entire hierarchy of angels. In Hinduism there are a number of other heavenly or spiritual beings, but they are not called angels, and the same goes for many other faiths.

Hazrat Inayat Khan, Rudolf Steiner and Aivanhov have all explained that there is a spiritual hierarchy. Aivanhov said that the archangels are highly evolved spirits that control human destiny. Dion Fortune maintained that the archangels are creatures of a different order from human beings; they are more like an organizing consciousness. She said that these are not beings with lives and consciousness as we imagine them, they are more related to the natural forces, but they are individualized, intelligent and goal directed.[309]

The first angels we meet in the Bible are the Cherubim with a flaming sword and which turned this way and that way. They were set to guard the way to the Tree of Life. Then the Seraphs are mentioned (who were present when Isaiah was called as a prophet), as well as the archangels and the ordinary angels. As 'messengers of the Lord' the angels appear frequently in the Bible; the first time when 'The angel of the Lord' asks Hagar, Abraham's second wife, to return to her mistress Sara (Gen. 16.9). According to Matt 18.10 Jesus said:

"See that you do not despise one of these little ones. For I tell you that their angels in heaven always see the face of my Father in heaven." This can be taken to mean that we all (or perhaps only those who believe?) have a special angel – a guardian angel that watches over us. The angelic hierarchy is described in a publication from the 5th century by the Athenian philosopher Pseudo-Dionysius the Areopagite with the title *The Celestial Hierarchies*.[310] The descriptions of the hierarchy of angels and the angels' names vary, however, in different sources. I have found the following ranking (please note that it is only Rudolf Steiner and Dionysius who have mentioned three hierarchies):

Inayat Khan	Rudolf Steiner	Aivanhov	Dionysius
	The first hierarchy:		The first hierarchy:
Seraphim	Seraphim	Seraphim (The holy ones))	Seraphim
Cherubim	Cherubim	Cherubim (Wheels)	Cherubim
Thrones	Thrones	Thrones (Lions)	Thrones
Mights		Mights (The shining ones)	
	The second hierarchy		The second hierarchy
Forces	Kyriotetes *(Gk. Lordships)*	Powers (The fiery ones)	Lordship
Powers	Dynamis *(Gk. Might/Virtues)*	Virtues (Kings)	Authorities
Principalities	Exusiai *(Gk. Authorities)*	Principalities (Gods)	Powers
	The third hierarchy (sunbeings)		The third hierarchy
	Archai / Indigenous forces		Principalities
Archangels	Archangels	Archangels (God's sons)	Archangels
Angels	Angels	Angels (The strong ones)	Angels
		Saints (Human beingsS)	

Figure 11. Variations on the Angelic Hierarchy

There are many angels and there are many names for the angels, and sometimes one angel may have multiple names. The names that are known in the West are Hebrew and end with EL (which symbolizes the word God). Henricus Cornelius Agrippa (1486-1535), who wrote about the occult teachings in medieval times, mentioned that the name of each angel symbolizes its task, as human beings are unable to understand the nature of the angels, it is not possible to give them names that reflect their inner being. He explained that the angels manage the heavens, the planets, the elements, the winds, the sky directions, the months, the days, and much more.[i] In a book that was found among the Dead Sea Scrolls at Qumran are mentioned seven archangels, respectively (see 1 Enoch 20):[311]

(The animal designations given in the parentheses are used by Helena Blavatsky. She believed that what Ezekiel saw as wheels, must have been the four cosmic angels.)

Michael	–	Israel's guardian (the Lion)
Raphael	–	Guardian of the human beings' spirit (the Dragon /human being)
Reguel	–	God's avenger towards the world of light
Remiel	–	Guardian of the souls in the underworld
Sariel	–	God's avenger towards those who are sinning in spirit
Uriel	–	Guardian of the underworld and the head of the celestial host, often associated with earthquakes and lightning storms as well as prophecies and mysteries (the Bull)
Gabriel	–	Ruler of Paradise and of the Seraphims and the Cherubims (the Eagle)

Bible references:

The Seraphims are mentioned only in Isaiah 6.2. They had each six wings.

Cherubims and Seraphims are mentioned in The Old Testament, as well as the angels Gabriel and Michael. According to Gyldendal's encyclopedia (1959) the word cherubim is of Assyro-Babylonian origin and is used in The Old Testament to denote God's messengers and guardians of sanctuaries. The Cherubims are mentioned in Genesis 3.24 as guardians with flaming swords, as well as in Exodus 25.18 and 1st Kings 6 and 8.7. Ezekiel (1st chapter) described four living beings (probably Cherubims) with four faces, respectively the face of a human being, a lion, an ox and an eagle. All had four wings. In Revelation 4.6 f. they are described with only one face each, but with one of the just mentioned faces. In Exodus it is said that the carpets of the Tabernacle shall show pictures of the Cherubims.

Gabriel is an archangel mentioned by name in the Bible (the name means God's man). Gabriel helped the prophet Daniel to interpret his visions (the Book of Daniel 8.16 and 9.21). He also appeared to Zacharias, the father of John the Baptist, and told him that he was going to be a father (Luke 1.19), and he came to Mary and told her of her coming

---

i. Henrichus Cornelius Agrippa von Nettesheim, (usually just referred to as Agrippa) was best known for his three books of occult philosophy, although he held many lectures and also published other works. Already in 1509, he was appointed professor of theology at the University of Dole, the Netherlands, but had to abandon this position after a year and became instead a diplomat for the German Emperor Maximilian I for a time. One of his many curious commissions was the post as physician at the court of the Duke of Savoy.

pregnancy (Luke 1.26). According to Islamic teachings it was Gabriel who revealed both the Quran and God's true nature to Muhammad. He is mentioned three times in the Quran.

Michael is mentioned in Revelation 12.7 as the one who along with his host of angels was fighting against the Dragon. Also, see the Epistle of Jude 1.9.

Raphael is mentioned in a document from the Qumran-discoveries – the Book of Tobi, which is not included in the Bible.

Thrones, dominions, principalities and spirit powers (from the Norwegian Bible text – in the New International Version it only mentions thrones or powers or rulers or authorities) are only referred to by St Paul (Col. 1.16) in the Bible. In earlier Norwegian Bible translations the word authorities was used in place of spirit powers (in the English King James version it is just 'powers'). In Eph 1.21 St Paul mentions all rule and authority, power and dominion. In Eph 6.12 he writes of a struggle "against the rulers, against the authorities, against the powers of this dark world and against the spiritual forces of evil in the heavenly realms." In Col. 2.15 is mentioned that Jesus disarmed the powers and authorities. It cannot have been helpful spirits that was meant by these terms.

Revelation 4.4 tells of the twenty-four elders who sat around the throne of God on twenty-four seats. In front of or below these are the seven spirits of God, and first after those are mentioned the four beasts. There are then the seven angels who stand before God (Rev. 8.2). These are equipped with trumpets, and each time such an angel blew the trumpet an awful catastrophe took place. God's judgment was fulfilled when the seventh angel blew the trumpet. It is possible that these are the archangels.

Aivanhov has said that the leaders of the angelic hierarchies, from the top down, ten in all, are:

Metatron*	–	who was standing next to the Throne
Raziel*	–	God's secret / God's splendour
Tzaphkiel*	–	God's contemplation / God's watcher or eye
Tzadkiel*	–	God's righteousness / charity
Chamael*	–	God's wish / incense burner
Michael*	–	God's likeness
Haniel	–	God's grace
Raphael*	–	God's healer
Gabriel*	–	God's man or God's power
Uriel	–	God's light or fire
Sandalphon*	–	The dark angel

Sandalphon is mentioned by Dion Fortune as Malkuth's archangel.

This name is mentioned by Aivanhov as another name of Uriel.

There is a certain difference between Enoch's list and Aivanhov's. Dion Fortune mentioned that the archangels that here are marked with an asterisk (*), which are all but Haniel and Uriel, are related to the different sephiroth, which are the ten power centres on the Tree of Life, Kabbalah's symbol. However, according to her, the sephirah Netzach has no archangel.

What then did the angels look like – if they actually were seen? God revealed himself to Moses several times, once as a flaming fire in a thorny shrub (Exodus 3). Later the Lord led the Israelites through the wilderness in the form of a pillar of cloud during the day and a pillar of fire by night (Exodus 13.21-22). In the Book of Daniel 10.5 a person of the over-world, who in the preface to that chapter is believed to be "the Son of God", is described as follows:

> I looked up and there before me was a man dressed in linen, with a belt of fine gold from Uphaz around his waist. His body was like topaz, his face like lightning, his eyes like flaming torches, his arms and legs like the gleam of burnished bronze, and his voice like the sound of a multitude.

Otherwise the angels are not described as fear-inducing. The Gospel of Matthew says that an angel of the Lord came down from Heaven and rolled away the stone in front of the Tomb. "His appearance was like lightning, and his clothes were white as snow." (Matt 28.3). The Gospel of Mark tells of a young man who sat inside the grave in a white robe (Mark 16.5).

According to the Gospel of Luke two men were seen in shining clothes at Jesus' burial place on Easter morning (Luke 24.4). John's Gospel tells of two angels who sat in white clothes inside the grave (John 20.12). (It should be noted that Barbara Thiering, among others, maintained that these were not angels, but physical human beings.)

The paintings and sculptures of angels found in the Western Christian culture mostly follow the Biblical descriptions but it is only Isaiah who has described wings on the revelations he saw. (Isaiah is believed to have lived around 700 BCE.) Heavenly and mythical beings have, however, been equipped with wings since time immemorial. It is natural to think that this is because they should be able to move in the air. Presumably also souls needed wings in order to be able to go to the next world and to return to this one. Many mythical creatures were considered a combination of several forces, such as the griffin (with an eagle's head on a lion's body with wings, found depicted on the walls of the Knossos Palace on Crete, which was destroyed around 1400 BCE). In the tomb of Tutankhamen (from 1323 BCE) images of the goddesses Isis and Neftys were found with wings, but whether these were grown out from the body or only attached to the arms are difficult to say. Other mythical creatures with wings were also depicted in ancient Egyptian tombs, but many of these are in the form of birds. Among the mythical beings from Greek antiquity which are depicted with wings are the gorgon Medusa and the horse Pegasus (described among others by Hesiod around 700 BCE). The god Mercury is depicted with wings on his heels. The victory goddess Nike is equipped with large and impressive wings on the beautiful Greek sculpture 'Nike from Samothrace' (from around 200 BCE) which is in the Louvre, but not on the famous sculpture of Paionios from 424 BCE which is in the museum in Olympia. People in the West who believe they have seen angels, often experience a vision of glowing figures. Whether they also have wings, is uncertain.

I cannot mention angels without also mentioning the devil, but this I will come back to later.

Spirit beings described in the other great religions

In Islam you hear about angels and demons and this may be explained by the fact that Islam also accepts The Old Testament. Allah is carried on a throne by four angels. These are symbolized by a human being, an ox, an eagle and a lion (as the description in *Revelation)*. Furthermore Cherubims and four archangels are mentioned. The angel Gabriel, known as Jibril in Arabic, and the angel Michael are the same as in Judaism and Christianity. Gabriel is the angel of revelations. Michael is the angel who sees to the human beings' needs and knowledge. Izra'il is the angel of death, and Israfil ensures that the soul returns to the body after death, at the judgment day, when the last trumpet sounds. There are also lower degrees of angels and guardian angels. Satan (Shaytan) is the tempter or the devil. He is also known as Iblis. He was originally one of God's angels, but refused to comply with orders to respectfully bow before Adam, and was therefore ejected from Heaven.

In Islamic mythology there is also a group of second class spirits called *jinni* (plural form is *jinnie*). They can assume human or animal form, although they consist of air or fire. It is said that they live in rocks, trees and old buildings. They have human bodily needs, but have no physical limitations. They may avenge themselves on people who hurt them or who have disturbed them, but they can also be exploited by people who understand the use of magic. There are even lower spirits. These are called *ifrit (ifritah* is the female form), *marid* and sila. They are strong and smart, sometimes helpful, but usually evil. They live in social groups underground. They are large, winged creatures that appear as clouds. They cannot be damaged by physical matter, but they can be killed, captured, and be kept prisoners by the use of magic. Aladdin's lamp spirit is a typical ifrit. A *ghul* is a different kind of evil spirit, who prefers to stay in deserted places or burial sites, and is said to be descendant of the devil Iblis. The ghuls are said to often feed themselves on dead or living people. They can be distinguished by the ass's hoof in whatever guise they appear. Lone walkers in the desert especially risk an encounter with a ghul, who then often appears in the form of a beautiful woman.

Helena Blavatsky wrote that the Hebrew angels that you meet in the Bible and in the abbalah have parallels in other religions. The archangels correspond to the *Dhyan Chohans* in Hinduism, also called devas (i.e. gods) or rishis. The seven rishis are said to be the patriarchs of all life on Earth. Blavatsky mentioned that other divine and heavenly powers in Hinduism are called *pitris, suras, asuras, danavas, daityas adityas*, and *gandharvas*, and more, and said that these correspond to the biblical thrones, dominions, principalities, powers, virtues, seraphim, cherubim and demons. Eastern art does not show angels, but in Hinduism there is a plethora of gods as depicted in their sculptures and paintings – though they are all manifestations of the one divinity.

Also within Buddhism there is a variety of spirit beings, both good and evil. *The Tibetan Book of the Dead* tells of forty-two peaceful and fifty-eight furious deities, which may be met after death – in the bardo of dharmata. If, when we encounter them, we understand that they represent our own thoughts and imaginings, we will be able to acquire wisdom. According to Tibetan Buddhism there are also many positive and negative forces that people experience or meet in their lives, some invisible and some of very different shapes. These are categorized as gods, spirits and demons. Among other things, there are supposedly eight classes of heavenly spirits or helpers, respectively devas, nagas, yakshas, gadharvas, asuras, garudas, kinnaras and mahoragas. There should also be eight classes of earthly spirits, which can be both of help and of harm to people, respectively ging, mara, tsen, yaksha, raksha, mamo, rahula and naga. These classes can be seen as subtle positive or negative manifestations of the eight types of consciousness. The negative manifestations can cause illness or other injury.

Revelations of the Virgin Mary

There are many people in different places in the Roman Catholic-Christian world who believe that they have seen the Virgin Mary in a vision. The most famous places of such revelations, all of which have become central places for veneration, are probably the following:

Lourdes, France: In the year 1858, it was a fourteen-year-old girl, Bernadette Soubirous, who witnessed many visions of the Virgin near Lourdes, France, over a period of five months. The visions took place at a cave. Pope Pius IX declared the visions as authentic in 1862, and a source of water in the cave, was revealed to Bernadette, as having healing powers. It is said that now more than five million people visit this place every year.

Fátima in Portugal: On the 13th May 1917 three shepherd children at Fátima in Portugal, Lucia dos Santos (10 years old), Francisco and Jacinta Marto, had a vision of a female figure. The woman said she was the Rosary-Lady. She appeared on the 13th of each of the subsequent months until October, with the exception of August, when the sighting was on the 19th. The date for the vision the children had learnt from the lady. She promised them that they would see a miracle on the 13th October that year. A large crowd was therefore assembled at the site – it is said to have been about 70,000 people. Immediately after the children witnessed the vision of the woman that day, the crowd experienced an astonishing solar phenomenon; it looked as if the sun fell to the earth. On the 13th October 1930 the children's experiences were declared to be visions of the Virgin Mary and the place declared holy. On the 13th May 1967, the 50-year anniversary of the first vision, Lucia dos Santos, who had become a Carmelite nun, followed Pope Paul VI to Fátima, along with approximately one million pilgrims.

The Coptic Church of Zeitoun, near Cairo: In 1968 and during the three following years the Virgin Mary, sometimes also the Virgin together with Joseph and the infant Jesus were seen on top of, and sometimes above, the Coptic Church of Zeitoun, near Cairo. The sightings were observed almost weekly, and over a period of several hours. They were seen and photographed by thousands of people. (*see figure 12 below*)

Medjugorje, Bosnia-Herzegovina: On the 24th June 1981 six children experienced several visions of the Virgin Mary in the sky. They reported that she revealed images of Heaven and Hell, as well as messages about coming world events. Pilgrims were asked to pray for peace. These sightings have, however, not been accepted by the Roman Catholic Church.

Figure 12. The Virgin Mary in Cairo.
Photo: Jerome Palmer, OSB. (From the book by Palmer: **'Our Lady returns to Egypt'**. *Reproduced in David Scott Rogo's book* **'Miracles'**.*)*

Villa de Guadalupe Hidalgo: This town located near Mexico City, is the most important religious centre in Mexico with visits from hundreds of thousands of pilgrims each year. It is said that here in December 1531 the Virgin Mary appeared twice to a native Mexican named Juan Diego and demanded that a church was built there. In 1754, the Virgin of Guadalupe, by a Papal decree, was declared patron of the New Spain. The Virgin became an icon for the Mexican independence movement in 1810.

The term 'The Holy Ghost' in The New Testament

The term 'The Holy Ghost' or 'The Holy Spirit' is used many places in The New Testament where the stories concern spirit. One should, according to the Christian creed, believe in the Holy Ghost as part of the 'triune God'. But what is this 'Ghost/Spirit'? The term is for many people quite unclear.

> Then John (the Baptist) gave this testimony: "I saw the Spirit come down from heaven as a dove and remain on him. And I myself did not know him, but the one who sent me to baptize with water told me, 'The man on whom you see the Spirit come down and remain is the one who will baptize with the Holy Spirit.' I have seen and I testify that this is God's Chosen One." (John 1.32-34)

John's Gospel (20.22) says that Jesus "*breathed on them and said, 'Receive the Holy Spirit'.*" when he revealed himself to the disciples a few days after the crucifixion. According to Acts 1.5 Jesus told his disciples on one of the times he showed himself to them before he ascended to Heaven on what we call Ascension Day (40 days after the crucifixion): "*For John baptized with water, but in a few days you will be baptized with the Holy Spirit.*" Furthermore, we learn that everyone in the Church of Jesus was filled with the Holy Ghost on Pentecost day:

> Suddenly a sound like the blowing of a violent wind came from heaven and filled the whole house where they were sitting. They saw what seemed to be tongues of fire that separated and came to rest on each of them. All of them were filled with the Holy Spirit and began to speak in other tongues as the Spirit enabled them. (Acts 2.2-4)

In the letters of St Paul we can read this:

> ... these are the things God has revealed to us by his Spirit. The Spirit searches all things, even the deep things of God. (1 Cor 2.10)

> Don't you know that you yourselves are God's temple and that God's Spirit dwells in your midst? (1 Cor 3.16)

> There are different kinds of gifts, but the same Spirit distributes them. There are different kinds of service, but the same Lord. There are different kinds of working, but in all of them and in everyone it is the same God at work. Now to each one the manifestation of the Spirit

is given for the common good. To one there is given through the Spirit a message of wisdom, to another a message of knowledge by means of the same Spirit, to another faith by the same Spirit, to another gifts of healing by that one Spirit, to another miraculous powers, to another prophecy, to another distinguishing between spirits, to another speaking in different kinds of tongues, and to still another the interpretation of tongues. All these are the work of one and the same Spirit, and he distributes them to each one, just as he determines.
(1 Cor 12.4-11)

In the Augsburg Confession (from the year 1530) we can read this (in article III, IV and XX.10):

> Christ might) ... forever reign and have dominion over all creatures, and sanctify them that believe in Him, by sending the Holy Ghost into their hearts, to rule, comfort, and quicken them, and to defend them against the devil and the power of sin.
>
> Also they teach that men cannot be justified before God by their own strength, merits, or works, but are freely justified for Christ's sake, through faith, when they believe that they are received into favour, and that their sins are forgiven for Christ's sake, ... And because through faith the Holy Ghost is received, hearts are renewed and endowed with new affections, so as to be able to bring forth good works.

Father Laurence Freeman has explained that in Christian terminology The Holy Spirit is the counsellor that Jesus promised to send to the Earth after his death. He said further that The Holy Spirit is Jesus' personal power or God's love. This power Jesus gave to his disciples after the ascension, but it is also present in all of existence. This often results in supernatural events, such as St Paul's ability to heal. (See Rom 15.19; 2 Cor 12.12 and 1 Tes 1.5.) According to Acts 19.6 St Paul mediated such a power of God on one occasion.

Marvellous healings also happen today. A recurrent feature of the people who have healing abilities is that most of them feel that they themselves are not the cause of the healing. The impression I have is that those healers experience themselves as mediators of a power that comes from the outside: A type of channelling of a cosmic love and healing energy, an energy that makes whole. When, therefore, in a Church context, the talk is about The Holy Spirit, I understand this as the cosmic power of love, an energy that a human being can receive and transfer to others. This power of love can also, sometimes and in special situations, be experienced by what we might call 'ordinary' people, people who have not come very far along the way of cosmic consciousness or faith in God. The question which then must be answered is whether this power of love is a kind of consciousness which we can relate to and which may affect our lives, or whether it instead must be considered as a heat source. For St Paul, it was clearly enough a consciousness that he could relate to, namely Christ. This may be so for anyone who considers themselves as Christian. But non-Christian people may also find that a consciousness outside of themselves is helping in one way or another in time of need.

Martinus said that "the full divine or cosmic consciousness" is what in the Bible is referred to as The Holy Spirit. He argued that spirit and consciousness are the same as thoughts – i.e. the individual's inner world. This inner world's reflection or creation in the outer world is what we experience as the world, nature, our fellow creatures, and also ourselves. But we have yet to realize that beings other than humans have such an inner world; our sense is not sufficiently developed. We are all creatures and creators; we are together with our fellow human beings creating the world. Martinus believed that the expression The Holy Spirit applies only to the gradient of the spiritual matter's occurrences.[312]

In certain cases it seems that a person has greater capabilities than those he or she was apparently equipped with from birth. This can happen without some special cause, but it can also be procured by intense spiritual work. Extraordinary abilities can occur when we are in contact with the Divine ONE or with something or someone on a higher consciousness level. It is this which, in my judgment, is described as being 'filled with The Holy Spirit'.

9.3. Evil spirits

We find stories about evil spirits in most religious traditions and mythologies, and in different forms. They cause everything painful to happen to people, and are depicted and described in the worst possible forms. The witches, who travelled to Bloksberg at the witches' sabbath to celebrate together with the devil, are a familiar motif in European folklore. The tales about the shamans, who had to fight demons in order to help sick people and thereby often risking their own lives, are told in stories from most shamanistic cultures. The Norwegian folktales are full of descriptions of trolls, troll-ladies or wood-nymphs (huldra, pl. huldre), gnomes (nisse, pl. nisser); and most of these must be considered as evil spirits. The trolls live in the mountains. Huldra is seen in the forest and on the heights. The dwarfs are largely underground. In lakes and waters there are water-trolls (nøkken), and in addition to those we can experience other types of nymphs (undines and naiads). In all the world's mythologies and folklore you find corresponding powers and beings, but with various descriptions of how they are seen or experienced. In Greek and Roman mythology nature is full of gods and half-gods. The half-gods are a result of intercourse between the gods and human beings. Many people report having seen such creatures. Not all supernatural creatures are evil, but they often do the opposite of what people want.

In fairytales there are often a number of evil and negative forces that appear in the form of human beings. Most people know the story of Count Dracula, the blood sucking vampire that during the day was a fairly ordinary castle owner in Transylvania, but that at night was a cannibalistic monster with facial features similar to a bat. Robert Louis Stevenson's narrative about the split personality Dr Jekyll and Mr Hyde has something of the same theme. In England there is a term for an evil spirit which feeds on corpses, namely the ghoul, which probably comes from the Islamic word ghul, already mentioned. I do not know of a corresponding term in Norway.

In the Bible the serpent is mentioned several times. The serpent was considered to be the devil in disguise, best known from the story of Adam and Eve. In the Book of Job it is said that Satan is one of the sons of God. In Revelation 12.9 and 20.2 the great dragon is mentioned (i.e. the old serpent, also known as the Devil) and Satan with his angels. These were thrown out of Heaven and down to Earth, there to be cast into the Lake of fire. Jesus was tempted by the devil as he fasted in the desert. According to Rudolf Steiner the luciferic spirits belong to the hierarchy of angels and archangels. They are fallen spirits. Their task is to give the human beings autonomy, the ability to make mistakes and go astray, and thereby also the possibility to do evil. According to some medieval sources in Europe, there were seven archdemons (archdevils), which actually were fallen angels. They represented the seven deadly sins, respectively:[i]

Lucifer	pride
Mammon	greed
Asmodeus	lasciviousness / lust
Satan	anger
Beelsebub	greed
Leviathan	envy
Befegor	laziness

Hildegard of Bingen painted what she saw in her visions – there were both angels and devils, and the devils look as we would expect them to look, for we know them from many pictures from the Middle Ages. For her the devil was real – she was often battling him in order to save souls and she could smell his presence. Caterina of Siena also told of battles with evil spirits when she sought to help those in need or those who were sick. It is reported that she became famous for her ability to expel evil spirits, although she did this reluctantly because the evil spirits would then bother her.[313] For example, she made an evil spirit leave a little girl named Lorenzina. When Lorenzina was 8 years old, she started to have fits with cramps. Under such fits she apparently spoke Latin fluently and discussed learned topics as if

---

i. In the Tibetan Buddhist teachings there are only six strong negative emotions, respectively pride, jealousy, desire, ignorance, greed and anger. (Sogyal Rinpoche p. 112.)

she was a University graduate. The last time Caterina commanded the demon to disappear from Lorenzina, it replied that it would possess Caterina instead. But by the grace of prayers it disappeared entirely. Padre Pio was also constantly fighting demons; and although these were not seen by other people, they sometimes heard fierce noises and heard Padre Pio's movements in his cell as if he were in a fight. Padre Pio said that the demons came to him, both in terms of monsters or evil men, but also as friends and superiors. But Pio saw through them because he felt a certain form of disgust when they appeared. In order to test them he demanded that they should praise Jesus; if they refused to do so, Pio presumed they were demons and not his friends.[314] Their experiences fit the following description in the Bible:

> When he arrived at the other side in the region of the Gadarenes, two demon-possessed men coming from the tombs met him. They were so violent that no one could pass that way. "What do you want with us, Son of God?" they shouted. "Have you come here to torture us before the appointed time?" Some distance from them a large herd of pigs was feeding. The demons begged Jesus, "If you drive us out, send us into the herd of pigs." He said to them, "Go!" So they came out and went into the pigs, and the whole herd rushed down the steep bank into the lake and died in the water. (Matt 8.28-32)

The question that remains unanswered is what it is that is actually seen, and what is actually perceived, when people tell stories about spirit contact.

9.4. Explanations of spirit beings

There are many types of spirit beings and, as we shall see, different explanations of what these animating entities really are. There are many who believe that they have contact with 'human beings' on 'the other side', beings who previously have been physical people. Some say that the world where they are located, functions much like the physical world. One may then wonder how long a being is located in such a physical-like existence. What has been written about death and the various consciousness levels can explain some of this, but not all. It should be noted, however, that not everything that is perceived as 'spooks' refer to spirit beings. It may be electric or magnetic fields, or other types of fields that cause temperature changes and atmospheric changes, which in turn can give motion to the floor or the walls. This can be experienced as if something is passing by, or something that sounds like steps or voices.

Medieval witch-hunting, with burning of large numbers of alleged witches, cannot be explained otherwise than as a collective psychosis, due to fantasies and hallucinations. In addition there is a good deal of strong emotions such as hate, aggression and desire for vengeance, not forgetting the Church's almighty righteousness. People who did not conform to general attitudes, who had special abilities or who were cast out of the so-called good society, were easily stigmatized. In 1692 witch hunting was very intense in the city of Salem in Massachusetts in the United States, which is described in detail in the city's legal documents.[315] The same type of documentation exists in most places where such persecution took place. The court documents describe, inter alia, what people believed to have seen or heard; stories that often were supported by confessions obtained under torture. Today, hopefully no one believes in the veracity of these stories, beyond that they are good evidence of human folly and the desire to be of importance; and what people may believe they are experiencing.

Three of the founders of the Society for Psychical Research in England, F.W.H. Myers, Edmund Gurney, and Frank Podmore, published a book in 1886 with the title *Phantasms of the Living*. Here they related more than a hundred stories they had received, in which people told of experiences of apparitions of people who were still alive. This was thus not some sort of spirit contact. The authors believed that the phenomena was caused by some kind of mental projection, as the apparitions were often seen shortly after the observer had thought about the person or tried to imagine the person then seen.

Lyall Watson has referred to a collection of data relating to the appearance of apparitions collected by Celia Green (b.1935), PhD, of the Institute of Psychological Research in Oxford.[316] He pointed out that the conclusion of this survey must necessarily be that the vast majority of cases of apparitions are caused by hallucinations or day dreaming, where what one expects will happen does happen. It is often people we know or have known who are seen in their usual surroundings and doing quite ordinary things, such as we are familiar with from earlier meetings but he pointed out that there are some cases that cannot be explained in this way – namely where there are several people who at the same time all see the same. This frequently occurs when the person, they are seeing, has recently died. On the other hand, Watson wrote that it seems that in all apparition phenomena related to a physical person – there must be a particular living person present. He also mentioned the curious point that all the apparitions have clothes on; and that the clothes should even survive physical death or destruction, he found peculiar. However, this may be explained in that the discarnate individual is able to materialize both its self and its clothes that fit the situation.

However, Lyall Watson found the teaching of the spirit Seth both logical and factual, and he thought that Edgar Cayce must have had a very special ability to give proper information.

He thought the same should apply to some other mediumistic statements but he found many such statements kitschy and in line with the medium's own thoughts and knowledge, and within what people of our times are concerned with (such as the fact that the UFO sightings were only reported after the Second World War, while the people of former times often were spellbound by the sub-earthly trolls and spirits), or by what is mentioned in available literature. The statements are also often vague and difficult to interpret. Watson pointed out that most statements have a dreamlike quality, and that often certain recurring themes are addressed. He related this in connection to Jung's archetypes. Watson further mentioned that in sleep we often goes beyond time and space and may produce knowledge that is unbelievable; in addition to that, all of us can have telepathic dreams, as well as dreams concerning the past, and dreams about the future. He thought something similar occurs when an individual goes into a trance and brings information from the spirit world. Although Watson accepted that Seth and Jane Roberts were not the same personality, he is not convinced that it is the same personality that is behind all statements given in the name of Seth. Watson thought that we are not fully acknowledging the capacity and the opportunities that consciousness can provide, and he suggested that we here probably have before us the same phenomenon which the multiple personalities present. As example he mentioned a session with the well-known Irish medium Eileen Garrett (1893-1970), in which her spirit contact lost breath and did not give an answer when it simply was asked what it had done since the last séance.

Michael Talbot, who in the book *The Holographic Universe* has written about some of the revelations of the Virgin Mary, believed that such visions are due to holographic projections created by people's unconscious thoughts. He said that the same probably applies to sights of most apparitions. The visions are in the beginning usually seen in a strong light, which then slowly weakens. In many cases not only people, but also objects such as a horse with carriage (and clothing) are seen. This, Talbot thought, indicated that it is not dead people that appear for the living.

Dion Fortune maintained that angels are embodied ideas rather than real beings. She said that they can be defined as cosmic energy, appearing for the consciousness in a form created by the human imagination. (This must probably be considered the same as holographic projection.) She said further that originally people imagined that the nature forces were embodied beings, and so people began to honour and worship these beings. Thereby these forces developed as astral images and the more people fantasized about these images, the more did they take form. Dion Fortune called these astral images the created beings' creations, i.e. man-made creatures. And she said that when psychic people are seeking to understand a life-form's spiritual nature and inner being, they will see these astral images and believe that they are real. Through generations of worship of these images, when people were starting to look at them as gods, the images became more and more manifest; so they become magical objects capable of independent actions. The image you are seeing is, however, only a symbol, she said, that will be animated and can be energized by the power people give it. (Just consider the effect many people attribute to the crucifix of Jesus or the depictions of the Virgin Mary.)

It is this phenomenon, she said, that is the key to talisman magic and many mysterious things that happen around people, for which we do not have any explanation. I consider Dion Fortune's explanations about embodied ideas very interesting. It fits in with Alexandra David-Néel's tale of her constructed phantom monk in Tibet, and Dion Fortune's own and others' construction of phantom figures. It also fits with what Michael Talbot wrote about holographic projections. But, according to my judgment, this explanation does not cover all the phenomena that the human beings encounter.

Dion Fortune explained that the devil is the opposite of the archangels, the demons are the equivalent of the angel choir, and the underworld is equal to the sephiroth sphere. She said that in the Kabbalah the symbol the Tree of Life has a negative side, called *qlifot*, and that it is there we meet these negative forces. She described those forces as the extreme aspects of each sephirah. If you think that the tree is located on the front of a balloon, any sephirah energy that goes out in the extreme will come to the back of the balloon, and it is this side that is called qlifot. Thus, each sephirah has a dark side. This can be said to correspond to the extremes of any activity: the Sun's heat is a good thing, but if it is too hot, it will be scorching and burning; water is vital, but too much in terms of rain causes flooding and floods, etc. If a large number of people are expecting something to happen, perhaps because of someone's dreams or predictions, or if the expectation of some kind of doomsday is spreading because of ominous signals or events, thought forms like the ones I have discussed above, may occur. Often phantoms can be seen at places where there has been some violence or gruesome events, indicating that there are emotional conditions which create the apparitions. Some people are sensitive to what has happened in a house, some are proficient in psychometry, some can 'read' an article and tell where it comes from or what it has been. Some houses have a good atmosphere, while others have the opposite. If something dramatic has happened in a house, this may still be 'in the walls'. That is, a particularly sensitive person may be able to see or feel what has happened on the spot, no matter how much time has elapsed since the incident took place. Some people are so sensitive that they will be able to see or relive the event, others experience only fragments. Anna Elisabeth Westerlund was in a way able to make a property 'tell' its history. She believed that this was the explanation to many of the ghost stories told. This might be explained by the theory of holographic projection.

Some people with a strong imagination can project their deeper thoughts or dreams into a hallucinatory vision or feeling. In environments with a certain hint of mystery, anxiety or fear can easily result in such experiences. If one is tired or exhausted and almost on the way into a dream state, the imagination can easily make figures of fog or voices from the sound of the wind. Perhaps this is what lies behind the experiences of meeting different spirits of the woods or mountains, such as trolls. As the public imagination has through many centuries told stories of strange adventures in forest and mountains, this may have created a kind of archetype that attracts energy from such attention. Additionally, if there is a strong focus on strange happenings in specific places, this will provide a concentration of energy or thought images at these sites, which in turn will give people the feeling that these places are special. Such fantasies can fit the theory of embodied ideas or holographic projections.

Thomas Lethbridge specialized, as previously mentioned, in the use of the pendulum, and he could locate water, metals and more with this. He also thought he had found the explanation for the phenomenon of *ghouls*. Leathbridge discerned, however, between ghosts and ghouls, as he used the word ghoul for a sense of something disgusting that one can experience at some places, such as a freezing feeling in a particular small area or a depressing feeling at such a place. A ghost on the other hand, is something one can see or hear. The phenomenon that some objects in a way can 'talk' if a person holding the article is sensitive enough or otherwise have some sort of contact with it, which is psychometry, caused Lethbridge to think that there is a type of force field around the object (the psi field?) were the information the article has received in some way or other is stored. The closest comparison he could think of was a photographic plate, which is able to store impressions (holograms?). By using the pendulum, he found that in places where in particular one experienced a sense of something disgusting, often there was an underground water source there. Since all objects can be considered having a force field, that probably also goes for water. Strong emotions or happenings may have impregnated themselves into such a force field. This may be the explanation when people have seen water-nymphs or other nature spirits, who are particularly seen near or in lakes. Sensitive people often pick up some of the things that have been recorded in such fields, or in such surroundings – i.e. psychometry or holographic projections. Maybe water or closeness to water provides extra sensitivity.

The phenomenon of St Elmo's fire – a glowing discharge of electricity, which often occurs during lightning storms around a ship's mast or a church spire – may be the cause behind the visions of the Virgin near Cairo in 1968. It has been suggested that such phenomena occur prior to earthquakes – and there was in fact an earthquake in the Cairo area in 1968.

In the early 1980s Guy Lamberts investigated some poltergeist phenomena that occurred in London. He claimed to have found a correlation between these phenomena and the river Fleet, which was in an underground drain, as well as in rain showers.[317] However, it is not only near this river that poltergeist phenomena happen.

The British eye specialist Anne Arnold Silk has collected a large amount of material on apparitions, light balls, and more *(see end-note 317)*. She thought that this demonstrates that such phenomena occur near fracture lines in the bedrock. She suggested that experiences of these phenomena can be linked with the so-called piezo-electrical energy (quartz under pressure), which affects the eyes and brains of those who observe the phenomena. Moveable magnetic fields are also said to have a subjective effect on the brain through the formation of magneto-phosphenes, which behave as beacons.

The British parapsychologist Serena Roney-Dougal, PhD, has in the book *Where Science and Magic Meet* suggested that close to fracture locations in bedrocks, so-called fault blocks, paranormal phenomena occur most frequently. She referred to a number of events where such context is proven. She and several other scholars also refer to special energy lines or fields around the Earth, and that it is particularly along these lines that paranormal phenomena, such as ghosts occur. These lines, the so-called *ley-lines*, are described by Thomas Lethbridge and Stephen Jenkins as well as others. At a place in England where several such lines meet, at different times visions of a Roman army have been observed, on several occasions. At another place, several people, also at different times, have seen and heard a great battle that took place at that site during the English civil war (1649-1651).[318]

The American/Norwegian medium Susan Sibbern has in her autobiography, published with the Norwegian title *Stifinner i grenseland – en bok om å være synsk* (Pathfinder in Borderland – a Book about being Psychic), mentioned what she refers to as battlefield energy. That is energy at places where there have been dramatic or painful events, and where the visitors through the ages have imagined what has happened. These people have in this way held the images intact, and it is these visions which sensitive people later can pick up. As an example, she mentioned that she feels unwell when she visits fortresses or comes into rooms where gruesome events have taken place. It seems to me, however, that this is not the full explanation. Some people seem to be able to pick up the story of an event happening at places where no one, other than the people directly involved, has been.

Colin Wilson's comment on Lethbridge's theories is that ghosts sometimes can act as intelligent beings, and that a person actually may experience a fight with such a non-materialized being. Wilson re-tells several such stories in this connection, including one where Lethbridge experienced being knocked down at a certain place by something invisible. As mentioned before, Padre Pio also had equivalent experiences, and he expressed that he was fighting with the devil. Some people have stated that revelations of the Virgin have been followed by inexplicable healings, ref. the water source in Lourdes, although this may be explained by the placebo effect.

People who channel information are very reluctant to consider such contact solely as a holographic projection, as is suggested by some; it is impossible to interpret all channelling as this kind of projection. For example, certain mediums chat with a spirit and convey information that neither the medium nor people nearby are familiar with – in certain cases it has been confirmed that this is knowledge that only the spirit could possess.

However, it is possible that the medium has retrieved all the information from the Akashic archive.

In some cases animals respond to paranormal phenomena, often with fright. Obviously they see or perceive something that people are not sensing. It has happened that animals have become sick and died of unexplainable causes in places with a lot of weird happenings, such as a machine that starts by itself; lamps that fall down or a bulb that flashes or lights up. In some cases for example, people experience, that electrical equipment stops working or that objects fly through the air. This gives the impression that it is a non-physical being who is the cause of what is happening. However, these last mentioned events are often physical poltergeist phenomena related to physical persons – but is it a physical person alone who is then causing the phenomena? Some people might want to explain all the spirit phenomena as poltergeist activity – but that presumes that all the phenomena can be linked to a living person, who preferably is present. Some ghost activities are said to be due to people who have lived at the site previously, but who are not known to the current residents. People with special abilities explain that they see deceased people at such places or get a feeling for what has happened, or that they with the help of friendly spirits can explain these happenings. These spirits can often also assist in order to achieve peace from the negative forces that have been residing in that place. Helena Blavatsky explained, however, such phenomena as the interplay of nature spirits with the astral light.

As mentioned above, a human being consists of several consciousness bodies, respectively the physical, the etheric, the astral, the mental, the causal or spiritual, and above those are the cosmic field and the field of oneness. When the physical body dissolves, the etheric, the astral and the mental body will exist for some time in the state that the Theosophists call *kamaloka*, and in the form that these call *kamarupa*. In kamaloka the astral form of the human being (which they call the *eidolon*[i] or phantom) is said to remain until passions have burnt out and the bond with the physical world has ceased. This phantom has no physical senses, no spirit and no higher mental activity (the Self has moved on). It will slowly dissolve, depending on the bond with the physical world. This phantom is what the Theosophists call the *elementals*.

Geoffrey Farthing explained that the *elementals* are phantoms or ghosts which are remnants of deceased people. When the higher Self has separated itself from its lower consciousness bodies, respectively the physical body, the life force (the etheric), the astral body and the mental body, then those psychic principles will become an empty shell.[319] Such a shell is a human

---

i. Freke and Gandy wrote in the book *The Jesus Mysteries* that the ancients used the word *eidolon* in a slightly different way. They explained that the human being consists of two parts, the physical part who suffers and dies (the eidolon) and the eternal spirit that is untouched by suffering (the daimon) and sees the world as an illusion.

being's astral corpse, without consciousness and without positive impulses. It usually dissolves quite quickly, but can in the meantime appear as a ghost. A *vitalized shell* is a more advanced and/or a more spiteful elemental – and may also appear as a ghost. This shell has for a short period of time a kind of self-awareness, and it can extend its existence if it manages to draw life energy from a physical person or through a medium from a group of people who participate in a spiritist séance. In special cases, such an elemental can suck almost all energy out of a physical human being. These animating entities are invisible, although a clairvoyant person might be able to see them according to what has been recorded. This may be what Edgar Cayce called thought-forms from retarded or undeveloped souls. Joan Grant said, as mentioned earlier, that a ghost or an apparition is a dissociated fragment of a personality with a limited amount of energy.

Geoffrey Farthing rejected in general that it is possible for dead people to contact the living, in part because of his understanding of what happens when a human being dies, and partly because of the experiences the Theosophists had with spiritism and ghost phenomena. It is only after a sudden death or suicide that the deceased for a short time can contact their living relatives. However, he explained that a Self, which exists at the causal plane, will be able to communicate with a physical human being who is in a state of higher consciousness. Possibly, there are such beings which some people in a near-death situation experience to meet. Sri Yuktesvar – Yogananda's deceased teacher – was apparently on the astral plane, when Yogananda happened to see him again after he had passed over, as his task was to help individuals who were there to proceed to the causal plane.

Helena Blavatsky explained that there also exist what she called *elemental spirits*, which are found in earth, air, fire and water.[320] She mentioned that they are called respectively gnomes, sylphides, salamanders and undines by the Kabbalists. They can be understood as nature forces, and in some cases they can be manipulated by beings that have lived on the Earth or by people who understand the use of magic. She pointed out that these are not the same as the elementals. Blavatsky further explained that these nature forces could intercept whatever is written in the astral light (the Akashic archive), and in some way animate the prints there of people and animals, and reproduce their actions or appearances. They can then represent not only a certain person's personality, but also retrieve their memories, thoughts and speech. She wrote that it is this that lies behind what is happening in séances and by special spiritistic poltergeist phenomena. But these elemental spirits are not able to do anything themselves apart from this. She explained that these nature beings are closely related to mankind's karma, as they unconsciously capture whatever people exude. That is, as long as people do not show love for nature and the eco system, these powers mirror the attitude of people, and they will therefore not work to the favour of mankind. But this will change if and as soon as people develop love and understanding for the whole creation, she said. An apparition or a ghost may, according to Helena Blavatsky, be an image which the medium sees in the astral light or the Akashic field. This image the medium may be able to project into its own astral field so that others will be able to see it – a holographic projection. But it can also be caused by what Blavatsky called its *kamarupic* shell, which has been the astral field that surrounded a living person. She explained that this field will dissolve shortly after the physical body's dissolution. The question then will be how long it is since that person died.

If you happen to see famous deceased people, the explanation given is that you then draw the thoughts and images from the people that are physically present, either the medium or others. However, such images can also be called forth from nature spirits – the elementary spirits. In this case there is such a spirit that is involved in the phenomena and not some higher entity from a dead person. Elementary spirits can be controlled by a superior intelligence, and this can be either the medium or another of those present. Blavatsky thus explained that many parapsychological phenomena may be due to the activity of the elementary spirits or in co-operation with them (as example can be mentioned the story of Findhorn and the devas there). Because we do not understand how they work, we consider everything that does not have an acceptable physical explanation as abnormal.

Many such phenomena can also be caused by people's clairvoyant or psychometric abilities according to Blavatsky. Such capabilities can also be explained by the reading of the astral light/the Akashic archive, where you can see everything that has been and also an indication as to all that may come. The astral plane is part of the astral light. This plane is also called the chimerical world, because most of what can be experienced there is self-created.

You can see and experience what you want. It is only those who are highly spiritually aware who have the ability to see through this plane. Others will take what is experienced there as reality. Blavatsky also explained that anyone with the ability to speak an unknown language or retrieve information that is otherwise hard to obtain or which is hidden, is identifying his or her self with a person whose image and life story can be read in the astral plane. It should be noted that both Arthur E. Powell and Geoffrey Farthing refer to Helena Blavatsky's teachings, but Powell is in addition using material gathered from Annie Besant and C.V. Leadbeater. There is not always consistency between these writers. But all that Blavatsky explained seem to confirm the theory of holographic projection and the psi field.

Arthur E. Powell explained that there are many types of beings on the different spiritual planes, which can communicate through a medium.[321] He mentioned that this could be:

> The medium's higher consciousness or Self
> Shadows or shells (remains of human beings – their astral corpse)

- Vitalized shells (elementals according to Blavatsky)
- Nature spirits (elementary spirits according to Blavatsky)
- Deceased human beings existing on the astral plane
- Deceased human beings existing on the causal plane
- Adepts (advanced spiritual beings or masters)
- Nirmanakayas (still higher spiritual beings)[i]

Powell explained the concept of the shadow as a soulless bundle of a human being's lowest qualities, which can remain in the Earth's atmosphere after the being's physical death. The vitalized shell can be said to be the remains of a human being that is left on the astral plane – in kamaloka – when the spirit that animated this proceeds to a higher consciousness plane. Both shadows and shells are animated or revived by thought vibration or by a living human being's magnetic radiation, and this is what happens during the spiritualistic séance. Powell also discussed the vampire phenomenon, but suggested that this pretty much is physical living people with very weak egos or self-knowledge that seek to suck energy out of other people, thereby enhancing their own ego – that is seeking to dominate other people.

Powell further explained that some spirit beings can take over or take hold of a physical human being or materialize in some other way. These spirits can be constructive or destructive. He described how a so-called adhesive spirit could work. This is the astral body of a departed person using the etheric body of a living person for example to make this person get drunk, so that the spirit can 'possess' this person and thereby experience the feeling of alcohol through the incarnate person (as I have already quoted). These are beings who cling to the earthly life after the physical death, and who do not accept that death has occurred. They are likely to remain near their earthly existence. This behaviour can occur when some of the etheric substance hangs on to the astral body, which will exclude the being from the astral world – the astral plane. It is these beings that may become adhesive spirits or that may come to possess a physical individual.

Something similar is happening, according to Powell, when a spirit presents itself through a medium. In certain cases, the spirit can use both the etheric and the astral body of a physical person and in this way appear visible to living people. He explained that in a medium a separation between the etheric body and the physical body can easily happen, which may result in serious danger for the medium. (This was apparently what happened with Edgar Cayce according to his biographer, when a person stretched his hand across Cayce's body while Cayce was in a trance. It resulted in a violent physical reaction in the 'sleeping' Cayce and he had great problems getting back to normal consciousness. His life was actually at stake.) Powell strongly

---

i. According to Tibetan Buddhism a nirmanakaya is a Buddha incarnation, either in a physical body or as an apparition, which seeks to influence and to be of help to physical beings.

stressed the dangers when a physical human being is exploited by a spirit in this way, or when a medium lets the etheric body become separated from the physical body. The natural life force, also known as *prana*, cannot circulate properly during such a séance and the medium will therefore be losing energy.

Powell said that the medium's awareness, capabilities and understanding, as well as the communicating spirit's consciousness with its knowledge and understanding, will affect the messages conveyed. No spirit being can convey more than its capabilities indicate. The lower spirit beings can often pretend to be a famous personality or a relative of those who are listening to the message, in order to make the message more trustworthy. Powell wrote that one should never blindly believe in a message that comes from the astral plane. Such a message is not more accurate than information you receive from living beings. One should use good judgment and a critical sense in the review. But many have received important information from channelled messages, so we must not simply reject all such information.

Nature spirits are a kind of awareness found in plants and animals. Powell has written that there are many classes of nature spirits, all of which have etheric bodies of different degrees of solidity. In the lowest classes are the elves and dwarfs and gnomes. On the face of the Earth are the fairies (a more advanced form of elves), sylphides, naiads and air spirits. The next stage of the nature spirits are the angels. As the etheric material is plastic, these spirits can assume the shape they want, on condition the wish is sufficiently strong, although they have their own specific basic shapes. Powell further explained that anyone with etheric capabilities has an enhanced ability to see, hear, or smell. That is, he or she has the ability to perceive vibrations that belong to other planes of consciousness than the physical. He mentioned that the Earth to a certain extent is transparent for the etheric seeing ability, so the person who has this ability can see a good way down into the Earth. Such a person can also see right through physical bodies and objects.

Dion Fortune has explained that when we hear voices or receive help in a difficult situation, which we believe is coming from our guardian angel, it is our own higher Self that takes action.[322] This was also the conclusion reached by Eileen Caddy after long-term guidance from what she in the beginning thought was God – that it was her own higher Self that gave the information she needed in order to develop the Findhorn community.

Martinus wrote that some communication may be the result of a discarnate being (a spirit) which creates a physical body, the so-called materialization.[323] All human beings have to a greater or lesser extent the possibility to materialize. But a spirit can also take over the physical body of a living human being – a medium. In the latter case the medium's physical appearance may change completely (which happened to some of the mediums mentioned above). Such a process can only last a short while, according to Martinus. If it lasts for a longer time, the medium's physical and mental body may change and may also be destroyed. This indicates that the medium must not be disturbed as long as the séance lasts. If it is disturbed its life may be in danger. Therefore Martinus warned against playing with such a process. During materialization the spirit is able to talk, hear and see on the physical plane. It will be able to emerge as a normal human being (see section on Ectoplasm chapter 3). But Martinus pointed out that a spirit cannot communicate anything to the human world other than what this spirit has experienced or learnt. Since such communication requires a strong concentration of mind from the spirit, the spirit is not at the same time able to participate in complicated philosophical or religious discussions or to give comments about the persons physically present (as in the case of Eileen Garrett's spirit contact, mentioned earlier).

The Danish author Asger Lorentsen has explained, in the same way as Rudolf Steiner and other mystics, that there are many different levels of existence in the Cosmos.[324] Those who are channelling or have light experiences are in contact with one of those planes. He maintained, inter alia, that most clairvoyants do not have contact with a high level, although they often believe they have. This is not a problem as long as other people can get some help from them. He pointed out that there are many spiritual universes and many spiritual beings that will help human beings. The spirit beings have specialized functions, and it is not certain that a spirit being can help a physical being, or that the clairvoyant's spirit contact is the right being for helping you.

Also through people who channel information from the *other side* we hear about beings of light that reside on different celestial levels, different planes of consciousness. These beings do not always consider themselves as archangels or angels, as it often is suggested that the archangels and angels reside on the lowest levels. When people are seeking contact with celestial beings, they should therefore seek contact with the highest beings of light. All beings of light on the *other side* want to help people, but their ability to do so varies.

Seth has pointed out that each consciousness has its own protection – which might be what we understand as a guardian angel but whether this can be said to be one's own higher Self or another entity is not clear to me. Though how my higher Self is able to get another person to act unwisely, in a way which favours me in the long run – which is what I have experienced, I cannot explain other than that he or she must have been influenced by my guardian angel, unless my subconsciousness or the superconsciousness is so forceful that it is able to make such a manipulation (see chapter 7.9 about the power of thoughts).

Aivanhov explained that there is a plethora of evil forces just as there are a lot of good ones.[325] But God is beyond good and evil. The devil does not exist as an entity that is God's counterpart. The devil can be said to be a collective force that is sustained and strengthened by the human beings' negative thoughts, feelings and actions. Aivanhov said that the human being is made up of millions of micro beings who work constructively and disruptively – i.e. for good and evil. You can run the risk that the evil ones take the upper hand, so that they take control of a human being. Aivanhov calls them "the elementals, worms, unwanted powers and sub-earthly spirits". The crucial thing is that you must not give them space – do not allow them to gain the upper hand. These negative forces can steal a human being's power, take its inspiration, ideas, the will to live and more, and instead promote lust for such things as sex, alcohol or intoxicating substances.

Arthur J. Ellison refers in his book *Science and the Paranormal* to a variety of contacts with spirits through mediums. What is particularly interesting in this material are the explanations given about the spirits' problems in getting the correct information through the medium. The spirit-contact Frederick Myers, (ref. the section about the Cross-Correspondences in chapter 3.11) mentioned, inter alia, that there are seven planes or levels in the spiritual world and that he, during this contact through the medium, was located on the third plane. Ellison pointed out that this corresponds with eastern and theosophical philosophy, which Myers knew well. The Myers-spirit was, at the time when this channelling took place, still strongly linked to the physical, but it said it could not continue in this way much longer as it needed to proceed further on in the spiritual world. The Myers-spirit explained that his ability to present himself in his own likeness, for physical beings, would be more difficult as time passed, as he was beginning more and more to forget what he looked like on Earth. Furthermore, this spirit contact explained that when a spirit sends thoughts and words to a medium, the medium has to try to express those on the basis of his or her understanding. The speed of thoughts is completely different on the spiritual plane (much faster) than that of the earthly plane, so that much of what the spirit desires to convey is not always caught or understood by the medium's subconsciousness. That is why the medium often talks incoherently or in symbols. In addition, the medium's mind may be involved in the given messages and distort these or present its own material. If the medium's subconscious becomes tired, this can also complicate the communication. The spirit can also become tired when struggling to get the desired message through the medium.

It is also worth noting Arthur Conan Doyle's comment, after his twenty years of study of paranormal phenomena, that "it cannot be too often repeated that the mere fact that a message comes to us in a preternatural fashion is no guarantee that it is either high or true. The self-deluded, pompous person, the shallow reasoner, and the deliberate deceiver all exist upon the invisible side of life, and all may get their worthless communications transmitted through uncritical agents. Each must be scanned and weighed, and much must be neglected, while the residue is worthy of our most respectful attention. But even the best can never be final and is often amended, ..."ⁱ

Rosemary Altea said that the world which people perceive is full of sensory deception, something we will understand when we develop our consciousness further. We know that atoms are mostly empty space. We believe that ghosts or apparitions have no substance because we see that they go through walls and objects. Rosemary Altea asked whether the ghost might be more real than a concrete wall. What she, with her clairvoyant ability, sees of non-physical bodies are human beings and not spirit beings. But she sees them in their astral bodies. We, according to her, retain the astral body associated with the last life in the astral sphere until reincarnation. This astral body will be a fully developed adult body, not the age imprinted body that many have when they die, and that astral body has the same shape and size as the physical body, but the astral body is indestructible. She said also that the soul grows and evolves when in the astral body after physical death and that anyone who dies as a child will develop a fully grown astral body eventually.

Rosemary Altea wrote further that she senses the discarnate individual's thoughts. She talks about thought waves rolling back and forth in a kind of a two-way process. She feels as if she becomes one with them. She explained that sometimes spirit-rescue is required when a person dies in a traumatic way, because he or she then often refuses to accept the new situation. This is work that may be dangerous and challenging for the medium, because the spirit beings must use the medium's body, thoughts and feelings to express their thoughts and feelings. Such an activity requires that the medium has sensible and safe people as aides at his or her side. An important aspect of spirit-rescue is that the soul, that is being helped, gets the opportunity to relive its own death process. Often it is only when this happens that the deceased accepts the situation, understands that it is only the physical body that is gone, and so can continue the journey to the next level.[326]

Norwegian Anne Brit Sylvareik (her former name was Thoresen Peters) has in an article in Parapsychological Notices no. 45 and 46/1998 with the title *Spiritisme i går, kanalisering i dag* (Spiritism yesterday, channelling today) given a brief overview of mediums and channelling through the millennia, and has sought to define the term channelling. She believed that we live in an open system, where the physical is formed of condensed thoughts that many can access. She thought that existence is a tremendous universal consciousness where everything is a part of us and we are part of everything (cfr. the theory of the psi field and the holographic universe). This explanation fits the different opinions that everything can be found in our consciousness, and that we can have access to someone else's consciousness but it says nothing about whether there are different

---

i. Arthur Conan Doyle, The History of Spiritualism (complete), p. 107.

dimensions of existence or beings in other dimension than the physical, which many of the quoted statements above indicate.

9.5. Is help available?

I have often experienced that I have a helper (or several helpers), and I often feel that I am being directed to do certain things and I am not alone in having such experiences. Who, for example, has taken control of my car, or control over me, and made the car drive just as it had to in order to avoid a collision in cases where there must surely have been one? I was not aware of what I should do. What caused me to behave in a certain way in a specific situation that made other people react to my disadvantage, but which gave the result that in the long run was to my advantage? Why do I meet just *that* person in certain situations? Who is whispering a warning in my ear when I am on the way towards a precipice in thick fog or prevents me from taking a bus or airplane that later has a serious accident? Many such experiences have been written about and described.[327]

A good example of such helpers is given in Fridtjof Nansen's description from that part of his polar expedition which began when he and Hjalmar Johansen left the ship *Fram* on the 14th March 1895. They went on foot on the ice cap as far north as to 86° 4' N and 133° 37' E.[i] On the 8th April 1895 they had to turn round due to the ice conditions. They came to Franz Josef Island where they had to spend the winter. Three times were Nansen and Johansen prevented by different conditions from setting out on the open sea in their kayaks; a voyage they would hardly have survived. Twice it was bad weather which stopped them. The third time when they were at the southernmost tip of the archipelago and apparently had no choice but to traverse the ocean they were attacked (and in fact rescued) by a walrus. The walrus tore a gash in the kayak which forced them back on dry land. Shortly after they heard dogs barking and found Frederick Jackson's expedition, which later brought them safely back to Norway.

We all probably know the concept of *providence* – we like to say that providence interfered when something inexplicable happens to our advantage. In the Old Norse mythology the term *hamingja* or the more familiar *fylgja* were well-known, both words can best be translated as guardian angel. One's fylgja would help in a difficult situation. All mythologies have stories about gods interfering in human lives and affecting them – such as in Homer's epics *The Odyssey* and *The Iliad*. Or is it my own subconsciousness or superconsciousness that makes other people come to my aid or cross my path? Was it the subconsciousness of Nansen and Johansen which in the aforementioned case directed the walrus, which certainly saved them from certain death? Or is it the highest spirit of the

---

i. Described in *Fram gjennom Polhavet* (Fram through the Arctic Ocean) by F. Nansen. The description of the voyage is available in English via the internet as *Farthest North*.

human being – the Self – that is this guardian angel; and which also can direct the nature forces as in the Fridtjof Nansen case? Or are there actually some other beings? Padre Pio is said to have explained that all people have their own angel – a guardian angel. (Ref. Matt 18.10: *"... For I tell you that their angels in heaven always see the face of my Father in heaven."*) If a person sought his help and begged the angel to contact Padre Pio, he would see this angel as clearly as if he saw a human being.[328] Padre Pio was able to send his angel to others to help them – or maybe just to remind a monastic brother about his tasks and it is said that his angel was in constant contact with the angels of the people who sought his help, those whom he considered as his spiritual children – his parishioners.

Do all human beings have a guardian angel? If we are to believe Padre Pio, the answer is yes. In certain traditions it is claimed that every human being is awarded an angel at physical birth. However, many people find this difficult to accept when they see all the misfortune which affects people, and all the difficulties most people are struggling with. If everything is predestined, so that people in some way are governed by their inherent desires and lust and what they need to learn, based on previous incarnations, there must be something or someone that makes sure, that whatever shall happen, this also happens. There must then be something that manages each human being's destiny. Many people experience spirit beings as something real that they can relate to, which sometimes can be seen and which can help. However, this controller can also be the super ego or the Self.

The Self seems to have a plan for this human life. If you do not want to follow your intuition, but want to let your ego decide, you will either experience crises or that something will affect you so strongly that you will be forced to change course. The ego is comparable to a forest wanderer who refuses to use a compass or read the map. Either you will go astray or you will be going in a circle, because you do not take into account the environment or the signs that tell you what you should do. It is only when you stumble or become alarmed that you begin to look around and are willing to correct your direction – and often quite a strong influence is required. I believe that what Eileen Caddy was told in this regard is correct.[329] The voice told her that she must accept what was happening, that everything had a meaning. There was a pattern in what was happening, and she would eventually learn that the greatest difficulties were the biggest blessings for her future development. She only had to accept this and have confidence. Later, Eileen Caddy came to the following conclusion: this voice was actually the highest ego, the immortal soul, or the Self, which is in compliance with the All. 'Our angel in heaven', whether we are big or small, is our Self, even though we at times believe we are getting help from other beings. This Self is said to see the Deity and knows the divine world order. It will therefore always see 'the heavenly Deity's face'. If we are in contact with this Self, we will always know what to do.

Who is it then that I am communicating with when or if I pray to God? Is it the guardian angel which is my closest spiritual helper, or is there a higher being? Aivanhov has said that it is difficult to pray to a God you do not have a clear picture of or some clear understanding of what it is.[330] He said that God is the power, wisdom and love. God is the source of life, as manifested in the form of light (the Son) and heat (which is the Holy Spirit). What else is manifesting itself as the life giving power of light (wisdom) and warmth (love) than the Sun – consequently Aivanhov recommended us to use the Sun as a symbol for God. We should relate to the Sun and feel its power, heat and light, and see that these three effects represent the Holy Trinity.

The next question then is: who is it that answers me when I feel that I get an answer or assistance from 'above'? Master Eckhart said that God is not something outside of us which speaks to us, but something within us.[331] The Kingdom of Heaven is within us. Thus, it is only our thoughts that can give us access to the Divine. Our thoughts keep us in touch with what goes under the concept of God – that is our own personal conception of the Divine – the divine emanation (radiance) towards the individual human being. Eileen Caddy has in her poems expressed this and also in her explanation about the Voice that gave her advice during many difficult years.[332] Eileen Caddy told of the inner voice that it sounded like a loving father who spoke to his child. In the beginning it also started its comments with "my beloved child". Later it went on to say "my dear child" and then finally only "my dear". Eileen Caddy felt a very strong love for this voice. She eventually realised that there was not an entity that was separated from her that gave her advice through the voice, although she did not understand what was going on. Then one day she realized that it was she herself who was the voice – there was no separation. God was inside her. It was the highest part of her or her being, an inner God, who was her mentor. She explained that we must search for the deep spiritual truths in ourselves instead of reading or studying different teachers. There you will find what you need.

What Eileen Caddy has said here, is confirmed by the experiences many Christian mystics have had. They say that we *do have* access to the actual Source, and that the angel inside of us sees God's face. By going deep into our own minds we will find answers to all the questions we can think to pose. It is our own innermost being (the Self) which answers – which has contact with the All or the One, even though we are projecting a response to the outside, to someone we consider as God, Jesus, an angel, a master or a guru. This is also confirmed by the research Stanislav Grof has done with holotropic breathing. However, we cannot expect to get all the help that our 'I' or Ego wishes. Perhaps we must have to experience pain, suffering, losing someone or darkness in order to make further progress in our personal development. "Nothing human shall be foreign to us." Neither are we going to have eternal life in the physical body we now have, although our 'I' may have difficulties accepting that. For the 'I' this may feel to be more than it can take, but it is not the 'I' that is the core of our being – it is the Self or something even higher. But if it is our higher Self that helps and controls us, does that mean that there is no spiritual world with spiritual beings?

9.6. Comments

Parapsychological phenomena such as telepathy, clairvoyance, psychometry, psychokinesis, retro-cognition, precognition and poltergeist-activities are related to physical people and show the amazing capabilities a person may have. Many happenings such as seeing ghosts or apparitions, automatic writing, channelled information and the like, can be due to images and data that are accessible by the subconscious of the medium and not from a spirit being. Psychologists are constantly experiencing that the psyche can exceed time and space. Many such stories may be attributed to the holographic consciousness and the Akashic archive. Potentially, we have access to all information. Sensitive people may pick up an article's history. Some events can be caused by hallucinations and fantasies, and some poltergeist phenomena can be caused by a physical individual. Channelling information may be achieved by the medium's ability to read a person's history from the aura, or read from the Akashic archive. This is also the conclusion reached by German professor Hans Bender (1907-1991), from his experience with parapsychology and Spiritism. Bender referred to several mediumistic cases which have been carefully followed by parapsychologists, similar to the stories told by Rosemary Altea, and other related phenomena.

In connection with a medium's description of a house that she had never seen, Bender stated that this could be due to telepathy or clairvoyance. He believed that neither unexplainable voices coming in on audio tape or figures seen on photographs or films, prove that they originated from non-living beings, but are more likely from living people's psyche. (This he wrote at a time when communication with the *other side* by means of electronic equipment, see chapter 3.11, had not been thoroughly investigated.) Although he did not find it probable that such mediumistic communication came from non-living beings, he would not claim that it could not be so.[333]

I wrote earlier in this chapter of Helena Blavatsky's explanation of a child who could speak a language that it never learned and discuss at a high level of expertise, (ref. the story of the girl Lorenzina, who was healed by Caterina of Siena). In the case of Therese Neumann she used words from the time of Jesus and described scenes as if she was really experiencing them (see chapter 3.3). When people experience seeing and hearing a spiritual being, which in the Western world one would identify as Jesus or the Virgin Mary, others may think that it is Buddha or the Indian god Shiva they are in contact with, depending on their religious and cultural backgrounds. These can be holographic projections, but it cannot be ruled out that all these phenomena might be caused by beings from another dimension. We should not ignore that there may also exist non-physical entities that are close to the human beings in order to help them, either individually or collectively. These helpers do not necessarily exist physically on our planet.

That the astral body is said to be a fully developed adult body, according to Rosemary Altea, is hard to believe. But the astral body may perhaps be said to be the individual personality's prototype or 'constructural drawings' – which is created anew for each physical existence and prevail until the next physical birth. It is also said that disease and any flaws you have in the physical life do not occur in a discarnate being, which seems obvious since the physical body is decaying.

That which Rosemary Altea wrote, however, does not fit especially well with what is explained in the Tibetan teachings about what happens when a human being dies, or that which Jes Bertelsen seemingly teaches. Neither the Tibetans nor Jes Bertelsen seem to believe in a life after death, to be anything like the life that people are living on the Earth, or in a deliberate continuity from one life to another. *The Tibetan Book of the Dead* explains, however, the necessity of guiding the deceased through certain stages in an after death existence, which is said to be a dream-like existence. It is possible that that which the various sources are referring to are different stages of existence after the physical death. Contact with a deceased might be possible in the very first period after the physical death, but when the mental death occurs and you go on to the causal plane, it is maintained that it is no longer possible to make contact, such as the so-called cross-correspondences indicate – although this went on for more than thirty years.

But can there be any other explanation for some of the stories mentioned above than that there are indeed souls from the *other side* that influence people's lives, or that there may be an interaction between such beings and physical persons? Who or what are the voices or individualities which appear through mediums in the form of materialization or channelling, or who is causing miracles? Did Yogananda's old guru Sri Yuktesvar really appear as a physical figure after his death? Is the materialization of objects or bodies possible? What about spirit possessions where a physical person completely changes character and actually also the way he or she looks? Were Emanuel Swedenborg and Rudolf Steiner only on a thought-flight to the psi field, or did they actually meet the deceased persons with whom they maintained they had communication?

There is much that indicates that there is another dimension with conscious beings, as many mystics have maintained. Both Seth, the Myers-spirit, John and Sri Yukteswar describe the existence in other dimensions in a way that indicates that not all channelled information is coming from our physical dimension. Arthur E. Powell's and Rosemary Altea's descriptions of the phenomenon of spirit give an explanation of a spirit world – a world that might be in physical contact with human beings, no matter how hard it is to relate to for those who are bound to the physical everyday existence. What they explained appears to be that which best covers all the known phenomena linked to spirit beings. The same applies to the research which Gary Schwartz has conducted, as well as the electronic transcommunication trials and the ectoplasm phenomenon. The near-death experiences which have been published lately also suggest that there is actually a spirit world of conscious beings.

Geoffrey Farthing said, as mentioned, that it is not possible for dead people to contact the living except in very special cases, but the mystics from all religions and from all corners of the globe believe that people are something more than the physical body and the mind.

Although much of what has been reported about miracles and conversations with the spirit world easily can be said to be due to human imagination and special abilities, I think it is hard to ignore that there are people who have contact with an existence other than the physical.

Their testimony I find so convincing that I have come to the conclusion that there must be other forms of existence than the physical world. This non-physical existence I will term a spiritual existence, which can have different levels. But as we have seen, there is great controversy over what the existence, on these different levels, is like, and there is also the unanswered question whether all is actually in existence at the same time.

With whom or with what we are in contact when a human being believes to have spirit contact, is, of course, uncertain. But if we consider the theories and the experiences that have been discussed above, the phenomenon that is behind a spirit experience is one of the following:

1. The observer's experience of having several existences at the same time.
2. The observer and/or the medium may have
   - been experiencing natural phenomena such as energy fields and the like
   - multiple personalities
   - had hallucinations, dreams and fantasies
   - used the power of thought / wishful thinking / a form of autism
   - picked up collective thoughts / battle field energy
   - seen holographic projections
   - used etheric abilities such as psychokinesis or psychometry
   - had an out-of-body experience – either one's own or seeing other's
   - had a near-death-experience
3. The observer and/or the medium may experience being on another plane or having contact with an individual on such a plane, which may be
   - the astral plane
   - the mental plane

- the causal plane – the Self
- higher consciousness, the Mary- or Christ-consciousness

4. Etheric beings that might be
   - nature spirits (elementary spirits)
   - shadows or shell (rests from human beings – their astral corpse)
   - vitalized shell (elementals)

5. Beings from the astral plane
   - deceased human beings
   - other beings from the astral plane

6. Beings from the higher planes
   - beings on the mental plane
   - beings on the causal plane
   - advanced spiritual beings or masters – adepts
   - still higher spiritual beings – nirmanakayas

10. Death

Now this is eternal life: that they know you, the only true God, and Jesus Christ, whom you have sent. (John 17.3)

10.1. Introduction

Death is a serious and difficult subject to write about and there is plenty of literature on this topic. It is not easy to pick out which fits the context here, as there are many approaches to the subject. Nevertheless, it can be said that all religions really are about one thing, namely, what lies behind this life and what happens when we die. These are the questions which writers attempt to answer in eschatology (the study of the last things). Most people seek an explanation through the religion in which they have been raised, if they accept it. If they are not bound by the learning from childhood, they can as a starting point search among the most well-known religions. In the three-volume work *Dødsrikets Verdenshistorie* (The World History of the Realm of the Dead) Olav O. Aukrust has tried to describe the views on death as found in the various religions and denominations, not just the best known. Aukrust was an Anthroposophist and sixth of the last of the volumes describes the eschatology of Anthroposophy.

I would expect to find that if there is a life after this, it would be described fairly equally in all religions and by anyone who maintains that they know. If reincarnation is a reality, I had also expected a mention of this in all the main religions. Such a concurrence does not appear to be the case if we consider only the written texts and are not seeking to interpret the images or parables used. But if we go to the mystics and the mystic traditions within each religion, the image is quite different. Mystery or mysticism is not something that stands out within the different religions, and I wonder why. It may be because the mystic experience is difficult to grasp for people without such experience, and most religions are based on conclusions and/or dogmas one is expected to accept without further question.

In the following pages I will first present some of the stories told by people who while alive believe having seen something of the next stage, through the so-called near-death experiences. Secondly, I will give you some of the descriptions I have found about what happens when a human being dies. Finally, I will try to see if there are any stories that seem to be more true than others, or if there is any similarity in what is described. However, already now, I will say that if this life is having a meaning, it must in my opinion, as well as for many others, have a continuation.

I think it is fairly obvious when I look back at my own life that we are undergoing a certain amount of development in this life which indicates that it has a meaning. People have believed from time immemorial and in all cultures that the human being has a soul that survives the physical body, but *what* it is that continues is another question. I must, however, mention that I cannot see that there is any necessary correlation between what happens after death and reincarnation. It might be possible to have a kind of spiritual existence after this physical life without a reincarnation on the Earth and it is unsatisfactory to talk about death without considering the theories or thoughts on world order or that which is called cosmology.

Many people reject the possibility that there is a spiritual world. Why is there such a tight wall between this life and the spiritual world – if it exists? A possible answer to this question is that the 'I' is so concerned with everything that happens in this world that it fails to capture signals from another dimension. Those who speak about a spiritual existence are saying they have reached beyond this highly concentrated 'I' (or perhaps a totally distracted 'I') – to a higher form of consciousness, that is, to the Self or maybe something higher. It seems that if we achieve a higher level of consciousness, we will also know what happens when the physical body dies. By consistent training it should be possible for all people to raise their levels of consciousness. According to Martinus, humanity is now in its darkest period because it does not have the awareness of the spiritual dimension and relates only to the material world. Slowly but surely, however, we all will develop the required receiving apparatus for this contact.

Jes Bertelsen has said that nature seems to have covered both birth and death with taboo, in part because birth is such a tremendous stress-forming event for the body that it would engender strong trauma if remembered. In order to remember what happened before birth, it is necessary to find out what happened during birth. The problem is that the 'I' was not then established. For a person to gain awareness of the spiritual plane, the ego must be transcended. That is, the consciousness must get past – get beyond – the ego. It is only when people get in touch with their spiritual essence, the Self, that they understand the meaning within physical life.[334] The Theosophists believe that there is a dense shell between the physical and the astral plane, otherwise an ordinary human being would be overrun by astral impressions, and all manner of astral adventures would be experienced by the human brain.[335] This shell can, however, be damaged or destroyed by strong emotions, consumption of drugs or similar damaging happenings, and a person may then have astral experiences.

10.2. Near-death experiences

There are many stories about people who have had a near-death experience (NDE). These are experiences that people have had while being declared clinically dead, but who then revived.

A person is declared clinically dead when the breathing has stopped, the heart has stopped beating and the brain signals have ceased. Also some people, who have been in a very traumatic situation or have had a holotropic breathing séance (cfr. Grof), may, however, have had such experiences. The experiences are strangely similar, regardless of culture and country. One of the best documented cases concerns a woman who is known under the name Pam Reynolds. She underwent a brain operation at Barrow Institute in Phoenix, Arizona, in 1991. Her eyes and ears were fully covered, she was in full narcosis and all life functions had ceased. Afterwards, she could still describe what was happening in the operation room. Also in the BBC programme in which Pam Reynolds and the doctors who operated on her described what had happened, there was an interview with a woman who was born blind, and strangely enough she could *see* what happened during the operation and give the details afterwards.[336] In addition to individuals telling of having had such experiences in recent times, come myths, fairytales and stories, which one must assume to have had their origins in experiences from another reality than the one in which we live. The most famous story of an old near-death experience in Norway is perhaps the poem *Draumkvedet* (The Dream Poem). In my opinion it fits well with the rest of such stories. Most Norwegians are well acquainted with the last line in each verse of the poem: "For månen skin'e og vegjine falle så vide" (So the Moon shines and the roads are so long). No one knows for sure when and how this poem was made. It was first recorded in the Norwegian district Telemark in the 1840's, but it is assumed that it at least is not later than around 1700.[337] The poem tells of Olav Åsteson who went to sleep on Christmas Eve and woke up thirteen days later. When he woke up he spoke about a journey through the realm of death, from hot hell past *Våsemyran* (a marsh) and *Gjallarbrui* (a bridge), to a part of Heaven. He had been given an insight into the life of the human beings and the fate of the souls after death. He saw the connection between sin and punishment, purification and grace. "For the tongue speaks and the truth is answering on Doomsday" (For tunga talar og sanning svarar på domedag), which is the final sentence in the poem.

In the reports about Shamanism we hear about shamans travelling to the realm of death and to other places on the Earth. He or she may experience great hardships, have to fight life-threatening strange beings and dangerous animals, and risk not getting back to a normal life. These trips were undertaken to bring a dying person's soul back to this life, or to heal diseases.[338] Joseph Campbell has recounted that, according to shamanistic theory, disease is either caused because a foreign body has entered the body of the sick, or that the soul has left the body and has been trapped in one of the spirit regions, which may be above, below or beyond this world.[339] Descriptions of the shaman's travels may not be totally comparable to the near-death experiences, but they are about visiting the realm of death, and the stories told are often consistent with the near-death experiences. However, it may seem that the shaman's travels better fit the descriptions of astral travels, that is, the consciousness on the astral plane in which the imagination plays a stronger role than what otherwise would be the case. Shamanic travels are perhaps closer to out-of-body experiences than the near-death experiences.

A very interesting description of a near-death experience is provided by the American doctor George G. Ritchie.[340] Ritchie was head of the psychiatric department at the Towers Hospital, Charlottesville, Virginia. Raymond A. Moody jr. has designated Ritchie's report as one of the three or four best and most fascinating stories about the experience of dying. Ritchie was declared clinically dead in 1943 and had, while in this state, an incredible experience of seeing his own body lying dead in bed. Ritchie met an individual of intense light, which he identified as Jesus. This figure radiated an unconditional love which included acceptance of all Ritchie's poor qualities, which he knew everything about. Simultaneously Ritchie experienced – as if happening in that moment, the whole of his life – everything he had experienced, in full detail. Jesus asked him to follow him, not with words, but as a telepathic order. They moved with the speed of light. They visited a city, which Ritchie registered as one of today's US cities. It was full of people, but he saw that quite a few of them were people with no physical substance, even if they looked like ordinary people. Those people, whom he understood were dead, seemed to think that they were still alive and related to the living as if they were, but since they had no substance, they were not seen by the living, nor could they do the same as when they lived. Nevertheless, they desperately continued to act as if they were alive – trying to drink beer, trying to perform the tasks they did previously, arguing with their fellow beings, reproaching their living children, etc.

Ritchie sensed the reason behind these dead people still being where they were, they still had their hearts on earthly matters. Ritchie then saw some people out on a moor. They were fighting, full of rage and frustration. But they did not have any substance and were not able to destroy each other. These people seemed to be locked into their passions, obsessed with violence, hatred, lust and destructive thought patterns. Everything they thought, they did. Ritchie sensed that it was not Jesus who had abandoned them, but that they had locked themselves inside their own emotions. But then he saw a lot of light shapes trying to help and he realized that such figures or angels had also been present to help people at the other places he had been, even though he had not seen them there. He was suddenly aware that there was a common denominator behind all the scenes he had been shown, and that was that those dead people lacked the ability to see the light or Jesus. The reason behind this inability was that the individuals were still greatly focused on earthly conditions. Ritchie's description is both incredibly beautiful and ugly. The battle scenes fit well with what we know from the Norse mythology about Valhalla – and one may ask how that myth occurred. Can Ritchie's story be true? Is it possible to remember and refer all that Ritchie tells us here from a near-death experience? Is it reality or is he out on a dream trip? We will probably never get an answer. Nevertheless, it is interesting to learn what others have experienced and have said about their near-death experiences.

Carl Gustav Jung had a near-death experience at a critical phase of an illness, during the Second World War. He felt that he was outside his physical body and went far out into space, from where he saw the Earth at more than a hundred miles distance, and he could accurately describe how the Earth looked from out there and it was very much as what we today are familiar with in pictures from space expeditions.[341] He said that he did not want to come back to the Earth – "this fragmented, limited, narrow, almost mechanical life," as he put it.

There are a number of people who have investigated out-of-body experiences and the lives of people before and after they have had these experiences. One of the most famous is Raymond A. Moody and his book *Life after Life*, which was published in the US in 1975.[342] It was a result of five years research based on patients' experiences having been declared clinically dead, experiences they reported after having returned to life. He noted significant similarities between the different stories and mentioned the same key elements in the experiences as those Elisabeth Kübler-Ross has described, which I will refer to below.

Kenneth Ring is another researcher who has examined the near-death experiences.[343] He interviewed 102 patients who had been in a near-death situation. Forty-eight per cent of these had a NDE. He has looked at the implications of these experiences and found they were very profound. The patients' lives were completely changed, and many developed paranormal abilities. Phyllis M.H. Atwater has investigated near-death phenomena since 1978, and has published several books on the subject.[344] She has interviewed more than 3000 people, many of whom were children. She has pointed out that there are many different types of experience, and they are not always nice. Some have almost hell-like experiences. Her descriptions are quite similar to those Elisabeth Kübler-Ross has described.

The Swiss American psychiatrist Elisabeth Kübler-Ross M.D. (1926-2004) has written several books about death, based on her knowledge as a doctor and psychiatrist, and on interviews with many people who have had near-death experiences, as well as on discussions and seminars she arranged.[345] What she has written, is similar to George G. Ritchie's experiences and coincides with what other scientists have found. Elisabeth

Kübler-Ross explained that the immortal body of a person is set free from the physical shell when it dies. The physical body is more like a cocoon. She described the death process as consisting of four distinct phases:

> In the first phase you will have an etheric form. You are out of the physical body, although you are very close to it, and will know what is going on with it and around it. This happens without any sort of panic, fear or anxiety. You experience your etheric body which is identical to the physical body, but without any of the handicaps the physical body had at the time of death. You will be totally conscious, but this is a higher form of consciousness, which also includes being fully conscious about everything that goes on in the surroundings where the physical body is left – what people close to the body think, any pretext they are using in order to lie to themselves and that sort of thing. (Is this the *etheric plane – the 2nd plane?*)
>
> In phase two you can move with the speed of thought, you are only spirit and energy. *You have your own identity and your special energy pattern.* Kübler-Ross said she has seen these energy patterns, reminiscent of shimmering, pulsating series of snowflakes. We meet an angel or guide who loves us, who is protecting us, and trying to direct and help us on the path we must follow in order to fulfil our own destiny, and we will be reunited with our deceased relatives. (Is this the *astral plane – the 3rd plane?*)
>
> In phase three you will firstly find yourself as in a tunnel or another form of transition. Then you will meet a bright light that is perceived as unconditional love, or Jesus if one is a Christian. It is a light that cannot be described. People who have seen this light, have within a second had a glimpse of all knowledge. Unfortunately this knowledge is forgotten when they return to the physical world. In the presence of this light you are faced with the responsibility for everything you have done. And then you will see how often you did not make the right choice, and how you have had to suffer the consequences of the choices made. You will understand that every thought, every word, every action and choice in your entire life has had an impact on other people. Then you will understand that the absolute only thing that matters is the pure love. (Is this the *mental plane – the 4th plane?*)
>
> In phase four you will no longer need the etheric form, you are only spiritual energy. This is the form that people have when living between their physical lives, and when they no longer are to be reincarnated.

Rune Amundsen (b.1952), Norway, is a specialist in clinical psychology and has published books about death and reincarnation.[346] He has also arranged seminars about these topics. He relates in his books several near-death experiences reported by Americans and Norwegians, which strongly resemble the description given by George G. Ritchie above. He has also referred to the American minister, physician, and psychiatrist Walter N. Pahnke (1931-1971) and some others, who have pointed out similarities between various mystics' experiences through the ages, which show that these experiences can be compared with other mystic experiences of unity with the Divine. Rune Amundsen emphasized the following as basic corner stones:

> The essence of the human being is its consciousness.
>
> The body is a vehicle for the consciousness when the human being is living in the physical world of time and space.
>
> When the body dies, the consciousness is liberated and passes to a world beyond this world of arranged time and space.
>
> The near-death experiences constitute the first phase of the transition to the life beyond.

Stanislav Grof's research, from séances with holotropic breathing and the use of hallucinogenic drugs (mentioned above) as well as what he reports about psycho-spiritual crises, has shown that people can have experiences during such situations which are almost identical to the near-death experiences. He has reported that the individuals may experience pain and despair in situations where they have a feeling of dying. Furthermore, they can experience hell, meetings with a deity or divine being, and they are seeing events from this and also from previous lives.[347]

Jes Bertelsen has said about the near-death experiences that people who have had such experiences are not actually dying. Their consciousness has taken them to the fifth plane, the plane of the Self, and there the events are mostly ecstatic and positive. He has stated that these experiences can be worth listening to, although they are coloured by the belief – or religious preconceptions – of the narrator. Consciousness, which is attached to the physical body, is still intact in these cases. Jes Bertelsen pointed out that when a person truly dies, the consciousness loses its connection to the body and to the energy field that surrounds the body, and then a totally different process takes place. He maintained that the consciousness' impersonal form (that which is not attached to any personality), which is the real consciousness, also goes on existing after death.[348]

Sogyal Rinpoche has said that stories about near-death experiences have been told throughout history in all mystic and shamanistic traditions, as well as by philosophers and authors such as Plato, Gregory the great, Tolstoy and Jung.[349] He has found that there is a specific core in all the NDE-stories, even if no two stories are exactly the same. His description of this core is consistent with what is related above as Elisabeth Kübler-Ross' conclusions. He said that those who have had such experiences have become deeply religious, in the sense that they see the meaning of life, the fear of dying disappears, and they become focused in the now and love-filled. He said that these descriptions often are in accord with what the *The Tibetan Book of the Dead* tells of the existence in the bardo of rebirth (*the Bardo of Becoming*).

In this state the mental body experiences visions and signs from different levels of existence, as well as many other types of visions. Those experiences can be both scary and uplifting. Sogyal Rinpoche pointed out, however, that there are marked differences between the near-death experiences and the Tibetan teaching about the bardo states. The major difference, he pointed out, is that the NDE's have been told by people who *did not die*, they have only been *close to death*. They cannot tell what actually happens when a person dies. People can have such a spiritual experience without being close to death. Tibetan teachings claim to be able to tell what actually happens when a human being dies. Sogyal Rinpoche warned therefore against believing that the NDE provides a correct description of what happens when death occurs. He maintained that it cannot be that simple. Death is not an unconditional peaceful and blessed process. Everything that we are living through during our physical life is part of a process that continues after death. Everything has a purpose. If we are not working purposefully in this physical life, we will face the problems again, either in the next state or in the next life.

Seth explained that the human being exists simultaneously in a physical world and in a spiritual world, and that we are active in the spiritual world when the physical body sleeps.[350] In this spirit existence we will have many of the same experiences as those we get when we die. It is to what a person directs its attention which is essential. After-death experiences will not feel so strange if we are aware of this. Seth's explanation fits the near-death experiences. He recommended that we should prepare for death by practising near-death experiences. Also in the dream world a kind of continuity of the experiences is experienced, in the same way as in the physical world. The experiences there are just as true for the dream ego as the daily life is for the physically conscious ego and if we do not believe in our dream life, it is because the physical conscious ego has convinced itself that it is just a dream. Because we do not remember the most important parts of a dream or understand how they should be interpreted, we experience them as chaotic and weird.

Although both Jes Bertelsen and Sogyal Rinpoche have stressed that the near-death experiences are not from people who actually have been dead, the stories fit well with Rudolf Steiner's and Emanuel Swedenborg's reports regarding the existence after death on the astral plane. They also fit Sri Yukteswar's story about the lower astral spheres and with Martinus' account of life after the first death, the physical. Also, in my opinion, Elisabeth Kübler-Ross' summary of the NDEs fits well with the descriptions of life on the different spiritual planes. Her description is, however, exclusively positive and does not include the awful stories which George G. Ritchie and others have told, and there is every reason to include those in order to make the picture complete. Sogyal Rinpoche suggested that people rather want to remember the positive experiences from such an event and not the negative ones. David Scott Rogo has referred some NDE-cases where the person concerned actually can be said to have been in hell. Both Dr Maurice Rawlings (1923-2010), a cardiologist in Tennessee, and Dr Charles Garfield, a psychologist at California University, have received such reports from their patients, although they have also been told of positive experiences. It should be noted in this context, that these doctors have received information at an early stage, a short time after the patients have return to normal consciousness. Rawlings said that unpleasant memories are fairly quickly banned from the memory.[351]

Some experiences like these have also been produced in laboratory experiments. The Norwegian TV channel NRK1 showed a BBC production, on 8th November 1999, about the human body's aging process where people were exposed to a strong centrifugal force. They experienced euphoria and felt then as though they were in a tunnel and saw a bright light at the end of the tunnel. It happened when the test person was on the verge of losing consciousness. The explanation was that when the blood was withdrawn from the brain, the ability to see would be changed so that it saw the light further and further away, just as though at the end of a tunnel. During some laboratory trials specific points in the brain have been stimulated, and the test person then achieved a dream-like state similar to those experiences with the use of drugs. As mentioned, Stanislav Grof has spoken of people who during holotropic breathing séances or under the influence of hallucinogenic drugs have had experiences similar to the NDE stories.

The question of whether the near-death experience is real or if it only is due to a stimulus of certain brain cells, is (in my opinion) unanswered. Certainly, these stories correspond fairly well to the Theosophical teachings about an astral existence and an existence after the physical death. However, even though such stories have been told many times, and with almost identical explanations, it is not proven that they say something real about life after the physical death. Michael Talbot has written that many scientists, particularly Kenneth Ring, are more and more leaning towards the theory that this can be explained as holographic experiences of the holographic brain. They are in particularly emphasizing the accounts regarding the strong light experiences and those where one seems to be outside time and space, and the experience that here one apparently has a physical adult body in the best of fitness and form. The experiences can be explained as the interaction of thought structures based on our beliefs and our expectations. It should also be added here that experiences from the operating room which the patients relate, having come back to consciousness, can be explained as telepathy, clairvoyance or psychometry.

10.3. Stories told about what happens when a human being dies

The ancient Egyptians' death cult is well-known. When you are in Egypt, you get the impression that their whole culture only concerned death, about what meets the deceased at the entrance to the realm of death, and about the importance of preserving the body for later use. Many people may also have read *The Egyptian Book of the Dead* or heard it discussed. One can easily think that this book is something like *The Tibetan Book of the Dead* but the two books are so different that a comparison has no purpose. *The Egyptian Book of the Dead* is a series of texts written on papyrus, found in mummies' chests and dating from about 1500 BCE and later. The texts were collected and published in 1842 by Richard Lepsius. These, together with texts found on walls and chests in older tombs and inscriptions in temples, are the foundation of what we today know of Egyptian mythology. It will, however, take too much space here to describe the Egyptian mythology and what the Egyptians believed would happen when a person dies, also because the mythology changed through the millennia in which the ancient Egyptian civilization existed. Religions historian Arthur Versluis has in his book *The Egyptian Mysteries* described the Egyptian gods, death cults and cosmology.[352] This description seems to be in agreement with much of what I have understood of many mystics' view of life. In order to understand this we must remember that the images are symbols of the forces of nature. It ought to be sufficient here to refer to Olav O. Aukrust's books. He said that the Egyptians did not consider death as the end of existence, but as a premise for a new existence and the transition to this. It was important to know what hazards one would meet on the other side, in order to be able to overcome them.

The ancient Greeks also believed in a life after death and reincarnation. The Greek poet Pindar (c. 518-438 BCE) has in a poem said: "The body follows death's decree, the soul lives in eternity." I think there is good reason also to quote Joseph Campbell's reference to the Greek philosopher *Heraclitus* (c. 540-480 BCE) (known for the phrase: *Everything is floating*) which shows that Bob Moore's description of what happens when a person dies (reproduced below), is not something new in an historical perspective.[353]

> For that alone comes from the gods, from there comes and to there it returns; not in body, but when it is freed and separated from it, and when it is completely clean and cleaned and without meat: for the most perfect soul, says Heraclitus, is a dry light rocketing out of the body like a bolt of lightning from a cloud; for that which is dirty and defiled by the body is like a rough incense, late to ignite and to rise up.

Plato's world view was based on, as previously mentioned, that beyond the world of our senses is a world consisting of norms, patterns and role models for thinking and action – a world of the invisible spirits. In addition he pointed to a spiritual existence. Socrates says in *Phaedo*, just prior to having to empty the cup of poison, that there is no reason to weep, because where he is going he is expecting to meet new friends and rulers, which are better than those he has met here in this world.

Yogananda conveyed in his autobiography his master Sri Yukteswar's explanation of the existence, an account the latter communicated after his physical death, according to Yogananda.[354] Yogananda recounts that the master on this occasion appeared in his old body of flesh and blood. The master explained that he really was on the astral plane, and that he lived on an astral plane. On that plane are the spirits of advanced individuals. The master explained further that the human soul is enveloped in three bodies, respectively an idea – or causal body, a subtle astral body, which is the seat of the human sense, and a crude physical body. When the physical death occurs, the individual loses its physical consciousness and becomes conscious of its astral body. But there is also an astral death, where he or she goes back to the physical world, unless the person has been so enlightened that the next stage is the idea-and-causal world. The human being, as an individualized soul, belongs to the causal world. As long as the human soul is enveloped in one, two or three bodies, which are closed due to ignorance and lust, the human being is not able go up into the Spirits' Ocean. When the rough physical container is dissolved, there are still two other bodies that prevent the soul uniting itself with what is known as "Everywhere-present life". He said:

> When the no-wishes state is achieved through wisdom, its power will dissolve the remaining two containers. The little human soul rises up, finally free, united with the Unmeasureable Plains.

When it comes to *Buddhism's* belief about death, everyone has presumably heard about Nirvana, which one can obtain through right behaviour and attitude. In Norway we hear mainly about the Tibetan form of Buddhism, and therefore I will mention something about that. This is partly due to Sogyal Rinpoche's book about the Tibetan belief of life and death, where he seeks to explain *The Tibetan Book of the Dead*. Padmasambhava, who lived in Afghanistan and came to Tibet around the year 750 CE, is said to have been the author of this book.[355] The texts were supposedly hidden and only found many hundreds of years later. The book consists of a series of instructions on what to say to a dying person to help this person to be prepared for what she or he meets when life in the body is ebbing out. If the dying one manages to retain what is said and remember it in death, it is possible to ensure that the usual return to earthly life ceases. That is, one can then reach a blessed state.[356] The most commonly used name of *The Tibetan Book of the Dead* is Bardo Thødol. The word *Bardo* means state, or rather the indeterminate state. The book describes the six states of Samsara or the cycle of existence, namely:

The most important states are the four transitional states (the bardo of dreams and the bardo of meditation do not belong to these). Sogyal Rinpoche has explained that the first two states are something like this:

Chikhai Bardo – the bardo at the moment when you are dying.

Dharmata Bardo – the period of death. The word dharmata means the real essence of things or reality, and dharmata bardo is the period when enlightenment occurs. Dharma is truth, but also reality.

The reincarnation's bardo.

The birth's and this life's bardo.

The dream's bardo.

Sam'di Bardo or the meditation's bardo. Sam'di is the state of meditation where the difference between subject and object disappears, the deepest form of meditation.

The first Bardo, the moment when you die, is very important. Then you will get a glimpse of the first enlightenment (*The first Luminosity*) – the essence of reality. How long this state will last may vary, depending on the level of development of the dying. For most people it is hardly more than some tenths of a second. It is important that you recognize this essence, the basic enlightened stage of existence, in order to evolve further. If you do not recognize this first enlightenment, you will experience the second enlightenment (*The second Luminosity*) and get another chance to be freed from your karma. If that does not happen, you will pass to the next bardo state, the Dharmata Bardo.

In Dharmata Bardo (that is the death period – the stage between death and a new birth) it is important that you recognize everything that happens as your own projections, and understand that you do not need to be afraid. The dying person may meet a lot of terrible creatures and gruesome experiences but it is again and again underlined that this is not due to intrinsic evil, but ignorance, unconsciousness and projections. The basic cause of sin and suffering is the belief that there is an 'I' or an ego that is the centre of existence. Because of this incorrect perception we are not able to see reality as it really is. The dying must be constantly reminded that whatever is experienced by terrible happenings, he or she has to realize what it really is, namely one's own projections. Furthermore, we must learn to recognize the beings who are our real helpers, who usually appear in such a strong light that it is almost unbearable to see, instead of the beings one can be tricked by, who appear in a dimly comfortable light. Dharmata Bardo is said to last for forty-nine days. *The Tibetan Book of the Dead* provides an accurate description of what you may meet on the different days, and from whom you will be able to get help. It gives recommendations with regard to what the bereaved should say to the dead to help him or her on the way. It is important that we are prepared as to what we meet after death, and that we have a guide who knows these stages. If we are completely prepared, perhaps we can avoid the burden of reincarnation, or at least get easier issues to battle against in the next life.

Sogyal Rinpoche claimed that the source of the doctrine of bardo is the fully enlightened mind, which is what the mystics within the Tibetan tradition have learnt in their meditations.[357] These mystics are bearers of a tradition that goes back to Buddha. But he also emphasized that *The Tibetan Book of the Dead* is difficult to understand for those who do not know the Tibetan tradition transmitted from master to student. He also said that life is a continuous dance of births and deaths, and that it would be impossible to learn to know death if it only happened once. Death brings us back to the original state, the true nature of mind, an empty space.

The Christian Apostolic Creed about death, which is used in The Norwegian Church, has the following wording: "I believe in the Holy Spirit, a sacred public Church, the Saints' society, the forgiveness of sins, the resurrection of the body and the eternal life." Christianity is thus based on the belief in a life after the physical. But what does the statement about the resurrection of the body mean or the concept eternal life? It is maintained that Jesus arose from the dead. Does it mean that his physical body was preserved? According to legend, his body was not in the grave when Mary Magdalene arrived there (John 20.1). Does this indicate that the body was still intact? Huston Smith has written the following about Christianity:[358]

> After death human life is transferred to the supernatural domain, but not even in earthly life is it quite isolated from that. This all sections in Christianity have agreed upon. The difference lies in the degree to which Christians try to take part in the supernatural life while they live on Earth. The Catholic Church asserts that the Trinity lives in every Christian soul, but that its presence usually cannot be noticed. Prayers and penitential exercises can make a soul inclined to receive exceptional supplies of supernatural grace, but strictly speaking the soul does not have any right to the mysterious stages in this life; they will come (in time) as gifts. The Orthodox Church actively encourages its members to take the initiative towards the mystical life.

Olav O. Aukrust has referred to the Catholic dogma which says:[359]

> ... the body that the soul will get on judgment day, is the same as the body it had in the earthly life and those two together constitute one single human being. The dead will be resurrected with numerically (what concerns numbers) the same body as they have had on Earth.

Aukrust also wrote that how this dogma is to be understood, the Church has not elaborated further. Aukrust referred in his work to the discussions that have taken place within the Church over the centuries regarding the understanding of these dogmas. There is no clear consensus. Both the immortality of the soul and the immortality of the body are thus witnessed in this credo, although soul and body are not considered the same. This belief has probably its origin with St Paul:

> But someone will ask, "How are the dead raised? With what kind of body will they come?" (1 Cor. 15.35)
>
> So will it be with the resurrection of the dead. The body that is sown is perishable, it is raised imperishable; it is sown in dishonor, it is raised in glory; it is sown in weakness, it is raised in power; it is sown a natural body, it is raised a spiritual body. If there is a natural body, there is also a spiritual body. (1 Cor. 15.42-44)
>
> Listen, I tell you a mystery: We will not all sleep, but we will all be changed – in a flash, in the twinkling of an eye, at the last trumpet. For the trumpet will sound, the dead will be raised imperishable, and we will be changed. For the perishable must clothe itself with the imperishable, and the mortal with immortality. When the perishable has been clothed with the imperishable, and the mortal with immortality, then the saying that is written will come true: "Death has been swallowed up in victory." "Where, O death, is your victory? Where, O death, is your sting?" The sting of death is sin, and the power of sin is the law. (1 Cor. 15.51-56)

When it comes to the Islamic standpoint, the following comment from Huston Smith is interesting:[360]

> The Quran depicts life as a short-lived but immensely valuable opportunity that offers us a choice once and for all. From here comes the intense message that permeates the whole book. The chance to return to life for only a single day to make good use of the possibilities is something 'the losers' on doomsday would put it even higher than anything they ever desired while they were alive.
>
> Depending on how the soul will make it on doomsday, it will go to heaven or hell. ...
>
> As a last point: If all this talk about punishment mainly seems to assign God the role of the punitive one, we can refer to the verses in the Quran that exempt Allah entirely for direct involvement. In these verses the souls are condemning themselves. Death burns away the protective defence works, so you are forced, with total objectivity, to realize how you have lived your life. In the uncompromising light from this vision, where no dark rooms are allowed, it is your own actions that arise to accuse or confirm. When the 'I' first has been extracted from the realm of lies, the untruthfulness it has armoured itself behind changes to flames, and the life it has lived there changes to a Nessos-shirt.[i]

Emanuel Swedenborg's description of the death realm coincides remarkably well with George G. Ritchie's near-death experience. Swedenborg explained that the first existence after death is a spirit world

---

i. A Nessos-shirt kills anyone who puts it on.

without borders.³⁶¹ This spirit world exists between the region of heaven and the region of hell. But there are a variety of spheres, each representing different degrees or levels that represent the various spiritual conditions possible to humankind. Each person is automatically judged by the totality of his or her life works. The true human mind is something other than the outer-borne mask or persona. This first period will be characterized by the relations of the mask, because existence is still exterior. You believe that you are still in the physical world, as the societal makeup is much like the Earth plane with houses, churches, assembly halls, and even palaces where those in charge would reside. This sphere was once called "Summerland" by the famous American medium Andrew Jackson Davis (1826-1910) when in trance.³⁶² It is the thought that direct the experiences and time does not actually exist. But Swedenborg also pointed out the same as is written in *The Tibetan Book of the Dead*, that in a short moment after the physical death has occurred, the angels do everything they can to help the deceased, but often this one does not realize this. How long you actually stay in this first existence will depend on how much time you need to lay off this outer mask and understand life and obtain harmony in the mind. In the next stage you will appear as your innermost mind really is. It is your thoughts and desires that govern existence. The thought is your will's tool. If the thoughts are negative, you will be drawn towards the lower regions and vice versa. Swedenborg pointed out that if you are cruel or acting or think evil, you are automatically pulled downwards towards personalities with the same type of mind. The penalty is that evil powers take control of you. Those who are not morally good enough will be purified and cleaned in this existence. When you have been cleaned of all that is negative in connection with your mind, you will come to the next stage, which is a preparation or apprenticeship before you can enter into Heaven. Here there are helping angels. It can be seen from the orientation that all souls are afraid of the unknown. That is, they are afraid to leave the level where they are and move on to the higher stages, in the same way as human beings in the physical existence are afraid to die. But what is underlined about the next existence is that spiritually related individuals will come in contact with each other and that in the higher existences all are good and close friends.

Rudolf Steiner has said that physical decay is spiritual birth. He has further explained that when the physical death occurs, the etheric body, the astral body and the mental body leave the physical body. It is the spiritual part of the human being who wakes up in the spiritual world. This is the opposite of what happens at birth, as consciousness then dies in the spiritual world and starts living in the physical. A person who has attained clairvoyance will be able to experience the spiritual world from his or her physical stage in the same way as a person who is dead, and will be able to go around in the spirit realm of the dead. Steiner has said that for him the spiritual world was a reality, and that he could follow a departed person over into the spiritual world. Olav O. Aukrust, refers to this statement of Steiner's, saying that Steiner's vision was that people are not on Earth just to gather physical valuables for a few short years, but to send something up into the world above the physical that only can be created and won on the physical plane. He further said that when Anthroposophy really gets a place in the hearts of people, it will bridge the cleft between the physical and the spiritual world.[363] In order to understand Steiner we must also try to understand what passes on into the spiritual world and later returns to a terrestrial existence. He explained that the human being in the period between the physical death and new birth lives through the spiritual world's realities. Aukrust wrote that there is only an extract of the etheric body and the astral body that goes on (both of these bodies disintegrate, but at different times), while the 'I' (the spiritual) continues. "Immortality is not a question whether the 'I' exists or not, but whether it is conscious of itself.

Immortality for the 'I' that is to be found in the human being's ordinary consciousness, is contradicted by each night's sleep, because then this 'I' is simply extinguished." Aukrust said that only the initiated ones or the seers can get an idea of this 'I' and then we might be in line with what Jes Bertelsen has explained.

There is not much we know about *Marcello Haugen's* view on death. The biography only states that he saw death as another form of life.[364] He recommended that we send dying people good thoughts and feelings, because this will help them during a difficult transition.

Martinus wrote that the living being has to be considered immortal since it has no beginning and never will cease to exist.[365] He explained that death is a remarkable encounter with God's primary consciousness and the godhead's biggest surprise for the human beings. Death is something that only concerns the physical organism. This has a limited time of service, and the individual must therefore renew it periodically in that part of existence which is spent in the physical life. Death is just a separation of the ego from its physical body. The other five bodies which form the 'I''s overall energetic organism, exist fully after the physical death, and are adequate as a foundation for the 'I''s eternal continuation. The 'I' has the ability to again create a physical body, whereby it carries on previous experiences, now transformed into talents, abilities and consciousness-bodies. The experience itself is only temporary, transient colour impressions, vibration and reactions – which ought to be understandable when we think of how we, for example, experience a journey. Martinus explained further that at the physical death of the organism the physical form of existence is replaced by a purely 'paraphysical' one. This spiritual type of existence spans a shorter or longer period of time, depending on the type of being concerned, as well as the being's consciousness level. Martinus also stated that the beings pass through the higher divine worlds in a sort of guest existence between the physical incarnations. In common with all beings on these high levels they radiate an absolutely harmonious flame of love; they express love and are perfectly in harmony with the laws of life. All types of hate and animosity have been left at the entrance to this world. Martinus' description of death must, however, be seen in context with his explanation about the living being and reincarnation.

When it comes to the question of why human beings are on Earth – why they have to come into physical matter, Martinus took as a starting point what he called the *talent-seed principle*. Through creative activity, the being will be enhanced with more and more talent-seeds, which contain the being's all knowledge and experience storage, as well as everything the being has at its disposal in order to maintain an organic structure – physically as well as paraphysically. The talent-seeds exist in what he called the living being's superconsciousness. (The term 'the living being' implies for Martinus something more than the physical human being. The same applies to what he terms as the 'I'.) In order to achieve cosmic consciousness the living being must pass through the earthly life, because here it will be able to have experiences which it otherwise is not able to acquire. It is mainly through earthly lives that we may learn wisdom. In order to acquire wisdom, we must be familiar with the difference between good and evil, and that can only be learned where matter offers resistance to movement and influences, and where it causes pain and discomfort when there is wrong thinking and action. Acting wrongly happens when one is in conflict with the laws of life and nature. Per Bruus Jensen, who has written about Martinus' teachings, said that the physical world can, with this backdrop, be seen as a school for wisdom and the art of living.

When it comes to the description of a person's death and what happens afterwards, Martinus has split the process in two. In the first part death is freeing the person from the physical organism. When this has happened, instead of receiving impressions through the physical body, the being will receive impressions from a world of paraphysical matter. In this state it will be the being's spiritual structure that serves to convey impressions and this we may say is now taking over the being's day-awareness. Martinus explained that this also applies to animals, but not to plants. The world the being meets after this first death will be very similar to the world it has left behind. The details that occur in the paraphysical world are created by the being itself. This is a world of volatile and light invisible matter that only becomes visible and gives form to the extent that the being itself, by using its spiritual structure or thought, adjusts and shapes it. The description further, which explains that the being still believes that it has an earthly existence, is totally in line with George G. Ritchie's near-death experience and Swedenborg's explanation.

The contact between the beings in the spiritual world is *mental*. The beings must be spiritually related in order to interact. That is, whoever you get in touch with depends on the spiritual level where you now are. However, it takes too much space here to give Martinus' descriptions in detail. I will only mention that the cultivation of physical interests and selfishness or egocentricity during the physical life period may cause problems for your life in the spiritual world. The only consolation is, however, that assistance can and will be given to those who have problems. It is also possible to cultivate positive interests and experience joy and inspiration in this world, and in this way achieve a kind of ideal existence. Martinus highlighted that in this sphere it is important to remain free from conflicts and adapt to the laws of the new existence. This means that the driving force behind what you think is your willingness to bring joy and blessing to others and to the totality. However, a new death will occur, which is a form of liberation from the lower nature in the being's psyche, a sort of purification. In this transition the being is freed from all that is low, base and primitive in its nature. Then it comes to a new zone (through a new birth) of the spiritual world that best may be described as Paradise or the Kingdom of God. There there are beings of a high spiritual level (guardian angels) that assist with this transition. Also in this sphere charity is the basis of existence and meaning, at the same time as it is a place for spiritual interests. The beings you meet here have incredible wisdom, intuition and cosmic knowledge. This elevated world is denoted by Martinus as 'God's primary consciousness'. All beings will, before they are born again in the physical world, reincarnated, have the opportunity to stay for a period in this sphere.

Edgar Cayce has explained that the conscious mind disappears when the physical body dies.[366] But the subconsciousness continues to exist, because it is not dependent on the physical substance. It is this part that becomes the soul's conscious mind after death, and it works as such until the soul takes residence in a new body. But human beings also have a higher consciousness, and at death this part takes over the functions of the subconscious, so this then becomes the soul's subconsciousness. When the soul is born again, this is reversed. This higher consciousness, which some people may, in very special cases, come in touch with, as Edgar Cayce did under his self-induced hypnosis is the human being's subconsciousness, the databank, which contains all previous experiences. The ordinary consciousness ought to listen to the subconsciousness – the small inner voice. Cayce has further explained that the new human being is building on what was achieved in previous incarnations, and there is a direct continuity from the last past life to the present. You may then experience the new life from the opposite side of the previous life; so that now there is a possibility that you may be the victim of actions of the same nature as you previously inflicted on others. But there is always a chance for repentance and grace, and good deeds now can offset earlier bad ones.

Laurens van der Post has commented on *Carl Gustav Jung's* statement that death is most difficult when you are on the outside of it, but that you will experience such a strong peace that you do not want to turn back when death is approaching.[367]

Anna Elisabeth Westerlund argued that when a person was dead, it could not come back to life.[368] She maintained that out-of-body experiences and experiences of previous incarnations could be explained by telepathy and psychometry. She did not find the existing documentation in regard to a life after this particularly credible.

Bob Moore has said that he has seen many people dying and followed their death process.[369] These have for him been rewarding experiences which have taught him much about what it is to live, because he has seen that the dying in a way is feeling high, which especially happens when the energy reaches the heart and is resting there. Then it moves up to the head and from there to what he calls the individual point, which is above the head. Then it disappears. Bob Moore believes that when the energy reaches the heart, the dying get the opportunity to feel, to accept and to open up to what is happening. He has emphasized that in this respect it is especially important how you think, and he is very sorry that some religions or theorists frighten people with their stories of death and hell. His experience from being present at deaths is that the death event is wonderful, because it releases restricting structures. The physical is limited, which means that we cannot easily reach beyond it. We have therefore lost contact with the deeper levels we have known, and we are prevented from understanding the relationship between conception, birth and death. We should look at death as something to be looked forward to, because then we would consider the physical life process differently. Then we will understand that we all have a deeper, richer contact with each other and that we are all connected, although we are individuals. We have our individual souls, which will grow. There is a development plane behind the physical that is important.

Jes Bertelsen has described the death process in his books, and he has also sought to explain the human beings' spiritual side. He has had close contact with Tibetan lamas and is well informed about the Tibetan form of Buddhism but in order to understand what he has written about death, we must first learn how he views the human being. He has said that all individuals have a lower awareness and a spiritual awareness, and the meaning of life is to develop love and higher awareness. The stage between death and the next life is an intermediary stage – here we are in the three inner planes. While we are on the physical plane, it is only by training and awareness that we can manoeuvre within these inner planes. The vision of a tunnel during a near-death experience corresponds to the transition to the fifth plane (the transition from the mental to the causal or spiritual plane). Bertelsen has written this:[370]

> However, when a human being really dies, then the attachment to the physical body is lost, as well as to the breath, to the astral and to the mental. And so the liquidation process through the fifth and the

sixth planes goes with lightning speed, because the delay from the identification and the anchored context with the lower planes is simply ending.

The ordinary consciousness is living and expanding in the first four consciousness levels: the physical-bodily, the etheric-energetic, the astral-emotional and the mental plane. These four levels and perception strategies cover and disguise the three inner planes, the spiritual, the cosmic and the unity consciousness. Death looks very different depending on whether it is experienced from the three external planes or from the three inner planes. The fourth plane, the heart's and the ordinary consciousness' mental level, seems to follow either the external plane's modus of happenings or the perspective of the internal planes. The understanding of Death as a termination, an ending and a disappearance, is real on the first four planes. The physical body dies, decays and disappears. The substance continues in new circles. The vital energy, life, likewise dwindles in death; normally it ends with the last breath. The astral-emotional, that is all the emotions, personal recollections, images and dreams, disappear in death. The archetypical collective, the astral matrix still remains, but on a collective unconscious and impersonal level. In the mental the content of the consciousness disappears. The swarm of words, fantasies and personal thoughts, of which I have spoken, heard and thought in my life, spread like a cloud and disappear in death. The consciousness' impersonal form, the proper consciousness, stays on. It is the consciousness in and of itself that is just the way to the inner planes. The three internal planes are normally relatively latent in a human life. They are like seeds, ready for germination, but often they do not ferment. The inner planes are present in all humans, but they are hidden, the consciousness is normally not awake in its internal planes.

The purpose of the exercises, prayers and meditation is to become awake on the inner consciousness planes. If a human being is awake, which means it has discovered and activated its spirituality, then such a human being will experience that which we call the level of the Self's continuity. Certainly, it is not possible to be conscious at the fifth plane without having experienced the progressive karma; we will see that the consciousness, from a more superior and impersonal plane, again and again reincarnates or is explicit through the mental, the astral, the vital and the body, and in this process the spiritual consciousness-continuum creates its individuality and restriction, and this encapsulated individual prerogative has a price, which is the death of the individual. But at the fifth spiritual plane – when it is awake and realized – death is rather the same as a sleep filled with dreams is for the 'I'. I go to bed and fall asleep. There are dreams and there is the deep sleep's vegetative continuum. But in the morning I am still – rather strangely – myself again – remembering continuity is continuous. For the 'I' at the fourth plane sleep is a breach in the consciousness, but within a superior continuity. Anyone being awake at the fifth plane 'will not taste death'.

From the awake perspective of the three inner consciousness planes there is no death understood as termination, ending or disappearance. As Bob Moore once said: 'There is no such thing as death.' Death is a transition or a modification in a superior consciousness-continuum or when looking from the perspective of the unity consciousness, there is neither birth nor death; the unity consciousness transcends even the phenomenon of time. A human being without the decisive spiritual praxis is not able to recognize the meeting with or the infolding in the unity consciousness. The rest of the process from the moment of death and until the next birth will therefore take place partly – as when fainting, partly in a dreamlike condition that changes between a blessed and a nightmare dream without the possibility of influencing or manoeuvring the process to any degree.

The enlightened consciousness, the naked essence of the consciousness, is hidden in the ordinary consciousness – within and from the self-image, within and from the image of the world – in the same way as a 3-D picture is hidden in a two dimensional computer picture. Meditation and prayer are basically, actually another way of seeing. The ordinary consciousness cannot straight away see its own higher or inner planes of functioning. The actual ordinary consciousness covers, through its basic functions,(instinctive consideration, focusing, activities and language) the inner consciousness functions (the spiritual, the cosmic and the unity consciousness). The purpose of wordless prayers and meditative contemplation is to de-learn the ordinary way of the 'I''s use of the consciousness, in order to, in this de-learning process, discover the higher consciousness levels, from where completeness, spiritual fellowship and compassion streams spontaneously.

Ken Wilber has, from a different point of view, shown that human beings have a transcendent Self. This Self is actually one and the same for everyone and is what may be called God.[371] When a human being is able to understand this, he or she will also get a feeling of eternal life but most people are concentrated around their own body, their own ego or persona, and have the strong wish that it is this 'I' that must survive the physical death. Ken Wilber underscored however that neither the mind, nor the ego or the body has eternal life. He pointed out that the body is constantly changing, and that also the emotions change through the years. The same goes for memories, because even if we have memories about events that have happened, is this not the same as remembering what we experienced in the way things actually happened. We have to live in the moment now. There is a feeling deep inside every person which is not memories, thoughts, mind, body, experiences, surroundings, emotions, conflicts, sensing or moods, because all of this is always changing. The innermost feeling is the Self, or that which Ken Wilber calls the transpersonal Witness. It is God alone that sees through our eyes, is listening with our ears and talks with our tongues. Wilber has maintained that this is the message given by Carl Gustav Jung, by saints, mystics and sages from all cultures, whether these are American Indians, Taoists, Hindus, Islamists, Buddhists or Christians. He has referred to sayings by Master Eckhart and St Clement from among the Christian mystics as well as several of the most outstanding mystics from other traditions. He has explained that when the Self (the soul), which is an individuality or an expression of a distinct person, obtains contact with the spiritual existence and becomes a clear spirit, it loses the illusion of separateness. When death occurs, the physical body will go up into the mental. When the mental body goes up into the soul, the life lived will be checked and evaluated. When the soul goes up into spirit, there will be a total liberation and transcending. When reincarnation occurs, this process will be almost reversed.

Seth explained, inter alia, that the human being does not consist only of matter. Death is the beginning of another existence.[372] When Seth was describing physical death and what happens thereafter, he took as a starting point the fact that we are living at the same time as millions of cells in our body are dying and at the same time being replaced. He said that the same happens with our consciousness; it is like a firefly that blinks on and off continuously. The consciousness is not continuous; it blinks on and off and is never totally turned off so, even if we are not aware of the fact, we may say that we very often are 'dead', even in the middle of the glorious life our consciousness is experiencing. By using the term that the consciousness is *on* or *alive*, Seth wanted to indicate that it is focused on the physical life and the physical reality. When it is *dead*, it is because the consciousness has its focus some other place. All living beings have such an on/off existence but the periods of *on* or *off* are different for the different structures, from atoms and molecules to other structures. Our ordinary consciousness does not sense this rhythm and even if our body has changed a lot compared with what it was say ten years ago, there is always an image with which we identify. Even when the consciousness leaves the physical body, the atoms and molecules of which this body is composed will continue to exist, but in another structure. Death is thus only a state where the consciousness has withdrawn from the physical body in such a way that this changes (disintegrates) but all its constituencies will continue to exist. Seth further explained that human beings are themselves forming their surroundings, both the physical and the spiritual. How we experience the next existence is therefore dependent on how we think. We will translate the happenings according to what we believe. There is never one given solution but we will meet guides who will explain what is happening. Some of those may be earthly individuals, who, with the help of out-of-body travels, can meet the deceased in its existence, although they do not necessarily have to remember those nightly trips.

We will find ourselves in a different form in the next existence. This would seem physical, but we cannot act as in the physical life. We must understand how the spiritual life is functioning. Here there are completely different laws than on Earth. We can meet kindred on the other side, but it can also be people we have met and been committed to in previous lives. Life there can be much more intense and joy-filled than on Earth, although we cannot expect a lazy life. Seth said that not only will we have to use our abilities; we will also be confronted with those we did not use in our last earthly existence.

Seth further explained that people, who believe in a life after death, will face the new life a lot more easily than others. We can prepare for this existence and we will then have a much better starting point than what we would otherwise have had. We can practise out-of-body travels and thereby experience the spiritual existence. We have such trips when we are sleeping, even if we do not remember them. There are methods for remembering dreams and other mental disciplines that help to remember other dimensions. At the moment we die, we may easily be confused and not understand what is going on. We can see our body lying lifeless, but may refuse to acknowledge that we cannot make contact with the surroundings. Thoughts and feelings affect the realities we face. That is, if we believe in hell and Purgatory, we will evoke this by our thoughts and feelings. It will be helpers there, who can help if we trust them. These assistants may take the form of what we believe in. If we believe in Jesus, for example, we will experience that Jesus is such a helper. We will then experience a period of self-scrutiny. Then we will have to review our attitudes, abilities and weaknesses, and have to consider whether to come back to the physical existence or not. Seth said that there is also a kind of body after death, and although this is not a physical body, it may look like one. It cannot be seen by physical people. It can do everything we can do in dreams. But it cannot hold on to physical objects; it goes straight through physical objects if necessary – for example; it passes easily through a wall and it follows the thought, so that in a fraction of a second it can be located somewhere else on the planet, if we think we are there. Moreover, its form depends on the thought, so that it looks the way we think we look. This body of death also exists when we are in our physical body, then it is woven through the physical body. Seth said there is no particular world to reside in after death because everything is thought, so the 'reality' we meet could be anywhere. We are where our mind is set. This is a kind of energy field. But Seth states that our perception of space is so flawed that it is difficult to explain this in an understandable way. For example, distance does not exist.

For *Rosemary Altea* contact with dead people is quite natural, she sees and hears the deceased as if they were real people. The only difference that she can see is that there are more vivid colours associated with the deceased. She sometimes experiences the spirit world as more real and of firmer fabric than the human world. What she has expressed is largely in accordance with

Emanuel Swedenborg's story and it fits well with George G. Ritchie's account.

Ambres explained that the astral and mental bodies of the human being continue their existence after the physical death of the body.[373] Then in the astral world the astral body will in a way be dissolved, which is a kind of school of liberation from desires, and the mental body will be exposed to the same in the mental world. When the body dies, the Rider (or soul) still remains. In the astral existence you will find that everything you previously created, were illusions. Matter is in this existence easily changeable and is influenced by thought. You exist in the way you are thinking. How long you will stay in this existence depends on what you want and what you are thinking. You will meet the people you wish to see. You can do what you want, go to school, work or whatever. The astral and mental bodies are in a way attached to each other, according to Ambres. You will go to the mental plane when the astral world is no longer attractive. From the mental plane you can see everything in the astral plane and in the physical world. Those who are on the mental plane can serve as guides for those who are on the astral plane. Heaven is what you want it to be. After you have freed the astral and the mental bodies, the Rider will arrive at the causal (spiritual) plane. On this plane it is free from subjective gradations. It reconsiders what it has learned and how it will evolve further – where it will next incarnate.

Jens Bertelsen's statement about Rudolf Steiner ought to be noted, namely that he was not an enlightened person. Rudolf Steiner, on the other hand, maintained that Emanuel Swedenborg's visions were very special and only mirroring reality, a mirror image in the etheric sphere of spiritual beings and activities, but mirror images that only showed their own activity. Thus this can be considered a hologram, but a hologram of a spiritual existence.

In the books *Journey of Souls – Stories about life between lives* by Michael Newton and *The Road to Immortality* by Geraldine Cummins there are fairly similar descriptions of life on the other side, which are in accordance with the explanations given above. They describe an existence that indicates a clear awareness of what is experienced there, about education and spiritual development, and about assistance from more developed souls, as well as about social gatherings with like-minded individuals according to our needs. The Myers-spirit explained that every time a soul goes from one level of existence to another, it will experience a kind of death where the soul has a period of preparation. He called these periods Hades. He described Hades as a sleep for the soul or as a period to prepare for what is coming, where there is a kind of liberation from the old consciousness body. This liberation process is comparable with the butterfly's effort to get out of the cocoon. How the existence in this period is experienced depends on your state of mind when you die. Where you are going will also depend on your attitude – if you are mainly materially biased (mostly animal) or whether you are mostly soul or spirit. You can return to the plane you just left or to an equally dense or denser, energetic plane; or you can go to a more advanced (more subtle) existence. On all the planes of existence you are meant to evolve spiritually, whether you are going back to a previous or equivalent existence, or to a more advanced level.

10.4. A summary of what has been expressed about death

What Rosemary Altea and other mediums have said about contact with deceased souls or non-incarnated spirits does not fit, according to my judgment, especially well with what can be learned from Tibetan teachings. The Tibetans do not seem to believe in a conscious life after death that may be something similar to the life people are living on Earth. Jes Bertelsen and Ken Wilber seem to be of the same opinion. Both Jes Bertelsen and *The Tibetan Book of the Dead* say that we should prepare for death, and that the deceased should be guided through the first stages of death. Moreover, they both maintain that part of the spirit life period, the period between physical death and rebirth, is like a dream, alternating between nightmare and happiness. How this is possible without some kind of 'I'-awareness, I do not understand. If you first have reached the level of the Self, I assume you have left behind everything that was related to the 'I' – both the ability to think, your imagination and memory.

Jes Bertelsen explained that a person, who has its consciousness on the level of the Self or above, who are awake into the collective unconscious, does not experience any spiritual death. He also stated that the advanced mystic could be said to exist at a higher level (maybe by this he means the causal plane) between its incarnations – if I understand him right. It must be said that I find it difficult to understand the Tibetan Buddhism, and therefore also Ken Wilber and Jes Bertelsen. These two have an understanding of existence which must be considered almost identical to Tibetan Buddhism. They both explain that there is a part of the human being which continues after the physical death, and refer to *The Tibetan Book of the Dead* when it comes to the physical death and what happens afterwards. But they also state that everything that is related to the ego, such as memories and memory, disappear with the physical death. I have problems with that as I try to follow their explanations – because what is then the purpose of preparing this ego in this life, or to meditate and strive to attain Nirvana in order to avoid being reborn? It does not matter to me if there is something from my life now that will be reborn, if there is no 'I'-awareness or memory attached to such a rebirth. Then I cannot see that there is some sort of spiritual world, which many, such as the Theosophists, Yogananda, Aivanhov, Rudolf Steiner, Rosemary Altea and many spiritualists, as well as Emanuel Swedenborg, tell us about. However, a distinction should perhaps be drawn between the ego required for a person to be able to live in this world, and to identify entirely with this ego.

One can also wonder whether the people I have referred to here have read each other's explanations and influenced each other, which may be why some of the explanations are quite similar. All that I have recorded here is to be found in various books, and what I have read other people may also have read. But I do not think the answer is that simple. I do not think Swedenborg was known by Jane Roberts, who channelled Seth, or by George G. Ritchie, although this cannot be said for certain (unless Seth knew Swedenborg's experiences from the spiritual side). But we can at least rule out the opposite. Jes Bertelsen has worked closely with Bob Moore, so that could explain the connection between these two. Martinus was also Danish and that Bertelsen studied Martinus can be seen by the references in Bertelsen's books. It is also likely that Bertelsen has studied the Seth material. He has further referred to Ken Wilber in some of his books. More questionable is whether Yogananda knew Seth (Yogananda died in 1952, while Jane Roberts began the channelling in 1963) or Swedenborg. So a clear answer cannot be given to this question.

It is difficult to make a comparison of the explanations that makes sense, because the same words are not always used for the same terms but if we try to categorize the explanations given, according to the consciousness planes discussed above, it is easier. Then we will see an odd likeness in the stories, even if they do not completely overlap. Most mystics mention that there are several stages in the existence we meet after the physical death process, when the physical death is final. These seem to be an existence on the different consciousness planes, which we have studied already but *The Tibetan Book of the Dead* seems to see the existence in the death realm as having only one stage, unless we are so far advanced that we do not reincarnate, and then we might find ourselves in the causal world or higher. Jes Bertelsen seems to share this view.

Swedenborg has a description of four stages in death, of which the fourth seems to be similar to what we would call Heaven. He claimed that he at any time was able to connect with the dead on the different levels. Both Rudolf Steiner and Emanuel Swedenborg claimed that they could be in this spiritual world. Rudolf Steiner mentioned also that a human being gets a spirit form after death. This form is constantly changing, and expresses the human being's moral and spiritual inner being.[374] During this period, human beings obtain contact with angels, archangels and primeval forces – what Steiner called the third hierarchies' beings. They are experienced as sun figures. At this level we have contact with people we are connected to, through our destiny. Steiner called the place where we are between death and birth as the *etheric world*. But at the same time he said that the human being passes into another world – the sensible super-physical world, which is the second hierarchies' world where we will meet the beings he called *exusiai, dynamis and kyriotetes* (see chapter 9.2). Finally we arrive in the sun-existence, where we are associated with the first hierarchy, which are *the thrones, the cherubs and the seraphs.* Almost all the persons referred to above have mentioned, as we have seen, several stages after the physical death. These we shall take a further look at now.

About the moment of death

The Tibetan Book of the Dead describes carefully what happens physically at the moment the body dies. So also does Sogyal Rinpoche. I have not found comments from the other referenced mystics about this process. The death process itself is normally not easy; anyone having been at a deathbed or followed a person's illness and death knows that. Some of the difficulties through the death process are due to the human being's fear of dying and the dying person's reactions to the relative's sorrow and despair. But once the process has progressed so far that it is just before death occurs, the dying seem to relax and to have gone beyond pain and concerns. In some cases, the dying person experiences pleasant encounters with deceased relatives.

About the physical death process

If we are to believe Rosemary Altea and some other reports, as the body is abandoned the dying will experience the same as when a living person has an out-of-body experience, and the person will not understand that death has occurred. As long as the etheric body is intact, the dead will be attached to its earlier physical existence, and it is also possible to keep this attachment with the help of the astral body. As mentioned earlier, Rosemary Altea has helped many deceased individuals to come to term with their new existence. That is also why *The Tibetan Book of the Dead* considers it important to explain to the deceased what has happened, so that the deceased may finish its connection to the living, and continue on the road that leads to a purely spiritual existence. Jes Bertelsen also places great emphasis on this, which he has explained in a series of lectures, also presented in the book *Døden og Dødsprocessen* (Death and the Death Process). Some people also explain that if those left behind are expressing strong grief, this will make it harder for the dying or the dead to leave them.

It can take anywhere from a few hours (which is most common) to weeks before the etheric body also is dissolved, after the physical body is decomposed. According to the Theosophists, who seem to recommend a quick cremation, the etheric body always disappears when the physical body is cremated. Martinus, on the other hand, believed that the body should decompose naturally since that is the natural process of all life. Then all of the micro organisms that exist in the physical body will have time to finish their physical existences. Steiner said, however, that it does not matter how the dead body is disposed of. He indicated that that takes from two to four days, and that it is in this period that a person's total life experiences passes in revue – before everything disappears. Steiner said that the memories are dissolved and taken up by the Cosmos in this period but then the soul will get a spiritual review of all that it has learned during sleep or when unconscious. One then gets a spiritual evaluation of one's earthly life, everything one has experienced and the impact one's life has had on the Earth itself. In earlier times in Norway it was the custom to perform what was called *likvake* (which was to keep watch over the corpse for several days), usually for three days. Although there are different opinions as to why one should keep watch over the corpse, the explanation that it can take from two to four days before the etheric body dissolves – and that before this happens the deceased still has a close connection to the physical life – fits with the view that the deceased has a need for the relatives left behind to remain close to the corpse (in order to make the deceased understand what has happened).

The Tibetan Book of the Dead, Sogyal Rinpoche, the Theosophists, Bob Moore and Jes Bertelsen have all maintained that the first thing that happens when we die seems to be that the energy of the body is concentrated in a point near the heart and that it then rises up to the head and proceeds further out. There are several people who have seen a strong light field around the just-dead person's head, which has remained around the head for a while and then disappeared. This is believed to be the body's energy. Jes Bertelsen has said that the actual death moment is very important, as the soul (for want of a better word), at the moment when the consciousness leaves the physical body, gets a glimpse of the three highest levels of consciousness. If the soul is aware of this, it may get a kind of enlightenment – in the form of a light experience – which is of vital importance for its future development. In this glimpse one comes into the divine consciousness level, which is perceived as an intense light source. One should strive towards this source. If you do not understand this when it happens, you will miss an important educational experience. It is therefore essential that we are prepared for this.

Sogyal Rinpoche and Jes Bertelsen explained that when we die, the physical body will dissolve, the vital energy, the emotions and the memories will disappear, and the ordinary consciousness and the ego will be gone. This also includes images and dreams. Everything connected to the 'I'-personality disappears.[375] The first four consciousness levels, that is the physical, the etheric, the astral and the mental, are connected to the physical person and will leave when we die. We can all see the physical life disappearing. Once the process has gone so far that one can probably no longer register any death process, what is then left is the higher consciousness, which is on a kind of inner plane such as when we are in dreams or in sleep. This is a kind of absence of thoughts. Jes Bertelsen has said: "The 'I' dies, but simultaneously with the 'I' there is the spiritual or the Self. This consciousness function or observation function is continued and dies not." Sogyal Rinpoche and *The Tibetan Book of the Dead* say, however, that once we have gone further into death, the ability to remember will return, we will be conscious and will not know whether we are dead or not. If we are conscious on the spiritual plane, we will experience a consciousness continuum even if the ego is dead.

Rudolf Steiner explained it this way, that when death occurs, the etheric body, along with the astral body and the ego, leave and only the physical body will be left.[376] Physical dissolution is spiritual birth, for in a physical existence only very special people are able to have connections with the spiritual world.

Seth explained that the consciousness recedes from the physical world into a kind of energy field.

Arthur E. Powell wrote that during the death process the etheric body separates from the physical body, but remains associated with this by a cord of etheric substance.[377] At the moment of death this cord breaks. In Theosophical terminology that means that the buddhic life web with the life force or *prana* frees itself from the physical substance and contracts, first around the heart, then it rises up to the brain and from there to the back of the skull, and then lastly completely leaves the physical body. In this terminology there is talk about a permanent atom that is enclosed in the causal body and remains there until reincarnation occurs.

After the physical death occurs, we will experience a new existence or a new form of life according to Marcello Haugen, and we will receive help from spirit beings in this transition phase. Also Emanuel Swedenborg stated that we will receive help from angels immediately after the physical death is final.

Martinus said that death is not the destruction of life, but a carrying on of 'The Eternal Sovereign Something' which each individual really is. Martinus explained that death is a freedom from physical matter, the spiritual structure takes over and you receive impressions from paraphysical matter. Death is the liberation of energy or substance, a change from previous bindings. That such a change can take place – or for creation to happen at all – there must be something or someone who has thought about this and wanted it – that is a consciousness. Death is the best solution when the physical body is tired, because it is only through the physical death that the individual (or the being as he called it) may have a continuous uninterrupted expression of life.

The first stage – the astral existence

Swedenborg, Steiner, Seth, Martinus and Arthur E. Powell, all seem to argue that when we die, we get a *conscious astral existence* connected to the earlier physical existence. It is this existence the Theosophists and Steiner called *kamaloka*. Steiner stated that the kamaloka-existence lasts one third of the time the earthly life lasted. These mystics said that it is the individual and from what it believes. If you do not know any better, you will believe that you are still in the physical matter. You will meet other individuals and get in touch with them, but only if they are on the same spiritual level as yourself. If you believe in hell or have evil thoughts, that is what you may experience. You are constantly confronted with yourself and your own thoughts and past experiences, that is, you are forced to self-scrutiny. There are spiritual beings around that want to help if you are willing to receive this help. Also Marcello Haugen has explained that we might get help from spirit beings in this existence and if you are prepared for what you will meet, you will more easily be able to adapt and to grow. These mystics said that we should prepare for such an existence. Martinus referred to *The Tibetan Book of the Dead*. What has been discussed above fits well with what we can read there.

Emanuel Swedenborg has provided a description of the three stages before the fourth stage, which can be said to be Heaven. Stage two and three of his description is a kind of purging and training process, which might be the same as the first stage (the astral plane) as described by the others referenced above. During the purging process we may meet evil spirits, but these are our own projections. The same applies to the suffering we may experience in a kind of hell. But we can get help and training from good angels, and it is up to ourselves to accept such help.

John (David Spangler) explained that the consciousness of most people goes to the astral or the lower mental realm when they leave their physical bodies, to continue further development there. He said that these worlds (at least in its human aspect) are quite like the physical world we know, although they do not have the same limits in regard to matter, energy, time and space. We can get in touch with these worlds through certain psychic (spiritual) experiences.

Rosemary Altea mentioned that souls grow and develop further after death, when they are in the astral body. That is, a person who dies as a child develops an adult astral body eventually. Presumably is this so at least until also the astral body disintegrates because of the transition to the mental plane.

Sri Yukteswar has told of his existence on the astral plane. The fairies, mermaids, fish, animals, gnomes, dwarfs, half-gods and spirits he experiences there, are presumably Earth spirits, water spirits, air spirits and etheric spirits, spirits that in popular imagination have been perceived as such, (ref. Arthur E. Powell's explanation[378]). Sri Yukteswar's description of the astral plane is otherwise reasonably equal to Powell's description. Also like these, what Seth, Martinus and Swedenborg have described of this first stage, fits very well with the near-death experience of George G. Ritchie and with other people's near-death experiences, even if the descriptions are not completely congruent. The duration of this stage is not mentioned, but the time as we know it on Earth is hardly a relevant factor.

The Tibetan Book of the Dead tells, as mentioned, about the existence in dharmata bardo – the death period – which is said to last for forty-nine days. Sogyal Rinpoche said, however, that these days are not earthly days. But what are they then? Jes Bertelsen's description corresponds otherwise to the Tibetan.[379] He maintained that at this stage it is important that the 'I' is willing to let go of its physical senses, its identity and give itself over to the new existence. Furthermore, we must try to relate completely neutrally to whatever we meet, whether that is gods, angels or demons, because all are only projections of our thoughts.[i]

Death's second stage – the mental realm

Some mystics mention an astral death, where the astral body dissolves and goes on to a new, higher spiritual stage. Jes Bertelsen has, however, as far as I can see, not mentioned this stage in his description.

Arthur E. Powell explained that all souls go to a level higher than the astral plane. This plane is called the *mental plane* or *Devachan*. He said that this plane is what the Christians call Heaven. On this plane the soul will be polished and the ability to love all fellow beings will be developed. All that was valuable from the human being's moral and mental experiences will become capabilities that are carried on into the next incarnation.[380] On this plane there are no obstacles between the souls, but they have only contact with soul friends – those they are mentally related to. Only sympathetic mind- and heart-ties can bring people together in the heavenly world. Furthermore, we are in contact with those who are more advanced than us, to the extent that our capabilities allow us to contact them. Similarly, we can get in touch with those who are less advanced than us, so far as they can communicate with us.

According to Martinus, we must pass through a kind of purification before we can go from the astral plane to the next plane. We must be released from the lower natures in the psyche before this happens, and there angels will be of help. On the next plane the development of the ability to feel compassion is the most important. This stage Martinus describes as a kind of paradise or the Kingdom of God. We are then in God's primary consciousness field. We all visit this sphere, before we again come down into a new physical birth.

On Swedenborg's fourth stage, which perhaps may be compared to the mental plane – what he called Heaven – there are also many levels, depending on the individual's psychological development. The inner mind must be refined in order to go on from one stage to the next. Rudolf Steiner also mentioned several spiritual regions which the soul would pass through before a new reincarnation occurs. The kamaloka period he terms the Moon's spiritual sphere. After staying there the soul will continue to the Sun's

---

i. Cfr. what has been written about Buddha's experiences during his meditation before he reached Nirvana.

When Buddha was sitting in deep meditation under a tree, he was first exposed to attacks from troll-like beings and other gruesome creatures. He sat completely still and did not let them affect him. Since this had no effect, he was exposed to earthquakes, storms and floods. He was still totally unmoved. Eventually, he was exposed to being seduced by beautiful women, beautiful moods and beautiful music. He was equally unaffected. Then he achieved Nirvana.

spiritual realm, where it will be working at creating the spiritual seed for a new physical body.³⁸¹

Death's third stage – the causal world

Sri Yukteswar has told us that the next stage after the astral plane is the causal plane, and that only the more advanced will go there. He did not mention any mental plane, but it is possible that what he described as the astral plane includes what others have described as the mental plane. Sri Yukteswar said about the causal plane: "There you will see all created things – fixed, fluid and gaseous substances, electricity, energy, all beings, gods, humans, animals, plants, bacteria – as consciousness-forms; just as a human being can close its eyes and know that he or she exists, even though the body then is invisible to the physical eyes and only exists as an idea."

Most Buddhists as well as the Theosophists mention the causal world. Individuals living there have an idea- or causal body. On this plane there is, according to what the Buddhists explain, no individuality in the sense we understand it. It may be possible that the beings living there are those that no longer reincarnate on Earth.

10.5. When is a human being dead?

And what happens at organ transplantation?

Previously we thought that a person was dead when the heart stopped beating, and there no longer were any traces of activity in the brain. This is termed clinical death but people who have been declared clinically dead, and who have come back to life, have been able to recount what happened around their physical body while they were without detectable awareness, as in the case of Pam Reynolds mentioned above. In one case a person was revived after being clinically dead for about five hours. So when is a person really dead? That is a question we are probably not able to answer today. The best known cases where people have come back to life, albeit rare, show that people who have met all criteria for physical death, were not actually physically dead. That seems to confirm that consciousness is not located in the brain, in other words, that there is a difference between mind and brain.

A lot of people in recent years have replaced sick and exhausted organs with organs from other people, and now some stories have come out which indicate that some organ recipients also get some new character traits or other specificities, which seems to come from the organ donor.

Stephen E. Braude has told of some cardiovascular/pulmonary transplants with such consequences.³⁸² He mentioned a case in which the recipient began to prefer food she had not previously liked. In addition, during the first few months after surgery she had dreams where she met a man who looked like the donor. In another case, the recipient became interested in classical music that he had not previously enjoyed. His attitude towards coloured people also changed for the better – it turned out that the donor was coloured. A third case concerned a seven-months-old child, who sometimes acted as the sixteen month old donor, and who several years later recognized the donor's father and called him dad, although he had never before seen him. This organ recipient then explained that the deceased was with him and sometimes spoke through him (as a spirit attachment). This last case reminds me of cases concerning split personality.

During spiritualistic séances it can happen that information is provided that has no connection to any of the participants. Then it seems as if an outsider spirit is forcing its way into the conversation to promote its special interests. One well-known case concerning such a situation is of particular interest in relation to organ donation and relic-practice.[383] The Icelandic medium, Hafsteinn Bjornsson (1914-1977) was during a period given information from a spirit who said his name was Runolfur Runolfsson, nicknamed Runki. It turned out that Runki had drowned in 1879. His corpse had been washed up on shore, but when it eventually was found, one leg was missing. The leg bone was found embedded in a house nearby, thanks to information that came forward during the séances where Runki participated. It turned out that Runki had been buried in the local cemetery without the leg bone. When the leg bone was placed in the same grave, Runki seemed satisfied and thanked the participants for help. He became a good spirit helper in Bjornsson's later séances.

It is claimed that there have been many such spirit contacts where the deceased does not seem to find peace in the spirit world before its physical remains have been given a proper burial. One explanation for such cases may be the deceased's belief in the resurrection of the body – that the body will not be able to re-emerge in its complete version unless all parts are buried together, and that it will not obtain peace in the spirit world before this has happened. But such thinking may raise impossible questions in relation to issues such as organ donors. Will their charitable action outweigh potential problems since the physical remains have not been properly buried? And what happens when a person is cremated instead? We may then also ask questions regarding all the relics of saints and other mystics found in the world. Is the deceased still bound to those remnants, and if so – for the better or worse? Many believe that to possess a relic, such as a bone from the skeleton of a saint, gives spiritual protection of this saint.

These thoughts made me think of the ritual practised by the Aztecs in Mexico when a person was sacrificed to the gods. The victim would be skinned, whereupon the priest dressed himself in the skin of the victim in order to be given some of the victim's power. This practice has parallels in some shamanic activities where the shaman dresses either in an animal's skin or takes on a mask that represents a particular animal, in order to possess some of the animal's strength and senses. The use of a talisman or an amulet has the same purpose. Such rituals could not have occurred without conscious intention, which may be based on an experience that one actually can acquire power and capabilities in this way. For the time being, organ transplantation is not so prevalent that there exists much research material concerning the consequences. A question which also arises in this connection is whether or not those consequences are registered only as a result of heart transplants or whether other forms of organ donation affect the recipient likewise. Another question is whether the donor's effect on the recipient is permanent or whether it will disappear after some time. Stephen E. Braude suggested that the effects can have different forms and be of varying strength, scope and duration. A possible explanation for some of these effects is that the donor's etheric, astral and mental bodies still are attached to the part of the body that remains in the physical sphere. The rest of the body will, as we know, disintegrate or be destroyed when the donor dies. The deceased might through these bodies influence the physical remains, in the same way as when various personalities appear in one physical person, or as in the channelling cases. But what happens if you get a pig's organ, which allegedly is a reality today? That remains to be seen.

10.6. Suicide

Many people have been in a crisis situation without finding any acceptable solution. For some the despair can be as fierce and the death-wish so strong that they choose to end their lives. It is one thing to choose to end one's life before the proper time has come, but it is quite another to know what you actually are doing. Is life thus ended? Is it only this physical life once and for all, and so no more? Can you be sure that you will not be thrown back into a similar situation? If so, nothing is gained.

Plato makes Socrates say in *Phaedo* that the only law to which there is no exception is the law that a human being must not commit suicide. Socrates said that people can be said to be the slaves of gods, and the gods will punish the person who commits suicide without permission, regardless of what this person is subjected to in regard to suffering. It is only the person who gets a call, as Socrates got when he had to empty the cup of poison, who has the right to do it.

Plotinus, however, seems to have accepted suicide, but only on the condition that there is no longer any further possibility for the soul's moral advancement.[384]

Sogyal Rinpoche wrote that whatever you did not learn to cope with in this life, you will meet again. It is impossible to run away. Whatever you try to avoid, you will meet again, and maybe then to a greater degree.[385]

Rosemary Altea also maintained that suicide does not solve any problems, and that we will only take the problems with us further. This also applies to disease. She explained that the purpose of life on Earth is to learn about our true spirit, and therefore that it is our mental state that determines how insurmountable the difficulties we face will be.[386]

In Theosophical teachings, according to Arthur E. Powell, a suicide has great karmic consequences, as a suicide might have an effect on the person's next physical life.[387] He wrote that a suicide is a horrible mistake that implies that you refuse to accept the karma you have been given at birth in this incarnation. It only delays the problems, and in addition the suicide itself will give the individual a new heavier karmic burden. It is said that it is a person's duty to make the best out of this physical existence, and preserve life as long as the circumstances allow it.

In a slow aging of the physical body, and during the death process, the astral body will be released from the physical body, and the lower mental passions and desires erased. According to the Theosophists among others, the state of the mind at the moment of death, will determine the person's subsequent existence on the astral plane. A person who is exposed to sudden death, as in a car accident or being murdered, will often not be aware of what happened – unless he or she has come so far in the spiritual development that the situation can be understood. Jes Bertelsen has said that it is important to help the victims of a car accident, for example, by sitting down and meditating to seek meditative contact with the deceased, thereby helping them to understand the situation, so that they manage to continue in the new existence. The mental horror and interference that many times follow a sudden death, may follow the deceased into the astral life, and may have a detrimental effect on the reincarnated personality.

Also in all Eastern philosophy where the law of karma is considered an absolute reality, it is maintained that suicide does not solve any problem.[388] It is only the physical body that dies at a suicide. The self and its karma will continue. Suicide only increases the karmic burden.

Nevertheless, it is a fact that some people will be exposed to such great hardships and sufferings that they see no other way out than to end this life. This can be due to violent pain, extreme handicap, mental illness or loss of the closest kin. In relation to these cases you have to wonder whether what is said about the law of karma can be correct. Plotinus' attitude to suicide must, in my judgment, therefore be acceptable.

In Norway we have The Society for the Right to a Dignified Death ("Foreningen Retten til en verdig død"). This society's aim is that the life of a patient who has no hope of recovery is not prolonged. A declaration stating that you do not want doctors seeking to save or prolong your life when it is hopeless cannot be considered as suicide.

11. Reincarnation

11.1. Introduction

Within most religions or faiths, such as Buddhism, Hinduism, Confucianism, Manichaeism and many more, there are beliefs about people being reincarnated on the Earth. The ancient Egyptians were preoccupied with life after death. That they found it necessary to mummify the dead bodies indicates that they believed in a return to the same physical body. Many people have experiences which they interpret as meaning that they have lived on the Earth before, that they have had a physical human existence before this life. Many believe that the soul incarnates in a variety of physical bodies through its development or existence. A soul, spirit or essence, may, however, have incarnated (come to the Earth 'in the flesh'), without necessarily having been reincarnated (that is to have lived on the Earth once or several times before).

Joseph Campbell has said that the difference between Eastern and Western way of thinking is that people in the West believe that each human being has a soul who gets a birth, a death and a destiny, and eventually a form after death which a clairvoyant person can recognize.[389] In the East on the other hand, they do not believe in the continuity of the personality, but in something that Campbell described as a monad or the reincarnated jiva. This something has no individual properties. It passes from one persona to the next, as a vessel through the waves. It can be a worm in one life period and a king in another. In this connection it can be noted that a temple near Bikaner in Rajasthan in India is dedicated rats, because the congregation there believes that all members of a particular family are reincarnated as rats. However, in the *Bhagavad Gita* the god Krishna describes to the warrior Arjuna that they both have been born many times; the difference is that Krishna remembers his past lives, while Arjuna does not.

When we read about the research that Ian Stevenson, among others, has done in regard to the question of reincarnation, especially from countries where people believe in reincarnation in one form or another, the picture is more nuanced than in Campbell's explanation.

What about the interests, characteristics and capabilities I have? Are they the result of pure coincidence; are they only a product of the heritage and the environment in this life; or are they the sum of what I have acquired through study, experience, dedication and interest in previous lives? And is it really possible to remember any previous life? In order to provide answers as to whether reincarnation is a real phenomenon, we must also provide answers as to what it is that is reincarnating, and we have to find the conclusion as to what consciousness really is. I refer to what has been discussed earlier about consciousness and planes of consciousness, about death and what happens to the human being during the death process and after physical death. But what actually survives physical death?

In this regard it is interesting to remember Colin Wilson's thought that it is life that invented death.[390] He points out that the pre-cambric creatures discarded worn out cells and allowed new ones to grow. The same still happens in the human body, where the cells are constantly renewed without the exterior structure being much changed. Life invented death, so that the entire body could be renewed. Wilson pointed out that variety then could replace uniformity as the basic law of existence – without total renewal, no variation.

The theory of reincarnation was prevalent among the ancient Greeks from long before Plato's time. Plato commented upon this in several places. In the dialogue *Phaedo* Plato refers the imprisoned Socrates' conversation about the soul's immortality, and he also portrays Socrates' death. In this conversation Socrates says that the living are evolving from the dead in the same way as the dead are evolving from the living.[391] The souls of the deceased must exist somewhere before they reincarnate. He argues that if not everything was going in a circle, but in a straight line, development would finally stop by itself and if all that is alive should remain dead, then eventually everything would be dead. Elsewhere, Socrates says that it is the 'trace of knowledge that the soul has collected in the course of its timeless journey' that he looks for in a person. In *Phaedo* Plato describes the principles behind his thoughts about reincarnation. There is a place beyond Heaven where pure knowledge, the truth, may be learnt. Here, every soul will be able to gain experience, but it will only be able to take in that which it is ready to understand. And that will be essential for the life to come, into which the soul will reincarnate. Those who have lived their past lives righteously will get a better fate next time; while others will have to pay for their incorrect way of life. This may be equivalent to what the Eastern philosophies teach about karma.

Plotinus believed that life follows life, and that each individual will get a destiny adapted to everything that has happened before. One cannot blame it on a power that gives reward according to what one deserves.

In the following we will consider more of what some others have written about reincarnation. The people and theories I am presenting here have not used the word reincarnation for exactly the same phenomenon, and they have not always used the same words and phrases when they describe their belief.

It is easy to get confused when we compare the descriptions. I have tried to group the different statements as best I can.[392]

11.2. The Bible and the teachings of Christianity

The Pharisees believed in reincarnation, but not all the Israelites in the olden times did.[393] In The Old Testament there is only one statement that may imply reincarnation. This is the following:

> Malachi 4.4-5: Remember the law of my servant Moses, the decrees and laws I gave him at Horeb for all Israel. See, I will send the prophet Elijah to you before that great and dreadful day of the LORD comes.

In The New Testament, the following stories may allude to reincarnation:

> About the reincarnated Elijah: Matt 16.13-14 and 17.10-13, Mark 8.27-28 and Luke 9.18-19 and 1.17.
> About those born blind, see John 9. Here Jesus does not reject the question as irrelevant, which may indicate that he accepts the reincarnation possibility.
> About Herod, who was saying that Jesus must be John the Baptist, who is raised from the dead. Matt 14.2.

Some may argue that the story about the Pharisee Nicodemus also is referring to reincarnation, since Nicodemus asks how someone who is old can be born again – for a second time to get into his mother's womb. (John 3.) But this story is explicitly referring to a spiritual birth, not reincarnation.

Sogyal Rinpoche wrote that Origen (c. 185-254) taught reincarnation of the soul, as he shall have maintained that all souls bring with them their victories or defeats from previous lives.[394] Although Origen wrote about the soul's transmigration and rejected that anything was written about this in The New Testament, he probably did not teach reincarnation, according to Wikipedia. Origen is considered one of the greatest Christian theologians, but he was declared a heretic because he did not believe that anyone would be tormented forever.

Also St Clement of Alexandria (c. 150-215) and St Jerome (c. 347-420) taught about reincarnation. (Jerome's theology influenced his contemporaries very strongly; he founded a monastery in Bethlehem and he translated many important writings into Latin.) St Augustine (354-430) on the other hand maintained that it shows a lack of piety if you believe that souls who have reached the highest bliss with God must return to life's misfortunes and inconvenience.[395] St Augustine believed that reincarnation was a metaphysical impossibility and he rejected the idea that human beings consisted both of a body and of a soul as a spiritual entity independent of the body. He believed that the soul was what gave the body form. St Augustine's view seems to have won within the dogmatic Christian philosophy.

One explanation as to why Christians do not accept reincarnation, is given by Noel Langley, who wrote that our version of the New Testament does not go back further than the fifth Ecumenical synod of Constantinople in 553 CE.[396] One of the purposes of this synod was to condemn the platonic inspired writings of Origen and his followers, as well as reincarnation. Emperor Justinian, who was invited to this meeting, was a weak emperor who was allegedly ruled by his wife Theodora (died 547). Theodora has been compared to the psychotic Roman emperors. Noel Langley claimed that Theodora wanted to make the Christian Church an eternal monument to her memory. When Theodora died, Justinian sought to make her divine, and he also continued her policy. Langley maintained that the basic idea of reincarnation about cause and effect, which suggests that one has to take the consequences of one's way of life in a later life, was so repugnant to a tyrant who wanted eternal life in the same style as he had lived, that the concept was declared heretical at the synod, and no church meeting since has managed to reconsider what was then decided.

The Danish lector and theologian Lars Bo Bojesen (b.1946) believes, however, that the main arguments against reincarnation are probably that such an idea will involve a denial that the human being is a totality of both soul and body (which was taught by Augustine, among others); it would also be a repudiation of the individual human being's eternal value for God, as reincarnation would be synonymous with self-redemption (redemption not by God's grace).[397]

A central Christian dogma, as in the creed used by the Norwegian Church, concerns the resurrection of the physical body: "*I believe in the resurrection of the body and eternal life*".

This dogma is not compatible with a human being living several lives, where a new body necessarily is created for each new life. Another part of the Norwegian Christian creed says: "*I believe in Jesus Christ ... sitting at the right hand of God the Father, and from there to come again to judge the living and the dead.*" Many people will think that this suggests reincarnation at least for the person Jesus. Matt 24.27 says, however: "*For as lightning that comes from the east is visible even in the west, so will be the coming of the Son of Man.*" (See also Luke 17.24 ff where the text is somewhat different.) And again in Matt 24.30: " *... when they see the Son of Man coming on the clouds of heaven, with power and great glory.*" (As in Mark 13.26 and Luke 21.27). It does not say that he will be reborn as a human being. According to John 14.19 Jesus says: "*Before long, the world will not see me anymore, but you will see me. Because I live, you also will live.*" (See also John 16.16).

In this regard, it is also interesting to note the text in Luke 24.36 ff according to which Jesus himself stood in the midst of the disciples after his resurrection. He asked them to look and feel his hands and feet, so that they could see that he was still of flesh and bones, and therefore was not a spirit. He also took something to eat to further emphasize this. Only then did he disappear. (See also John 20.19 ff about doubting Thomas.) None of these stories provides any proof for that which we generally associate with reincarnation. The closest explanation for this phenomenon is, in my judgment, that Jesus materialized; that is that he exchanged spiritual energy with physical matter and thereby was able to appear in his former human body – if he really was dead.

11.3. Buddhist doctrines and related explanations

Buddhism, as previously discussed, is not a clearly defined philosophy or religion, and there are many (partly contradictory) theological orientations within Buddhism – and these include the question of reincarnation. A Thai Buddhist teacher, Buddhadasa Bhikkhu, has dismissed the whole question of reincarnation. He has said that this question has nothing to do with Buddhist teachings. In the Theravada-Buddhism (mainstream in Cambodia and Sri Lanka among other places) there is supposedly no clear teaching regarding reincarnation. Ajahn Amaro, who belongs to this branch, has explained, however, that Buddha described the process of being reborn, and that this happens at different levels of existence.[398] Basically it is our habits that are reborn, he said – that is everything that the mind is clinging to, all the things we love, hate, or want to own or have opinions about. What makes rebirth cease is non-attachment, which is the letting go of thoughts, feelings, perceptions and beliefs. How we are reborn depends on what we are attached to.

According to several sources Buddha answered neither yes, nor no in regard to a concrete question of whether there is a personal core of being. The reason Buddha did not give a concrete answer to the question was in consideration for the requester, whom Buddha presumed would have problems either way he answered.[399] Buddhism teaches the way to the non-self, *anatman*. This is the opposite of the idea that there is a self or atman. It is the belief in *atman* that is causing suffering. The causal principle is essential in Buddhism. Everything is connected; everything has a cause, with the exception of the first cause. If everything is connected and interdependent, there cannot be any real inherent essential core in any entity. In addition to the understanding that everything is connected, the teaching points out that everything is under constant change. In Buddhist scriptures it says the Buddha taught:

> "Men have, O young man, deeds as their very own, they are inheritors of deeds, deeds are their matrix, deeds are their kith and

> kin, and deeds are their support. It is deeds that classify men into high or low status" (Majjhima Nikaya 3,202)

This is understood as the karma that goes from one life to another, as a flame is transferred from one candle to another. It is just a causal link, no transfer of individuality.

Huston Smith has said that the question whether there is a personal core of being, refers to the human 'I'. He explained that Buddha did not accept some kind of a mental ball that passed from body to body – the image of a wave on the beach is a more apt explanation. Thus there is a causal relationship, but no physical or mental substance. At the very highest plane (the seventh), there is no duality according to the Buddhists, no division.

There is only The One. Here there is no being's inner core. This is Nirvana.

Both Rudolf Steiner and Sogyal Rinpoche refer from King Milinda's conversation with the sage Nagasena, where the king is being taught as to whether individuality exists in a human being or not.[400] Although they do not use the same one of Nagasena's many different explanations for the phenomenon, it seems that the point each time is that the new consciousness is not the same as the one before, but it is neither a different one. The clearest explanation is, in my judgment, the one where Nagasena states that the fruit on an almond tree has little other than the name and the shape in common with the seed from which the tree originated. Others explain that consciousness can be compared to a river. The water in the river is always there, but it is constantly changing, although it is up to the source (the human being) whether it should be clean, dirty or poisoned.

When the 14th Dalai Lama, during the John Main seminar in England in 1994, was asked the question – what is being reborn, he passed the question on to the panel participants without answering it. Sogyal Rinpoche, however, gives the Dalai Lama's view on reincarnation in his book.[401] He explained that according to the Buddhist view the idea of rebirth is based on the continuity of the mind, as the mind is explained within Buddhism. The Buddhists do not believe in anything concrete surviving the death of the body, in that a thing can go from one Earth life to the next. It is not like pearls on a string, where one can say that the thread which keeps the pearls together is the soul. What goes on from life to life is rather what the Christians call grace – a kind of blessing. But consciousness does not arise from nothing. It is caused by a substance on the very deepest and finest level. This substance permeates each life. Sogyal Rinpoche compares it to that of dice that are placed on top of each other. Each dice is separate from the one below and the one above. But they are functionally connected – they are dependent on each other, they are upholding each other.

The designation of a lama is often explained in this way: a person, who has mastered the law of karma and having been so-called *'realized'* has reached Nirvana, and can choose to come back to Earth to help people there. A realized master will often, before his death, be able to provide some indications as to where the rebirth will take place, and the reborn will be able to recognize objects that the deceased master had in use. (This does not mean a direct continuation of the late master's personality, but that the new master, because of his clairvoyance, intuitively knows that certain objects have belonged to the old master.) The Tibetan lama Tulku Urgyen Rinpoche (1920-1996) has explained that a master can reincarnate in a number of people who are living at the same time, and also that one person can be the reincarnation of a number of earlier masters.[402] In Michael Newton's book *Souls Travels* chapter 10, case 22, where his clients, under hypnosis, tell of the existence after the physical, the story of a client is recorded which talks about divided souls – that is, a soul incarnate in several people at the same time – the soul energy will be split into several different sections. This confirms Tulku Urgyen Rinpoche's statement that a lama can incarnate in more than one person at the same time. As mentioned in chapter 7.15, this was also Plotinus' view. He explained that no living creature will ever cease to exist, but many individuals may be incarnations of the same soul. That is, a physical person is not necessarily one individual soul. It further shows that it must be the qualities that continue, not the personality. Sogyal Rinpoche wrote, however, that Buddha remembered up to a hundred thousand different existences when he achieved Nirvana, with their different experiences and characteristics.

The Tibetan Book of the Dead says that there is something that will survive death, a kind of consciousness or mental body. It explains that you have a mental body consisting of instincts (verse 12). This cannot die, although you are nothing – a natural form of emptiness and this Nothingness cannot be damaged or destroyed. The deceased – or rather the awareness of the deceased – should not be afraid of dangerous or scary happenings. This consciousness exists between two incarnations – in the bardo state. But the consciousness will at birth lose all contact with the former existence, so it is not possible to remember anything from a previous physical life.

Ken Wilber, who is close to Tibetan Buddhism, has mentioned that the mystics of all traditions accept the migration of souls.[403] He referred to, among others, Sri Aurobindo's teaching and to what he designated as the *perennial philosophy*. Human beings have a transcendent self, which is a kind of spiritual awareness. They, therefore, have an intuitive feeling that there is an existence after the physical. He explained that according to the Buddhist/Tibetan soul-teaching the individual's psyche or consciousness consists of two difference essences or particles – what the Tibetans call *tigle*. These are located in the heart centre, the heart-chakra. One particle exists only in the individual's physical life. The other particle, *the indestructible drop* or light-entity *(luminosity)*, can be said to be an inner layer of the first and exists until the Buddha-consciousness is achieved. That is, it transmigrates – going from one physical life to the next. Wilber sometimes calls this perpetual, transmigrating particle – the soul, but he uses also the term the *psychic/subtle* being for this entity. He also calls these two particles respectively the frontal awareness that develops through a physical life and the deeper mental consciousness which transmigrates. The highest level of consciousness development a human being can achieve through a physical life will be brought into the next life through the eternal particle. The higher the level the eternal particle achieves, the less it is engaged in the physical life. And this continues until the stage which Wilber calls the *radical enlightenment.*

Wilber has pointed out that people are so concerned with their 'I', their persona, their play character or existence, which is what he calls the centaur (half human (thinking) and half animal (instincts)), that they believe that the *individual* 'I' will live eternally. The human being cannot imagine any non-existence but most people do not have contact with their true Self, which is immortal. They believe that it is the ego or the 'I' that is immortal, but as Buddha has already pointed out, anything that has been created – put together – will die or dissolve, which means that it will change. Reincarnation does not mean that your 'I' is going from one earthly existence to another; it is the transcendent Self that is the one and only transmigrant. That is, only the transcendental Self is immortal, without time, without history, not the individual 'I'. Because the typical adult human being identifies itself only with its separate 'I', the intuition, which otherwise is correct in knowing that the transcendent Self is immortal, becomes corrupted and changes to the desire that the personal 'I' is immortal. Because of this, the human being fears that death is the end of everything, and therefore will not consider this idea further. Immortality exists, however, at the bottom of the consciousness, but on the other side of the 'I'-death.

Ken Wilber explained further that when death occurs, the physical body will go up into the mental body. When the mental body goes up into the soul, we will have our lives examined and reviewed. When the soul goes up into spirit, it is a radical liberation and transcendence. At reincarnation, this process is almost reversed. You generate a soul from spirit, then the mind from the soul and so a physical body out of the mind and then all the previous steps are forgotten when one is born into a physical body. He pointed out that *The Tibetan Book of the Dead* offers the most comprehensive description of this process. As the frontal consciousness evolves in the baby, the deeper psychic consciousness' (the soul's) accessibility will slowly melt down into a sort of oblivion (a memory loss or amnesia, as he called it). This process can take from a few weeks to a couple of years. It is only when the frontal consciousness development in the baby approaches the level of the Self (the psychological level) that the individual has the possibility to call forth, in the mind, experiences from around birth or from the pregnancy period, or possibly from earlier existences, but very few people have the chance to get this far in their physical life.

Jes Bertelsen, who in his mystical understanding also is very close to Tibetan Buddhism, seems to be on par with Ken Wilber on the question of reincarnation.[404] He has also said that there is no 'I' that reincarnates. Most people know only the 'I', not the Self. The awareness that he calls the Self, will, according to him, never die but it will have been present in the lives of other 'I's. These 'I's represent the Self's development path, and the Self will remember its dreams from one life to the next. He explained that the Self's process is that the consciousness slowly loses its identity and concentration in the body to instead establish an alternative centre outside the 'I'. He further said that the consciousness is both in the 'I' and in the Self, and in the *Open Field* and in the *Unity Field*, although the form of the stages differs. The Self is undergoing a slow consciousness process, through a variety of different 'I-body-lives'. This is the process of the Self, as progressive karma. (As far as I understand him, the consciousness will perceive itself as an individuality both on the fifth plane [the Self's] and on the sixth plane [the Christ consciousness], but at reincarnation the Self will get another personality – where personality is understood as the physical, the etheric and the mental energy fields. The word 'I' then means the personality, not the individuality.)

Bertelsen has mentioned four types of karma: The *compensative karma* (from the astral plane, which corresponds to the 'I' level); the *progressive karma* (from the spiritual plane, which corresponds to the level of the Self); the *collective karma* (in the open field) and the *karma's termination or transcendence* (corresponding to the highest level). Both of the two first mentioned types of karma will emerge in a new physical individual. A human being leaves an imprint on the astral plane, an astral pattern. A new individual may bring this imprint into the new Earth life – the *compensative karma*. That is, the new human being must live a life that seeks to compensate for the negative in the astral pattern created by the previous individual. Bertelsen has referred to Steiner and Martinus when he pointed to the cosmic law which says that all the energy that is triggered from one consciousness entity, returns to that *same* entity. (With the use of the words consciousness entity, Bertelsen must, in my understanding, mean that which Martinus has called the living being – the part that exists forever.) The *progressive karma* will give the new individual, a *spiritual* potential, as it will bring along a spiritual quality which the previous 'I' accrued earlier, in its physical life.

It is not the 'I's (the personalities) that are living over and over again. They are included only as parts in a pattern, a pattern that extends over several successive lives; lives which the individual 'I' is unable to see. But the consciousness on the inner or higher plane (from the Self's level and higher) understands these patterns and the karmic continuity. On the highest plane these lives will be parts in a progressive *spiritual* development. Jes Bertelsen has mentioned, however, that on the seventh plane, these successive lives are actually contemporary lives. (Here, we should remember some mystics' explanations that we live several lives at the same time.) Bertelsen has referred to Tulku Urgyen Rinpoche, who has explained that reincarnation is only a phenomenon of faith for most people, because there is only a consciousness rooted in *rigpa* (pure consciousness), that can obtain real information regarding reincarnation, which can be said to be continuous. Such a pure consciousness is first achieved on the fifth or sixth consciousness plane. The teaching regarding karma must not be misunderstood. Many dreams, visions or regression experiences have no connection with the Self's previous 'I'-structures. These experiences can just as easily be astral fantasies, what Jes Bertelsen has designated as archetypal symbols, mythology-like symbols of more personal undetermined stuff.

Christmas Humphreys has explained that rebirth is a reality, but that it is the inner mind, the soul or the immortal essence of the pure mind, which is the reincarnating entity.[405] This is not the part of the mind that can see, hear, smell or touch and react according to that, but the higher mind that is the intellect, which has an overall perception of the ego. On the highest plane is

The Universal Mind, the Entity. Remembrance is a property of the mind, not of the brain. The brain is new in each new incarnation. We recall, if anything, only certain things. We could not stand to remember everything painful that we have done or experienced. Those who claim to remember their past lives will usually get their impressions from the Akashic archive. The human being's ability to interpret the psychic world, which is a world of illusions, is limited. The inner mind is collecting everything it needs to get on with its development. The karmic remembrance is the conscience. Humphreys further said that that which reincarnates is not an immortal soul, but a bundle of attributes called the character. This is the product of previous lives. Every life is a spark of the whole on the way back to the whole. He thought that the Self exists and does not exist; it is immortal, but it changes all the time. He also referred to the comparison with a flame that passes from one combustible material to another. The material decays, but the flame is passed on and is in a sense the same all the time, although the light it emits is not the same. If we compare this with human beings, we can imagine the human body as the combustible material in this example, the light as the personality or human character – or the 'I', and the flame the spirit that goes from individual to individual.

11.4. The teachings of Hinduism

Hinduism is based on the idea of an immortal, immaterial soul, which passes from one Earth life to the next – governed by karma. Yogananda explained that human beings reincarnate on the Earth until they reach the state as sons of God.[406] Here are some of the explanations given by Huston Smith:

The individual souls have come into the world in a mysterious way; we can be confident that this is due to God's power, but how and why we are not able to detect completely. They start as souls of the simplest forms for life, but they do not disappear when their original body decays.

According to the Hindu view, the spirit is not dependent on the body where it stays than the body is dependent on the clothing it wears or the houses in which it lives. 'Worn out clothing is thrown away by the body / Worn out bodies are thrown out by the resident". (Bhagavad Gita). ... Each inner life's present condition – how happy it is, how confused or how clear it is, how much it sees – is exactly a product of what it has wished and done in the past. In the same way, its present thoughts and decisions determine its future experiences. Each action directed towards the world is a reaction to oneself and gives it a hammer-blow that forms its final destiny.

This view of a complete moral universe imposes on the Hindu complete personal responsibility. It produces no foothold for psychological projection (that is, to place the blame on others for one's own difficulties) or use excuses about a lack of luck. However, it is not fatalistic. Karma determines that any decision must get its unforgiveable consequences, but the decision in itself is taken completely freely. The stack of cards that the player takes up from the table, has been given in a previous life; now, he is free to play them the way he wants. The course a soul follows is drawn up from its desires and deeds in each of the stages of the travel. ... In the course of this pilgrimage the human spirit is never alone. From start to finish its core is Atman, the inner God, seeking deliverance as a jack-in-the-box – or in a chaotic meaning: God is one's eternal companion, the Friend who understands everything.

11.5. Theosophical teachings

Arthur E. Powell has explained that in each human being there is something he called a monad (ref. Leibniz' use of the term mentioned above), which is a unit of consciousness, actually consciousness plus matter.[407] He defined the word monad as a fragment of the divine life, which is a separate being, but so quaint that it is impossible to explain the context (however, he made a good attempt). This fragment wants to live, it is self-motivated and self-determined. The individual monad's evolutionary process is its own free choice. It is the same as the life-force; the will to create and which provides joy by being alive. How the monad occurs in a physical body is described by Powell, but it takes too much space to render even a summary of this here.

The monad is the source of the desire to be expressive, to be conscious and to feel alive – which is the same as the ability to receive impressions and experiences. It also contains the wish to be creative. This is the desire (*kama*), which is the cause of reincarnation. What it desires depends on what it has learnt and what it wants to experience. The monads who desire the material will go for this in their next incarnation. Those who desire spiritual activities will search for this. If it has lost all desire for the physical world, it will not be reborn into it, but into a different world. There are many different types of worlds. Those who have practised meditation may come to a mental world. It should be noted that no desire can be overcome by force. If it wants to go ahead with its existential development, its desires must be transformed so that it is not reborn to the same kind of existence as the one it now has in this physical world. The reincarnating soul will be born from a combination of different circumstances, depending on what it needs in the coming life for further development. It has brought with it the essence of its good and bad deeds from previous lives. It must come up against relationships to other souls, which may be unfinished. Strong emotional bonds, such as love or hatred, it will meet again, but perhaps in another form.

The soul (Powell called it the ego, which is confusing when comparing with other people's use of the term ego) will bring along with it material qualities, sensory perceptions, abstract ideas, special wishes and mental abilities. These will sometimes be embedded in the causal body, partly in the mental body. At birth everything that has happened before is forgotten, but before birth the soul sees the reason behind this incarnation and the possibilities this will give it. Each incarnation is known to be a step in the development from the material to the spiritual, to the final union with the Divine. It has also been said that a soul may wish to undertake a very difficult life to promote its development.

Powell wrote that Buddha often spoke against the idea that the persona continues, which was a common theory in his time, but at the same time he explained the human being's continuous life. Powell said that the true meaning of the Buddha's teachings was that the outer and temporary part of the human being is not permanent, but the rest survives, and it is this that is the real human being. And this human being is inseparable from the Universal Self. There are the many and The One. It is the Self that puts on a variety of 'I's, personalities or masks. Through each Earth life the Self is always reaping experiences, which the personalities take part in, so that they become carriers of ever better qualities. Finally, the personality's quality will become so that it only has the Self's consciousness – which means that there is only one consciousness. A personality that manages to raise its consciousness to the level of the causal body (the level of the Self) will not experience the death of the physical body as an end. Neither the astral body's nor the mental body's death will then be experienced as the end of existence.

According to Geoffrey Farthing, *Helena Blavatsky* underlined that it is only the spiritual essence – i.e. the memory of all that is well and good – which is said to be immortal.[408] It is only the higher Self (the ego in her terminology) that exists in Devachan. She said that there are many deaths: the death of the physical body, the human being's animal soul's (the desire's) death, the death of the astral body (which she called the *Astral Linga Sarira*), and the Self's metaphysical death which is happening at each new physical birth. The worst that can happen to a human being is that the soul dies while he or she is still physically alive. Then there is nothing from this person that goes on, and it becomes what in a moral view will be considered as a living corpse. At the Self's metaphysical death it will send a beam of itself down into a new personality, and this beam will carry the karmic consequences from previous personalities. But the new personality will be unable to remember anything of what the Self experienced in Devachan or earlier. She indicated that what a person believes to remember from past lives are probably pictures or happenings taken from the astral light or the Akashic archive.

Helena Blavatsky has in her book *The Key to Theosophy* a chapter with the heading *On the Mysteries of Reincarnation*. Here she tries to answer several questions as regards reincarnation, one of her answers is the following: "Reincarnation means that this Ego will be furnished with a *new* body, a *new* brain, and a *new* memory. Therefore it would be as absurd to expect this *memory* to remember that which it has never recorded as it would be idle to examine under a microscope a shirt never worn by a murderer, and seek on it for the stains of blood which are to be found only on the clothes he wore." ... "The Ego which re-incarnates, the *individual* and immortal – not personal – "I", the vehicle, in short, of the Atma-Buddhic Monad, that which is rewarded in Devachan and punished on earth, and that, finally, to which the reflection only of the *Skandhas*, or attributes, of every incarnation attaches itself." ... "'attributes' among which is *memory*, all of which perish like a flower, leaving behind them only a feeble perfume."

11.6. Contemporary lives?

In most of the so-called readings that *Edgar Cayce* gave, he mentioned the person's previous lives, often as far back as to the Atlantis-period. Noel Langley has published a book about some of these reincarnation cases. There were more than 2500 descriptions of reincarnation among the more than 6000 people to whom he gave readings.[409] In the cases that have been published, there are certain points that seem to be of relevance in most of the cases of interest when comparing them with other reincarnation reviews. One point is that a person does not seem to change sex, even when lives as far back as to the Atlantis-period are retold. Another is that there are usually several hundred years between the lives that are addressed, or the life which is said to have had the greatest influence on the person's current life and character. Furthermore, there seems to be a certain level of development of a person's character and abilities, or at least a certain relationship between the present life and its possibilities and the past lives.

In light of the research that Ian Stevenson has done, it is of interest to note Edgar Cayce's comments in regard to people whom he said had been victims of a sudden or violent death in a previous life. He explained that people who have suffered a violent death might be so confused that they fail to leave the astral plane and move on towards the light or a higher level. They will have a tendency to wish a speedy return to the Earth. Noel Langley referred to the Irish psychic author Joan Grant who has told of many similar cases, where previous war-children came back fairly quickly. In a case from Cayce's readings that is mentioned in the book, the reincarnation took place before nine months had passed. It was suggested that the reason for this quick reincarnation was that the individual was seeking some kind of protection against the horrors of war, which in the astral world were still attached to the astral body as fantasy images or thought forms.

Edgar Cayce is supposed to have said that our subconscious remembers past lives, while the conscious mind does not. One reason for this is that we are so heavily involved in our current existence that we do not have space in our minds when we are awake to think of earlier existences. Another reason is more obvious. We could not manage to live with the burden there would be if we remembered everything negative we had done through all our existences on the Earth. If we also had to live with the knowledge that we will suffer for all the evil we have inflicted on others through the ages, we would hardly be able to bear this life, but the law of karma is not brutal and avenging. You will not be subjected to greater trials than you can bear, and there is always an opening for salvation. Each new life is an opportunity for the soul's progress and is built on what the soul brings with it from past lives, of good and bad. We do not have to remember, because we are the sum of all we have experienced. It appears in our habits, in our capabilities, in what we like and dislike, in our feelings, in our strength and in our weaknesses. If we listen to our inner voice, our conscience, we will always know what is right and what is wrong and how we should live our lives, according to Cayce.

Cayce explained that a person's current mental state or temperament is also connected with the lessons the soul has acquired in its existences in the spheres between the earthly lives, although the innate behaviour pattern necessarily will be shaped in the environment and the culture where it grows up.[410] In existences between the earthly lives the soul will be in spheres of special interest depending on what it was, or wanted to be, engaged in (something also that Rudolf Steiner and some Greek philosophers taught). Cayce used the names of the planets in these spheres of interest (which Steiner also did). For example, Mercury represents the mental sphere or intellect.

In the Cayce biography Bro explained that Cayce's view on reincarnation was not that a life was lived through and completed before the next life began, and so on, as if they were pearls on a string. No life is ever finished, he explained. We live all our lives at the same time, with some lives in the foreground. He stressed that it is the main values and dynamics from each life that is carried over into the present time, in the sub-personalities that may come forward or recede on the consciousness' scene, depending on its growth, needs and preferences. (How there can then be some extra-terrestrial periods between the earthly lives in which the soul might develop further, is for me unclear.) Bro pointed out that the most important thing that we can learn by considering these different lives is that it is the spirit that is life, while the thought is the builder and the physical existence is the result. If the energy and the purpose of what we are undertaking is not of spirit, then we will not achieve what we are striving for or are seeking. The term 'the life's continuity' as used by Cayce showed that everything we have done has consequences both for the present life and for all the other lives we have lived. The souls have great freedom in what they do, although everything in existence has a direction, namely towards the fullest potential of all creation. The souls will therefore get the chance to evolve by again and again meeting conditions that will contribute to their proper development. You will, however, not get more out of a certain life period than what you put in to it. Everyone is connected to the divine source, and the soul will always try to find the right way. What is important for the individual is to train itself in self-knowledge, acknowledging that you have a covenant with God and that there is a creative common spirituality. By being aware of unusual information and inspired happenings and by training in such awareness, you will be able to obtain help in your development so that you become more in accordance with the Spirit of the Universe. The Universe is created so that the Divine is always ready to answer the individual's efforts to exercise love.

When *Seth* was explaining the existence and the context of what we call reincarnation, he took as a starting point the view that time is a non-existent phenomenon, but a solution people use to deal with the reality that is around them in their three-dimensional existence.[411] People need to split up everything that happens to be able to grasp some of it. The human being can only manage a small piece of the existence at any time, but there is no beginning or end. Seth used the term *entity* or the being's energy source for that which exists eternally. The entity can be said to be multi-dimensional, and it exists in a way on the outside of the physical human being. The entity falls into and out of the three-dimensional time/space-system and receives physical experiences where it touches this system. There it leaves a life track. It is not so that one life track arises before another; all individual life tracks exist simultaneously. These tracks are connected through electromagnetic energy patterns, since they are coming from the same entity. This is a kind of psychic connection. But a single life track, that is the individual physical being, can only perceive one track at a time, which is considered as one physical life. The superior unit is at the same time separated from, but still part of the various life tracks and these life tracks can appear in what, in the time/space axis, are seen as different ages. So even if a physical human being sees life as following a straight line from birth to death, the other existences are just as real within their time/space-understanding. Another century exists just as much as this one. All the life tracks that arise from one entity affect each other. A person's perceptions and actions affect others' experiences and actions, in the same way that each of these, in their existences will affect the former. Nevertheless, each life track is special and independent. Seth compared this with the fact that an individual is part of a family and therefore stands in a dependent relationship to the family, in the same way that a city is part of a country. The individual tracks are as life roles in a play, in which each actor has a specific task to be worked through but no text or solutions are given; each actor has complete freedom within certain limits, albeit within a parent theme. Here he mentioned as an example that great artists exist in a particular time period of specific reasons, suitable for their own goals.

Important periods in the history of humanity will occur because then there is an intense mental and spiritual focus on specific goals, in a desire to actualize an intuitive truth. Thus, progress has nothing to do with time. Seth said that it is wrong to believe that actions from a previous life have effects on later lives. The law of karma he did not accept, as he pointed out that all lives are lived at the same time. The entity is experiencing all life tracks or physical lives at the same time. He referred to it as instantaneous communication or a return message system. The entity is affected by the different life track's experiences because it is through these that it gains experience and can affect the life tracks in return. But using the terms cause and effect on these exchanges is incorrect because that presumes the time/space dimension and that the experiences are coming in a historical sequence. To explain this on the basis of usual rational thinking is impossible, he said.

Seth explained further that development happens in all directions at once without necessarily involving newer and higher development stages. The entity is a kind of centre that explores and involves itself in creative activity. In order to better explain what is said here, Seth elsewhere compared existence as being like a web that extends in all directions without beginning or end, so that there is a plethora of small squares or cubes. Each cube constitutes a level of existence but the special inherent property is that each cube can move into other cubes without affecting those who reside in the individual cube. And all the cubes are located inside other cubes. One cannot see through them, but the cubes can move through each other. Seth called this activity for the fifth dimension (since we live in a three-dimensional world with time as the fourth dimension). In reality there are no structures or rooms or walls, this is only something the physical life has constructed according to its senses. Seth can move through the physical constructions. And if we can consider this web field as something moving, constantly vibrating and lively, which contains all that exists in the Universe and at the same time is a projection of the Universe, we are approaching an understanding of the Universe.

What Seth said about time is also important in order to understand his explanation of reincarnation. He said the same as Master Eckhart said around the year 1300 about the term 'time', namely that everything in the Universe exists at the same time, as there is no beginning or end. There is no past, present or future. It only seems so for our limited mental ability, but there is a part of the physical individual – the entity – that is not locked inside the physical reality and which knows that everything is an eternal now. What people can experience as former incarnations, said Seth, can be compared with experiences some individuals have in the form of multiple personalities, as described in the book *The Three Faces of Eve*, where there are different personalities within a single individual's psyche, which appear at different times in the person's outer personality. Because many life tracks are parts of the same entity, some of their experiences may flow over from one life track to another.

The starting point for what *Ambres* conveyed about reincarnation is that the human being is not created at birth. It is only the physical human body that begins at conception.[412] He distinguished between the human beings and the physical bodies, as he considered the physical body to be the medium through which the human beings express themselves. In every individual there is a divine spark, which he designated the Rider or the basic personality. This is a synthesis of everything that has been achieved in previous incarnations. You may occasionally experience an impulse, an intuition or a certainty that originates from this basic personality. Ambres explains it this way – a human being consists of a physical body, an astral body (where feelings are created and stored) and a mental body (where the thoughts are created and stored). However, only the Rider reincarnates. The Rider creates an etheric substance around the physical body, and it is in this substance that the astral and mental bodies occur. This etheric substance, the etheric body, attracts knowledge through the child's conditioning and the attention the environment gives a child. Thereby feelings grow and form the astral body. Thought activity begins and forms the mental body. These bodies are embedded in the physical body using etheric threads that convey information to the physical body. The bodies are affected by the karma that the Rider carries with it from earlier incarnations. The Rider is often buried deep down in the mind due to the adaptations the child must make in order to fit into the society, the family and the environment in which it grows up. It is important to dig out this basic personality. All the experiences we have from previous incarnations are lying as a synthesis in the cell memory and as a shadow around the body. The problem is that people are so concerned with the outer physical world that they do not see this incarnation shadow. We must turn inward into ourselves in order to see it.

The Rider will carry along experiences from one incarnation chain at a time, first a chain as a man and so a chain as a woman. The Rider itself has no gender. Ambres explained, however, that in the transition between these chains there may occur incarnations that do not follow the pattern. In the cell memory there may therefore be strong remnants from a masculine body, which will show up in the new feminine individual (and vice versa). This explains homosexuality, because due to this cell memory a person may have sexual attraction towards its own gender. Ambres said that one should therefore not condemn homosexuality. But it should not be followed up, because then you risk bringing this tendency with you into several later incarnations. He pointed out that each gender has the opposite sex latent within and also this gender's properties. It is important to use both the masculine and the feminine aspect in yourself in order to create balance. But Ambres also stated that we are not only living here and now, we are living all the existences, all the way back to the gaseous form, at the same time. And everything, including minerals and plants, has a form of consciousness.

Rune Amundsen has suggested that people seem to have a database inside, which partly consists of past lives.[413] Many are struggling with mental health problems and these can often be traced back to happenings in earlier lives, as they emerge through regression therapy. He said that there seems to be a form of righteousness where we have to account for everything we do, so what we are doing against others, on a deeper level we are doing against ourselves. This presupposes an existence after death and a form of reincarnation. But his thoughts on reincarnation are not based on a linear time model. He also stated the opinion that everything exists simultaneously here and now, without past or future. The human beings, however, are experiencing only the now.

Elisabeth Haich has written the book *Initiation* which is about how she experienced living in the Second World War Germany at the same time as she also lived in Egypt in pre-Christian times. Her description fits perfectly well with what Seth, Ambres and Cayce have told that we are living several lives at the same time. She wrote that we simultaneously experience cause and effect – it is all a complete and perfect present.[414]

Another story about existing simultaneously in two different time periods was shown in a television program in Norway around 1990. The film presented there was based on the book *An Adventure* published in 1911 written by Charlotte Moberly (1846-1937) and Eleanor Jourdain (d. 1924). It is about two English college teachers who visited Versailles as tourists. Suddenly they both had the experience of being at the court of Louis XVI. Everything around them was, as they later learned, just as it was at that time but the people around them did not heed them, and went also straight through them. They heard a melody being played and as they both had a good ear for music, they later wrote the melody down. For a long time they were not able to find the composer, but several years later, they found the notes to the melody and it turned out to be from the eighteenth century.[415]

The Mazatec shaman Maria Sabina, who lived in Mexico around 1950, has described how she saw all the past and the future at the same time, as one single event that had already occurred. She saw her son's life from beginning to end, how he would be killed, the face of the man who would kill him and the knife that would kill her son.[416]

11.7. Reincarnation stories

Many people have experienced regression – that is to be taken back to possible earlier lives through hypnosis or deep relaxation. Lyall Watson has referred to a case where a person apparently is reliving events that happened during the civil war in Spain.[417] This person had been taken back to a previous life, and what he was able to describe from that life might be an explanation to his behaviour in this life. Watson's comment to such experiments was that the conscious mind is using abilities that lie in the unconscious, to be able to bring forward fantasies that seem incredibly convincing as reports from a former life, but he has a suspicion that much of it is coming up due to telepathy. Watson also referred to a statement from Ian Stevenson, who supposedly has said that what appears can be a mixture of the test person's personality, his or her expectations of what the hypnotist wants; thoughts on how an earlier life might have been, and perhaps also something paranormal. But Watson will neither disregard the possibility that such regression experiences may be due to possession by others, rather than reincarnation, as the person often presents both its own current character traits as well as the characteristics of the one he or she is experiencing to be. It has been written a lot about such regression experiences. Some stories are often retold. Some of the best known are the following:[418]

In 1956 the book *The Search for Bridey Murphy* by Morey Bernstein caught attention and caused much debate. A lady, Mrs. Tighe, under hypnosis came forward with a lot of information about her existence in the nineteenth century as an Irish girl named Bridey Murphy, and she was able to give many details about life in Ireland at that time. According to Colin Wilson (in 1973) a lot of publicity and negative comments surrounded the case. It was claimed that most of what was told matched with Mrs. Tighe's own experiences and what she had heard or read.[419] Apparently it was not claimed that it was a deliberate attempt at fraud, just a mix of fantasy and reality. Noel Langley has in his book about Edgar Cayce and reincarnation (from 1967) researched the case very thoroughly. His conclusion about the Bridey Murphy case is that her tales of her former life must have been real. If one checks the documents and listens to the audio tapes used during the séances, one will be convinced. Both Wilson and Langley refer to Curt J. Ducasse (1881-1969), professor of philosophy at Brown University, Rhode Island, who studied the matter and discussed his investigations in his book about reincarnation. Ducasse's conclusion provides full support to Bernstein and Tighe.

The story of the English psychiatrist and his patient who found out that they had known each other as Cathars living in the 12th-13th century is perhaps the most remarkable. The doctor, Arthur Guirdham (his real name is

Francis Eaglesfield) has discussed this in the book *The Cathars and Reincarnation* (1970). The patient came up with an amazing amount of details about the Cathars which later historians could mainly confirm. Some of these details were not known at the time of the consultations.

Jenny Cockell has written a book about her experience of having previously existed as the Irish woman Mary Sutton, who died in 1932, about 20 years before Jenny Cockell was born.[420] Mary Sutton had seven children, and her eldest son believed to see in Jenny Cockell the person who was his deceased mother. (On the CSICOP website there is a very critical comment to this book.)

11.8. Spirit possession, Spirit attachment or Telepathic takeover

According to some reincarnation stories children have been able to express themselves in an unknown language. Also adults, who are taken back to previous lives, have sometimes spoken an unknown language. Being able to use a foreign language during hypnosis is called xenoglossi. In a case from Blackpool in 1927 a young girl named Rosemary began to speak a language that was identified as ancient Egyptian. She said that she received messages from a spirit who had lived under pharaoh Amenhotep III, around 1400 BCE. Several experts in old Egyptian were consulted, and they all confirmed with amazement that the language was old Egyptian. Lyall Watson, who has retold the story, considered this case as very good evidence of continuous life.[421] David Scott Rogo has referred to Joel Whitton, former professor of psychiatry at the University of Toronto Medical School, who performed experiments in 1976 with a colleague as the test person. The test person participated in several séances. In one of them he spoke the ancient Norse language, in another he wrote texts in a language that was used in Mesopotamia around 650 CE.[422] I cannot, however, accept these stories as proof of reincarnation, they may rather be examples of telepathic takeover (*overshadowing*), ref. the story regarding Caterina of Siena and the girl Lorenzina.

In some cases, a child has suddenly changed character and maintained that it is a completely different person. Such cases cannot be evidence of reincarnation when the person it claims to be died after the child was born. A possible explanation in such cases is that it has become 'possessed' by a deceased person who still exists as an earthbound spirit being. Another explanation may be that which Helena Blavatsky mentioned, that one identifies with an individual whose life story can be found on the astral plane.

The following cases can also be understood as telepathic takeover, overshadowing, by a deceased personality. A three-year-old Indian boy named Jasbir suddenly changed personality and claimed that his name was Sobha Ram. This occurred after Jasbir had been seriously ill of smallpox and in a coma. Sobha Ram died approximately at the same time by poisoning at the age of twenty-two years. Jasbir had strong memories of Sobha Ram's life and claimed that Sobha Ram died when Jasbir was sick, and that he – Sobha Ram – now had taken over Jasbir's body.[423]

An eighteen-year-old girl named Lurancy Vennum, born 16th April 1864, suddenly changed personality while under hypnosis. The hypnosis was used in an attempt to cure her of a mental disorder that had lasted for many years. She then claimed that her name was Mary Roff. Mary Roff had died 5th July 1865 at the age of eighteen years. This was a little more than a year after Lurancy Vennum was born. Lurancy Vennum could report many aspects that were linked to Mary Roff's personality, things she could not have had knowledge of in the normal way. This change of personality lasted for approximately three months. The Mary Roff personality then disappeared. Lurancy Vennum did not remember anything of this episode.[424]

11.9. Several people remember the same previous life

The French professor, Reverend Father François Brune, has in an article from 2006 with the English title *Towards a new interpretation of the signs of reincarnation* mentioned one case, without giving further details, in which two different children, who lived at the same time, told the same stories from past lives.[425] It would be interesting if research could find more such cases and with many more details that would indicate that both could have been that person (or both overshadowed by the same deceased person). It would imply that there are other explanations of such memories than reincarnation.

Ian Stevenson discovered two children (Sleimann Bouhamzy and Imad Elawar) who both had many memories of the life of Said Bouhamzy, who died in a traffic accident in Lebanon 8th June 1943. Sleimann Bouhamzy was born six months later the same year. He was the nephew of Said Bouhamzy. He gave many details about the accident and about Said Bouhamzy's life, details that could not have been acquired in a normal way. Imad Elawar was born fifteen years later (i.e. in 1958). He lived in a very different place from Said Bouhamzy and had no connection to that family. He could also give many details about Said Bouhamzy and about the traffic accident, which could indicate that it actually was Said Bouhamzy's personality from which he got these memories. But Stevenson believed that, based on the rest of the information given, that these memories seemed to come from the cousin of Said Bouhamzy named Ibrahim Bouhamzy, who died in 1949.

11.10. Research

Ian Stevenson has carried out in-depth studies around many reported reincarnation cases, especially from India. He has investigated almost 2600 cases in all. He has referred to these surveys in several books he has published. In these he tells of contact with the families of the children who claim that their parents are not their real parents. Those children can name people who they maintain are their proper parents. They say that they live or have lived in another location which is also frequently named. They can provide details from the lives of the persons they claim that they have been. The persons they believe they have been are dead, and as a rule, they have had a sudden or violent death. A term for this kind of memories is extra-cerebral memory.

In his book from 1997 – *Where Reincarnation and Biology Intersect* – Stevenson has cited cases where there are physical characteristics, such as birth marks, deformities and other similarities between what a child says it experienced, or looked like, in a previous life (or how the person, with whom the child is identifying, looked in its life) and how the child's body is in this life. There are a couple of cases of major malformations that Stevenson mentions especially and pictures of these are included in the book, which are almost identical with the marks or malformations on the previous person's body. The person, who lived the previous life, has in some cases been identified and the stories verified, partly by using hospital records. Stevenson has further reported from some cases where relatives of the deceased have given the deceased certain marks just after death; or blood spots or other liquid has appeared on the corpse in connection with the death. A child, who claims to be the deceased, may then have birth marks or some damage to the skin that corresponds to the damage which was inflicted on the body of the deceased.

There seems to be a common feature for these stories. The children are usually between two and five years of age when they start talking about the other person, and that during this period they are constantly coming back to this and this person's experiences. Moreover, it seems that the previous person, in most cases, has had a sudden and often violent death, and that this happened only a few years before the child was born. The children cannot give any total picture of this other person or his or her situation, only some images – that are told again and again. When the child becomes a little older, these memories will cease and are often soon forgotten. The children often behave like small adults. It must be emphasized, however, that not all the stories given by the children can be verified, and not everything that is said is found to be correct – to the extent where it has been possible to verify the stories. But in most cases there is an incomprehensible consistency between the previous person and the present child, and with what the child reports from the previous person's life.

On the basis of what some mystics have claimed, it should be noted that in several cases (ten featured in Stevenson's book) the child maintains that it has had a different gender in the previous life. It has had trouble in adapting to the new gender and often has characteristics of the previous gender. In most of the cases mentioned, it is a girl who says she has been a man, although one would expect an even distribution. Another point to note is that the length of time between the previous and the current life can be very short. In some cases this period was from just nine months to about one and a half years, although most cases seem to be from five to ten years. In one case the period between the two lives was as short as fourteen days (case of Semir Taci).

Ian Stevenson has suggested a definition of reincarnation, as being the 'survival of the physical death and then a return to the physical life'. To be able to recognize a personality from one life to another, however, requires not only that a person has knowledge of certain things, but also that they have knowledge of how certain things are done.[426] It is in only a few of the cases which Stevenson has discussed that the child turns out to have the same special abilities that the former personality had, such as a facility for singing and music, or – in one case – special technical insight. But no new Mozart or other Western prodigy has, as far as we know, claimed to remember past lives. Stevenson concluded that the only adequate explanation he could find regarding the cases he had examined is reincarnation, although all cases have certain shortcomings. An alternative explanation, such as extrasensory perception, also has its shortcomings. However, he begins the last mentioned book with descriptions of parallel cases, which have nothing to do with reincarnation. These are:

> *Stigmata*, such as the wound marks Francis of Assisi had, similar to those Jesus suffered on the cross. Stevenson thought that this can be explained due to an intense identification with Jesus and his wounds, so that one indirectly applies those to oneself through the psyche (mental images).
>
> *Hypnosis*. By using hypnosis, it is possible to affect another person's psyche. One instructs the hypnotized patient to create mental images. (It is perhaps something similar that is happening during healing – and also through what we term the placebo effect.)
>
> *Telepathy*. In many cases a person has the feeling that something is happening with a related person, and perhaps experiences pain equal to what the other person is feeling. The typical case is a mother's feeling that her child is having an accident when this is actually happening at another place.
>
> *Maternal impression*. A mother's psychic experiences may result in damage to the embryo. A well-known such example that can be found in Norwegian literature and rural legends is the pregnant woman that sees a hare and then bears a child with cleft lip and palate, which today is rejected as pure superstition. Ian Stevenson wrote, however, that he has found approximately 300 such cases by reading medical reports from Europe and the United States.

Professor Erlendur Haraldsson (b.1931), Iceland, has studied and described similar cases from India and Lebanon respectively similar to those reported by Ian Stevenson. He noted that the studied cases essentially occur in cultures where people believe in reincarnation. He has, however, also knowledge of a parallel case from Iceland. Similar stories are also told by others. Both Sogyal Rinpoche and Aivanhov have described such stories in their books when they write about reincarnation, reports from Tibet and Bulgaria respectively. It can also be noted that in the biography of Edgar Cayce, a case is referred to in which a five-year-old child, who happened to meet Cayce, claimed to have known Cayce in a previous life.[427]

Professor, psychiatrist, *Joel Whitton* in Canada, has collected a variety of reports regarding experiences of past lives, experiences that were related by people he had hypnotized. He was then also told stories from the existence between the physical lives.[428] Contrary to what many mystics have said, people have often reported to have had a different gender in the previous life. In some cases, a trauma in this life seemed to have arisen in a former life. This is also what many regression therapists observe.

The psychologist *Helen Wambach* (1925-1988) PhD, United States, did much research on the life before this life, and has published several books about her findings.[429] She has had many groups of people lying relaxed on the floor, and taken them back to previous experiences, also to lives before this life, through so-called light hypnosis. She has then handed out questionnaires to the participants. All in all, she received almost 750 completed forms, in which she, inter alia, had asked the participants what they had experienced during the hypnosis, about past lives, how it was to be born and the feelings associated with this. Almost everyone was able to write about the feelings and sensations both before and during their birth, about previous lives, about why they chose to be born in the twentieth century, that they chose their own gender, and that they to some extent had chosen to live again. It is worth noting that her interview objects usually replied that it was they who chose the sex with which they were born. Another interesting thing was that 89% of the 750 who had responded, stated that they were not part of the embryo before this was about six months old. Moreover, many said that they were not completely bound to the embryo from this time, as they could go in and out of the embryo's body at will and in some cases up until the birth.

Previously we have considered some of what *Edgar Cayce* is supposed to have said about the cause behind people's problems and about reincarnation. He frequently gave information from a previous life as explanation for present circumstances. When exploring reincarnation, one must also consider the readings Edgar Cayce gave throughout his life, and the work that has been done in order to verify his statements. In a few cases this has given positive results, as it has been possible to find historical people whose life descriptions match that which Cayce told people now living about their past lives.[430]

Stanislav Grof has proven that people have access to a massive database through unusual consciousness states, which can be achieved through trance, circular breathing, or by the use of drugs. In such a trance state, one can experience being almost anything that it is possible to imagine, whether from real life or from imagination. He has described an episode which may have significance for the understanding of the reincarnation question.[431]

A young woman, who was born after the Second World War, experienced during a séance that which her father (who was still living) experienced during the war. She felt that she was her own father as a soldier in a very realistic war scene, where she was shot so that the ball touched her cheeks and ear. Her father later confirmed that this had happened, something she did not know beforehand. Grof has said that many people experience past lives when in a trance state, and that such experiences can have healing effect. Sometimes one may be introduced to the law of karma and learn to take responsibility for past actions, while at the same time get insight into what should be done to be freed from the karmic obligations. This does not require that one believes in reincarnation. Grof stressed that such experiences often give surprisingly accurate information about times, places and customs that the individual could not have known about in advance. Furthermore, it has shown that such experiences often are associated with different emotions, psychosomatic or interpersonal problems that the person has in the present life.

Another strange aspect of earlier life experiences that Grof wrote about, are cases of synchronicity. For example, when a man during a séance is reliving what is perceived as an episode from a previous life, he will often meet in that episode a person with whom he has a difficult relationship in this life. If during this séance he is able to forgive or to resolve an issue in relation to this person, the remarkable happens – the problems in this life will also be solved. To the extent that Grof was able to verify such experiences, it turned out that the other person also often experienced a profound change – and that this usually happened at about the same time, despite great distances between them. The change could come in the form of a sudden new view of the other; new information could emerge from an independent source or through specific events. Grof mentioned that he did not feel convinced that such episodes really stemmed from previous incarnations, as much of what was reported could be explained in another way. But he pointed out that such experiences cannot be explained by the scientific methods we are familiar with today.

He further said that in mythical traditions where reincarnation is accepted, it is not believed that an individual actually comes back as such. The advanced reincarnation theory maintains that all borders or divisions of the existence are illusory, so that ultimately it is only the creative principle or the cosmic consciousness that is.

11.11. Various statements about reincarnation

Rudolf Steiner claimed that the human being undergoes many incarnations. He said, inter alia, that the purpose of these incarnations is that people should work with their self-development, so that they finally may reach the highest form of consciousness and become spiritual beings. But when they get that far, the Earth will have become another type of planet. Steiner explained that it is the human individuality that goes through one incarnation after the other, like a red thread that is outside the physical, the etheric and the astral body. This life-thread is always separated from the outer Cosmos, also in the period between two lives. But there is still a part of the astral body that follows the 'I' in this in-between period, which Steiner has called the kamaloka period. This is a kind of power body which contains that which has been experienced of moral, intellectual and aesthetic values. There is also an extract of the etheric body that is brought forth from incarnation to incarnation. This extract is the sum of the thoughts and feelings we are left with when we are given a retrospective on the life we have lived, immediately after the physical body has been abandoned. And he said that what is real progress in one incarnation, is brought over to the next – along with the 'I' (the Self in Bertelsen's terminology), which he said is the basic eternal. Steiner further explained that in regard to the physical body, that which disappears at death are only the substances of the body, while the form will remain. The clairvoyant seer will still see an etheric body, an astral body and an 'I' (the mental body). Later, the seer will see the etheric body depart from the rest and dissolve, except for the above mentioned extract. Still later many will see that there is an extract of the astral body that stays on, while the remainder is dissolved, but something important still remains from the physical body, and that is its shape, or that which Steiner called the phantom. He has further explained that an ordinary human being is unable to remember its past lives. It is only a person with clairvoyant abilities or one who has reached the higher 'I' (the Self), who can recognize memories of past incarnations. It is only this higher 'I' that passes from one Earth life to another, and who is conscious through death.[432]

Martinus' starting point was what he called the living being.[433] This is a something that is experiencing life – it is not energy, as energy in itself cannot perceive. Energy or motion is without life. Since everything that is has been created, it must be something behind creation. There are myriads of creatures composed of organisms or whose bodies are complex organisms. These are evidence that there is a something that created them, for they could not have created themselves. This something is identical to that which in each living creature is experiencing existence. This something has not been created; it is there from eternity to eternity. Martinus said that all existing living beings are immortal. Every living creature has five manifestation bodies, and on the earthly plane it is the physical body that is prevalent. At death we leave the physical body, but the other bodies will still exist, and the living being will experience existence through these bodies.

Martinus has a long description of the reincarnation principle, which is difficult to understand and, therefore, difficult to render here. The most important point to be noticed is the individual's need for a physical body in order to live on the Earth. The need to remain on the Earth is due to the fact that it is only here that the individual has the opportunity to evolve towards higher consciousness states. The individual must therefore attach itself to a new physical structure, when the old structure disintegrates due to old age, injuries or illness. The individual has a paraphysical nature that leaves the physical organism at death, and which then attaches itself to a new physical organism. Between the physical existences the living being will have a spiritual existence of shorter or longer duration. Its (unconscious) desires to return to the physical life will determine the duration of the spiritual existence. This unconscious desire influences the ability to associate itself with physical matter. A certain selection principle will be active at the same time.

Martinus maintained that human destiny is not a question of sin and forgiveness, but a matter of cause and effect. Reincarnation is, according to his statement, a non-debatable fact. One cannot atone for bad deeds by means of sacraments and grace. As you sow, you will reap. There is therefore only one way to go, and that is to work with yourself in order to become a better human being. To do that you need to know yourself, the reason why you have done what you have done, and your reactions. Meditation is a way to go inward, into yourself. On the basis of the present research results about reincarnation it should be noted that Martinus wrote that the human being's memory ability and intuition are not very well developed at the stage where humanity is now; normally we can therefore not remember past lives. He rejected as well (like Ambres and Cayce) that we cannot change gender from one life to the next. The change of gender is a process that spans a long time, according to these mystics.

Aivanhov explained almost the same as Martinus and Steiner.[434] He also said that reincarnation is a fact, and the only solution that provides an acceptable explanation of life. If we do not understand the reincarnation principle, we will never understand our present situation or the experiences that shape our lives. But he also stated that it is of no purpose to research past lives through regression, as that does not teach us anything. We have to accept that what is happening to us has its cause in earlier events, but what they actually were plays no role, for we have to take responsibility for what has happened anyway. However, we will understand that we can no longer blame others for our problems and accidents, and that revenge has no purpose. People need to work on improving themselves, so that the next incarnation will be better than the current one. The most important thing is to learn to love other people, helping them and educating them without expecting anything back.

Gurdjieff's starting point was that a human being with a fully developed consciousness consists of four bodies.[435] These are organisms of ever finer substance, which partly penetrate each other. Such a person will be able to live after death and to reincarnate. As regards other people, he expressed that they hardly could be said to exist, as they mainly only responded to external circumstances – so how could you then say that they lived on? Also Gurdjieff's disciple, Peter Ouspensky[i] (Pyotr Demianovich Ouspenskii) (1878-1947), said almost the same when he was asked about reincarnation. If you have not developed any of the four bodies, you cannot know if you are reincarnating – and that is the case for almost all of today's people.

Bob Moore has pointed out that the human beings are born with certain qualities.[436] He believed that these are a manifestation of how the individual has evolved in a variety of physical and non-physical life periods. For example, the development of consciousness is a quality that is carried on. It is these *qualities* that he termed soul. For the soul to unfold, it must have both a physical mechanism in order to express itself through a physical existence, and a non-physical development (the soul level). It is this exchange that can be said to be the individual's incarnations.

Milan Ryzl believed that our known consciousness which is related to time, in the sense that its form of thinking consists of a series of individual, successive visions or statements, cannot contain the spirit that is beyond time.[437] From a timeless spiritual component's standpoint reincarnation is not a concept, since all lives are only aspects of the same existence. Then it will have neither a start nor an end. Ryzl asked if the consciousness we know today will be able to survive the death of the body, since the body's consciousness so strongly is associated with the physical.

The Indian-American author and physicist *Amit Goswami,* PhD, a researcher at The Institute of Noetic Sciences, USA, has in his book *Physics of the Soul – The quantum book of living, dying, reincarnation and immortality* explained the soul, the various consciousness bodies and the spirit world from the quantum theory of the physicists. His explanation as to how the soul takes residence in a new physical body is fairly similar to Arthur E. Powell's description.

Ervin Laszlo said that in the psi field we may find holograms for everything that is and has been. These holograms can be brought forth to see if we are able to adjust ourselves to the wave patterns which the holograms create. Therefore he did not think that what goes under the designation reincarnation-experience is something that is related to a specific individual. Anyone having such an experience has only caught another individual's story. We are all leaving tracks in the psi field, so in that sense he thought we are immortal.

Lyall Watson has considered some of Ian Stevenson's surveys and drawn conclusions based on his own experiences as a biologist and researcher of

---

i. Ouspensky was a journalist in a Moscow newspaper, later also a writer. He has written the books *A New Model of the Universe* and *The Strange Life of Ivan Osokin*. He was a disciple of Gurdjieff after the two met in 1915, and worked later to spread Gurdjieff's teachings.

paranormal phenomena.[438] He found that the cases examined so far do not give us evidence of reincarnation, and that we today (this was written before 1974) do not have the opportunity to know what happens after the physical death but he acknowledged that consciousness, the day consciousness and the unconscious, seems determined by processes that are at least not in their entirety localized in the physical brain; that consciousness may not be physical at all. Watson referred to the infinite amount of information that is stored in our genes and in each cell of the body, and the unconsciousness' amazing ability to capture and store information. He thought the reason why we do not hear of more of the so-called reincarnation cases, in spite of the possibilities that ought to be available from the unconscious, had a biological explanation. Otherwise, there should have been many more souls who would have made themselves known through reincarnation than those that have been found through research. Watson mentioned the possibility also that young children can develop multiple personalities, and that the mentioned reincarnation cases might have biological causes. He also referred to the fact that many people have access to an unimaginable amount of information that does not have any direct relation or is of any benefit to our day-to-day life. His basic question in this regard is why. Why do we have this ability, how can it be used? Does it have some survival significance?

But then, what about the matching bodily scars and marks that have been found on some people? Is it possible to telepathically pick up the story of a deceased person who accidentally had a similar bodily error? Or can you develop an injury due to a strong identification with another human being – in the same way as Francis of Assisi's stigmata? This seems unlikely, considering that these children were born with those deformities – so they must have occurred already in the embryo. Maybe it is not completely implausible that the mind may have been influenced telepathically, even at the embryonic stage. See the discussion in the previous chapter regarding extraordinary phenomena and abilities, about the manifestations of mind images on the body (chapter 3.12). It should be noted that the aforementioned cases of reincarnation applied to people who lived within small geographical distances.

Lyall Watson has suggested that the mind can control the body's genetic system.[439] He has discussed treatments with hypnosis, in which the patient is hypnotized and ordered to heal his or her self. Watson specifically mentioned that Brocq's disease, an awful disease of the skin that is caused by a mutation in a gene, and until 1951 was considered incurable, has been cured in this way. Stan Gooch has told of a case in which a woman, who had had a sadistic father who had cruelly beaten her, developed big bleeding wounds on her body just by remembering the battering. And Watson further mentioned that several cases of large birth marks caused by congenital errors, have also been cured through hypnosis. If you can change a gene code through the use of the mind, or affect it in order to get rid of an illness or injury, it may give reason to believe that the mind may also do the opposite.

Hypnosis experiments show that the mind is in control of the body's physical and chemical processes, but that the day consciousness does not know about this or is not able to use this ability, unless in very special cases – such as the yogi's control of the body. And the mind must have existed in one form or another ever since the first cell stage.

In this context Watson also mentioned the out-of-body experiences. He believed that so many cases have been reported that they must be regarded as a reality. These experiences demonstrate that consciousness cannot be locked to the physical body. On the other hand, he suggested that the organizing field, the bioplasma field or energy body, which is believed to contain the individual's memory and experience characteristics, must depend on energy, and he believed that such energy can best be provided by a living body. One explanation of spirit beings may be that this field, which can remain a short time after the physical death, in some cases may affect another living body, which will give this person the idea of having seen or felt a spirit being. But such an energy body that operates independently of the physical body does not seem to be able to make any changes and seems very simple minded; and without supply of energy from the living body it will soon be dissolved. Supply of energy to this bioplasma field may come only from a person who is sufficiently mentally divided or from someone else who is sufficiently receptive. Watson suggested that this field can be drained by the use of holy water or through exorcism. This description may, according to him, also provide an explanation of accounts of vampires and werewolves, as well as of other creatures that are a mixture of humans and animals – in the way that also animals have bioplasma fields. (Such an explanation from a biological standpoint fits well with the Theosophical theory about the existence of an etheric double.) Watson took this idea one step further. He started with the fact that discharges of electrical energy can be printed in the wax on a gramophone disc and that magnetic impulses can be transferred to a tape and later replayed. Then he did not find it unlikely that patterns of bioplasmic energy can be preserved in the crystals of precious stones and metal with which this energy has been in contact. He took this reasoning a step further when he said that it is not unlikely from a biological point of view, that the energy from a charged living body will be able to reincarnate if it finds a suitable living substrate in the correct state of responsiveness, provided that it does not take a too long time until this happens.

Lyall Watson has also said that the best indication that reincarnation is a reality, had to be if one could prove that a now living person had the same mind as a particular departed one. He referred to Professor Curt Ducasse's statement about the difficulties of proving that an old person is the same as a young person, which can only be overcome if it can be proved that the young body has become the old one. The same ought to be applicable in a presumed reincarnation case; it must be the mind from the previous person who has become the mind of the present person. That is, the previous person's subjective experiences must be found in the present mind as memories. Watson believed that this is impossible to verify. But if it can be proved that a now living person has information that no other now living person possesses (although this may be caused by spiritual possession or by reading the Akashic records), he will be able to accept it as second best evidence. As an example of such a proof he mentioned the Rosemary reincarnation case. She could speak the old Egyptian language.

Colin Wilson observed that there are fundamental different opinions between spiritualists as to whether reincarnation is a real phenomenon.[440] He pointed out that the so-called channelled information does not provide any confirmation of reincarnation. But he pointed out that the present evidences for reincarnation are just as trustworthy as those who tell of a life after death. However, in his review of reincarnation cases he drew a parallel to a number of strange phenomena, such as split personality, spirit possessions (including the case where a Brazilian farmer became possessed by a personality who claimed he was a German physician, and the farmer thereafter carried out many successful operations)[i], UFO experiences, hypnosis and manifestations of unknown personalities. Perhaps there is a correlation in all this.

Georg Hygen and Jon Mannsåker, both prominent members of the Norwegian Parapsychological Society, in 1990 published articles about the reincarnation question.[441] Georg Hygen's article was a presentation of his lecture on reincarnation at a meeting that year in the Norwegian town of Florø. He commented on the reincarnation material which had been collected up to that date, which consisted of stories about apparitions, mediumistic statements, out-of-body experiences, death-bed visions, near-death experiences and brain-physiological studies. Georg Hygen's conclusion was that reincarnation was not proven, although there was extensive anecdotal material; but he also noted neither could the question be said to have been refuted, as no natural explanations had been found for these phenomena. Jon Mannsåker commented on the research done by Ian Stevenson and Helen Wambach. His conclusion at that time was that the results presented allowed for a reincarnation interpretation, but he also thought that this could indicate a different form of consciousness after the physical death.

The following commentary from *The Other Side* as received by Anabela Cardoso is however interesting. It said: "Reincarnation happens only occasionally and only when there is no other possibility."[442]

I have read several books lately about outstanding English mediums, but in none of the books do I find that the spirits who present themselves through a medium mention anything about their own previous incarnations on Earth. There is, however, one interesting exception to this lack of comments. In the book about Isa Northage (1898-1985) it is recorded that during a séance held

---

i. It should be noted that Stan Gooch in the book *The Paranormal* (1978) maintained that the farmer (Arigó) was cheating. See further about Arigó in chapter 15 about healing.

by that extraordinary English medium, Helena Blavatsky, who died in 1891, appeared and delivered a long explanation in regard to the question of reincarnation[i]. She stated that reincarnation is not true and said, inter alia, the following: "They told me in spirit that I could not reincarnate. I have tried and tried to come back to be somebody else but could not. We cannot reincarnate; we progress, we do not come back. Some may say this is not Madame Blavatsky, but do not doubt it; it is." She said that during her lifetime she had advocated the idea of reincarnation, which she found was truth and justice, as she then believed that everyone ought to come back to learn and experience. Her explanation now was as follows: "Memories of past lives are revived by spirits bringing such thoughts that represent the lives they had lived and their experiences are impressed on your mind as your own. You then think you remember your past. When you study Theosophy you develop your mind and live in an atmosphere of mind; you remove yourself as much as possible from the physical, becoming sensitive and aware of spirits around you. They speak to you by impressions[ii] and their past will be like a panorama; you feel it and live their past over again. This you mistake for the memory of former incarnations."

There are, however, some interesting facts in regard to this statement. One I have included earlier in this chapter (11.5) from her explanations as to what happens when we die, that there is only a *beam* of the Self/monad that will form a new personality on Earth. It is not the individual person that is reincarnating; from which follows that an earthbound spirit is never able to reincarnate (but may be able to possess a human being). Why should her spirit now say the opposite? Was this spirit really the personality of Helena Blavatsky? It is interesting that almost the same statement, part of it with exactly the same wording, is to be found in Carl Wickland's book *Thirty years among the Dead,* from 1924.[iii] The date for Isa Northage's experience is not given. Her book was first published in 1960. Presumably Carl Wickland was the first one to record the visit by Helena Blavatsky in spirit – the séance he is referring was held in 1922. So, did the spirit of Blavatsky appear twice, or was some other spirit repeating her sayings at the second appearance? It is also possible that both appearances were a spirit pretending to be Blavatsky, or that she did not quite remember what she actually taught about reincarnation during her lifetime (which I find unlikely). I do not believe that the author of the biography of Isa Northage has copied the story from Carl Wickland's book without saying so. But this story shows that we must be fairly careful as regards spirit communication.

---

i. See *A Path prepared – the Story of Isa Northage* by Allan MacDonald, pp. 38-39.

ii. One of the guides of Minnie Harrison impressed her that she knew a village in France when she had never left England - see Tom Harrison, *Life After Death: Living Proof,* p. 231.

iii. See more about this book in chapter 3.11 in the section about documentation of spirit contacts.

11.12. Comments

The researchers have not found any adequate explanation for the strange phenomena that may be considered as reincarnation stories. But if we take a closer look at the cases in which children claim to be a different person and the circumstances related to this other person, there are a number of more or less plausible hypotheses (apart from impressions):

> Accounts of past lives have sometimes matched well with stories of parents, grandparents or great grandparents. These stories may be confused with one's own experiences.
>
> By the use of telepathy or intuition infants can (maybe even in the embryo stage) somehow get hold of another person's life and strongly identify with this.
>
> A mother's experiences or visual impressions may be so strong that they are picked up by the embryo, so that the mother's impressions put their mark on it (*maternal impression*).
>
> If the child is mentally very open or weak, a discarnate creature – a departed spirit, if such one exists – might have been able to take over the child's consciousness, i.e. a kind of possession.
>
> Multiple personalities in the psyche might be a possibility, but that, however, says nothing about why the child identifies itself with a particular departed person. This might be explained by the psi field.
>
> A person may acquire information from the psi field. This can also be explained in the way that a mind has access to an infinite knowledge bank, so that all that is and has ever been is available for everyone. The problem is to be able to tune into this common consciousness.
>
> The brain operates holographically – it has access to all information, ref. the psi field or the Akashic archive.

Helen Wambach's experimental results may partly be explained by these hypotheses. But it is also possible that the imagination creates stories that are remembered as one's own experiences. If any of these explanations is the right answer, none of the cases that have been subject to investigation can be said to be proof of reincarnation. If possession or impression is the explanation, this indicates that there is a life after death. None of these solutions explain, however, the aforementioned cases of deformities which seem to have been transferred from a departed to a living person. Perhaps Lyall Watson's suggestion that consciousness can influence our genes, so that the child intuitively picks up another individual's fate, may be the explanation. Stanislav Grof's experiments with LSD and holotropic breathing show that the mind's ability is amazing and incomprehensible. Many people experience that they have been a famous personality in a previous life during such a séance and it has happened that two or more persons have identified themselves with the same personality.

However, Ian Stevenson's reports leave a big question – why would a new individual get deformities corresponding to those of a former individual? Why would a new individual get birth marks or similar skin lesions like those suffered by a departed person? Is it possible to find a logical explanation for this? Even if we were to accept the law of karma and reincarnation; that does not explain the cases in which a victim of violence transfers its sufferings to a new individual. (The performer of the violence is said to have lived on in some of those cases.) It may imply that the physical body's experiences are retained by the astral and mental bodies, and therefore also by the causal body, so that everything is passed on and transferred to a new physical individual – who does not need to have any direct relationship with the deceased. As we have seen previously, thoughts are able to influence matter in such a degree that this might cause deformities in the body; but why are there then not more people born with such characteristics? A common characteristic in the cases Ian Stevenson considered was that the previous individual suffered a sudden and often violent death. Maybe an unexpected death has the consequence that the soul in some cases is unable to escape the physical life and the physical body, so that what happened marks it too strongly. But with today's many car accidents and other disasters in which people perish, it is strange that we do not hear more about such cases than those Stevenson has found.

The cases mentioned here should imply that there are both physical and mental qualities, including not least – memory, which is transferred from a departed person to a new incarnated personality. However, Sogyal Rinpoche, Jes Bertelsen, Ken Wilber, Martinus and Rudolf Steiner, all argue that the memory dies with the 'I' and does not survive physical death. They all seem to believe that it is only the Self that can carry properties or qualities on from past lives, but that the memories from such lives cannot be transferred. All that is related to the 'I', that is, the physical, etheric, astral and mental, according to these mystics, dissolves at the physical death or at each new birth at the latest.

Many believe that the strongest evidence of reincarnation is cases where a child is found to have special skills, ref. Curt Ducasse's commentary rendered above by Lyall Watson. Ian Stevenson refers to several possible reincarnation cases where a child is extraordinarily gifted with a particular skill, whether this may be mechanics, dance, music or language. The mother's language is something a child slowly learns while learning to talk. There is a lot more difficult to learn another language later. But the skill of talking a different and unknown language sometimes occurs with adults in trance.

What is repeatedly seen in the surveys of Ian Stevenson is that a new little individual can have memories, abilities and physical markers that correspond to a previous individual's experiences, abilities and physical body. Is it this that constitutes a personality? And why do they lose the memories after a few years? Do those still remain in the child's unconsciousness and influence its behaviour later on? I cannot see any clear coherence or similarity between the different reincarnation testimonials or between these and the above mentioned research findings and strange tales. I barely remember what happened yesterday; is it then any reason to believe that I will bring with me all the events that have happened in my life now into a later life? I have some mental images from my childhood, which for me is like looking at a picture book. It should be me, but I feel no connection to the images. On the other hand, I know that some dramatic experiences (such as war experiences in childhood) reside far inside my emotional system and those emotions might pop up under certain circumstances. I have no conscious control over those emotions and neither am I able to remember the events. So I cannot disregard that I am influenced by those early experiences in one way or other. I am undergoing changes all through my life, physically, mentally and spiritually. Everything that I am doing or thinking today is based on what I have previously learned and what I have experienced. What I have experienced is influencing the way I today am acting and reacting, which is very different from before. This is not something external that can be measured. It is a synthesis of qualities or a lack of such.

Who am I then? Who is behind the thoughts that arise in my mind? Who controls the functions of my body? The teaching of several mystics is that if we ask ourselves the question 'who am I', we will find out that there is no 'I'. It has been said that here is no unchangeable nucleus in any being. If I try to meditate – that is, to stop the thoughts – I find that I still am, but I am then not doing anything and nothing happens. What are we if we are not acting, not being active in some way, either physical or thought-wise? Our activity is related to the physical body, which we are unable to take with us through death. Would anyone recognize me if I did not have a recognizable body through which I can express myself?

Occasionally I have felt like a chameleon – instead of having to change colour, I change the way I am behaving depending on to whom I am talking or in who's company I am. So who is then the true 'I'? However, I find that other people have not changed much through the years. People with whom I went to school seem almost exactly the same twenty or fifty years later – they have only become older by appearance. What we recognize in others are the facial features, their voice and their way of moving. If we for example dress ourselves differently from what we did before, change hair colour, change body shape or the way we move, we are not so easily recognized. But if we then share common memories and experiences when we meet again, we easily come back to our old way of contact. We are recognized, but if we do not have memories in common, we are as strangers to each other. Again I must ask: what is this 'I' that is supposed to be unchangeable? I find myself unchangeable, but that is because changes happen so slowly that I do not register them, because I do not see the changes from one day to the next. However, there seems to exist a pattern that was given us when we were born – or which we brought with us, because the cells die and are renewed all the time and adapt to the given whole. This pattern seems unchangeable throughout the individual's physical life, even though the specific pieces repeatedly are changed. But what is this pattern? Does it pass on to the next life? Is this the essence that some people call the Self? Or is it just a temporary structure that applies to this physical life?

Rune Amundsen used the term databank about that which is collecting experiences and linking the various lives together. Ambres used the terms the Basic Personality and the Rider.

Seth said that we have a variety of different egos that all are part of one being, with which we have contact at a place within us, that we are a multidimensional personality. Martinus talked of the living being, which goes down in one Earth life after another in order to gain experiences and lessons learned, and which – just as a human life – is evolving with the acquired experiences and knowledge. These different terms fit the concept of the Self.

The only logical explanation of what we hear about reincarnation seems to me to be what many mystics teach about consciousness, that there are several consciousness bodies. These are, as mentioned earlier, the physical, the etheric, the astral, the mental, the causal and the spiritual. Above this is the One – the All. We see that the physical is abandoned when death occurs. We do not see the other bodies, although some mystics do. However, if it is the etheric that provides the basis for biological life and keeps the physical together, we will no longer have any use of that when the physical disappears. The astral and the mental are our experiences, fantasies and thoughts. Do we need these further on? What we need is presumably only the synthesis of what we have experienced and learned – in order to build on this in the next existence, wherever that may be. Here, I find it important to emphasize what Plotinus said about memory, that when the individual soul parts split off, each soul part soon forgets that which the other part was concerned with. The human related part of the soul will only remember that which happened in this human life.

If something is going to continue, it must be the causal body (the Self) which can be said to be the synthesis of what has been gathered through the four lower consciousness bodies. This Self will participate in several physical lives, if it creates new physical lives, and will then be able to gather experience from them all. Whether this happens as successive lives or contemporary lives will depend on how we define the concept of time. Seth, Cayce and Ambres, all said that all beings are living several earthly lives at the same time. But this may perhaps only mean that we must not use an earthly perspective, since this time perspective is limited. However, it is tempting to ask why do I need to work with myself or adjust myself to others if my behaviour does not have any consequences for myself – that is, to my

'I'? Eat, drink and be happy will easily become the way of life if the 'I' cannot see the harmful consequences of egotism. Martinus' answer to this question is perhaps the only answer. He said that all beings (all Selves) want to experience, experiment and learn, but that you easily get tired of everything you do, whatever it is, and therefore you will seek change. Both extreme violence as well as extreme joy is sought by all beings, but everything is a transition to other stages. He also said that the rule of destiny entails that one harvests as one sows. If it will be the current or the next 'I' or the Self, that must take the consequences, is unclear. Whether we will be meeting our sins in this life, in death, on the death bed or in a later life, as far as I know, he did not say.

Martinus, Ambres and Cayce, all said that we will not in one life be a male, while in the next life maybe a female. There are long cycles where we either will be the one or the other, but some transitions can create gender confusion. When such a transition happens – when one cycle is completed – is not clear for me. However, if this is correct, the stories told in which a person experiences having the opposite gender in its previous life, or can choose its gender before coming into this life, can hardly be a reincarnation experience. But what is it then? On the other hand, a change of gender may explain homosexuality, transvestism and the need for gender change – that is that one clings to the physical body and the psyche from an earlier incarnation.

Jes Bertelsen has said the existence after the physical death is a dream-like state. That is perhaps the key word. There is no awake consciousness after death, but experiences as in a dream and maybe we are bringing these dreams with us to the next existence. For example, when I in a past life regression session experience being a priest or an American Indian, that might not be something that I have experienced. But in my subconsciousness I have some experience material which in a dream might manifest as if I were that person, and as such thought and worked in a particular way. Perhaps this experience material also is reflected in the genes, so that physical damage is transferred from one individual to another, although this to me seems very unlikely.

Reincarnation to a new physical existence on Earth is one question to which I have not found any clear answer; although the explanations given that it is the Soul and not the personality that reincarnates, indicates that any remembrance a personality may have of a previous life must find its explanation in something other than what we normally think of when using the word reincarnation. Whether there is another existence than the earthly one is another question. There seems to be some sort of a conscious existence after the physical during which the personality continues to be aware of its former self and to develop – at least for a certain period. The evidence for this is overwhelming, as shown in the chapters 3.11 and 10.4 above. Since there is such an existence, there must in each individual be a core or consciousness with a form of awareness of this existence during this period, although at the very highest plane there might not be such a core – only the One.

To sum up – to me the picture seems to be: When you leave this physical life you go to the astral world, called Summerland by some, which is very close to and very similar to life on Earth. There you, as a personality, exist according to how you think. You will still have your astral body and also retain the subtler bodies. You may from there get in contact with the physical world. However, if you are so earthbound that you do not quite believe that you have passed over you will be in limbo. In very special cases the entity may then go back to Earth as a reincarnated being. One cause for going back may be a sudden death, as for example being murdered, when your experience leaves imprints on mind and soul that can only be worked through in a physical body. If you are able to adjust to the surroundings in the astral world and accept the assistance you will find there, you may get enough help to stay on that plane or proceed to other planes on that side. Then the personality will slowly lose the feeling of being a personality and accept being part of the 'group soul' – or the higher Spirit. The fragment is then back where it belongs. This fragment will not come back to Earth.

There seems to be a plan within our earthly existence, and if so, there is reason to take a further look at some related questions that have engaged people throughout time. All the mystics I have read or read about, highlight one issue as the most important thing in life, namely, that people must learn to develop their ability to love. This is said to be vital for how the existence in the first after-life period will be experienced and for the further development of the soul. What that means, we shall now consider.

12. Love –
The Goal of Humanity

> And now these three remain: faith, hope and love. But the greatest of these is love. (1 Cor 13.13)

> And people are here to adopt the Godhead's warm love, to develop and repay it. And the only way that they can do this is to become self-aware ego-beings. Only then can they repay the love. ... At the end of the Earth's evolution people shall reach that stage where the ego, which then is independently in the inner part of the human being based on full devotion, gets the impulse to do right and good. When love is so spiritualized that nobody wants to do anything other than to follow this impulse, it has consummated that which Christ Jesus brought into the world. For that is one of the secrets of Christianity that it teaches: 'Look to Christ, fill you with his figure's power, try to be like him, to follow after him; then that which is the innermost 'I' will be freed, so that it does not need any law in order to do what is good, the right thing.' Thus Christ is the one who brings the impulse to freedom from the law, so that what is good will be done, not because of the law, but as an impulse from the love that lives in the interior.
> *Rudolf Steiner* [443]

> That which exists as pleasure in this world, all comes from the desire to make others happy. And any suffering that is, is caused by the desire to make myself happy.
> *The Buddhist master Shantideva (685-763), (see next footnote)*

> If you are trying to suppress your selfish motives – anger etc. – and instead seek to promote more kindness and compassion for others, then in the final round it will be yourself that is getting the most benefit from it. So therefore I sometimes say that the wise selfish person should practice this. Stupid egoists are always thinking of themselves, and the result is negative. Wise egoists are thinking of others, are helping others as far as they can, and the result is that they also benefit from it.
> *The 14th Dalai Lama* [444]

Love is a misused word in our society. It is used about falling in love, about physical attraction, desire and good feelings. Love has absolutely nothing to do with sexual relationships. It would provide a better understanding if people showed respect for this word and only used it about the almost holy feeling which can endure and withstand everything, and which is not selfish. Everyone has a yearning within and believes that this yearning is to experience the love from another human being and also to love another person. We believe that this kind of love is the most important thing in life. Then we experience a love affair and think that this is real love, only to experience deep sorrow when this illusion bursts – and we start looking for another human being where we can hide or with whom we can hide. Anyone who knows what love is – the divine love – does not need another person in order to get a feeling of one's own value. Anyone knowing what the divine love is, no longer needs to search, but knows that life is to be lived as it is, and have peace of mind and heart.

But to show such love does not mean that we must allow other people to do as they please, or that you have to help and save them from any difficulty or danger. Many people are like small children, there must be limits as to what they can do because they must show consideration to others. They have to face difficulties in order to grow – mentally as well as spiritually. In this context, I will refer to a conversation I once had with some friends, which might contribute to an understanding of what love really means. The starting point for the discussion was my report on a course with Matthew Manning, where we did an exercise where we were to experience the difference between positive and negative thoughts. The exercise was the following:

> We were two together. Person A was to walk towards person B with the eyes closed and stop as soon as he/she felt any type of resistance. B was, at the same time, going to think either positive or negative thoughts. For instance, the thought could be that A was welcome and that B was fond of him/her. If this was the case, A experienced in most cases that he/she could come so close to B that there was a collision. If B sent out negative and dismissive thoughts, A usually stopped at one or two metres distance away. (A would not in advance know which option B chose.)

This shows some of the power thoughts can have. You should never send out negative thoughts, because it is registered by someone in one way or another. My friends had difficulties understanding how it is possible to send out positive thoughts if you do not like a person. Eileen Caddy has said that in such a situation she said to herself: 'I love you, I bless you, I see the divinity in you.'

However, not many people manage to do this. When they dislike someone, they are not able to see anything positive in them. For example, if a person does something which one does not find acceptable, as a rule it is almost impossible to avoid looking at them negatively or with disgust, but it is important that we distinguish between a person and the person's *action*. Even if we dislike a person's action, then the person might still be worthy of love, because he or she acted appropriately based on his or her situation. That does not mean that bad deeds are not to be prevented or commented upon. Obviously we have to set limits for other people's expansion if it causes harm to others or to other people's property or something similar. In the interaction between people we must have rules for everyone to follow, but that is not the same as one not feeling love towards a person who breaks the rules. It is important to send loving thoughts so that he or she will feel welcomed and thereby be more receptive to the restrictions that must be followed. I am left with the feeling that the reason why we humans are so afraid of each other is due to the fact that we have not learned what love really is. Neither do we understand the impact of thoughts. How can we follow the words of Jesus about love when we do not understand them?

How to convey to people that love is the most important thing in this world, and that this is what we are here first and foremost to learn? How can we learn what love is, if we do not have love for ourselves, and we do not know the difference between positive and negative thoughts? How can we get a better world when we believe that a person who does something wrong against us must be punished for this action so that we have peace in our emotional lives? Why is vengeance so important? It has nothing to do with love. That leads only to the opposite. Why is it so difficult to forgive?

We had several examples and exercises in Matthew Manning's course that showed the importance of thoughts.

> In one example, MM called on a strong young man. He had to hold his weakest arm horizontally out from the body and think of something positive and enjoyable. MM failed to pull down the arm. Then the man should hold his strongest arm horizontally and think of something sad. MM pulled down the arm without effort.
>
> In another exercise we first sat together three and three, and had to sending energy to each other while we were holding hands. When we had done this for a while, we had to feel each others' hands. Then we had to stand up and try to notice each others' energy radiation by slowly bringing our hands up and down each side of each of the partner's body from the head down, and so in the same way in front of and behind the body. Then we should give each other a good hug. Thereafter we had to go out on the floor and mix with the rest of the participants (there were fifty-five people there in all). We were then told to close our eyes and find our two partners with closed eyes. Strangely enough, I and my two partners found each other. Almost all the other groups managed this as well.

This report was written at the beginning of November 1993, just after the course. In December the same year, I suddenly had a situation where I really was tested, where I felt so severely threatened by a person that I became almost physically ill. Was this a mere coincidence, or was there some unknown power behind it? On the basis of what happened, I am tempted to believe the latter. Fortunately, the situation resolved itself after a few months, but how do we practice love in such a situation? We risk having to live with an insane person as our closest relative or neighbour, or one who is only acting from his or her own needs, perhaps for the rest of our life. Do we manage this psychically? Jesus and all the other great spiritual personalities explain that love is the most important issue. Perhaps it is this that we are supposed to learn from such a situation.

Rudolf Steiner has said:[445]

> Our Earth is love's cosmos. Therefore, our development goes in the direction of bringing people together in love. When the Earth sometime in the future will dissolve – after the seventh trumpet has sounded, when the Earth loses its physical substance and is changed into an astral celestial body, then love will have taken hold of the entire human genus, the power of love, as it has evolved by all that is worldly. It is the Earth's task to let this force of love flow into and penetrate humankind, just as the power of wisdom has imbued our environment everywhere.

But it is not easy if we are to follow Bob Moore, who has said: '*Do not resist evil*'.[446] He further said:

> The only possibility you really have is to try to reach a level which is beyond aggression, which is beyond the level of emotions, and by the help of the force from this level to try to bring forward whatever you can to humanity's total development. And I am sure that in our century there is in fact a growing recognition of this. I think that this is a process that it is actually very nice to get involved in, because in our time all life's rhythm, the life energy has become very much quicker.

It is no small challenge to follow his recommendation. How can I manage to show love for a person who threatens me, when I am in a situation where I feel afraid, very afraid? But maybe that is just such a situation that is needed for me to be tried. One can do as Eileen Caddy did when she was faced with a person she did not like. Jesus also said: '*Father, forgive them, for they do not know what they are doing.*' (Luke 23.34)

If it is so that life has a dimension which goes beyond this life and the essence of what we are and do on this Earth will be with us further, Jesus' words must be very important, even for the situation I was in. The conclusion must be that I must not destroy my development by doing something that provokes or makes what has been done badly worse. But if life's solution is that everything is happening at random and that everything is ending with death, it may be tempting to let the consequence be that I must win over you, otherwise you will win over me. The answer as to why we live ought to be known before we choose the last solution.

There is only one solution, namely to believe that the power of thought is greatest. That is, if I manage to avoid being controlled by my emotions, and am able to feel love – even in such a situation – and can send loving thoughts to the wicked person, the problem will be resolved. The well-recited advice to people to send such thoughts in the form of a white light – as if you used a torch light, for if you are sending love in the form of good thoughts, one's emotions may get too heavily involved; white light is clean, free of emotions and thoughts. As an example of the latter I refer to Phyllis Krystal's story told in her book about the Indian (highly controversial) guru Sai Baba.[447] Phyllis Krystal was on board an aircraft when it was hijacked. Silently she prayed for help from Sai Baba and mentally she experienced that he said that she should send loving thoughts to the hijackers. With Sai Baba's mental help she felt love flowing from her to the hijackers. The miracle happened, if we are to believe the story. She noted that the hijackers became more and more insecure and disoriented. The aircraft landed in Amsterdam, the doors opened and everyone was allowed to go out. The hijackers also went out, and the only thing that happened was that they set fire to the aircraft before they surrendered.

> The more individual a human being becomes, the better he/she can be a carrier of love. ...
>
> Love is slowly changing to spiritual love, which is passing from soul to soul and which ultimately will include all of humanity with a common bond of common brotherly love. But Christ-Jesus, as he appeared in the story and seemed to behave for outer eyes, is the power, the living force, which for the first time in human history made the brotherly ideal behaviour into a social reality and people will learn to perceive the ties of this brotherly love as the fulfilled, spiritualized Christianity.
> *Rudolf Steiner* [448]

Marcello Haugen has in a short memo written as follows:[449]

> The Earth's mission is to develop the principle of love. Therefore, love – the love for your fellow beings – without any form of jealousy, discontent or egoism – contains the right temperature in our sphere and produces health in the body and truth in the soul at the right portion to our organism's development opportunities as they now are. ...
>
> Among the disciples John represents love – one of the twelve faculties in the human being. When this faculty in the human being is called and invoked in single truth, the consciousness of elevated love will awake and bring clarity to love's true character. On a daily basis we should therefore meditate on love's idea in a universal spirit, so that we always can be in connection with our own individual and cosmic rhythm. There should be moments of quiet spiritual consideration and dedication in this sublime idea, which then, through this sublime mood will be living in the solar plexus. When the human being can bring forth the positive force of love, this force will dissolve all bitterness, all hate. But how does the love for our fellow human

being arise? If we are able to love our fellow human being as ourselves, we must be saturated with divine love – to ourselves.

Love is the law's fulfilment.

There is nothing here in the world, neither wealth nor rank, position or might that so easily can make a person conceited and foolish, than when it thinks it owns more spiritual wisdom than others, and if anyone has become conceited – as a Pharisee – due to such thoughts, then he or she cannot make progress. He/she is then glued to where he/she is, for the foundation for spiritual perfection is to forget oneself. A human being considers itself as "something" or "nothing". In the consideration of one's own "nothingness" lies spirituality. Those who have just a small bit of understanding of nature's inner laws, knows that even the most secret thought, such as: how good I am, how generous or knowledgeable, what great influence and great appeal I have; even the most secret thought of this nature will dull the ability to acknowledge the so-called super-sensible world, an acknowledgement that belongs to our physical possibilities in our time. The road is so easy to find and yet so difficult to walk.

Sogyal Rinpoche has written the following as answer to the question why it is so difficult to give love:[450]

> There are many who are stuck because they have not received love. The problem is not that they cannot give love, but that they do not know how to give it. Their parents did not know it, and they are are themselves at risk to transfer this curse to their children. Therefore, it is so important to open the heart. When you read the Buddhist teachings and understand how much kindness, compassion and love that they contain, you will develop gratefulness, and that is the beginning of affection and love. A love where you truly understand your fellow being's needs, is what the dying person needs most of all. This is also what we all need when we are going through changes, crises and suffering and sorrow, for the dying can teach us to take care of those who are living as well.

Sture Johansson has referred the following commentary which he received from another dimension:[451]

> Yes, was his answer. Of course they have known it and the result of the lives they are now living is only that they have a new round to go in order to even out this of 'no use' existence. Please remember my friend, that we must understand the law of karma and we must learn the law of love.
>
> Take the road that suits you and let others take their road. People are not alike, but give them the ability to wonder as a start. Let them usethis as a bridge. Think of love, give them love – this is the basic principle in Cosmos.
>
> – Yes, I thought, love is the word, love is the key, but a word is not

> important – it is what it means that is everything. I saw this portal, while the word and the feeling seeped into me as into a spacious room. LOVE, LOVE, LOVE! Love is to understand and understanding is love. Yes, everything is love – depending on how the human beings themselves understand it.

We need to understand the consequences of our thoughts and actions. They affect others, but they also hit back at us. We must acknowledge the law of karma. Maybe we then better understand the following biblical sayings:

> But I tell you, love your enemies and pray for those who persecute you, that you may be children of your Father in heaven.
> (Matt 5.44-45)
>
> And the second is like it: 'Love your neighbour as yourself.'
> (Matt 22.39. See also Romans 13.9)

My problem in the threatening situation in which I found myself was to see the conditions within me that needed clarification. It was possible that that was the core of aggression and rage that I sometimes expressed in my thoughts. Or was it perhaps rather my egotism, which I here met but in an enhanced version in another? But how should I improve my weaknesses? With that I needed help. My solution was firstly to ask for help – from the spiritual powers that surrounded me. And then I tried to understand the person whom I felt was threatening me, and to send him love. The end of the story was that the person after a few months disappeared from my life – and I had learnt an important lesson. Perhaps we are now in a better position to understand St Paul when he wrote the following in 1 Corinthians chapter 13:

> If I speak in the tongues of men or of angels, but do not have love, I am only a resounding gong or a clanging cymbal. If I have the gift of prophecy and can fathom all mysteries and all knowledge, and if I have a faith that can move mountains, but do not have love, I am nothing. If I give all I possess to the poor and give over my body to hardship that I may boast, but do not have love, I gain nothing. Love is patient, love is kind. It does not envy, it does not boast, it is not proud. It does not dishonour others, it is not self-seeking, it is not easily angered, it keeps no record of wrongs. Love does not delight in evil but rejoices with the truth. It always protects, always trusts, always hopes, always perseveres. Love never fails. But where there are prophecies, they will cease; where there are tongues, they will be stilled; where there is knowledge, it will pass away. For we know in part and we prophesy in part, but when completeness comes, what is in part disappears. When I was a child, I talked like a child; I thought like a child, I reasoned like a child. When I became a man, I put the ways of childhood behind me. For now we see only a reflection as in a mirror; then we shall see face to face. Now I know in part; then I shall know fully, even as I am fully known. And now these three remain: faith, hope and love. But the greatest of these is love.

This is the unselfish love which endures everything, and it is our attitude and our thoughts that must contain it. We can begin to practice it by letting our spouse, closest friend or children go their own ways and have freedom of choice – also to take stupid decisions. They should not be bound by their closest relatives or friends – they have their own road for development. If we are able to cope with losing a spouse, child, house or other assets, whether it is ever so painful, we have perhaps started on the path where we shall go on to acknowledge what real love is. For without that recognition we have not come particularly far in our spiritual development.

> If it is true, as I have tried to show, that love is the only true and fully valid answer to humanity's life problem, any society that excludes or restricts the development of love, will in the long run perish, because it goes against human nature's deepest needs. *Erich Fromm*[452]

Martinus described cosmic love in this way:[453]

> Only the beings, who love their fellow beings as themselves, which means: to love everyone and everything, have an unshakeable peace inside, a peace, through which the endless source 'the Holy Spirit' or 'the cosmic consciousness' unimpeded will reveal itself and substantiate the total love with the Divine's own knowledge and thereby ultimately let the being think the Almighty's eternal thoughts; and so that the being is initiated in a total understanding of the object, that which it, in the form of everything and everyone for a long time since has embraced and included in the love. Only in this being, in whose bosom love stimulates the heart, pulses for the benefit of the whole world, or for the benefit of all other living beings, can the intellect's or the understanding's clear light shine, so that everything dark has to leave.

13. Evil, Angst and Conscience

> Everything is very well. *Martinus*

> Without opposition, no progress. Sympathy and antipathy, thought and action, love and hate are necessary for the human being's existence.
> *William Blake*[454]

> In every deed, also the evil ones, in the evil of punishment just as well as in the evil of fault, God's glory can be seen and felt in the same degree.
> *Master Eckhart*[455]

> And so what of virtue and evil? ... Virtue is founded in us by the soul; evil is caused by the soul's intercourse with the outside world.
> *Plotinus*[456]

> Amor Fati – Love your destiny.

> One day the angels came to present themselves before the LORD, and Satan also came with them. The Book of Job 1.6

Everything painful that Job suffered, according to the account in the Bible, was caused by Satan, but with the Lord's permission. The reason for this permission was that Satan challenged the Lord by maintaining that Job would tell the Lord 'goodbye' if he was subjected to severe hardship, directed, initially, towards everything he owned and had cherished, and then (when this was not sufficient) also to Job's own body. The question was whether Job would fear God no matter what happened to him, and not make any claims against the Lord.

The story of Cain and Abel can be found in Genesis chapter 4. Despite the fact that Cain killed Abel, the Lord decided that anyone who killed Cain, because he had killed his brother, was to be punished and suffer revenge seven times. (And Cain was considered to be the forefather of all who keep livestock and everyone who plays the harp and the flute.) Judas Iscariot fetched the guards who arrested Jesus according to the Bible's story, but Jesus knew that one of the disciples would to do this. He said to Judas during the last supper: *"What you are about to do, do quickly."* (John 13.27.) This might indicate that they had agreed on this in advance. He did not prevent Judas, but allowed Judas to play the role that has given him the designation 'traitor' ever since. Was Judas then really lost forever? Some researchers believe that Judas was Jesus' closest confidant. He was entrusted with the group's purse (John 12.6 and 13.29), and he must have been sitting next to Jesus during the last supper because he dipped his bread in the same bowl as Jesus (Matt 26.23).

The New Testament tells us that Jesus was tempted by the devil. According to the Gospels (Matt 4.1, Mark 1.12, Luke 4.1 – the Gospel of John does not mention this event) Jesus was led by the Spirit out into the desert to be tempted there by the devil. (The term Satan is used in other versions.) Also Buddha is said to have met the devil (Mara) at the time of his religious awakening, when the devil took on all kinds of figures and shapes in order to scare or entice Buddha to abstain from his intent.

In nature we see that everyone is struggling for their existence, which necessarily becomes a battle against others, whether those are prey of a different species or of the same kind. The strongest ones survive. Pierre Teilhard de Chardin has pointed out that the world has become what it is by coincidence and fumbling. How many unsuccessful attempts are there for just one successful one – how many accidents are there for one of good luck – and how many sinners for a saint, he asked.[457] He thought that evil is located not only in disorder and failure, in dissolution, in loneliness and in anxiety, but also in progress in terms of work and effort. Evolution is a dual process – it is rolling outwards at the same time that it centres on itself. The Universe works very hard, it is sinning and suffering, but there is an evolution towards greater consciousness. The adventurous path of humanity reminded him of the way of the Cross – which might have a meaning we do not see. There can be no denying that existence contains destructive as well as constructive forces; without growth, no development; without destruction, no renewal; without changes, there will be stagnation.

The human beings throughout time have discussed evil and why there is so much pain and difficulty in the world. In the chapter about spirit beings, we considered the phenomenon of evil spirits. According to Rudolf Steiner they exist in order to teach people independence. Others believe they are necessary as the driving force for human development – without resistance, no development. In astrological teachings the planet Saturn is a force that creates problems, but it is also considered as the great teacher. Aivanhov explained that there is a plethora of evil forces, just as many as there are good powers. Dion Fortune said that the good is the balance between opposing forces in the world.[458] Evil is a power that is not in balance. She was of the opinion that the Tree of Life and the Kabbalah explain the forces that exist in the Cosmos and how they interact with each other.

That which is evil is one thing but that which hurts is something else. All of nature alternates between growth and decay. Both growth and decay must necessarily happen with pain. The question is whether the destructive forces or illnesses and accidents, which apparently strike at random, are due to evil forces, in the form of satanic spirits. In all religions we encounter, however, the notion of divine powers that influence the human beings or cross their will, or are considered to help the one or the other party in a conflict. Thus, according to the Greek poet Homer, the gods participated on both sides in the Trojan War. That leads us to the question whether whatever is painful happens with the Lord's knowing consent, ref. Job's and Jesus' experiences – so that everything, including accidents and crimes, can be said to have a meaning. If this is the case, there must be a meaning that is not apparent to the individual human being; neither to anyone creating damage nor to those affected by a crime or accident. At a higher level, which the human mind is not able to understand, there might be a purpose. But then a different question arises, namely whether the purpose is only of group importance, that is, as it applies to mankind in general or to one's community, or whether it also includes the affected individual. The Norwegian author and poet Henrik Ibsen seems to have touched on this in his dramas. Especially it has expression in the play *The Emperor and the Galilean*. The main character in the play, Julian seems to be appointed by providence both to become emperor and to serve the Spirit. He has all the prerequisites to be a Galilean, that is, one who follows Christ; but in order to serve the Spirit he must submit to 'the Wrath of Necessity', in the same way as Cain and Judas. He becomes emperor, but then rejects the Galilean and provides thereby the pretext for hatred and aggression especially against the Christians. He is killed after only a few years as emperor. Ibsen shows, however, that Julian by going against the development of Christianity in fact drives humanity's development towards the light – towards the third realm, which Ibsen describes as the land of light and happiness, which is the spiritual light – God's love, *Deus Caritatis* as it is referred to in the play *Brand*. As for Julian, this is what is said in the play:

> '... but great and glorious it dawns on me that this is the Lord's wonderfully broken tool. ... The Emperor Julian was an instrument for punishment – not to death but to redress. ... You human soul who has gone astray, if you had to go astray, this will surely be reckoned to your good on the great day when the mighty is coming in clouds of judgment of the living dead, and over the dead that are alive!'

Ambres said this:[459]

> There are two power systems, one that is constructive and one that is destructive, where the destructive force, if the human being only uses this one, becomes worse. At first it may appear to be constructive but quite soon it turns out that it is decreasing and the more advanced the technology gets, the stronger it accelerates, so that eventually the constructive force cannot offset the destructive one. The human being must wake up! The force of love works long-term, but theopposite, the negative force works short-term and is hard. In its aggression it may live for a long time and build even greater and greater oppositions, so that

it even may kill the power of love.

> Sometimes people say 'God is evil. God creates war. How could God allow weapons of destruction? How could God allow hunger?' – cannot people see that it was themselves who created the wars in their fear of living, in their negative force! Can they not see that they themselves created the famine, that they created the different cultures, the traditions! They created the different religions that contradict each other.

The Swedish author Marianne Fredriksson makes one of the characters in one of her books say the following:[460]

> As regards the Devil, she understood that she had met him in her own heart, that he was with her as he was with all people, only exceptionally denied and hidden. ... But now she knew that what Petter had said was that evil can be found inside the human being, inside every human being, and that it is only with this understanding that evil can be understood and fought.

Human beings in their first years of living must necessarily fight for life in order to become a personality, in order to assert themselves in society and to evolve. But the more insecure a person feels, the stronger it will often try to assert itself. As Marianne Fredriksson makes another character say:

> I also believe that a personality mainly is a defence. That is why mine is so strong and distinct.

Here it is said that evil is manmade and not caused by external forces. Suffering is partly man made, partly a natural necessity. If there is a spiritual continuation, everything we encounter ought to have a meaning, suffering as well as the evils we experience. This means that we must face the evil in our own mind, before we can go out and save the world. As long as evil is inside us, we will attract external events that reflect this evil.

From where does this evil come? It seems to me that it is desire in human beings which is the quality that develops malice and inflicts pain on other people. But desire is also a necessity for a person to be able to evolve. A child must learn to assert itself, to strengthen its character, to learn to resist others who seek to influence him or her. That is, it must seek independence, it must covet knowledge and education in order to get something to live by, covet a profession. It has to try to find the ways and means in order to get food, clothing and housing, and last but not least, it must look for a sex partner in order to be able to have a family and thus contribute to the preservation of the species. But if we cannot at the same time learn to set limits on our own desires, we will soon exceed the boundaries of what would be a fruitful interaction with other people. And even if we take the latter into consideration, the desire could still exceed what we really need – and then instead of contributing we are depleting the Earth. Without desire there is no progress, but too much lust is devastating. The human beings must have compassion, understanding and moderation in their claims, if not overreaching desire will take control, and we risk developing evil to a greater or lesser degree.

In Theosophical teaching it is said that evil does not come from the human being's higher self, but from a shortcoming in the higher self. There can be no evil in the causal body neither in the ego (the Self). Arthur E. Powell has written:[461]

> But where there is a blank spot in the causal body, there is always the possibility that the lower bodies can cause an evil action of one sort or another. In this way the astral elemental can for example possess a human being and make him or her participate in a crime. In such a case the ego is not sufficiently awake to intervene and prevent it, or is otherwise unable to understand that the astral body's passion or greed can force the lower self to commit a crime. Evil does not come from the higher self; it comes from a lack in the higher self; for if the ego was more advanced, it would stop the human being as soon as the evil thought arose, and the crime would not take place.

Plotinus said that all kinds of differences give people reason to complain, but this is because they do not understand that owning a lot of things, or to be more powerful than any other, is of no importance.[462] The wise one thinks of the spiritual realm, while everyone else is concerned with this world. Among the latter, there is a group that has certain memories about virtue and therefore has some contact with the good, while the great masses do not have that. In the case of failure and errors, as well as murderers or those who are slaves of passions, he pointed out that most people are like undeveloped children. Life is a training camp where there are winners and losers. Does it matter if you are unfairly treated in one life if you are immortal, Plotinus asked. And he further indicated that if you are killed, you get your wish fulfilled – if the earthly life becomes bothersome, you are not bound to it. A human being's only task is, according to Plotinus, to seek to make yourself perfect, and only the individual itself can do this. There are people who have reached the height of goodness and we have to accept the goodness of the heavenly spirits.

G.W. Leibniz' thoughts about evil are restated by Carl Grimberg (see endnote 287) in this passage:

> But why has God allowed so much pain and abnormality here in this world? In answer to this, Leibniz responds that evil, relatively, is something, somewhat less good. Evil is the negative prerogative for the good, especially because it evokes reaction and thereby predominantly has good consequences. 'Need is the mother of invention', and evil is an inspiration for good. Without inspiration, people are easily dulled. 'Without The Tarquinier's crimes and Lucretia's suicide the Roman

> republic, which had nurtured so many heroes, would not have been created.' Evil is, as Goethe's Mephisto, part of the force whose task it is always to want evil and always works for the good.
>
> For those who can get an overview of the whole, the evil has the same task as the shadows in a painting. How quite different is the impression, is it not, if one is looking only at a little part of a master's painting compared with considering the entire work of art, as Leibniz said it. In the first case you are seeing only a few colours with no meaning, in the latter case it is an admirable expression of a great artist's genius. In the great world-harmony the evil fades and dissolves itself as do the disharmonies in a symphony. So for Leibniz the entire existence is like a beautiful symphony, a work of art that has come from the hand of God. And even if the evil and destructive powers may sometimes seem to dominate, we must not let that lead us astray in our assessment of this 'the best of all worlds', for from this chaos something new and better will slowly arise.

Martinus explained that human beings must acquire wisdom in order to achieve cosmic consciousness. And in order to achieve wisdom, people must face the resistance that only the physical world can provide. It is only in the physical world that we can learn the difference between good and evil. It is only there that thinking wrongly or acting wrongly causes pain and discomfort; or rather to think and act in a way that is contrary to life's and nature's laws.[463] Aleister Crowley (1875-1947) was world famous for practising black magic. He did not have a happy life, rather the opposite. He was a heavy drug addict at the end of his life. He is thus an example of how not to use one's abilities.

But why do we risk being exposed to evil if we ourselves are working for the good? Perhaps we all have to be exposed to evil so that we can learn what that is – and in the end maybe we all are so well acquainted with the consequences of evil that everyone only wants to do what is good. Nothing human shall be foreign to me, as it is said.

About angst

All human beings possess an existential anxiety – angst. For many species this is like the anxiety of death, for others it is an anxiety of life. The existential angst is something other than a phobia (fear), such as fear of the open space, fear of other people, dogs, spiders and similar. The latter, however, can be an emergence of the deeper-lying existential angst. The Danish philosopher Søren Kierkegaard (1813-1855) has described the existential angst and called it 'the angst for nothing'. This angst can be defined as 'the pure angst, the metaphysical angst; the basic element in the human soul'.[464] Such angst causes narrowness or constriction. We dare not open ourselves up to life. We become like the people Plato described who are only seeing the shadows from life on the cave wall and do not dare to turn around, although they then will see the light.

Ken Wilber wrote that seclusion creates anxiety but also that where there are others, there is fear. As long as the child feels at-one with the mother, it feels safe, but when it begins to feel itself a separate individual, it becomes afraid – afraid of the separation.[465] This fear follows us throughout life, unless we come so far in our acknowledgement that we realize that there is no separation – we are a part of the All. The fear expresses itself in the fear of death, the fear of letting go of the 'I', the ego. In order to develop spiritually, we must meet this angst – the dark night of the soul, as St John of the Cross called it. *'Through darkness to light'*, as Ibsen expressed it in the play *The Emperor and the Galilean*. Some people face life's difficulties alone in their own mind. Others are faced with suffering caused them by others, by nature's fierce forces or as a result of congenital flaws – or all of it at the same time. We cannot understand why existence is so unjust, and why someone is hit in one way while others get it in a different way. One kind of explanation have I sought to give in the chapter about diseases, but without the assumption that life has a deeper meaning, and that the sufferings we have on this Earth will give our spiritual qualities an opportunity for development, which we unconsciously might choose ourselves, we may easily give up and despair. In this context, it may be opportune to remember the symbol that Elisabeth Kübler-Ross saw everywhere on the walls of the Nazi death factory Maidanek in Poland, namely the butterflies.[466] It gave the doomed the hope that their stay here on Earth was like the cocoon stage, and that they soon would come out like the butterflies.

About conscience

Why do some people have a strong conscience and the basic view that we should live so that we are not doing any harm or damage to others, but, on the contrary, strive to help others as much and as best we can? Other people, however, seem to be devoid of such an attitude, and some appear to be pure sadists without a bit of empathy or compassion. In many cases conscience seems to be hidden behind a religion or philosophy that excuses any type of action, no matter how crazy or evil it might be. Is it the will of gods or satanic forces behind the one or the other attitude? Is the human being excused even if it does something wrong – like Cain, Judas and Emperor Julian?

This latter question cannot be answered, but what I am citing here may perhaps give a sufficient answer for some:

> But I tell you, love your enemies and pray for those who persecute you, ... (Matt 5.44)
>
> Jesus said, 'Father, forgive them, for they do not know what they are doing.' (Luke 23.34)

The most difficult thing might be to forgive ourselves if we had the ability to see all the consequences of our thoughts and actions. We should not disregard that that is possible, from the numerous stories that are told, that we will see a revue of our life just before we lose consciousness in a deep crisis. Love and forgiveness are two sides of the same coin. Self-love requires that we see all sides of ourselves and forgive ourselves. Master Eckhart once said:[467]

> You could quickly, just now, and with all force and real disgust turn away from all sins, and just as strongly turn towards God, although you may have committed all the sins that ever have been committed since the time of Adam and that will be committed in the future; those He entirely would forgive along with the penalty, so that you, if you died at this moment, would be placed in front of God.

Ambres and Martinus have both expressed that people do not need to seek forgiveness for their negative or evil actions, because they are acting according to the best of their capability in the situation they are in – even in such a simple action as to sneak a free ride on a bus or tramway. People will act negatively until they have experienced so much negativity that they begin to seek what is good, and have learnt to understand the consequences of their thoughts and actions.

It is important to remember that to help ourselves or others requires that we understand ourselves and others. However, it is necessary to set limits, both for our own and for other people's activities if this activity goes beyond the boundaries of what is required for a society or family to function properly. We have to be told what is allowed and what is not allowed. And we must often be reminded about what rights we can have or cannot have, if we do not have the ability or willingness to see this for ourselves. In extreme cases, we must, if necessary, be restrained from what we want to do or are on the threshold of doing. On the other hand, there must be some individual freedom in order to evolve. The individual must not be completely restricted from action. The frontiers here may be difficult to draw. Dion Fortune noted that too much mercy is a fool's work, and that too much patience is a coward's mark.[468] This is because it often is a necessity for the promotion of health and happiness to take on a burden and she further said that the diet for a sick person who wants to recover health might evoke disease in someone who is healthy. She believed that Christianity is too one-sided as it ignores the rhythm of life. Its dualisms are more antagonistic instead of providing equilibrium. We must acknowledge life's strict side in a world in development. We need both Vishnu and Shiva.

14. Destiny and Free Will

Karma

> Whoever sheds human blood, by humans shall their blood be shed; for in the image of God has God made mankind.   (Genesis 9.6)

'A nemesis is passing through life' is a phrase many think they have seen confirmed. If, for example, I cheat you, let us say for 100 pounds, I might later experience that someone either cheats me, takes something from me or does some damage, costing ten times the amount. Or I experience a very difficult situation and can later experience a similar difficult situation, but then with myself in the opposite role. There are many who believe that such a nemesis passes through several lives, but it is not for the sins committed by a previous generation that a child will suffer. It is maintained that it is your own sins you will be confronted with. The evil you meet is of your own origin, whether something you have done in this life or in an earlier one. This is karma.[469]

Karma is understood as an action and the effects of that action. Any action would, apart from the objective consequences, also have subjective consequences for the person involved. You will be marked by the actions you perform. Good actions will leave good and positive feelings in the mind. Negative or evil actions will leave unpleasant mental states. These may not be noted or acknowledged at the time of action, but sooner or later the actions will be remembered and cause anguish and anger. Those who believe in reincarnation think that they will meet the consequences in a later existence. But in order to understand fully what is said about karma, we have to understand what is thought about soul and spirit. Within Hinduism and Buddhism the doctrine of karma is central. This doctrine is close to the teaching regarding cause and effect, or the causality principle. However it is not only within the Eastern way of thinking that the principle of karma is accepted.

Martinus has explained that every thought and action sooner or later will come back to the sender. That is, evil actions will be repaid – an eye for an eye, a tooth for a tooth. The repayment will not necessarily come from the one who suffered your negative action, but often quite unexpectedly from another place and perhaps with double strength. The problem is that you do not see and do not realize the context unless you are completely conscious of your actions and what happens later. Without response to an action, people would not learn the effect of their thoughts and actions, and would thus fail to obtain experience and wisdom. But at the same time Martinus pointed out that no sinners are subjected to the avenging wrath of a god. All individuals act according to their abilities and sense, such as those are at the time of action; and if people have not developed sufficient love and good sense, that they understand the consequences of their actions, they cannot be said to have sinned. Human destiny is not a question of sin and forgiveness, but about cause and effect. Reincarnation and karma are irrefutable facts according to his statement. One cannot, as has been said, atone for bad deeds by means of sacraments and grace. As you sow, you reap.

Aivanhov also explained that you will reap what you sow – that is the law of cause and effect.[470] This law applies both on the physical, the mental and the spiritual plane but normally you will meet the consequences only at the beginning of the next existence. The way you live in this earthly existence provides the framework for how the next earthly existence will be.

Edgar Cayce has also said that the law of karma is the law of cause and effect. But it must be put in context with the correct understanding of destiny. Karma can be compared to the body's reaction to food. The food will affect every cell in the body, and in the same way, every thought and action will affect the mind.[471] You will not be subject to greater trials than you can take, and there is always an opening for salvation. Karma must be understood so that it will take effect when we fail to live up to what we know we should do. But each new life is an opportunity to the development of the soul and is based on what the soul brings along from past lives, of good and bad. And there is always the possibility of grace.

Jes Bertelsen mentioned that it seems to be a law within the energy-economy of the totality.[472] This is the law of karma. Karma is the unconscious consequences of the actions of the 'I'. He explained that energy is always returning, and that whenever an 'I' is acting it will cause changes in the balance that is in the totality and thereby also in the structure and power lines of the unconscious.

Plotinus also said that there is a system of law and punishment.[473] Virtue has its profit and evil its appropriate shame. The human being's only task is to strive to be better – seeking the heavenly goodness. The more perfect a person becomes, the more benevolence towards fellow human beings it will have and the more humble it will be. Plotinus maintained that the wise one does not consider as unjust that some are poor and others are rich, for those who have wealth do not necessarily have better lives than the poor. However, we must not consider karma as something that forces us to do what is good.

Christmas Humphreys wrote that if we do not realize that the most important principle of existence is the law of love so that we are only doing good in order to avoid reprisals or because we feel compelled to it, then we have not followed the law of love. Then, we have not improved our karma. When the living being understands the law of love and has come far enough in wisdom and love, it will of necessity act with love. Then it cannot avoid doing what is good, and it will not incur negative karma.

Some mystics have explained, however, that a living being can undertake a heavy karma created by others and thereby contribute to the development of one or more people. This is what many believe that Jesus did – he transferred the disciples' karmic burden to himself so they could receive the Holy Spirit. But others argue that one cannot relieve another's karma, one can only provide support.

In order to understand what Seth taught about karma, we must know what he said about reincarnation and about contemporary life.[474] He maintained, inter alia, that painful and difficult experiences are not situations that happen to us accidentally, but because we unconsciously choose them. He said that it is incorrect that actions from a previous life take effect in a later life. The law of karma he did not accept as he pointed out that all lives are lived at the same time. The consequences of an act cannot be considered as punishment, but as experience – it enables development. To use the terms cause and effect of these exchanges are incorrect because that assumes the time/space dimension and a historical order of the experiences. Progress has nothing to do with time, he said.

What Seth explains here, is what I feel is closest to reality. It is only by considering the living being as more than the personality, that I get a reasonable understanding of the existence. That is, there must be an entity that creates its own reality through the different personalities by which it enters into life, and thereby also carries the consequences of those physical lives. Otherwise I cannot see any sense in that an individual (i.e. the individual personality) is born and dies in for example a concentration camp, or has to live its life here on Earth as an invalid, if the physical existence is to be experienced only once. When (or if) each of the different personalities develops its consciousness so that it can get in touch with the essence in itself (the actual living entity), it will understand the context or see that the choices were made on a deeper level.

Predestination and predictability

> (Jesus said to Peter.) "Very truly I tell you, when you were younger you dressed yourself and went where you wanted; but when you are old you will stretch out your hands, and someone else will dress you and lead you where you do not want to go." (John 21.18)

I refer to what is written above about divination in the chapter concerning strange events. Is it really possible to predict the future? Ken Wilber has rejected the possibility of precognition. He maintained that if precognition is a reality and an absolute possibility, all events have to be predestined for all time. Then such a thing as free will or real creativity (what he called *true free emergence*) cannot exist, nor could there be something like Heisenberg's uncertainty principle. Then the Universe through all times and at all levels had to be a deterministic machine, which he cannot accept.[475]

In contrast, Aivanhov argued that all is predestined.[476] He said that everything is controlled from above as it is the heavenly hierarchies that determine, right down to what the individual is eating and drinking, and nothing can be created without it being in harmony with the All. There is a kind of cosmic computer where everything is planned and calculated, and there are spiritual beings that makes sure that everything goes as it is destined. Everything happens so that each individual shall have experiences from the Earth. Nothing can be changed in the present life, but thoughts, beliefs and prayers can influence conditions in the next, he said.

There are countless stories of people who have had dreams that came true. Inter alia, it has been told many dreams concerning Titanic's fate, coming before the catastrophe. But whether this is sufficient evidence that the future always is predestined, is another question. We have no way to find out how many people actually dreamed about Titanic before it began its voyage – it may have been a considerable amount because the ship received enormous media coverage. That a handful of people then dreamt about an accident with the ship, is not sufficient evidence that these are actually true dreams. However, a novel about a comparable disaster, which was published fourteen years ahead of the Titanic disaster, was marvellously close to the real event.[477] But this can have been only a strange coincidence. Some people may have disaster warning dreams because they expect accidents and disasters, and so they think that they actually have true dreams when an accident occurs. The fact that people cancel an air flight, because they have negative feelings about it, is not sufficient evidence of precognition if the trip ends in disaster. It might as well be a random coincidence.

The Norwegian psychics, Karl Tandstad and his daughter Olga Tandstad Skaue, could predict the future of people – it is referred and admitted many such stories in the book about them. Marcello Haugen gave the exact time of his death two days before it occurred.[478] How did he know? Many people have had visions and dreams of circumstances that occur later. Many have also been predicted events which have occurred later, although just as many people have experienced that the predictions did not come true. There is also something called self-fulfilling prophecy – that is a prophecy that comes true because the person receiving such a prediction adapts his or her behaviour accordingly.

Padre Pio is said to have been of the opinion that not everything is predestined.[479] He has said that some events cannot be changed because they are subject to God's eternal plan, while other conditions may be subject to human prayers and virtues, or the lack of such. It is our duty to do whatever we can to help ourselves and for example seek professional medical help when we are sick, if this can help. Miracles can only happen where human intervention may not give good results, he said. He could not always help a person.

That some people have certain capabilities that allow them to see into the future, skills that others do not have, is obvious. Bob Moore has said that the clairvoyants who can tell the future are using a mental ability that is associated with the astral level.[480] This phenomenon is baffling the scientific knowledge of the world today, although some theories as explanation of the phenomenon have been presented. Michael Talbot wrote that a famous psychic American – Ingo Swann[i] (b.1933) – considered the future as crystallized opportunities. He further referred to statements by Dr David Loye, clinical psychologist and co-director of the Institute of Future Forecasting in California, who has spent many years examining predictions and the mental abilities that are associated with these. Loye has said that the theories of David Bohm and Karl H. Pribram about the holographic mind, provide the best explanation for the phenomenon. Many psychic people experience future images in the same way as the past is experienced. Loye suggested that reality is a giant hologram where both past, present and future are given – up to a certain point. It needs not be only one hologram – there may be multiple holograms, that go into each other or around each other, possibly as parallel universes. From this follows that we should take the phenomenon of future prediction seriously even if the individual prediction does not always occur.

About free will

> For I do not do the good I want to do, but the evil I do not want to do – this I keep on doing.   (Romans 7.19)

In the play *The Emperor and the Galilean* the author Henrik Ibsen uses the term the wrath of necessity and he writes there that some people, such as Cain, Judas and the Emperor Julian, *must* follow a path that the world order has designated for them, no matter how wrong the result. But what about us? Do we have to live the life we are given? We may for example have a congenital or later acquire a disorder that ultimately makes life so awful that we do not see any other possibility than to end it. This apparently is to select the lesser of two evils. But do we have a real choice in these cases? Is not the situation rather that we do not have any choice? Aivanhov has said that there is nothing that can be called free will in the single human life since

---

i. Ingo Swann was used as a psychic in the Stargate Project, which was financed by the U.S. Federal Government and was active trough 25 years from the 1970s. Especially "remote viewing" was in focus for the project – where the psychic person was trying to "see" potential sites of military interest for example in Russia.

everything is predestined. But he also said that everything good and positive we can get out of the present life will affect our life in the next physical life. So the free will consists in the ability to improve oneself mentally and spiritually, so that the next incarnation will be better than the current one.

According to the Bible Adam and Eve ate the apple taken from the tree of knowledge and thereby acquired the ability to distinguish between good and evil. It was not knowledge in itself that was essential, but that they obtained the understanding of the good and the evil. If this means that they thereby got the ability to choose between doing good and doing evil, we have to accept that they had free will. Animals normally do not understand the consequences of their actions, although I have seen dogs behave clearly guilty when they know that they have done something wrong, even before it is discovered. People, even the very young ones, are as a rule aware whether they are doing anything good or evil (but that is not the same as doing right or wrong). Rudolf Steiner has maintained that it is only the human beings and some of the angels who have the freedom to choose between good *and* evil.[481] He further said that true love has freedom as a prerequisite.

When discussing the concept of free will, it is important to distinguish between to do evil or to do good, and to do what is right or wrong. In both cases, there may be questions about the lesser of two evils (one must occasionally resort to a white lie). But we must know what is evil or good, or what is true or false. If we do not know the difference, we cannot choose what is correct or act properly. But are we acting out of necessity or of free will? To answer that question we have to decide who or what is making us act as we do. Here I find it necessary to distinguish between that which Jes Bertelsen calls the 'I' and the Self. The 'I' thinks that it is acting because the 'I' is not aware of any other. But who or what made the decisions in for example the following happenings:

> I am going to a specific place and think I know the way. Then I make a detour because I take the wrong road in an intersection. I am reaching my destination but this road is somewhat longer. And then it turned out that the short way was blocked so I would have had to turn around and take the road I took. Who was actually taking the decision at the crossroad?
>
> I was driving a car and suddenly I was in a situation where the risk of a collision was really great. But then I unconsciously made the exact manoeuvres so I avoided the collision, although my driving skills cannot explain the reaction. Who made me do that?
>
> I am suddenly being treated so badly at my work place that I feel compelled to seek another job that was just then coming up. I got the job and thereby changed my environment and got new challenges – which in the long run turned out favourably. Actually I had begun to feel a need for change, but had not yet dared to do it. Who was behind this behaviour from this new boss?

> Without any special reason one night I became occupied with a specific problem. After some hesitation, I took a book from my bookshelf to find the answer to the question. Out of the book fell an important voucher that belonged to my sister (who had borrowed the book many months earlier). The voucher was needed for her final accounting, which had to take place the next day because of the tax-return deadline. Who made me think of the problem in the first place?

By the so-called synchronous experiences or what we call coincidences (concurrent events), it is natural to wonder what it is that makes me acting at the right moment and in a way that allows this to occur? For example:

> I am going out of my door to fetch something from the outside at the same moment a friend comes to see me.
>
> I was reading something of interest in a book. Accidentally I was reading another book a little later the same day and found something more about the same subject, although this was not the main subject in any of the books.
>
> I started to practise a new yoga exercise, and then it was precisely that exercise that was taught in the next gymnastic lesson, which was not a yoga lesson.
>
> I am offered a new challenging job just at the time when my private situation was such that I could accept the offer.
>
> I am being offered to purchase an apartment just when I was visiting a person who immediately offers me a loan, which I otherwise would not have known how to obtain.

Is it really the 'I' that decides what I should do or not do, or is there someone behind the 'I' – for example the Self or a spirit helper, who makes me act as I do? Is the 'I' only a zombie? What can be said to be certain is that there are several, shall we say personalities that govern me. For example, if I respond irrationally it is not the 'I' that reacts, but often someone behind the 'I' – someone the 'I' cannot control. A strong crying reaction or a fierce anger can have its cause in forgotten experiences from years before, perhaps from early childhood. Sometimes I have had such crying bouts without any knowledge as to why I was crying. In such cases it is the subconscious that takes over the 'I' consciousness. At other times, I believe there must be my Self that is governing me. Does the 'I' then have a free will? Or rather, maybe I should be regarded as a character in a play, for which all the sayings, costumes and décor are given in advance. In that case, it must be the Self that is the actor – that is an actor who appears once in one play and at another time in another. It is important then to know that it is not a question of being fully identified with the role, but to understand that it is a play from which to gain experience, and that it is the attitude of the mind that is important. But again: does this mean that everything we do is predestined, and that we are only living according to a given script?

Erik Dammann posed this question to the German professor of psychology Hans Jürgen Eysenck (1916-1997) who lived most of his life in England.[482] Eysenck's answer to Dammann's questions was that he did not believe in free will, and in addition he said that he really did not understand what it meant. He believed the term is anachronistic and meaningless, but that people are programmed so that they have an illusion of having free will. Whatever a person does is determined by his or her genetic equipment and former environment. No action occurs without cause, and the cause is determined by the person's genes, culture, upbringing, needs, desires, etc. If this was not the case, the action would be a mere coincidence, and then it would not be as a result of free will or free choice. Also David Bohm was asked by Erik Dammann about free will. And he answered that without a certain restricted order freedom was meaningless. If we are not bound by background and upbringing etc., which in a way make us prisoners, we do not have freedom to choose something else. And if we are not aware of this, freedom is an illusion. Professor of physics Geoffrey Chew (b.1924) at Berkeley University in California answered Dammann by saying the idea of determinism or predestination requires a conception of time, and he then asked what time really means. The Norwegian brain researcher, Professor Per Andersen believed, as previously mentioned, that there are no other ways to understand consciousness than as a result of electrical impulses in the brain. But if everything is obtained by random impulses, what becomes then of the free will?

It is virtually impossible to give a clear answer to the question of free will in my judgment, for it requires first and foremost an answer to the question of *who* is having this free will. The Self (the super consciousness) may have a free will, since it is in control of what it wants the 'I' to experience. But not always does it find reason to intervene. That seems to depend on what the Self wants to experience. The 'I', however, is too dominated by its subconscious and by its background, with everything that that means, to be able to have much free will. It is only in exceptional cases that the 'I' is conscious of the Self. To me, the 'I' seems more like a puppet on a string for the Self.

Martinus believed that a being has free will. He said that the being must evolve from the deepest darkness to the lightest and most delightful level of existence. It has to go through all good and evil – nothing human must be unknown. It must learn the difference between good and evil, and it must learn to understand that only by being in compliance with the fundamental tune of the Universe, which is love, will it be able to approach the light. Therefore, Martinus said that everything in our destiny that deviates from this basic tune is due only to our own being, and is the real cause behind any event. But the being is not able to understand more than it has experienced, therefore it must go through a series of experiences so that the soul will be moulded and shaped, and that which Martinus called experience and talent cores will come forth. This will imply that we in a certain sense can be said to have free will. But if this free will applies to that which Martinus called the living being, which probably may be said to be the Self, the 'I' will not necessarily have a free will. I am not sure if he distinguished between the 'I' and the Self.

We are all facing hardships on our way through life; without setbacks, no growth, but we live our lives differently, and the problems we face may seem to be nothing for some people, but insurmountable obstacles for others. Why does Destiny discriminate in this way? Is everything due to karma from this and previous lives? Is this only of importance for this our life now? Hardship is a necessity for existence. Without feeling the pain we would not take our hand away from the oven, and the hand would become useless. The body we grow into is a prerequisite for a life on the Earth. Without resistance from our environment we would not learn to adapt to it. But there is a lot of hardship that is absurd, at least from the point of view of the 'I'. When I look back on my own life, has all the hardship I have had to face been of any use for my personal development, even though it may have taken me ten to twenty years to realize that? Sometimes the right person has appeared exactly at the time when I needed help to get me out of a swamp, or I have received support during a difficult period. Sometimes someone has even given me a kick when I needed that to change course. Those who have become shamans or mystics have often had very traumatic experiences, which has totally changed the personality and given them supernatural and sometimes healing capabilities.

In The Old Testament we read about Jacob's fight with God, although he did not know that it was God with whom he wrestled. Do we have a meeting with the divine in existence when we are subjected to difficulties – also such problems that we are unable to tackle? Perhaps such difficulties are due to a conflict between the personality and the Self – the personality's desire to be independent, independent of the Self? This is the opposite of the phrase: 'Not my will, but Thine'. Some people say that the personality does not meet harder challenges than what it can manage, and the purpose is growth.

15. Disease and Healing

Researchers have now found that every cell in the body can be said to have consciousness, in regard of both their special needs and communication with other cells in the body.[483]

Every thought forms chemical reactions in the brain cells and later also in other cells in the body. Trials have shown that a cell can react to thoughts, even after it has been removed from the body where the thought arose. Ervin Laszlo has reported on lie-detector expert Cleve Backster's (b.1924) trials with cell cultures taken from the mouth of a person, which showed responses when the test person was stimulated emotionally – and even when the cell culture was placed several miles away.[484] Furthermore, Laszlo also referred to Dean Radin's trials with what is called sympathetic magic – that is performing magic on a substitute for the person you want to influence. The experiments showed that such influence is possible, something the shamans have used throughout time. This is also practiced in voodoo, which is black magic – attempting to harm a person by such methods as sticking needles into a doll.

Michael Talbot has said that the amazing ability of the mind to control the body, both to inflict disease and to encourage self healing, as well as the individual's ability to heal others, can be explained by the fact that the physical body is only one of the levels of the human energy field. Because disease often can be observed by clairvoyant people long before it shows any physical symptoms, many people believe that the disease occurs in the layers of the energy field that is surrounding the physical body. That means that the energy field is more basic than the physical body, and that is perhaps where we find the blueprint or the architectural drawing of the physical. The American doctor Richard Gerber, whom Michael Talbot has referred to, has studied the consciousness bodies' energy fields for many years. He has suggested that it is the etheric body that is responsible for growth and development of the physical body. He said that the physical body is subordinate to the etheric, which in turn is subordinate to the astral, which in turn is subordinated by the mental body, and that each superior body is serving as a pattern or template for the lower. That means that it is the thought or the mental which is the superior, which content has consequences for the physical.

We are composed of a psychogenic system (psyche and body) that seems to be functioning everywhere at the same time. Body and mind are entangled. The body's cells are made up of molecules, and it has been found that molecules are affected by the mind, for example by producing stress hormones. It is well-known that many diseases are psychically caused, such as stress. By *reprogramming* the emotions, or using positive thoughts instead of negative ones, we can enhance the body's immune defence system. We know that if we are heavily involved in something mentally, we forget the bodily ailments. The body's posture and effectiveness depends on our mood. Falling in love may get a depression to disappear and the body to work better. A great sorrow may kill a human being. Medicine men/women and shamans are taking advantage of the mental states when trying to heal a person. Some witchdoctors are, unfortunately, doing the opposite. Yogis can get their body to perform in the most awkward ways: they can control their breathing, the pulse, the digestion, their sex organs, the metabolism and the kidney functions. By self hypnosis or self-inflicted ecstasy we can make the mind not to feel pain inflicted on the body. When the mind is able to get the body to act positively, the mind is also able to get the body to work adversely, as shown in Stanislav Grof's experiments with hallucinogenic drugs, where the test persons during a hallucination could have violent pain or spasm attacks, increased heart rates and many other physiological symptoms.

A salamander has the ability to make a severed feet or tail grow back. All organisms, including humans, have evolved from a single cell. In this cell, there is a *something* that causes it to divide, and again a *something* which determines that some cells are later to become brain cells, while others shall be bone cells, etc. What is this *something*? And why cannot this *something* help us when we lose a leg or when something is damaged within the body? Why does a salamander have so much better contact with its regeneration equipment than human beings? Or is it possible that we have the same capabilities latent somewhere? How comes that bears and other hibernating animals can sleep through a long winter or under other extreme conditions and survive without eating and drinking, with reduced bodily functions? One thing is the physiological processes that are involved, but what is it that allows them to be reprogrammed according to the circumstances while human beings cannot, at least not today?[i]

And why do we become sick? Let us have a look at some sayings about illness.

Padre Pio is said to have expressed that the will of God does not require that everyone can claim to have a healthy and good life.[485] Illness can be a

---

i. Two research teams, from Japan and the United States respectively, have taken skin cells and changed them into stem cells, so called induced pluripotent stem cells. This is a type of stem cells that can become almost any type of cell. The results were published in November 2007. Researcher George Daley thinks that this is the largest medical breakthrough of the decade. (The Norwegian Broadcasting Company - NRK 21.11.2007)

part of God's plan for human development. By accepting our suffering we can contribute to the salvation of other people, just as Jesus' suffering is said to have contributed to the salvation of mankind. Many people seeking Padre Pio's help were not quit their suffering, but experienced a spiritual healing instead. However, if someone experienced physical healing (a miracle), it was God who should be honoured and no other, according to Padre Pio.

Ken Wilber has written something that I find of importance:[486]

People have physical, emotional, mental, existential and spiritual dimensions, and I would presume that problems on one or all of these levels will contribute to disease.

> - Physical reasons: diet, environmental poisoning, radiation, smoking, genetic predisposition, etc.
> - Emotional reasons: depression, rigid self-control, over-independence.
> - Mental reasons: constant self-criticism, constant pessimism, especially depressions which seems to affect the immune system.
> - Existential reasons: excessive death anxiety that causes excessive life anxiety.
> - Spiritual reasons: failing to listen to one's inner voice.

Ken Wilber wrote that we first must decide to which dimension a person's problems belong, and then treat the problem from the point of what is applicable for this level. He meant that good mental health is to be in accord with Cosmos. That is, a Cosmos that includes matter, body, mind, soul and spirit. Anything that is not in such an accord is unhealthy. A culture that is not in such an accord is a sick culture. He believed that if Plato, Plotinus and the vast majority of the world's most prominent wise, which also were philosophers, were right, and since all of these dimensions (matter, body, mind, soul and spirit) are available to all women and men, then not to honour and give heed unto these dimensions may be compared to malnutrition. And that is the same as disease. As example he mentioned the mental problems. He believed that the various psychological theories and therapies have not been able to distinguish between the different states of consciousness levels in the human beings. Eastern theories of psychotherapy are roughly dealing with the higher levels of the psyche, while the Western therapy forms are concerned with the lower levels in general. He is also of the opinion that psychologists who work with the lowest levels of the psyche, has no contact with the higher levels, and therefore reject the theories put forward by people who work with these levels. In the book *Transformation of Consciousness* he mentions the various mental development stages that a person is passing through during its early years. He has demonstrated potential psychopathologies that may occur on the different levels and which techniques are best to use at these levels to correct the distortions in the psyche. He operates with nine stages in the development of the human beings' consciousness. Each of the nine levels has their special characteristics, their opportunities for development and their particular possible pathologies. Wilber considered Sigmund Freud as the most typical representative for theories dealing with the 'I'-level (this level contains several of the stages that have been dealt with in the book *Transformation of Consciousness*). Wilber recommended the transactional analysis theory as the best tool at this level. Among theories dealing with the existential level (the level Wilber also calls the centaur level), Wilber especially recommended gestalt therapy and certain forms of yoga (Hatha yoga). At this level, it is important to accept the bodily changes that occur, and also whatever other changes that occur in life. He could also accept certain forms of bioenergetic analysis, but stated that one must avoid therapy forms which do not verbalize the experiences or are not using what he calls *mental-egoic* insight (he uses the concept *egoic* about the self conscious 'I').

When it comes to the transcendental level, Wilber recommended Carl Gustav Jung's works (which Sigmund Freud never accepted, and which many psychologists today also reject).

Wilber referred to that the modern, educated Western people today have lost touch with this level due to a lack of awareness of the spiritual in the existence, which in turn is a result of lack of religious belief. This is in the West compensated for by an interest in yoga, meditation, New-Age stuff etc., or by experimenting with the shadow sides of the spiritual such as occultism, black magic and the use of psychedelic drugs. It is at this level that Jung's theories of archetypes are particularly relevant. The archetypes do not belong to the level of the 'I', but are transcending the individual consciousness. By integrating the archetypes that occur in our dreams or fantasies, we will avoid being controlled by daily life, as we will begin to see that everyday experiences are of no importance in the larger context, and that the deeper Self is not influenced by those. Thereby, we can obtain contact with the still, inner source – the Self – which is separated from our mind, body, emotions and thoughts. Wilber also called this transpersonal Self for the Witness. It is on this level that we can come in contact with the real love – the compassion for everything and everyone in existence. Ken Wilber was actually saying, very broadly referred, that all people have a spiritual goal and are using their energy to obtain this goal. But this will be manifest in different ways, according to the individual's level of consciousness.

- At the material level - as hunger
- At the biological level - as sex
- At the mental level - as a wish to exchange thoughts
- At the spiritual level - as a wish to obtain contact with the Divine

But he also pointed out that people have a desire in the opposite direction, namely the death wish, or what he called *thanatos*. This is the desire to return to the mother's womb. Dreams need to be interpreted according to the dreamer's development stage. Especially in psychotherapy it is important to be aware of this, so that when interpreting a dream one starts on the lowest level, and then move on up if necessary.

In the great meditative systems, such as the systems that Hinduism and Buddhism are based on, the idea that each level has its specific help-bearing energy or *prana* (also known as wind or breath in these systems) is an essential element. If you can gain control over this energy at one level, you can transcend, or rise above, this level. And since the mind controls this energy (the mind rides the wind), the energy will assemble where the thoughts are concentrated. It follows that if one, for example, concentrates the thoughts and focuses intensely on one particular chakra, the energy tends to gather there (and if one is dying, may be dissolved there). By the help of the mind we can be in control of these energies.

Francis of Assisi and Caterina of Siena were often ill and had strong physical ailments.

However, as long as they lived they did not give much consideration to the body. Maybe that had some special reasons. Irina Tweedie (1907-1999), who wrote a book about her apprenticeship with an Indian Sufi mystic, has given a possible explanation for this.[487] She consulted this mystic for the first time in 1961 and quickly became his disciple. She called him Bhai Sahib or only Guruji. Guruji explained to her that when one was in the Self (the higher consciousness), the body hardened and one lost contact with it. This has also happened with many saints and other mystics and when they are in ecstasy or in trance. He further explained that when one was in the Self one would have so strong vibrations that the physical body could not sustain the voltage. The body would be damaged and at a certain point be continuously sick. The more spiritual one becomes, the less significant is the body, and the ability to take care of the body will diminish.

Many believe that disease is caused by a person's psyche. But even if mind and body is entangled, we must not feel guilty when we are sick and do not understand our illness. Disease can, as we have seen, be associated with conditions in past lives that we have brought with us into this life in order to try to develop spiritually. But disease can also be caused by reactions in this life – reactions we have not released, but on the contrary drawn into the body, without the conscious 'I' being involved. It is therefore not the conscious 'I' that is the cause of the disease. It is only the person being in contact with the higher spiritual levels that have the opportunity to understand the deeper relationship between mind and body.

Seth's comments in regard to disease and suffering are, in my opinion, a good explanation as to why we become sick.[488] These statements must be seen in context with his comments about reincarnation and about what physical life really is. He said among other things that suffering is a source to obtain higher awareness and is actually a sign of vitality, because death is not the end of existence. The events we are exposed to, we have ourselves arranged, possibly in unconscious cooperation with our parents. A further design of the life we are going to experience in future incarnations, will take place also after the physical death. It is therefore important to understand the relationship between thought and reality. We must learn to transform energy and ideas into experiences, since the reality we will experience in the future is based on experiences from many lives. We are ourselves shaping our environment, we choose our parents and we choose where and when we will be born. Illness can be a result of emotions gone astray or withheld. The mind will then push these into specific body parts and create disease there. But illness can also be something we choose to help for example parents or others to an understanding of life or reality's innermost core. By having a handicapped child parents may be led to knowledge and an understanding they would not have been able to find on their own. Seth also said that disease may have a creative effect. The personality can release a disease, a crisis, or seek out a disastrous situation in order to gain experience with the forces of life and death. It could then experience that the crisis was mobilizing a deeply hidden survival instinct or some other unconscious ability or power.

In some cases, a deadly disease will also be an unconscious attempt to withdraw from this life – a kind of escape attempt. Such a subconscious desire may be behind some types of serious illnesses – and is a possible explanation why some elderly spouses die within a short time of each other; the surviving partner simply does not manage to live alone. The 'I''s use of artificial stimuli such as liquor, tobacco and drugs are also an escape from reality, as the 'I' is well aware that this may cause disease on body and mind.

By becoming better at observing our own emotions, and by being better to come in contact with our subconscious, we will be able to get a better understanding of how our body works and even reacts. That could then help us to get rid of physical ailments, for example by the use of self hypnosis. What we should always try to do, whether by ourselves (self hypnosis or active consciousness development) or by the help of others (doctors or healers), is to seek to become aware of our physical, psychological or mental problems, and by that way – maybe – get rid of the disease or reduce the suffering. Such awareness can either apply to the actual physical behaviour or by the way we tackle the disease. *But we should always remember that the Self may find that the strongest trial is needed in order for the 'I' to get ahead with its cosmic development.* In this connection I refer to Seth's comment that suffering is a source to obtain higher awareness, which only scares that part of the consciousness that believes that death denotes the end of everything. We are all going to die, and there is no guarantee that that will happen quickly and painlessly. Many reports are indicating that the stronger pain we are willing to take on here on the Earth, the more will our mind be purged, and the further will we advance in our karmic process.

Some saints have, however, been healed after long-lasting and life-threatening diseases.

Teresa of Avila's illnesses lasted many years with much pain and paralysis and sometimes also unconsciousness. She wrote that it was only after she had turned to St Joseph (Jesus' father) with prayers for help that she slowly recovered. Therese Neumann was also for several years very sick (blind and paralyzed after a car accident). She was healed thanks to prayers to St Therese of Lisieux (who died before Therese Neumann was born), and she then got supernatural powers. This confirms that the 'I' should not try to end its physical life – to commit suicide – in a difficult situation, because the 'I' does not understand the necessity of suffering. But that should not prevent us from seeking medical assistance where that is possible, or to try prayers, self hypnosis, or, if a physician cannot help, to seek a healer.

> He said to her, "Daughter, your faith has healed you. Go in peace and be freed from your suffering." (Mark 5.34)
> Wisdom in the soul is necessary in order to cure the body.
> *Hildegard of Bingen,* from the diary of 18th Oct. 1152

The word healing is normally used about self healing or for healing others through the laying on of hands, through prayers, through hypnotism or through self suggestions. Edgar Cayce was healing many persons while he was in a self induced hypnotic state, by giving instructions on medications that should be used, or by referring to specific doctors, or by explaining the patient's health condition and how the patient could improve his or her life. The Norwegian Healer Association (founded 1994) defines healing as follows:[489]

> Healing is a traditional and totally oriented process between human beings, whereby one through the laying on of hands, energy balancing, prayers or some similar spiritual oriented method seeks to help people to better health and life quality both physically, psychically and spiritually. Healing is a natural ability which can be developed and strengthened. The Norwegian Healer Association recognizes a common source behind the healing life force, a source which represents love, intelligence, truth and wisdom. The spiritual and non physical dimension of consciousness is considered as a natural and integrated part of life's existence.

The Norwegian healer Ottar Myhre (1928-2004) has explained that various types of healing are practiced, such as the laying on of hands, energy transfer to a patient's aura, healing by prayer, remote healing, self healing and psychic operations. His experience was that just about any type of ailment is suitable for healing, but that not everybody can be healed in this way. He has given the following definition of a healer:[490]

> A person who has a natural ability to give or transfer energy or the vital force which can promote an inner balance and healing process is a healer.

In the above quoted verse from the gospel of Mark, Jesus does not claim to have done the healing, but said that the woman did the healing herself. This indicates a type of self hypnosis – which might be the same as healing through faith. Is it possible that others can influence a person to self hypnosis? Or is it really possible for others to influence a person to become healthy without this being self hypnosis? What is actually happening?

> Very truly I tell you, whoever believes in me will do the works I have been doing, and they will do even greater things than these, because I am going to the Father. (John 14.12)

It has been said that whoever does not live with fear, will stay healthy in body and soul. That is, we have to believe in ourselves, in our own centre that can be called the god centre or heart centre. In the same way, those who seek healing must believe that it will help otherwise they will not remove the fear in their own minds. It is only by removing the fear that we will be able to receive healing. That one's faith does work is shown by the many cases of miraculous healing at religious cult sites such as Lourdes in France. In some such places crutches, bandages and other forms of evidence that such articles no longer are of any use and have been left behind, can be seen. Those items show that a patient has recovered after having been there and have prayed or touched the shrine. There is a possibility that we in the deepest of our being have the ability to regenerate any organ in the body.

Within some church communities prayers have regularly been practiced with the hope that this will heal a sick person. In some such communities there is a form of mass suggestion during such prayers, and it has been claimed that some people actually get rid of diseases in such séances. The American journalist Michael Schmicker has in his book *Best Evidence*, from 2000, mentioned a number of healing trials at hospitals where some patients were prayed for and others were not. The patients did not know about the trials. He wrote that the patient groups which were prayed for became well faster than the group which were not prayed for. However, the Norwegian journalist Ingrid Spilde wrote in an article in 2005, which can be found on the website forskning.no, that research in America regarding the effect of prayers for patients who were having heart operations, was discouraging. Vinjar Fønnebø, Norwegian professor of preventive medicine at the University of Tromsø and the head of the National Research Center in Complementary and Alternative Medicine (NAFKAM), mentioned in a lecture in Oslo in 2007 during a conference under the auspices of the Norwegian Parapsychological Society, the results from surveys made under the control of the Cochrane Organization[i]. Those surveys were looking at

---

i. This is an international, non-profit and independent organization that was founded in 1993, named after the British epidemiologist, Archie Cochrane. The Cochrane collaboration aims to develop up-to-date and accurate information about the impact of health interventions and to make this available to the world. Everybody have access to the research results that this organization produces, which are published on the organization's website.

the effect of organized prayers to God regarding diseases. One such trial, which concerned dying patients, gave significant positive results. When meta-analysis was used, the results were more uncertain, but the authors of the analysis maintained that the results were interesting. Another analysis concerned pregnancy obtained through test-tube treatment, which indicated that prayers gave greater probability for the egg to be attached to the uterus than for those that had not been prayed for. A question that was raised during the trials was whether it was preferable that the patient knew that she was prayed for.

The results indicated that knowledge of the praying gave a negative effect. Fønnebø pointed out, however, that it is difficult to draw any clear conclusion from these results. It is problematic to create satisfying blind trials.

In our time everyone ought to accept that some people have the ability to heal or alleviate others suffering. The Norwegian mystic Marcello Haugen was well-known due to his ability to help other people, even people that he was not in direct contact with. Another well-known Norwegian healer, Joralv Gjerstad (b.1926), was awarded the King's merit medal for his charitable activity through fifty years. In our days there are many people who are practicing healing. The British healer Matthew Manning was often in Norway with lectures and healing circles during the 1990s. There are many people who have got a better life thanks to him. During many of his visits to Norway Manning managed to heal persons with demonstrable injuries. He then used the laying on of hands. He has participated in scientifically arranged trials, where his abilities were tested. These trials are mentioned in Matthew Manning's autobiographies. He has told how he has influenced cancer cells (the cells were placed in lead cages). These trials show firstly that self hypnosis is not the only way to activate healing and further that a cure through healing is a reality. This last statement is further confirmed by the fact that healing works on animals – who hardly understand what is going on.

Harry Edwards (d.1976) practised healing through the laying on of hands and worked at a spiritual healing centre in England, for more than forty years. He wrote many books, including *The Evidence of Spirit Healing*, in which more than a thousand cases are referred, supported by medical data. George Chapman (1921-2006) was a psychic surgeon who worked in England for about 50 years. He worked in trance. There were a number of witnesses who attended the sessions and thorough investigation took place over long periods. J. Bernard Hutton wrote the book *Healing Hands* (1966) about Chapman, where more than a hundred healing cases, all of which were thoroughly investigated and attested, are mentioned. The extraordinary English trance medium Isa Northage (1898-1985), called Dr Isa by her grateful patients, materialized a spirit by the name of Dr Reynolds. He performed psychic operations while materialized, could help patients without materializing and gave medical advice.[i]

Professor Bernard Grad (b.1920) at McGill University in Montreal, Canada, experimented with the germination ability of barley grain. Some crops were given water which a healer first had held in his hands for 30 minutes. The water was in sealed glass bottles while held by the healer. The barley grains had much better germination ability than the control grains which were given regular water. Lyall Watson, who is recounting this experiment, thought that water is composed of unstable molecules held together by chemical bonds, which have only ten percent of the strength of those found in most other contexts. These bands seem to be easily influenced by a healer. Bernard Grad also performed healing experiments with mice, and found that injured mice held by a healer, were healed quicker than mice held by others. Sister M. Justa Smith, PhD, at Rosary Hill College, New York, also mentioned by Lyall Watson, has experimented with enzymes. It was noted that there was a noticeable change with enzymes in a sealed bottle when a healer held it in his/her hands for seventy-five minutes, in comparison to other enzymes that the healer had not been near. Justa Smith shall also have reached the conclusion that human thoughts alone can bring forth a healing effect.[491]

Lyall Watson also wrote about the Brazilian farmer and healer José de Freitas (Arigó) who died in 1971. He treated more than two million people. In most cases he could diagnose and write out the right prescriptions by just throwing a glance at the patient and without looking at what he wrote. He explained that he was told what he should do by a voice in one of his ears. For a period he also undertook complicated operations with knife and scissors under non-sterile conditions and without any narcosis, but for this he was jailed as he was not licensed as a physician. Some of these operations have been videotaped and various control measures were taken in order to prove that he was cheating. But it was never possible to catch him cheating, and no-one has been able to explain the results, which, according to Watson was total healing of the patients. Much information about Arigó can be found on the Internet and in John G. Fuller's book *Surgeon of the Rusty Knife* (1974). (As mentioned earlier, Stan Gooch maintained that Arigó was an imposter.)

Edivaldo (c. 1930-1974) was another psychic surgeon from Brazil. His full name was Edivaldo Oliveira Silva. He is one of several psychic surgeons described in the book *The Unknown Power* (1975) by Guy Lyon Playfair (b.1935). Edivaldo helped more than 65,000 people and performed psychic surgery on approximately 10,000.

Lyall Watson also wrote of similar operations carried out by a number of Philippine healers who belonged to the spiritist community Union Espiritista

---

i. See *A Path Prepared – the Story of Isa Northage* by Allan MacDonald

Democracy de Filipinas on the island of Luzon. Lyall Watson attended hundreds of such operations and had the opportunity to make further investigations, without being able to see that what happened was fraudulent. He could neither explain what was happening. He also referred to other Western scientists who attended such operations. No one has been able to prove fraud according to Watson. But it is striking that it has not been possible to get pictures from the operations. Anyone who tried came home with black films. And samples of gallstones or other tissues from the operation had inexplicably disappeared between the time the sample was placed in a sealed box and the box was opened again. Stan Gooch mentioned that Mike Scott made a documentary film about those healers that proved that everything that happened was faked. However, Lyall Watson has not changed his opinion on the operations in spite of this film.[492]

Lyall Watson also commented upon acupuncture and some of the research done on this method. Acupuncture is based on the existence of twelve main channels or meridians in the body, where energy flows. It is said to be more than seven hundred points on the body that can be manipulated by the use of needles in order to improve health. But these points or channels provide no known physiological pattern. A patient in Japan that was particularly sensitive to these points, however, could tell exactly where these meridians were, as he maintained that he felt an echo along the meridians when touched by a needle at the acupuncture points. Lyall Watson referred to surveys from different places in the world confirming the existence of the acupuncture points and the meridians.

Today there are many alternative healing methods and systems, such as homeopathy, reflexology, iris diagnostics etc. However, it is not a purpose for this book for taking a closer look at those. What is of interest in our context is that all those systems are based on that a human being consists of more than the physical body. This is supported by the fact that a human being's mental state strongly can influence how the physical body functions.

Most people know, presumably, the so-called placebo effect – that is, a group of patients that does not get medicine, but pills they believe are medicine, will recover just as well as the persons in a group that get medication. We also hear of patients who recover because they believe that they have received healing, while the healer in reality is not in activity just then. This implies that the result just as much is due to the patient's own expectation as to someone else's efforts. Then we may remember Jesus' words: "*Your faith has saved you.*" It is then reasonable to ask whether it is only the self hypnosis that makes one recover, or whether other factors also are at work. The word placebo comes from Latin and means 'I want to please'; the opposite is nocebo – 'I will hurt'. Magicians, who are using black magic – voodoo – to injure, are making use of the nocebo effect. If we are expecting that something or someone is injuring us, deterioration may easily be the result. To understand why healing works, we must be aware of how strong a belief or the power of thought is, and how important this can be in a healing process.

Thelma Moss (see chapter 6) used a high-frequency device on a healer to see if there was any measurable change in the energy body while he was working.[493] It recorded dramatic changes in the aura, which was described as glowing. Stan Gooch believed, however, that there is nothing supernatural occurring in connection with healing. He argued that what happens when someone seeks to heal another by the laying on of hands or by prayer, is that the body's own normal healing process was thereby accelerating and strengthening. That such healing occurs, he believed was documented beyond doubt, although many scholars still do not accept that this is true. The registering done by the HeartMath Institute, USA, and elsewhere to see if the heart can affect the brainwaves of another person, shows that a person can affect another through warm sentiments – perhaps this is a form of psychokinesis.

In laboratory experiments it has been shown that bacteria will be affected by magnetic fields. When the field is changed, the bacteria change the direction of their movements. That is, the bacteria will be influenced by the structure or pattern of the field. Water also has a structure. Perhaps the human body has a structure that has not yet been proven – maybe the meridians or the etheric body or aura are part of such a structure. In this case, it is natural to assume that it is this that will be affected through healing. There may be a defect somewhere in this field that causes disease or injury. If the structure is a kind of energy field that can be affected by the power of thought, maybe a change in the pattern of this field can heal the defect. Then the healer is tuning into the patient's wave pattern or interference pattern and seeks to change that. When a person has a mental imbalance, to a greater or lesser degree, it is a possibility that this may affect the structure of the energy field around the body. And later, perhaps after many years, this disorder will surface in the form of a disease or a deterioration of the body. For example, many people were not accepted as war invalids after the Second World War because their injuries were not registered until many years later. What causes an imbalance or why this has not been repaired earlier is actually of no interest. The cause may perhaps have been forgotten a long time ago. But the change in the structure is there and might possibly be reversed, if it is not so extensive that it is beyond repair.

There are many who believe in the importance of visualizing a white light, which one draws down from Cosmos and directs to the sick person or to the injury. We can also do this when we are doing self-healing. Or we can get help from another person, the healer, who is visualizing that the white light is drawn in from Cosmos, passing through his or her hands and into our body. If the white light is a kind of cosmic energy, which can change the sick person's energy field, then this may be the explanation as to why healing takes place. Lyall Watson has mentioned Shafica Karagulla's experiments in the 1970s with a person named Diane. Diane said she saw an energy body that supported and infiltrated the physical body as a tissue of light rays (compare this with Rudolf Steiner's description of the etheric body). She could also see straight through people's physical body and was able to describe the inner organs. She saw swirls of energy in this energy body similar to what others have described as chakras. If these flows were abnormal or missing, or the energy body was irregular or had an abnormal form, then it was likely that it was an illness or injury in the body at this location. Watson wrote that Diane, and others who have the same ability, undoubtedly are seeing energy patterns around the physical body. This is what the yogi philosophers described as *prana*, which is what the acupunctural system is based on, and that which the high-frequency apparatuses are registering as bio-plasma.

Watson further told about tests arranged by Japanese Hiroshi Motoyama PhD (b.1925), clinical psychologist, at the Institute of religion-psychology in Tokyo, which showed that the brainwaves during a healing performed by the Philippine healer, Tony Agpaoa, were alpha waves, and that the galvanic skin response increased and that the blood pressure changed rhythm, which indicated that the para-sympathetic nervous system was affected. (It is this system which, according to Aivanhov, communicates with the chakra points.) This suggests that the healers in some way are able to control a force that affects the field in the energy body which surrounds the physical body. Watson wrote that he could not give any meaningful explanation regarding the kind of psychic surgery performed by healers. However, one explanation could be that behind all life is a blue print or a meaning, a plan in that space which is Cosmos. Motoyama is also said to have developed a technique that can measure electrical signals from the chakras.

The Norwegian doctor and healer Audun Myskja PhD (b.1953) has written a book about the effect of music on people.[494] He writes there about the American biologist Sharry Edwards, (named Scientist of the Year in 2001 for her work in BioAcoustic Biology) which has put forward the hypothesis that all people have their own sound and frequency (called the signature sound), which are associated with his or her mental and physiological state. During disease or during a stressed or depressive mental situation this sound will change, but by listening to certain low-frequency sounds one may be able to normalize the conditions. Audun Myskja's own research on sound and his experience as a doctor has shown that by using sound one will be able to locate the affected site, and possibly enhance or heal the problem area by the use of sound. Maybe healing really consists in tuning into another person's energy frequency, reveal discord, and then to affect the patient's frequency by using one's own radiation. Audun Myskja refers to the experiments that were performed more than 300 years ago by the great Dutch scientist Christian Huygens (1629-1695) regarding the phenomenon that is known as coupled oscillation. Huygens discovered that if several pendulum clocks were set in motion with different rhythms, they would eventually get the same rhythm. Myskja mentions that this is probably caused by one impulse which is stronger than the others, and therefore pulls the others along. Moreover, Myskja refers to more recent trials with sound and colour where the purpose was to find out how they influence body cells. The results indicated that different tunes can evoke different colours around the cells, and that the cells also can be influenced to change form when different frequencies are played. Some have compared such synchronicity with what happens when a tuning fork is put into vibration and makes another fork to vibrate in the same way. In a similar way people are also found to synchronize their activities when together frequently. This is seen under different conditions, such as when playing golf, as previously mentioned in chapter 6 in connection to the research performed by the Institute of HeartMath. This is thought-provoking à-propos that which Myskja reports.

Arthur E. Powell has commented the concept *prana*, which denotes the life force or the breathing in every creature.[495] He said that it is the prana that keeps the body together. However, a too large portion of this energy in the nervous system can lead to disease, in the same way as too small an energy can cause exhaustion. It is this energy that builds the body, creating cells and provides the ability to feel pleasure, despair and pain. Powell stated that prana is both in the physical, mental, astral and etheric body. Everything suggests that nervous weaknesses are caused by damages in the etheric layer. Some people have stronger prana than others and this radiation can be exploited by others in that they are able to pull it towards themselves. Since energy can be affected by the will, anyone that knows how to control it can let the energy go wherever they want, and also reinforce the radiation. Someone with a weak prana may be able to be strengthened by obtaining energy from another person, and thereby be able to make bodily or mental weaknesses in their system healed. A healer will be able to enhance the effectiveness of their prana by visualizing the sick organ, and imagine that the organ is healed by the power of thought. By putting oneself in a sort of meditative state, one may, for example, imagine the person one has consented to attempt to heal. By visualizing that one is entering this person's body and trying to locate the pain, and then visualising that one is restructuring the cells at this point and thereby removing the pain or the sick tissue, maybe one can heal this person.

Science has shown that it is an electrical voltage in each cell and that the cell membrane is leading electricity, as the voltage is different on the inside and the outside of the membrane. Any change is due to the transport of neurobiological ions between nerves, between nerves and muscles, and between nerves and glands. Ions are positively or negatively charged molecules – and it is the interaction between these that creates electricity. Lyall Watson has mentioned that changes in the electrical field in the human body can be the cause of irritability, tiredness, dizziness, headaches and changes in the heart rhythm and the blood pressure.⁴⁹⁶ Watson claimed that all air contains ions. He referred to a variety of experiments that have shown that people who are exposed to negative ions feels better than people who are exposed to positive ions, and that a surplus of positive ions causes more illness, more accidents and other negative reactions than normal.ⁱ There are many people who feel better when being at the seaside or in the mountains, where there are more negative ions than in the lowlands. This may be the cause of many people's change of moods when there are changes in the weather. The fohn-wind, for example, makes many people depressed. Can this be the explanation why some people have stronger healing powers than others? They may have a stronger field of negative ions around them.

Some people claim that they are being tapped for powers when they are giving healing, while others say they are being positive charged so they can provide more. Also when you are visiting the old or sick, or when you have contact with people with whom you communicate poorly, after the visit you may find that you have been depleted of energy. Vice versa, you may feel an increase of energy by close contact with small children. Matthew Manning has said that when he gave healing, he was being positively charged, and had plenty of energy thereafter. Therefore he never gave healing in the evening, in which case he could not manage to sleep. We should learn to understand this effect of energy exchange. If we understand what is going on, maybe we can learn to stop this draining of energy, learn how we can get more and how we can share it with others without being drained.

Hildegard of Bingen has described how she experienced giving healing by prayer and by laying on of hands.⁴⁹⁷ First she had to ask for God's protection, as she was anxious that the patient's disease could be transferred to her. She mentioned one such event where she thought that she took over the patient's demons and allowed their vapour form to sink into her own being, as she said it. But it could also be that the impact was not as strong as a demon possession. She explained that the difference between a demonic possession and an ordinary disease was that during a demonic possession both the soul and the body were involved. She then told of a case in which she healed a man with a big lump in the head which he got from a fall. She sent him energy by the laying on of hands, and slowly she felt through her hands that the lump flattened. First she held her left hand above his chest, while she stroked his back with the other hand. Then she placed the right hand above his heart, because she felt that this area was warmer than

---

i. An article from 2003 found on the website *www.forskning.no* tells about experiments with equipment which produces negatively charged ions. In the intensive care department at a British hospital they have been able to bring to an end repeated infections caused by the bacterium acinetobacter thanks to the use of such equipment. Ionizing equipment can be a powerful weapon in combating hospital infections, according to Clive Begg at the University of Leeds. The article also mentions that according to *The New Scientist* previous research under the auspices of the electronic company Sharp has demonstrated that positive and negative ions produced by their air conditioner can inactivate viruses, including influenza.

elsewhere, and focused all her awareness on this palm, while she prayed for him. The right hand tickled and trembled while she was holding it in this way, so she believed that it received something. The lump disappeared.

Many healers are feeling that there is a sort of energy coming from the outside that is causing the healing, so that the healer is only a medium. This can be due to benevolent spiritual powers, the so-called helpers. Some believe that there are no such helpers, but that it is we ourselves who have strengths and weaknesses, and that we sometimes are better at using the one side than the other. Many healers have said that it is important that the healer has the awareness focused on the sick spot or at the patient. Some are visualizing colours during the session, or they are praying, or, if applicable, are harmonizing their breath with that of the patient. Good emotional connection between patient and healer is required. The healers must also have genuine compassion or love ability and be totally bodily relaxed. An old tenet from Epidaurus[i] stated that only a wounded doctor can perform healing, and only as far as he has healed himself. Carl Gustav Jung is supposed to have said that only a doctor, who is strongly affected by the patient, can heal.[498] Possibly, this is what is meant when we talk about being on the same wavelength as another human being – we must try to understand and tune in on the patient's level of vibration.

In order to heal oneself or help others the key is to have contact with our own feelings and reactions, and – not the least – that we are able to register other person's mood. But people have different energy emission and the ability to have contact with others varies. As we all know, some are good at making contact, exchange experiences, feelings, thoughts and ideas, while others are locking themselves in, are hiding in a black tent which does not emit any light. This may be because they are not present in the now and therefore do not register other people or the reactions from those people, nor anything that surrounds them. It can also be caused by fear of other people, and perhaps also a hidden fear of themselves. Some people have very little contact with their own being and therefore they do not get good contact with others either. A good healer must have good energy radiation and openness towards others.

We must acknowledge that we have a kind of energy field around us, and that it is we ourselves who manage this field's exchange with the environment. That means that we need to be present in ourselves, but not locked in ourselves. We have to be aware what is happening around us. That applies not only in relation to other people, but also to what happens in nature, what is happening around us here and now. We must notice our own wounds, but we must not remain in them, just accept that they are there. Only then can we proceed and only then can we help others. But the most important thing – if we want to help another human being or ourselves – is

---

i. Epidauros was the medical centre in Greece in the old times, dedicated the god of healing - Asclepius.

to be open for the cosmic energy and seek to be the channel that conveys this energy to the person (or animal) we want to help.

I think it is important to consider what Ken Wilber mentioned, that we have different levels of consciousness – physical, emotional, mental, spiritual and existential – and that we must consider how we are functioning on these different levels when we are trying to understand our own reactions, frustrations and possibly psychic bindings and pathologies. Wilber speaks of the senses of the body, the senses of the mind, the senses of our thoughts and the senses of the spirit, and that it is important to be aware of which of these senses are used in a given situation. For me it gives meaning to think of the chakra energies. If I am responding emotionally in some situation (I am for example being moved by something, or angry or happy), I should consider why this happens and from what chakra it is I am responding. Maybe a restructuring of the energy in the affected chakra can free the bindings there and thereby perhaps lead to better health.

It is important that all the chakras are in balance. The energy radiation must not be too strong from a single chakra, but neither must it be too weak. If you have too much energy concentration in one chakra, there will be too little in another. Many men tend to use too much of their energy in the solar plexus chakra (outward going activity) which may take energy away from the heart-chakra (compassion) or the chakra in the forehead (the pineal – intuition). Many women use too much energy in the heart chakra and almost none in solar plexus. Without a good balance in all the chakras we will not be able to meet our fellow human beings in a good way. For example, we will not have adequate sensitivity to understand other human beings when mostly using the solar plexus energy, and they will then easily feel overpowered and react dismissively. Or we will appear vague and unclear if we do not have enough solar plexus energy, so that other people have problems dealing with what we are saying and doing, because then they do not quite understand us.

Everyone should work with their root chakra by exercising the body so it becomes flexible and pliable, for example by using yoga or some other gymnastic method; manipulate the navel chakra (hara) and solar plexus by trying to understand one's desires, feelings and emotions by using psychotherapy or other similar therapies, and by learning one's own sexual feelings and needs, if applicable, for example in conversation with a sexologist; manipulate the heart chakra and throat chakra, for example in conversations about existential questions and by training one's sensitivity to other people's feelings and needs; manipulate the forehead chakra and crown chakra by the help of meditative or other spiritual exercises, preferably with the help from a spiritual teacher. Jes Bertelsen has in his books described a number of energy exercises aimed at improving the energy circulation in each chakra point. These are to be recommended. But when it comes to illness and healing, it is important to remember that not all physical pain or disease can be cured. We will all die; the question is when and how. It is said that suffering is the safest path to spirituality. The suffering you have may be due to your karma, or maybe they are the consequences of the life you are now living. Maybe you voluntarily have agreed to take on those sufferings in this life in order to go ahead with yours or the Earth's spiritual development. That does not mean that you should accept your sufferings as such – you must do what you can to improve yourself, in order to get on better with your spiritual development.

16. Prayer, Meditation, Forgiveness and Spiritual Development

16.1. Prayer and meditation

The difference between prayer and meditation is that in prayer I am talking to God, while in meditation God speaks to me. To meditate is to listen to your inner voice. To pray is to communicate with the inner voice.

> As we are going to hear much about the joy the Lord gives to those who stay in prayer, I will not say anything about it here. I can only say that prayer is the door to the great spiritual gifts which He has given me. *Teresa of Avila*[499]

> Ask and it will be given to you; seek and you will find; knock and the door will be opened to you. (Matt 7.7)

> This, then, is how you should pray: "Our Father in heaven, hallowed be your name, your kingdom come, your will be done, on earth as it is in heaven. Give us today our daily bread. And forgive us our debts, as we also have forgiven our debtors. And lead us not into temptation, but deliver us from the evil one. (Matt 6.9-13)

The translation from Aramaic to English of the prayer Our Father in Heaven, which was first translated from Aramaic to Greek is as follows:[500]

> O Birther, Father – Mother of the Cosmos.
> Focus your light within us – make it useful,
> create your reign of unity now –
> your one desire then acts with ours
> as in light, so in all forms.
> Grant what we need each day in bread and
> insight, loose the cords of mistakes bindingus
> as we release the strands we hold of others' guilt.
> Don't let surface things delude us
> but free us from what holds us back.
> From you is born all ruling will
> the power and the life to do
> the song that beautifies all
> from age to age it renews.

> Truly – the power to these statements
> – may they be the ground
> from which all my actions grow.

The Christians also often use the litany *Kyrie Eleison* (Lord, have mercy on us) or the Rosary prayer *Ave Maria*, which begins as follows:

> Ave María, grátia plena, Dóminus tecum. Benedícta tu in muliéribus, et benedíctus fructus ventris tui, Jesus.
>
> Hail, Mary, full of grace, the Lord is with thee, blessed art thou among women, and blessed is the fruit of thy life, Jesus.

In Islam the prayer *la ilaaha ill-Allah* (only God deserves worship) is used. This I have also seen written *la ila'ha illa-l-la'h* (which I have used in chapter 2.2) and which is said to mean 'there is no God besides Allah'. In addition, a frequently used expression is *Allâhu Akbar* (God is great).

In Buddhism and Hinduism, the word OM is a word often used in meditation and prayer:

> "Brahman is", thus says the seer of Brahman.[i]
>
> "Brahman is the door", thus speaks the man of austere harmony whose sins have been washed away.
>
> "OM is the glory of Brahman", says the man of contemplation forever thinking on Brahman.
>
> It is therefore by vision, by harmony, and by contemplation that Brahman is attained. Maitri Upanishad 4.4.[501]

Martinus in a short paper about prayer said that the prayer *Our Father in Heaven* is the best prayer we can use, and he has given an in-depth interpretation of what each line of the prayer actual says. Master Eckhart is supposed to have said something similar to this: that sounds create images and images create matter. When we are in contact with our frequency, we are in harmony – are still – and in this stillness comes the Divine.

What happens when we are praying?

As can be seen from what is cited here, and at which we are going to take a closer look in this chapter, the importance of praying is emphasized in all religions. But what happens when we are praying and how should we pray? What is the difference between prayer and meditation? Prayer is the term the Christians use, while meditation in particular is an Eastern phenomenon. The border between prayer, meditation, visualization and self-hypnosis can be difficult to see, although it is maintained that the power of thought is without borders for those who have a strong visualizing ability.

---

i. Brahman is the creator of the Universe.

The purpose of prayer and meditation is to make the consciousness open and receptive for the inner impulses. There are many examples that show that people who are praying or meditating regularly, have a more harmonious mind and a better life than those who do not pray or meditate. This should therefore be something that everyone, no matter what you believe in or have as a philosophy, should practice regularly. Both forms are a means to turn the mind inward, into itself, to get to know yourself and your Self. Only by becoming familiar with your own feelings and reactions and the reasons why you react as you do, will you achieve peace of mind. The feeling of safety creates harmony and peace in your existence, and strength to face the difficulties in life. In return, thanks to meditation and prayer you may reach an acceptance of existence; you may come to see how important it is to have a good relationship with your surroundings, and you get a completely different and better understanding of death. You will become familiar with your real 'I'.

If we believe that life has a meaning, we should seek to find or understand this meaning, then we will better understand how we should live and it will be easier to accept death. (It is maintained that those who are looking will find. But you might find only that which you have already been looking for, unless you are willing to be open to what you find and give it critical scrutiny.) One way to go is to seek out other people and to learn from them, either by their example or through a meaningful dialogue, but that requires that you either find people of confidence who have something to teach, or that you are so prone to learning that you learn by studying others, regardless of how they are. Another way to learn is to search in available literature. However, many argue that one can only learn by having an experienced teacher or guru. The problem is that there are many who appear to be gurus – but who can we trust to lead us on the right path? It has been said that the teacher will be there when we are ready. Maybe we do not need an external teacher. We may find what we need inside ourselves, as a kind of higher or more refined 'I', namely the Self. In this case, meditation or prayer is the way to get in touch with this Self; to try to come in contact with the Self is what I call the spiritual path.

A Catholic once said to me that by constantly repeating the Rosary prayer, in an almost meditative way, she often accordingly turned her thoughts towards the Divine and towards God's revelation on Earth, which is Jesus Christ; and she then felt that she made contact with the great wonder through Jesus Christ. Some Christian mystics have – thanks to intense prayer (without other guidance than the Bible and sometimes a confessor) – achieved access to inexplicable supernatural powers and experiences, but one does not have to be a Christian to work with self-development or to search for a meaning to life, or to obtain supernatural powers. Prayer or meditation is practised within most cultures on the Earth. Below you will find some testimonials from people who possibly have extensive experience and wisdom in this regard.

Jes Bertelsen has said that the very best thing for a person to do is to develop higher consciousness so that one can be beneficial for others as well as for oneself.[502] The meditative process leads to increased self-understanding; but the most significant price is that it brings one into a relationship with something higher, to something spiritual, and ultimately to the Divine. He has hinted that people have a built-in longing for contact with the Divine. This longing may be seen during crises or peak experiences, which he considers as part of a natural individuation process. He maintained that the same can be experienced during treatment with self-development strategies. Often, however, this desire will not be satisfied by such processes alone. Then one will understand the necessity of spiritual training as a daily discipline, and the need for a coach. He has suggested that by a daily exercise for hours through fifteen to twenty years, one might expect to come in touch with the level of the Self – The Mary-consciousness, but this is hardly possible for any but the very few. Everyone else should be able to get some benefit from just being more aware of their own actions and thought patterns.

Sogyal Rinpoche has said that it is important that we all are familiar with the real nature of the mind while we are here on the Earth. Then we will be prepared when this nature reveals itself at the moment of death, and thereby we will finally be released. Only through meditation will we gradually be able to acknowledge and stabilize the nature of the mind, and thereby understand human development through rebirth and karma. Meditation is the road to recognition of who we really are, and to enlightenment. Our daily lives are filled with activity, competition and struggle, while meditation is the opposite. Through meditation we learn to let go of emotions, needs and concepts which occupy the mind. Meditation is to bring the mind home.

Martinus wrote that we, through prayer and meditation, can trigger a great magical power, provided it is done correctly.[503] But at the same time he warned against seeking to achieve mystical abilities by trying Spiritism or going to occult schools. He said that those who tried to acquire clairvoyance or other mental abilities might risk spiritual derailment and decline, and that by using this way it was just as impossible to achieve cosmic consciousness as it is for a child suddenly to become adult. The necessary internal organs that are required for spiritual consciousness need time to develop. There is only one way to develop these, and that is by practising charity through several Earth lives. He further said that to join a monastery, which according to him was to leave humanity to care for itself, has nothing to do with selflessness. He believed that without practising charity through one's daily behaviour, meditation, such as recommended by Oriental religions, is an artificial way which is an unjustified intrusion into the Most Holy.

Per Bruus Jensen explained Martinus' thoughts on prayer on the basis that it is quite common to ask other people for help, but, he said, because people do not believe in God, they see no purpose in praying to God. But God's existence is for Martinus indisputable, and the person who does not ask is therefore cut off from prayer's possibilities – which are to ask the greatest power in existence for help. Martinus believed that a spiritual channel is opened up through prayer and there you may contact divine guardian angels. He said that there is no limit to the help you can get from the Divine, if you are open to the spiritual and the request is not violating the laws of existence. By using prayer we can prepare for the next existence and take away some of the unpleasant thoughts or ideas we may have when passing the threshold of death. We can thus seek to reduce the stay in what can be termed the purgatory fire – the purging process the souls must undergo before they can go on to the spiritual realm. This can be done by, every evening, considering what has happened during the day and how things can be improved, as well as asking for inspiration and the strength to do things better the next time.

Dion Fortune wrote that the Kabbalah is a system for spiritual development. The Tree of Life symbol is used by the initiated as a means to lead the thoughts towards the unseen and the incomprehensible, as she expressed it, and not only to obtain certain thoughts or emotions. She maintained that this symbol is the best for a Western mind, as this mind is very different from the Oriental one. A person who is meditating on a symbol that has been in use by mystics for a long time, will acquire the ideas that the symbol has been associated with without having this explained.

Erich Fromm[i] (1900-1980) has written about how to practise the art of love. In order to practise love exercise is a necessity, as for any type of craft. And in order to practise you need discipline, concentration and patience. He further stressed that in order to practise an art the most important of all must be to master that art – which means that you have to be completely dedicated. To practise discipline, concentration and patience are meditation exercises, and Erich Fromm has given instructions for some such exercises.

Ken Wilber has very strongly emphasized that meditating is not a narcissistic withdrawal from the world. It is a simple and natural continuation of the evolutionary process, where to look into yourself means that you go beyond yourself towards a larger whole and understanding.[504] He said that the more one looks into oneself, towards one's own self, and can reflect on oneself, the less one becomes egocentric. Being self-conscious is normally considered the same as to highly appreciate yourself – having a big ego, but to be conscious of your own Self is to see yourself on an equal footing with any other human being. And in order to be conscious of your own Self, you have to work on yourself – learn to see yourself from the outside, from other

---

i. Erich Fromm was a German Jew who lived in the United States from 1934 to 1950, then he moved to Mexico City, and then to Switzerland in 1974. He was a psychoanalyst, PhD, and professor at Bennington College in Vermont, at the Yale University and at the University of Mexico City. He wrote many books.

people's perspective. He said that to meditate means to go even further into yourself and that when going beyond the usual 'I' – you will experience a completely new and expanded consciousness and identity. Meditation is therefore one of the strongest counterweights to ego-centricity and narcissism, and therefore also a counterbalance to what he calls geo-centricity (the need to belong to a specific location), socio-centricity (belonging to a particular ethnic group) and anthropo-centricity (belonging to a particular people). You will instead feel greater connection to the world and the world's people – a world-centricity.

I find that Ken Wilber's thoughts about meditation are the essential with meditation – that meditation is one of the strongest counterweights against ego-centricity and narcissism. Every human being should work with its self-development; first and foremost to obtain a good life while here on Earth, and to be able to endure the difficulties one necessarily will encounter through life without being crushed, but also in order to meet the fellow human beings in the right way, and to become a true global citizen, and not a person driven by desire, tradition and indoctrination.

How to meditate or pray?

The term meditation is today used for various techniques to calm the mind; that is to try to empty the mind of thoughts. You should just be. Then you learn to let troublesome stuff go, to minimalize your needs; and you will seek to open up for the numinous, the incomprehensible, the Divine. If you are lucky and have tried long enough, you will perhaps in this way experience contact with Cosmos and the spiritual. However, the term meditation is also used for exercises that intend to rebalance the energies of the mind. That is, to try to restructure and improve the way we use our abilities, as well the physical (the root chakra), the instinctive (the hara-chakra), the emotional (the solar plexus-chakra and the heart chakra), and the mental (the throat-chakra) capabilities. Balance in the chakra system is needed to obtain peace of mind, and is the first step towards concentration and contemplation. Meditation is first and foremost concentration, to clear the head for everything that swirls around in it. Only when we are completely empty of thoughts and bodily tensions and emotions, can we experience a feeling of being one with Cosmos – everything that surround us. Only then can we sense the divinity in the existence. Then we get a sense of what the reality is, not just a belief. Through prayer and meditation we can enhance our spiritual consciousness.

If you have difficulties, pain, conflicts and the like or something similar that are occupying your mind and thoughts, prayer may be the solution in order to clarify what is happening.

Prayer may help you to see things from another perspective, or bring you help from higher powers (if you believe in them) so that changes take place. By expressing your experiences in words (or writing about them) you may see that negative feelings and frustrations are reduced or disappear; you may get greater clarity of what you are experiencing, and thereby calming your mind. By turning to God or a spiritual entity, you have the possibility to complain about the situation to someone, have someone to ask or have someone to blame. There are many who have given instruction on meditation and prayer; now we shall look at some such sayings.

Sogyal Rinpoche has described what he called the alchemy of dedication, which is an important aspect of prayer and meditation. He wrote that it is important to have a teacher or a role model to look up to with affection and respect, and a longing to become like this model. To follow a real spiritual master is the only way to achieve enlightenment. And he explained that if you relate to your teacher as to a buddha you will experience the blessings of a buddha, and the right teaching will come to you. If you consider your master as an ordinary human being, you will only get blessings from a human being, and the correct teachings might not reach you. This description is completely in accordance with what Irina Tweedie learnt during her apprenticeship with the Sufi master Guruji. She has, however, pointed out how difficult it is for a person with a Western cultural background to give full devotion. If we in our culture are to follow Sogyal Rinpoche's guiding and choose Jesus as the master we want to give our devotion and whose words of wisdom we want to follow, then we must see the importance of worshiping him as a God, even if we believe that he was just a human being and not a god. And perhaps this is what lies behind the position of Jesus as established in the Christian world. If I consider the Christian mystics' lives and the descriptions of the way they have prayed and the devotion they have given to God and Jesus, I understand what is said here. Sogyal Rinpoche also said that the important thing is to practise attention – we must be present in whatever we are doing. We will then gradually be able to drop all the negative thoughts and gradually achieve more peace of mind.

Marcello Haugen has in his little book *Betragtninger over en dag* (Considerations regarding a day) given recommendations about how to pray.[505] Since he is considered by many as Norway's greatest mystic, that is a good reason to reprint some of what he has written:

> There are three requirements you should give yourself every day.
>
> Firstly: The day must start with a harmonious wakening of body and soul. These are both expressions for our life and must after being awake from sleep be given a consistent rhythm so that the day can begin in harmonious unity. The lack of understanding of this can be seen with most people – the relationship between body and soul on the one hand and the spiritual higher activities on the other. The harmony between body and soul must be regained. Strong natures know this secret. ... Life is infinitely rich. Open up your soul, let your life flourish. ...
>
> But do you know that only a confirmation of all your life's phenomena

– a confirmation of body and soul can lead you to harmony? ...

You should daily use some time on thoughts within yourself.

You must through devotion, stillness and awe try to obtain release for your soul through considerations about life itself from the deepest part of your being. Try to visualize your inner nature as a holy god essence, wherein your being's core has its origin, and from where the life-giving holy elements come to you as nourishment for your soul.

Sit in such moments silently in your small chamber, free from all thoughts and ideas from the outside as well as from the inside. Let your sensory sensations be as in a vacuum, listening and waiting until you feel that a holy joy fills your mind, a joy not of this or that external goods, but an immediate joy, real joy of life, because you feel you are participating in life itself, and still are in time.

In such a moment the holy spiritual warmth will come into your soul and give it the right temperature, the balance which in turn is born in the body as a normal body temperature and passes it on to the whole organism. It is this normal internal temperature, which determines whether a body is sick or healthy. ...

Know that all your life statements are symbols of your innermost being. ... Let us start working with ourselves just now and thus always this just now, day by day.

Marcello Haugen has also given the following recommendation in a memo:

To be read now and then
I am in our subjective mind.

Let us try to stop creating sprouts of disease by not having thoughts about disease, but by turning our awareness to higher things. Make love alive by thinking of love. Create the light of wisdom in the world by verifying the creator's omnipresent omnipotence. Let us in our minds see the creator's pure substance. This is the way to transform the microbes. This is the counterbalance to the sprouts of disease.

The real and enduring created things can be brought into visible form in this simple way. It is so easy that a person with a big intellect (systematic thinking) might pass it by, and it is so easy that even the most foolish can understand it. No special education is required to achieve the sacred connection to the creating spirit. We do not need to know of anything other than a simple attention to the Creator. It does not need long and tired years of study. No diving into in the depths of difficult theories and speculations, but only a simple child-like attention towards the omnipresent spirit, and a heart filled with love and kindness for everything and all things. Our suffering comes from our small personal self. It is only the holy might that produces what is good and only that will last forever.

Teresa of Avila has in her book *The Interior Castle* described the importance of prayer and given instructions as to how one should begin to pray, of which the most important thing is to collect the mind and to think of God. She wrote that to pray is so important and such a good thing that no one should take away this benefit, because God gives the one that prays great joy and great gifts, even if one is only advancing small steps at the time. And there is nothing to fear. She explained that when practising prayer, this practice will pass through four main stages. However, everything becomes easier when practising. These four stages can be compared to four different ways of watering a garden. She explained that we can water in the following four ways: either by the help of our arms to fetch water from a well, which is heavy work; or by using paternoster equipment where we have a water bucket that is lowered up and down in the well by means of such equipment, which is much easier and provides more water; or we can take water from a river or stream through a channel or pipeline, which gives even more water; or we can hope for rain. When it rains, it is God that is watering and we do not have to do anything. Some of what Teresa further described, regarding the result of the different watering methods, is very similar to the near-death experiences. This is especially true for what she called the enchantments, which she experienced during the third way of watering.

She explained that the first thing you notice when you start to pray is comparable to *the hard way* to fetch water. It is heavy work. You have to try not to see and neither to listen to the sounds you hear. You have to be by yourself and you must start with thinking about your life, and in a way trying to put it behind you. Teresa suggested that you begin with thinking about Jesus' passion. You have to imagine the sufferings Jesus underwent, his loneliness, his pains and whatever else you can imagine. She wrote that this is a form of prayer that anyone can start with, and that it is a safe way until the Lord leads you to the supernatural. *The second way* to fetch water, which is happening when you are getting used to pray, she called the Prayer of Silence. Then you have come so far that your will and the soul's abilities are starting to work, although they are joined together in God. You will be filled with peace and a great joy, even though she found that the mind is a bothersome spirit that is presenting you with images and thoughts which disturb your peace. But this nuisance must be rejected by means of the will. *The third way of watering* is the next step in the development of prayer. When we let the water run directly from a river or a source, we need to control the water along the way, but it does not require any work to let the water stream. At this stage the abilities of the soul will be sleeping, and they will not understand how they are working. The pleasure and joy is greater than at the preceding stage. She described the emotions as matching those that one can imagine someone has, when with a light in the hand is close to dying the death that he or she is yearning for. It is like a death from the world, where you are only enjoying God. Teresa wrote that it was like delightful folly and a divine madness, in which you are learning to know the true wisdom. *The fourth way of watering*, which is the final stage of the prayer's development, is a divine union and is experienced as pure bliss, not as work. But she could not describe this state with words, nor did she actually understand what was happening, and she could therefore not explain what it was. She was not aware of the difference between soul and spirit, or what one understands by the mind. Neither could she say how long such a condition lasted, but suggested maximum half an hour. The only thing she could say clearly was that she had a sense of being with God, and that she had a clear certainty about this condition.

Levi H. Dowling has given a similar description of prayer. In the book *Den nye tidsalders evangelium om Jesus Kristus* (The New Age's Gospel about Jesus Christ) he wrote:

> God sings for us through birds and harps and human voices; He speaks to us through the wind and rain and thunder. Why should we not bend down and honour him at his feet. God speaks to the hearts which are separated from him, and the hearts turned away from him must speak to him. This is prayer. It is not prayer to shout for God, nor to stand or sit or kneel and to tell him all about the sins of humanity. It is not prayer to tell The Holy One how great he is, how good he is, how tall and compassionate. God is not a human being that can be bought in human ways. Prayer is the burning desire that every life form must be light; that every action must be crowned with goodness; that every living thing must obtain well-being with our help. A charitable action, a helpful word is a prayer, a deep-felt effective prayer. The source of prayer is in the heart; by thought, not by words, is the heart carried to God, where it is being blessed. Then let us pray.

David Spangler has referred the following explanation from the spirit called John:[506]

> We would not deny communication, though, to someone who earnestly seeks it in order to enhance his or her capacity to serve. However, you must remember that we do not always communicate in words. Sometimes it is in qualities and flows of energy. Sometimes it is in a spirit of encouragement or peace, a flash of insight or inspiration. There may be reasons in the structure of the individual's personality why a verbal contact and communication may not be right, but this does not mean a communion cannot take place between us. Indeed, it is this communion that we treasure most.
>
> To create this communion, we suggest that you develop a practice of prayer and meditation.
>
> Do not, though, direct it specifically towards us. Let your attention go to God, for, as I have said, it is in the divine presence that we may meet. The very fact that you acknowledge us and are aware of our efforts on behalf of the Earth gives your consciousness an openness

that reaches to us and connects us with your life.

There are many kinds of prayers and meditations. I would suggest you investigate the possibilities and choose what is right for you. Remember, though, that we commune most powerfully in acts that resonate. Be a spiritual world to your world, and you can be sure we will be present assisting. To offer you a place to begin, however, I will outline a possible meditation. Begin in comfort, acknowledging, appreciating, and giving blessing to your physical surroundings and conditions. Anchor yourself through such acknowledgement and appreciation in your humanness and in your environment. Then, turn your thoughts toward God. In this, I recommend that you contemplate and fill your mind and heart with the qualities that you associate with God. Invite the divine presence into your being and be aware of his power already within you as the very source of your life. If you do nothing else than this, filling yourself with awareness of your closeness to the Beloved, and if you can carry that awareness as a radiance into your daily affairs, you will accomplish much. A further step is to then invite into your imagination a sense of what the divine spirit seeks to accomplish upon the Earth. You are not asking for specific directions, however. You are seeking to attune to a flow, a process, a sense to what God wishes the Earth to become, particularly the physical world of which you are a part. I have already mentioned our vision of the Earth's destiny as a planet upon which synthesis is learned. What does synthesis means in human terms? What kind of civilization and culture could develop that would best fulfil this destiny?

Let your imagination be open to considering these questions. In time, though, ask yourself how might these visions or images of planetary destiny, of the flow of God's spirit within the world, be best implemented within your own life. What small and specific steps might you be able to take that would resonate with that spirit and its direction? Take the larger vision and personalize it in ways you can deal with in your life at the moment. Be a world saviour in the quality of your responses to life, not necessarily in the quantity of vastness of your actions. ... Finally, in seeking the spiritual worlds, remember what you truly seek is your oneness with God. We are not a substitute for divinity. We are colleagues, if you wish, in the endeavours of earthly evolution; we wish to be friends. However, contact with us is less than it could be if it takes the place of a spiritual path to the Beloved. Put God first, then we can meet in the mutual embrace of her spirit.

Master Eckhart speaks in his sermons about how God or the Deity is to become yours. A good help to understand this is given in the following statement:[507]

> A liberation from all motives and intentions in which the self can hide itself – and from all the thoughts and concepts, notions and ideas, whereby the imperfect human sense down here has tried to express and objectified the human being's basic experience: GOD.

Continue in prayer, said St Paul (Col. 4.2 and Eph. 6.18). But how is that possible and how do we pray? An explanation of this statement can be found in the book *A Russian Pilgrim's Report*.[i] Here it is said that the most important prayer is '*Have mercy on us, O Lord*'. It was something like this that the two blind men said when they begged Jesus for healing. (Matt 20.30, Mark 10.47 and Luke 18.38.) It is maintained that if you get into the habit of continuously repeating this prayer, you will experience such a great bliss that you cannot be without it – and the prayer will eventually be permanently within you. To begin with you pronounce the prayer with your lips, shaping the words. Later it is enough just to have them in your thoughts, for finally to imagine the prayer in your heart – in which case it eventually will be manifested in each heartbeat. You start gently by saying the prayer a few hundred times per day. Later it can be expanded to a thousand times or several thousand times. This is heavy work at first, but becomes more and more joyful. This practice should give the person praying inner peace and love for everything created.

You need no special prayer or meditation method if you manage to rest in pure consciousness, but very few are capable of this without having practised for a long time. The German diplomat, psychotherapist and Zen-master Karlfried Dürckheim (1896-1988), who has written a book about meditation and how to meditate, has said that much has been called meditation.[508] He has strongly emphasized that meditation should be an instrument to penetrate into one's innermost being, and being a so-called initiation exercise. He explained the word initiate (from the Latin word *initiare*) as opening doors to the hidden, that is, to our innermost being. The purpose of his book was to show how we can experience the supernatural, the Divine in existence, that which lies behind everything spiritual. If you are working towards such an experience, your personality will change. His starting point was that all human beings are suffering from a personal distress, namely that which occurs when we realize that we cannot understand everything with our common sense, and that our real being has not been expressed. Meditation is, according to his view, a way to liberation. It may be that you only need to practise in silence or just to be silent or you maybe should try to visualize a holy picture or word in order to understand its message, and thus find a means for obtaining spiritual depth.

---

i   The book is the report from a nameless Russian wanderer seeking answers to this question from various spiritual teachers. Probably it was written just before 1860, and it was published in Russia for the first time in 1881. The wanderer is told that he can find the answer to his questions in a book called Filokalia. This book is originally from the monastic communities on the peninsula Athos in Greece, and consists of a collection of explanations given by 24 prominent church leaders up through the ages – from as far back as around the year 200 and until the middle of the 18th century. Filokalia was first published in Venice in 1782. It was translated into Russian and published there in 1793, and was later much regarded in Russia.

Sogyal Rinpoche said that Buddha taught 84,000 different meditation methods, although he thought that one of the following three methods is best today:
- To follow your breath
- To look at an object or at a picture of a Master
- To recite a mantra

Jes Bertelsen has in his books explained that there are many methods that may concentrate the different forces of the mind. Silence is a good starting point. That means that you must have no thoughts, no pictures or any other disturbing impulses. The consciousness must learn to register this silence. What you then may experience is moments of emptiness or blessing or light. What is to be understood as silence is thus a non-verbal presence.

A mantra is a Sanskrit expression that is thought to have a divine power which is to be used in meditation. There are many different mantras. This may either be a word, a phrase or a verse. A steady repetition of a mantra during meditation may lead to a reprogramming of the mind, something like self-hypnosis, which may turn the stream of thoughts from something negative to something positive. But we do not have to use a mantra in order to meditate. However, many are recommending the use of a mantra, although for different purposes. The Maharishi movement is using a mantra in what is called a transcendental meditation teaching. Another meditation organization in Norway, Acem, which does not have any religious attachment, explains how meditation with the use of a methodical sound makes you feel well and reduces stress. This seems to me very much the same as a mantra.

Sogyal Rinpoche has explained that the definition of the word mantra is "that which protects the mind", since a mantra is laden with energy which is transferred to the person using it. The mantra that he has recommended is *"OM AH HUM VAJRA GURU PADMA SIDDHI HUM"* (the Tibetans say: Om Ah Hung Benza Guru Péma Siddhi Hung), which is said to be Padmasambhava's and all enlightened beings' mantra. This mantra is said to have the very best effect for peace, healing and change. The words *"Om mani padme hum"* is also said to be one of the most forceful mantras in Buddhism. It means "Oh you who has a Jewel in the Lotus". Sogyal Rinpoche said that this was the mantra used by Avalokiteshvara, the compassionate Buddha, which purges all the negative emotions which are the cause of reincarnation. The word AOM or OM, which is the first word in this mantra, is said to be just as strong when standing alone. The explanation for this is given in *The Upanishads*.[509] The following citation is taken from *Prasna Upanishad*:

> The Word OM, O Satyakama, is the transcendent and the immanent Brahman, the Spirit Supreme. With the help of this sacred Word the wise attains the one or the other.

OM, or AUM, has three sounds. He who rests on the first, his meditation is illumined thereby and after death returns speedily to this world of men led by the harmonies of the *Rig Veda*. Remaining here in steadiness, purity, and truth he attains greatness.

And if he rests his mind in meditation on the first two sounds, he is led by the harmonies of the *Yajur Veda* to the regions of the Moon. After enjoying their heavenly joys, he returns to the Earth again.

But if, with the three sounds of the eternal OM, he places his mind in meditation upon the Supreme Spirit, he comes to the regions of light of the Sun. There he becomes free from all evil, even as a snake sheds its old skin, and with the harmonies of the *Sama Veda* he goes to the heaven of Brahma wherefrom he can behold the Spirit that dwells in the city of the human body and which is above the highest life. There are two verses that say: "The three sounds not in union lead again to life that dies; but the wise who merge them into a harmony of union in outer, inner and middle actions becomes steady: he trembles no more."

With the harmonies of the *Rig Veda* unto this world of man, and with those of the *Yajur Veda* to the middle heavenly regions; but, with the help of OM, the sage goes to those regions that the seers know in the harmonies of the *Sama Veda*. There he finds the peace of the Supreme Spirit where there is no dissolution or death and where there is no fear.

In Katha Upanishad we can read this:

When the wise rests his mind in contemplation on our God beyond time, who invisibly dwells in the mystery of things and in the heart of man, then he rises above pleasures and sorrow. ...

I will tell you the Word that all the Vedas glorify, and self-sacrifice expresses, all sacred studies and holy life seek. That word is OM.

That Word is the everlasting Brahman; that Word is the highest End. When that sacred Word is known, all longings are fulfilled.

It is the supreme means of salvation: it is the help supreme. When that great Word is known, one is great in the heaven of Brahman.

Atman, the Spirit of Vision, is never born and never dies. Before him there was nothing, and he is ONE for evermore. Never-born and eternal, beyond times gone or to come, he does not die when the body dies.

If the slayer thinks that he kills, and if the slain thinks that he dies, neither knows the ways of truth. The Eternal in man cannot kill: the Eternal in man cannot die.

Concealed in the heart of all beings is the Atman, the Spirit, the Self; smaller than the smallest atom, greater that the vast spaces. The man who surrenders his human will leaves sorrows behind, and beholds the glory of the Atman by the grace of the Creator.

> Resting, he wanders afar; sleeping, he goes everywhere. Who else but my Self can know that God of joy and of sorrows?
>
> When the wise realizes the omnipresent Spirit, who rests invisible in the visible and permanent in the impermanent, then they go beyond sorrow.

In the chapter about God, Yogananda referred to the description of the sage Patanjali, who was said to meditate on the word Aum, because Patanjali meant that this sound represented God. Yogananda said the following in this connection:[510]

> **Aum** is the Forming word, the mumbling from the Vibratory Motor, the witness of the Divine's presence. Even the person starting with Yoga will hear the astonishing sound of **Aum** in the inner ear. Through this blessed encouragement the seeker of God will be convinced that he is in connection with the super-earthly realms.

In a footnote in connection with this, we find in the autobiography of Yogananda the following comment:

> "These things saith the Amen, the faithful and true witness, the beginning of the creation of God; (Revelation 3.14.) ...
>
> "In the beginning was the Word, and the Word was with God, and the Word was God. ... All things were made by him (the Word or Aum); and without him was not anything made that was made." (John 1.1-3) The *Aum* of the Vedas became the holy word *Hum* of the Tibetans, the Muslims' *Amin*, and the Egyptians', the Greeks', the Romans', the Jews' and the Christians' word *Amen*. Its meaning in Hebrew is certain or loyal.

Everywhere in the Bible, we can find words of wisdom, truth, words that comfort and words for reflection, but without a belief that there is a greater spirituality and something more than our physical world, there are many who find it difficult to enjoy these words. This is also one reason why many people have difficulty using prayer or a mantra-meditation. But work on self-development will help anyone in their everyday life. If you do not want to use prayer or are finding mantra meditation too complicated, there are other techniques you can use. There are many different methods for relaxation training or training in self-awareness. Each one of those seeks to exploit the alpha level of the brain. You can increase your sensitivity and thereby also your mental abilities and your self-esteem by concentrating on the breath, which also is recommended as a meditation exercise. What you then are seeking to achieve is to set the body in a kind of sleep, so that your breathing becomes heavy and quiet as when you are sleeping, while the consciousness is awake. This is also called autogenic training. In addition, if your thoughts can become still so that your consciousness is in a kind of vacuum, you can become more awake and obtain increased energy. Then you have reached a kind of meditative state and can get in touch with your own deeper consciousness.

Carlos Castaneda said that his Mexican teacher Don Juan taught him how to use the drug mescaline in order to reach higher consciousness, and thereby to make contact with the spiritual world, and he described the effect this poison had on him. It is well-known that using drugs such as LSD, morphine, cocaine and heroin can help one to achieve other consciousness states than the one we consider to be normal. However, the use of such substances is very dangerous for the psyche and is absolutely not to be recommended.

The subconsciousness has access to a much larger information bank than the waking consciousness. In addition, it is able to communicate the body's physical problems and might provide a solution if the body or mind has difficulties. Some people obtain contact with the subconsciousness through movements (such as tai chi, qigong, yoga or similar exercises), through touch massage, aromatherapy or the like, or just by being physically still and trying to stop the thoughts. Interpretation of dreams is also a way to get in touch with the unconscious. The same applies to psychoanalysis, free-association therapy, automatic writing, bio-feedback etc. Concentration on the chakra points is a form of training that provides a better flow between the various consciousness bodies and strength to the weakest energetic areas. A simple method that is recommended by many is self-hypnosis. It is, as mentioned, a form of mind control where one tries to reprogram the mind with exercises that aim to make the brain activity function on the alpha level. This is often very similar to meditation. Such a practice is this one:

> Start with three deep in breaths. While breathing try to relax first your eyes, then the body and then you should try to release all tensions.
>
> Then you count backwards from one hundred and down to zero, a number for each out breath. Then take three deep in breaths. Feel that you are relaxing all your limbs, face and body. Then you visualize a rainbow, approach it, be on it, and then let yourself fall through the different layers/colours in it, and down to the white, healing light. Here you give yourself suggestions for how you want your life to be, what is wrong and what needs to be addressed. Then you return to normal consciousness taking the same path in reverse order.

The Silva method shows a different way to get down to the brain's alpha level and for reprogramming the mind. An exercise, which I learned at a Silva course, is as follows:

> Sit a while quietly with your eyes closed. Try to concentrate on making your breathing slow and check that you are sitting correctly, so that your back is as straight as possible, and your legs and arms are resting well. You can sit on a chair or for example on a bench or settee with your legs crossed.

When you feel ready, take a deep in breath and visualize the number three in front of you three times on an out breath. Then do the same with the number two and so with number one. Then you should have reached a nice, quiet level of the mind. To get even deeper, you should calmly count down further, from ten to one, but you must first tell yourself that you are doing this to come down to an even quieter and deeper level. Now you should be in a totally relaxed state and you should try to be like this as long as possible – as long as you find it comfortable. Then you can program yourself to tell yourself what you want to achieve of positive things, or you can try to get the mind to be completely still. When you feel finished, go back slowly, first count from one to ten, and then start again, from one to five.

Maybe the simplest way is to make use of the HeartMath techniques when one wants to teach larger groups as a whole to achieve greater harmony in life. The Institute of HeartMath has, as mentioned, shown the heart's energetic or cardio-electromagnetic communication with other organs in the body, not least with the autonomic nervous system that is controlled from the brain. The Institute has developed techniques that make the heart affect the brain so that it can be re-programmed, so that negative emotions and relationships do not tap into the body for energy. These techniques are called, respectively, Freeze Frame, Heart Lock-In and Cut-Thru. The Freeze Frame technique is to concentrate the consciousness in the heart and so to seek to achieve positive states such as the feeling of love and of caring. Heart Lock-In is to lock these positive feelings inside the heart, by focusing attention on the heart area. Cut-Thru helps reprogramming the mind from the negative to the positive, especially at the moment when we are experiencing stress. These techniques have been tested on a variety of jobs and in schools. Very positive results are reported both in attitudes and in physiological conditions. Also reported is an increased sensitivity to others, better tackling of negative feelings as well as increased co-operation, better concentration and learning abilities. These programs can best be described as a kind of heart meditation.

A variety of experiments with people who meditate or who are practising other stress-fighting methods over longer periods, have shown physiological changes such as improving blood pressure and the immune system, improvement in concentration and learning abilities, moods etc. Brain scans, which have been used by Andrew Newberg, University of Pennsylvania, and Richard Davidson, University of Wisconsin, have shown distinct differences in the activity in different parts of the brain during meditation and otherwise.[511] By using a special technique called the Hemi-Sync-technique, developed by the Monroe Institute in Virginia, USA, and with the use of an advanced sound system, it is possible to make a person go directly from an awake state right into a deep meditative state. There are specific sound frequencies that bring forth this state in a test person, who lies isolated in a small cage in order to be able to concentrate one hundred percent on the sound. Others have shown that Zen Buddhist monks in trance, who have spent many years trying to obtain deep meditation, can accomplish synchronized fluctuations of their brain waves, between the left and right halves of the brain. The same has been obtained with the use of the Hemi-Sync-technique[i] and with the same effects as the Zen Buddhist monks obtained.[512]

There does not seem to be any great differences between the various methods for prayer and meditation. In all the methods the goal is to calm the thoughts, obtain better contact with the body and dissolve the body's physical tensions, which are often due to the fact that we are clinging to certain thought structures. Whatever the technique, you have to practise often and for a long time so that the brain is reprogrammed, in order that you no longer are controlled by the programmes you learned during childhood, youth, or from the environment etc. Stan Gooch believed that meditation is a practice where you get more in touch with your subconsciousness; you learn to be alone and to be quiet. However, he rejected that you thereby will come in contact with a higher reality or something divine, neither did he seem open to the existence of a spiritual dimension. But no matter what you might think about that, by working with your consciousness, through prayer, meditation, or any other form for self-development (development of the Self), you will open yourself to non-physical impressions. You will obtain greater sensitivity and intuition, improve contact with your own and others' feelings and reactions, you even might be receptive to extrasensory impulses (ESP), perhaps even to spiritual impulses. You might begin to approach the consciousness level of the Self and adopting a better – and possibly happier – attitude towards life.

16.2. Sin and forgiveness

In relation to the discussion about prayer I would like to mention some other central concepts used in Christianity, concepts which many find difficult to understand. The term sin, so often used in the preaching of the Church, is especially provoking. As an example, see Psalm 51 in the Book of Psalms in the Bible, where the word sin is prominent. Verse 5 says: "*Surely I was sinful at birth, sinful from the time my mother conceived me.*" The Catholic Church requires its members to confess their sins, and preferably this should be done every day. Thus it is maintained that the conscience will be wakened and the human being's attitude to life will be changed. But what does it really mean to be a sinner? The original language of the New

---

i. Hemi-Sync is a shortening for hemispheric synchronization. The technique consists in submitting two slightly different audio frequencies, one for each of the receiver's ears. This will create a third frequency in the brain which produces an altered consciousness state. This can give paranormal experiences and out-of-body experiences.

Testament was Greek. The Greek word that is translated with the word sin actually means to be hitting the side of the goal or to miss it. If the words in John 8.11: "*Go now and leave your life of sin*" is translated in line with this meaning, the right translation should be "go away and keep your own centre", that is, be in yourself. But this interpretation does not fit particularly well in the aforementioned verse in the Psalms.

> Sin is separation from God.   *St John of the Cross*[513]

> When he comes, he will prove the world to be in the wrong about sin and righteousness and judgment: about sin, because people do not believe in me;   (John 16.8-9)

> ... your existence is a sin that is not comparable with any other. Because to exist is to separate yourself from something, which in this case is God; the existence itself implies separation.
> *Rab'ia*, a Sufi mystic and saint, ca 700 CE[514]

> The Hereditary sin is the consciousness ingrained tendency to approach the sensible with lust and without love.
> *Jeremi Wasiutynski*

> A great sin is to lose courage, in which case I doubt God. It is a sin to turn away from that which God has called me.
> *Sister M. Kristin Riosanu*[515]

The Augsburg Confession of faith, written in 1530, says this: (Article II):

> Also they teach that since the fall of Adam all men begotten in the natural way are born with sin, that is, without the fear of God, without trust in God, and with concupiscence; and that this disease, or vice of origin, is truly sin, even now condemning and bringing eternal death upon those not born again through Baptism and the Holy Ghost.

St Julian of Norwich said that not to think of God is the cause of all sin.[516] If the human being thought of God continuously, it would not have ill feelings or desires which lead to sin. She maintained that Jesus in a revelation assured that sin is as it should be, and that this term includes everything that is not good. People must undergo purification; and that means that everyone will have to be made to naught, as Jesus was, both in flesh and in all of our innermost feelings that are not good. Jesus' love helped people through suffering. Suffering is something temporary. It is letting us know ourselves and finally to ask for mercy. And everything will eventually be well.

St Caterina of Siena constantly accused herself of ingratitude and for being a sinner. I wonder whether St Caterina was in contact with the very highest Heaven, and that she knew that if not all of the errors (small and large) she had committed in this life – and maybe even in earlier lives, were regretted and forgiven by *herself*, she would not reach this Heaven. Perhaps that was why she prayed so intensively.

The Norwegian author Carl Fredrik Engelstad (1915-1996) has in his book about St Joan of Arc, *De levendes land* (The Land of the Living), emphasized the Church's teachings about how important it is that you confess your sins before you die and obtain forgiveness for your sins. St Joan of Arc, who according to the view of the Church was a great sinner, was burnt on the stake because she refused to confess her sins (which she probably did not understand, since she only had followed the advice of her inner voices). But the book's (and reality's) big devil in human form at the time, baron Gilles de Rais, escaped the fire because he appeared as a repentant sinner.

Also Martinus has commented those words in John 8.11: "Then neither do I condemn you," Jesus declared. "*Go now and leave your life of sin.*" His starting point was that every human being at any given time is at the peak of their development and is acting (for good or evil) according to the abilities and insight they possess at that time. They are not sinners when they do not know any better. When Jesus said that one's sins were forgiven, that was an encouragement to the person who believed himself or herself to be a sinner. Jesus preached unto people so that they – according to their experiences – could have peace of mind. He spoke to people who believed themselves victims of an avenging and punitive God and who did not have the understanding or knowledge enough to understand the real world view (which Martinus believed he had explained).[517]

Ambres has said almost the same as Martinus. There is nothing to regret, neither anything for which to request remission of sins, as long as you were acting according to the best of your ability, such as you had to act, at the time you acted – if something went wrong, it was because the capability could do no better.[518] If you later realized that you should have acted differently, that is not the same as to condemn yourself for what you have done.

Edgar Cayce constantly stressed in his readings that one had to be aware of the three important universal laws. The first is the law of love. The second is the law of cause and effect: do unto others what you would have others do unto you; we are ourselves responsible for what is happening to us, both the good and the bad things – there is no avenging God. And the third law is the law of grace. A soul can always mitigate the effects of evil or bad actions by compensating with good actions – unselfish actions for the benefit of other people. He meant that the free will was always stronger than fate. The situation in which a human being finds itself was chosen by its own free will. If a soul is regretting and asking for mercy, this will be given. It is always possible to reduce the effects of a bad karma by the help of other people's prayers, provided that one sees and regrets one's actions.[519]

Irina Tweedie's Sufi master one day requested her to write down her sins, absolutely everything she could remember, right from childhood. She had to include all secrets. The reason was that if she did not do this now, God would one day demand this of her. She had great difficulties deciding what she should write and she felt that much of what she put on paper was silly, if not shameful and embarrassing. But she finished the task and delivered the master the paper. He did not cast even a glance at the paper, tore it into pieces and threw it away. The intention was achieved – it was she who should evaluate herself.

These opinions and attitudes I understand better when I hear stories about people who are about to die, and at the moment they believe they are dying, they see their life passing in revue. Then they are presented with the wrongs they have thought and/or done, when it is too late to do anything about it in the life that now is reaching its end. We ought to be more aware our actions and thoughts, so that we are not hurting or damaging anyone. If every evening we making a habit of reviewing the day's events and thinking about what has happened – what we have done, said or thought, and what we could have done differently – then we may obtain peace of mind and a more harmonious life. But that does not prevent the law of karma (if it is real) taking its effect, if you have inflicted pain or suffering on other people. Such an effect we should seek to avoid, if nothing else, by asking, for example, for forgiveness while we can. That may save us from painful thoughts and regrets later in life, especially when the time comes for us to leave this world.

This is in line with what the Theosophists have explained: when the etheric body is losing contact with the physical body, the Ego (which in Theosophical terminology is the higher mental body) is reliving its total life – all details are displayed. Emanuel Swedenborg too mentioned an existence where the deceased was in a sort of purging and training process for a period of time. From the near-death experiences we have learnt that we will be held responsible for everything we have done, in the sense that we ourselves must acknowledge what we should have done differently and how our actions have affected others. This is also in accordance with the Islamic and Christian teachings about the Judgment Day, and with the Christian teachings about purgatory (purification), and the Christians emphasis on repentance, penitential exercises and remission of sins.

The Egyptian Book of the Dead explains that the deceased's heart is weighed on arrival to the Kingdom of Death, to check if the deceased is worthy of entry. *The Tibetan Book of the Dead* describes, as we have seen, what to say to the dying and the dead at different times, to help them through the experiences they will meet. Jes Bertelsen's book *Døden og Dødsprocessen* (Death and the Death process) is about some of the same, and includes also how to prepare for death. The Dalai Lama has said that in order to get a good death, we need to live a good life. We cannot hope for a peaceful death if our lives and our thoughts are full of emotions.[520]

Most people have a conscience, and may be this feeling is actually a reminder of what a human being might meet at the gate of death. But if we are to be judged, it seems that it is we ourselves who are our strictest – and only – judge. Undoubtedly, it will be of help to ask forgiveness for our actions before we die, in order to get peace of mind and to facilitate the transition to the spiritual life, but the best will of course be to adapt our life the best way possible so that we do not have a bad conscience. What seems most important is to ask ourselves that which is highlighted in the NDE reports– what could we have done differently to ease life for our fellow human beings and other living beings?

16.3. Spiritual development

Throughout time there have been some individuals who have mentally reached above the physical world of the senses and ultimately gained insight into the spiritual world. They have tried to describe those experiences and the accounts, whether they are from America, Asia, Africa or Europe, are strangely alike despite their cultural diversity. In ancient Egypt and in the Greek culture there were cults and mystery schools – of which the schools of the Dionysian cult and the Pythagoras cult are among the best known from Greece. In these schools one could be initiated in the mystics' secret teachings. The Order of the Free Masons, which we encounter in Mozart's opera *The Magic Flute*, also uses an initiation procedure. Rudolf Steiner called these initiations a 'way to knowledge' about the higher worlds. Jes Bertelsen has explained that self-development is to expand, integrate and balance the personality in an ecological and cyclic togetherness with other people and with the Earth. Some designate this as an individuation process. But anyone who wants to reach the unity consciousness of the Divine must renounce experiences and identity. One will then find that the feeling of personal identity is replaced by a compassionate feeling for other people. Both Jes Bertelsen and Sogyal Rinpoche highlight the necessity of having a personal teacher (guru) in this endeavour.[521]

The Danish theologian and priest Lene Højholt has interpreted John's Gospel as a description of the way to become Jesus' equal – Jesus' friend, – note the words in John 15.15: *"I no longer call you servants, because a servant does not know his master's business. Instead, I have called you friends, for everything that I learned from my Father I have made known to you."* She believes that the Gospel describes six stages on this road, respectively:[522]

The phase of calling	-	chapter 1, 2 and 3
The phase of decision-making	-	chapter 4, 5 and 6
The phase of accepting	-	chapter 7, 8 and 9
The phase of discipleship	-	chapter 10 and 11
The phase of serving	-	chapter 12 and 13
The phase of friendship	-	chapter 14 and 15

That means that the disciples in the final phase have obtained the Christ consciousness – have become equal to Jesus. A similar interpretation can be made from the Gospel of Thomas, one of the Gnostic Gospels found at Nag Hammadi. Most of the Jesus' words here may indicate a spiritual guidance through these phases. See, for example, verse 14 where Jesus says to Thomas: "*I am no longer thy master; for thou hast drunk, thou art inebriated from the bubbling spring which is mine and which I sent forth.*" This can be understood so that Thomas has been inaugurated so he has got the Christ consciousness (the bubbling spring). And in verse 112 Jesus says: "*He who drinks from my mouth will become like me. As for me, I will become what he is, and what is hidden will be revealed to him.*"[523]

Many people are today working with self-development, and some are also seeking spiritual development. Many people are offering help with such work, but it is not easy to know where to go or who gives guidance you can trust. It is said that you will always come to the right places and meet the people you need to meet in order to get ahead – you might need difficulties and opposition. But it might be a good thing to have a certain base from where to start when deciding where to begin. Firstly it is important to consider what you primarily want to obtain, and what you need to work with. Some schools are working mainly with the physical (which corresponds to the root chakra), others are mainly working with the emotional, that is the feelings (the abdominal/hara chakra, the solar plexus and the heart chakra), others again are working on the intellectual plane (the throat chakra), and a few provide actual spiritual guidance (the pineal chakra). Either way, whatever work is done with one chakra will also affect the other energy centres in the body, and ultimately dissolve bodily and emotional blocks. Sheer physical training, where the emphasis is placed on the body, breath and awareness of movement, may be the way to go as a first step. Gestalt therapy, emotionally-based massage and special techniques for connecting with the subconsciousness may be the gateway to awareness of the feelings and emotions. Many meditation methods can, in my judgment, be more intellectual approaches, and require strong concentration and determination of the individual. But all types can be combined, which is also being done in some schools – perhaps with the most exciting results. Surely it is both inspiring and giving, in relation to spiritual development, to meet other people in a group who dare to give of themselves and with whom one can share one's experiences.

Teresa of Avila has described her way towards god-consciousness as follows: She called her mind the little butterfly, and described the progress towards unity with the Divine as a seven-step staircase, or like going through seven Houses.[524] The first three steps apply to the ordinary mind or the ego, the manifest world of thoughts and sensing. The first House she called *humility*. There the ego is still associated with other beings and to the comfort outside the castle (the inner awareness). It must therefore submit to a long and difficult period with strict discipline in order to be able to turn inward. In the second House, which is the practice of prayer, intellectual studies, constructive actions (*edification*), and good company will strengthen the desire and the ability to go inward. In the third House, the House of a perfect life, discipline and ethics are necessary for what is to come. In the fourth House, using what she called the *Prayer of Recollection and the Prayer of Quietness*, a natural or transpersonal grace will be felt. Here you will achieve peace; the activities of the mind such as memory, thoughts and sensing will automatically be lowered, thereafter you will begin to open up for the inner room with the related grace (as Teresa called it). This is the level of spiritual reassurance, because you find that the self is soothed, albeit without the 'I' becoming transcended. In the fifth House you experience through the *Prayer of Oneness* a spiritual unification, where the soul directly experiences the Spirit that is living in the very soul of the heart. In the sixth House are the Lover and the Beloved, that is the butterfly and God, the soul and the uncreated Spirit, one. The experience in the fifth House will last only for a short moment, possibly up to half an hour in the case of Teresa. In the sixth House the experience may last for longer periods of time. Here the soul is completely absorbed in the Divine, and when separation happens – when the soul consciousness returns to the physical body – this is experienced as a fierce sorrow or pain. The tool for being able to follow this path forward – to be able to experience these stages – is what Teresa described as prayer. In the seventh House a veil will be removed from the soul's eye, so that "in a peculiar way, it now sees and understands something of the wonderful, which it receives in this House through an intellectual vision. By an unfailing presentation of the truth, the Holy Trinity shows itself, all three persons, as a fire, who throws its light into the spirit, like a shiny bright cloud."

Master Eckhart has said this about the spiritual unification:[525]

> Whatever comes to you in this manner gives you pure existence and durability; but what you are seeking or loving outside of this, is destructive. You can take this in whatever way you want and wherever you want, but it perverts everything. This birth alone gives however, pure existence, everything else perverts. Nevertheless, in this birth you will get a share in the Divine influence and all of its gifts.

Jes Bertelsen describes in his book *Hjertebøn og Ikonmystik* (The Heart Prayer and Icon Mysticism) the mysticism of the Eastern Christian Church, and also elements from the mysticism of Western Christianity.[526] His starting point is especially the practice of meditating on icons. Icons are painted with the purpose of being an aid for the different levels of consciousness. You must use the type of icon that applies to the level of consciousness where you are, if such a meditation shall be of any use. The icon's colour scheme is important in that regard. Jes Bertelsen wrote that colours are fluctuations that have symbol values. He mentioned that:

Red	represents	passion and suffering
Black	–	death and transformation
Green	–	trust and pregnancy
Blue	–	transcendence
White	–	eternity
Gold	–	the uncreated light

In this book Jes Bertelsen offers a guide to what he calls the heart prayer. He has pointed out that all the major traditions have a heart prayer practice, where the stages and the introductions are very similar. Within Buddhism, this prayer is often built up around a mantra of the Buddha's name, in Islam around the name of Allah and in the Christian tradition around the name of Jesus Christ. The essence of the heart prayer tradition is to bring God's name into the heartbeats. It is only in the first, perhaps five to ten years, that it is necessary to use words. The prayer will eventually be placed in the heart, and follow the heart sound. Then the words will disappear and there comes a kind of non-linguistic awareness. Bertelsen mentioned that some of the monks at the mountain Athos in Greece practised the heart prayer for eight/ten hours every day for five/ten years, and then they visualized Mary, Jesus' mother, for five to ten years. Only then were they ready to work on the highest level, the Christ level, in their meditation. At the higher steps of the meditation process one is also trying spiritual visualization, which differs greatly from the visualization used in self-development work. Jes Bertelsen has warned against going into such a practice without the guidance of an experienced teacher.

Rudolf Steiner argued that in every human being there are abilities that can help humanity to achieve recognition of the spiritual worlds.[527] Anyone who obtains contact with those abilities will also be able to participate in and testify to the existence of the spiritual worlds. At all times there have been mystery schools where it has been taught that which the spiritual sciences teach. We will not have the power to develop towards something higher if we do not first develop the feeling that there is something greater than ourselves. This requires that we develop awe, worship and admiration. This is done by being full of love towards the fellow beings, which requires a continuous spiritual process. Humanity's task on Earth is to be co-creating. That is, one has to have contact with the spiritual world and bring the creative forces that are to be found there, into the earthly existence. Steiner further explained that thoughts and feelings are real facts. An incorrect thought may be just as devastating for other's thoughts as a rifle bullet which can destroy a physical object. So we must almost be more careful with what we say and think, than with what we do in our physical actions. People must be aware of their soul and their spirit, not just the body. To acquire knowledge of the higher worlds – to penetrate the secrets of existence – Rudolf Steiner called spiritual science. He explained that insight into a higher world depends on the etheric body and the astral body having managed to develop the higher organs that this requires. Through meditation, concentration and contemplation, the astral body will transform itself.

Steiner explained that the Christians' initiation of old contained seven emotional experiences or seven steps. These he described as follows:

> 1. Washing. The human being must be able to look back at the lower realms in nature, and also on anyone who is lower in the social hierarchy, and bow to them in appreciation and say "I owe you my life". When the physical body is thoroughly trained in this, it will affect the soul (compare Jesus' washing of the disciples' feet).
>
> 2. Scourging. The human being must imagine that it carries all the sorrows and sufferings of the world, but still able to stand upright.
>
> 3. Coronation with thorns. The human being must imagine that its holiest values are being covered with ridicule and derision, but still able to stand upright.
>
> 4. Crucifixion. The human being must imagine that its body is as alien as a coat or a piece of wood. It must not connect its 'I' with its body.
>
> 5. Hell. This is also called the mystical death. One experiences diving down to the ancient ground of evil, pain, sorrow and suffering. Everything that lives off the evil at the bottom of the human soul must be felt.
>
> 6. Resurrection. The human being feels here at one with the Earth body, and that it belongs together with the whole Earth.
>
> 7. Ascent to Heaven. This condition cannot be described with words. Here one obtains knowledge. One is accepted in the spiritual world, but has the opportunity to return to the physical world.

Steiner claimed that this initiation process would affect the astral body through conscious daily activity. The astral body is then so transformed that it can look into the higher worlds. The last stage, and the most difficult, is to instil in the etheric body the organs which the astral body has acquired through this process, so that one can obtain communication between the spiritual existence and the physical, which means that the human being then has become enlightened.

Ken Wilber believes that the Tibetan Buddhism is the best guide for the development of higher consciousness, because it relates to the various states of consciousness, which Wilber describes as respectively psychic (this is not the abilities of the psyche, but the first level of higher consciousness), subtle, causal and the highest or the outermost *(the ultimate)*. This form of Buddhism has three stages on the spiritual path, which are known as Hinayana, Mahayana and Vajrayana.[528] On the lowest step, Hinayana, one uses a form of meditation in which one is to focus on nothing, just accept whatever is popping up in the mind. One shall not consider it, reject it or follow it. One shall only witness that it is coming, and then let it go. The next step, Mahayana, aims to achieve individual enlightenment, but one is thereby disregarding that also others should be enlightened. It is only by seeking enlightenment for all beings that one comes beyond one's own ego. And that is the purpose of the final step, Vajrayana. A form of meditation at this stage is called *tonglen*, which is said to be a practice that is so powerful and transforming, that it said to have been kept secret until relatively recently. In this meditation you shall try to imagine or visualize a person you know and like and who you know is having a hard time. When you breathe in, you shall try to imagine that everything this person has of sufferings and hardships is stitched to a thick tar-holding cloud, which you then inhale through your nose and let sink into your heart. All this pain is then held in your heart. When you then exhale, you shall send all sorts of good thoughts to the person in the form of a healing, liberating light. And then you do the same with the place where the person lives, with that special city, with that particular country and in the end with the whole globe. This is done because you recognize that there is only one Spirit, and everyone is part of this Spirit.

Among the Gnostic scriptures from Nag Hammadi, there are texts that describe how to proceed in order to achieve spiritual enlightenment, something the historian in religion Elaine Pagels (b.1943), professor at Princeton University, writes about in the book *The Gnostic Gospels.* An author of such a text, Zostrianos, has explained that you first must stop all desire, which probably needs to be done through asceticism. Secondly you have to stop the chaos of thoughts, and then search for peace of mind by the help of meditation. The advanced student will then experience receiving the Light, in which the mind opens up to the eighth heaven with the souls and angels there, singing hymns to the ninth heaven and its powers. Elaine Pagels maintains that many Gnostics claimed that it was ignorance and not sin that caused human suffering. Knowledge was received if one had self-insight. Elaine Pagels says that according to the Gospel of Thomas Jesus said that if you manage to know that which is inside you, it will save you. If you do not, it will destroy you.[529] That is, one must work with one's self in order to gain spiritual insight, in the same way as if you were in psychotherapy. This is lonely work. Anyone who achieves such insight, called gnosis, will no longer be a Christian, but has become Christ.

This is why Gnosticism was considered dangerous by the Orthodox Church fathers. Gnosticism had a religious perspective that entailed a strong contrast to the kind of Christianity that became the early Christian Church. The Gnostics, who would be Christ like, would not submit to the Church's institutional structure, with its bishops, priests, creeds, canonical writings and rituals, that maintained it was the absolute authority and required blind obedience. Submission was only one point where Gnosticism was in opposition to the early Orthodox Church fathers. The most important was probably that the Gnostics did not see Jesus as God, but as a teacher. Neither did they accept that the salvation of mankind would come through

Jesus, as an event that would come to the human beings from the outside. This was something that had to come to the individual from within, through a spiritual awakening. Finally, in her book Elaine Pagels asked the question – where one might find the source for religious authority. She said that for a Christian the answer would have to depend on whether it is one's own experience or the Scripture, the rituals and the priesthood that are most important.

Huston Smith wrote that the Sufis – the Muslim mystics – wanted to come closer to God. To reach this goal, they devised three different methods, respectively the way of the heart, the way of ecstasy and the intuitive ability to distinguish.[530] By devotion, probably in the form of prayer and meditation, one could experience "God's love in the centre of the Universe", as Huston Smith said it. The highest bliss is to experience this love and to give it on to others. But also through ecstasy, which normally could be obtained through dancing, one could obtain contact with the Divine.[i] The last way demanded long spiritual training, which Huston Smith did not further elaborate. But he explained that the mysticism of love would give knowledge of the heart, that the ecstasy or the trance would give visual or visionary knowledge and that the intuitive mysticism would give direct acknowledgement of the Divine. According to my understanding, this means that the knowledge of the heart will make you understand your fellow beings and give you compassion; that visionary knowledge will give you astral experiences where the fantasy must be used to interpret the symbols you see, hear or feel; and that the last type will give you a mental understanding – the knowledge of the Self, which is a spiritual understanding.

Martinus explained that the resurrection of Jesus at Easter morning was not the most important happening in the life of Jesus.[531] He called this resurrection the second resurrection. The most important message was the preaching and the demonstration of the "Heavenly realm" that was to come, as something within the human beings. By this he meant the ability to live in contact with the laws of the Universe, an ability to be of help and a blessing for the totality, the ability to be – not as someone bothering others or other living creatures in their existence, on the contrary being an inspirer, life-giver and happiness promoter and through this serve as a life source for all beings, as Martinus expressed it. This new consciousness attitude is "the new birth of spirit", and that is the great resurrection and revelation in the coming of Jesus on Earth. This is a cosmic consciousness attitude, which makes up the Heavenly realm's kingdom on Earth. It is only possible to obtain this resurrection and to make it exist as the total result of the most perfect love for all beings, and through this be the only true Christianity or

---

i. I have attended a Sufi dance – a whirling meditation, so-called dancing Dervish (dhikr) from the group called the Mawlawis. The dancer had a long, white, wide dress and he was whirling around himself on a small spot not bigger than his feet. I counted more that 300 circlings without stop. I believe he stopped at about 350 circlings. He had then complete control of himself and walked slowly out of the room without any sign of dizziness.

the saviour of humanity. In order to come closer to this cosmic consciousness, one has to work with one's own spiritual development.

The Bulgarian mystic *Peter Deunov*, who later used the spiritual name Beinsa Douno (1864-1944), and his disciple *Aivanhov* taught how one should work in order to gain greater love ability, as well as wisdom and harmony in existence.[532] They also taught attitudes toward food and physical training, as well as meditation and visualization techniques. The philosophy of Deunov was that it was love and wisdom that created life, and that these energies also have the power to reshape the world, our lives, our society and our homes. If we accept love and wisdom, truth and righteousness will come. Deunov taught that God is the innermost principle of Love, Wisdom and Truth, as well as the essence of the Universe and life and the actual reality. God is manifest through the human beings as the light of our spirits. The purpose of life is fellowship with God or with those principles.

Some people have a strong urge to get close to the Divine. It is this urge that made saints such as Francis of Assisi and Teresa of Avila devote so much of their time to intense prayer and meditation. Such mystics are experiencing something that others only may get a glimpse of, a timeless and peaceful mood, a blissful state, something similar to using drugs. With today's medical terminology one might say that they are getting a strong dose of endorphins in this way, and if you have experienced it once, you will have to have more. Eventually, the interest and engagement in the outside world is withering, and one wants only to proceed deeper and deeper into the mind. However, Teresa of Avila never lost contact with the outside world. On the contrary, she was very active as head for a monastic movement. Francis of Assisi had a strong compassion with the outer world, but ignored, as mentioned, his own physical needs and lived so intensely into Jesus' woes that he got the stigmata. He ate very little and exposed himself to cold. Francis became eventually physically weakened and plagued by diseases.

Also some of the great Hindu mystics believed that the starting point for spiritual development was the desire to be freed from sorrow, joy and all manner of worldly benefits.[i] I then have to ask whether it is appropriate to withdraw from the outside world in this way. If we shall manage to take care of God's gifts, we must also take care of our body and necessarily adapt to the world in which we live.

When I had read Jes Bertelsen's book *Hjertebøn og Ikonmystik* (The Heart Prayer and Icon mysticism), where he writes of the Greek monks who meditated many hours each day during most of their lives but only managed to get a few glimpse of the Divine, I wondered whether what I have written above is correct. If such meditation does not give my Ego any advantage, why should I employ such self-control? And if there are no consequences

---

i. See *Spiritual Instruction by Sri Ramana Maharshi*, instruction no 2: "An intense longing for the removal of sorrow and attainment of joy and an intense aversion for all kinds of mundane pleasure."

for me neither in this life, nor in the next, why should I follow this ascetic life? However, both Jes Bertelsen and Sogyal Rinpoche have said that it is important to be prepared for dying. Higher consciousness will make this meeting easy. Both these two and also others, as Martinus, highlight that this also will facilitate one's karma in the coming life. There is therefore only one way to go, and that is to work with oneself to become a better human being. To do that you need to know yourself, know the reasons why you are doing that which you do, and your reactions. Meditation is a major help to go inward into yourself. If you want to be more satisfied with life, or want a better physical and mental existence, meditation is the way to go. And if thought has the power to heal a person, perhaps our thoughts also create the reality around us, both for the good and for the bad. Marcello Haugen's words, which are referenced in the chapter on meditation, are easy to follow.

I shall not go further into the different steps or different ways of initiation. Anyone who is interested may search available literature. However, that there is a process to follow which provides extraordinary capabilities is witnessed not only from what I have written here. We find it, in what Rudolf Steiner has mentioned, in similar stories in all cultures, as well as from our own time. Mircea Eliade has written about the shamans in general, and the Norwegian assistant professor Brita Pollan has described the Sami way. Joseph Campbell has described such initiations in his books on mythology. Irina Tweedie has described her learning period with a Sufi master. Yogananda has written about his development. Sogyal Rinpoche has described the Tibetan way. Among the Christian saints and mystics we find the same story, although with somewhat different ways of development. And not to forget Jes Bertelsen who has written extensively about consciousness and the liberation of the consciousness.

Anyone working with his or her own spirituality, as well as the person who is or becomes psychotic, will, initially, obtain contact with the same spiritual field. The first field one meets is the astral field. The psychotic will not understand what is happening and will often be thrown out of it or will be mentally lost in this field. It is very important to have a strong 'I' and a proper foundation when embarking on the spiritual road. The myth of the Minotaur – the man-eating monster, part human and part animal, in the Cretan labyrinth, where Theseus, thanks to the help of Ariadne's thread, found his way back to the world – is perhaps a picture of the difficulties one might encounter on this path, and how to find the way out of the problems. The first step on the spiritual path is, therefore, to work with the 'I' and with the body. You must have a good grounding. A strong 'I' requires good contact with the body, and that is obtained if you have a good 'I'.

We must be conscious of our limitations, our dependence on the rest of the world and of the limitlessness which the existence seems to be. We must be conscious that our thoughts and feelings in certain cases can be perceived by our surroundings and also affect the environment – and then in turn also ourselves. And we must be aware that time is a relative term and that all things may be happening right now, at one and the same time. If we do not take into consideration that the human being is something more than matter and biological or chemical processes, and are working to further develop our 'I', we will not get a deeper understanding of the human being nor of other living organisms, nor of this life.

17. Myths, Symbols and Rituals

Myths are one form for communicating what people know – or perceive – about our mystical existence. Storytelling is another form, which is closer to the human experience, and often also provides a metaphorical representation of the human psyche. Religion, as I see it, is a further refinement of myths. What can be said to be the same in religions and myths is that they tell, in parables (as in the Bible), of people's experiences or images that are understandable in the culture where they have their origin. People of today are often not aware of these cultures and such pictorial language, and will therefore have difficulty understanding the stories. Religion and myth frames and structures a community. Institutionalized symbols and rituals, religious or secular, will ensure that significant events are remembered (such as a Christmas celebration in memory of the birth of Jesus), or help individuals to deal with life's joyful or difficult events (such as baptismal, wedding and funeral rituals). They tell stories that may help you to understand what you are experiencing.

If you need to work on your individuation process, the use of symbols is an essential aid.

We find symbols and signs everywhere, in language, in mathematics, in religion and in art, but also in the form of advertisements for goods and products. Not least in our dreams we meet symbols as images of our innermost feelings and desires. Human beings need symbols to express feelings and fantasies that not so easily are communicated in words, and in order to be able to relate to the incomprehensible. The word symbol means characteristic or mark. It represents something other than what it seems to be at first. A cross, for example, which consists of two lines that intersect each other at a right angle, can express many different things, depending on the context in which it is presented. Christians will immediately see it as representing the cross on which Jesus was crucified, but it is also a symbol for Christianity, so the person wearing a badge in the shape of a cross is demonstrating that he or she is a Christian. Ken Wilber distinguished between symbols and signs. He considered that a symbol is transcending and representing something higher than what it looks like, something that cannot be rendered directly, while a sign represents something juxtaposed; something at the same level. Stanislav Grof also described symbols in this way, referring to Jung's understanding of them. Jung believed that symbols represented a higher level of consciousness – a transcendental reality. In daily speech, however, the terms are often used interchangeably.

A Greek Orthodox priest once pointed out that when we worship an icon, it is not an image of the deity, but the human face of the Godhead that people worship. The Godhead itself cannot be depicted, because a human being cannot imagine the nature of the Godhead. Symbols as images of the Divine or creative forces have been used through all times.

However a symbol does not necessarily have to be a picture or an object; it might well be a living creature, a tree, a plant, or a mountain. Cows are, as we know, sacred animals in India. In ancient Egypt the gods were depicted with animal faces or bodies. The Egyptian goddess Hathor was depicted with the horns of a cow and had the cow as her characteristic sign. Animal worship was at its highest in Egypt with the sacred bull, Apis, worshiped at the god Ptah's temple in Memphis. Apis, which was chosen to be sacrificed at specific religious holidays due to its special appearance, was honoured as a God, because people saw it as a reincarnation of Ptah. After the sacrifice it was considered as Osiris, the god of the underworld. Dion Fortune explained that images that people visualize, such as images of pagan gods, always have their basis in a natural force.[534] Due to peoples' visualization abilities, a symbol will eventually be animated and activate the power that people give it. She maintained that this power is very real. It is the key to talisman magic and to rituals performed to consecrate artefacts, as well as to obtain cooperation from the gods or the forces of nature through for example music, rhythm, smell or colour.

A cross, where all the arms are of equal length, is said to be the oldest of humanity's symbols, as traces of it are found everywhere. The horizontal bar is often representing matter or the Earth, and the vertical bar the Sky or the Spirit. The four endpoints of the cross stand for the four Earth corners. This equal-armed cross has been changed through the ages and in the different cultures. The pharaohs of ancient Egypt are pictured with the ankh symbol, where one arm of the cross is transformed into something close to a circle. This sign symbolizes peace. In discoveries in Turkey from the bronze ages, from about 3000 BCE, we find the wheeled cross, where the equal-armed cross is surrounded by a circle. From India around 2500 BCE and from Assyria around 1800 BCE there came the swastika symbol, in which the outer half of all the cross's arms are bent. When bent with an angle to the right it represents the masculine principle and to the left it represents the feminine principle. This symbol has had different meanings in different cultures. For some people the cross was a symbol of the creative forces, for fertility and for the Sun.

In some cultures, however, fertility was connected with the Moon (the lunar cycles and the menstruation periods in women is almost of the same length), and the symbol of fertility has often been something like the Moon. Mircea Eliade has shown that one such symbol is the ox's horns.[535] A crescent-shaped horn clearly refers to the Moon. Two horns facing each other represent the entire lunar period. Eliade believed that wherever the ox's horns are used as a symbol, it represents The Great Goddess or Magna Mater. Animals that disappear for a period are identified with the Moon. Eliade mentioned as examples snails (which disappear into their houses), bears (which hibernate in wintertime) and frogs (which disappear into lakes and later resurface). Also snakes are considered as a symbol of the Moon because they often disappear, but also because they shed their skin and thus are considered to be immortal and reincarnating. The snakes are often found lying in one or multiple rings, and it is said that the number of rings are equivalent to the moon-days. (Rings are considered as lunar qualities.) The Moon gives fertility, knowledge and immortality, and all of the aforementioned animals are associated with these qualities, although the snake or serpent perhaps is the strongest symbol in this regard.

We find the serpent as a symbol in many contexts. In Genesis in the Old Testament, it is the serpent that tempted Eve with the apple from the Tree of Knowledge with the result that Adam and Eve were expelled from Paradise. The serpent is smarter than all other animals and is a seducer. In some places it is equated with Satan or the Devil (as in Rev. 20.2). In some religions and cultures it is, however, a sign of wisdom. The Caduceus – the Mercury wand which is the symbol of the God Mercury (Hermes in Greek) – is adorned with two snakes, although these are said to have been olive branches originally. The two snakes, which twine around each other and around the wand, are said to symbolize the masculine and the feminine aspect of existence. These are the eternal alternating forces of the Universe – the outgoing and the recipient energies. Snakes have also been connected to medical science since antiquity as they were the symbol used by the Greek physician Asclepius, considered the God of healing. The symbol was a wand with a snake. In Epidaurus, there was a snake enclosure where patients were placed, because it was believed that this would heal them. In ancient Egypt the pharaohs had a cobra figure in their headdress as symbol of wisdom.

Holy numbers

According to both Pythagoras and the Jewish tradition numbers are holy, and each number has its special meaning. But should any number be extra holy, it ought to be the irrational number 1.618033 ... with an infinite number of decimal places. This is the number of the so-called golden ratio and is called *phi*. *Phi* is a Greek letter and is written Φ. It describes the relationship when a line of a particular length,'ac', is divided into two ('ab' and 'bc'), so that the entire line's relationship with the longest part is equal to the longest part compared to the shortest part, as follows: (ac/ab = ab/bc). Furthermore, a rectangle may have such a golden ratio, when the ratio between the longest and shortest side is equal to phi. If you create a square out of the shortest side of such a rectangle, the rest will be a golden rectangle. When this is done again and again, and the corner points then are connected with a curved line, we will get a so-called phi-spiral or a logarithmic spiral. This relationship and this spiral pattern we find many places: in architecture as in cathedrals, in pine cones, in sunflower seeds, in shells, in the crown leaves of flowering plants, and strangely enough also in the design of galaxies. Already during the construction of the first great pyramid in Egypt – Zoser's step pyramid in Zakkara, from the third dynasty, from around 2650 BCE – the golden ratio was known. (Imhotep is believed to have been the architect. He was later declared divine.)[536] Colin Wilson has written in his book about Atlantis that there is a phi-relationship between the three pyramids in Giza. Euclid (300 BCE) is said to have given an accurate definition of the golden ratio.

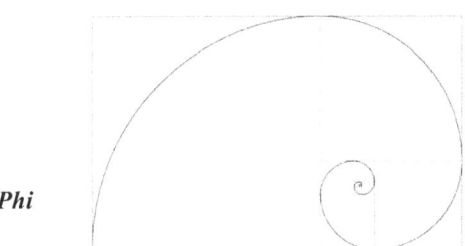

Phi

Another magic number is 3.14 ... also with an infinite number of decimal places. This irrational number (is called *pi* and is written π. It expresses the ratio between a circle's circumference (c) and its diameter (d), so that $c/d = \pi$. A circle's area (a) is calculated to be $a = \pi r2$, where r is the circle's radius. But *pi* is also used in other mathematical formulas, as in the calculation of certain movements, vibrations and waves. This number has also been known since antiquity. In the tomb of Hesy (also a person from Egypt's third dynasty, around 2650 BCE) descriptions and articles have been found indicating that the people must have known the number pi and been advanced in other mathematical calculations. Also Archimedes (around 250 BCE) knew the number, even though he has not left behind a calculation with as many decimal places.

In ancient Egypt the number ten seems to have been special. The Jewish Kabbalah is built on the number ten as there are ten sephiroth, though some argue that it also can be seen as built over the number seven, see the comparison with the chakras as mentioned below. We find the number seven in myths and in religious explanations about the creation of the world. This is a very old symbol that is attributed particularly great importance. The creation story, as told in Genesis, explains that the Earth was created in seven days. Revelation tells us about the seven spirits of God, the seven churches, the seven stars and the seven candlesticks. In the book *Talking with Angels* the number seven is often mentioned. Also Martinus and Ambres referred to this number several times. Gurdjieff explained the law of the number seven and the law of the octave in his teachings, which are ideas that also Pythagoras taught.[537] According to these laws all processes in the Universe are vibrating in seven successive steps. Helena Blavatsky pointed out that numbers are holy and have specific meanings in most mystical traditions, and that the Jewish Kabbalah, the Egyptian mysteries and the Hindu teachings are in accordance in regard to the importance of numbers. She explained that the number seven has a special occult meaning which she did not elaborate further, and that seven is life's number.[538] Thus it is no wonder that even in exoteric (published and known, non-secret) writings the number seven appears in many contexts. Blavatsky has devoted a chapter in the book *The Secret Doctrine* to describe the use of the number seven in old books, such as the Indian Puranas and Vedas, the ancient Egyptian writings and the Kabbalah. The number seven is also found in the verses that Blavatsky called *The Book of Dzyan*. Blavatsky claimed that this book is part of Gautama Buddha's esoteric teachings (the teachings for the initiated). Here are listed the seven sublime men, the seven truths, the seven sons, the seven eternities, etc. Pythagoras is supposed to have declared that the number seven is convenable and agreeable to holy and divine things.[539]

But a common explanation as to why the number seven has been ascribed special importance as a symbol is that in antiquity there were observed seven wandering stars in the sky (compared with the other stars that stood firm – the fixed stars). These seven wanderers were the Sun, the Moon, Mercury, Venus, Mars, Jupiter and Saturn. All were attributed divine qualities, and were eventually also worshipped as gods. The seven days of the week are said to have been attributed to these seven planets as far back as the old Babylonians (about 6-700 BCE). And as most people may know, the names of the weekdays are inspired by these gods (although it should also be noted that the Romans had another division of the months and other terms for the days):

Norwegian	*English*	*French*	*Planet or God:*
Mandag	Monday	Lundi	Moon or Luna
Tirsdag	Tuesday	Mardi	Mars or Tyr (German god of war)
Onsdag	Wednesday	Mercredi	Mercury or Odin
Torsdag	Thursday	Jeudi	Jupiter or Tor
Fredag	Friday	Vendredi	Venus or Frøya
Lørdag	Saturday	Samedi	Saturn (french: sabbati dies – the day of the Sabbath)
Søndag	Sunday	Dimanche	Sun (french: dies Dominicus, the day of the Lord)

Another explanation as to why the number seven has special significance, is the Moon's orbital period around the Earth (29 days, 44 minutes and 2.9 seconds) and women's menstruation cycle (about 28 days), which are both approximately four times seven. Neither the Moon nor the planets, however, have a turnaround time that gives an exact number by dividing with seven. Mercury uses 88 Earth days to go around the Sun, which corresponds to 7 x 12.57 days. Venus uses 224.7 Earth days = 7 x 32.1 days. Mars uses 687 Earth days or approximately 1.88 years = 7 x 98.14 days. Jupiter uses 11.86 years = 7 x 1.69 years. Saturn uses 29.46 years = 7 x 4.21 years. Some of the most prominent star constellations have seven visible stars. This is especially the Plough [Big Dipper] (Great Bear – Ursae Major), which is a marked constellation as it turns around the Polar Star (Alpha Ursae Minoris – the celestial north pole). But this is the situation now in our time. When the pyramid of Cheops (Khufu) was built (ca. 2650 BCE), the star Thuban (Alpha Draconis – in the star constellation the Dragon) was the polar star. The constellation the Pleiades, or the Seven Sisters, is near the ecliptic; and the Sun and the planets which are all following the same path across the sky, the ecliptic, will periodically come close to the this constellation. In Greek mythology the Seven Sisters are said to represent the seven daughters of the Titan Atlas, although it is difficult to see more than six stars with the naked eye. This star group has in time immemorial been linked with the maritime and the agricultural seasons' beginning and end, as it is in the Eastern sky in the spring mornings and in the Western sky in the mornings in the autumn.

In music, the scale which is mainly used in the West is composed of seven whole tones, the tones C, D, E, F, G, A and H. when we also include the next tone, the higher C (C') we have an octave (8 tones). The relationship between C and C' is such that the largest of these has an audio frequency vibration the double of the first. However, not all cultures or all types of music are using a scale with seven tones, and not all seven tone scales are equal. But in the West, as well as in India and Iran, it is mainly the seven tone scale that is used in music, so here too the number seven is prominent.

When we consider the colours, the white light that shines through a prism is split in seven main colours: red, orange, yellow, green, blue, indigo, and violet. This is also the main colours of a rainbow. Mircea Eliade has said that in many cosmologies the rainbow has been regarded as a bridge between Heaven and Earth, and that the rainbow's seven colours reflect the seven heavens. He referred to that the use of this symbol can be found both in India and Mesopotamia, and in Judaism.[540] Actually, there are not seven distinct colours, but a gradual transition from one shade to the next, both in a prism and in the rainbow. It was Isaac Newton who first split the light through a prism. It is said that he used the seven main colours of the spectrum, which he then could see, paralleling the notes in the scale.

But probably the most important argument for giving the number seven special significance is that people who are clairvoyant see the energies that are found around the human body centred in seven main chakras, and that the mystics talk about seven heavens (see the mystics' explanations about consciousness bodies and consciousness planes with seven main levels). Also in Martinus' cosmology there are seven levels and the Theosophists talk about seven root races in the development of the world. Stan Gooch believed, however, that wherever the number seven appears in explanations or statements, there is reason for scepticism.

More about myths, stories and fairy tales

How do you explain something you do not fully understand? Why is children told the story that babies are brought by the stork or that Mr Sandman helps us to sleep? How to explain why people sometimes behave irrationally? Or how to explain how people and the world have been created and evolved? All cultures have their creation stories, more or less varied. When Charles Darwin presented his evolutionary explanation, he attracted fierce resistance. The same type of resistance met Galileo Galilei when he said that he could prove that the Earth was spinning. Why do people find it so difficult to accept a different explanation for the phenomena of the Universe than what they have been brought up to believe? And why do they become so angry, yes almost hateful towards whatever is new? Then obviously it is safer to use myths, stories and fairy tales, which seem not to be true, but still have a high degree of truth in them – maybe a hidden truth. Then you do not have to accept the realities.

When I was a child, we were told stories about what the parent generation experienced during the Second World War. For me this was fairy tale. I was unable to relate to it as reality. Where is the boundary between fairy tales and actual history? Sometimes this boundary is blurred out, as in the explanations as to how we were created, how our psyche works, and what happens when we die, and why we should behave in one way instead of another. We are told stories about wicked witches and trolls, so we can learn to look after ourselves. Many of these tales, fables and allegories (parables) are not rooted in the real world, but it is easier to tell such stories, because we then do not have to deal with actual people or events. Using fairy tales as explanations when it is something we do not quite understand or are reluctant to speak of in clear text, is neutral and safe. I think that is why there are so many similar fairy tales found around the World. Many fairy tales are almost identical, whether they are told in the East or the West. The Brothers Grimm's fairy tale collection from the German-speaking areas contain many of the same stories as those the researchers, Asbjørnsen and Moe, collected in Norway. It has been shown that many fairy tales and stories actually are describing the human psyche.

Myths are almost the same as fairy tales, but are often presented as having historical roots.

According to some dictionaries the myths and stories are about the life and fate of gods and semi-gods in bygone times. Often these gods and semi-gods have once been strong or prominent persons who have been declared divine, such as Imhotep – the architect of the step pyramid in ancient Egypt (which is assumed to be built before the pyramid of Cheops), or the emperor

Augustus in the Roman Empire. The gods and goddesses and their stories and character properties are actually images of human types and human problems. The stories give people some pointers to help solve problems they encounter in their own lives. The tales about the Nordic gods – the *Aesirs* – can be understood as tales of the first people, or the first group of people, who settled in Scandinavia and who (maybe) came from Asia. As time goes by, they are given supernatural powers and more and more considered as heroes. But the myths may also explain the creation of a people, a country or the entire World.

People need to know where they belong, who they are and where they come from. Most people want to know their roots. (However, preferably they want to know that they are of a good breed.) Then it is good to have a nice family story to refer to. But one thing is the family; we would also like to know where we belong, and that we are accepted by our environment and the country in which we live. Then a common language and a common culture are important. The use of rituals is of importance in order to keep a family, a community or a country together, and they are essential for a religious community. The use of symbols often serves the same purpose. A country's history is important for its self-esteem, as the relation of the Jews to The Old Testament, and a family's story will bind the members of the family together. Many stories may also reflect problems that occur between people and the way the psyche reacts. A classic tale which has been the source of a wide range of psychological theories, and also given its name to the concept of the Oedipus complex, is Sophocles' (496–406 BCE) tragedy about King Oedipus. King Oedipus, who had been removed from his closest family as a small child, unconsciously commits incest with his mother by marrying her, and unconsciously commits patricide by killing his father. When he realizes what he has done, he blinds himself – sacrificing his eyes. Jeremi Wasiutynski, who has analyzed the story from a psychological point of view, was of the opinion that this story tells of the difficulties that people meet on their way to ego-consciousness.[541] The story can be understood as an individuation process, as a process of the inner soul-life to find the true self. The mother-binding must be broken and the father-binding likewise. One must be blind to the material temptations and turn to the original in oneself. To blind oneself usually means turning the consciousness inward, on itself which will give increased wisdom. The story of the blind seer and fortune-teller from ancient times, Teiresias (a mythical figure who is said to have lived in Greece at the time of Oedipus) confirms that the inward-looking attitude gives wisdom. Teiresias was blinded by the goddess Hera because he said to Hera and her spouse, the god Zeus, that a woman's joy over a sexual intercourse could be said to constitute nine tenths while the male's pleasure only accounted for one tenth. Zeus gave him the prophecy-ability (and the ability to understand the speech of birds) as compensation for being blinded, and the privilege (?) to live for seven human generations.

Peer Gynt, the drama by Henrik Ibsen, may also be understood as the endeavour of the personality or the 'I' to find the true Self. The symbolism here is easier to understand, because the symbols used are so baroque and refers to national and universal human weaknesses – with the Hall of the Trolls and the Insane Asylum in Cairo as well-known examples. Ibsen added also a clear message in the mouth of the button-moulder: "To be oneself, is: to kill oneself." But also with the drama *Brand* Ibsen seems to have given a picture of the individuation process – Brand must discharge everything that binds in order to proceed further. A physical death, with which the play ends, can also be understood as a psychical death, which is needed to find one's Self.

More about rituals

All human beings and all cultures have their rituals. The term ritual is often connected with a religious act, something spiritual. But in Japan this has been developed to include everyday activity – such as the tea-ceremony according to the *zen*-method. Daily tasks that are often repeated are usually denoted routine. The boundary between a ritual and a routine may be difficult to draw. If the routine is executed in a manner which reminds us of our divine life, I will consider it a ritual more than a routine.

In daily life it is a good thing to have routines. It allows certain activities to be performed without further thought, such as getting up in the morning, brushing the teeth, cleaning the house and the like. The action goes without thought, because we have done it so many times before. This means that we feel at home where we are. But activities that we do regularly, but less frequently, and especially in interactions with others, are rituals. In the Christian part of the World the celebration of Christmas and Easter are typical rituals that bind the family together. A ritual is also something as simple as greeting the next door neighbour, either by a nod or by shaking hands. It provides cohesion and is a sign of friendliness. It helps us to feel at home in the neighbourhood. A slightly clearer form of ritual is when the neighbours gather on certain days, so as to work together, celebrating midsummer eve or something similar. When this is recurring over the years, it becomes a ritual that brings the neighbourhood a feeling of togetherness. Similar rituals are used to bind a nation together. The 17th May is a typical ritual day for Norwegians. That day we think of ourselves as one people, and consider ourselves different from anyone not displaying the Norwegian flag or speaking Norwegian.

Religious rituals are important instruments linking believers together. But religious rituals are also used to remind us that there is a spiritual dimension of life, and to honour those who are born, those who become adults, are getting married or are dying. Such transitional rituals have been used throughout time and by all peoples. People in the industrial part of the world often smile at the rituals people living in more primitive cultures are using to relate to what they do not understand, or to invoke the spiritual and the supernatural forces. But also in the industrialized world similar rituals are used. We light candles in memory of our loved ones who have died. In a baptism we pour water over the infant's head. We hoist a flag on certain holidays, which actually are memorial days.

However, rituals to commemorate that which we do not understand are becoming fewer in our part of the world. We are no longer so good at highlighting important transitions in our lives as before. Albeit in some countries a father may now be present at childbirth, a lot of people are dying in solitude, mainly in hospitals. We are not familiar with death as a part of life, and we react with shock when one of our nearest dies. Young people do not get a sense of being accepted in the community, with similar responsibilities and obligations as adults, when they come of age. They are not experiencing a clear marking that they have reached a point in life where they must assume responsibility for their own lives and for their surroundings. Rituals are, therefore, important. They increase the sense of cohesion. Their aim is to facilitate and enhance life's transitions, while reminding us of everything that we do not understand. Especially because of this, perhaps a stronger emphasis on life's transitional phases would give us greater reverence for our fellow human beings and for life. More emphasis on rituals will help us to see that a belief in a spiritual dimension is a good guide for life.

The Kabbalah

The Kabbalah is a Jewish mystical religious philosophy which flourished particularly in the years from 600 to 1700 CE. The word basically means tradition.[542] Colin Wilson wrote that the Kabbalah provides more plausible responses to an understanding of the human psyche than any other modern explanation system, Carl Gustav Jung's explanations included.[543] Its fundamental principle is the acknowledgement of the human being's different self-levels, or consciousness levels. These levels lead up to the Deity, the All, and they are described by the use of a symbol in the shape of the figure called the Tree of Life. The human beings have all the levels latent in them, but they are trapped in the physical level – which is our Universe.

It is not possible to understand existence by means of thoughts alone. However, by using symbols the mind can begin to meditate on what these represent and thereby achieve some understanding, although this cannot be expressed by words. The Tree of Life, with its ten sephiroth (sephirah is the singular word) and the twenty-two paths between them, is one such way of meditation. By learning what the individual symbols in the figure stand for and what the connection between them means, when meditating on them one might establish a philosophic standpoint in regard to an understanding of existence.

From the twelfth century onwards several books have been published about the Kabbalah. According to the website Wikipedia the main work is *Sefer Yetzirah* (also termed The Book of Creation), which many believe was

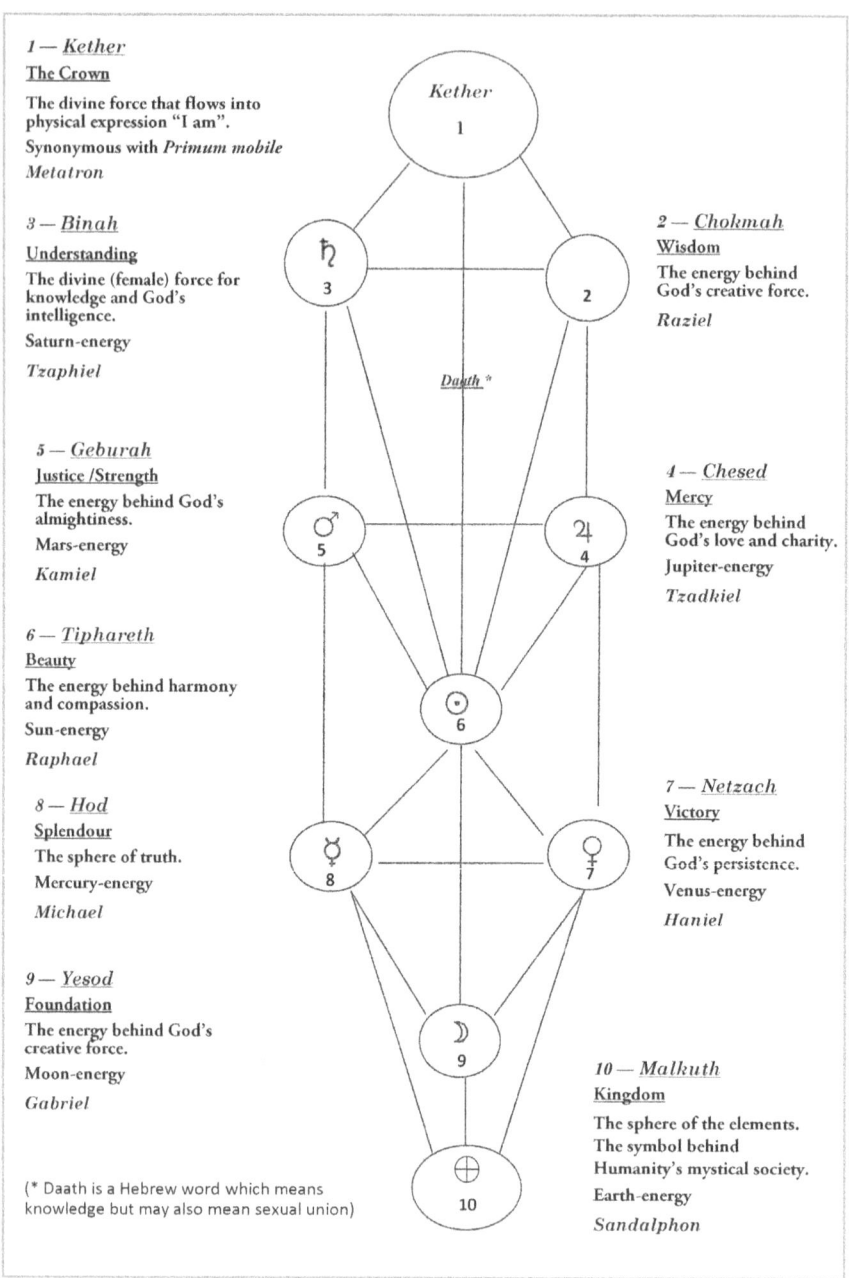

Figure 13. *The Tree of Life of The Kabbalah*

written between the years 300 and 600 CE. It describes the thirty-two ways to esoteric wisdom. That is, the ten sephiroth plus the twenty lines between them, corresponding to the twenty-two letters of the Hebrew alphabet. Another book, *Sefer Ha-Zohar* (The Book of Radiance), was published in Spain around 1280 and is by some equated to the books of Moses (the Torah). It was written by the great Jewish rabbi Moses de Leon. For Dion Fortune the Kabbalah was a living system of spiritual evolution, not a historical curiosity. (Much of what is said here is based on her description.) Aivanhov has explained it mainly in the same way.[544]

Dion Fortune wrote that the system is far older than the twelfth century, but only then was it written down. It is said to be the archangel Metatron that gave the mystics within Jewish society the Kabbalah. She mentioned, inter alia, that the final sentence in the prayer *Our Father in Heaven*: "yours is the Kingdom , the power and the glory ..." is purely cabbalistic, and that the words in the prayer are symbols used in the Kabbalah.[545] Ken Wilber has considered the Kabbalah as an expression of consciousness, as the various signs on the Tree of Life represent the different levels of consciousness, from the material level to the highest spiritual level.

As shown in the drawing, the Tree of Life is made up of ten signs, the so-called sephiroth, each with a short descriptions and text. Each sephirah has a name. These are, respectively, Kether, Chokmah, Binah, Chesed, Geburah, Tiphareth, Netzach, Hod, Yesod, and Malkuth. The sephiroth are in different ways associated with each other – as shown below, there are twenty-two lines between them. An entire cosmogony and psychology can be expressed by the symbol the Tree of Life. Each sephirah in the Tree of Life, its location and the context in which it is inserted, is said to provide insight to psychology, philosophy and theology. Dion Fortune called the Kabbalah the yoga of the Western World. By meditating on the Tree of Life one may achieve union with the divine will. By concentrating on the individual shapes in the Tree of Life one may be able to obtain information about that which previous generations have acknowledged. The sephiroth represent the nature forces, while the paths represent the consciousness levels. Each sephirah has a triple aspect, respectively philosophical, psychological and magical.

The Tree of Life, showing only the ten sephiroth and the twenty-two roads between them, is depicted in Figure 13 on the previous page.

The Tree of Life may be seen as appearing on four planes or worlds. These account for the four worlds or manifestation planes consisting of ever denser matter. They are called respectively:

> Atziluth – The plane of emanation (the divine world). Here the divinity is working directly .
>
> Briah – The plane of creation (the spiritual world).
>
> Yetzirah – The plane of formation (the psychological/thought world).

Assiah – The material plane or plane of action (the physical world). Here the divinity is working through the chakras, the planets, the elements and the signs of the Zodiac.

According to Dion Fortune, the Tree of Life may be interpreted in different ways and there are different schools of interpretation. One school considers these worlds as linked to specific sephirah. Another school interprets the Tree of Life so that the system exists in each of these planes. That means that the lowest sephirah – Malkuth – at the highest level (Atziluth) will be the highest sephirah in the next plane (Briah). Dion Fortune writes:

> "We must always bear in mind that the planes do not tower up one above another into the empyrean like the storeys of a building, but are conditions of being, states of existence of different types, and though they developed successively in time, they occur simultaneously in space; existence of all types being present in a single being, as we realize when we remember that the being of man is made up of a physical body, emotions, mind, and spirit, all occupying the same space at the same time."

One should also note that in addition to the four above-mentioned manifested planes, there are three unmanifested planes in existence. In my judgment, the first four planes may be compared to the causal plane, the mental plane, the astral plane and the physical plane. The three unmanifested planes will then be the cosmic field, the unity field as well as the All.

There is seen to be full consistency between that which the Tree of Life symbolizes and the Tarot cards, and also between these and the Chinese divination system *I Ching*. Dion Fortune also maintained that astrology is connected with the Tree of Life, and that it is only on the basis of an understanding of the Tree of Life that it is possible to see that astrology is a philosophical system. When using the Tarot cards, an understanding of the four card colours, respectively the sword (spades), the chalice (hearts), the wand (clubs) and the pentagram or the five-stars (diamonds), is required. The sword is related to fire, which corresponds to the plane of Atziluth in the Kabbalah. The chalice is linked to water, which corresponds to the plane of Briah. The wand is attached to air, which corresponds to the plane of Yetzirah. And the pentagram is related to earth, which corresponds to the plane of Assiah. Furthermore, each ace is related to Kether, the card number two to Chokmah, the number three to Binah, etc. When one is aware of this context, and what the associated elements as well as what each sephirah stand for, one will more easily be able to interpret the different Tarot cards when they are displayed.

The ten sephiroth can further be arranged in seven departments, also termed castles by Dion Fortune. The first castle consists of Kether, Chokmah and Binah, and the seventh of Yesod and Malkuth. The five middle castles consist of each sephirah. The meaning of the various planes one will only be able to understand through extensive studies of the different levels. It is not possible to explain in words the higher forms of existence, and the knowledge about these cannot be achieved by thought. The consciousness must therefore transcend thought in order to understand what these forms of existence mean. By concentrating on one sign at the time on the Tree of Life, the seeker will be making a step by step ascent towards an understanding of life.

Both Dion Fortune and Aivanhov explained that the sephiroth also represent the hierarchy of angels. Dion Fortune mentioned further that there are four variants of the Kabbalah. These are the practical Kabbalah, which is about talismanic and ceremonial magic, the dogmatic

Kabbalah, consisting of the cabbalistic literature, the literal Kabbalah, which is about the use of letters and numbers, as well as the unwritten Kabbalah, which consists of an understanding of the symbols on the Tree of Life. It is this last meaning that Dion Fortune has tried to explain in her book. This book is recommended if you want to obtain a better understanding of the symbols. Some people (among them Caroline Myss [546], who has worked as a healer in the US since 1983) maintain that the Tree of Life reflects the chakras, and that the Christian sacraments have their parallels here:

Sacraments	*Chakras*	*Sephiroth*
Baptism	Root	Malkuth /Sekina
Eucharist	Hara	Yesod
Confirmation	Solar plexus	Hod and Netzach
Matrimony	Heart	Tiphareth
Penance	Neck	Chesed and Geburah
Holy Orders	Pineal	Binah and Chokmah
Anointing – Last rites	Crown	Kether

18. The Universe and Evolution

In order to obtain a good attitude toward life and death, it is not enough to look at what the mystics and others are saying about what happens when we die, and about possible reincarnation. It is also – in my judgment – important to have some understanding of the creation and the purpose of existence. In this chapter I will therefore take a look at what has been said in this regard.

Astrological considerations

The Earth's axis does not have a stable direction. Its north pole will in the course of a period of 25,920 years be making a round tour in the sky – a circle – and the result is that the Polar Star (Alpha Ursae Minoris), which is where the axis is pointing today, not always will be – or has been – the pole star. This round is called the Platonic world year because Plato described this in his book *The Republic*. As mentioned before, astrology divides the Ecliptic, the Sun's path across the sky, into twelve zones, the so-called star signs. This path is also known as the Zodiac. (As mentioned, the star signs and the star constellations are not the same, as the star constellations which are the images which the constellations seem to form; or seemed to form in antiquity, at the time when they got their names – perhaps as far back as 5000 years ago or more. The star constellations have changed a great deal since then. The changing of the Earth's axis leads to changes in the Sun's position, changes relative to the starry sky behind. This position moves in the opposite direction from the astrological star signs. The Sun is within the same twelve-part zone of the sky for 2160 years. Rudolf Steiner called those 2160 years a cultural period.[547]

Our current calendar establishes the year so that the spring equinox always is on the 20th/21st of March – which is where the astrological sign of Aries (the Ram) begins. There are many people who argue that we are now living through a paradigm shift because the Sun at the spring equinox, astronomically, is about to pass from the sign of Pisces to the sign of Aquarius. Aquarius is by astrologers considered as the sign of spiritual development, and many believe that we, because of this culture period transition, are entering into a whole new understanding of the world, where human charity and spiritual acknowledgement is central. But to claim that we are coming into the period of Aquarius, presumes that we are dividing the twelve zones of the Ecliptic, and in particular the border between the sign of Aries and the sign of the Pisces, as they did 2000 years ago. Then the spring equinox was around zero degrees Aries, while today it is closer to zero degrees Pisces.

Astrologically, however, the equinox is still placed at zero degrees Aries. An interesting point in relation to the age of Pisces, which is maintained to have been the last 2000 years, is that this period began when Christianity began. As I have previously mentioned, the star sign Pisces was by some regarded as the star image of Israel and the star image of the coming Messiah. The first Christians used this symbol as the symbol of Christianity.

Other considerations

I will now briefly consider the thoughts some philosophers and mystics, whom I previously have mentioned in this book, have expressed about our existence, the future and the world development. The astrological world view has not been of importance among these, although both Helena Blavatsky and Rudolf Steiner believed that the Earth's development passes through several cultural periods.

Ervin Laszlo has written that there are many things indicating that behind our universe there are other universes – perhaps a cosmic 'womb', which has been named a *meta* universe.

Maybe our universe is part of a series of earlier universes, which has given impetus to the universe we see today. And that when this universe collapses, it will again encounter a new universe, which will build on the experiences that today's universe has acquired.

Plotinus is said to have maintained that to ask why the World's Soul has created the Cosmos, is the same as asking why there is a Soul in the first place, and why the Creator creates.[548] The question implies that there is a beginning to the eternal, and also a creative act performed by a changeable being that turns from one thing to another. But he sees no logic in this. The All which has become life, is no amorphous structure. The Universe is organized, efficient, complex, all comprehensive, and it displays an inconceivable wisdom.

Helena Blavatsky has explained that there are four other dimensions of existence, beyond the three we have considered here.[549] We will understand this better, when humanity has developed further. At the next stage in this development human beings will have six senses and function in four dimensions. Later, human beings will have seven senses and function in five dimensions. Today it is not possible to understand what this means, but she gives an indication by mentioning that the sixth sense will enable people to see through what we call solid material. This is perhaps the etheric sense that some individuals already have developed. Blavatsky said that the nature spirits, those she called elementals, and also the elementary spirits, can operate in the fourth dimension. This is not time, since that term does not exist in this dimension. It is difficult to explain, but it relates to the earthly dimension.

Rudolf Steiner argued that there are several cultural periods following each other, and that at a given point in time our era will also disappear, in order to make room for a new one.[550] He had an extensive explanation about the development of the world and what he called the different cultural eras. In our time, he said, we are deepest down in matter. But the human beings will evolve into a spiritual existence. This requires that the 'I' is consciously working with its development, which most people do not. The task of human beings while on Earth is, according to Steiner, to develop the spiritual Self. Self-love will no longer occur. Then there will be no falsehood or aberration, nor illness and death. The human beings must take up in them what he called the Christ impulse. To look to Christ's personality, to be run through and strengthened by this Christ impulse will evoke the ability to make such a transformation in oneself. Then the human being will eventually be master of the physical body. The last goal of the development is to overcome death, and people will receive help from higher beings in this regard. Steiner claimed that the Earth goes through what he called seven incarnations. These were, respectively, Saturn, Sun, Moon, Earth, Jupiter, Venus and Vulcan. Saturn has given humanity the building blocks for the physical body, the Sun has given the etheric body, the Moon the astral body, and the Earth has given it the 'I'. Jupiter, Venus and Vulcan have as tasks the design of the higher or spiritual bodies.

Martinus explained that we are all immortal beings with an infinite chain of experienced lives behind us. We are all developed from simple, primitive forms, and our current level is only part of a development scale up to more advanced planes of existence and greater spiritual development. The Universe is one big organism consisting of minerals, smaller organisms, plants, animals or humans, and everything is present as organs of the Universe. But there are many kinds of worlds, and not all are good. The good worlds are populated by beings with very advanced morals and harmony. There are worlds with lower morals, with sickness, misery and barbarism. It is the being's development and qualifications that determine the type of world or what kind of existence it will come to after this physical life. Martinus has through his books tried to describe the existence and the world's development. It is difficult to briefly describe his cosmogony. Some of it has been included in some of the chapters of this book. What is most important is perhaps his stressing that everything is in development, and that everything that is sent out eventually will return to the sender. The individual being – and he said there are myriads of beings – is following a predestined development. How fast the individual is developed depends on him or herself. He said that the goal of the creation process is that humankind shall obtain cosmic consciousness.[551] That means a consciousness that will help people understand the purpose of the world and then also the creation process. When they have come that far, human beings will know how to manage and distribute the Earth's products, so no-one will starve any longer, freeze or behave wrongly towards others. Moreover, everyone will then also understand life's problems as steps in an educational process initiated by providence, leading towards the world plan's final goal culminating in love. Then we will understand that any motion, vibration or action is a manifestation of God, and there is light and love for all living beings.

Aivanhov explained that the cosmic intelligence envisions the development in two directions – towards matter and towards spirit.[552] Human beings were allowed to descend into matter in order to develop in the world of senses, to learn to know it and to work on it. The spirit of the human being must go so deep into matter that it forgets its origin – its heavenly home where it once lived. The goal of the earthly existence is to take fully into its possession the body's capabilities and to use them to manipulate the outer world. It requires a descent into matter, an involution. But as soon as people have achieved sufficient self-control and control of their possibilities, they will start to rediscover the forces they once possessed and begin on their spiritual development. Aivanhov said that the human beings are still under the influence of involution, but that some will have come so far that they are working with their spiritual development.

In the book *Talking with Angels* Gitta Mallasz refers what one of the Angels was explaining about the Cosmos and existence.[553] This it is difficult to convey without citing everything in the book, and even then is it difficult to understand. However, the number seven is strangely central as shown by the following:

> This message is for you, for your heart has asked.
> Every organism consists of Seven Flames.
> Above each of the Seven there is a peak: the guide.
> Alone this guide would be of little value:
> but it is part of a new circle of Seven with a new crown.
> Thus each Flame knows both serving and guiding.
> Without a wick, the candle could not burn.
> Without a body, there would be no Individuality.
> The Heart of Light beats high above.
> If your gift or self reaches it, heavenly Grace flames up.
> THUS: ONLY THROUGH THE HUMAN BEING
> CAN GRACE DESCEND.
> The Seventh – the highest GUIDE – teaches you.
> Thus from infinity comes space and from space comes infinity,
> From eternity is born the temporal and from the temporal: eternity.
> May the Strength of the Seven Forces be with you. Burn!

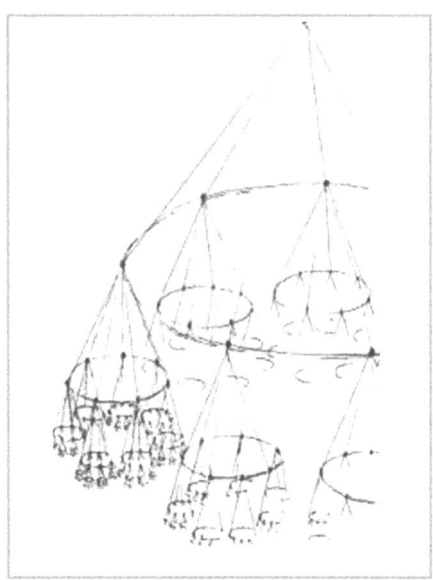

Figure 14. Sketch from the book: 'Talking with Angels' by Gitta Mallasz, p. 424

Ambres has exactly the same presentation of the deity.[554] Ambres explained that God, who is the origin of everything and who is in everything, is a dreamer initiating a process in order to experience itself. God has multiplied in several planes downwards, in a hierarchy that leads down to the human beings. First, he created the seven gods, who are images of him or herself. Each of these seven gods then has its dream, which it makes real in the form of seven new creatures, and so on down in infinity.

David Bohm has said that people's problem is their many dimensions, respectively an individual, a social, a cultural and a cosmic dimension.[555] The Eastern religions have, according to him, emphasized the individual and cosmic side, while the Western religions have laid emphasis on the social and cultural. In the West one seeks to master the material, although the individuals are not able to master themselves. If people could begin to change themselves and their social connections, and renew the culture, this may lead to a change in the spirit of the time. It takes more imagination to see that the future is not necessarily determined by the knowledge one has, or of what happened in the past.

Jes Bertelsen wrote that the goal of development is 'the essence or the higher self'.[556]

When you have come that far, you will have a kind of higher consciousness, in this consciousness you will find yourself in the collective field and you will be open to others. This means that you are what you are saying. There is no difference between what you are saying and doing on one side, and what you are on the other side. One has become what Bertelsen calls transparent. Transparency depends on that the human being accepts itself and that it constantly illuminates its being with consciousness. This is explained thus: when a transparent human being functions, it works in two dimensions simultaneously; partly in the dimension of the daily consciousness through speech, information, movement and gestures; partly in the dimension of the higher consciousness by immediate dissemination of information. Higher consciousness is a transgression of the 'I', in glimpses or permanently. It is open and accessible for everyone. There are no preferences, no emotional judgment or consideration. No exclusion. Spiritual guides are seeking to help the individual human being to achieve such transparency.

Jeremi Wasiutynski believed that it is not possible to speak of an objective world, since only that which a person can acknowledge can be determined.[557] Subject and object cannot be separated from each other as they are the two opposites of consciousness. He then wrote:

> An adequate theory of the creation of the All and the continuing creative evolution must therefore be seen as a universal consciousness theory that includes both subject and object. The original, persistent, even timeless Subject is only rarely available at the bottom of our sensing and our will. But it is the only real Being. The original Object is the absolute, unobjectifiable great void. By an alternating effect between these two spheres creation occurs.

He said that it not only involves a physical creation, an outer process, but at the same time – and originally – a psycho-mental process. His explanation of the creation of the world is complicated, and those who are interested must read his book. The following explanation can give an indication as to his understanding of reality:

> Above we have outlined the existing evidence that the entire reality can be derived à priori from the relationship between the pureSubject and the just as unthinkable and unsubjectifiable Object which is the great Void. In the light of our considerations the physical universe has proven to be constructed on contradictions.
>
> But this is not the whole truth. In their original forms as stated in creation's simple laws, all equations in physics are pure *identities*. If the world had been only physical, we would have been able to call it a soap bubble of illusions. But life's presence and the creative evolution are changing the situation. The qualities that life have attached to the abstract structures of physics, have transformed the identities to laws, and they have given us a foretaste of the absolute values.
>
> As suggested above, the absolute values can be regarded as basic dimensions for the four pre-physical worlds as can be seen by the pleroma through the rise of subordinate matrix components. The absolute Goodness, Beauty, Truth and Holiness cannot be observed by us directly, but they can, in principle at least, be made known to us through a sort of inspection. They represent four independent dimensions in the way they are created in the higher worlds, that is in

> the movement towards the creator of the All, the pure Subject, in psychological literature sometimes referred to by the rather diffuse and ambiguous term the Self.

The goal of humanity is to get back to this Self, to the All's creator. The 'false facade of easy adaptions to the world must be broken down, and the real, albeit complex based, ousted inner personality must come up in daylight'. He wrote further:

> By now several billion years have passed since the world was constituted by a disastrous limitation of consciousness and existence. ... But a creation process cannot end in pure matter, for also matter carries a proof for its spiritual lineage in the form of its creation matrix. In other words: the matter's nascent returning process to the Self must have started the process we call life. We are ourselves its products. ...
>
> The process of becoming self-confident is only part of a comprehensive, cosmic process of return to the original One, to The Highest Self. ... But in the long run, the universal correlation between all organisms makes itself felt, and then the species that are not adapted to the long-term goal, which is to serve life as a whole, will go under, either because they indirectly are harming the organisms they depend on, or because they cannot live in changed environmental conditions, or for other reasons. ...
>
> From now on, the human being seems to have to search for the holy in itself, beyond anything that it has identified itself with so far. ... That is, that life on Earth is about to be mature enough to become Earth's consciousness-carrying body. ...
>
> Thereby, we will arrive at a new phase of humanity.

Wasiutynski maintained that the human being's task is to become itself. It is to realize a purpose, an inner, hidden pattern that each person is carrying within. Knowledge of oneself, that is, to one's inner and outer personality is in this context not sufficient. You have both to acknowledge and in a creative way to develop your relations with the All, the outer as well as the inner, since we are inextricably linked to the Universe, and since it is only in the whole of the Universe that we find ourselves. This is the living, creative way of life. Then the latent capabilities will be developed, which in the beginning are the not fully developed ordinary capabilities. But when approaching the full, normal humanity, there are also certain supernormal capabilities. He said further:

> The road to absolute individualization – to the full realization of the individual human being's possibilities – goes through the abandonment of personal goals – through the annihilation of the 'I' in the service of the All – and vice versa. ... The trick to be one's self – an individual in its entirety, inextricably connected with the All – has always been the core of human wisdom teaching, but today it is almost forgotten. ... When the time has come when a dedicated minority has

resolved this paradox in practice in its own life and trustingly is followed by the rest, then the foundation is laid for a new civilization, and life on Earth will be renewed.

Also *Pierre Teilhard de Chardin* has philosophized about life's development. With his background as geologist, palaeontologist and theologian, he had thorough insight into the Earth's development to date, which should give a good background for further drawing of major development-lines. He described the creation of the Earth through different layers, which he called the geo-genesis (the Earth's formation), bio-genesis (the living being's creation), and ultimately into the psycho-genesis (the creation of the psyche). But with the ability to think or to reflect a higher function in the human being occurring, namely the birth of the spirit and its further development, the process he called noo-genesis was born. He believed that this activity of thought is reflected in a separate layer of the Earth which he called the noo-sphere, which is located outside of and above the biosphere. In an essay entitled *Some Reflections on Progress* (The Norwegian title was *Notat om fremskrittet*) he wrote that everything in nature has always been under transformation and is in continuous transformation.[558] The biological evolution has always moved in the direction of a larger brain, that is, toward a higher level of consciousness, and he asked himself whether or not this indicates that it is a fundamental force in the organic growth of life towards the need to acknowledge and to think. He asked further whether the fact that this special branch, where the human being is, on the tree-trunk of development, with the ability to think, has had the consequence that all other species have halted in their development. Does that mean that the species that obtained a higher consciousness have cost the development so much that the available forces were so to say absorbed in them? We have got a growing understanding of the human being's internal cohesion and the individual's responsibility for the whole. This, he said, is to begin to realize the Universe in our consciousness. "Progress is ... awareness about everything there is and everything imaginable."

Pierre Teilhard de Chardin outlined, in the book *The Phenomenon of Man*, humanity's creation through millions of years. He pointed out that what specifically makes the human being different from other creatures is its capacity for reflection – to see itself, to think. Furthermore, he pointed out that which is extra special with humanity, namely, that it is the only species that has not changed, has not adapted physically to the environment in which it finds itself, and neither has it split into different branches, as has happened with all other species. On the contrary, the human beings, particularly in recent years, have approached each other and mixed with each other. Mentally the human beings have not changed, except that they have managed to acquire more knowledge, during the last, approximately, 8-10,000 years. He wrote that people are individuals who have transcended their pure organic individuality to knowingly participate in a community with others. For all life's different species the uniting of individuals is very important, but they do not thereby lose their personality. The parts are made perfect and are fulfilled in any organized whole. The consciousnesses cannot be mixed, they need to be united. He emphasized that many confuse individuality with personality. If we are seeking to separate us as much as possible from others, we will tear the world apart and it will perish. But by a convergence towards everyone else, towards others, we will contribute to the world's structure of development. "*The true Ego grows in adverse relation to egoism.*" And he further said:

> "The more everyone is becoming 'the others', the more they are 'themselves'." ... "Among the various forms for psychic connections that spiritualize the noo-sphere, we must before all others acknowledge, acquire and develop energies that will go from centre to centre, if we really want to give our contribution to the development progress within us – and by that fact we are here brought to the problem of love."

Ken Wilber believes that the holistic system that he has worked out is a useful index for a categorization of the different world views and the different philosophies, religions and scientific explanations.[559] If we should seek to create a world view, in Wilber's opinion we have at least to use the system he has developed, with the four quadrants, the different consciousness levels and stages, the many development lines, types and areas. He has sought to compare more than a hundred different theories, and even though this comparison necessarily will have to be fairly superficial, he thought that that was better than no comparison. He has also commented on a number of these areas, and has demonstrated that many people focus only one-sidedly on one of the four quadrants in his system. One way to classify a worldview is in his opinion by using the chakra system. As an example, he referred to the materialistic world-view that was put forward by Thomas Hobbes and Karl Marx, which he finds is related to the root chakra or the first chakra. Vitale and prana-based world-views, as for example in Freud's and Bergson's views, relate to the hara-chakra or second chakra. Power-based views, as Nietzsche's, is related to the third chakra or the solar plexus. Rational worldviews, such as Descartes', are related to the fourth chakra or the heart chakra. Nature mysticism, as Thoreau's, is related to the fifth chakra or the throat chakra. The God mysticism, as Teresa of Avila's, is related to the sixth chakra or the pineal chakra, while formless mysticism, such as Master Eckhart's, is the seventh chakra or the crown-chakra. However, Wilber stressed that one must be aware that if anyone is presenting a worldview, for example connected to the root chakra, the person will be doing this on the basis of rational thinking, i.e. from the fourth chakra or the heart chakra, while he or she has all the attention directed towards the root chakra.

On the basis of his classification in quadrants, lines, levels, types and areas, Wilber thinks that the time now is ripe to use this approach to shape an integrated Constitution for a World civilization. It should rest on a fundamental moral intuition that protects and promotes all levels. The Constitution must also include a directive that promotes the totality throughout the development cycle, without giving privileges to a specific group. Furthermore, it must be a careful pusher for a conversion of the full spectrum of human potential, by encouraging people to develop and grow to their full potential.[i] To promote these ideas for development towards a World Facilitation Federation, he believes is the main task for this millennium.

Henrik Ibsen must have been a mystic otherwise he could not have written the dramas he wrote. He considered the play *Emperor and Galilean* (1873) as his main work, written shortly after the plays *Brand* and *Peer Gynt*. The latter two can be read as the battle which the outer ego has in order to arrive at the inner real self and can therefore be considered to describe an individuation process. *Emperor and Galilean* is about spiritual development, and the main character's development through pain and suffering is a key part of the play, based on historical events. The Roman Emperor Julianus (Flavius Claudius, nicknamed the Apostate – Apostata) came to power in the year 361. He was killed after only two years of reign, at thirty-one years of age. He was the nephew of Emperor Constantine, who recognized Christianity as a religion in the Roman Empire, but who was not baptized until at his death bed. Julianus succeeded his cousin Constancios to the throne. Constancios, who also accepted Christianity, had killed all of Julianus' closest relatives, including according to some rumours his own sister Helena who was married to Julianus. Besides being a frugal and industrious person, Julianus was a philosopher and left several writings. In the play he is greatly influenced by the mystic Maximos from Ephesus. Maximos is an important character in the drama. It is Maximos who is presenting Ibsen's vision of the development of the world.

The Norwegian high school teacher Gunhild Hoem, who has written an analysis of the drama, believed that the drama is about light's struggle to overcome darkness; the spiritually enlightened reality in combat against the spiritually darkened reality, and that the individual human being is carrier of a spiritual and divine reality. She has explained that Julian's task according to Maximos is 'to found the Kingdom'. To achieve this he must go the way of necessity and liberty, as Ibsen describes it. Maximos points out that there are three kingdoms: The first was founded on the tree (by Adam's fall) and what Ibsen called 'the lust of the flesh'; then the kingdom that was based on the Tree of the Cross (by Jesus) which Ibsen calls 'the kingdom of the spirit';

---

i. "Beyond that, in my estimation, it would be guided by the Basic Moral Intuition (protect and promote the greatest depth for the greatest span), which itself embodies both the prime directive (facilitates the health of the entire spiral of development without privileging any particular wave) and a gentle pacer of transformation for the full spectrum of human resources (inviting people to grow and develop their full potentials – interior and exterior – to the best of their abilities)."

and finally the third and coming kingdom – which will be founded on the tree of knowledge and the Cross together: " ... because it hates and loves them both, and because it has its living sources under Adam's garden and under Golgotha. Those two kingdoms will be devoured by the third, which now is coming; the spirit will in this kingdom be saturated by matter and matter by the spirit – then the goal is reached. ... The created will be one with the creator. ... Logos in Pan – Pan in Logos." Maximos thought that this last kingdom was very close and thought it would be founded by Julian, though he eventually, when Julian was dead, had to acknowledge that there would be still a long way to go, but: "The third kingdom will come! The human spirit will reclaim its inheritance." The Emperor Julian was described as a tool for disciplining the human beings – not to death but to renewal. He was like Cain and Judas, 'a wonderful, broken vehicle'. Julian was one of 'the three keystones of the wrath of necessity', one of the 'three great helpers in denial', where Cain and Judas were the other two. Gunhild Hoem wrote:[560]

> The human being's life and development process is burdensome and difficult, but the goal of the process is the realization of the spiritual qualities in the human being itself. ... When the human beings as individuals have realized God's image in themselves and thus become 'god-emperors' and 'emperor-gods' in their own inner kingdom and thus have reached up to the 'the emperor's seat', then the individuals together constitute the humanity which will be living in freedom and in the light for which 'the third kingdom' stands as a symbol. 'The third kingdom' is therefore a condition in the individual human being.

Ibsen makes Julian say that he, with his 'body changed to spirit' had –

> "been deep into the paradise gardens; the angels had been singing their praise for me; I had beheld the light in the middle ... Do you know how the spirit of acknowledgement filled me? – It happened one night during prayer and fasting. Then I sensed that I was taken far away – far out of the room and out of time; although the day was sunny and shiny around me, and I was standing by myself on a ship with flat sails in the middle of the brilliant Greek sea. The islands were towering, like light sheet of clouds, far away, and the ship was lying heavily as if in sleep, on the fine blue surface. ... Behold, this surface became more and more transparent; lighter, thinner; finally, it was no more, and my ship hung over an empty terrible deep. No greenery, no sun down there, only the dead, mucous, black sea bottom in all its abominable nakedness. But above, in the infinite vault that before had seemed to me so empty – there was life; There the invisible took forms, and silence got tones. – Then I understood the great releasing knowledge. ... That which is, is not; and that which is not, that is. ... That which in the human being's slavery filled hope is behind death, that is exactly the great secret's goal to pass on to all fellow knowledgeable human beings here in our earthly life. This is the restoration that Maximos and his apprentices are seeking, – that is the forfeited likeness with the deity."[561]

What Ibsen has written here is quite similar to that which we have seen described as near-death experiences, and may indicate either that Ibsen had such an experience or has had the knowledge that such experiences can occur. It can also resemble the Unio Mystica experience. The coming kingdom will thus be founded on the tree of knowledge and the tree of the Cross combined. This can be understood so that it is intelligence and compassion, i.e. the ability to love that is required. This is precisely that which gives wisdom according to Martinus, and which is a prerequisite for spiritual development.

19. Conclusion

What conclusion can we draw from the rich and, in truth, diverse material I have tried to gather and have presented here to the readers of this book? Some of it will immediately be considered speculative, unlikely and perhaps scary to the unprepared reader, but hopefully also a spur to further reading and reflection on the insights I have tried to convey. If I were to summarize what I believe to have learned and understood by all this, it is first and foremost that we must acknowledge that there is a spiritual world and that we can get help from the beings in that world. This last requires that we believe in them and relate to them, which can be done by *asking for help* – not as I want (i.e. not what the superficial ego wants), but as you want (i.e. as the divine evolution indicates). Maybe this help will come from our own higher Self, who has contact with everything that happens. To pray may be a way to obtain contact with this Self.

Furthermore, we must remember this: *The cosmic spiritual law* is LOVE. The Cosmos is love. The divine principle is love. Everything that happens has a purpose, namely to develop each individual to greater understanding, to stronger compassion, to be and to show the all-encompassing love, which does not discriminate and that can withstand everything.

Our Life's mission is to experience, to create, to learn, to evolve and to work. Many people explain that you have chosen to come into this physical life. You have chosen your *setting*, i.e. the circumstances into which you are born. *Make the best out of the life you have chosen* – that is, you work with yourself on the physical plane, on the psychic/emotional plane, on the mental plane and on the spiritual plane. To become yourself is to realize a purpose, an inner, hidden pattern that you have within you, as Jeremi Wasiutynski said it. In this perspective everything is a form of energy. People consist of energy. It is, as we have seen, an energy field in and around each human being – the aura. This energy field vibrates and transmits or attracts energy (such as the high pressure and low pressure which cause the changes in the weather). Thoughts and actions create energy structures that have effects on the surroundings. Energy exchange takes place especially through the chakras. If you have focused too hard on the energy in one chakra, you have perhaps neglected the energy in one or several other chakras, and because space is curved (everything goes in a circle), these structures will sooner or later come back to you. *The kind of energy that you are sending out to your surroundings will return.* If you think you are rejected by others, you will probably react to this idea, and then others will feel being rejected by you. In psychology, the term projection is often used. That is that you are projecting onto others whatever you do not like in yourself. In the terms of energy, this means that you, unconsciously, are aware that you are not using this energy properly, and because it is so easy to identify, this energy transfer is easily observed in everyone else. However, 'the beam in our own eye' we do not acknowledge. St Paul said (2 Cor 9.6): *"Remember this: Whoever sows sparingly will also reap sparingly, and whoever sows generously will also reap generously."* A well-known statement is: *"What you sow you shall receive back tenfold."*

Before the negative energy comes back it might have attracted other structures that strengthen it. "What you are doing against the others, the others might to do unto you" – applies both in negative and in positive ways. The term 'eye for an eye and tooth for tooth' means that you will get back what you inflict on others – but not that the others have any right to avenge themselves. It serves only to confirm the saying 'There is a Nemesis passing through life!'

Remember that you can mitigate the consequences of your wrong thoughts and actions by recognizing them, by thinking about them and see if you could have thought or acted differently. This is a form of self-examination and confession. I*t is NEVER too late to reconsider an action.* You do not have to tell this to others, it is for you to see it. You should consider all thoughts and actions, even those that seem completely irrelevant. In order to implement such a self-search of everything you do, you have to do it daily; otherwise something might easily be overlooked and forgotten, although it might show up much later. But then it may be too late to do anything about it, if anything can be done then. You must ask forgiveness if you have done something wrong, even if it concerns a deceased person. Either you need to take it up with yourself or with the person concerned (if another person is involved), or you have to ask the deity or the spirit world for forgiveness. This is to ask for MERCY. In this connection it is also important to know that when you acted as you did, you did it from the assumptions and abilities you then had. You shall not condemn yourself for what you should have done differently. And others have no right to condemn you for what you have done.

Buddha and Jesus are two of the few individuals we know from world history who are said to have had direct contact with the spiritual world and who understood the cosmic world order, i.e. the divine principle. They had God consciousness. This means that in everything they did, they followed the divine main principle – they practised love. Other people cannot do this; a few (such as the mystics) may perhaps practise it now and then. *Not to be conscious of the Divine is considered as sin.* One does something that is not as it should be if one is unable to be in contact with the divine principle –

which is to practise the all-embracing love. This means that almost all people are sinners to a greater or lesser degree. But everyone is doing the best they can. This should, however, not prevent us for always trying to do better.

"*Remember to live while you are doing it*", said the Danish poet and gruk author Piet Hein.

But remember also *why* you are living. According to the mystics, we are in this world to develop ourselves and to learn, but to do so, we must recognize the fundamental cosmic principles. In addition to that, all that happens is governed by the principle of love, everything is bound together, and you are yourself responsible for your own development – consciously or unconsciously. To live is to be present in the moment; to live with love for everyone and everything; to forgive others for the injustices they might do to you; to see every day as a gift that is given to you so that you can develop yourself; and the goal is to feel and experience the divine life and the divine love.

Why should we learn to use our inner strength? What will that do for *me*? Does that matter in this life if there is no conscious continuation? This question I hope to have answered in the foregoing.

If reincarnation is a reality or there is a life in another dimension – and there is continuity in the human consciousness, so that we can remember earlier lives under certain circumstances and perhaps also are conscious of our individuality in the period when we are in the next Bardo (to use the Tibetan term) – we should strive to become better human beings. There is a meaning to life – as all mystics are saying. Maybe there is a meaning in our individual lives – and this meaning we should strive to understand. There is every reason to be aware of our daily activities, thoughts and reactions. If we are looking closely at what happens, we might perhaps see a pattern. We are ourselves the cause of most of what is happening in our physical life. If we want a good life, we should try to act for the best of everything and everyone, not just to satisfy our own desires. Martinus said that living beings have only themselves to blame for what happens to them throughout life; this the great spiritual leaders of mankind have emphasized over and over again.[562] This can also be seen from the following citations:

> ... when people learn to use their inner powers and abilities – the spiritual perception's powers and abilities – then they can penetrate into the secrets of existence, to what is hidden in the spiritual world behind the sensory world. *Rudolf Steiner* [563]

> The Button-moulder: To be yourself is: to kill yourself. However, for you this explanation is wasted; so therefore, let it be called: everywhere to toil with the Master's meaning on the signboard.
> Peer Gynt: But what about he that never learnt what the Master wanted of him?
> The Button-moulder: This he should be sensing. *Henrik Ibsen*

The next question is how to live. We cannot all live in a convent or become like Mother Teresa. We cannot all try to save the world. Most people must be where they are, be the small wheels in the machinery that maintains the mundane tasks at work and at home. Without them, the whole machinery would come to a standstill. There are many who have given recommendations as to how to live and how to develop. Not everything that is easy to understand. But to work with yourself, with your ego instincts, your feelings and thoughts, is essential in order to progress, and to achieve greater joy in this life and perhaps lay the foundation for a possible later life. We must practise self-discipline, questioning why we think, act and react as we do. The only person who is freed from selfish motives and desires and who wants to live in harmony with the divine principle, which is goodness and love, is truly free. Most individuals, however, are only living as a reaction to external demands and circumstances; they are not present in themselves in what they are doing.

In the book *The Celestine Prophecy* by the American author James Redfield (b.1950), BA in sociology and MA in counselling, I found a description of a person's potential development that fits well with the thoughts I have got through working with this book. Redfield's book is about nine insights that, when they are experienced and understood in the proper order, can be seen as steps in a spiritual development that can lead to cosmic understanding. This is in accordance with Rudolf Steiner's vision. I shall in the following attempt to give a brief summary of the nine insights. They may be a good supplement to the Buddhist Four Noble Truths and the Eight Paths to enlightenment as rules of life.

The First Insight is that we must be aware that life is something other than what we daily observe. Much of society's restlessness and disease happens because we are striving and struggling too much, as we do not understand what we should do and how to do it. When we have become aware of this, we have the first insight. It means that we are embarking on a revaluation of the inherent mystery that governs our lives on this planet. Then we begin to realize that coincidences do not happen randomly, but have a meaning, a spiritual significance; perhaps are due to something spiritual seeking to influence us in a certain direction.

The Second Insight helps us to wake up, to see that our fears, our intuition, tell us something about reality. The historical development that the Earth and the human beings have undergone is not just a technological development, but is also a spiritual development. By studying and understanding the development that has taken place, we can more easily understand why we perceive the world as we do today, and it will also be easier to see what our contribution can be to the further development of civilization. Now is the time to try to understand what is behind the life on this planet, and why people are at the stage of development they are now.

The Third Insight shows that everything physical in the Universe is just energy, and that this energy reacts to how we think. When we have reached this insight, our understanding of the physical universe will be changed and we get a whole new type of existence. We will then be conscious of how we behave towards others – both towards people, animals and plants – and how we think. What we think is reflected in our aura. As we learn to see this energy – the aura – we will understand how other people's lives are, what they think and feel, and we will learn how to help them. By using this energy properly, for example, by growing useful food plants, by giving the plants energy and by eating the right food, we will be given more energy.

The Fourth Insight shows how people today are fighting to get energy. The human beings have shut themselves off from the cosmic energy source. Instead, they seek to steal energy from each other, an outright power struggle. When we learn to understand this, we will also learn how to avoid being robbed of energy, and we will then relate to each other in a completely different way. A typical way to steal energy is to bully another person. All quarrels within a family or at workplaces or war between nations are aimed at giving the victor energy. Those who win will be feeling high and strong. Those who lose will be feeling depressed and drained of energy.

With *The Fifth Insight* we have learned to open up for the cosmic source and to get supplies from there, and then we experience that love flows through us. We will then also be able to open up for the mystical experience. Many people have had glimpses of such experiences during meditation or prayer. A very few are able to experience this more than as glimpses. To get such a mystical experience and to obtain being filled with cosmic energy, we must be open to the surroundings, we must see the beauty everywhere and to feel love for everything in nature. When we are really seeing the beauty in all things and the uniqueness of all there is, we will also experience the love of everything. When we are sending love to all there is, such as a tree or a plant, we will receive energy back from it all. It sounds incredible that we can receive cosmic energy, but some people may, as we have seen, actually subsist on such energy alone.

The Sixth Insight shows how we unconsciously control others, and teaches us not to do that anymore. In childhood we learn to play certain roles, which we continue with the rest of our life – or until we learn to change that behaviour. The child learns such a game in order to get attention, or energy, from the parents. We are not behaving honestly when using such a game; we are then not communicating as we should with our surroundings and we will often miss the fine compassionate contacts or important information that other people may give us. We will then be losing the opportunity to get help with our spiritual development. James Redfield describes four such key roles, respectively the investigating judge, the oppressor, the king (the sublime and removed), and the submissive (the poor guy). Each individual will often be a combination of the roles their parents played.

The Seventh Insight concerns dreams. It explains that we must compare our dreams (including thoughts and daydreams) with the actual situation we are in. Often dreams tell us something important about what will happen or how to deal with what is happening. We must ask why we have had these thoughts or dreams, what we first thought that triggered them, and what connection they have with life's problems as they currently are. We must deal with this as an observer. Thus we are dropping the control and are instead participating in a development. If we are getting frightening images in the dream, these must be stopped. Instead we should consciously try to imagine a pleasant scene. If we are still getting scary images, even though we are trying to change them into nice pictures, we must try to accept them, but we do not have to follow them. The world is a mysterious place which provides us with what we need if we follow the right path.

The Eighth Insight shows how people should learn to relate to each other, how to give each other energy and how to avoid being dependent on each other. It is important to relate properly to children. They need the adults' constant, unconditional attention or energy. They must not be deprived of energy, which often happens when adults correct them. They have to learn about the world from adults and not from other children. It is therefore important to talk to them in a language they understand, and to tell them the truth. When we understand the energy relationships, we also understand what happens when we cease being in love or when a marriage ends in quarrelling and divorce. When two people fall in love, they are unconsciously giving each other much energy, so that both feel uplifted and thriving. Because they expect that all this energy is coming to them from their partner, they are cutting off the cosmic energy supply. So when they in the long run are not receiving enough energy from the partner, they will by force be seeking more by using the learned games from childhood. It is important to understand that we very often are looking for our lost inner partner in another person. Instead of being a whole person when entering a partnership, we will often consist of two half persons.

That can be compared to a person with two heads and two wills, and can result in a fight about whom should follow whom, when to prioritize between all daily living activities and opportunities. If we are a whole person and are entering a partnership with another whole person, that partnership becomes a super person. However, both parties must have full right to follow their own development. That requires that both are honest and true, and that both are willing to be completely open about what they do and why. If both people are equally open and know how to give each other energy, both will feel uplifted. The same can happen in a group of people who are working together and are open to each other.

The Ninth Insight shows the future of human development. As a result of altered consciousness, people will voluntarily reduce population growth. Eventually, the working hours will be reduced. People's essential needs will be met by using machines, and natural resources will be better utilized. Our intuition will guide us, and all will be harmony. Our need for meaning will be satisfied when we work with our own development. We will reduce the pace of activity. Everyone will be more alert and on guard not to miss the next meeting which may be of importance for one's development. Through every meaningful exchange with other people we will feel better and more inspired. The Ninth Insight ends with suggesting that when people have the right attitude and understanding, they will vibrate at a higher level.

Martinus said that the inner core of the human being knows the divine life and longs for it; it is the basis for all religious feelings. Jes Bertelsen explained it in this way:[564]

> Everyone seems to be born with such an open and compassionate heart. But for most people childhood gives occasions for so much disappointment, rejections, abandonment and abuse that the natural heart closes in protection. This closure sits like a psychosomatic block in the muscles and tendons and in fibres around and within the heart. Normally it requires a long and difficult therapeutic work and self-development to be conscious of those closures and blockages. The heart contains lots of crying not cried out, lots of wounds in the soul and in the emotions that are not healed. Each time the heart did not get the nurture of love, the heart contracted. Each time the love that was sent out was not received, the heart suffered. Normally it takes a long time to restore the natural heart.

'Know thyself' was a well-known saying among the ancient Greeks[i]. It was written on the Temple of Apollo at Delphi. The message is just as relevant today. But we cannot know ourselves until we have reasonably managed our relationship with our inner, unconscious forces and our relationship to our surroundings – that which affects us from without. Perhaps when we understand this, will we be able to be less ego-centred, less judgmental and more concerned about fellow human relationships, and also about how we treat this planet on which we reside. But this requires, as the nine Insights explain, that we are open to other thoughts than those to which we have been trained, open to other cultures, open to others' theological ideas and others' ways of practising their religious beliefs. Buddhism and its Four Noble Truths were for me good guides. I hope that this book can help other seekers in finding their way.

---

i. The right translation might rather be: "Know thy Self".

Or maybe we should rather listen to the Ecclesiastes' advice as it is written in the Bible (12.12-14):

> Be warned, my son, of anything in addition to them.
> Of making many books there is no end,
> and much study wearies the body.
> Now all has been heard;
> here is the conclusion of the matter:
> Fear God and keep his commandments,
> for this is the duty of all mankind.
> For God will bring every deed into judgment,
> including every hidden thing,
> whether it is good or evil.

Reference notes

A book's title is given in Norwegian when the Norwegian book or edition is used as reference (the English title or a translation of the Norwegian title is then given in parenthesis.) Please note that all dates are given according to an English standard, that is day, month, year.

Where a book title is abbreviated to initials in the Notes please see the Bibliography under the author's surname for details.

To chapter 1

1. Cited from Helge Hognestad's text in the program for the Norwegian society *Møtested Høvik* (the Høvik Meetingplace), written in August 1991. Helge Hognestad (b. 1940), PhD, was priest in the Norwegian Church. He was the founder and leader of the society *Møtested Høvik* which was a forum for discussions and existed in the period 1985-2003. He has authored several books.
2. Bertelsen SV p. 135.
3. Wilson, *The Man and His Vision* pp. 106 and 114.
4. Johansson, *Resan til Ljuset* (The Voyage to the Light) p. 84.

To chapter 2

5. Johansson, *Møte med Ambres* (Meeting Ambres) p. 16.
6. *Dalai Lama læser Evangeliene* (The Dalai Lama reading the Gospels – English title *The Good Heart*) p. 89.
7. Schjelderup, *Hvem Jesus var* – (The Man Jesus –).
8. Illustrert Vitenskap no 8/94 p. 5. See also Wikipedia – *Human language*.
9. Campbell PM. A detailed description of the grotto paintings and the interpretation of these are given by Graham Hancock in the book *Supernatural – Meetings with the Ancient Teachers of Mankind*.
10. Jacobsen, *Hyllest til Gudinnen – visjon and tilbedelse av hinduismens store gudinne* (Tribute to the Goddess – vision and worship of Hinduism's great Goddess). See especially pp. 11, 17, 23, 26, 83 and 85.
11. Much of what is said here is taken from the book *Dalai Lama læser Evangeliene* (The Dalai Lama reading the Gospels). Other sources used are Alan W. Watts, *The Way of ZEN*, and Huston Smith, *Verdens Religioner* (The World's Religions), as well as other translations of the Four Noble Truths. Huston Smith has authored many books about religion.
12. The background for the descriptions in this chapter is Chaim Potok's book, *Wanderings – History of the Jews*. About the origin of the Talmud, see especially p. 313 about 'The academy of Sura i Babylon'. The edition Misjna was terminated around the year 200 CE. Chaim Potok is an American Jew of Polish descent. See also Werner Keller, *The Bible as History* p. 441.

13 Potok, *Wanderings – History of the Jews* p. 86.
14 Kapelrud, *Dødehavsrullene* (The Dead Sea Scrolls) p. 95. Arvid Kapelrud (1912-1994) was professor at the University of Oslo, his main subject being The Old Testament.
15 Finkelstein and Silberman, *The Bible Unearthed,* citation from the book's introduction chapter.
16 Smith, *Verdens religioner* (The World's Religions), p. 157 and 158.
17 *Dalai Lama læser Evangeliene* (The Dalai Lama reading the Gospels) p. 17. Father Laurence Freeman, who wrote this book, has worked with distributing the Christian meditation tradition and was the leader of 'The World Community for Christian Meditation' when the book was published. He has explained many Christian concepts in the book. See also Evelyn Underhill's explanation about the Trinity in her book *Mysticism* p. 109 and 110.
18 For further interest, see the book *Sigrid Undset* by the Norwegian author Tordis Ørjasæter p. 192.
19 Steiner, *Johannesevangeliet* (The Gospel of John) p. 119 f.
20 Bertelsen HI pp. 18 and 20.
21 Skarsaune, *Den ukjente Jesus* (The unknown Jesus) p. 114 f.
22 Ehrman, *Misquoting Jesus – The Story Behind Who Changed the Bible and Why.* Bart D. Ehrman 'chairs the Department of Religious Studies at the University of North Carolina'.
23 Eisenman, *James, the Brother of Jesus* p. 65 f., and *The New Testament Code.* See p. 579 in the last mentioned book about the prophets.
24 About the Gnostic writings and the Dead Sea Scrolls, see Doresse, *The Secret Books of the Egyptian Gnostics;* Pagels, *The Gnostic Gospels*; Kapelrud, *Dødehavsrullene* (The Dead Sea Scrolls), and Baigent/Leigh, *The Dead Sea Scrolls Deception.* Jean Doresse (b. 1917) was a French archeologist with special interest for egyptology and papyrology.
25 Plotinus, *The Enneads* 2.9.10.
26 Mack, *The Lost Gospel – Q, The Book of Christian Origins* p. 108, 114, 216, 224/225. Skarsaune, *Den ukjente Jesus* (The unknown Jesus) pp. 146 and 143.
27 Marcus, *Mester Eckehart, prædikener and traktater* (Master Eckehart, Sermons and Articles) p. 61. Aage Marcus (1888-1985), Denmark, was a historian specializing in religion and art.
28 Steiner, *Johannesevangeliet* (The Gospel of John) p. 11.
29 See as example *Thomasevangeliet* (The Gospel of Thomas) verse 105.
30 Aschehoug's encyclopedia of 1958 about Christology and the edition of 1961 about the Trinity.
31 Keller, *The Bible as History* pp. 364 and 358.
32 Leivestad, *Hva vet vi om Jesus* (What do we know about Jesus).
33 Maier, *Josefus' hovedverk* (The main works of Josephus) p. 269 with footnotes, and pp. 271 and 281.
34 Eisenman, *James, the Brother of Jesus*, p. 65 f. See also Freke and Gandy, *Jesusmysteriene* (The Jesus Mysteries) p. 174 with footnotes.
35 Skarsaune, *Den ukjente Jesus* (The Unknown Jesus) p. 233.
36 Tacitus, *The Annals of Imperial Rome* p. 365 – probably written after the

year 100 CE.
37　Fasola, *Peter and Paul in Rome* p. 14.
38　Potok, *Wanderings – History of the Jews* p. 371.
39　Campbell, *Hero* p. 353.
40　Lindholm, *Innsyn i Nordiske Gudesagn* (Insight in Nordic God Legends).
41　Thiering, *Jesus the Man.* She was assistant professor in theology in Sydney, Australia, from 1967 to 1993. See also her book *The Book That Jesus Wrote – John's Gospel.*
42　Bertelsen BI p. 167.
43　Eisenman, *James, the Brother of Jesus* and *The New Testament Code.*
44　Mack, *The Lost Gospel – The Book of Q* p. 217.
45　Martinus LB III p. 1069 f.
46　Steiner, *Johannesevangeliet* (The Gospel of John) pp. 203 and 205.
47　Yogananda II p. 73.
48　Aivanhov, *Mennesket, herre over sin skjebne* (Man, Master of his Destiny) p. 173.
49　From *Seth materialet* (The Seth Material) p. 67 and Seth Speaks p. 408.
50　Martinus LB I p. 57.
51　Dowling's book was first published in 1907 in the US. He maintained that the material was taken from the Akashic archive.
52　Marcus, *Mester Eckehart, prædikener and traktater* (Master Eckhart, Sermons and Articles) p. 16.
53　Yogananda I p. 194.
54　Steiner, *Apokalypsen* (The Apocalypse) pp. 74 f. and. 80.
55　Wyller, *Johannes Åpenbaring* (The Revelation).
56　Blavatsky, *The Secret Doctrine* II p. 618.
57　Wilber II p. 428 – *Up from Eden*. This is also to be found in the book by Campbell OrM p. 86.
58　Yogananda I p. 62, citation from the sayings of a sage.
59　Ken Wilber, VIII p. 266 – T*he Marriage of Sense and Soul.*
60　Mahatma Gandhi – See the journal *Alternativ Nettverk,* January 1997.
61　*Dalai Lama læser Evangeliene* (The Dalai Lama reading the Gospels) p. 39.
62　Juan Mascarós, pp. 12 and 31.
63　Augustin, *Confessiones* p. 230. Written around 397-398 CE.
64　*Dalai Lama læser Evangeliene* (The Dalai Lama reading the Gospels) p. 39.
65　Hildegard of Bingen, *Book of Divine Works, with Letters and Songs* p. 276.
66　*Dalai Lama læser Evangeliene* (The Dalai Lama reading the Gospels) p. 39.
67　Marcus, *Mester Eckehart, prædikener and traktate*r (Master Eckhart, Sermons and Articles) p. 16 and Wetlesen, *Mester Eckhart – Å bli den du er* (Master Eckhart – To become what you are) pp. 288/289, as well as the latter's translation of Master Eckhart's sermon no. 58, 4th section. See also Aasmund Brynildsen (1917-1974), *Mester Eckehart – Taler til under-visning* (Master Eckhart – Speeches for Teaching) p. XVIII-XIX.
68　Bertelsen HI s. 113.
69　See Julian of Norwich, *Revelations of Divine Love*, LT, section 5.

70 Kullerud, *Hans Nielsen Hauge* pp. 186 and 255.
71 Schjelderup, Veien jeg måtte gå (The Road I had to walk) p. 106.
72 Laurens van der Post, *Jung and the story of our time* p. 216.
73 Yogananda book II p. 34 and 270 and book I pp. 206, 28, 179, 183 and 278.
74 Wilber V pp. 27 and 95 – *Grace and Grit.*
75 Bruus Jensen p. 433 and 435, and Martinus MK p. 5.
76 Plotinus, *The Enneads* 2.9.9.
77 Aivanhov, *You Are Gods* pp. 150 and 468.
78 Mallasz, *Samtaler med engler* (Talking with Angels) p. 207.
79 *Seth Materialet* (The Seth Material) pp. 164 and 168.
80 *Dalai Lama læser evangeliene* (The Dalai Lama reading the Gospels) p. 168.
81 Underhill, *Mysticism* pp. 97 and 99. See for later references p. 71. This book is considered as one of the classics in regard to the study of mysticism.
82 *Seth Materialet* (The Seth Material) pp. 164-168.

To chapter 3
83 Bergh and Edvardsen, *Mannen som stoppet hurtigruta* (The Man who stopped the Norwegian Coastline ferry).
84 Parmann, Marcello Haugen, and the book *Mystica Eterna*. The last mentioned book has some notes and stories written by Marcello Haugen. See also the book *Betraktninger over en dag* (Considerations for a Day) from 1930. These two last books were published by the Norwegian publishing firm Mystica Eterna in 2003.
85 Westerlund, *Telepatiens gåte* (The Enigma of Telepathy).
86 Myklebust, *Synske hjelparar i hundre år* (Clairvoyant Helpers through one hundred Years).
87 Bertelsen DCM p. 81.
88 Wetlesen's translation of Mester Eckhart's sermon no. 58.
89 Wilber book V p. 22 and 25 – *Grace and Grit.*
90 Stace, *The Teachings of the Mystics* p. 9. The later references from this book are from pp. 14, 20, 24, 25. Stace was professor in philosophy at Princeton University, USA.
91 Part of what here is written about Hildegard is based on the book *The Journal of Hildegard of Bingen* by Barbara Lachman. This book consists of parts from Hildegard's diary, notes made on Sundays in the year 1152. The diary was originally written in Latin and it was not until 1960 that the text was translated into German. See also the book *Hildegard of Bingen's Book of Divine Works with Letters and Songs.*
92 From Caterina's biography written by the Norwegian Nobel Laureate, author Sigrid Undset (1882–1949), who converted to Catholicism in 1924.
93 Teresa of Avila's autobiography. See the Danish edition p. 141 f. See also her book *The Interior Castle.*
94 Ruffin, *St Pio – The True Story*, p. 158 about stigmata.
95 Yogananda book II p. 246.
96 West, *The Devil's Advocate,* 1959, is recommendable in this connection. It

tells about the canonizing process in the Catholic Church. The proper title for the devil's advocat is 'promoter fidei'.
97 Yogananda II p. 64.
98 Louise Marie Frenette, *Aivanhov – A Biography* p. 234 f.
99 Rinpoche p. 100.
100 Steiner, *Fra Jesus til Kristus* (From Jesus to Christ), 3rd lecture p. 46.
101 Aivanhov, *Et nytt lys på evangeliene* (The Gospels in a new Light), the chapter about Jesus calming the storm. See also the book *Mennesket, herre over sin skjebne* (Man, Master of his Destiny) p. 171 f.
102 Eliade, *Shamanism*. See also Pollan (assistant professor in history of religion at the University of Oslo), *Samiske sjamaner – religion og helbredelse* (Shamans among the Sami people – Religion and Healing).
103 *Illustrert Vitenskap* no. 1/2003. See also Dammann p. 274 and Wilson, *Mysteries* p. 506.
104 Manning's experiences have been told by himself at several meetings I have attended, and they are also described in detail by Dammann in the book *Bak Tid and Rom* (Behind Time and Space) p. 167 f., and by Wilson in the book *Mysteries*. See also Manning's own books, such as his autobiography *Med en fot i stjernene* (One Foot in the Stars).
105 Indridason's story has been retold by Georg Hygen in *Parapsykologiske Notiser*, see no. 28/1989, no. 29/1990, no. 30/1990 and no. 32/1991. His story is also to be found on Internet.
106 See report from the lecture given by William Roll in Oslo in 2003, published in *Parapsykologiske Notiser* no. 57/2004.
107 Professor Roger Nelson, Princeton University, has demonstrated that thought can influence a swinging pendulum, see article in Aftenposten 3.12.1995 with the title *Tankesvingende pendelforsøk* (Thought swaying trials with pendulums). Also Michael Talbot has mentioned this in the book *The holographic Universe*. Jane Henry's book Parapsychology contains several articles by well known researchers concerning different parapsychological phenomena. Meta-analysises of RNG-tests have been performed by Dean Radin and is described in the book *Entangled Minds*. See also Fotini Pallikari, *Purported Evidence and Feasible Interpretations* of *Retrocausation*, 2006, and her lecture given at a meeting arranged by Norsk Parapsykologisk Selskap (The Norwegian Parapsychological Society) in Oslo 17.1.2008.
108 Richard Wiseman's doctoral thesis about fraud, commented upon by Paul McKenna in the book *Vår mystiske verden* (Our Mysterious World) p. 89 f. See also Sybo A. Schoutens article *Quantitatively judged Trials with Mediums and Paragnostics* published in Norwegian in the journal Parapsykologiske Notiser no. 35/1993. See also Eysenck and Nias, *Astrology, Science or Superstition* pp. 42 and 39.
109 Fuchs, *Nostradamus*, 1982.
110 This story has been taken from the book *Dramaet om Mexicos erobring – Cortés and Montezuma* (The Drama about the Conquest of Mexico - Cortés and Montezuma) by Maurice Collis.
111 Rolf Manne is professor at The Chemical Institute at the University of Bergen, Norway. See article in Aftenposten 11.1. and 23.2.1999.

112 Schmicker, *Best Evidence*, p. 119 f. about the use of the pendulum. He refers to the publication by Hans-Dieter Betz, *Unconventional Water Detection, Field Test of Dowsing Technique in Dry Zones*, Journal of Scientific Exploration, 1995. Furthermore, he recommends the book *The Divining Hand, The 500-Year Old Mystery of Dowsing* by Christopher Bird, Atglen, Pa., Schiffer Publishing 1993.

113 Lethbridge was during a period of thirty years leading the excavations for 'The Cambridge Antiquarian Society' and for 'The University Museum of Archaeology and Ethnology' and was very interested in the use of the pendulum, cfr. his books *Ghost and Divining Rod* (1963) and *The Power of The Pendulum* (1976).

114 Hawking, *Univers uten grenser* (A Universe without Borders. The English title is: A Brief History of Time) pp. 71 and 19.

115 Aivanhov, *You Are Gods* p. 388.

116 Nelson, *Shortwave Radio Propagation Correlation with Planetary Positions*, RCA Review 12; 26, 1951.

117 Addey, *The Search for a Scientific Starting Point*, Astrological Journal 3:2, 1967 and 5:1, 1969.

118 Eysenck and Nias, *Astrology, Science or Superstition*. Some of these trials have also been reported by Lyall Watson in his book *Supernature* and by Colin Wilson in *Mysteries* (p. 448). Wilson refers also to the tests performed by John Gribbin and Stephen Plageman. Hans Jürgen Eysenck (1916-1997) was professor in psychology at the University of London as well as leader for the psychiatric department at Maudsley Hospital, England. He has authored many books and articles.

119 The Norwegian journal *Psykisk Helse* (Psychic Health) has quoted this statement from Lingjærde according to an article in Aftenposten 5.1.1999.

120 See the article *Parapsychology, The Science of Unusual Experiences*, presented by Ron Roberts and David Groome. See also Shawn Carlson, *A Double-blind Test of Astrology* (1985), and article in *Nature*, 318, 419-425.

121 Wilson, *Mysteries* p. 581 f.

122 Plotinus, *The Enneads* 2.3.1-6.

123 From the book *Marcello Haugens egen lærebok – Inayat Khan, I en østerlandsk Rosenhave* (Marcello Haugen's own book for teaching – Inayat Khan, in an Eastern Rose Garden) p. 174, published by Jan-Erik Kvamsdahl.

124 Yogananda book I p. 197 f.

125 Laurens van der Post, *Jung and the story of our time* p. 242.

126 Rudolf Steiner, *Apokalypsen* (The Apocalypse) p. 68.

127 Ken Wilber VIII p. 64 – Introduction, pp. 441, 617, 619 – *One Taste*.

128 Colin Wilson, *Mysteries* pp. 292 f., 430, 449.

129 Aivanhov, *Mennesket, herre over sin skjebne*, (Man, Master of his Destiny), the chapter about reincarnation.

130 Richard Wilhelms, *I Ching eller Forvandlingens bok* (I Ching or The Book of Change).

131 This is mentioned in Stan Gooch's books *The Double Helix of the Mind and The Paranormal*. Everything mentioned in this book as coming from Gooch

are taken from those books by Gooch (he has detailed references). He has also written several books about the paranormal, about psychology and about brain research.

132   Colin Wilson, *The Occult* p. 100.

133   See the book *The Wisdom of the Tarot* by Elisabeth Haich as well as *Illustrert Vitenskap* no. 7/97 and Dion Fortune, *Kabbalah* pp. 72 and 100.

134   Dion Fortune's real name was Violet Firth. Colin Wilson has said that she was one of the greatest among the modern occultists. She founded the society 'Fraternity of Inner Light' in 1922, which later changed its name to 'The Society of Inner Light'. She has written several books about psychology, among which is the book *Psychic Self Defence* (1930) about the mind's transcendent powers. However, after having studied occultism, she mainly wrote about this subject. Here the references are to her book *Kabbala – den mystiske tradition afdækket and forklaret* (The Kabbalah – the Mystic Tradition revealed and explained).

135   Colin Wilson, *Mysteries* p. 368.

136   See C. G. Jung, *Synchronicity, An Acasual Connecting Principle*, 1960. See also Hans von Noorden about the definition of this term in his book *Parapsykologiens revolusjon av verdensbildet* (The Parapsychological Revolution of the World Image) arranged by Frank-Thore Nilsen p. 67 f.

137   Lyall Watson, *Lifetide* p. 362 and *Heaven's Breath* p. 325.

138   This has also been described by Erik Dammann p. 269 f. See also David Lorimers book *Thinking Beyond the Brain*. In an article in this last mentioned book, Michael Grosso, professor in philosophy at the Jersey City State College, has attested an out-of-body experience where he was visited by another person's phantom body. Michael Talbot has in his book *The Holographic Universe* also a chapter dealing with this phenomenon.

139   See also the article by David Moorehouse about 'Remote Viewing' in *Alternativ Nettverk* no. 5/1999 p. 7. He and some others were trained by CIA so that they only by the use of their mind could 'see' certain places. An article in *Parapsykologiske Notise*r no. 48/1999 p. 7 tells of 'a letter that was not sent'. The author, Thomas L. Aall, experienced to 'see' a female friend writing a letter to him while he was out walking in the woods. The letter was, however, burnt and not sent. See also Lyall Watson, *Lifetide* p. 324 f. and *The Romeo Error*, chapter 6.

140   See the book *At the Hour of Death – A New Look at Evidence for Life after Death* by Karlis Osis and Erlendur Haraldsson. The book is a report regarding death-bed visions. The authors have analyzed doctors and nurses reports about sayings from dying patients.

141   Raymond A. Moody jr., *The Light Beyond – about 'empathic death experiences'*, p.x. Rider 2005.

142   David Scott Rogo, *Liv etter døden* (Life after Death). Rogo had a special interest in parapsychology. He was director of Research for the Society for Psychic Research, Beverly Hills, California, and a member of the Graduate Faculty at John F. Kennedy University, Orinda, California.

143   Colin Wilson, *Mysteries* p. 444.

144   Mentioned by Stephen E. Braude in his book *Immortal Remains, the*

Evidence for Life after Death.

145 Laurens van der Post, *Jung and the Story of our Time* p. 256.
146 From the book *H. P. Blavatsky* by Mary K. Neff. Colin Wilson has written about Blavatsky in his book *The Occult.*
147 Geoffrey Farthing, *Exploring the great Beyond.* Farthing was chief commercial engineer for the Yorkshire Electricity Board, England, and became director of The European School of Theosophy when he retired.
148 See *The Seth Material.*
149 From the cover of the book *Stjärnöga* (Star Eyes) by Sture Johansson. Johansson has also written the books *Møte med Ambres* (Meeting Ambres) and *Resan til Ljuset* (The Travel to the Light) which are referred to several places in this book.
150 Shirley MacLaine, *Its all in the Playing* pp. 127 f. and 195 f. (about Kevin Ryerson).
151 Øyvind Solum, Article in the journal *Alternativ Nettverk* no. 2/1997.
152 See article in *Illustrert Vitenskap* no. 9/1999 about J.Z. Knight. See also description of Ramtha in the book *Beyond the Bleep* by Alexandra Bruce.
153 Both the citations from Charles Richét and from Peggy Barnes are taken from John R. Crowley's article, *Ectoplasm: A Report from Experiences,* www.freewebs.com/afterlife/articles/crowley.htm. John R. Crowley was in 1988, when the article was written, a member of the Board of Trustees of ARPR. He is Associate Prof. Emeritus, Department of English, State University of New York at Brockport.
154 Rosemary Altea, *Ørnen and Rosen* (The Eagle and the Rose). Also other books have been published in Norwegian about how it is to be born as a medium, such as Marion Dampier-Jeans, *Mitt liv med åndene* (My life with the Spirits) and Susan Sibbern, *Stifinner i grenseland* (Pathfinder in Borderland).
155 Most of the information about Carl Wickland is found on Internet. Both his books can be downloaded. The citation from the last book mentioned is from page 24.
156 Arthur J. Ellison tells about this in the book *Science and the Paranormal.*
157 Gary E. Schwartz, *The Afterlife Experiments.*
158 Ray Hyman is one of the founders of CSICOP. He has been heavily critizised because of his negative attitude to ESP in books authored by Adam Mandelbaum and Dean Radin.
159 See more about this project on the website: http://veritas.arizona.edu/papers/Smith.pdf. See also Susy Smith, *The Afterlife Codes – Searching for Evidence of the Survival of the Soul.* Susy Smith has written many books about her activity as a medium. Inter alia, she has maintained that she has channeled information from William James (died in 1910 – professor of psychology at Harvard University), see her book *The Book of James.*
160 See *Den hellige Teresa af Avilas liv fortalt av hende selv* (Vida), p. 228. The sculpture of Teresa's mystical experience by Giovanni Lorenzo Bernini (1598-1680) can be seen on Wikipedia.
161 Michael Talbot, *The Holographic Universe.* Talbot has written quite a lot about

mysticism and physicist theories. See also David Scott Rogo, Miracles.
162 See I.M. Owen & M. Sparrow, *Conjuring up Philip*; Lyall Watson, *Lifetide* p. 357; Colin Wilson, *Mysteries* p. 556; Arthur J. Ellison, *Science and the Paranormal* p. 102 f. and Colin Wilson, *The Occult*. Dion Fortune describes her experience in her autobiography *Psychic Self Defense* and in the book *Kabbala* p. 230 f. Arthur E. Powell built essentially on the theory that the Theosophists Annie Besant and C. W. Leadbeater taught. His books were first published around 1920. Two books that describe the phenomenon of materialization are: W. Crookes, *Researches in the Phenomena of Spiritualism*, 1874, and C. Richet, *Thirty Years of Psychical Resarch*, 1923. Crookes was president of The Royal Society in England and Richet received the Nobel Prize in medicine and physiology.
163 Jane Roberts, *The nature of personal reality*, p. 137
164 Rupert Sheldrake, *Dogs That Know When Their Owners Are Coming Home*, 1999.
165 See Guy Lyon Playfair, *Twin Telepathy* and Dean Radin, *Entangled Minds*.
166 Noel Langley, Edgar Cayce – *On Reincarnation* pp. 20 and 134 f. and Colin Wilson *The Occult* p. 215.
167 Colin Wilson and Rand Flem-Ath, *The Atlantis Blueprint*.
168 Lyall Watson has in the book *Lifetide* commented upon the UFO-phenomena and expressed a negative attitude as to the belief that those are visits from outer space. Graham Hancock has in the book *Supernatural – Meetings with the Ancient Teachers of Mankind,* suggested a connection between the UFO experiences and the shamans' experiences.
169 Lyall Watson, *Lifetide* p. 238. Karl Pribram, *The Neurophysiology of Remembering* – an article in *Scientific American* of January 1969.

To chapter 4

170 Carl Sagan, *The Demon-haunted World – Science as a Candle in the Dark* p. 208 f. He has authored many popular scientific papers and was behind the TV-program about Cosmos, as well as authoring the book *Cosmos*, Random House New York 1980.
171 See the following books about levitation by Olivier Leroy, *La lévitation,* describing the levitation of several Christian saints, and *La Raison primitive*, about levitation in primitive societies. Mentioned also by Mircea Eliade in the book *Shamanism*, p. 481.
172 Ervin Laszlo, PhD, has authored several scientific books. He is from Hungary and lives in Italy. He has been teaching and researching at the New York State University, and has worked for the UN Institute for Training and Research (UNITAR) and for UNESCO. He was also founder of the Club of Budapest in 1993 – an international think tank. In this book Laszlo refers to several phenomena and research results which I have mentioned here and which I have also found in other sources.
173 Marlo Morgan, *Det virkelige folket* (The Real People – the English title is *Down Under*) p. 67 and Laurens van der Post, *The lost world of the Kalahari* pp. 236 and 21.

174 Erik Dammann, Norway, mentions in his book *Bak Tid and Rom* (Behind Time and Space) an interview with professor John Hasted. Daniel Dunglas Home is mentioned by Arthur J. Ellison in the book *Science and the Paranormal – Altered States of Reality.*

175 See inter alia Stanislav Grof, *The Adventure of Self-discovery and Psychology of the Future.* See also his article in David Lorimer's book *Thinking Beyond the Brain.* Also to be mentioned is Grof's book *Introduktion til Den Indre Rejse – Selvoppdagelsens Eventyr* (An Introduction to the Travel within – the Story of Self Discovery).

176 Edward F. Kelly et al. pp. 548, 549 and 569.

177 From Stephen W. Hawking's book, *Univers uten grenser* (A Universe without Borders), see p. 47.

178 Deepak Chopra, *Kropp uten alder. Sinn uten tid* (A body without Age. A Mind without Time) p. 286 f. Chopra, MD, is an ayurvedic physician and consciousness researcher. He lives in the US.

179 See Aage Marcus, *Mester Eckehart, prædikener and traktater* (Master Eckhart, Sermons and Articles) p. 118.

180 C. Bernard Ruffin, *St Pio – The True Story* p. 142.

181 Martinus LB book II p. 380.

182 *Illustrert Vitenskap* no. 1/2004. Article by Helle and Henrik Stub.

183 Olav Hilmar Iversen's article in Aftenposten 2.10.1994 with the title '*Kroppen er flyktig, bare sjelen er stabil*' (The Body is passing, only the Soul remains).

184 Fritjof Capra, *The Web of Life – A New Scientific Understanding of Living Systems* pp. 97, 243 and 295. He is probably best known for the book *The Tao of Physics* from 1975.

185 David Bohm, *Wholeness and the Implicate Order*. Mentioned by Erik Dammann pp. 118 f. and 110.

186 Michael Talbot, *The Holographic Universe.*

187 See note 183 about Iversen as well as David Lorimer's book *Thinking Beyond the Brain.*

To chapter 5

188 See article about Helena Blavatsky by Marianne Aga in the journal *Alternativt Nettverk* no. 5/1998, as well as Helena Blavatsky, *Theosophical Glossary*, Joseph Campbell OrM p. 233 and Geoffrey Farthing, *Exploring the Great Beyond.*

189 Arthur E. Powell AL p. 198.

190 Christmas Humphreys, *Karma og Genfødelse* (Karma and Reincarnation) p. 68.

191 Harmon Hartzell Bro, *Edgar Cayce – A Seer out of Season* p. 128. See also Noel Langley, *Edgar Cayce – On Reincarnation* p. 46.

192 Anna Elisabeth Westerlund, *Telepatiens gåte* (The Enigma of Telepathy) pp. 18 and 20.

193 Lynne McTaggart, *The Field – The Quest for the Secret Force of the Universe.* The citation is from Internet at: http://homepages.ihug.co.nz/~sai/McTag_field.htm.

To chapter 6

194 Carlos Castaneda has written many books about Don Juan. Don Juan was from the south west of the US and Castaneda met him for the first time in 1960.

195 Aivanhov, *Auraen og menneskets åndelige sentre* (Man's Subtle Bodies and Centres) and *You Are Gods*. Jes Bertelsen EB p.36.

196 See Lyall Watson, *Grenseløst liv* (The Romeo Error) pp. 162-178 and 226 as well as *Det er mer mellom himmel og jord* (Supernature - The Natural History of the Supernatural) p. 88 f. Serena Roney-Dougal has in her book *Where Science and Magic Meet*, a chapter about earth magnetism. She has also referred to the research done by Burr.

197 See the book *Science of the Heart*, 2001, from the HeartMath Institute. See also comments by Lyall Watson in the book *Heaven's Breath* p. 286 f. about the magnetic field around the heart which was registered in 1963 by G.M. Baule and R. McFee, and around the head by D. Cohen in 1972. Baule and McFee have written the book *Detection of the Magnetic Field of the Heart*.

198 Gary E. Schwartz, *The Afterlife Experiments* pp. 21 f. and 286.

199 See inter alia Arthur E. Powel's books and the book by Randi Olerud *Flammer til Liv* (Tongues of Fire making Life).

200 Colin Wilson, *Mysteries* p. 578. See also Michael Talbot, *The Holotropic Universe*. He has mentioned several such investigations that show the same. Shafica Karagulla was born in Turkey, was educated in Lebanon, worked in England and Canada, and became an American citizen in 1957.

201 This and the example mentioned in the next section has been reported by Lyall Watson in the book *Grenseløst liv* (The Romeo Error) p. 190 f. and by Colin Wilson in the book *Mysteries*.

202 Arthur J. Ellison was an engineer and professor at the City University in London. He was very interested in paranormal phenomena and was for two terms president of The Society for Psychical Research, London. This book, which was his last, was published after his death.

203 Article in Aftenposten 30.11.1997, with the title *Blinkende spor* (Blinking signs) by Morten Falck.

204 Aivanhov, *Auraen and menneskets åndelige sentre* (Man's Subtle Bodies and Centres). See also *You Are Gods* pp. 380 f. and 398 f.

205 Harmon Hartzell Bro, *Edgar Cayce – A seer out of season* p. 171.

206 See p.108 f. She bases her knowledge on the teaching of Swami Satyananda Saraswati, see his book *The Pineal Gland (Ajna Chakra)* (1972).

207 Colin Wilson, *Mysteries* p. 581 f.

208 See Jes Bertelsen EB p. 40 f. and Randi Olerud, *Flammer til Liv* (Tongues of Fire making Life) p. 101.

209 Ken Wilber book VIII p. 35 – the introduction.

210 Lyall Watson, *Grenseløst liv* (The Romeo Error) p. 139. Watson refers to articles in *American Anatomical Memoirs* 9:257, 1919.

To chapter 7

211 Jeremi Wasiutynski, according to an article in *Aftenposten* 13.9.1998 – an interview by Bodil Fuhr.

212 Mentioned by Erik Dammann p. 282. Eugene Wiegner was a Nobel price winner in physics. Said in 1979.
213 Pierre Teilhard de Chardin, *Fænomenet Menneske* (The Phenomenon of Man) p. 146.
214 Colin Wilson, *The Occult* p. 14.
215 Ken Wilber book VII pp. 662-664 – *The Eye of Spirit*.
216 Erik Dammann *Bak Tid and Rom* (Behind Time and Space) p. 283.
217 Of more recent books of interest concerning this theme, and which gives a good view of where the scientists stand today in regard to consciousness, is the book *Thinking beyond the Brain*, articles collected by David Lorimer, and the book *Irreducible Mind – toward a Psychology for the 21st Century* by Edward F. Kelly et al.
218 See *Parapsykologiske Notiser* no. 37/1994, an article about the Silva method by Steinar Johansen. See also Audun Myskja's book, *Den musiske medisin* (The Music Medicine) p. 82.
219 Colin Wilson, *Mysteries* p. 444.
220 Ken Wilber book VIII p. 348 – *One Taste*.
221 Jes Bertelsen Kp p. 11.
222 Lyall Watson, *Grenseløst liv* (The Romeo Error) pp. 250, 264 and 266.
223 Bob Moore's teaching is explained in Olerud's book *Flammer til liv* (Tongues of Fire making Life) p. 95 f.
224 Jes Bertelsen's teaching as referred to in this main section is taken fromthe following of his books, EB pp. 9 and 29 f., SV p. 162, HI p. 40 f., and Kp p. 11.
225 Rudolf Steiner's explanation mentioned in this chapter is taken from his books *Apokalypsen* (The Apocalypse) pp. 48, 58, 165-166 and *Fra Jesus til Kristus* (From Jesus to Christ), 5th and 7th lectures.
226 Aivanhov, *Mennesket, herre over sin skjebne* (Man, Master of his Destiny) p. 44.
227 Lyall Watson, *Grenseløst liv* (The Romeo Error) pp. 147, 161, 238, 239.
228 Arthur E. Powell ÆD pp. 7, 11.
229 Yogananda I p. 209.
230 Colin Wilson, *Mysteries* p. 335 f.
231 See the book *Gurdjieff – An Introduction to His Life and Ideas* by John Shirley, p. 151.
232 Lyall Watson, *Grenseløst liv* (The Romeo Error) pp. 123, 134 f.
233 Mentioned by Ørnulf Hodne in his book *Mystiske steder i Norge* (Mystical Places in Norway) p. 24.
234 Referred by Ken Wilber book I p. 297 – *The Spectrum of Consciousness*.
235 Astri Hognestad, *Livskriser and kreativitet – et Jungiansk perspektiv* (Life-crisis and creativity – a Jungian Perspective) pp. 57 and 62. Here she has mentioned some of the most important archetypes.
236 Sture Johansson, *Møte med Ambres* (Meeting Ambres) p. 50.
237 Ken Wilber V p. 212 – Grace and Grit, and VII p. 656 f. – *The Eye of Spirit*.
238 Thomas A. Harris, *Jeg er OK – Du er OK* (I am OK – you are OK) and Eric Berne's books *Games people play* and *What do you say after you say hello?*. Thomas A. Harris, MD, was one of the founders of Institute for

Transactional Analysis, Sacramento in California. Eric Berne (1910-1970) was a psychiatrist MD in Carmel in California and the author of several books about transactional analysis.

239 Jon Wetlesen, *Mester Eckhart – Å bli den du er* (Master Eckhart – To become what you are) p. 63.
240 Colin Wilson, *The Occult* p. 216 and *Mysteries* p. 447.
241 See Ken Wilber VIII pp. 547, 575 – *One Taste*, and Ken Wilber IV p. 219 f. – *Two Humanistic Psychologies*.
242 Montague Ullman/Nan Zimmerman, *Bruk dine drømmer* (Use your Dreams) pp. 41 and 68. In this chapter it is also referred to pp. 20, 22, 25, 36, 37, 53 f. Ullman (1916-2008) was an American psychiatrist, MD, and was professor in clinical psychology at Albert Einstein's College of Medicine, New York. He started The Dream Laboratory at the Maimonides Medical Center in Brooklyn, New York.
243 Martinus LB II pp. 414, 423.
244 From *Seth Speaks* p. 136 f.
245 Lyall Watson, *Lifetide* p. 231 f.
246 From Kristin Flood's book *Samtaler om gåtene i oss* (Conversations about the Enigmas within us) p. 129.
247 Sture Johansson, *Møte med Ambres* (Meeting Ambres), See note 2 to chapter 15 and pp. 12, 47, 48, 49, 50 and 51.
248 Harmon Hartzell Bro, *Edgar Cayce – On Dreams* p. 106 f.
249 Jeremi Wasiutynski, *Det kosmiske drama* (The cosmic Drama) pp. 20, 175, 176.
250 Jes Bertelsen DCM pp. 35, 29, 18.
251 Ken Wilber IV p. 154 – *Transformation of Consciousness*.
252 Lyall Watson, *Grenseløst liv* (The Romeo Error) p. 231.
253 Plotinus, *The Enneads* 4.3.27 f. and 4.4.2-5
254 Fritjof Capra, *The Web of Life* p. 243.
255 See the book *Thinking beyond the Brain*, arranged by David Lorimer - article by Charles Tart.
256 Sogyal Rinpoche p. 46 f.
257 Yogananda II pp. 176, 279, 280.
258 Barbara Lachman, *The Journal of Hildegard of Bingen* pp. 4 and 31.
259 Plotinus, *The Enneads* 4.8.1.
260 Stan Gooch, *The Double Helix of the Mind* pp. 126 and 218.
261 Huston Smith p. 174.
262 Evelyn Underhill, *Mysticism* pp. 81 and 85.
263 Jes Bertelsen HI – the introduction to the book.
264 See the reference given in chapter 4.3 above.
265 The journal *Flux* no. 25/26 – 2001 p. 17.
266 Edward F. Kelly et al *Irreducible Mind – toward a Psychology for the 21st Century*, See espesically pp. 618, 623 and 633.
267 *Seth – The nature of personal reality* pp. 137, 149, 153 and 363.
268 Martinus LB I p. 236, and LB III pp. 749, 1022.
269 Deepak Chopra – Article in *Alternativt Nettverk* no. 5/1998, from a lecture

270 given in 1991.
270 See article in Illustrert Vitenskap no. 4/98 and no. 1/2003 p. 48 f., and Dean Radin, *The Entangled Minds* p. 182 f.
271 See the book *Parapsychology – Research on Exceptional Experiences*, edited by Jane Henry p. 37 – the article by Jane Henry.
272 Ervin Laszlo, *Revolusjon i vitenskapen – Fremveksten av det holistiske paradigmet* (Revolution in Science – the Rise of the Holistic Paradigm) p. 47.
273 Lyall Watson, *Lifetide* pp. 312, 316.
274 Ken Wilber IV p. 271 – *Quantum Questions*.
275 Gary Zukav, *The Dancing Wu Li Masters – An overview of the New Physics* p. 54.
276 Noel Langley, *Edgar Cayce – On Reincarnation* p. 43.
277 Deepak Chopra – Article in *Alternativt Nettverk* no. 5/1998, from a lecture given in 1991.
278 Sogyal Rinpoche p. 46.
279 Colin Wilson, *Mysteries* pp. 265 and 266.
280 Juan Mascarós' translation pp. 60 and 61.
281 Deepak Chopra – Article in *Alternativt Nettverk* no. 5/1998, from a lecture given in 1991.
282 John Shirley, *Gurdjieff – An Introduction to His Life and Ideas* p.199, 'The laws which govern the Megalocosmos also govern the Macrocosmos ... down to the Microcosmos.'
283 Rudolf Steiner, *Johannesevangeliet* (The Gospel of John) p. 69 f.
284 Olav O. Aukrust I pp. 34-37.
285 Plotinus, CC p. 277 and the Enneads 4.3.5 f.
286 Jon Wetlesen, *Mester Eckhart – Å bli den du er* (Master Eckhart – To become what you are) pp. 55 f. and 73 f.
287 From Carl Grimberg, *Menneskenes Liv and Historie* (The Humanity's Life and History) book 14 p. 56. Gottfried Wilhelm von Leibniz (1646-1716) was for a period of 40 years in the service of the Elector of Hannover (in 1714 the Elector Georg Ludvig became king of Great Britain and Ireland as King George I). Leibniz was a universal genius with great knowledge in mathematics, philosophy, history, geology and economics. In the year 1700 he was elected life-long president of the Academy of Science in Berlin when this was established. Carl Grimberg (1875-1941) was a Swedish historian.
288 Martinus LB V pp. 1979-1980, 2013, 2052 and 2066.
289 Ken Wilber VII p. 460 – *The Eye of Spirit*.
290 The lecture is printed in *Parapsykologiske Notiser* no. 46/1998 p. 35 f. Milan Ryzl has lectured about parapsychology all over the world and written many articles and books about this phenomenon. See inter alia the book *How to Develop ESP in yourself and in others*, 1972. More information can be found on this website: http://mankindresearchunlimited.iwarp.com/whats_new_27.html.
291 Juan Mascarós' translation pp. 99-100.
292 Jon Wetlesen, *Mester Eckhart – Å bli den du er* (Master Eckhart – To become what you are) p. 102.

293   Rudolf Steiner, *Apocalypsen* (The Apocalypse) p. 48.

To chapter 8

294   See Rudolf Steiner, *Hvorledes Erverves Kundskap om Høiere Verdener* (How to obtain Knowledge about the Higher Worlds), p. 3.
295   See the historian of religions Arthur Versluis *Om de egyptiske mysterier* (About the Egyptian Mysteries) p. 52.
296   David Spangler, *Cooperation with Spirit – Further Conversations with John*.
297   See Aschehoug's encyclopedia (1958/62) about Plato.
298   Lecture given in Oslo in the spring 2000.
299   From *Seth Speaks* p. 16 f.
300   Gitta Mallasz, *Samtaler med engler* (Talking with Angels) p. 259.
301   Henrik Lauridsen-Katborg, *Et rør til himmelen – Personlighedens grænseland* (A Pipeline to the Sky – the Border Country of the Personality). Lauridsen-Katborg is head of the 'Institut for Somatisk Psykologi' in Denmark.
302   From the book *Parapsykologiens revolusjon av verdensbildet* (Parapsychology's revolution of the World Picture), edited by Frank-Thore Nilsen p. 74 f.
303   Lyall Watson, *Grenseløst liv* (The Romeo Error) p. 196 f.
304   Jes Bertelsen Ks pp. 183, 189, See also NH and HI – the Introduction in regard to what is written here.
305   Noel Langley, *Edgar Cayce – On Reincarnation*. See p. 234.
306   Evelyn Underhill, *Mysticism* p. 154 f.
307   Yogananda II p. 181 f.
308   Arthur E. Powell ML p.190.

To chapter 9

309   *Hazrat Inayat Khan og sufibudskapet* (Hazrat Inayat Khan and the Sufi messages) by Sirkar van Stolk and Daphne Dunlop p. 152. Olav O. Aukrust III p. 370 and 476-478, 611. Aivanhov, *You are Gods* p. 163 f. and *Et nytt lys på evangeliene* (A new Light on the Gospels) - the chapter 'Hvis dere ikke blir som barn igjen' (Unless you become like children again). Dion Fortune p. 96.
310   The publication can be found on the following web-site: http://www.tertullian.org/fathers/areopagite_13_heavenly_hierarchy.htm
311   See Agrippa, *Three Books of Occult Philosophy* p. 532 f. Here the names of the angels and the angelic tasks are discussed as well as the planets, the starsigns, the winds and the worlds that each angel rules. Many more names than those listed here are mentioned and there are references to and reports from many sources. The Book of Enoch is not included in the Bible. It is believed written in the second or first century BCE. Enoch had heavenly revelations and was shown the heavenly light sources by the angel Uriel.
312   Martinus LB I p. 57 and LB III pp. 1001, 1006.
313   See Sigrid Undset, *Caterina av Siena*, chapter 12 and 20.

314 C. Bernard Ruffin, *St Pio – The True Story* p. 85 f.
315 Mentioned by Carl Sagan in the book *The Demon-haunted World – science as a candle in the dark.*
316 Lyall Watson, Lifetide pp. 252, 341, 319, 320, 236 and *Grenseløst liv* (The Romeo Error) p. 211.
317 Mentioned by Arthur J. Ellison in an article published in *Parapsykologiske Notiser* no. 43/1997. He is here refering to a lecture given by Anne Arnold Silk in 1991 for the British Society for Psychical Research.
318 Mentioned by Colin Wilson in *Mysteries.*
319 Geoffrey Farthing, *Exploring the Great Beyond* p. 75 f. and chapter 10, where he also refers to H.P. Blavatsky's, *Isis Unveiled.*
320 See the book *H.P. Blavatsky* by Mary K. Neff p. 386.
321 Arthur E. Powell AL p. 167.
322 Dion Fortune p. 190.
323 Martinus LV p. 83.
324 Citation taken from *Alternativt Nettverk* no. 6/1998 p. 89, an article about Asger Lorentsen. Lorentsen has written many books about the star people and about the human being's inner universe, and is considered one of the most influential persons within the Danish new-religious movement of his day.
325 Aivanhov, *You are Gods* pp. 280 and 302 f.
326 Rosemary Altea, *Ørnen and Rosen* (The Eagle and the Rose) pp. 76, 117 and 69.
327 For example in the book by Helge Hognestad, *Morgendemring* (The Morning Twilight).
328 C. Bernard Ruffin, *St Pio – The True Story* p. 314.
329 Eileen Caddy and the book *The Magic of Findhorn* by Paul Hawken p. 101.
330 Aivanhov, *You Are Gods* p. 190 f.
331 See Aasmund Brynildsen, *Mester Eckehart – Taler til undervisning* p. XVIII (Master Eckehart – Speeches for Teaching).
332 Eileen Caddy, *Footprints on the Path,* pp. 140 and 147. See also the video *Opening doors within*, Findhorn Foundation.
333 *Parapsykologiens revolusjon av verdensbildet* (Parapsychology's revolution of the World Image) with Frank-Thore Nilsen as editor. In this book there is an article by Professor Hans Bender about Parapsychology and spiritism, a lecture that was given in Vienna the 5th April 1971 for 'Österreichische Gesellschaft für Parapsychologie'. Hans Bender was until 1975 professor in psychology at the university of Freiburg, Germany, and author of many books. He did a lot research on the poltergeist phenomenon.

To chapter 10
334 Jes Bertelsen DD pp. 12, 14 and 22.
335 Arthur E. Powell ED p. 72.
336 Mentioned by Michael Schmicker in the book *Best Evidence*, p. 204. The BBC's TV-program about NDE, with the title *The Day I died*, was shown on the Norwegian TV, NRK1, 10.01.2004. (Pam Reynolds is a pseudonym.)
337 From Dagne Groven Myhren's comments to the old Norwegian poem

Draumkvedet (The Dream Poem) in an article printed in Aftenposten 6.1.1994 and from the performance *Draumkvedet* at the Norwegian theater, Det Norske Teater, that was shown first time 19.1.1994.
338 Brita Pollan, *Samiske sjamaner* (Shamans among the Sami people). See inter alia p. 13.
339 Joseph Campbell PM p. 260.
340 George G. Ritchie, *Tilbage fra i morgen* (Return from Tomorrow). Raymond A. Moody jr. has written the introduction.
341 C.G. Jung, *Minner, Drømmer og Tanker* (Memories, Dreams and Thoughts), p. 206. Laurens van der Post's book *Jung and the Story of our Time* p. 248.
342 The Norwegian edition was published in 1977 by Dreyers Forlag with the title *Livet etter livet* (The Life after Life). Moody was an American psychiatrist, MD and with a PhD in psychology and philosophy. He has published many more recent books about the same. See also Alice Mürer's article in *Parapsykologiske Notiser* no. 21/1986.
343 Kenneth Ring, PhD., *Life after death* and *Heading towards Omega*.
344 See comments in *Alternativt Nettverk* no. 5/2002.
345 Elisabeth Kübler-Ross, *Døden er livsviktig* (Death is of Vital Importance) pp. 95 and 121 and *Livshjulet* (The Wheel of Life) p. 191 f.
346 Rune Amundsen, *Livets Speil, Opplevelser på dødens terskel* (The Mirror of Life, Experiences at the Threshold of Death), citation from note 12 p.15 and p. 19, and *Døden er en del av livet* (Death is a part of Life). Rune Amundsen is also refering to the book by Joel L. Whitton, *Life Between Life*. Dr. Whitton's most important discoveries started where the NDE's ended. Rune Amundsen also found the book by Stanislav Grof *Den Indre Rejse* (The Adventure of Self-Exploration) important. He further referred to the book by Walter Pahnke et al, *Implications of LSD and Experimental Mysticism*, J. Religion & Health, 1966. Rune Amundsen, Norway, begun as a clinical psychologist, and became later a psychoterapeut and author. In the book by Kristin Flood *Samtaler om gåtene i oss* (Discussions on the Enigmas within us) there is an interview with Rune Amundsen about death.
347 Stanislav Grof, *Psychology of the Future* p. 227.
348 Jes Bertelsen NH pp. 162, 168 and DD p. 14.
349 Sogyal Rinpoche pp. 319 f. and 333.
350 *Seth Speaks* p. 134 f.
351 D. Scott Rogo, *Liv etter døden* (Life after Death) p. 100.
352 Versluis *The Egyptian Mysteries*, see p. 52 about the human being's different spiritual levels.
353 Both quotations are from Joseph Campbell OcM p. 319.
354 Yogananda II p. 181 f.
355 See *The Tibetan Book of the Dead – the great liberation through hearing in the Bardo*, translated by Francesca Fremantle and Chögyam Trungpa. Olav O. Aukrust has also written about the Tibetan book of the Dead.
356 See also Jes Bertelsen's comments regarding the Bardo stages, Dp2 p. 86 f.
357 Sogyal Rinpoche pp. 13 and 33.
358 Huston Smith p. 227.

359 Olav O. Aukrust III p. 121.
360 Huston Smith p. 158.
361 Signe Torsvik, *Emanuel Swedenborg* p. 260 f.
362 From page 53 and 63 in the book *Talking to the other side: A History of Modern Spiritualism and Mediumship* by Todd Jay Leonard
363 Olav O. Aukrust III pp. 333, 388, 347, 403 and 404. See also Rudolf Steiner, *Johannesevangeliet* (The Gospel of John) pp. 12, 15 and 125 and *Apokalypsen* (The Apocalypse) p. 52 ; Jes Bertelsen DD p. 18; and Collin Wilson, *The Man and His Vision* p. 42.
364 Øistein Parmann, *Marcello Haugen* p. 237.
365 See Martinus MS p. 63; LB II pp. 388 and 492; LB III p. 895; and Bruus Jensen pp. 171, 173, 175, 182, 193, 196 and 254.
366 Noel Langley, Edgar Cayce – On Reincarnation p. 44 f.
367 Laurens van der Post, Jung and the story of our time p. 248.
368 Anna Elisabeth Westerlund, *Telepatiens gåte* (The Enigma of Telepathy) pp. 10 and 46.
369 *Conversations with Bob Moore* pp. 74 and 48.
370 Jes Bertelsen NH pp. 99, 168, 161-164, 167 and 173 and SV p. 154.
371 Ken Wilber I p. 552 – *No Boundary* and Ken Wilber IV pp. 342, 343 – *Death, Rebirth, and Meditation*.
372 From the book *Seth materialet* (The Seth Material) pp. vii and 10 f. and from *Seth Speaks* p. 116 f., especially pp. 123, 125, 127 and 131.
373 Sture Johansson, *Møte med Ambres* (Meeting Ambres) p. 62.
374 Olav O. Aukrust III pp. 475 f. and 335.
375 Jes Bertelsen NH pp. 162, 165 and DD p.16.
376 Rudolf Steiner, *Apokalypsen* (The Apocalypse) p. 52 and *Johannesevangeliet* (The Gospel of John) pp. 12 and 125.
377 Arthur E. Powell ÆD p. 79 f.
378 Arthur E. Powell AL p. 153.
379 Jes Bertelsen DD p. 69.
380 Arthur E. Powell ML pp. 150 and 149.
381 Olav O. Aukrust book III p. 354.
382 Stephen E. Braude, *Immortal Remains – The Evidence for Life after Death*, p. 236 f. Gary E.R. Schwartz and Linda G.S. Russek have heard of the same after extensive interviews with heart transplant patients over a period of ten years, cfr. article in *Illustrert Vitenskap* no. 15/2005 with the title 'Personligheten sitter i hjertet' (The Personality resides in the Heart), where several such examples are given.
383 The case is mentioned by Stephen E. Braude in the book mentioned above and by David Fontana in the book *Is there an Afterlife?* Fontana states that many such cases can be found.
384 Lloyd P. Gerson, *The Cambridge Companion to Plotinus* p. 321.
385 Sogyal Rinpoche p. 333.
386 Rosemary Altea, *Ørnen and Rosen* (The Eagle and the Rose) p. 138.
387 Arthur E. Powell AL p. 118 and KL p. 154.

388 See inter alia Christmas Humphreys, *Karma og Genfødelse* (Karma and Reincarnation) p. 84.

To chapter 11

389 Joseph Campbell OrM pp. 242 and 250.
390 Colin Wilson, *The Occult* p. 757.
391 See the book *Plato* by Harold North Fowler p. 249.
392 Those interested should also read the book *Reincarnation in World Thought* by J. Head and P.L. Cranston, Julian Press, N.Y. 1967.
393 Mentioned by Barbara Thiering, *Jesus the Man.* See also Jes Bertelsen, *Kristusprocessen* (The Christ Process) p. 22 about Jewish mysticism – the Kabbalah. The Pharisees were a Jewish sect that disappeared around the time of the destruction of Jerusalem's temple in the year 70 CE. St Paul was originally a Pharisee according to Acts 23.6.
394 Origen is mentioned by Sogyal Rinpoche p. 82.
395 This is the headline in *De civitate Dei,* 12th book 21st chapter, cfr. Lars Bo Bojesen, *Fænomenet Ånd* (The Spirit Phenomenon) p. 75.
396 Noel Langley, *Edgar Cayce – On reincarnation. The truth about people who have lived more than once – and what it means for you*, p. 179.
397 Lars Bo Bojesen, *Fænomenet Ånd* (The Spirit Phenomenon) p. 73.
398 *Dalai Lama læser Evangeliene* (The Dalai Lama reading the Gospels) p. 39 and p. 100. Ajahn Amaro (his real name is Jeremy Horner) is a member of the organization Ajahn Sumedho and lives in the Chithurst monastery in England. This is a Buddhist society of the Theravada Buddhism.
399 *Dalai Lama læser Evangeliene* (The Dalai Lama reading the Gospels) p. 113. And about causality p. 198. See also description of the same story to be found in the book by Christmas Humphreys *Karma og Genfødelse* (Karma and Reincarnation) p. 60; and by Huston Smith p. 77.
400 Rudolf Steiner, *Fra Jesus til Kristus* (From Jesus to Christ), 5th lecture and Sogyal Rinpoche p. 91.
401 Sogyal Rinpoche pp. 89, 98, 99, and 82.
402 *Blazing Splendour – The memoirs of Tulku Urgyen Rinpoche.* See pp. 396 and 397.
403 Ken Wilber IV pp. 342-343 – *Death, Rebirth, and Meditation*, and Wilber I p. 625 – *Where It Was, There I Shall Become*, and VII p. 582 – *The Eye of Spirit.*
404 Jes Bertelsen SV p. 115 f. ; EB pp. 112-113; Kp p. 33; DD pp. 16 and 21; NH p. 171 and BI pp. 171 and 142.
405 Christmas Humphreys, Karma og Genfødelse (Karma and Reincarnation) pp. 59, 61 and 68.
406 Yogananda I p. 209.
407 Arthur E. Powell KL pp. 14, 16, 140, 149, 150 and 206.
408 Geoffrey Farthing, *Exploring the Great Beyond,* see, inter alia, p. 76. See also Helena Blavatsky, *The Secret Doctrine.*
409 See Noel Langley, *Edgar Cayce – On Reincarnation.*
410 Harmon Hartzell Bro, *Edgar Cayce – A seer out of season* pp.132, 172, 183, 185

411 *The Nature of Personal Reality* p. 388; *Seth Speaks* pp. 49 and 237; *Seth-materialet* (The Seth Material) pp. 19 f., 95 and 96.
412 Sture Johansson, *Møte med Ambres* (Meeting Ambres) pp. 17, 18, 23, 34 and 64.
413 Kristin Flood, *Samtaler om gåtene i oss* (Discussions on the Enigmas within us) pp. 69 and 88.
414 Elisabeth Haich, *Initiation.* See especially p. 534.
415 The story is also mentioned by Colin Wilson in *Mysteries* p. 357 (but he does not mention the music) and by Michael Talbot. Charlotte Moberly and Eleanor Jourdain were both leaders of St. Hugh's College, Oxford, England, Moberly from 1886 to 1915 and Jourdain from 1915 to 1924.
416 J. Halifax, *Shamanic Voices.* Mentioned by Stanley Kripner in the book *Parapsychology – Research on Exceptional Experiences*, edited by Jane Henry. See also the description of Maria Sabina in Graham Hancock's book *Supernatural – Meetings with the Ancient Teachers of Mankind.*
417 Lyall Watson, *Grenseløst liv* (The Romeo Error) p. 231.
418 The stories mentioned here are taken from Colin Wilson's book *The Occult* and Lyall Watson's book *Lifetide.* They have taken them from other sources.
419 Colin Wilson, *The Occult.* See also Noel Langley, *Edgar Cayce – On Reincarnation.*
420 See *Parapsykologiske Notiser* no. 54/2002 p. 17 f. and the book *Yesterday's Children* by Jenny Cockell.
421 Lyall Watson, *Grenseløst liv* (The Romeo Error) p. 235.
422 David Scott Rogo, *Liv etter døden* (Life after Death) p. 200.
423 Ian Stevenson, *Where Reincarnation and Biology Intersect.*
424 Lyall Watson, *Grenseløst liv* (The Romeo Error) chapter 8.
425 See *ITC - Proceedings of the Second International Conference on Current Research into Survival of Physical Death with Special Reference to Instrumental Transcommunication* p. 41.
426 Lyall Watson, *Lifetide* p. 321 f.
427 See Noel Langley, *Edgar Cayce on Reincarnation* p. 30.
428 Joel L. Whitton and Joe Fisher, *Life between Life.* Also Michael Talbot has mentioned this in the book *The Holographic Universe.*
429 Helen Wambach, *Life before Life,* and *Reliving past Lives.* Wambach was a practicing psychotherapist in the US from 1955.
430 Noel Langley, *Edgar Cayce – On Reincarnation* p. 208.
431 Stanislav Grof, *The Adventure of Self-Discovery* p. 80. See p. 86 about reincarnation.
432 Rudolf Steiner, *Johannesevangeliet* (The Gospel of John) p. 29 and *Fra Jesus til Kristus* (From Jesus to Christ) 3rd, 5th, 6th and the last part of the 7th lecture. See further Olav O. Aukrust III p. 405 and the references mentioned above concerning Aukrust.
433 Martinus MS p. 33 and Bruus Jensen pp. 173, 175 and 182.
434 Aivanhov, *You Are Gods* p. 244 f.
435 See Colin Wilson, *Mysteries* pp. 340-341 – from the book by Ouspensky

The Strange Life of Ivan Osokin.
436 From *Conversations with Bob Moore* pp. 79 and 87.
437 Milan Ryzl, *Søken etter erkjennelse av høyere dimensjoner og en annen verden* (The Quest for Recognition of the higher Dimensions and a different World), referred in Parapsykologiske Notiser no. 46/1998 p. 35 f.
438 Lyall Watson, *Lifetide* pp. 321, 207 and 302.
439 Lyall Watson, *Grenseløst liv* (The Romeo Error) pp. 239 and 234.
440 Colin Wilson, *The Occult* p. 687. See especially p. 673.
441 See Parapsykologiske Notiser nr. 29/1990 and 30/1990.
442 See *ITC - Proceedings of the First International Conference on Current Research into Survival of Physical Death with Special Reference to Instrumental Transcommunication* p. 104. ITC Journal, 2004.

To chapter 12
443 Rudolf Steiner, *Johannesevangeliet* (The Gospel of John) pp. 48 and 75.
444 From the book by Sogyal Rinpoche.
445 Rudolf Steiner, *Apokalypsen* (The Apocalypse) p. 138.
446 *Conversations with Bob Moore* p. 28. He is here citing from the Bible, Matt 5.39.
447 Phyllis Krystal, *The Ultimate Experience* pp. 100 f. Satya Sai Baba (b. 1926-2011) lived in Bangalore in India and was considered by many as a wise man and a guru. He is said to have been able to perform all the miracles that the Bible reports that Jesus could do. Professor Erlendur Haraldsson (b.1931), Iceland, has observed Sai Baba as he has had the opportunity to spend some time with him, and he has confirmed the many astonishing feats performed by Sai Baba and has written books about him. Howard Murphet, who also has written a book about Sai Baba, confirms this, according to Lyall Watson, see his book *The Romeo Error*. Many people, who have spent some time in close contact with Sai Baba, have written books about their experiences. However, it should also be mentioned that Sai Baba has been accused of cheating and sexual abuse of young boys, and has probably been jailed because of this. This was maintained in a video film that was shown on the Norwegian TV channel NRK1. Stan Gooch does not approve of him.
448 Rudolf Steiner, *Apokalypsen* (The Apocalypse) p. 27.
449 Marcello Haugen, *Betragtninger over en dag* (Considerations for a Day), p.56, 60.
450 Sogyal Rinpoche according to an article in Aftenposten 6.4.1997.
451 Sture Johansson, *Resan till Ljuset* (The Voyage to the Light) pp. 83 and 106.
452 Erich Fromm, *Om kjærlighet* (About Love) 1956 p. 133.
453 Martinus KB p. 20.

To chapter 13
454 Citation from Aftenposten 14.04.1997. William Blake (1757-1827) was an English painter and mystic.
455 Citation from Jes Bertelsen's book HI p. 111.

456 Plotinus, *The Enneads* 2.3.8.
457 Pierre Teilhard de Chardin, *Fænomenet Menneske* (The Phenomenon of Man) p. 281.
458 Dion Fortune p. 224.
459 Sture Johansson, *Møte med Ambres* (Meeting Ambres) p. 11.
460 Citation taken from Marianne Fredriksson's book, *Simon og eiketrærne* (Simon and the Oak Trees) pp. 285 and 270.
461 Arthur E. Powell KL p. 188.
462 Plotinus, *The Enneads* 2.9.9.
463 Bruus Jensen pp. 179 and 180.
464 Citation from F.J. Billeskov Jansen's book about Søren Kierkegaard, mentioned by Gunhild Hoem in the book *Under forvandlingens Lov – En studie i Henrik Ibsens dramatikk* (Under the Law of Change – a Study in Henrik Ibsen's dramatic writings). What is mentioned here is also from Gunhild Hoem's book, se p. 16. See also her article in *Parapsykologiske Notiser* no. 34/1992 pp. 126 f.
465 See Ken Wilber II p. 201 – *The Atman Project.*
466 Elisabeth Kübler-Ross, *Livshjulet* (The Wheel of Life).
467 Citation taken from Jes Bertelsen's book HI p. 111.
468 Dion Fortune, p. 170.

To chapter 14

469 See inter alia Humphreys, *Karma og Genfødelse* (Karma and Reincarnation) p. 84 and Helena Blavatsky's comments regarding Karma, as well as other theosophists' writings.
470 Aivanhov, *You are Gods* p. 217.
471 Noel Langley, *Edgar Cayce – On Reincarnation* pp. 38 f. See also pp. 239 and 247.
472 Jes Bertelsen EB p. 109.
473 Plotinus, *The Enneads* 2.9.9.
474 *Seth Materialet* (The Seth Material) pp. 70-89 and 95-96.
475 Ken Wilber III p. 325 – *Eye to Eye.*
476 Aivanhov, *Mennesket, herre over sin skjebne.* (Man, Master of his Destiny). See the chapter about reincarnation, especially p. 187.
477 Morgan Robertson, *Futility,* F. Mansfield, N.Y. 1898. Mentioned by Erik Dammann p. 274.
478 Øystein Parmann, *Marcello Haugen* p. 237.
479 C. Bernard Ruffin, *St Pio – The True Story* p. 342.
480 Randi Olerud *Flammer til Liv* (Tongues of Fire making Life) p. 107.
481 Olav O. Aukrust III p. 613.
482 Erik Dammann pp. 180, 117 and 289.

To chapter 15

483 Deepak Chopra – Article in *Alternativt Nettverk* no. 5/1998.

484 See Ervin Laszlo p. 67.
485 C. Bernard Ruffin, *St Pio – The True Story* p. 344.
486 Ken Wilber V p. 61 – Grace and Grit; IV p.154 – *Transformation of Consciousness*; IV pp. 219 f. – *Two Humanistic Psychologies;* VI 0p. 238 and 616 f. – *Sex, Ecology, Spirituality*; and IV p. 353 – *Death, Rebirth, and Meditation.*
487 Irina Tweedie, *The Chasm of Fire – A Woman's Experience of Liberation through the Teachings of a Sufi Master*, p. 147. Tweedie was born in Russia, was educated in Vienna and Paris, and then settled in England. In 1961 she went to India and became an apprentice with an Indian Sufi master (he died in 1966).
488 *Seth-materialet* (The Seth Material) pp. 14 and 67-89 as well as *The nature of personal reality* pp. 365-367.
489 See the Society's laws § 3. See www.healing.no.
490 See *Parapsykologiske Notiser* no. 46/1998.
491 Lyall Watson, *Grenseløst liv* (The Romeo Error) p. 246 f. See also the website http://www.williamjames.com/Science/PSIONIC2.htm
492 See Stan Gooch, *The Paranormal*, 1978, and the exchange of letters between him and Lyall Watson, included in Stan Gooch's book *The Double Helix of the Mind.*
493 Lyall Watson, *Grenseløst liv* (The Romeo Error) pp. 146 p. 250, 264 and 266. Shafica Karagulla and Hiroshi Motoyama are also mentioned by Michael Talbot in his book *The Holographic Universe.*
494 Audun Myskja, *Den musiske medisin* (The Music Medicine) pp. 216 and 218 f. Stanislav Grof has also mentioned that music has a healing effect, which has been documented through his special form for research.
495 Arthur E. Powell ÆD p. 84.
496 Lyall Watson, *Heaven's Breath* p. 287 f.
497 Barbara Lachman, *The Journal of Hildegard of Bingen* pp. 49 – 50.
498 Laurens van der Post, *Jung and the story of our time* p. 128.

To chapter 16
499 *Den Hellige Teresa af Avila's liv, fortalt av hende selv* (St Teresa's autobiography) p. 62.
500 Citation from *Alternativ Nettverk*, an article about Christian mysticism.
501 Juan Mascaró's translation, p. 101.
502 Jes Bertelsen Dp3 pp. 155 and 157 and BI p. 56.
503 Martinus LB pp. 2313 and 2308 f. as well as Bruus-Jensen pp. 429, 431, 438, 439, 268 and 269.
504 Ken Wilber VI p. 263 – *Sex, Ecology, Spirituality.*
505 Marcello Haugen, *Betragtninger over en dag* (Consideration for a Day) pp. 21, 47, 50, 55, 56 and 63, as well as *Mystica Eterna* p. 95.
506 David Spangler, *Cooperation with Spirit – Further Conversations with John* pp. 21 f. and 31.
507 Citation from Aasmund Brynildsen, *Mester Eckehart – Taler til undervisning* (Master Eckehart – Speeches for Teaching) p. XXIII.
508 Karlfried Dürckheim *Meditera – vägen til förvandling* (Meditation – the Road to Change).

509 Juan Mascarós' translation pp. 73 and 59.
510 Yogananda I p. 278.
511 Some of these trials have been mentioned in the book by Daniel Goleman, *Destruktive Følelser – Hvordan kan vi håndtere dem?* (Destructive Emotions – How to handle them?) See also the article in *Illustrert Vitenskap* no. 9/2004 about the positive effects of meditation as seen in resent research.
512 See *Illustrert Vitenska*p no. 12/1994 and W. Adam Mandelbaum, *The Psychic Battlefield*. Mandelbaum was an American lawyer and investigation officer with extraordinary psychic abilities. He participated inter alia in the project 'Remote Viewing' which was financed by the American State through CIA (The Central Intelligence Agency).
513 Alain Gugno, *St. John of the Cross* p. 125.
514 Huston Smith p. 174.
515 Sister M. Kristin Riosanu. From an interview in Aftenposten 4.10.1998 p. 3.
516 Julian of Norwich, *Revelations of Divine Love*. See LT, sub chapter 27 f.
517 Martinus LB III p. 1072.
518 Ambres' explanation in a lecture given in Oslo 23.5.2000.
519 Noel Langley, *Edgar Cayce – On Reincarnation* p. 47.
520 Mentioned by Sogyal Rinpoche.
521 Jes Bertelsen NH p. 46.
522 Lene Højholt, from a lecture given at a meeting arranged by Møtested Høvik 19.04.2001. Cfr. her book *Vejen* (The Road).
523 From Jean Doresse, *The Secret Books of the Egyptian Gnostics.*
524 Mentioned by Ken Wilber, See VI p. 302 – *Sex, Ecology, Spirituality.* Teresa of Avila, *Sjælens Slot* (The Interior Castle), see p. 161 about the seventh house.
525 Mester Eckhart, sermon no. 58, in Jon Wetlesen's translation.
526 Jes Bertelsen HI pp. 13, 34, 36 and 82.
527 Rudolf Steiner, *Hvorledes Erverves Kundskap om Høiere Verdener* (How to obtain Knowledge about the Higher Worlds). Citation from pp. 3, 8-10, 36, 50 and 179. See also his book *Johannesevangeliet* (The Gospel of John).
528 Ken Wilber V p. 286 – *Grace and Grit,* and II p. 47 f. – *The Atman Project.*
529 Elaine Pagels, *The Gnostic Gospels* p. 135. The Gospel of Thomas is one of the Apocryphal Gospels. See verse 70 in The Norwegian Book-club's edition of 2001.
530 Huston Smith pp. 171-172.
531 Martinus LV p. 102.
532 Peter Deunov founded 'The Brotherhood of Light'. This is a religious society that is in contact with 'The White Brotherhood' – which is the spiritual world's brotherhood with the goal to serve God, based on divine love, divine wisdom and divine truth, and which is striving to give the Earth spiritual impulses. He is described in the book *Prophet for our times* by David Lorimer, Element Books Ltd., UK, 1991.

To chapter 17

534 Dion Fortune pp. 214-215.

535 Mircea Eliade, *Patterns in Comparative Religion* p. 164.
536 Lucie Lamy, *New Light on Ancient Knowledge – Egyptian Mysteries* pp. 71 and 70.
537 John Shirley, *Gurdjieff – An Introduction to His Life and Ideas*, p. 157 f.
538 Helena Blavatsky, *The Secret Doctrine II* p. 622.
539 Lucius Apuleius, *The Golden Ass*, Worldworth Classics 1996, p. 185.
540 Mircea Eliade, *Shamanism p. 134.*
541 Jeremi Wasiutynski p. 79.
542 Chaim Potok, *History of the Jews* p. 446.
543 Colin Wilson, *Mysteries* p. 397.
544 Aivanhov, *You Are Gods* p. 155 f.
545 Also in Agrippa's book there is an overview of The Tree of Life and the meanings of the different symbols.
546 Caroline Myss, *Ånd og Energi* (Spirit and Energy) p. 293.

To chapter 18
547 Olav O. Aukrust III p. 353.
548 Plotinus, *The Enneads* 2.9.8.
549 Geoffrey Farthing, *Exploring the Great Beyond* p. 105.
550 Rudolf Steiner, *Apokalypsen* (The Apocalypse) pp. 62 f. and 80 f. and *Johannesevangeliet* (The Gospel of John).
551 Martinus KB p. 36.
552 Aivanhov, *Auraen og menneskets åndelige sentre* (Man's Subtle Bodies and Centres) p. 21.
553 Gitta Mallasz, *Talking with Angels* pp. 422-423.
554 Sture Johansson, *Møte med Ambres* (Meeting Ambres), Sturid forlag 1996 p. 71.
555 Erik Dammann pp. 118 and 110. From a conversation in 1985.
556 Jes Bertelsen DCM p. 82, f.
557 Jeremi Wasiutynski pp. 32, 43, 44, 46, 50, 57, 58 and 15.
558 Pierre Teilhard de Chardin, *Om menneskets fremtid* (The Future of Man) where the article mentioned is included. See especially pp. 31 and 37. See also his book *Fænomenet Menneske* (The Phenomenon of Man), especially p. 231.
559 Ken Wilber VIII pp. 33, 36, 63 and 77 – *The Marriage of Soul and Sense*.
560 Gunhild Hoem, *Under forvandlingens Lov – En studie i Henrik Ibsens dramatikk* (Under the Law of Change – a Study in Henrik Ibsen's dramatic writings). See also her article in *Parapsykologiske Notiser* no. 34/1992.
561 See the third act of the play. The citation is based on the edition published by Gyldendal in 1972 p. 336-337.

To chapter 19
562 Bruus Jensen pp. 386 and 389.
563 Rudolf Steiner, *Johannesevangeliet* (The Gospel of John) p. 5.
564 Jes Bertelsen NH p. 79.

Bibliography

Addey, J.M., *The Search for a Scientific Starting Point*, Astrological Journal 3:2, 1967 and 5:1, 1969
Aftenposten – a Norwegian daily newspaper
Agrippa, *Three Books of Occult Philosophy,* arranged by Donald Tyson, Llewellyn Publications 2003
Aivanhov, *Mennesket, herre over sin skjebne* (Man, Master of his Destiny), Prosveta Forlag 1992
  - *You Are Gods*, Prosveta p.A., France, 2002
  - *Auraen og menneskets åndelige sentre*, (Man's Subtle Bodies and Centres) Prosveta Forlag 1993
  - *Et nytt lys på evangeliene* (A new Light on the Gospels) Prosveta Forlag
Altea, Rosemary, *Ørnen og Rosen* (The Eagle and the Rose), Hilt & Hansteen Forlag 1996
Alternativ Nettverk, January 1997, the article about Mahatma Gandhi
  - no. 2/1997, interview with Kevin Ryerson
  - no. 5/1998, article about Helena Blavatsky
  - no. 5/1998, article about Deepak Chopra
  - no. 6/1998, article about Asger Lorentsen
  - no. 5/1999, article about 'Remote Viewing' and David Moorehouse
  - no. 9/1999, article about J.Z. Knight
  - no. 5/2002, article about some Christian mystics
Amundsen, Rune, *Livets Speil, Opplevelser på dødens terskel* (Life's Mirror, Events at Death's Threshold), Aventura Forlag Oslo 1987
  - *Døden er en del av livet* (Death is a Part of Life), Kilde Forlag 1992
Apuleius, Lucius, *The Golden Ass*, Worldworth Classics 1996
Aschehoug's encyclopedia 1958 and 1962
Augustin, *Confessiones*, Penguin Classics 1961
Aukrust, Olav O., *Dødsrikets Verdenhistorie* (The World History of the Realm of the Dead) book I, II and III, Dreyer Forlag A/S, 1985
Baigent, Michael and Leigh, Richard, *The Dead Sea Scrolls Deception*, Jonathan Cape, 1992/1991
Baigent, Michael, Leigh, Richard and Lincoln, Henry, *The Holy Blood and The Holy Grail,* Arrow Books 1996/1982
Bergh, Richard and Edvardsen, Erik H., *Mannen som stoppet hurtigruta* (The Man who stopped the Norwegian Coastline ferry), Grøndahl forlag 1990
Berne, Eric, *Games people play*, Penguin Books 1975/1964
  - *What do you say after you say hello?* Corgi Books 1979/1974

Bernstein, Morey, *The Search for Bridey Murphy*, 1956
Bertelsen, Jes, Dp2 - *Dybdepsykologi 2* (Depth psychology 2), Borgen Forlag 1985/1979
- Dp3 - *Dybdepsykologi 3* (Depth psychology 3), Borgen Forlag 1986/1980
- DCM - *Drømmer, chakrasymboler og meditation* (Dreams, Chakra Symbols and Meditation), Borgen Forlag 1986/1982
- EB - *Energi og bevidsthed* (Energy and Consciousness), Borgen Forlag 1985
- SV - *Selvets Virkelighed* (The Reality of the Self), Borgen Forlag 1988
- Ka - *Kvantespring* (Quantum Leaps), Borgen Forlag 1988
- Kp - *Kristusprosessen* (The Christ Process) Borgen Forlag 1989
- BB - *Bevidsthedens befrielse* (The liberation of the Consciousness) Borgen Forlag 1991
- NH - *Nuets Himmel* (The Heaven of the Now), Borgen Forlag 1994
- DD - *Døden og Dødsprocessen* (Death and the Death Process), Vækstcenteret 1995
- HI - *Hjertebøn og Ikonmystik* (The Heart Prayer and Icon mysticism), Borgen Forlag 1998
- BI - *Bevidsthedens Inderste – Dzogchen* (The Innermost Consciousness – Dzogchen), Rosinante Forlag A/S 1999

Billeskov Jansen, F.J., *Søren Kierkegaard*
The Bible. The New International Version(UK 2011) is used here
Blavatsky, Helena P., *The Secret Doctrine*, The Theosophy Company, 1947/1888
- *The Key to Theosophy*, The United Lodge of Theosophists, LA, California 1920/1889.
- *Theosophical Glossary*, The Theosophy Company 1930/1892
- *Isis Unveiled*, The Theosophy Company 1931/1877

Bohm, David, *Wholeness and the Implicate Order*, Routledge & Kegan Paul, 1982
Bojesen, Lars Bo, *Fænomenet Ånd* (The Spirit Phenomenon) p. 73, Gyldendal Danmark 1993
Bond, Frederick Bligh, *The Gate of Remembrance,* 1918
Braude, Stephen E., *Immortal Remains, The Evidence for Life after Death,* Rowman & Littlefield Publishers, Inc. 2003
- *The Gold Leaf Lady and other Parapsychological Investigations*, The University of Chicago Press, 2007

Brennan, Barbara Ann, *Hands of Light – A Guide to Healing through the Human Energy Field,* Bantam Books 1988
Bro, Harmon Hartzell, *Edgar Cayce – On Dreams*, The Aquarian Press, 1989/1968
- *Edgar Cayce – A seer out of season,* The Aquarian Press, 1990/1989

Bruce, Alexandra, *Beyond the Bleep*, Disinformation Company Ltd. 2005
Brune, François, *Towards a new interpretation of the signs of reincarnation,* ITC Journal Centre for Investigation, 2006
Bruus Jensen, *X - En komplet indføring i Martinus' kosmologi* (A Complete

Introduction to Martinus's Cosmology), book 2, Nordisk Impuls 1987

Brynildsen, Aasmund, *Mester Eckehart – Taler til undervisning,* (Master Eckehart – Speeches for Teaching) Dreyers Kulturbibliotek 11

Burr, Harold Saxton and Northtrop, F.S.C., *The Electrodynamic Theory of Life,* ca. 1930

Caddy, Eileen, *Footprints on the Path*, The Findhorn Press 1988/1976

Campbell, Joseph, - PM - *Primitive Mythology*, Penguin Books 1976
- Hero - *The Hero with a Thousand Faces*, Princeton University Press
- OrM - *Oriental Mytholgy*, Penguin Books 1976
- OcM - *Occidental Mythology*, Penguin Books 1976

Capra, Fritjof, *The Web of Life – A New Scientific Understanding of Living Systems*, Anchor Book 1996

Carlson, Shawn, *A double-blind test of astrology*, article in Nature 1985

Carter & McGrey, *Edgar Cayce – On Healing*, edited by H. L. Cayce, Aquarian Press 1991

Castaneda, Carlos, *The Teachings of Don Juan - A Yaqui Way of Knowledge*, Penguin Books 1982/1968

Chase, Truddi, *When Rabbit Howls*

Chopra, Deepak, *Kropp uten alder. Sinn uten tid,* (Ageless Body, Timeless Mind, 1993) Grøndahl Dreyer forlag 1996.

Cockell, Jenny, *Yesterday's Children*. See also Parapsykologiske Notiser no. 54/2002

Collin, Rodney, *The Theory of Celestial Influence* (1954)

Collis, Maurice, *Dramaet om Mexicos erobring – Cortés og Montezuma* (The Drama of the Conquest of Mexico - Cortés and Montezuma), Dreyer Forlag

Conan Doyle, Arthur, *The History of Spiritualism, 1926* – Complete two volumes, The Echo Library 2006

Cummins, Geraldine, *The Road to Immortality*, Pilgrims Book Services 1984/1932

Dalai Lama læser Evangeliene, Borgen Forlag 2000 (English title: The Good Heart - A Buddhist Perspective on The Teachings of Jesus, 1996)

David-Neel, Alexandra, *My Journey to Lhasa*, 1927

De Apokryfe Evangelier (The Apocryphal Gospels), De norske bokklubber 2001

Detering, Hermann, *The Falsified Paul: Early Christianity in the Twilight,* translated from German by Darrell J. Doughty and published by Institute for Higher Critical Studies, 2003. It can be found on Internet. The title of the original is *Der gefälschte Paulus: das Urchristentum im Zweilicht,* Patmos Press, Düsseldorf, 1995

Doresse, Jean, *The Secret Books of the Egyptian Gnostics*, Inner Traditions International Ltd, 1986/1958

Dowlings, Levi H., *Den nye tidsalders evangelium om Jesus Kristus*, Spinxh forlag, København. The first edition published in 1907 in the USA

Dürckheim, Karlfried, *Meditera – vägen till förvandling* (To meditate – the Road to Change), Proprius Förlag, 1985. The first edition published in 1976 in Germany under the title *Meditieren – wozu und wie*

Edwards, Harry *The Evidence of Spirit Healing*, Sanctuary Trust, reprint 1978
Ehrman, Bart D., *Misquoting Jesus – The Story Behind Who Changed the Bible and Why*, HarperCollins 2005
Eisenbud, Jule, *The World of Ted Serios,* William Morrow & Company, 1967
Eisenman, Robert, *James, the Brother of Jesus*, Watkins Publishing, London 2002
- *The New Testament Code – The Cup of the Lord, The Damascus Covenant and The Blood of Christ,* Watkins Publishing, London, 2006

Eliade, Mircea, *Shamanism – Archaic techniques of ecstasy,* Bollingen Series LXXVI, 1974/1951
- *Patterns in Comparative Religion*, Sheed & Ward Ltd. 1997/ 1958

Ellison, Arthur J., *Science and the Paranormal*, Floris Books 2002
Elkin, A.P., *Revolusjon i vitenskapen – Fremveksten av det holistiske paradigmet* (Revolution in Science – the Emergence of the Holistic Paradigm), 2003
Engelstad, Carl Fredrik, *De levendes land* (The Land of the Living) Ashehoug 1986
En russisk pilegrims beretning,1860 (The Way of a Pilgrim, SkyLight Paths Publishing 2001)
Eysenck, H.J., and Nias, D.K.B., *Astrology: Science or Superstition*, Penguin Books 1988
Falck, Morten, article in Aftenposten 30.11.1997, *Blinkende spor* (Sparkling Tracks)
Farthing, Geoffrey, *Exploring the Great Beyond*, The Theosophical Publishing House 1978
Fasola, Umberto M., *Peter and Paul in Rome*, Vision, Rome, 1980
Fechner, Gustav Theodor, *Zend Avesta,* 1851
Filostratos, Flavius, *Life of Apollonius*. See Internet.
Finkelstein, Israel, and Silberman, Neil Asher, *The Bible Unearthed: Archeology's New Vision of Ancient Israel and the Origin of Its Sacred Texts,* The Free Press, 2001, USA.
Flood, Kristin, *Samtaler om gåtene i oss* (Discussions on the Enigmas within us), Tano Forlag 1992
Flux nr. 25/26 – 2001, article by professor Per Andersen
Fontana, David, *Is there an Afterlife?*, O Books 2005
Fortune, Dion, *Kabbala – den mystiske tradition afdækket og forklaret* (The Kabbalah – the mystic tradition unvailed and explained), Sankt Ansgars Forlag i 1990/ 1935
- Psychic Self Defence

Fowler, Harold North, *Plato*, William Heinemann Ltd. 1960
Fox, Matthew, *Hildegard of Bingens Book of Divine Works, with Letters and Songs*, Bear & Company, Inc, 1987
Frazer, James, *The Golden Bough*, Wordsworth Editions Ltd. 1996. His works were first published in 12 books during the period 1890-1915. The first one volume edition was published in 1922.
Fredriksson, Marianne, *Simon og eiketrærne* (Simon and the Oak Trees), Ex Libris Forlag 1995

Freke, Timothy & Gandy, Peter, *The Laughing Jesus – Religious Lies and Gnostic Wisdom*, O Books 2006
- *Jesusmysteriene – Var den opprinnelige Jesus en hedensk gud?*, Emilia forlag 2007. (The Jesus Mysteries – was the original Jesus a pagan God?)
- *Jesus and the Lost Goddess – The secret Teachings of the original Christians*, Three Rivers Press 2001

Fremantle, Francesca and Trungpa, Chögyam, *The Tibetan Book of the Dead, the great liberation through hearing in the Bardo*, Shambhala, Boulder & London, 1975

Frenette, Louise Marie, *Aivanhov – A Biography,* Suryoma, Ltd. 1999

Fromm, Erich, *Om kjærlighet (*About Love, 1956), Dreyer Forlag 1969

Fuchs, Eberhard, *Nostradamu*s, 1982, Bogan forlag, Denmark

Fuller, John G., *Surgeon of the Rusty Knife* (1974)

Gardner, Laurence, *Bloodline of the Holy Grail*, HarperCollins Publishers 2002/1996

Gerson, Lloyd P., *The Cambridge Companion to Plotinus*, Cambridge University Press, 1999/1996

Goleman, Daniel, *Destruktive Følelser – Hvordan kan vi håndtere dem?* (Destructive Emotions – How to handle them), Borgen 2003

Gooch, Stan, *The Double Helix of the Mind,* Wildwood House Ltd. 1980
- *The Paranormal*, Fontana 1979

Goswami, Amit, *Physics of the Soul – The quantum book of living, dying, reincarnation and immortality*, Hampton Roads 2001

Grant, Joan, *Far Memory*, Ariel Press, 1985/1956
- Kelsey and Grant, *Many Lifetimes*, 1967

Grimberg, Carl, *Menneskenes Liv og Historie* (Humanity's Life and History) book 14, Cappelen forlag 1977

Grof, Stanislav, *The Adventure of Self-discovery,* State University of New York Press, 2000
- *Psychology of the Future*, State University of New York Press, 2000
- *Introduktion til Den Indre Rejse - selvoppdagelsens eventyr* (Introduction to the Inner Voyage – the Fairytale about the Discovery of the Self), Borgen Forlag 1987

Gugno, Alain, *St. John of the Cross*, Burns & Oates Ltd. Kent, 1982

Guirdham, Arthur, *The Cathars and Reincarnation*, 1970

Gurdjieff, George Ivanovitch, *Beelzebub's Tales to his Grandson*, Routledge & Kegan Paul 1981

Haich, Elisabeth, *The Wisdom of the Tarot*, Unwin Paperbacks 1985/1969
- *Initiation*, Unwin Hyman Limited, London, 1988/1960

Halifax, J., *Shamanic Voices*, New York, E.P. Dutton 1979. Commented upon by Stanley Kripner in the book *Parapsychology – Research on Exceptional Experiences,* edited by Jane Henry, Routledge 2005

Hancock, Graham, *Supernatural – Meetings with the Ancient Teachers of Mankind*, Arrow books 2003

Harris, Louie, *'Alec Harris: the full story of his remarkable physical mediumship,*

Saturday Night Press Publications (SNPP) 2009
Harris, Thomas A., *Jeg er OK – Du er OK* (I am OK – You are OK), Tiden Norsk Forlag 1973
Harrison, Tom, *Visits by our Friends from the Other Side*, 1989/2011, Saturday Night Press Publications(SNPP)
- *Life after Death: Living Proof – A Lifetime's Experiences of Physical Phenomena and Materializations through the Mediumship of Minnie Harrison,* 2004/2008, Saturday Night Press Publications (SNPP)

Hasted, John, *Metallbøyerne* (The Metal Benders)
Haugen, Marcello, *Betragtninger over en dag* (Consideration for a day), 1930, forlaget Mystica Eterna, 2003. See also the book *Mystica Eterna*, 2003
Hawken, Paul, *The Magic of Findhorn,* Fontana/Collins 1990
Hawking, Stephen W., *Univers uten grenser* (A Universe without Borders. - The English title is: A brief History of Time), Cappelen Forlag 1993
Head, J. and Cranston, p.L., *Reincarnation in World Thought*, Julian Press, N.Y.1967
Hildegard of Bingens Book of Divine Works, with Letters and Songs, Matthew Fox, Bear & Company, Inc, 1987
HeartMath Institute, USA, *Science of the Heart*, 2001
Henry, Jane, *Parapsychology – Research on Exceptional Experiences*, Routledge, 2005
Hodne, Ørnulf, *Mystiske steder i Norge* (Mystical Places in Norway), J.W. Cappelens Forlag a.s. 2000
Hoem, Gunhild, *Under forvandlingens Lov – En studie i Henrik Ibsens dramatikk,* (Under the Law of Change – a Study in Henrik Ibsen's dramatic Writings). Solum Forlag 1997
Hognestad, Astri, *Livskriser og kreativitet – et Jungiansk perspektiv* (Life crisis and creativity – a Jungian Perspective), Notam Gyldendal 1997
Hognestad, Helge, *Morgendemring* (Morning Twilight), J.W. Cappelens Forlag 1989
Humphreys, Christmas, *Karma og Genfødelse* (Karma and Reincarnation), Hernov forlag 1983
Hunt, Valerie et al, *A Study of Structural Neuromuscular Energy Field and Emotional Approaches.*
Hutton, J. Bernard, *Healing Hands*, Paperback Library Inc. 1966
Hygen, Georg, Vardøger. *Vårt paranormale nasjonalfenomen* (Vardøger. Our Paranormal National Phenomenon), J.W. Cappelen Forlag A/S, 1987
- *Telepati.Vår medfødte mobiltelefon* (Telepathy. Our inborn Mobile Telephone), J.W. Cappelen Forlag A/S, 1988

Højholt, Lene, *Vejen*, Borgen 2006
Ibsen, Henrik, *Keiser og Galilæer*, Gyldendal's edition 1972 – a Fakkel book
Illustrert Vitenskap no. 8/1994, about the ability to speak.
- no. 12/1994 about W. Adam Mandelbaum
- no. 7/1997, about Elisabeth Haich
- no. 4/1998, about Dean Radin
- no. 9/1999, about J.Z. Knight (Ramtha)
- no. 1/2003, about Dean Radin

- no. 1/2004, about the Universe
- no. 9/2004, about Daniel Goleman
- no. 15/2005, an article with the title 'The Personality sits in the Heart'

ITC *Proceedings of the First International Conference on Current Research into Survival of Physical Death with Special Reference to Instrumental Transcommunication.* ITC Journal 2004
- *Proceedings of the Second International Conference on Current Research into Survival of Physical Death with Special Reference to Instrumental Transcommunication.* ITC Journal 2006

Iversen, Olav Hilmar, an article in Aftenposten 2.10.1994, *Kroppen er flyktig, bare sjelen er stabil* (The body is passing, only the Soul remains)

Jacobsen, Knut A., *Hyllest til Gudinnen – visjon og tilbedelse av hinduismens store gudinne* (Tribute to the Goddess – vision and worship of Hinduism's great Goddess), Emilia forlag 2007

Jacobsen, Nils-Olof, *Liv etter døden?* (Life after Death?), Gyldendals Kjempefakler 1972

Johansson, Sture, *Resan til Ljuset* (The Voyage to the Light), RAM-Stiftelsen, Stockholm 1984/1974
- *Møte med Ambres* (Meeting Ambres), Sturid forlag, 1996/1985
- *Stjärnöga* (Star Eyes), Sturid Forlag 1994

Julian of Norwich, *Revelations of Divine Love,* Penguin Books 1998 – translation by Elizabeth Spearing

Jung, Carl Gustav, *Synchronicity, An Acasual Connecting Principle,* 1960
- *Minner, Drømmer og Tanker* (Memories, Dreams and Thoughts), Gyldendal Norsk Forlag 1990

Kapelrud, Arvid, *Dødehavsrullene* (The Dead Sea Scrolls), Universitetsforlaget, 1971

Keller, Werner, *The Bible as History*, Bantam Books 1982/1965

Kelly, Edward F. et al, *Irreducible Mind – toward a Psychology for the 21st Century,* Rowman & Littlefield Publishers Inc, 2007

Kharitidi, Olga, *Inn i sirkelen* (Into the Circle), Hilt & Hansteen forlag 1997

Koestler, Arthur, *The Sleep-walkers – A History of Man's Changing Vision of the Universe*, Pelican Books, 1968/1959

Krystal, Phyllis, *The Ultimate Experience*, Element Books 1990

Kullerud, Dag, Hans Nielsen Hauge – mannen som vekket Norge (Hans Nielsen Hauge - The Man who awakened Norway), Forum Aschehoug 1996

Kvamsdahl, Jan-Erik, *Marcello Haugens egen lærebok – Inayat Khan, I en østerlandsk Rosenhave* (Marcello Haugen's own book for teaching – Inayat Khan, in an Eastern Rose Garden), eget forlag 1993

Kübler-Ross, Elisabeth, *Døden er livsviktig* (Death is of Vital Importance), Ex Libris Forlag 1993 (første utgave på engelsk 1991)
- *Livshjulet* (English title: The Wheel of Life. A Memoir of living and dying), Gyldendal Norsk Forlag ASA 1998

Lachman, Barbara, *The Journal of Hildegard of Bingen*, Bell Tower, 1995/1993

Lamy, Lucie, *New Light on Ancient Knowledge – Egyptian Mysteries,* Thames and Hudson, 1994/1981

Langley, Noel, *Edgar Cayce – On reincarnation.* The truth about people who have lived more than once – and what it means for you, The Aquarian Press 1989/1967
- *Edgar Cayce – On Reincarnation* edited by H. L. Cayce, Aquarian press 1989

Laszlo, Ervin, *Revolusjon i vitenskapen – Fremveksten av det holistiske paradigmet,* Flux forlag 2003. (The English title is Revolutionary Science. The Rice of the Holistic Paradigm.)

Laurens van der Post (see Post)

Lauridsen-Katborg, Henrik, *Et rør til himmelen – Personlighedens grænseland* (A pipeline to the Sky – the Border Country of the Personality). Modtryk Forlag, Danmark, 1995

Leivestad, Ragnar, *Hva vet vi om Jesus* (What do we know about Jesus), Forum Forlag 1996

Leroy, Olivier, *La lévitation*
- *La Raison primitive*

Leonard, Todd Jay, *A History of Modern Spiritualism and Mediumship, Universe, Inc., 2005.*

Lethbridge, Thomas C., *Ghost and Divining Rod,* 1963
- *The Power of the Pendulum,* 1976

Lindholm, Dan, *Innsyn i Nordiske Gudesag* (Insight in Nordic God Legends), Dreyer forlag 1987

Lingjærde, Odd, as said to the journal *Psykisk Helse* (Psychic Health) according to an article in Aftenposten 5.1.1999

Lilly, John, *The Centre of the Cyclone,* 1972

Lorimer, David, *Thinking beyond the Brain,* Floris Books 2001
- *Prophet for our times,* Element Books Ltd., UK, 1991

Mack, Burton L., *The Lost Gospel – Q, The Book of Christian Origins,* Harper SanFrancisco 1993

MacLaine, Shirley, *It's all in the playing,* Bantam Books 1988

Maier, Paul L., *Josefus' hovedverk* (The Main Works of Josephus), Hermon Forlag 1998

Mallasz, Gitta, *Talking with Angels,* Daimon Verlag 1988

Mandelbaum, W. Adam, *The Psychic Battlefield,* St. Martin's Press, 2000

Manne, Rolf, articles in Aftenposten 11.1.1999 and 23.2.1999

Manning, Matthew, *Med en fot i stjernene* (One Foot in the Stars), Eikstein Forlag 2000

Marcus, Aage, *Mester Eckehart, prædikener og traktater* (Master Eckehart, Sermons and Articles), Sankt Ansgars Forlag 1983

Martinus - LB - *Livets Bog* (The Book of Life) (consisting of seven books – which also have the title The Third Gospel), Martinus Institut 1985
- LV - *Livets Vej* (The Way of Life), Borgen Forlag 1988
- MK - *Martinus Kosmologi – en introduksjon* (Martinus's Cosmology – an Introduction), Martinus Institut 1997
- MS - *Menneskehedens skæbne* (Humanity's Destiny) from 1962, Martinus Institut 1995
- KB - *Kosmisk bevidsthed* (Cosmic Consciousness), Martinus Institut 1950

Mascarós, Juan, *The Upanishads*, The Penguin Classics 1965/1979. Translation from Sanskrit to English.
Mauthner, Anne & Alexander, *Conversations with Bob Moore*, Switzerland 1992
MacDonald, Allan, *A Path prepared – the Story of Isa Northage*, Saturday Night Press Publications, 2012
MacKenna, Stephen, *Plotinus's The Enneads,* 1960
McKenna, Paul, *Vår mystiske verden* (Our mystical World), Grøndahl Dreyer 1998
McTaggart, Lynne, *The Field – The Quest for the Secret Force of the Universe,* HarperCollins Publishers Inc. 2001
Menzies, Gavin, *1421,* Bantam Books 2002
Moberly, Charlotte and Jourdain, *Eleanor, An Adventure,* 1911
Moody jr., Raymond A., *The Light Beyond*, Rider 2005
- *Livet etter livet* (The Life after Life), Dreyers Forlag 1977
Morgan, Marlo, *Det virkelige folket* (the English title is Down Under), Gyldendal Norsk Forlag 1995
Müller, Bente, *Gjennom Lysmuren* (Through the Light wall), Dreyer 1986.
Myers, Frederick W.H., *Human Personality and its survival of Bodily Death,* 1903, a shortened issue published by Dover Publications, Inc. 2005/1961
Myhren, Dagne Groven - omtale av Draumkvedet (comments to the Dream Poem) in an article in Aftenposten 6.1.1994
Myklebust, Oddbjørn, *Synske hjelparar i hundre år* (Psychics' Helpers for a hundred years), Nabogarden Forlag 2000
Myskja, Audun, *Den musiske medisin* (The Music Medicine), Grøndahl Dreyers Forlag 1999
Myss, Caroline, *Ånd og Energi* (Spirit and Energy), Hilt & Hansteen 1997
Nansen, Fridtjof, *Fram gjennom Polhavet* ('Fram' through the Polar Sea)
Neff, Mary K., *H. P. Blavatsky - hendes egne og andres erindringer* (H.P. Blavatsky – her own and others' Memories), Sankt Ansgars Forlag 1990
Nelson, J. H., *Shortwave Radio Propagation Correlation with Planetary Positions*, RCA Review 12;26, 1951
Newton, Michael, *Sjelereiser – Beretninger om livet mellom livene* (Soul Travels – Tales from Life between Lives), Damms forlag, 2005. The original title is Journey of Souls – Case Studies of Life between Lives. 1994
Nilsen, Frank-Thore, *Parapsykologiens revolusjon av verdensbildet* (The Parapsychological Revolution of the World Image, Aschehougs forlag 1977
Olerud, Randi, *Flammer til Liv – Et skjebnemøte med helbredende hender* (Tongues of Fire making Life – A life-changing meeting with healing Hands), Dreyers Forlag 1979
Osis, Karlis and Haraldsson, Erlendur, *At The Hour of Death – A New Look at Evidence for Life After Death*, Hastings House 1997/1977
Ouspensky, Piotre Demianovich, *A New Model of the Universe and The Strange Life of Ivan Osokin*
Owen, I.M. & Sparrow, M., *Conjuring up Philip*, Fitzhenry and Whiteside, 1976
Pagels, Elaine, *The Gnostic Gospels,* Penguin Books 1979
Parapsykologiske Notiser (the journal Parapsychological Notices issued by the

Norwegian Parapsychological Society):
- no. 21/1986, article by Alice Mürer about Raymond A. Moody jr.
- no. 28/1989, no. 29/1990, no. 30/1990 and no. 32/1991, articles by Georg Hygen about Indridi Indridason
- no. 34/1992, report from a lecture given by Gunhild Hoem
- no. 5/1993, article by Sybo A. Schouten
- no. 37/1994, article by Steinar Johansen about the Silva-method
- no. 43/1997, an article by Arthur J. Ellison where he mentions a talk given by Anne Arnold Silk in 1991 for the British Society for Psychical Research
- no. 46/1998, about healing by Ottar Myhre
- no. 45 and 46/1998, articles by Anne Brit Sylvareik (previously Thoresen Peters) with the title *Spiritisme i går, kanalisering i dag* (Spiritism yesterday, channeling today)
- no. 46/1998, om Milan Ryzl, *Søken etter erkjennelse av høyere dimensjoner og en annen verden* (The Quest for Recognition of the higher Dimensions and a different World)
- no. 46/1998, article by Sverre Martinussen about Emanuel Swedenborg
- no. 48/1999, a comment from Thomas L. Aall about a letter that was not sent
- no. 54/2002, article about Jenny Cockell
- no. 57/2004, report from a lecture given by William Roll in Oslo in 2003
- no. 58/2004, a story about the phenomenon vardøger experienced in the USA

Parmann, Øistein, *Marcello Haugen,* Dreyers Forlag A/S 1985/1974

Penrose, Roger, *The Emperor's New Mind*, Oxford University Press 1989

Playfair, Guy Lyon, *Twin Telepathy,* Vega, London 2002
- *The Unknown Power,* 1975

Plato, - *The Republic*
- *Phaedo*

Plotinus, *The Enneads,* see Stephen MacKenna.

Pollan, Brita, *Samiske sjamaner – religion og helbredelse,* (Shamans among the Sami people – Religion and Healing) Gyldendal Norsk Forlag 1994/1993

Post, Laurens van der, *Jung and the story of our time.* Penguin Books 1983
- *Farlig ferd til det indre,* Gyldendal Norsk Forlag 1956 (Venture to the Interior, Penguin Books 1983/1952)
- *The lost World of the Kalahari,* Penguin Books 1982/1958

Potok, Chaim, *Wanderings – History of the Jews,* Fawcett Crest Books, New York, 1983/1978

Powell, Arthur E., - AL – *Astrallegemet* (The Astral Body), Sankt Ansgars Forlag 1993
- ÆD - *Den Æteriske Dublet* (The Etheric Double), Sankt Ansgars Forlag 1997
- ML - *Mentallegemet* (The Mental Body), Sankt Ansgars Forlag 1993
- KL - *Kausallegemet* (The Causal Body), Sankt Ansgars Forlag 1997

Powell, Diane Hennacy, *The ESP Enigma. The Scientific Case for Psychic Phenomena*, Walker & Company, 2009

Radin, Dean, *Entangled Minds,* Paraview Pocket Books 2006
- *The Conscious Universe*, HarperCollins 1997

Redfield, James, *The Celestial prophecy,* Bantam Book 1994 (The Norwegia title is *Den niende innsikt*)
Ring, Kenneth, *Heading towards Omega – In Search of the Meaning of the Near-Death-Experience,* 1984
- *Life after death – A Scientific Investigation of Near-Death-Experiences* 1980
Riosanu, Sister M. Kristin, from interview in Aftenposten 4.10.1998
Ritchie, George G., *Tilbage fra i morgen* (Return from Tomorrow), Jupiter forlag, Danmark, 1984/1978
Roberts, Ron and Groome, David, *Parapsychology, The Science of Unusual Experience,* Arnold 2001
Roberts, Jane, *The Nature of Personal Reality - a Seth Book,* Bantam Books 1988/1974
- *Seth-materialet* (The Seth Material), Hilt & Hansteen Forlag 1990
- *Seth Speaks - The Eternal Validity of the Soul,* an Amber-Allen Book, New World Library 1994
Robertson, Morgan, *Futility,* F. Mansfield, N.Y. 1898. Mentioned by Erik Dammann
Roney-Dougal, Serena, *Where Science and Magic Meet,* Vega 2002
Ruffin, C. Bernard, *St Pio – The True Story,* Our Sunday Visitor Publishing Division, Indiana, USA, 1991
Sagan, Carl, *The Demon-haunted World – Science as a candle in the dark,* Headline Book Publishing 1997/1996
Schjelderup, Kristian, *Veien jeg måtte gå* (The Road I had to go), Aschehoug 1962
- *Hvem Jesus var – og hvad Kirken har gjort ham til* (The Man Jesus – and what the Church made of Him), 1924.
Schmicker, Michael, *Best Evidence,* Writers Club Press 2002
Schwartz, Gary E., *The Afterlife Experiments,* Atria Books 2002
Scott Rogo, David, *Liv etter døden* (Life after Death), Cesam Media A.S. 1988
- *Miracles,* New York, Dial Press, 1982
Sheldrake, Rupert, *Dogs that Know when Their Owners are Coming Home,* 1999. (The Norwegian title is *Uforklarlige krefter hos dyr*)
- *The Hypothesis of Morphic Resonance – A New Science of Life,* 1981
Shirley, John, *Gurdjieff – An Introduction to His Life and Ideas,* Penguin 2004
Sibbern, Susan, *Stifinner i grenseland – en bok om å være synsk* ((Pathfinder in Borderland – a book about being psychic), Indre Ledelse Forlag 2003
Skarsaune, Oskar, *Den ukjente Jesus* (The Unknown Jesus), Avenir Forlag 2005
Smith, Huston, *Verdens religioner i tekst og bilder* (The World Religions in writings and pictures), Hilt & Hansteen Forlag 1995/1958
Smith, Susy, *The Afterlife Codes – Searching for Evidence of the Survival of the Soul,* Hampton Roads Publishing Company Inc. 2000
Sogyal Rinpoche, *The Tibetan Book of living and dying,* Random House 1992 / Rigpa Fellowship
Spangler, David, *Cooperation with Spirit – Further Conversations with John,* published at Findhorn
Stace, Walter T., *The Teachings of the Mystics – Selections from the great mystics and mystical writings of the world,* an introduction, edited with

interpretative commentaries and explanations, A Mentor Book USA 1960

Steiner, Rudolf, *Johannesevangeliet* (The Gospel of John), Vidarforlaget 1974. The Book has also been published with the title *Verdensordet og Jorden – Johannesevangeliets hemmeligheder* (The World Order and the Earth– The Secrets in The Gospel of John), Antroposofisk Forlag 2002
- *Johannes Apokalypse* (The Apocalypse of John), Vidarforlaget 1992/1911
- *Hvorledes Erverves Kundskap om Høiere Verdener* (How to obtain Knowledge about the Higher Worlds), Vidarforlaget 1979, a reprint of the sixth edition from 1914
- *Fra Jesus til Kristus* (From Jesus to Christ), Forlaget Jupiter, Odense, Denmark, 2000/1911

Stevenson, Ian, *Where Reincarnation and Biology Intersect*, Praeger Publishers, 1997

Stolk, Sirkar van and Dunlop, Daphne, *Hazrat Inayat Khan og sufibudskapet* (Hazrat Inayat Khan and the Sufi Message), Sankt Ansgars Forlag 1975

Tacitus, *The Annals of Imperial Rome,* Penguin Classics 1971

Talbot, Michael, *The Holographic Universe,* Harper Collins Publisher 1996/1991

Teilhard, Pierre, de Chardin, Fænomenet Menneske, (The Phenomenon of Man) Jespersen og Pios Forlag, 1958/1947
- *Om menneskets fremtid* (The Future of Man), Dreyer 1968

Teresa of Avila, *Vida di Santa Teresa de Jesús,* (The Danish title is Den Hellige Teresa af Avila's liv, fortalt av hende selv, Sankt Ansgars Forlag 1982. The Norwegian title from 2003 is *Boken om mitt liv*)
- *Sjælens Slot*, Sankt Ansgars Forlag, København 1992. (The Norwegian title is *Den indre festning* – [The Interior Castle])

Thiering, Barbara E., *Jesus the Man*, Corgi Books 1993
- *The Book That Jesus Wrote – John's Gospel,* Corgi Books 1998

Thigpen and Cleckley, *Evas tre ansikter* (The Three Faces of Eve)

Torsvik, Signe, *Emanuel Swedenborg*, Sankt Ansgars Forlag 1984

Tompkins, Peter Chr., *The Secret Life of Plants*, 1989

Tulku Urgyen Rinpoche, *Blazing Splendor – The memoirs of Tulku Urgyen Rinpoche,* as told to Erik Pema Kunsang and Marcia Binder Schmidt, Rangjung Yeshe Publications 2005

Tweedie, Irina, *The Chasm of Fire – A Woman's Experience of Liberation Through the Teachings of a Sufi Master*, Element Classic Editions 1993/1979

Ullman, Montague and Zimmerman, Nan, *Bruk dine drømmer* (Use your Dreams), Dreyer forlag, 1982

Underhill, Evelyn, *Mysticism – a Study in the nature and development of Man's spiritual consciousness,* New American Library – a Meridian book, 1955 /1911

Undset, Sigrid, *Caterina av Siena,* H. Aschehoug & Co 1996/1951

Versluis, Arthur, *Om de egyptiske mysterier* (About the Egyptian Mysteries), Arkana Paperbacks 1988/1959

Wambach, Helen, *Life before Life,* Bantam Books 1979
- *Reliving past Lives*, Arrow Books 1980

Wasiutynski, Jeremi, *Det kosmiske drama* (The Cosmic Drama), Pax Forlag 1998

Watson, Lyall, *Grenseløst liv*, Ernst G. Mortensens Forlag 1975. (The English title is *The Romeo Error*, 1974)
- *Det er mer mellom himmel og jord,* Ernst G. Mortensens Forlag 1974. (The English title is *Supernature - The Natural History of the Supernatural*, 1973)
- *Heaven's Breath,* Coronet edition 1984
- *Lifetide,* Coronet edition 1983/1979
- *Lightning Bird,* Coronet edition 1982/1983

Watts, Alan W., *The way of ZEN,* Penguin Books Ltd. 1980

Wests, Morris L., *The Devil's Advocate*, 1959

Westerlund, Anna Elisabeth, *Telepatiens gate* (The Enigma of Telepathy), Aschehoug 1986

Wetlesen, Jon, a translation of Master Eckhart's sermon nr. 58
- *Mester Eckhart – Å bli den du er* (Master Eckhart – To become what you are), H. Aschehoug & Co, 2000

Whitton, Joel L., and Fisher, Joe, *Life between Life,* 1986

Wilber, Ken, Eight books from Shambala, London/Boston:
- I – *The Spectrum of Consciousness*, 1977
- I – *No Boundary*, 1979
- I – *Where It Was, There I Shall Become,* 1980
- II – *Up from Eden*, 1981
- II – The Atman Project, 1980
- III – *Eye to Eye*,1983
- IV – *Death, Rebirth, and Meditation*, 1983
- IV – *Transformation of Consciousness*, 1986
- IV – *Two Humanistic Psychologies,* 1986
- IV – *Quantum Questions*, 1986
- V – *Grace and Grit,* 1991
- VI – *Sex, Ecology, Spirituality,* 1995
- VII – *The Eye of Spirit,* 1997
- VIII – *The Marriage of Sense and Soul,* 1998
- VIII – *One Taste,* 1999
- *A Theory of Everything,* Shambala 2001.

Wilhelms, Richard, *I Ching eller Forvandlingens bok* (I Ching or The Book of Change), Strubes Forlag, Denmark, 1981

Wilson, Colin, *The Man and His Vision, a biography of Rudolf Steiner,* The Aquarian Press, 1985
- *Mysteries,* Granada Publishing Books, 1979/1978
- *The Occult*, Granada Publishing 1978/1973

Wilson, Colin, and Flem-Ath, Rand, *The Atlantis Blueprint*, Delta Trade Paperback 2002

Wiseman, Richard, his doctoral thesis about fraud, mentioned by Paul McKenna in the book *Vår mystiske verden* (Our mystical World), Grøndahl Dreyer 1998

Woje, Svein and Klepp, Kari, *Jesus døde ikke på korset* (Jesus did not die on the Cross), Borglund Forlag 2003

Wyller, Egil A., Johannes *Åpenbaring* (The Revelation of John), J.W. Cappelens Forlag A/S 1986

Yeats, William B., *A Vision*

Yogananda, *En yogis selvbiografi,* Borgen forlag 1997 (the first edition published 1946 under the title: *Autobiography of a Yogi*). This Norwegian edition consists of two parts and is referred here as Yogananda I and Yogananda II.

Zukav, Gary, *The Dancing Wu Li Masters – An overview of the New Physics*, Fontana/Collins 1980

Ørjasæter, Tordis, *Sigrid Undset,* Ascehougs Forlag 1993

Index

A

Abhidhárma 24
Acem 407
Addey, John 94, 466,486
Adonis 42
Agpaoa, Tony 389
Agrippa I, King 40
Agrippa, Henricus Cornelius 247-8, 475, 486
Aivanhov, Omraam Mikhael 46, 47, 58, 76, 77, 93, 100, 136, 163, 170, 171, 246, 249, 269, 270, 274, 303, 337, 340, 361, 369, 371, 372, 389, 423, 437, 439 443, 463, 464, 465, 466
Akasha/Akashic 82, 160-1, 241-2, 264-66, 275, 323, 326, 344, 346, 463
Akhenaton 18, 26
Alexander the Great 18
Altea, Rosemary 122, 124, 271, 275-6, 301, 303, 305, 308, 312, 468, 476-8, 486
Amaro, Ajahn 318, 47
Ambres – see Sture Johansson 11, 112, 114-5, 190-2, 202, 209, 228, 239, 302, 330-31, 340, 349, 350, 362, 367, 414, 429, 444, 461, 468, 472-3, 478, 480, 482, 484-85, 492
Amenhotep III 18, 333
Amundsen, Rune 477, 486
Anatman 24, 318
Andersen, Per 220, 375, 489
Angela of Foligno 74
Annas, chief priest 41
Apollonios of Tyana 44
Apuleius, Lucius 485-6
Aquinas, Thomas 53, 60
Arigò 344, 386
Aristeas' letter 27
Aristotle 15, 64
archetypes 145, 173, 201-3, 212, 241, 260, 380, 472
Archimedes 42, 429

Arthur, British king 12
Asbjørnsen and Moe, fairytales 432
Asclepius 181, 392, 428
Assurbanipal 18
Astral Linga Sarira 325
Athos 192, 406, 419
Atkinson, Mike 186
Atlantis 49, 115, 136, 326, 429, 469, 498
Atlas 16, 431
Atma 187, 236
Atman 24, 51, 226, 234, 318, 324, 408, 482, 484, 498
Aton 18, 26, 57
Attis 41
Atwater, Phyllis M.H. 283
Augsburg – the Creed 38, 51, 255, 413
Augustine 52, 203, 316, 317
Augustus/Octavian, Emperor 18, 20, 433
Aukrust, Olav O. 21, 228-9, 279, 291, 294, 474, 475, 477-8, 480, 482, 485-6
Aum – see OM
Aurastar 2000 169
Avalokiteshvara 76, 407
Ave Maria 396
Aztec culture 20

B

Ba – see also Ka 228-9, 277
Babaji 45, 76
Bacchus 42
Backster, Cleve 377
Bacon, Francis 64
Baigent, Michael 35, 44, 462, 486
Bardo 252, 285-6, 289, 290-1, 308, 320, 454, 477, 490
Basa, Teresita 110
Begg, Clive 391
Beloussov, Lev 223

Bender, Hans 275, 476
Bergson, Henri 448
Bernstein, Morey 332, 487
Bertelsen, Jes 11-13, 31, 48, 53, 67, 107, 163, 173, 185, 187-92. 194, 197, 211, 220, 227, 241, 243-4, 276, 280, 285-6, 294, 297, 302-6, 308-9, 313, 322-3, 339, 347, 350, 369, 373, 393, 398, 407, 415-6, 418-9, 423-4, 444, 458, 461-4, 471-3, 475-9, 482-85, 487
Besant, Annie 11, 12, 266 469
Betz, Hans-Dieter 89 466
Bhagavad Gita 22, 51, 242, 314, 324
Bhai Sahib – see Guruji
Bhikkhu, Buddhadasa 318
Bikaner's rat temple 314
Binah 437-39
bio-genesis 447
bioplasma/mic 189, 343
biosphere 447
Bjornsson, Hafsteinn 311
Blackmore, Susan 141
Blake, William 481
Blavatsky, Helena P. 11, 12, 50, 82, 84-5, 112-3, 126, 132, 136, 160, 248, 252, 264-7, 325-6, 333, 345, 430, 441, 463, 468, 470, 476, 479, 485-7, 494
Bloksberg 256
Bohm, David 132, 155-6, 180, 372, 375, 444, 470, 487
Bohr, Niels 68
Bojesen, Lars Bo 317, 479, 487
Bond, Frederick Bligh 111, 487
Boshier, Adrian 80
Bouhamzy, Sleimann, Said and Ibrahim 334
Boyers, David 169
Bradley, Raymond Trevor 186
Brahma 22-3, 56, 408
Brahman 22, 51, 57, 216, 396, 407-8
Brand 362, 434, 449
Braude, Stephen E. 130, 135, 142, 310, 312, 467, 478, 487
Brennan, Barbara Ann 167-8, 487
Briah 437-8
Bro, Harmon Hartzell 65-6, 160-1, 171, 327-8, 470-1, 473, 480, 487
Brocq's disease 342
Brother Klaus 74
Broglie, Louis de 68

Brown, Rosemary 111, 332
Bruce, Alexandra 468, 487
Brune, François 334, 487
Brynildsen, Aasmund 53, 178, 463, 476, 483, 488
Buddha, Gautama Siddharta 15, 23, 48, 50-1, 76, 216, 244, 275, 291, 309, 318-21, 325, 361, 407, 453
buddhi 187, 236
Burr, Harold Saxton 99, 164, 189, 471, 488
Button-moulder 434, 454

C

Caddy, Eileen 124-5, 268, 273-4, 353, 355, 476
Caddy, Peter 124-5
Caduceus – also Mercury's wand 428
Caiaphas, chief priest 41
Campbell, Joseph 14, 16, 41, 59, 160, 281, 314, 424, 461, 463, 470, 477, 479, 488
Capra, Fritjof 150-1, 215, 470, 473, 488
Cardan, Jerome 138
Cardiff Poltergeist Case 83
Cardoso, Anabela 128-30, 344
Carlson, Shawn 98, 466, 488
Castaneda, Carlos 163, 410, 471, 488
Caterina of Siena 71, 74, 122, 257-8, 275, 333, 381, 413, 475, 497
Cayce, Edgar 65, 99, 115, 136, 141, 160-1, 171, 210-11, 218, 224, 241, 259, 265, 267, 296, 326-8, 331-2, 337, 340, 349-50, 369, 383, 414, 469-71, 473-5, 478-80, 482, 484, 487-8, 493
Celestine Prophecy, The 133, 455
Chaffin Will case 110
Chalcedon, Synod of 38
Charles V, Emperor 88
Chase, Truddi 197, 488
Cheops – Khufu 17, 431-2
Chephren – Khafre 17
Chesed 437, 439
cherubim 246
Chew, Geoffrey 375
Chiron – Kheiron 181-2
Chokmah 437-9
Chopra, Deepak 148-9, 157, 222, 224, 226, 470, 473, 472, 482, 486, 488
Clark, Vernon 98
Claudius, Emperor 39-40
Clement of Alexandria 69, 300, 316
Cleopas – Cleophas – Cephas 46

Cleopatra 18
Cochrane, Archie / Organisation 384
Cockell, Jenny 480
Collin-Smith, Rodney 95
Conan Doyle, Arthur 120-2, 271, 488
Confutse/Confucius 15, 19
Constantine, Emperor 20, 449
Conti, Emma 111
Cornelius 45
Cortés, Hernán 88, 465, 488
Crabtree, Adam 143
Croesus, King 87
Cronos 20, 92-3
crop circles 136
Cross-Correspondences 126, 270, 276
Crowley, Aleister 77, 365
Crowley, John R. 119, 468
CSICOP 127, 142, 333, 468
Cummins, Geraldine 130, 240, 302, 488
Culture periods 49
Curran, Pearl 111
Cyrus, King 18, 87

D

Daimon 264
Dalai Lama 23, 76, 170, 243, 319, 352, 415, 461-4, 479, 488
Daley, George 378
Dammann, Erik 180, 375, 467, 470, 472, 482, 485, 496
Dampier-Jeans, Marion 468
Darwin, Charles 432
David, King 18
David-Néel, Alexandra 132, 488
Davis, Andrew Jackson 293
deadly sins 257
Death, Right to a dignified, Society 313
Delphi 87, 485
dervish 422
Descartes, René 175, 178, 448
Detering, Herman 32, 488
Deunov, Peter 46, 423, 484
Deva 124-5, 252, 266
Devachan 243, 309, 325,326
Dhyan Chohans 252
Diane – see Shafica Karagulla 167, 471, 483
Díaz de Castillo, Bernal 88

Dickinson, Emily 111
Dionysus, the god 42
Dionysius, the Areopagite 247
Djoser 17
Don Juan, a Yaqui-Indian 163, 410, 471, 488
Doresse, Jean 462, 484, 488
Douno, Beinsa – see Peter Deunov 423
Dowling, Levi H. 48, 161, 404
Dracula 257
dragon 181, 248, 249, 257, 431
Drake, Frank 137
Draumkvedet, The Dream Poem 281, 477, 494
Driesch, Hans A.E. 241
Ducasse, Curt J. 332, 343, 347
Dunne, Brenda 85
Durga 23
Dürckheim, Karlfried 406, 483, 488
Dürer, Albert 111
dynamis 304

E

Eaglesfield, Francis 333
Eckhart 37, 48, 52-3, 68, 149, 192, 203-4, 229, 235, 274, 300, 330, 360, 367, 396, 405, 418, 448, 463, 464, 470, 473-4, 484, 498
Ecclesiastes 26, 459
École Biblique 27
ectoplasm 115-6, 118-20, 122, 130, 269, 277, 468
Eddington, Arthur 68
Edwards, Harry 385, 488
Edwards, Sharry 389
Ehrman, Bart D. 33, 462. 489
Eidolon 264
Einstein, Albert 68, 148-9, 168, 473
Eisenman, Robert 33, 35-6, 39, 44-5, 49, 462-3, 489
electronic voice phenomena 128
elementals 132, 190, 264-5, 267, 270, 278, 441
elemental spirits 132, 265
Eliade, Mircea 79-81, 424, 427-8, 431, 465, 469, 485
Elizabeth of Rent 74
Elkin, A.P. 143, 489
Ellison, Arthur J. 169, 270, 468, 469, 470, 471, 476, 489, 495
Elmo's fire, St 262
Empedocles 42, 218

Emperor and Galilean 362, 366, 372, 449
Encyclopedia Britannica 2001 171
Engelstad, Carl Fredrik 414, 489
Epidauros 392, 428
EPR-paradox 149, 161
Euclid 429
Eusebios 39
exusiai 304
Eysenck, Hans Jürgen 96-7, 375, 465, 466, 489
Ezekiel 171, 248

F

Farthing, Geoffrey 113, 160, 190, 264-6, 277, 325, 468, 470, 476, 479, 485, 489
Fasola, Umberto M. 40, 463, 489
Fátima, Portugal 252-3
Fechner, Gustav Theodor 240, 489
Filostratos, Flavius 489
Findhorn 114, 124-5, 266, 268, 476, 488, 491, 496
Finkelstein, Israel 27, 462, 489
Flem-Ath, Rand 136, 469, 498
Fontana, David 83, 118, 129-30, 478, 489
Fortune, Dion 104-5, 132, 246, 249, 250, 260-1, 268, 361, 367, 399, 427, 437-9, 467, 469, 475-6, 482, 484, 489
Francesco Forgione – see Padre Pio
Francis of Assisi 70-73, 110, 131, 216, 336, 342, 381, 423
Frazer, James 9, 10, 489
Fredriksson, Marianne 363, 489
Freeman, Laurence 30, 59, 255, 462
Freitas, José de – see Arigò
Freke, Timothy 32, 35, 39, 41-2, 264, 462, 490
Freud, Sigmund 158, 211-2, 380
Fromm, Erich 399, 481, 490
Frøyland, Jan 89
fulcrums 182, 211-12, 227
Fønnebø, Vinjar 384

G

Gabor, Dennis 155
Gabriel, archangel 28, 217, 248-9, 251
Gaia 20, 154, 222
Galilei, Galileo 64, 154, 161, 432
Gallienus, Emperor 69
gamma-rays 94, 166
Gandhi, Mahatma 50, 77, 117, 463, 486

Gandy, Peter 32, 35, 39, 41-2, 264, 462, 490
Ganesh 23
Garab Dorje 44, 203
Gardner, Laurence 18, 44, 490
Garfield, Charles 287
Garrett, Eileen 260, 269
Gauld, Alan 143
Gauquelin, Michel 96-7
Gebelin, Antoine Court de 104
Geburah 437, 439
Geller, Uri 84
geo-genesis 447
Gerber, Richard 377
Gerson, Lloyd P. 70, 478, 490
ghoul 257, 262
Gilgamesh 17
Gilles de Rais 414
Giuliani, Veronica 131
Gjerstad, Joralv 385
Goethe, Johann Wolfgang von 365
golden ratio 428-9
Gold Leaf Lady 135, 142, 487
Gooch, Stan 103, 108, 137-8, 169, 172, 218, 342, 344, 386-8, 412, 432, 466, 467, 473, 481, 483, 490
Goswami, Amit 341, 490
Grad, Bernard 386
Grant, Joan 189, 265, 327, 490
Green, Celia 259
Gregory the Great 285
Greyson, Bruce 143
Grimberg, Carl 364, 474, 490
Grimm's fairytales 432
Grof, Stanislav 107, 144-7, 224, 226-7, 274, 281, 287, 337-8, 426, 470, 477, 480, 483. 490
Groome, David 98, 466, 496
Grosso, Michael 143, 467
Guadalupe Hidalgo 254
Gugno, Alain 484, 490
Guirdham, Arthur 332, 490
Gurdjieff, George Ivanovitch 77, 196, 341, 429, 472, 474, 485, 490, 496
Gurney, Edmund 259
Guruji 381, 401
Gyatso, Tenzin – see Dalai Lama 23

H

Hades 93, 302

Haich, Elisabeth 331, 467, 480, 490, 491
Hamingja 272
Hammurabi 17, 19, 215
Hampton, Judith Darlene – see Ramtha
Hancock, Graham 461, 469, 480, 490
Han regime 19
Hansen, Jan-Erik Ebbestad 54
Hanuman 23
Haraldsson, Erlendur 336, 467, 481, 494
Harappa 18
Harris, Alec 116, 490
Harris, Thomas A. 472, 491
Harrison, Minnie 118, 345
Harrison, Tom 118, 345, 491
Hasted, John 143, 470, 491
Hatha yoga 380
Hathor 427
Hauge, Hans Nielsen 54, 464, 492
Haugen, Marcello 9, 63, 65-6, 99, 163, 307-8, 356, 371, 385, 401-2, 464, 478, 481-3, 491, 495
Hávamál 41
Hawken, Paul 125, 476, 491
Hawking, Stephen W. 93, 466, 491
healers 79, 255, 382, 386-7, 389, 392
Hein, Piet 454
Heisenberg, Werner 68
Hemi-Sync-technique 411-2
Henry VIII 111
Henry, Jane 85, 474, 480, 490
Hera 433
Heraclitus 218, 288
Hercules 42, 136
Hermes Trismegistus 59, 92, 428
Herod Antipas, Tetrarch 41
Herod the Great 18, 26, 38
Herodotus 87
Hesy's tomb 429
Hieronymus – see Jerome, St
Hildegard of Bingen 53, 70, 217, 257, 383, 391, 463-4, 473, 483, 489, 491, 492
Hinayana 24, 420
Hobbes, Thomas 448
Hod 437, 439
Hoem, Gunhild 449-50, 482, 485, 491, 495
Hognestad, Astri 201, 472, 491
Hognestad, Helge 59, 461, 476, 491
Home, Daniel Dunglas 143, 470

Homer 362
Hope, William (Billy) 120
Humphreys, Christmas 160, 323, 370, 470, 479, 491
Hunt, Valerie 168, 172, 187, 491
Huygens, Christian 389
Hygen, Georg 143-4, 344, 465, 491, 495
Hyman, Ray 127, 468
Hyslop, James Hervey 111-12
Højholt, Lene 416, 484, 491

I

I Ching 19, 103, 438, 466, 498
Ibsen, Henrik 362, 366, 372, 434, 449-51, 454, 491
Inca empire 20
Ignatius of Loyola 72
Iliad 272
Imad Elawar 334
Imhotep 429, 432
Indridason, Indridi 83-4, 495
Inge, William Ralph 55
Institute of HeartMath 165, 186, 390, 411
instrumental transcommunication 128, 130, 480, 481, 492
Irenaeus, Bishop 34
Iversen, Olav Hilmar 149, 150, 157, 220-1, 470, 492

J

Jacobsen, Nils-Olof 128, 461, 492
Jahn, Robert G. 85, 223
James, Willliam 111-12, 221, 241, 468
Jasbir 333-4
Joan of Arc 414
Jeans, James 68
Jenkins, Stephen 263
Jensen, Per Bruus 57, 295, 398, 464, 478, 480, 482, 483, 485, 487
Jerome, St 316
John the apostle 32, 37-8, 42, 45-7, 49, 61, 72, 77, 109, 112, 250, 254, 279, 291, 316-18, 356, 360, 361, 370, 384, 409, 413-4, 416 462, 474, 478, 480, 497, 499
John of the Cross 72, 366, 413-4, 416, 462, 484, 490
John the Baptist 29, 39-41, 248, 254, 316
John XXII, Pope 48

John Paul II, Pope 53
John, a spirit – see David Spangler 237-8, 242, 276, 308, 404, 475
John Main-seminar 319
Johannes, a monk 111
Johansen, Hjalmar 272
Johansson, Sture –see Ambres 472, 495
Johnson, Ken 169
Josef of Cupertino 72
Joseph, Jesus' father 38, 217, 253, 383,
Joseph, son of Jacob 18, 38, 208,
Josephus 33, 39-41, 45, 462, 493
Joshua 40
Jourdain, Eleanor 331, 480, 494
Judas, gospel of 34, 45
Judas Iscariot 45, 360-2, 366, 372, 450
Judge, William Q. 11
Julia Domna, Empress 44
Julian of Norwich 53, 413, 463, 484, 492
Julian, Emperor 362, 366, 372, 449-50,
Julianus (Flavius Claudius), Emperor 449
Jung, Carl Gustav 10, 13, 55, 99, 100, 103, 106, 111, 147, 158, 197, 201-3, 210-12, 260, 283, 285, 296, 300, 380, 392, 426, 435, 464, 466-8, 472, 477-8, 483, 491-2, 495
Justinian, Emperor 317

K

Ka – see also Ba, 228-9, 277
Kaaven, Johan 65
Kali 19, 23
kama 191, 324
kamaloka 191, 241, 264, 267, 307, 309, 339
kamarupa/rupic 264, 266
Karagulla, Shafica 167, 388, 471, 483
karma 22, 24, 46, 77, 160, 233, 242, 265, 290, 298, 313, 315, 319, 322-4, 327, 329-30, 338, 347, 357-8, 368-70, 376, 394, 398, 414-5, 424, 470, 479, 482, 491
Keller, Werner 461-2, 492
Kelly, Edward F. et al. 143, 147, 221, 470, 472-3, 492
Kepler, Johannes 64, 97
Kether 57, 437-9
Khan, Hazrat Inayat 99, 246, 466, 475, 492, 497
Kharitidi, Olga 80, 492
Khirbet Qumran 26
Kierkegaard, Søren 12, 365, 482, 487

King Wên 103
Kirlian, Semyon and Valentina 168-9
Klepp, Kari 44, 498
Knight, J.Z. – see Ramtha
Knossos 250
Koestler, Arthur 205, 492
Kripner, Stanley 480, 490
Krishna 23, 76, 314
Krishnamurti, Jiddu 11, 132
Krystal, Phyllis 356, 481, 492
Kullerud, Dag 54, 464, 492
Kübler-Ross, Elisabeth 283-6, 366, 477, 482, 492
Kyriotetes 304
Køhn, Rosemarie 61

L

Lachman, Barbara 464, 473, 483, 492
Lahiri Mahasaya 45
Lakshmi 23
Lamberts, Guy 262
Langley, Noel 317, 326-7, 332, 469-70, 474-5, 478-80, 482, 484, 493
Lao Tzu 15, 19
Lateau, Louise 74
Lauridsen-Katborg, Henrik 239-40, 475, 493
Lazarri, Dominica 74
Leadbeater, C.W. 266, 469
Leibniz, G. W. 230, 324, 364-5, 474
Leigh, Richard 35, 44, 462, 486
Leivestad, Ragnar 39, 462, 493
Lemuria 136
Leonard, Todd Jay 478, 493
Leonardo da Vinci 64, 170
Lepsius, Richard 288
Lerner, Barbara 208
Lethbridge, Thomas C. 90-1, 196, 262-3, 466, 493
ley-lines 263
L-field 164
Lidwina of Schiedam 74
Lilly, John 195-6, 493
Lincoln, Henry 44, 486
Lingjærde, Odd 96, 493
Logos 47, 61, 450
Lonely Planet, TV series 111
Lorentsen, Asger 269, 476, 486
Louis XVI 331

Lourdes 73, 252, 263, 384
Loye, David 372
Lucia dos Santos 252
Luther, Martin 31
Lysanias, Tetrarch 41

M

Mack, Burton L. 36, 462-3, 493
MacKenna, Stephen 494, 495
MacLaine, Shirley 114-5, 468, 493
Maclean, Dorothy 124-5
Magna Mater 428
Mahabharata 23
Mahabhutas 235
Mahādevī 22
Maharishi-movement 407
Maharshi, Sri Ramana 423
Mahayana 24, 420-21
Malkuth 249, 437-9
Mallasz, Gitta 59, 113, 239, 443-4, 464, 475, 485, 493
manas 187, 236
Manne, Rolf 89, 465, 493
Manning, Matthew 83-4, 111, 183, 353-4, 385, 391, 465, 493
Mannsåker, Jon 344
Marcion 32
Mary Magdalene 32, 34, 44, 46-7, 109, 291
Mark Antony 18
Martinus 10, 12, 37, 46, 48, 57-8, 66, 74, 76, 149, 150, 181-2, 185-6, 192-3, 200, 202, 204, 207, 214, 222, 228, 230-1, 256, 268-9, 280, 286, 294-6, 304-5, 307-9, 322, 339-40, 347, 349-50, 359, 365, 367-9, 375-6, 396, 398-9, 414, 422, 424, 429, 431, 442, 451, 454, 458, 463-4, 470, 473-6, 478, 480-81, 483-5, 487, 493
Martinussen, Sverre 64, 495
Marto, Jacinta 252
Marx, Karl 20, 448
Masada 26, 45
Mascarós, Juan 51, 463, 474, 484, 494
Maturana, Humberto 150
Mauthner, Anna & Alexander 67, 494
Mawlawis 422
Maximos 449-50
Mayo, Jeff 98
McCraty, Rollin 186
McKenna, Paul 85, 87, 465, 494, 498

McPherson, Tom 115
McTaggart, Lynne 162, 470, 494
Medjugorje 253
Medusa 251
Mephisto 365
Menes 17
Menzies, Gavin 88, 494
Mercury's wand, see also Caduceus 428
Milinda, King 319
Minotaur 424
Mithras 42-3
Moberly, Charlotte 331, 480, 494
Mohenjo-daro 18
monad 228, 230, 233, 314, 324, 326, 345
Montezuma II 88, 465, 488
Moody jr., Raymond A. 282-3, 467, 477, 494-5
Moore, Bob 13, 67, 76, 173-4, 177, 186, 190-1, 288, 297, 299, 304, 306, 341, 355, 372, 472, 478, 481, 494
Moorehouse, David 467, 486
Morgan, Marlo 142-3, 469, 494
Moses 18, 25, 27-8, 40, 50, 215, 250, 316, 437,
Moses de Leon 437
Moss, Thelma 169, 388
Motoyama, Hiroshi 389, 483
Mozart, Wolfgang Amadeus 82, 336, 416
Muhammad Ibn Abd Allah 28
Murphy, Bridey 332, 487
Myers, Frederick W.H. 126-7, 131, 143, 221, 240, 259, 270, 276, 302, 494
Myhre, Ottar 383, 495
Myhren, Dagne 476, 494
Mykerinos – Menkaure 17
Myskja, Audun 389-90, 472, 483, 494
Myss, Caroline 439, 485, 494
Mürer, Alice 477, 495

N

NAFKAM 384
Nag Hammadi 34, 417, 421
Nagasena, sage 319
Nansen, Fridtjof 272, 494
Nebuchadnezzar 17-8, 208
Nefertiti 18
Neff, Mary K. 468,. 476, 494
Nehru, Jawaharlal 77
Nelson, John 94, 466, 494

Nelson, Roger D. 222, 465
nemesis 368, 453
Nero, Emperor 39
Nessos-shirt 292
Netzach 250, 437, 439
Neumann, Therese 73-4, 131, 275, 383
Newton, Isaac 64, 166, 431
Newton, Michael 130, 302, 320, 494
Nias, D.K.B. 96-7, 465, 466, 489
Nicholas of Flüe 74
Nietzsche 196
Nicaea, Synod of 38
Nicodemus, a Pharisee 316
Nirvana 24-5, 76, 187, 192, 220, 289, 303, 309, 319-20
nocebo 387
Noorden, Hans von 240, 467
Nordgard, Knut Rasmussen – see Vis-Knut 65
Northage, Isa 344-5, 385-6, 494
Norwegian Healer Association 383
Northtrop, F.S.C. 99, 164, 488
Nostradamus 77, 88, 105, 141, 465, 490

O

Odin 41, 76, 430
Odovakar 20
Odyssey 272
Oedipus 433
Olcott, Henry S. 11
Olerud, Randi 67, 174, 471-2, 482, 494
OM or AUM 396, 407-8, 420
Origen 316-7, 479
Osiris 42, 237, 427
Ouspensky, P.D. 77, 95, 341, 481, 494
Owen, George and I.M. 132, 469, 494

P

Padmasambhava 289
Padre Pio 71-4, 108-10, 131, 149, 217, 258, 263, 273, 371, 378-9
Pagels, Elaine 421-2, 462, 484, 494
Pahnke, Walter 284, 477
Pan 450
Paris, François de 134
Parmann, Øistein 66, 464, 478, 482, 495
Parvati 23
Patanjali 56, 76, 409

Paul VI, Pope 253
Paul, Saint 29, 31-6, 39, 43-6, 48, 107-8, 216, 249, 254-5, 291, 358, 406, 453, 463, 479, 488-9
Pauli, Wolfgang 68
Peek, Kim 81
Peer Gynt 434, 449, 454
Pegasus 251
Pentateuch 25
Phantasms of the Living 259
phi 428-9
Philip, Tetrarch 41
Philip, a thought form 132, 469, 494
Philo 40, 61
pi 429
Picasso 111
piezo-electrical energy 262
Pilate, Pontius 32, 39, 40, 45
Pindar 288
placebo 263, 336, 387
Planck, Max 68
Plato 15, 42, 64, 69, 130, 136, 203, 218, 239-40, 285, 288, 312, 315, 317, 365, 379, 440, 475, 479, 489, 495
Plotinus 34, 58, 69-70, 99, 189, 214, 218, 229, 312-3, 315, 320, 349, 364, 369, 379, 441, 462, 464, 466, 473-4, 478, 482, 485, 490, 494-5
Podmore, Frank 259
Podolski, see EPR-paradox
Pollan, Brita 424, 465, 477, 495
Pontoppidan, Erik 54
Porphyrios 69, 70
Post, Laurens van der 55, 111-2, 133-4, 143, 296, 464, 466, 468-9, 477-8, 483, 493
Potok, Chaim 461-3, 485, 495
Powell, Arthur E. 133, 142, 160, 174, 189-91, 237, 243, 266-8, 276, 307-9, 313, 324-5, 341, 364, 390, 469-72, 475-6, 478-9, 482-3, 495
Powell, Diane H. 143, 495
Prajapati 234
prana 168, 173, 189-90, 268, 307, 381, 389-90, 448
Pribram, Karl 156, 162, 180, 372, 469
Psalms, the Book of 26, 412-3
psychogenic system 378
Ptah 50, 427
Ptolemaios 18
Purusha 226
Pythagoras 15, 42, 416, 428, 430

Q

qlifot 261
quadrant 151-5, 448
Quetzalcoatl 88
Quirinius 38
Qumran 26, 35, 49, 248-9
Quran (Koran) 28-9, 217, 220, 249, 292

R

Rab'ia 413
Radin, Dean 86, 143, 377, 465, 468-9, 474, 491, 495
Raimondo della Vigne 72
Rakhmaninov 212
Rama 23, 76
Ramayana 23
Ramadan 28
Rameses II 18
Ramtha 115, 468, 491
Randi, James 141
Rasputin 77
Rawlings, Maurice 287
Redfield, James – (Celestine Prophecy) 64, 133, 455-6, 496
Reich, Wilhelm 168
Resch, Tina 84
Reynolds, Dr 385
Reynolds, Pam 281, 310, 476
Rhea 20
RIGPA/ Rigpa 170, 216, 323, 496
Rig-Veda 22
Ring, Kenneth 108, 283, 287, 477
Rinpoche, Sogyal 76, 170, 176, 216, 225, 257, 285-6, 289, 291, 305-6, 308, 312, 316, 319-20, 337, 347, 357, 398, 401, 407, 416, 424, 465, 473-4, 477-9, 481, 484, 496
Rinpoche, Urgyen 320, 323, 479, 497
Riosanu, M. Kristin 413, 484, 496
Rishi 22, 45, 252
Ritchie, George C. 122, 282-4, 286, 292, 295, 302, 304, 308, 477, 496
Roberts, Jane 48, 59, 112-3, 134, 260, 304, 466, 469, 496
Roff, Mary 334
Rogo, David Scott 110-1, 132, 253, 286, 333, 467, 469, 480, 496
Roll, William G. 84, 465, 495
Roney-Dougal, Serena M. 171, 263, 471, 496
Rosemary, a girl from Blackpool 333, 344
Ruffin, C. Bernard 71, 74-5, 464, 470, 476, 482-3, 496
Runki 311
Runolfsson, Runolfur – see Runki
Russek, Linda G.S. 127-8, 166, 478
Ruysbroek, Jan van 219
Ryerson, Kevin 115, 468, 486
Ryzl, Milan 232, 341, 474, 481, 495
Røine, Eva 209

S

Sabina, Maria 331, 480
Sagan, Carl 137, 141-2, 158, 469, 476, 496
Sahagún 88
Sai Baba 356, 481
sacrament 30-31, 340, 369, 439
Salem in Massachusetts 259
Solomon, King 18, 38
Sandia-laboratory 169
Saraswati, Brahma's spouse 23
Saraswati, Satyananda 471
Sargon I 17
Schjelderup, Kristian 14, 54, 61, 73-4, 461, 464, 496
Schmicker, Michael 384, 466, 476, 496
Schrödinger, Erwin 68
Schwartz, Gary E.R. 127-8, 137, 166, 277, 468, 471, 478, 496
Scott, Mike 487
Sefer Yetzira 435
Sefer Ha-Zohar 436
sephirah / sephiroth 250, 261, 429, 435-9
Serios, Ted 135, 489
Semir Taci 336
Septuagint 27
seraph/ seraphim 70-1, 239, 26, 248, 252, 305
Seth 48, 59, 61, 112, 114, 134, 136, 207, 221-2, 239, 259-60, 269, 276, 286, 300-1, 304, 307-8, 328-31, 349, 370, 381-2, 463-4, 468, 473, 475, 477-8, 480, 482-3, 496
Shakyamuni – see Buddha
Shang dynasty 19
Shankara 203
Shantideva 352
Shaw, George Bernhard 78
Sheldrake, Rupert 134, 143, 469, 496
Shiva 19, 22-3, 57, 216, 275, 367

Sibbern, Susan 263, 468, 496
Silk, Anne Arnold 262, 476, 495
Silva method 386, 410, 472, 495
Simon Magus 32, 40
Simon Peter (see also Cleophas) 42, 45
Simon the Zealot/Canaanite 45
Skarsaune, Oskar 32, 36, 39, 44, 462, 496
Skaue, Olga Tandstad 67, 371
Smith, Huston 28, 30-1, 219, 291-2, 319, 323, 422, 461, 473, 477-9, 484, 496
Smith, Justa 386
Smith, Susy 128, 468
Sobha Ram 333-4
Society for Psychical Research 126, 131, 142-3, 259, 471, 476, 495
Socrates 15, 69, 126, 288, 312, 315
Sophia 34
Sophocles 433
Solum, Øyvind 468, 491
Soubirous, Bernadette 252
Spangler, David (John, a spirit) 112, 114-5, 237, 242, 276, 308, 404, 475, 483, 496
Sparrow, M. 469, 494
Spilde, Ingrid 384
Sri Aurobindo 189
Sri Yukteswar 45, 110, 239, 242-3, 276, 308, 310
Stace, Walter T. 68, 219, 464, 496
Steiner, Rudolf 11-2, 31-2, 37, 46-7, 49, 76-7, 99, 109, 136, 177, 187-9, 191-2, 197, 227, 236-7, 241, 243, 246-7, 257, 269, 293-4, 302-5, 307, 309, 319, 322, 327, 338-40, 347, 352, 355-6, 361, 373, 416, 419-20, 424, 440-2, 454, 462-3, 465-6, 474-5, 478-81, 484-5, 497-8
Stevenson, Ian 122, 314, 326, 332, 334-7, 344, 347, 480, 497
Stevenson, Robert Louis 257
Sturluson, Snorri 79
Suetonius 39-40
Sutta/Sutra 24
Sutton, Mary 333
Swastika 427
Swann, Ingo 372
Swedenborg, Emanuel 12, 64-5, 109, 138, 276, 286, 292-3, 295, 302-4, 307-9, 415, 478, 495, 497
Sylvareik, Anne Brit 271, 495

T

Tabernacle 248
Tacitus 39, 462, 497
Talbot, Michael 132, 134-6, 142, 156-7, 163, 167, 198, 227, 260-1, 287, 372, 377, 465, 467-8, 470-1, 480, 483, 497
talisman magic 261, 427
Talmud 25, 210, 461
Tanakh 25
Tandstad, Karl 67
tan-matras 235
Tarot card 104-5, 438
Tart, Charles 473
Tauler, Johannes 48
Teilhard de Chardin, Pierre 178, 361, 447, 472, 482, 485
Teiresias 433
Teresa of Avila 63, 71-2, 131, 177, 383, 395, 403, 417-8, 423, 448, 464, 468, 483-4, 497
Tertullian 38-9, 475
Tertön Sogyal 170
Theseus 424
Tezozomoc 88
Theodora, Empress 317
Theodotus 34
Theravada-Buddhism 24, 318, 479
Thiering, Barbara 32, 35, 43-4, 250, 463, 479, 497
Thigpen and Cleckley 197, 497
Thompson, Frederic 111
Thomsen, Martinus – see Martinus
Thoreau, Henry David 448
Thuban 431
Tiberius, Emperor 39-41
Tiphareth 437, 439
Tighe, Mrs. 332
tigle 320
Tiller, William 169, 241
Titanic 371
Tiye 18
Toksvik, Signe 64
Tolstoy, Leo 285
Toltec culture 20
Tompkins, Peter Chr. 124, 497
tonglen 421
Torah 25, 437
Trajan, Emperor 39
transactional analysis 203, 380, 473
Tree of Knowledge 3, 373, 450-1
Tree of Life 104-5, 138, 246, 250, 261, 361, 399,

Tree of Life (cont) 435-9, 485
Tripítaka 24
Tutankhamen 18, 250
Tweedie, Irina 381, 401, 414, 424, 483, 497

U

UFO 136, 141, 223, 259, 344, 469
Ullman, Montague 206, 209-10, 473, 497
Underhill, Evelyn 60, 68, 78, 220, 242, 462, 464, 473, 475, 497
Undset, Sigrid 462, 464, 475, 497, 499
Unión Espiritista Democracy de Filipinas 387
Upanishad 22, 51, 219, 226, 234, 396, 407-8, 494
Urgyen Rinpoche, Tulku – see Rinpoche, Urgyen
Urim 210

V

Vajrayana 24, 420-1
vardøgr 144
Varela, Francisco 150
Vedanta 22, 48, 231
Vennum, Lurancy 334
Versluis, Arthur 288, 475, 477, 497
Vínaya 24
Vinci, Leonardo da 64, 170
Vishnu 22-3, 216, 367
Vis-Knut 65
Visva 65, 234
Vitruvius-man 170
Vulcan 442

W

Wambach, Helen 337, 344, 346, 480, 497
Wasiutynski, Jeremi 178, 199, 206, 209-10, 212, 413, 433, 445-6, 452, 471, 473, 485, 497
Watson, Lyall 80, 91, 94-5, 98, 106, 137, 164-5, 169, 175, 186, 189, 198, 207-8, 212, 223, 241, 259-60, 332-3, 341-4, 346-7, 386-91, 466-7, 469, 471-6, 480-1, 483, 498
Wawro, Richard 81
Weinberg, Steven Lee 115
Westerlund, Anna Elisabeth 66, 161, 261, 297, 464, 70, 478, 498
Wetlesen, Jon 204, 463, 464, 473-4, 484, 498
White, A. 98
White Brotherhood 484
Whitton, Joel 333, 337, 477, 480, 498
Wiegner, Eugene 178, 472

Wilber, Ken 12, 50, 57, 68-9, 77, 99, 147, 150-5, 157-8, 173, 179, 181-4, 187, 189, 192, 194-5, 202-3, 205-6, 211, 224, 227, 231, 243, 299, 300, 303-4, 320-22, 347, 366, 370, 379-80, 393, 399, 400, 420, 426, 437, 448, 463-4, 466, 471-4, 478-9, 482-5, 498
Wilhelms, Richard 466, 498
Wilson, Colin 11-2, 65, 77-8, 80, 84, 90-1, 95, 98-9, 100, 103, 106, 136, 164, 169, 179, 183, 196-7, 204, 225, 263, 315, 332, 344, 429, 435, 461, 465-9, 471-4, 476, 478-81, 485, 498
Woje, Svein 44, 498
Worth, Patience 111
Wyller, Egil A. 49, 463, 499

XYZ

Xavier, Francis 72
X-rays 117, 166
Yeats, William B. 100, 499
Yesod 242, 437-9
Yetzirah 437-8
Yogananda, Paramahansa 45-7, 49, 50, 55-6, 74, 76, 99, 110, 192, 216-7, 239, 265, 276, 289, 303-4, 323, 409, 424, 463-6, 472-3, 475, 477, 479, 484, 499
Yusuf of Yuha 18
Zeitoun (near Cairo) 253
Zen 12, 48, 139, 231, 412, 434, 461, 498
Zero-Point Field 162
Zeus 12, 19, 20, 92, 433
Zimmermann, Nan 210
Zodiac 42, 91, 98, 101, 437, 440
Zoroaster/Zarathustra 15, 46
Zostrianos 421
Zukav, Gary 224, 474, 499

Ørjasæter, Tordis 462, 499
Åsteson, Olav 281

www.ingramcontent.com/pod-product-compliance
Lightning Source LLC
Chambersburg PA
CBHW071642160426
43195CB00012B/1332